Readings in Planning Theory

Readings in Planning Theory

Edited by Scott Campbell and Susan S. Fainstein

Selection and editorial matter copyright © Scott Campbell and
Susan Fainstein 1996

First published 1996

Reprinted 1997 (twice), 1998 (twice), 1999, 2000, 2001

Blackwell Publishers Inc
350 Main Street
Malden, Massachusetts 02148, USA

Blackwell Publishers Ltd
108 Cowley Road
Oxford OX4 1JF, UK

Library of Congress Cataloging in Publication Data
Readings in planning theory/edited by Scott Campbell and Susan S. Fainstein
  p. cm.
  Includes bibliographical references and index.
  ISBN 1–55786–612–0 — ISBN 1–55786–613–9 (pbk)
  1. City planning. I. Campbell, Scott, 1958– . II. Fainstein, Susan S.
HT165.5.R43   1996   95–36047
307.1'216'0973—dc20   CIP

British Library Cataloguing in Publication Data
A CIP catalogue record for this book is available from the British Library

Typeset in Meridien
Printed and bound in Great Britain by T. J. International Limited, Padstow, Cornwall

This book is printed on acid-free paper.

Contents

Contributors

Robert A. Beauregard
Paul Davidoff
Jameson W. Doig
Norman Fainstein
Susan S. Fainstein
Frank Fischer
Robert Fishman
Richard E. Foglesong
John Forester
Ann Forsyth
John Friedmann
Peter Hall
David Harvey
Patsy Healey
Harvey M. Jacobs
Jane Jacobs
Jerome L. Kaufman
Richard E. Klosterman
Norman Krumholz
John M. Levy
Helen Liggett
Charles E. Lindblom
Bobbi S. Low
William H. Lucy
Beth Moore Milroy
Matt Ridley
Marsha Ritzdorf
Leonie Sandercock
Richard Sennett
William H. Wilson

Acknowledgments

We wish to thank our editor, Simon Prosser, for his support and suggestions and Hooshang Amirahmadi for making resources of th0e Department of Urban Planning and Policy Development at Rutgers University available for this project. We also thank Yi-Ling Chen, Antonia Casellas, Soraya Goga, and John Ottomanelli for their assistance.

Regarding the chapter titles listed in this reader's table of contents, we have retained all the original article titles. For book excerpts, we have generally used either the original book title, the chapter title, or a combination thereof. The texts are, whenever possible, reprinted in full. We have deleted short sections of the original text only when a book chapter excerpt refers to another chapter of the book not included in this reader. We have made minor editorial changes to achieve uniformity of style.

We are grateful to the publishers for their permission to reprint the following material:

Fishman, Robert. 1977. *Urban Utopias in the Twentieth Century: Ebenezer Howard, Frank Lloyd Wright, and Le Corbusier*. New York: Basic Books, pp. 3–20; 23–51; 64–75; 226–34. (excerpt: "Urban Utopias: Ebenezer Howard and Le Corbusier")

Wilson, William H. 1989. *The City Beautiful Movement*. Baltimore and London: The Johns Hopkins University Press, pp. 281–305. (excerpt: "The Glory, Destruction, and Meaning of the City Beautiful Movement")

Jacobs, Jane. 1961. *The Death and Life of Great American Cities*. New York: Vintage, pp. 3–25.

Sennett, Richard. 1990. *The Conscience of the Eye*. New York: Knopf, pp. 41–68. (excerpt: "The Neutral City")

Klosterman, Richard E. 1985. "Arguments for and Against Planning," *Town Planning Review*, Vol. 56, No 1, pp. 5–20.

Foglesong, Richard E. 1986. *Planning the Capitalist City*. Princeton, N.J. Princeton University Press, pp. 18–24.

Harvey, David. 1985. *The Urbanization of Capital*. Baltimore: Johns Hopkins University Press, pp. 165–84. (excerpt: "On Planning the Ideology of Planning")

Ridley, Matt and Bobbi S. Low. 1993. "Can Selfishness Save the Environment?" *The Atlantic Monthly*, Vol. 272, No. 3. pp. 76–86.

Beauregard, Robert A. 1989. "Between Modernity and Postmodernity: The Ambiguous Position of U.S. Planning." *Environment and Planning D: Society and Space* 7, pp. 381–95.

Healey, Patsy. 1992. "Planning Through Debate: The Communicative Turn in Planning Theory." *Town Planning Review* 63 (2), pp. 143–62.

Lindblom, Charles E. 1959. "The Science of 'Muddling Through'," *Public Administration Review*, Vol. 19 (Spring), pp. 79–88.

Davidoff, Paul. 1965. "Advocacy and Pluralism in Planning," *Journal of the American Institute of Planners*, Vol. 31, No. 4 (Dec.), pp. 544–55.

Kaufman, Jerome L. and Harvey M. Jacobs. 1987. "A Public Planning Perspective on Strategic Planning," *Journal of the American Planning Association* 53, pp. 23–33.

Krumholz, Norman. 1982. "A Retrospective View of Equity Planning: Cleveland, 1969–1979," *Journal of the American Planning Association* 48 (Spring), pp. 163–74.

Levy, John M. 1990. "What Local Economic Developers Actually Do: Location Quotients versus Press Releases." *Journal of the American Planning Association*, 56 (Spring), pp. 153–60.

Hall, Peter. 1980. *Great Planning Disasters*. Berkeley, Calif.: University of California Press, pp. 56–86. (excerpt: "London's Motorways")

Doig, Jameson W. 1987. "Coalition-Building by a Regional Agency: Austin Robin and the Port of New York Authority," in Clarence Stone and Heywood Sanders, eds., *Politics of Urban Development*. Lawrence: University of Kansas Press, pp. 73–104.

Ritzdorf, Marsha. 1992. "Feminist Thoughts on the Theory and Practice of Planning," *Planning Theory* 7/8, pp. 13–18.

Liggett, Helen. 1992. "Knowing Women /Planning Theory," *Planning Theory* 7/8, pp. 21–6.

Fainstein, Susan S. 1992. "Planning in a Different Voice," *Planning Theory* 7/8, pp. 27–31.

Milroy, Beth Moore. 1992. "Some Thoughts About Difference and Pluralism," *Planning Theory* 7/8, pp. 33–8.

Friedmann, John. 1992. "Feminist and Planning Theories: The Epistemological Connection," *Planning Theory* 7/8, pp. 40–3.

Sandercock, Leonie and Ann Forsyth. 1992. "Feminist Theory and Planning Theory: The Epistemological Linkages," *Planning Theory* 7/8, pp. 45–9.

Lucy, William H. 1988. "APA's Ethical Principles Include Simplistic Planning Theories," *Journal of the American Planning Association*, Vol. 54 (Spring), pp. 147–9.

Fischer, Frank. 1991. "Risk Assessment and Environmental Crisis: Toward an Integration of Science and Participation," *Industrial Crisis Quarterly* 5, pp. 113–32.

Forester, John. 1993. "Learning from Practice Stories: The Priority of Practical Judgment," in Frank Fischer and John Forester, eds., *The Argumentative Turn in Policy Analysis and Planning*. Durham, N.C.: Duke University Press, pp. 186–209.

Introduction: The Structure and Debates of Planning Theory

Scott Campbell and Susan S. Fainstein

Planning theory is an elusive subject of study. It draws on a variety of disciplines and has no widely accepted canon. The purpose of this reader is twofold: (1) to define the boundaries of this area of inquiry and the works that constitute its central focus; and (2) to confront the principal issues that face planners as theorists and practitioners. It is organized by the questions that its editors raise rather than by the chronological development of the field.

Compiling a reader in planning theory presents a tricky dilemma: One can either cautiously reprint the early postwar classics – thereby duplicating several past anthologies, including Faludi's popular 1973 reader – or else run the risk of prematurely elevating otherwise transient ideas. We take a different path; we have selected a set of readings – both "classic" and recent – that effectively address the pressing and enduring questions in planning theory.

We see the central question of planning theory as the following: *What role can planning play in developing the city and region within the constraints of a capitalist political economy and a democratic political system?* The emphasis is not on developing a model planning process but rather on finding an explanation for planning practice based on analyses of the respective political economies of the United States and Great Britain. Our effort is

to determine the historical and contextual influences and strategic opportunities that shape the capacity of planners to affect the urban and
regional environment.

What is Planning Theory?

It is not easy to define planning theory; the subject is slippery, and explanations are often frustratingly tautological or disappointingly pedestrian.
There are four principal reasons for this difficulty. First, many of the
fundamental questions concerning planning belong to a much broader
inquiry concerning the role of the state in social and spatial transformation. Consequently, planning theory appears to overlap with theory in all
the social science disciplines, and it becomes hard to limit its scope or to
stake out a turf specific to planning. Second, the boundary between
planners and related professionals (such as real estate developers, architects, city council members) is not mutually exclusive; planners don't just
plan, and nonplanners also plan. Third, the field of planning is divided
into those who define it according to its object (land-use patterns of the
built and natural environments) and those who do so by its method
(the process of decision making). Finally, many fields are defined by a
specific set of methodologies. Yet planning commonly borrows the
diverse methodologies from many different fields, and so its theoretical
base cannot easily be drawn from its tools of analysis. Taken together,
this considerable disagreement over the scope and function of planning
and the problems of defining who is actually a planner obscure the delineation of an appropriate body of theory. Whereas most scholars can
agree on what constitutes the economy and the polity – and thus what is
economic or political theory – they differ as to the content of planning
theory.

The amorphous quality of planning theory means that practitioners
largely disregard it. In this respect planning resembles other academic
disciplines. Most politicians do not bother with political theory; businesspeople generally do not familiarize themselves with econometrics; and
many community organizers do not concern themselves with social
theory. Planning as a practical field of endeavor, however, differs from
other activities in its claim to be able to predict the consequences of its
actions. Planners need to generalize from prior experience if they are to
practice their craft. In their day-to-day work planners may rely more on
intuition than explicit theory; yet this intuition may in fact be assimilated
theory. In this light, theory represents cumulative professional knowledge. Though many practicing planners may look upon the planning
theory of their graduate education as inert and irrelevant – and see in
their professional work a kind of homespun, in-the-trenches pragmatism
– theory allows one to see the conditions of this "pragmatism". Just as

Keynes warned of being an unwitting slave to the ideas of a defunct economist, we believe that it is also possible to be a slave to the ideas of a defunct planning theorist.

One of our prime motives in selecting the readings for this book is to enable practitioners to achieve a deeper understanding of the processes in which they are engaged than can be attained through simple intuition and common sense. We do not envision completely eliminating the gap between theory and practice; doing so would deny the power of each. Often decried, this gap can structure a powerful creative tension between the two. Nevertheless, we do believe that theory can inform practice. Planning theory is not just some idle chattering at the margins of the field. If done poorly, it discourages and stifles; but if done well, it defines the field and drives it forward. We have therefore identified a set of readings that address themselves to the questions planners must ask if they are to be effective, and we include case studies of planning in action with this purpose in mind.

Beyond this intention, we aim to establish a theoretical foundation that provides not only a field with a common structure for scientific inquiry but also a means for defining what planning is – especially in the intimidating company of more established academic disciplines. Theory allows for both professional and intellectual self-reflection. It tries to make sense of the seemingly unrelated, contradictory aspects of urban development and creates a rational system with which to compare and evaluate the merits of different planning ideas and strategies. It also allows planners to translate their specific issues into the language of more general social scientific theory so that planning may interchange ideas with other disciplines.

A well-developed theoretical foundation serves as a declaration of scholarly autonomy, often institutionalized in the form of a planning theory requirement for master's degree programs and professional certification in city planning. The relatively recent expansion of Ph.D. programs in planning goes hand in hand with the rise of planning theory. Such programs are used not only to increase research in planning departments; they also reflect the ability to develop the discipline's own theoretical foundations. A Ph.D. program also uses theory to distinguish and elevate itself from its larger counterpart, the professional master's program.

Our Approach to Planning Theory

Our approach is to place planning theory at the intersection of political economy and intellectual history. We do not see it, however, as mechanistically determined by these two forces. Those who misuse structural theory will inevitably fall victim to a sense of helplessness in the face of predestined social forces. Instead, the planner should use theory to consider how the local and national political economy, in addition to the field's own history, together influence the collective imagination of the discipline's possibilities, limitations, and professional identity. The challenge for this professional – and sometimes activist – discipline is to find the negotiating room within the larger social structure to pursue the good city.

We also place planning theory at a second intersection: that of the *city* as a phenomenon and *planning* as a human activity. Planning adapts to changes in the city, which in turn is transformed by planning and politics. This interaction is not a closed system. Planners not only plan cities; they also negotiate, forecast, research, survey, and organize financing. Nor do planners have an exclusive influence over cities; developers, businesses, politicians, and other actors also shape urban development. The result is that the discipline of planning is influenced by a wide variety of substantive and procedural ideas beyond its own modest disciplinary boundaries. Studies of planning refer to works in political science, law, decision theory, and public policy. Writings about the city draw upon traditions primarily in urban history, urban sociology, geography and economics. Though not always consistently, we use this practical distinction of substantive versus procedural theory to distinguish *Readings in Planning Theory* from its companion volume, *Readings in Urban Theory* (Fainstein and Campbell, 1996).

Debates Define Theory:
Six Questions of Planning Theory

No single paradigm defines the foundation of planning theory. Such a lack of agreement about planning priorities and planning ideologies is inevitable; yet this disagreement is mistakenly carried over into the classroom, leading to unnecessary disagreement over how planning theory itself should be taught. As a result, many departments shy away from developing a rigorous, unified theory program. However, agreement on how to teach planning theory systematically should be possible even without the questionable prerequisite that planning itself be either wholly systematic or consensual. On the contrary, the teaching of planning theory should explicitly explore the roots and implications of these long-standing disputes in the field. Planning is a messy, contentious field; planning theory should provide the means to address these debates and understand their deeper roots.

In this light, we view the study of planning theory as a series of debates. Here are six of the questions at issue:

1   What are the historical roots of planning?

The first question of theory is of identity, which in turn leads to history. The traditional story told of modern city planning is that it arose from several separate movements at the turn of the century: the Garden City, the City Beautiful, and public health reforms. Three basic areas characterized its subsequent history: (1) the formative years during which the pioneers (Howard, Burnham, etc.) did not yet identify themselves as planners (late 1800s–ca 1910); (2) the period of institutionalization, professionalization, and self-recognition of planning, together with the rise of regional and federal planning efforts (ca 1910–45); and (3) the postwar era of standardization, crisis, and diversification of planning (Krueckeberg 1983).

   This story, often repeated in introductory courses and texts, is useful in several ways. The multiplicity of technical, social, and aesthetic origins explains planning's eclectic blend of design, civil engineering, local politics, community organization, and social justice. Its status as either a quasi-, secondary, or pubescent profession is explained by its development as a twentieth-century, public-sector, bureaucratic profession, rather than as a late-nineteenth-century, private sector profession such as medicine (Hoffman 1989).

   At the most basic level, this framework gives the story of planning (at least modern, professional planning) a starting point. Planning emerges as the twentieth-century response to the nineteenth-century industrial city (Hall 1988). It also provides several foundational texts: Howard's *To-morrow: A Peaceful Path to Real Reform* (1898), Charles Robinson's *The Improvement of Towns and Cities or the Practical Basis of Civic Aesthetics* (1901), and Daniel Burnham's plan for Chicago (1909), as well as several defining events: the Columbia Exposition in Chicago (1893), which launched the City Beautiful Movement; the construction of Letchworth, the first English Garden City (1903); and the first national conference on city planning, held in Washington, D.C. (1909).

   Yet this tale of planning's birth is also problematic. As the years go by and the planning pioneers pass away, the story is simplified and unconditionally repeated. Contingent or coincidental events and texts are elevated to necessary steps in the inevitable and rational development of modern planning. Even the best of tellers can succumb to repeating this tale of the "great men of planning history". This uncritical acceptance of these early years of planning juxtaposes oddly with the soul-searching period following World War II, especially after the collapse of the 1960s Great Society and weariness of urban renewal created a crisis of confidence. The result is an essentialistic life-cycle model of planning's birth, growth, maturation, and midlife crisis – a model that largely excludes the political, economic, and cultural forces that continually transform planning both in ideology and practice.

One path out of this debilitating historicism is to bridge benign past folklore and current skepticism through a reassessment of planning history in which both past and present are retold with the same critical (and sometimes revisionist) voice. Richard Foglesong's *Planning the Capitalist City* (1986) and Robert Fishman's *Bourgeois Utopias: The Rise and Fall of Suburbia* (1987) are but two of the better examples. One can certainly fault some critical histories for also being narrow-minded, replacing the historical logic of capital with the heroicism of "the great men of planning history". The challenge is to write a planning history that encourages an accurate but also critical, subtle, and reflective understanding of contemporary planning practice. An effective planning history helps the contemporary planner shape his or her complex professional identity.

2   What is the justification for planning? When should one intervene?

Planning is intervention with an intention to alter the existing course of events. The timing and legitimacy of planned intervention therefore become questions central to planning theory: Why and in what situations should planners intervene? Implicit here is an understanding of the alternative to planning. Though it is most commonly assumed that the alternative is the free market, it could equally be chaos or myopic self-interest. Indeed, automatically assuming that we know the alternative to planning is dangerous. For some, the hope of rational planning was simply to equate the market with uncertainty and to believe that the logic of the plan would therefore replace the chaos of the market. Yet others hold the reverse belief: that the logic of the market should replace the chaos left by planning (Hayek 1944). Whereas the Great Depression seems to vindicate the former view, the collapse of Eastern European state socialism is frequently cited in support of the latter.

The duality between planning and the market is a defining framework in planning theory. A person's opinion of planning reflects his or her assumptions about the relationships between the private and public sectors – and how much the government should "intrude". The safe stance in planning has been to see its role as making up for the periodic shortcomings of the private market (Moore 1978; Klosterman, chapter 6, this volume). This approach creates a neat and tidy division between the public and private worlds, each with their unique comparative advantages. It treats planning as the patient understudy, filling in when the market fails but never presuming permanently to replace the market or to change the script of economic efficiency. This legitimacy significantly limits creative or redistributive planning efforts, but it does make a scaled-down version of planning palatable to all but the most conservative economists (Friedman 1962).

Nevertheless, not everyone sees the market-planning duality as so benign or well behaved. For some, the function of planning is to confront the private market directly every step of the way (Harvey, chapter 8, this volume); others see planning as helping the market along. (Frieden and Sagalyn 1989). This debate becomes even murkier when one challenges the tidy separation between the public and private sectors, either from a relatively upbeat (Galbraith 1967) or skeptical view (Lowi 1969). Public and private sectors no longer represent mutually exclusive sets of actors, interests, or planning tools. Privatization of traditionally public services has raised the question of whether only the public sector can serve the public interest. The rise of public-private partnerships in the wake of urban renewal efforts also reflects this blurring of sectoral boundaries (Squires 1989). The growing number of planners working in the private sector also upsets the traditional professional role that planners play in the battles between public and private interests. Public sector planners borrow tools developed in the private sector, such as strategic planning. The emergence of autonomous public authorities to manage marine ports, airports, and other infrastructures has created hybrid organizations that act both like a public agency and a private firm (Walsh 1978; Doig, chapter 19, this volume). Finally, the growing non-profit or "third sector" further demonstrates the inadequacies of viewing the world in a purely dichotomous framework of the government versus the market.

3 "Rules of the game": what values are incorporated within planning? What ethical dilemmas do planners face?

This growing complexity and uncertainty in the planner's stance between the public and private sectors also questions traditional ethical assumptions. As planners increasingly work in the private and quasi-private sectors, do their clients become privatized as well? A planner's loyalty is torn between serving employers, fellow planners, and the public. In this contested terrain of loyalties, what remains of the once accepted cornerstone of planning, serving the public interest?

This dilemma is further complicated by the expansion of planning's functions beyond merely technocratic goals to address larger social, economic, and environmental challenges. Within society at large the values of democracy, equality, and efficiency often clash. These conflicts are reflected in the choices planners must make as they try to reconcile the conflicting goals of economic development, social justice, and environmental protection. Despite the long-term promises of sustainable development, this triad of goals has created deep-seated tensions not only between planners and the outside world but also within planning itself (Campbell 1996).

Another ethical dimension arises from the difficulties surrounding the planner's role as expert. Questions concerning the proper balance between expertise and citizen input arise in issues like the siting of highways and waste disposal facilities, when particular social groups must bear the costs. They are played out, as Frank Fischer discusses (chapter 27, this volume), when experts seek to quantify risk, placing a monetary value on human life. They show up, as Martin Wachs (1982) argues, in the assumptions used by model builders when they forecast the future impact of public facilities. Critics of those purporting to use scientific expertise to justify policy doubt the legitimacy of their methods, arguing that technical language disguises the values being interjected and obscures who wins and who loses. But the development of technical forecasting methods nevertheless is necessary if planners are to fulfill their responsibility of designing policies for the long term.

4   The constraints on planning power – how can planning be effective with a mixed economy?

It is not enough to determine that planners should routinely intervene in the private market; that determination in itself raises the question of authority and power. Unlike some other professions, planners do not have a monopoly on power or expertise over their object of work. Planners work within the constraints of the capitalist political economy, and their urban visions compete with those of developers, consumers, and other more powerful groups. When they call for a type of development to occur, they cannot command the resources to make it happen. Instead, they must rely on either private investment or a commitment from political leaders. They also work within the contraints of democracy and of the bureaucracy of government (Foglesong, chapter 7, this volume). Their goals, however, often have low priority within the overall political agenda. Thus, despite the planning ideal of a holistic, proactive vision, planners are frequently restricted to playing frustratingly reactive, regulatory roles.

The most powerful planners are those who can marshall the resources to effect change and get projects built (Doig, chapter 19, this volume; Caro 1974; Walsh 1978). They bend the role of the planner and alter the traditional separation between the public and private sectors. The resulting public-private partnerships (planners as developers) make the planner more activist (Squires 1989); yet they also strain the traditional identity of the public planner and make many idealistic planners squirm. How else can one explain the uncomfortable mixture of disgust and envy that planners felt toward Robert Moses, who as the head of various New York City agencies had far more projects built than did all the traditional city planners he disparaged?

5   Style of planning: what do planners do?

The justification for planning is often comprehensiveness. Yet the ideal of comprehensiveness has suffered serious criticism. Standard accounts of planning theories explained comprehensive planning as the attempt to coordinate the multiple development and regulatory initiatives under-taken in a region or city. Success depended on a high level of knowledge and the technological capability to use it. The attempt was ostensibly worthy but it failed on two counts. First, comprehensive planning required a level of knowledge, analysis, and organizational coordination that was impossibly complex (Altshuler 1972). This critique led to the push for incremental planning (Lindblom, chapter 13, this volume). Second, it presumed a common public interest but in effect gave voice to only one interest and ignored the needs of the poor and the weak. This critique led to the call for advocacy planning (Davidoff, chapter 14, this volume).

The assault on comprehensive planning continued into the 1970s and 1980s. Strategic planning theorists rejected its impossibly general goals and instead embraced the "lean and mean" strategies from the business and military sectors (Swanstrom 1987). By contrast, equity planning emerged as a less combative form of advocacy planning that allowed planners to serve the interests of the poor from within the system (Krumholz, chapter 16, this volume).

There are problems with writing a tidy obituary for comprehensive planning, however. First, many planners continue to use the compre-hensive approach as the model for their work, both because they continue to believe in it and because they find the alternatives inadequate (Dalton 1986). The primary task for many planners continues to be the writing and revising of comprehensive plans for their communities.

If the death notice of comprehensive planning may thus be premature, such dismissal may also misunderstand the theory's actual rise and fall. Planning theorists at times presume a kind of naive, golden era of comprehensive rational planning during the early postwar years that may never have actually existed. In constructing the history of planning, planners arguably are guilty of after-the-fact revisionism in their labeling of comprehensive planning. Planners may have falsely interpreted the planning theory disputes since the 1960s as the fall-out from the schism of a once united field, rather than simply as a reflection of a young, diverse field seeking to define itself during a turbulent era.

This is not to deny the power of the comprehensive planning debate; but it should be seen as one of several important debates that shaped the identity of the young field of planning theory. Unfortunately, much of this debate over comprehensiveness took place inside a theoretical vacuum. Planners often argued about the proper role of planning based simply on the merits of the concepts themselves (for example, large versus small-scale; top-down versus bottom-up), while underestimating the larger political and economic forces that shaped and constrained planning. The articulation of and eventual challenge to comprehensive planning was thus part of a larger expansion of planning theory beyond land-use planning into social and economic policy.

6   The enduring question of the public interest

Thirty years ago, the engaging debates of planning theory involved the conflicts between comprehensive versus incremental planning, objectivity versus advocacy, centralization versus decentralization, top-down versus bottom-up leadership, and planning for people versus planning for place. These debates from the adolescence of planning now seem a bit tired and bypassed. It is not that they have been conclusively resolved but rather that the field is so broadly scattered that each pole lives on. This current eclecticism reflects the fragmentation of planning itself. Nevertheless, these debates were arguably necessary for the intellectual development of the field, and the student planning theorist still needs to read and understand these controversies.

What has endured is the persistent question of the public interest. Planners continue to face the central controversy of whether there is indeed a single public interest and of whether they recognize and serve it. Incremental planners claimed that the excessive complexity of the comprehensive public interest prevented the planner from directly serving it, while advocate planners argued that what was portrayed as the public interest in fact represented merely the interests of the privileged. More recently, postmodernists have challenged the universal master narrative that gives voice to the public interest, seeing instead a heterogeneous public with many voices and interests. Finally, the persistence of fundamentalist thinking and community identity based on religious rather than secular, municipal values undermines the ability to find a consensual public interest (Baum 1994).

Yet planners have not abandoned the idea of serving the public interest, and rightly so. Postmodernists provided planning with a needed break from its preoccupation with a monolithic "public" (represented by Le Corbusier's and Robert Moses' love of the public but disdain for people); yet a rejection of Englightenment rationality, shared values, and standards leaves the planner without adequate guidance to serve this fragmented population. Some have touted strategic planning, and others have borrowed private sector approaches as the practical path for planning; but these approaches neglect the "public" in the public interest. A belief in the public interest is the foundation for a set of values that planners hold dear: equal protection and equal opportunity, public space, and a sense of civic community and social responsibility. The challenge is to reconcile these benefits of a common public interest with the diversity (postmodern and otherwise) that comes from many communities living side by side. David Harvey (1992) looked to the generally held ideas of social justice and rationality as a bridge to overcome this dilemma. The recent emphasis on the planner as mediator may reflect a new approach to the public interest: an acceptance of the multiplicity of interests, combined with an enduring common interest in finding viable, politically legitimate solutions. Planners serve the public interest by negotiating a kind of multicultural, technocratic pluralism. The recent interest in communicative action – planners as communicators rather than as autonomous, systematic thinkers – also reflects this effort to renew the focus of planning theory on the public interest (Innes 1994; Forester 1989; Healey, chapter 11, this volume).

In the end, this question of the public interest is the leitmotif that holds together the defining debates of planning theory. The central task of planners is serving the public interest in the cities, suburbs, and country-side. Questions of when, why and how planners should intervene – and the constraints they face in the process – all lead back to defining and serving this public interest. Yet this public interest is changing. The restructured urban economy, the shifting boundaries between the public and private sectors, and the changing tools and available resources constantly force planners to rethink the public interest. This rethinking is the task of planning theory.

The Readings

We have selected the readings for this volume to represent what we think are the central issues in planning theory. In particular, they address the challenge and dilemma of planning as defined at the beginning of this introduction. *What role can planning play in developing the city and region within the constraints of a capitalist political economy and a democratic political system?* We approach this question primarily through texts that address specific theoretical issues. However, we have also included several case studies that provide vivid and concrete illustrations of this question. We do not attempt to outline a model planning process. Rather, our effort is to place planning theory within its historical context, its political economy, and the surrounding urban and regional environment.

Although planning theory is a relatively young field, one can already speak of "classic readings." Our guide has been to choose those readings – both old and new – that still speak directly to contemporary issues. Most have been written in the past ten years, though some articles from the 1960s are still the best articulation of specific debates. Most draw upon experiences in the United States and Great Britain, though hopefully their relevance extends far beyond these boundaries.

We have organized the volume into six sections, each prefaced with a short introduction to the main themes. We begin with the foundations of modern planning, including both traditional and critical views of planning history. We then turn to two interrelated questions: *What is the justification for planning intervention?* and *How should planners intervene?* Regarding the political and economic justifications for planning, we have selected readings that examine the neoclassical, institutional, and Marxist arguments. They place planners in the larger context of the relationship between the private market and government (both local and national). Regarding the style of planning, the readings examine the dominant planning approaches: comprehensive, incremental, advocacy, equity, and strategic planning. The readings also explore two emerging directions: postmodernism and communicative planning. The case studies presented in the fourth section illustrate both the opportunities and constraints affecting planners in the United States and Great Britain.

Gender has emerged as a powerful and transforming theme in urban planning in recent years. This issue has many facets, including the differing uses of urban space by men and women; the threats cities pose to women's personal safety; and the increasing number of women entering the labor force. The readings in the fifth section address the way in which emerging feminist ideas are changing planning theory. In particular, these readings examine how basic epistemological and methodological issues in planning theory should change to address their previous shortcomings.

The volume concludes with three readings on planning ethics, professionalism, community participation, and communication. Each addresses a shortcoming of the traditional, rational-comprehensive model of planning, whether its simplistic notion of serving the public interest, its lack of subtlety about ethical conflicts, its presumption of privileged expert knowledge, or its tendency to oversimplify and overgeneralize the causal relationships found in cities. The emerging stance for planners involves a greater familiarity with political conflicts, a proactive role in the communication of choices and risks, and the greater use of the rich complexity of storytelling.

Further Reading

Altshuler, Alan. 1972. "The Goals of Comprehensive Planning," in Fainstein and Fainstein, *The View from Below*, pp. 205–218. Boston: Little, Brown. (First published in 1965)

Baum, Howell S. 1994. "Community and Consensus: Reality and Fantasy in Planning," *Journal of Planning Education and Research* 13, pp. 251–62.

Caro, Robert. 1974. *The Power Broker: Robert Moses and the Fall of New York*. New York: Alfred Knopf.

Campbell, Scott. 1996. "Green Cities, Growing Cities? Ecology, Economics and the Contradictions of Urban Planning," *Journal of the American Planning Association*, forthcoming.

Dalton, Linda. 1986. "Why the Rational Paradigm Persists: The Resistance of Professional Education and Practice to Alternative Forms of Planning," *Journal of Planning Education and Research* 5 (3), pp. 147–53.

Davidoff, Paul. 1965. "Advocacy and Pluralism in Planning," *Journal of the American Institute of Planners*, Vol. 31, No. 4 (Dec.), pp. 331–8.

Doig, Jameson W. 1987. "Coalition Building by a Regional Agency: Austin Tobin and the Port of New York Authority," in Stone and Sanders, eds, *The Politics of Urban Development*. Lawrence: University of Kansas Press, pp. 73–104.

Fainstein, Susan S. and Scott Campbell. 1996. *Readings in Urban Theory*. Cambridge, Mass.: Blackwell.

Fainstein Susan S. and Norman I. Fainstein. 1971. "City Planning and Political Values," *Urban Affairs Quarterly*, Vol. 6. (March), pp. 341–62.

Faludi, Andreas, ed. 1973. *A Reader in Planning Theory*. New York: Pergamon Press.

Fishman, Robert. 1987. *Bourgeois Utopias: The Rise and Fall of Suburbia*. New York: Basic Books.

Foglesong, Richard E. 1986. *Planning the Capitalist City*. Princeton, N.J.: Princeton University Press.

Forester, John. 1989. *Planning in the Face of Power*. Berkeley, Calif.: University of California Press.

Frieden, Bernard, and Sagalyn, Lynne. 1989. *Downtown Inc. How America Rebuilds Cities*. Cambridge, Mass.: MIT Press.

Friedman, Milton. 1962. *Capitalism and Freedom*. Chicago: University of Chicago Press.

Galbraith, John Kenneth. 1967. *The New Industrial State*. Boston: Houghton Mifflin Co.

Hall, Peter. 1988. *Cities of Tomorrow*. Oxford: Blackwell.

Harvey, David. 1985. *The Urbanization of Capital*. Baltimore: John Hopkins University Press.

Harvey, David 1992. "Social Justice, Postmodernism and the City," *International Journal of Urban and Regional Research* 16 (4) pp. 588–601.

Hayek, Friedrich, 1944. *The Road to Serfdom*. London: Routledge.

Healey, Patsy. 1992. "A Planner's Day: Knowledge and Action in Communicative Practice," *Journal of the American Planning Association* 58 (1) pp. 9–20.

Hoffman, Lily M. 1989. *The Politics of Knowledge: Activist Movements in Medicine and Planning*. Albany, N.Y.: SUNY Press.

Howard, Ebenezer. 1898. *To-morrow: A Peaceful Path to Real Reform*. London: Swan Sonnenschein.

Innes, Judith E. 1994. "Planning Theory's Emerging Paradigm: Communicative Action and Interactive Practice." Unpublished manuscript.

Klosterman, Richard E. 1985. "Arguments for and Against Planning," *Town Planning Review*, Vol. 56, No. 1, pp. 5–20.

Krueckeberg, Donald A. 1983. "The Culture of Planning," in Krueckeberg, ed., *Introduction to Planning History in the United States*. New Brunswick, N.J.: CUPR Press.

Krumholz, Norman, et al. 1982. "A Retrospective View of Equity Planning:

Cleveland, 1969–1979" and "Comments," *Journal of the American Planning Association*, Vol. 48 (Spring), pp. 163–83.

Lindblom, C. E. 1959. "The Science of Muddling Through," *Public Administration Review*, Vol. 19 (Spring), pp. 79–88.

Lowi, Theodore J. 1969. *The End of Liberalism: Ideology, Policy, and the Crisis of Public Authority.* New York: Norton. (Reprinted in 1979 as *The End of Liberalism: The Second Republic of the United States*, 2d ed. New York: Norton.)

Marcuse, Peter. 1976. "Professional Ethics and Beyond: Values in Planning," *Journal of the American Institute of Planning*, Vol. 42 (July), pp. 264–74.

Moore, Terry. 1978. "Why Allow Planners to Do What They Do: A Justification from Economic Theory," *Journal of the American Institute of Planning*, Vol. 44, No. 4 (October), pp. 387–98.

Squires, Gregory D., ed. 1989. *Unequal Partnerships: The Political Economy of Urban Redevelopment in Postwar America.* New Brunswick, N.J.: Rutgers University Press.

Swanstrom, Todd. 1987. "The Limits of Strategic Planning for Cities," *Journal of Urban Affairs*, Vol. 9, No. 2, pp. 139–57.

Wachs, Martin. 1982. "Ethical Dilemmas in Forecasting Public Policy," *Public Administration Review* 29 (Nov./Dec.), pp. 562–7.

Walsh, Annmarie Hauck. 1978. *The Public's Business: The Politics and Practices of Government Corporations.* Cambridge, Mass.: MIT Press.

Part I

Foundations of Twentieth-Century Planning Theory

Introduction

The readings in this first section examine the foundations of modern planning. They offer both traditional and critical views of planning history. We begin with an excerpt from Robert Fishman's examination of three foundational figures in planning history: Ebenezer Howard, Frank Lloyd Wright, and Le Corbusier. Fishman goes beyond the standard account of the three to examine the social history behind their distinctive utopias. Although all three were reacting to the reality of grimy industrial cities, each took a fundamentally different path toward planning his ideal urban society. Corbusier's Radiant City was mass-scaled, dense, vertical, hierarchical – the social extension of modern architecture. Wright went to the other extreme: His Broadacre City was a mixture of Jeffersonian agrarian individualism and prairie sub-urbanism linked by superhighways. Howard's Garden Cities were scaled somewhere in between: Self-contained villages of 35,000 residents held together by a communal cooperative spirit. The three utopias symbolize fundamental choices in the scale of human settlements: Corbusier's mass *Gesellschaft*, Howard's villagelike *Gemeinschaft*, or Wright's American individualism. This excerpt focuses on Howard and Le Corbusier.

To complete the traditional foundation of city planning, we turn to William H. Wilson's analysis of the City Beautiful movement. With its origins in civic improvement, the Columbian Exposition of 1893 in Chicago, and Daniel Burnham's 1909 Chicago Plan, the City Beautiful movement was an important catalyst for the rise of planning commissions, public-private partnerships and civic aesthetic awareness. Yet the City Beautiful movement also became an easy target of criticism: it was elitist if not totalitarian, advocating the beautification of the city surface while ignoring the poverty and inequality inherent in the political and economic structure of the city. Wilson offers a refreshing and balanced view of the movement, recognizing not only these legitimate criticisms but also the enduring merit of its efforts.

Though these various foundations of intellectual planning history might represent distinctly different choices in imagining the ideal city, Jane Jacobs argues that they all suffer from a similar dangerous misconception of how real cities actually operate. She groups these classic planning prototypes together under the label of the "Radiant Garden City Beautiful." She sees in Howard, Burnham, and Le Corbusier a shared wariness that seeks to replace the rich complexity of a real metropolis with the abstract logic of an idealized planned city. We include here the introductory chapter to her landmark 1961 critique of postwar American urban renewal, *The Death and Life of Great American Cities*. This book arguably makes unfortunate oversimplifications about the evils of planning while both neglecting the destructive role of the private sector in urban renewal and romanticizing the capabilities of small, competitive, neighborhood businesses. Yet the book remains one of the most compelling and well-written arguments for encouraging diversity, dynamism, and innovation in big, dense, messy cities. It also signals the long transition of planning theory from an early faith in science and comprehensiveness to a more self-critical, incremental approach.

We conclude this section's readings with Richard Sennett's essay "The Neutral City," from his 1990 book, *The Conscience of the Eye*. Sennett views the development of the city from a distinctly different vantage: He examines how the city has been transformed in parallel with the spiritual transformation of society. The key to this transformation is the rise of neutral space – the urban extension of secularization. Sennett draws parallels to Max Weber's *The Protestant Work Ethic and the Spirit of Capitalism*, seeing this process of neutralization as part of the transformation from Catholicism to Protestantism.

Like Jacobs, Sennett deplores the vanquishing of diversity by modern planning. His vision of the historical American city, however, is bleaker than hers. Rather than celebrating an earlier urban form, he excoriates the grid plan that prevails in most U.S. cities and predates the superblocks that were the objects of Jane Jacobs's wrath. This grid erases the past, neutralizes the land, and denies the environment any inherent value in order to produce the commodification needed for efficient real estate transactions. The skyscraper, rather than reaching for the heavens, then emerges as the vertical expression of this neutral, horizontal grid. More recently, the loss of the city center and its replacement by neutral, bland "nodes" have enforced this neutralization of cities, allowing the American individual to withdraw and dwell in this bland environment.

2

Urban Utopias: Ebenezer Howard and Le Corbusier

Robert Fishman

Introduction

What is the ideal city for the twentieth century, the city that best expresses the power and beauty of modern technology and the most enlightened ideas of social justice? Between 1890 and 1930 three planners, Ebenezer Howard, Frank Lloyd Wright, and Le Corbusier, tried to answer that question. Each began his work alone, devoting long hours to preparing literally hundreds of models and drawings specifying every aspect of the new city, from its general ground plan to the layout of the typical living room. There were detailed plans for factories, office buildings, schools, parks, transportation systems – all innovative designs in themselves and all integrated into a revolutionary restructuring of urban form. The economic and political organization of the city, which could not be easily shown in drawings, was worked out in the voluminous writings that each planner appended to his designs. Finally, each man devoted himself to passionate and unremitting efforts to make his ideal city a reality.

Many people dream of a better world; Howard, Wright, and Le Corbusier each went a step further and planned one. Their social consciences took this rare and remarkable step because they believed that, more than any other goal, their societies needed new kinds of cities. They were deeply fearful of the consequences for civilization if the old cities, with all the social conflicts and miseries they embodied, were allowed to persist. They were also inspired by the prospect that a radical reconstruction of the cities would solve not only the urban crisis of their time but the social crisis as well. The very completeness of their ideal cities expressed their convictions that the moment had come for comprehensive programs, and for a total rethinking of the principles of urban planning. They rejected the possibility of gradual improvement. They did not seek the amelioration of the old cities, but a wholly transformed urban environment.

This transformation meant the extensive rebuilding and even partial abandonment of the cities of their time. Howard, Wright, and Le Corbusier did not shrink from this prospect; they welcomed it. As Howard put it, the old cities had "done their work." They were the best that the old economic and social order could have been expected to produce, but they had to be superseded if mankind were to attain a higher level of civilization. The three ideal cities were put forward to establish the basic theoretical framework for this radical reconstruction. They were the manifestoes for an urban revolution.

These ideal cities are perhaps the most ambitious and complex statements of the belief that reforming the physical environment can revolutionize the total life of a society. Howard, Wright, and Le Corbusier saw design as an active force, distributing the benefits of the Machine Age to all and directing the community onto the paths of social harmony. Yet they never subscribed to the narrow simplicities of the "doctrine of salvation by bricks alone" – the idea that physical facilities could *by themselves* solve social problems. To be sure, they believed – and who can doubt this? – that the values of family life could be better maintained in a house or apartment that gave each member the light and air and room he needed, rather than in the cramped and fetid slums that were still the fate of too many families. They thought that social solidarity would be better promoted in cities that brought people together, rather than in those whose layout segregated the inhabitants by race or class.

At the same time the three planners understood that these and other well-intended designs would be worse than useless if their benevolent humanitarianism merely covered up basic inequalities in the social system. The most magnificent and innovative housing project would fail if its inhabitants were too poor and oppressed to lead decent lives. There was little point in constructing new centers of community life if the economics of exploitation and class conflict kept the citizens as divided as they had been in their old environment. Good planning was indeed efficacious in creating social harmony, but only if it embodied a genuine rationality and justice in the structure of society. It was impossible in a society still immured in what Le Corbusier called "the Age of Greed." The three planners realized that they had to join their programs of urban reconstruction with programs of political and economic reconstruction. They concluded (to paraphrase one of Marx's famous *Theses on Feuerbach*) that designers had hitherto merely *ornamented* the world in various ways; the point was to *change* it.

The ideal cities were therefore accompanied by detailed programs for radical changes in the distribution of wealth and power, changes that Howard, Wright, and Le Corbusier regarded as the necessary complements to their revolutions in design. The planners also played prominent roles in the movements that shared their aims. Howard was an ardent cooperative socialist who utilized planning as part of his search for the cooperative commonwealth; Wright, a Jeffersonian democrat and an admirer of Henry George, was a spokesman for the American decentrist movement; and Le Corbusier had many of his most famous designs published for the first time in the pages of the revolutionary syndicalist journals he edited. All three brought a revolutionary fervor to the practice of urban design.

And, while the old order endured, Howard, Wright, and Le Corbusier refused to adapt themselves to what planning commissions, bankers, politicians, and all the other authorities of their time believed to be desirable and attainable. They consistently rejected the idea that a planner's imagination must work within the system. Instead, they regarded the physical structure of the cities in which they lived, and the economic structure of the society in which they worked, as temporary aberrations that mankind would soon overcome. The three planners looked beyond their own troubled time to a new age each believed was imminent, a new age each labored to define and to build.

Their concerns thus ranged widely over architecture, urbanism, economics, and politics, but their thinking found a focus and an adequate means of expression only in their plans for ideal cities. The cities were never conceived of as blueprints for any actual project. They were "ideal types" of cities for the future, elaborate models rigorously designed to illustrate the general principles that each man advocated. They were convenient and attractive intellectual tools that enabled each planner to bring together his many innovations in design, and to show them as part of a coherent whole, a total redefinition of the idea of the city. The setting of these ideal cities was never any actual location, but an empty, abstract plane where no contingencies existed. The time was the present, not any calendar day or year, but that revolutionary "here and now" when the hopes of the present are finally realized.

These hopes, moreover, were both architectural and social. In the three ideal cities, the transformation of the physical environment is the outward sign of an inner transformation in the social structure. Howard, Wright, and Le Corbusier used their ideal cities to depict a world in which their political and economic goals had already been achieved. Each planner wanted to show that the urban designs he advocated were not only rational and beautiful in themselves but that they embodied the social goals he believed in. In the context of the ideal city each proposal for new housing, new factories, and other structures could be seen to further the broader aims. And in general, the ideal cities enabled the three planners to show modern design in what they believed was its true context – as an integral part of a culture from which poverty and exploitation had disappeared. These cities, therefore, were complete alternative societies, intended as a revolution in politics and economics as well as in architecture. They were utopian visions of a total environment in which man would live in peace with his fellow man and in harmony with nature. They were social thought in three dimensions.

As theorists of urbanism, Howard, Wright, and Le Corbusier attempted to define the ideal form of any industrial society. They shared a common assumption that this form could be both defined and attained, but each viewed the ideal through the perspective of his own social theory, his own national tradition, and his own personality. Their plans, when compared, disagree profoundly, and the divergences are often just as significant as the agreements. They offer us not a single blueprint for the future but three sets of choices – the great metropolis, moderate decentralization, or extreme decentralization – each with its corresponding political and social implications. Like the classical political triad of monarchy – aristocracy – democracy, the three ideal cities represent a vocabulary of basic forms that can be used to define the whole range of choices available to the planner.

Seventeen years older than Wright and thirty-seven years older than Le Corbusier, Ebenezer Howard started first. His life resembles a story by Horatio Alger, except that Alger never conceived a hero at once so ambitious and so self-effacing. He began his career as a stenographer and ended as the elder statesman of a worldwide planning movement, yet he remained throughout his life the embodiment of the "little man." He was wholly without pretension, an earnest man with a round, bald head, spectacles, and a bushy mustache, unselfconscious in his baggy pants and worn jackets, beloved by neighbors and children.

Yet Howard, like the inventors, enlighteners, self-taught theorists, and self-proclaimed prophets of the "age of improvement" in which he lived, was one of those little men with munificent hopes. His contribution was "the Garden City," a plan for moderate decentralization and cooperative socialism. He wanted to build wholly new cities in the midst of unspoiled countryside on land that would remain the property of the community as a whole. Limited in size to 30,000 inhabitants and surrounded by a perpetual "greenbelt," the Garden City would be compact, efficient, healthful, and beautiful. It would lure people away from swollen cities like London and their dangerous concentrations of wealth and power; at the same time, the countryside would be dotted with hundreds of new communities where small-scale cooperation and direct democracy could flourish.

Howard never met either Frank Lloyd Wright or Le Corbusier. One suspects those two architects of genius and forceful personalities would have considered themselves worlds apart from the modest stenographer. Yet it is notable that Wright and Le Corbusier, like Howard, began their work in urban planning as outsiders, learning their profession not in architectural schools but through apprenticeships with older architects and through their own studies. This self-education was the source of their initiation into both urban design and social theory, and it continued even after Wright and Le Corbusier had become masters of their own profession. Their interests and readings flowed naturally from architecture and design to city planning, economics, politics, and the widest questions of social thought. No one ever told them they could not know everything.

Frank Lloyd Wright stands between Howard and Le Corbusier, at least in age. If Howard's dominant value was cooperation, Wright's was individualism. And no one can deny that he practiced what he preached. With the handsome profile and proud bearing of a frontier patriarch, carefully brushed long hair, well-tailored suits, and flowing cape, Wright was his own special creation. His character was an inextricable mix of arrogance and honesty, vanity and genius. He was autocratic, impolitic, and spendthrift; yet he maintained a magnificent faith in his own ideal of "organic" architecture.

Wright wanted the whole United States to become a nation of individuals. His planned city, which he called "Broadacres," took decentralization beyond the small community (Howard's ideal) to the individual family home. In Broadacres all cities larger than a county seat have disappeared. The center of society has moved to the thousands of homesteads that cover the countryside. Everyone has the right to as much land as he can use, a minimum of an acre per person. Most people work part-time on their farms and part-time in the small factories, offices, or shops that are nestled among the farms. A network of superhighways joins together the scattered elements of society. Wright believed that individuality must be founded on individual ownership. Decentralization would make it possible for everyone to live his chosen lifestyle on his own land.

Le Corbusier, our third planner, could claim with perhaps even more justification than Wright to be his own creation. He was born Charles-Édouard Jeanneret and grew up in the Swiss city of La Chaux-de-Fonds, where he was apprenticed to be a watchcase engraver. He was saved from that dying trade by a sympathetic teacher and by his own determination. Settling in Paris in 1916, he won for himself a place at the head of the avant-garde, first with his painting, then with his brilliant architectural criticism, and most profoundly with his own contributions to architecture. The Swiss artisan Jeanneret no longer existed. He had recreated himself as "Le Corbusier," the Parisian leader of the revolution in modern architecture.

Like other "men from the provinces" who settled in Paris, Le Corbusier identified himself completely with the capital and its values. Wright had hoped that decentralization would preserve the social value he prized most highly – individuality. Le Corbusier placed a corresponding faith in organization, and he foresaw a very different fate for modern society. For him, industrialization meant great cities where large bureaucracies could coordinate production. Whereas Wright thought that existing cities were at least a hundred times too dense, Le Corbusier thought they were not dense enough. He proposed that large tracts in the center of Paris and other major cities be leveled. In place of the old buildings, geometrically arrayed skyscrapers of glass and steel would rise out of parks, gardens, and superhighways. These towers would be the command posts for their region. They would house a technocratic elite of planners, engineers, and intellectuals who would bring beauty and prosperity to the whole society. In his first version of the ideal city, Le Corbusier had the elite live in luxurious high-rise apartments close to the center; their subordinates were relegated to satellite cities at the outskirts. (In a later version everyone was to live in the high-rises.) Le Corbusier called his plan " 'the Radiant City,' a city worthy of our time."

The plans of Howard, Wright and Le Corbusier can be summarized briefly, but the energy and resources necessary to carry them out can hardly be conceived. One might expect that the three ideal cities were destined to remain on paper. Yet as we shall see, their proposals have already reshaped many of the cities we now live in and may prove to be even more influential in the future.

The plans were effective because they spoke directly to hopes and fears that were widely shared. In particular, they reflected (1) the pervasive fear of and revulsion from the nineteenth-century metropolis; (2) the sense that modern technology had made possible exciting new urban forms; and (3) the great expectation that a revolutionary age of brotherhood and freedom was at hand.

Caught in our own urban crisis, we tend to romanticize the teeming cities of the turn of the century. To many of their inhabitants, however, they were frightening and unnatural phenomena. Their unprecedented size and vast, uprooted populations seemed to suggest the uncontrollable forces unleashed by the Industrial Revolution, and the chaos that occupied the center of modern life. Joseph Conrad eloquently expressed this feeling when he confessed to being haunted by the vision of a "monstrous town more populous than some continents and in its man-made might as if indifferent to heaven's frowns and smiles; a cruel devourer of the world's light. There was room enough there to place any story, depth enough there for any passion, variety enough for any setting, darkness enough to bury five millions of lives."[1]

The monstrous proportions of the big city were relatively new, and thus all the more unsettling. In the first half of the nineteenth century the great European cities had overflowed their historic walls and fortifications. (The American cities, of course, never knew such limits.) Now boundless, the great cities expanded into the surrounding countryside with reckless speed, losing the coherent structure of a healthy organism. London grew in the nineteenth century from 900,000 to 4.5 million inhabitants; Paris in the same period quintupled its population, from 500,000 to 2.5 million residents. Berlin went from 190,000 to over 2 million, New York from 60,000 to 3.4 million. Chicago, a village in 1840, reached 1.7 million by the turn of the century.[2]

This explosive growth, which would have been difficult to accommodate under any circumstances, took place in an era of laissez-faire and feverish speculation. The cities lost the power to control their own growth. Instead, speculation – the blind force of chance and profit – determined urban structure. The cities were segregated by class, their traditional unifying centers first overwhelmed by the increase in population and then abandoned. Toward the end of the nineteenth century the residential balance between urban and rural areas began tipping, in an unprecedented degree, towards the great cities. When Howard, Wright, and Le Corbusier began their work, they saw around them stagnation in the countryside, the depopulation of rural villages, and a crisis in even the old regional centers. First trade and then the most skilled and ambitious young people moved to the metropolis.

Some of these newcomers found the good life they had been seeking in attractive new middle-class neighborhoods, but most were caught in the endless rows of tenements that stretched for miles, interrupted only by factories or railroad yards. Whole families were crowded into one or two airless rooms fronting on narrow streets or filthy courtyards where sunlight never penetrated. In Berlin in 1900, for example, almost 50 percent of all families lived in tenement dwellings with only one small room and an even smaller kitchen. Most of the rest lived in apartments with two tiny rooms and a kitchen, but to pay their rent some of these had to take in boarders who slept in the corners.[3] "Look at the cities of the nineteenth century," wrote Le Corbusier, "at the vast stretches covered with the crust of houses without heart and furrowed with streets without soul. Look, judge. These are the signs of a tragic denaturalization of human labor."[4]

Howard, Wright, and Le Corbusier hated the cities of their time with an overwhelming passion. The metropolis was the counterimage of their ideal cities, the hell that inspired their heavens. They saw precious resources, material and human, squandered in the urban disorder. They were especially fearful that the metropolis would attract and then consume all the healthful forces in society. All three visualized the great city as a cancer, an uncontrolled, malignant growth that was poisoning the modern world. Wright remarked that the plan of a large city resembled "the cross-section of a fibrous tumor"; Howard compared it to an enlarged ulcer. Le Corbusier was fond of picturing Paris as a body in the last stages of a fatal disease – its circulation clogged, its tissues dying of their own noxious wastes.

The three planners, moreover, used their insight into technology to go beyond a merely negative critique of the nineteenth-century metropolis. They showed how modern techniques of construction had created a new mastery of space from which innovative urban forms could be built. The great city, they argued, was no longer modern. Its chaotic concentration was not only inefficient and inhumane, it was unnecessary as well.

Howard, Wright, and Le Corbusier based their ideas on the technological innovations that inspired their age: the express train, the automobile, the telephone and radio, and the skyscraper. Howard realized that the railroad system that had contributed to the growth of the great cities could serve the planned decentralization of society equally well. Wright understood that the personal automobile and an elaborate network of roads could create the conditions for an even more radical decentralization. Le Corbusier looked to technology to promote an opposite trend. He made use of the skyscraper as a kind of vertical street, a "street in the air" as he called it, which would permit intensive urban densities while eliminating the "soulless streets" of the old city.

The three planners' fascination with technology was deep but highly selective. They acknowledged only what served their own social values. Modern technology, they believed, had outstripped the antiquated social order, and the result was chaos and strife. In their ideal cities, however, technology would fulfill its proper role. Howard, Wright, and Le Corbusier believed that industrial society was inherently harmonious. It had an inherent structure, an ideal form, which, when achieved, would banish conflict and bring order and freedom, prosperity and beauty.

This belief went far beyond what could be deduced from the order and power of technology itself. It reflected instead the revolutionary hopes of the nineteenth century. For the three planners, as for so many of their contemporaries, the conflicts of the early Industrial Revolution were only a time of troubles that would lead inevitably to the new era of harmony. History for them was still the history of progress; indeed, as Howard put it, there was a "grand purpose behind nature." These great expectations, so difficult for us to comprehend, pervaded nineteenth-century radical and even liberal thought. There were many prophets of progress who contributed to creating the optimistic climate of opinion in which Howard, Wright, and Le Corbusier formed their own beliefs. Perhaps the most relevant for our purposes were the "utopian socialists" of the early nineteenth century.

These reformers, most notably Charles Fourier, Robert Owen, and Henri de Saint-Simon, drew upon the tradition of Thomas More's *Utopia* and Plato's *Republic* to create detailed depictions of communities untainted by the class struggles of the Industrial Revolution. Unlike More or Plato, however, the utopian socialists looked forward to the immediate realization of their ideal commonwealths. Owen and Fourier produced detailed plans for building utopian communities, plans for social and architectural revolution that anticipated some of the work of Howard, Wright, and Le Corbusier. Two themes dominated utopian socialist planning: first, a desire to overcome the distinction between city and country; and second, a desire to overcome the physical isolation of individuals and families by grouping the community into one large "family" structure. Most of the designs envisioned not ideal cities but ideal communes, small rural establishments for less than two thousand people. Owen put forward a plan for brick quadrangles, which he called "moral quadrilaterals." One side was a model factory, while the other three were taken up with a communal dining room, meeting rooms for recreation, and apartments.[5] His French rival Fourier advanced a far more elaborate design for a communal palace or "phalanstery," which boasted theaters, fashionable promenades, gardens, and gourmet cuisine for everyone.[6]

The utopian socialists were largely forgotten by the time Howard, Wright, and Le Corbusier began their own work, so there was little direct influence from them. As we shall see, however, the search of each planner for a city whose design expressed the ideals of cooperation and social justice led him to revive many of the themes of his utopian socialist (and even earlier) predecessors. But one crucial element sharply separates the three planners' designs from all previous efforts. Even the most fantastic inventions of an Owen or a Fourier could not anticipate the new forms that twentieth-century technology would bring to urban design. The utopian socialists' prophecies of the future had to be expressed in the traditional architectural vocabulary. Fourier, for example, housed his cooperative community in a "phalanstery" that looked like the château of Versailles. Howard, Wright, and Le Corbusier were able to incorporate the scale and pace of the modern world into their designs. They worked at the dawn of the twentieth-century industrial era, but before the coming of twentieth-century disillusionment. Their imaginations were wholly modern; yet the coming era of cooperation was as real to them as it had been for Robert Owen. Their ideal cities thus stand at the intersection of nineteenth-century hopes and twentieth-century technology.

The three ideal cities, therefore, possessed a unique scope and fervor, but this uniqueness had its dangers. It effectively isolated the three planners from almost all the social movements and institutions of their time. In particular, it separated them from the members of two groups who might have been their natural allies, the Marxian socialists and the professional planners. The three ideal cities were at once too technical for the Marxists and too revolutionary for the growing corps of professional planners. The latter was especially intent on discouraging any suggestion that urban planning might serve the cause of social change. These architect-administrators confined themselves to "technical" problems, which meant, in practice, serving the needs of society – as society's rulers defined them. Baron Haussmann, that model of an administrative planner, had ignored and sometimes worsened the plight of the poor in his massive reconstructions of Paris undertaken for Louis Napoleon. But the plight of the poor was not his administrative responsibility. He wanted to unite the isolated sectors of the city and thus quicken the pace of commerce. The wide avenues he cut through Paris were also designed to contribute to the prestige of the regime and, if necessary, to serve as efficient conduits for troops to put down urban disorders. Haussmann's physically impressive and socially reactionary plans inspired worldwide imitation and further increased the gap between urban design and social purpose.[7]

Even the middle-class reformers who specifically dedicated themselves to housing and urban improvement were unable to close this gap. Men like Sir Edwin Chadwick in London bravely faced official indifference and corruption to bring clean air, adequate sanitation, and minimal standards of housing to the industrial cities. Yet these philanthropists were also deeply conservative in their social beliefs. Their rare attempts at innovation almost always assumed the continued poverty of the poor and the privileges of the rich. The model tenements, "cheap cottages," and factory towns that were commissioned in the second half of the nineteenth century were filled with good intentions and sound planning, but they never failed to reflect the inequities of the society that built them. When, for example, the English housing reformer Octavia Hill built her model tenements, she kept accommodations to a minimum so that her indigent tenants could pay rents sufficient not only to cover the complete cost of construction but also to yield her wealthy backers 5 percent annual interest on the money they had advanced her.[8] (This kind of charitable enterprise was known as "philanthropy at 5 percent.") Not surprisingly, designs put forward under these conditions were almost as bleak as the slums they replaced.

Howard, Wright, and Le Corbusier were not interested in making existing cities more profitable or in building "model" tenements to replace the old ones. These views might have been expected to have attracted the sympathetic attention of the Marxian socialists who then controlled the most powerful European movements for social change. Indeed, the *Communist Manifesto* had already recognized the necessity for radical structural change in the industrial cities by putting the "gradual abolition of the distinction between town and country" among its demands. Nevertheless, the socialist movement in the second half of the nineteenth century turned away from what its leaders regarded as unprofitable speculation. In an important series of articles collected under the title *The Housing Question* (1872), Friedrich Engels maintained that urban design was part of the "superstructure" of capitalist society and would necessarily reflect that society's inhumanities, at least until after the socialist revolution had succeeded in transforming the economic base. He concluded that any attempt to envision an ideal city without waiting for the revolution was futile and, indeed, that any attempt to improve the cities significantly was doomed so long as capitalism endured. The working class must forget attractive visions of the future and concentrate on immediate revolution, after which the dictatorship of the proletariat would redistribute housing in the old industrial cities according to need. Then and only then could planners begin to think about a better kind of city.[9]

Howard, Wright, and Le Corbusier could therefore look neither to the socialists nor to the professional planners for support. Initially, at least, they were forced back upon themselves. Instead of developing their ideas through collaboration with others and through practical experience, they worked in isolation on more and more elaborate models of their basic ideas. Their ideal cities thus acquired a wealth of brilliant detail and a single-minded theoretical rigor that made them unique. This isolation was no doubt the necessary precondition for the three planners' highly individual styles of social thought. Certainly their mercurial and independent careers showed a very different pattern from the solid institutional connections of, for example, Ludwig Mies van der Rohe or Walter Gropius. Mies, Gropius, and the other Bauhaus architects were also deeply concerned with the question of design and society; yet none of them produced an ideal city. They had more practical but also more limited projects to occupy them.[10] The ideal city is the genre of the outsider who travels at one leap from complete powerlessness to imaginary omnipotence.

This isolation encouraged Howard, Wright, and Le Corbusier to extend their intellectual and imaginative capacities to their limits, but it also burdened their plans with almost insurmountable problems of both thought and action. They had created plans that were works of art, but the city, in Claude Lévi-Strauss's phrase, is a *"social* work of art." Its densely interwoven structure is the product of thousands of minds and thousands of individual decisions. Its variety derives from the unexpected juxtapositions and the unpredictable interactions. How can a single individual, even a man of genius, hope to comprehend this structure? And how can he devise a new plan with the same satisfying complexities? For his design, whatever its logic and merits, is necessarily his alone. In imposing a single point of view, he inevitably simplifies the parts that make up the whole. Howard, Wright, and Le Corbusier each filled his ideal city with *his* buildings; *his* sense of proportion and color; and, most profoundly, *his* social values. Would there ever be room for anyone else? The three ideal cities raise what is perhaps the most perplexing question for any planner: in attempting to create a new urban order, must he repress precisely that complexity, diversity, and individuality that are the city's highest achievements?

The problem of action was equally obvious and pressing. Deprived of outside support, the three planners came to believe that their ideas were inherently powerful. As technical solutions to urban problems and embodiments of justice and beauty, the three ideal cities could properly claim everyone's support. By holding up a ready-made plan for a new order, Howard, Wright, and Le Corbusier hoped to create their own movements. This strategy, however, led directly to the classic utopian dilemma. To appeal to everyone on the basis of universal principles is to appeal to no one in particular. The more glorious the plans are in theory, the more remote they are from the concrete issues that actually motivate action. With each elaboration and clarification, the ideal cities move closer to pure fantasy. Can imagination alone change the world? Or, as Friedrich Engels phrased the question: How can the isolated individual hope to *impose his idea* on history?

These two related problems of thought and action confronted Howard, Wright, and Le Corbusier throughout their careers; yet they never doubted that ultimately they could solve both. Each believed that if a planner based his work on the structure inherent in industrial society and on the deepest values of his culture, there could be no real conflict between his plan and individual liberty. Patiently, each searched for that harmonious balance between control and freedom: the order that does not repress but liberates the individual.

With equal determination, they sought a valid strategy for action. Their ideal cities, they knew, could never be constructed all at once. But at least a "working model" could be begun, even in the midst of the old society. This model would demonstrate both the superiority of their architectural principles and also serve as a symbol of the new society about to be born. Its success would inspire emulation. A movement of reconstruction would take on momentum and become a revolutionary force in itself. Rebuilding the cities could thus become, in a metaphor all three favored, the "Master Key" that would unlock the way to a just society.

The three planners, therefore, looked to the new century with confidence and hope. Against the overwhelming power of the great cities and the old order that built them, Howard, Wright, and Le Corbusier advanced their designs for planned growth, for the reassertion of the common interest and higher values, for a healthy balance between man's creation and the natural environment. It would seem to be an uneven contest. Nevertheless, the three planners still believed that an individual and his imagination could change history. The revolution they were seeking was precisely an assertion of human rationality over vast impersonal forces. They resolved that in the coming era of reconciliation and construction, the man of imagination must play a crucial role. He would embody the values of his society in a workable plan and thus direct social change with his prophetic leadership. For Howard, Wright, and Le Corbusier, this next revolution would finally bring imagination to power. "What gives our dreams their daring," Le Corbusier proclaimed, "is that they can be achieved."[11]

Ebenezer Howard

The ideal city made practicable

> Town and country *must be married*, and out of this joyous union will spring a new hope, a new life, a new civilization.
> Ebenezer Howard (1898)

Of the three planners discussed here, Ebenezer Howard is the least known and the most influential. His *To-morrow: a Peaceful Path to Real Reform* (1898, now known under the title of the 1902 edition, *Garden Cities of To-Morrow*) has, as Lewis Mumford acknowledged, "done more than any other single book to guide the modern town planning movement and to alter its objectives."[12] And Howard was more than a theoretician. He and his supporters founded two English cities, Letchworth (1903) and Welwyn (1920), which still serve as models for his ideas. More important, he was able to organize a city planning movement that continues to keep his theories alive. The postwar program of New Towns in Great Britain, perhaps the most ambitious of all attempts at national planning, was inspired by his works and planned by his followers.

In the United States the "Greenbelt Cities" undertaken by the Resettlement Administration in the 1930s owed their form to the example of the Garden City. The best recent example of an American New Town is Columbia, Maryland, built in the 1960s as a wholly independent community with houses and industry. In 1969 the National Committee on Urban Growth Policy urged that the United States undertake to build 110 New Towns to accommodate 20 million citizens.[13] The following year, Congress created a New Town Corporation in the Department of Housing and Urban Development to begin this vast task.[14] So far, sixteen American New Towns have either been planned or are under construction. The most fruitful period of Ebenezer Howard's influence is perhaps only beginning.

If Howard's achievements continue to grow in importance, Howard the man remains virtually unknown. The present-day New Town planners are perhaps a little embarrassed by him. They are highly skilled professional bureaucrats or architects; Howard's formal education ended at fourteen, and he had no special training in architecture or urban design. The modern planners are self-proclaimed "technicians" who have attempted to adapt the New Town concept to any established social order. Howard was, in his quiet way, a revolutionary who originally conceived the Garden City as a means of superseding capitalism and creating a civilization based on cooperation. Howard's successors have neglected this aspect of his thought, and without it the founder of the Garden City movement becomes an elusive figure indeed. He shrank from the personal publicity that Frank Lloyd Wright and Le Corbusier so eagerly and skillfully sought. Throughout his life he maintained the habits and the appearance of a minor clerk. He once said that he enjoyed his chosen profession, stenography, because it enabled him to be an almost invisible observer at the notable events he recorded. Even at the meetings of the association he headed, he preferred to sit in an inconspicuous position behind the podium, where he could take down the exact words of the other speakers. Frederic J. Osborn, one of his closest associates, remembered him as "the sort of man who could easily pass unnoticed in a crowd."[15] He was, Osborn added, "the mildest and most unassuming of men . . . universally liked, and notably by children."[16]

Nonetheless, Howard succeeded where more charismatic figures failed. In 1898 he had to borrow fifty pounds to print *To-morrow* at his own expense. Five years later his supporters were advancing more than £100,000 to begin the construction of the first Garden City. The rapidity of this turn of events surprised Howard and is still difficult to explain. The root of the mystery is Howard himself. He had reached middle age before beginning his work on city planning and had never given any indication that he was capable of originality or leadership. His book, however, was a remarkable intellectual achievement. He concisely and rigorously outlined a new direction for the development of cities and advanced practical solutions that covered the whole range of city planning problems: land use, design, transportation, housing, and finance. At the same time, he incorporated these ideas into a large synthesis: a plan for a complete alternative society and a program for attaining it.

Howard, moreover, proved to be a surprisingly effective organizer. He was an indefatigable worker who bent with slavelike devotion to the task of promoting his own ideas. At cooperative societies, Labour Churches, settlement houses, temperance unions, debating clubs – at any group that would pay his railroad fares and provide a night's hospitality – he preached the "Gospel of the Garden City" under the title "The Ideal City Made Practicable, A Lecture Illustrated with Lantern Slides." He possessed a powerful speaking voice, and, more important, he was able to communicate an overwhelming sense of earnestness, an absolute conviction that he had discovered "the peaceful path to real reform."

Mankind, he proclaimed, was moving inevitably toward a new era of brotherhood, and the Garden City would be the only fitting environment for the humanity of the future. His original supporters were not planners or architects but social reformers whose own dreams he promised would be realized in the Garden City. Patiently, he assembled a broad coalition of backers ranging from "Back to the Land" agrarians to George Bernard Shaw. Working constantly himself, he felt free to draw upon the resources and talents of others. He thus made his ideas the basis of a movement that, fifty years after his death, continues to grow. As one of Shaw's characters in *Major Barbara* observes, absolute unselfishness is capable of anything.

Inventing the Garden City

Howard never called himself a planner. His activities can be described in many words – theorist, organizer, publicist, city founder – and yet he always preferred to describe himself as an inventor. He was, he proudly proclaimed, the "inventor of the Garden City idea." The term is both appropriate and significant. In an image dear to the nineteenth century, Howard saw himself as one of those dreamers and backyard tinkerers who emerge from obscurity with one great idea, brave neglect and ridicule from the "practical" world, and finally see the skeptics confounded and the invention become an integral part of a better world. Howard in his moments of triumph was fond of comparing himself with George Stephenson, the self-taught engineer who built the first practical locomotive. The Garden City, he hoped, would be an equally significant innovation, revolutionary in itself and, like the early locomotive, capable of great improvement. It would be an engine of progress with the ability to unlock social energy and move society towards beneficent ends which even its inventor could not foresee.

The term "inventor" had one other meaning for him. As a devoted admirer of the great inventors and an occasional practitioner himself, he knew that the most important inventions were rarely the most original. They were, rather, uniquely serviceable applications of ideas that were already well known. This was precisely what Howard claimed for his innovation. In language borrowed from patent office applications he described the Garden City as a "unique combination of Proposals" that were already before the public. Howard was being truthful as well as modest. One can easily demonstrate that almost every aspect of the Garden City was borrowed from other schemes that were in existence at the time Howard began his work, some for the decentralization of cities, some for the democratization of wealth and power. This, however, would be to miss the point of Howard's achievement, for he alone saw the connection between the diverse ideas that went into his plan. With the ingenuity and patience of an inventor putting together a useful new machine out of parts forged for other purposes, Howard created a coherent design for a new environment and a new society.

Howard was able to assemble the disparate elements of the Garden City so successfully because he had a firm set of unquestioned beliefs that guided his actions. Unlike Wright and Le Corbusier, who were always emphasizing their own uniqueness, Howard was a remarkably typical product of his milieu. This prophet of decentralization was born in the center of London in 1850; his parents ran a small shop in the city. He left school at fourteen to become a junior clerk in a stockbroker's office. To better his prospects he taught himself the new Pitman system of short-hand and set up shop on his own.[17] He thus raised himself from the bottom of the hierarchy of clerkdom and joined that group of "little men" – petty entrepreneurs, commission salesmen, shopkeepers – who strug-gled to maintain a proud independence in the era before large organizations absorbed the white-collar class.

This success, however, never satisfied him. For Howard was touched by the great expectations of the nineteenth century. He wanted to contribute to the "unexampled rate of progress and invention" that he believed characterized his times. He started to tinker with gadgets: a keyless watch, a breech-loading gun, a typewriter that automatically allotted to each letter the space it occupied in print typography.[18] These projects, never successful, absorbed his attention and his ready cash. In his most unusual attempt to make his fortune he emigrated briefly to the United States, where a year spent as a homesteader in Nebraska convinced him of the virtues of stenography. He returned to London in 1876.[19]

After this episode his ambitions took a less material turn. While strug-gling to build up his stenography practice, he grew preoccupied with what was then called "the Social Question" – the origins and causes of all the poverty that daily surrounded him. Perhaps his own failure and temporary poverty in the United States had awakened his sympathy for the poor in his own country. The principles of moral duty he had learned in Sunday school and his own innate kindliness surely also played their part. In any case, he soon joined a series of reading and discussion groups with names like the "Zetetical Society." For him and the other members, these groups represented an opportunity to educate themselves in the great political and economic questions of the day. Together they taught themselves John Stuart Mill on political economy, Herbert Spencer on social science, Darwin and Huxley on evolution. There he met high-minded men and women with concerns similar to his own and was initiated into the world of middle-class London radicalism.

These genteel revolutionaries have rarely been appreciated or even understood in our time. They were amateurs and idealists in a field that has come to be dominated by professionals and politicians. Their plans for reconstructing society survive only in the pages of old pamphlets with titles in ornate type: *Brotherhood, Cooperation.* Photographs in these pamphlets show us their faces, which have no elegance and little humor but much hope and integrity; the men are in stiff white collars, the women in severely buttoned dresses. Under each picture is an identifying caption: "Secretary, Temperance Union and Cooperative Society" or "Spiritualist and Social Reformer." The Radicals had more than their share of cranks, but their movement was the home of much that was most humane in nineteenth-century British society, as well as the source of much that would prove most fruitful for the twentieth century. When Howard designed the Garden City in the 1890s, he followed unhesitatingly the social ideals he had learned as an obscure Radical of the 1870s and 1880s.

The Radicals believed that Victorian England was not the best of all possible worlds; that the economic life of the nation was corrupt, inhumane, inefficient, and immoral; and that political power, despite the appearance of democracy, was unjustly concentrated in the hands of a few. This concentration, they feared, would ruin the nation if allowed to continue. In the countryside the near-monopoly of landholding by large owners was bankrupting agriculture. Farm workers, deprived of any hope of owning their own land, were fleeing the land and swelling the urban slums. There they were easily exploited by "sweating" employers, whose sharp practices and monopolistic tactics were driving the honest "little person" out of business. If these trends were to continue, the result would be a society polarized between capital and labor. The Radicals were not Marxists, so they saw in this last prospect only violent conflict that would destroy both sides.

Their remedies for this dismal situation were democracy and cooperation. They wanted first to break the power of the landed gentry who controlled Parliament and to institute a thoroughgoing land reform. This would draw farm workers back from the slums and create a new class of yeoman smallholders, prosperous and independent. For the urban industrialized areas, the Radicals called for cooperation to replace large-scale capitalism. Profit sharing in production would gradually erase the distinction between worker and employer, thus ending class conflict. At the same time, cooperative stores would end profiteering and wasteful anarchy in distribution.

The Radicals devoutly believed in progress, and they held that humankind was evolving toward a higher stage of social organization – the cooperative commonwealth – in which brotherhood would become the basis of daily life. But while they were sure that humankind was capable of creating this better world, they had no definite strategy for achieving their goal. They rejected what were to be the two great engines of social change, government intervention and the labor movement. They rejected big government as a dangerous concentration of power, even if it were on their side. For the Radicals, independence and voluntary action were both means and ends. Nor did they support organizing the working class. As we have seen, they regarded class struggle as one of the evils of modern society.

Without a plan of action, the Radical movement alternated between long periods of discussion and short bursts of activity when the true path seemed to be found. One such burst accompanied the arrival in London in 1884 of Henry George, the American reformer whose proposal for a "single tax" of 100 percent of all rental income would, in effect, accomplish the Radical program of land reform at a stroke. George's ideas left their imprint on the Radical movement in general and, as we shall see, on Howard in particular, but they failed to win over the British electorate, and the enthusiasm subsided. Sometimes individuals or small groups would abandon their homes and businesses to form utopian colonies like Topolobampo in Mexico. There they hoped to create a "working model" of true cooperation to win over a skeptical world.

More frequently, the Radicals allowed themselves to hope that their small-scale cooperative enterprises might, through voluntary action alone, supplant their profit-making competitors. If the Trusts had grown great on the force of selfishness, why should not brotherhood prove even more powerful? Cooperative socialism could then prevail without any legislation. A good example of these hopes – and illusions – was a scheme propounded by two friends of Howard's, J. Bruce Wallace and the Reverend Bruce Campbell, to bring cooperative workshops and stores to the slum dwellers of London's East End. At the beginning of 1894 the co-ops, aptly named the Brotherhood Trust, had enrolled over one hundred customers. "Suppose," Wallace urged his supporters on February 1, 1894, "suppose one fresh customer gained monthly for every old customer." After some rapid calculations he was able to announce that by February 1, 1896, they would have over one hundred million enrolled. "In the third year the trade of the whole world would be in the hands of the Trust, for fraternal purposes."[20]

Wallace was quick to add: "I am not so sanguine as to believe that our little movement will actually spread with such rapidity."[21] Nevertheless, it was a revealing fantasy, the dream of a "little man" that his modest enterprise might one day change the world – without coercion. Slightly transposed, it was the same as an inventor's dream of worldwide success by virtue of having created a superior product. As we shall see, Howard's conception of the Garden City as "the peaceful path to real reform" combined elements of both dreams.

Throughout the 1880s, Howard continued to absorb both the principles and the problems of the Radical movement. He remained a follower, emerging from anonymity only once to deliver a speech on spiritualism at the Zetetical Society. His cogitations on interplanetary ether waves as the possible physical basis of spiritualist communication gave no hint of his coming concerns.[22] His period of quiescence ended suddenly, however, in 1888 with a single event that made him an activist for the rest of his life: he read Edward Bellamy's *Looking Backward*. Published in Boston in 1888, *Looking Backward* had won immediate popularity in the United States and exercised a profound influence over such men as Thorstein Veblen and John Dewey.[23] Written against the background of the industrial depression and growing labor unrest that engulfed both America and Europe in the third quarter of the nineteenth century, the book presented a graphic depiction of a society in which these problems had been overcome. The hero of the novel is a prosperous Bostonian who has the good fortune to sleep soundly from 1887 to 2000 and wake in a society organized on moral principles. Industry has been efficiently grouped into one government-owned cooperative Trust. Distribution has also been concentrated into one great Department Store, whose branches in every city and village sell everything the nation has produced. Competition has been replaced by centralized planning; poverty and unemployment are unknown; all citizens between twenty-one and forty-five occupy ranks in the "industrial army," and everyone receives an equal salary.

Although Bellamy's novel was only one of the genre of "utopian romances" that seemed as ubiquitous in their time as murder mysteries are in ours, it was by far the most effective in its critique of industrial capitalism and its imaginative demonstration that a better alternative could exist. *Looking Backward* was sent to Howard by an American friend. He read it at one sitting and was "fairly carried away." The next morning, as he later wrote

I went into some of the crowded parts of London, and as I passed through the narrow dark streets, saw the wretched dwellings in which the majority of the people lived, observed on every hand the manifestations of a self-seeking order of society and reflected on the absolute unsoundness of our economic system, there came to me an overpowering sense of the temporary nature of all I saw, and of its entire unsuitability for the working life of the new order – the order of justice, unity and friendliness.[24]

Howard was sufficiently enthusiastic to believe that many others would share his revelation. He was especially impressed with Bellamy's use of an imaginative portrayal of an alternative to demonstrate the "absolute unsoundness and quite transitory nature" of existing society. In the absence of any other viable movement for change, Bellamy's vision of a better future could become the standard around which men of goodwill would unite. Howard claimed that he was responsible for persuading an English firm to publish *Looking Backward* in London in 1889.[25] In imitation of the Bellamy Clubs then forming in the United States, Howard soon began meeting with small groups to discuss Bellamy's ideas. In 1890 he participated in the formation of the

English Nationalization of Labour Society, the counterpart of Bellamy's Nationalization Party in the United States.[26]

As *Looking Backward* won an enthusiastic readership in English Radical circles, Howard allowed himself the belief that the Nationalization movement was the plan for action the Radicals had been seeking. Even at the time of his greatest hope, however, he could not believe that the movement would have the power to take over the industry of Great Britain very soon. "This perception, naturally, led me to put forward proposals for testing Mr. Bellamy's principles, though on a much smaller scale."[27] Howard began to devise a model community of a few thousand people in which – as in *Looking Backward* – everyone would be employed by the community, whose directors would run every enterprise. If successful, this project would prove the efficacy of Bellamy's ideas to those who would not be moved by purely literary arguments, and thus speed the day when nationalization could occur on a national scale.

Characteristically, Howard's maiden attempt at planning was not an attempt to advance his own ideas but to adapt those of another. Nonetheless, as Howard began to work on the scheme, he came to realize that Bellamy's novelistic gifts had blinded him to the differences between his own goals and those advanced in *Looking Backward*. For Howard shared the Radical mistrust of all concentrations of power, whereas Bellamy made centralization the key to his reforms. Howard saw more clearly than many other readers that behind Bellamy's faith in control from above there was a strong authoritarian bias. Bellamy proudly compared his "industrial army" to the Prussian army. As for its leaders, he spoke grandly and vaguely of a small corps of managers who could plan the economy of the United States or any other nation in the year 2000. In his system, he claimed, the management of all American industry would be "so simple, and depending on principles so obvious and easily applied, that the functionaries at Washington to whom it is trusted require to be nothing more than men of fair ability."[28] Although Bellamy was realistic about the likely intelligence of the bureaucrats of the future, he had unlimited faith in their efficacy, a faith that Howard could not share. Bellamy had seized upon all the forces of concentration and centralization in late-nineteenth-century society and saw in them the possibility for a more humane order. Not only did Howard doubt the practicality of extreme centralization, but he also denied its desirability even if it could work.

Howard continued to work out the plan of a model community; now, however, it was designed to put forward and test his own ideas. The Garden City was not the simple result of Bellamy's influence on Howard. Rather, it grew out of Howard's attempt to correct Bellamy's authoritarian bias and to devise a community in which social order and individual initiative would be properly balanced.

He began with Bellamy's plan for "nationalization," the concept that the entire productive capacity of a nation could be managed as it if were one huge Trust, and all its stores and shops controlled as if they were branches of one great Department Store. In thinking about his own model community, Howard was particularly aware of the problems connected with farming. His own failure as a farmer had sufficiently sensitized him to the difficulties in that area, and he doubted that even a small community could successfully manage all its farms. He had, moreover, followed the decline of the Radical utopian colony in Mexico, Topolobampo, whose directors had controlled all productive activity. Their attempts at management had merely focused all the dissatisfactions of the colony on themselves and destroyed the experiment. Howard proposed, therefore, what would become the policy of the Garden City: that the community include both privately and collectively owned enterprise and leave to the citizens the choice of how they wished to work.

From this, Howard proceeded to an even more significant transformation: a critique of Bellamy's ideal of centralization. Bellamy believed that the industrial society of the future ought to be controlled by bureaucrats working from their command posts in the great cities. In opposing nationalization, Howard also began questioning the inevitability of centralization. Specifically, he began to modify his original view that the community he was designing was only a scale model of the centralized society of the future. Was the balance of individual society he was seeking possible in the metropolis? Or did the small decentralized community have an inherent value of its own?

In wrestling with this question, Howard was no doubt influenced by Peter Kropotkin, a Russian anarchist whose articles appeared in the widely read London journal *The Nineteenth Century* between 1888 and 1890.[29] These articles, later collected as *Fields, Factories, and Workshops* (1899), argued that while steam energy and the railroads had brought large factories and great cities, the dawning age of electricity would make possible a rapid decentralization. He saw the future in what he called "industrial villages," twentieth-century versions of the old crafts villages of the preindustrial era. There electrically powered, cooperatively owned cottage industries would turn out goods more efficiently than the old urban factories, while the workers' homes and gardens would be nestled in unspoiled countryside.

Kropotkin's views found a deep response in English Radical circles, especially his prediction that all the great urban concentrations of people and power were destined to disappear; his conviction that the future belonged to small-scale cooperators; and his belief that decentralization would make possible a society based on liberty and brotherhood. Howard, who called Kropotkin "the greatest democrat ever born to wealth and power,"[30] decisively abandoned his temporary infatuation with the centralized schemes of Edward Bellamy. Kropotkin had called his attention to the crucial importance of *scale* as a factor in social theory. "On a small scale," Howard proposed, "society may readily become more individualistic than now and more socialistic."[31] Conversely, he came to realize that the great city could never become the home of the co-operative civilization he was seeking. He was now ready to formulate the fundamental principle of the Garden City: *Radical hopes for a cooperative civilization could be fulfilled only in small communities embedded in a decentralized society.*

Howard thus turned to decentralization as a means of action, a way of voting with one's feet against the concentration of power and wealth that the cities represented. His anti-urbanism had nothing in common with the vague longings for a more natural life propagated by the "Back to the Land" movement, which was then enjoying one of its periodic revivals. He loved the excitement of London and deeply valued the social qualities of the great cities.[32] It was their economic and political role that disturbed him. "Palatial edifices and fearful slums are the strange, complementary features of modern cities."[33] Howard's identification of the metropolis with the extremes of wealth and power was the starting point of his analysis of the modern city and the real source of his antagonism toward it. He realized that the concentration of wealth and misery in the city would require an equally vast concentration of power to combat it. His favorite example of this was slum clearance. In a large city the inflated price of urban land and the vast numbers of slum dwellers meant that an effective program required a government with powers of taxation and confiscation that Howard, as a good Radical, shrank from even seeking. To accept the nineteenth-century metropolis as the inevitable context for modern life meant that either the force of vested interest would continue to prevail or an equally monstrous force based on class conflict would be raised to topple it.

Both alternatives affronted Howard's belief that mankind was moving to a higher stage of brotherhood. He drew the necessary conclusion: Large cities had no place in the society of the future. Surveying the "ill-ventilated, unplanned, unwieldy, and unhealthy cities – ulcers on the very face of our beautiful island,"[34] he proclaimed: "These crowded cities have done their work; they were the best which a society largely based on selfishness and rapacity could construct, but they are in the nature of things entirely unadapted for a society in which the social side of our nature is demanding a larger share of recognition."[35] Everything genuinely valuable in the social life of the city could and must be preserved in new communities designed so that the advantages of the town could be "married" to those of the country. "Human society and the beauty of nature are meant to be enjoyed together."[36] In communities of about 30,000 people based on small business and agriculture, everyone could enjoy the benefits of a healthy environment. Reduced to the scale of a Garden City, the gulf between capital and labor would be narrowed, social problems would become amenable to cooperative solutions, and the proper balance of order and freedom could be achieved.

How could this great social transformation be achieved? Howard summed up his response in his diagram of the "Three Magnets." Town and country were compared to magnets, each with its particular drawing power, its particular combination of attraction and repulsion. The town, with its excitement, high wages, and employment opportunities, suffered from high prices and poor living conditions. The beauty of the country-side was vitiated by its economic backwardness and "lack of amusement." The task for the planner would be to create a third magnet, the Town-Country magnet, the new community, which would have high wages and low rents; beauty of nature but "plenty to do"; "bright homes and gardens" along with freedom and cooperation.

In the diagram, "The People" are poised like iron filings between the magnets. This aspect of the metaphor is unfortunate, for Howard's point is that people will respond freely and rationally to the environment that gives them the most advantages. No one had been drafted into the cities. The great migration from the countryside, which in Howard's lifetime had brought seven million rural residents to the British urban centers, occurred without legislative compulsion. Similarly, the great exodus from the city to which Howard looked would require no coercive power.

What it required was planning. The Town-Country magnet had to be created consciously to yield the combination of physical and social benefits that were promised. This task Howard took upon himself. Although he had no training in architecture or city planning, he did have the inventor's confidence that he could find the better way. Working alone in the time he could spare from his stenography practice, he set out to give the Radical movement not only a new goal but the strategy for action it had been lacking. Building new towns, creating a new environment – that was the way to the cooperative commonwealth. Howard strove patiently to design that Third Magnet he called the Garden City, whose promise of a better life would draw people away from the urban centers into a new civilization.

Design for cooperation

Between 1889 and 1892 Howard created the basic plan for his ideal community. He envisaged his Garden City as a tightly organized urban center for 30,000 inhabitants, surrounded by a perpetual "green belt" of farms and parks. Within the city there would be both quiet residential neighborhoods and facilities for a full range of commercial, industrial, and cultural activities. For Howard did not conceive the Garden City as a specialized "satellite town" or "bedroom town" perpetually serving some great metropolis. Rather, he foresaw the great cities of his time shrinking to insignificance as their people deserted them for a new way of life in a decentralized society. No longer would a single metropolis dominate a whole region or even a whole nation. Nor would the palatial edifices and giant organizations of the big city continue to rule modern society. Instead, the urban population would be distributed among hundreds of Garden Cities whose small scale and diversity of functions embody a world in which the little person has finally won out.

Howard does not seem to have been familiar with the designs for geometric cities that utopian socialists had put forward earlier in the nineteenth century. Nonetheless the perfectly circular, perfectly symmetrical plan he devised for the Garden City bears a distinct resemblance to some of these, notably James Silk Buckingham's cast-iron Victoria (1849).[37] The explanation, however, lies not in direct influence but in shared values. For Howard had inherited that tradition in English utopian thought in which it was assumed that society could be improved just as a machine could – through the appropriate adjustments. A properly functioning society would thus take on the precise and well-calculated look of a good machine.

For Howard, therefore, there was nothing merely "mechanical" in the relentless symmetry of the Garden City. He wanted to make the design the physical embodiment of his ideal of cooperation, and he believed that his perfectly circular plan would best meet the needs of the citizens. He promised that every building would be "so placed to secure maximum utility and convenience."[38] This "unity of design and purpose" had been impossible in old cities formed, in Howard's view, by "an infinite number of small, narrow, and selfish decisions."[39] In the Garden City, however, an active common interest would make possible a uniform, comprehensive plan. With selfish obstructions removed, the city could assume that geometric form that Howard believed was the most efficient and the most beautiful. The symmetry of the Garden City would be the symbol and product of cooperation, the sign of a harmonious society.

The only relevant book he remembered reading was written by a physician, Dr Benjamin Richardson, and entitled *Hygeia, A City of Health*.[40] It was an imaginative presentation of the principles of public sanitation in which Dr Richardson depicted a city whose design would be the healthiest for its inhabitants. He prescribed a population density of twenty-five people per acre, a series of wide, tree-shaded avenues, and homes and public gardens surrounded by greenery. "Instead of the gutter the poorest child has the garden; for the foul sight and smell of unwholesome garbage, he has flowers and green sward."[41] Howard was happy to follow this prescription. The public health movement, of which Dr Richardson was a prominent representative, was a vital force for civic action; it had persuaded the public that there was a strong correlation between the health of a community and its political and moral soundness. Howard maintained that the Garden Cities would be the healthiest in the nation.

He incorporated the low population density, the wide avenues, and other features of *Hygeia* into the geometry of his own city.

The problem of health was especially important because Howard planned the Garden City to be a manufacturing center in which the factories would necessarily be close to the homes. In order to separate the residential areas and also to ensure that everyone would be within walking distance of the workplace, Howard put the factories at the periphery of the city, adjacent to the circular railroad that surrounds the town and connects it to the main line. Here one can find the enterprises appropriate to a decentralized society: the small machine shop, or the cooperative printing works, or the jam factory where the rural co-operative processes its members' fruits. As usual in the plan, physical location has a symbolic aspect. Industry has its place and its function, but these are at the outskirts of the community. Howard had little faith in the role of work – even if cooperatively organized – to provide the unifying force in society. This he left to leisure and civic enterprise.

There are two kinds of centers in the Garden City: the neighborhood centers and the (one) civic center. The neighborhoods, or "wards" as Howard called them, are slices in the circular pie. Each ward comprises one-sixth of the town, 5,000 people or about 1,000 families. Each, said Howard, "should in some sense be a complete town by itself" (he imagined the Garden City being built ward by ward).[42] The basic unit in the neighborhood is the family living in its own home surrounded by a garden. Howard hoped to be able to provide houses with gardens to all classes. Most residents would be able to afford a lot 20 by 130 feet; the most substantial homes would be arranged in crescents bordering Grand Avenue, a park and promenade that forms the center of the ward. In the middle of Grand Avenue is the most important neighborhood institution, the school. This, Howard commented, should be the first building constructed in each ward and will serve as a library, a meeting hall, and even as a site for religious worship. Churches, when they are built, also occupy sites in Grand Avenue.[43]

There are two cohesive forces that bring the residents out of their neighborhoods and unite the city. The first is leisure. The center of the town is a Central Park, which provides "ample recreation grounds within very easy access of all the people."[44] Surrounding the park is a glassed-in arcade, which Howard calls the "Crystal Palace": "Here manufactured goods are exposed for sale, and here most of that class of shopping which requires the joy of deliberation and selection is done."[45]

The Crystal Palace, in addition to providing an attractive setting for consumption, also permits the town, by granting or withholding leases, to exercise some control over distribution. Howard, as always, recommended a balance between individualism and central organization. He rejected the idea of one great cooperative department store run by the community, like the one in *Looking Backward*. Instead, he advocated that there be many small shops, but only one for each category of goods. If customers complain that a merchant is abusing his monopoly, the town rents space in the Crystal Palace to another shopkeeper in the same field, whose competition then restores adequate service. Whatever the merits of this solution, it aptly reflects the Radical ambivalence toward the trades that supported so many of them, the desire for economic independence without the self-destructive competition that accompanied it.

Important as consumption and leisure were in his system, Howard nonetheless reserved the very center of the Central Park to the second cohesive force, "civil spirit." He wanted an impressive and meaningful setting for the "large public buildings": town hall, library, museum, concert and lecture hall, and the hospital. Here the highest values of the community are brought together – culture, philanthropy, health, and mutual cooperation.

We might wonder what kind of cultural life a Garden City of 30,000 could enjoy, but this question did not bother Howard. He never felt the need of that intensification of experience – the extremes of diversity and excellence – that only a metropolis can offer. We must also remember, however, that Howard lived in a milieu that did not look to others to provide entertainment or enlightenment. The English middle class and a sizable part of the working class created its own culture in thousands of voluntary groups: lecture societies, choral groups, drama guilds, chamber symphonies. Here, as elsewhere, Howard disdained the kind of central-ization that focused the life of a nation on a few powerful metropolitan institutions. He looked to small-scale voluntary cooperation not only for the economic base of the community but also for its highest cultural attainments.

The Garden City occupies 1,000 acres in the middle of a tract of 5,000 acres reserved for farms and forests.[46] This "Agricultural Belt" plays an integral role in the economy of the Garden City; the 2,000 farmers who live there supply the town with the bulk of its food. Because transpor-tation costs are almost nonexistent, the farmer receives a good price for his produce, and the consumer gets fresh vegetables and dairy products at a reduced price. The Agricultural Belt, moreover, prevents the town from sprawling out into the countryside and ensures that the citizens enjoy both a compact urban center and ample open countryside. "One of the first essential needs of Society and of the individual," wrote Howard, "is that every man, every woman, every child should have ample space in which to live, to move, and to develop."[47] He added a new element to the rights of man – the right to space.

The Garden City in all its aspects expressed Howard's ideal of a coop-erative commonwealth. It was the Zion in which he and his fellow Radicals could be at ease, the environment in which all the Radical hopes could be realized. Yet the Garden City was more than an image of felicity for Howard had carefully wedded his vision of the ideal city to a concrete plan for action. Indeed, he devoted relatively little attention to the details of the new city and a great deal to the means of achieving it. He wanted to show that there was no need to wait for a revolution to build the Garden City: it could be undertaken immediately by a coalition of Radical groups working within the capitalist system. The first successful Garden City would be a working model of a better society, and those that succeeded it would decisively alter English society. Building the Garden City was itself the revolution. The planned transformation of the environment was the nonviolent but effective strategy that the Radical movement had been seeking. The Garden City was, as Howard put it, "the peaceful path to real reform."

Howard wanted the building of the first Garden City to be an example of voluntary cooperation, and he devoted most of his book to outlining and defending his method. The key to Howard's strategy was his contention that building a new city could be *practical*, i.e., that money advanced for its construction could be paid back with interest. Funds could thus be solicited from high-minded and thrifty Radicals with the assurance that they would be both helping the cause and earning a modest return for themselves. The germ of Howard's scheme could be found in an article written in 1884 by the distinguished economist Alfred Marshall.[48] Marshall had pointed out that the rail networks that covered Great Britain rendered the concentration of so many businesses in London economically irrational. Many businesses could be carried out far more cheaply, efficiently, and pleasantly where land was inexpensive and abundant. Marshall proposed that committees be established to buy up suitable land outside London and coordinate the movement of factories and working people. The value of the land in these new industrial parks would rise sharply, and the committees that owned them would reap a handsome profit.

Howard, who knew both the proposal and its author,[49] took up this suggestion and transformed it to suit his own ends. He began by asking the reader to assume that a group of his supporters – "gentlemen of responsible position and undoubted probity and honor," as he hopefully described them – had banded together to form a nonprofit company. They would raise money by issuing bonds yielding a fixed rate (4 or 5 percent), purchase 6,000 acres of agricultural land, and lay out a city according to Howard's plans. They would build roads, power and water plants, and all other necessities, and then seek to attract industry and residents. The company would continue to own all the land; as the population rose, the rents too would rise from the low rate per acre for agricultural land to the more substantial rate of a city with 30,000 residents. All rent would go to the company and would be used to repay the original investors. Any surplus that remained after the financial obligations had been discharged would provide additional services to the community.[50]

Howard proposed, in other words, that the Garden City be founded and financed by philanthropic land speculation. The scheme was speculative because it was a gamble on the rise in values that would result from attracting 30,000 people to a plot of empty farmland, and philanthropic because the speculators agreed in advance to forgo all but a fixed portion of the expected profits. The concept was not original with Howard. "Philanthropy at 5 percent" was a familiar feature in English reform circles, and activists from the Owenites to the Christian Socialists made use of fixed-dividend corporations to raise money for cooperative stores and workshops. The Reverend Charles Kingsley, a Christian Socialist, aptly illustrated the spirit of this reconciliation of God and Mammon when he exhorted his followers to "seek first the Kingdom of God and his Righteousness with this money of yours and see if all things – profits and suchlike – are not added unto you."[51]

Howard did add a new emphasis to this method. He stipulated that part of the rental income each year be placed in a sinking fund and used to purchase the bonds of the original investors. As the number of bond-holders decreased, the amount that the company had to pay each year to the ones remaining would also decrease. Meanwhile, income from rents would be constantly growing as the town grew; the surplus, as we have seen, was earmarked for community services. Eventually the Garden City would buy out all the original investors, and the entire income from rents could be used to benefit the citizens. Taxes would be unnecessary; rents alone would generously support schools, hospitals, cultural insti-tutions, and charities.[52]

The residents of the Garden City would thus continue to pay rent, but landlords would be eliminated. The private ownership of land for the benefit of individuals would be replaced by collective ownership for the benefit of the community. Howard placed tremendous emphasis on this change. He, like almost every other Radical, believed that the "land question" – the concentration of the ownership of land in Great Britain in the hands of a few – was, as he put it, the "root of all our problems."[53] As late as 1873 an official survey had shown that 80 percent of the land in the United Kingdom was owned by less than 7,000 persons.[54] The spread of Garden Cities would transfer land ownership on a large scale from individuals to the community, thus inaugurating an economic and social revolution.

Howard's analysis of the crucial importance of the "land question" derived from the writings of the American reformer Henry George, a hero of English Radicals in the 1880s. George was probably the most influ-ential man of one idea in nineteenth-century Anglo-American history. His panacea, the Single Tax (the appropriation of all rent by taxation) was based on his view that there was no real conflict between capital and labor. The "antagonism of interests," he argued "is in reality between labor and capital on the one side and land ownership on the other."[55] The great landowners used their natural monopoly to demand exorbitant rents and thus appropriate without compensation the lion's share of the increased wealth from material progress that ought to go to the workmen and entrepreneurs who actually produced it. This perversion of the economic order impoverished the proletariat, imperiled the manufacturer, and upset the natural balance of supply and demand. It was the real cause of depression, class conflict, and the spreading poverty that seemed an inevitable companion to progress.

Characteristically, Howard accepted everything in George's theory that pointed toward reconciliation and rejected everything that promised conflict. He rejected the Single Tax because he saw that it meant the expropriation of a whole class. He accepted, however, George's view that the solution to the land question would restore the economy to a healthy balance and create the conditions for a reconciliation of capital and labor. He believed he had found the solution to the land question himself. The Garden City, he wrote, "will, by a purely natural process, make it gradually impossible for any landlord class to exist at all." Private landholding "will die a natural but not too sudden death."[56] Building Garden Cities would accomplish all of George's aims "in a manner which need cause no ill-will, strife or bitterness; is constitutional; requires no revolutionary legislation; and involves no direct attack on vested interest."[57] The Garden City company would, in fact, enjoy all the privileges of a profit-making concern. The legal forms that landlords had designed to protect their own interests would now foster the creation of a higher form of society.

The powers extended to the Garden City company as sole landlord would be greater than the legal authority possessed by any nineteenth-century English municipality. Through its control of all leases it could effectively enforce the ground plan and zone the community without special legal authority. Howard was a firm believer in "gas and water socialism," and he stipulated that the town's board of management should provide all utilities on a nonprofit basis. He also thought the town might well establish municipal bakeries and laundries.[58]

Although the Garden City company would have the legal right to own and operate all the industry in the Garden City, Howard favored a balance of public and private control. The large factories on the periphery were clearly to be established by private industry, though Howard hoped that through profit sharing they would eventually take on a cooperative character. They still would be subject to the authority that the town as sole landlord could impose: No polluters or employers of "sweated" labor would be allowed.[59] The board of management would also share responsibility for public services with private citizens. Howard hoped that individuals would establish a large group of what he called "pro-municipal enterprises." These were public services whose necessity was not yet recognized by the majority of the citizens, but "those who have the welfare of society at heart [would], in the free air of the city, be always able to experiment on their own responsibility, . . . and enlarge the public understanding."[60] In addition to the more conventional charitable and philanthropic activities, "pro-municipal enterprises" included cooperative building and pension societies.

As income from rents grew, the municipality would gradually take over the services that voluntary cooperation had initiated. In industry, too, Howard believed that the evolutionary trend was toward greater public ownership and control. The most important principle, however, was that no one has the right to impose a degree of socialism for which the citizens were not ready. The elimination of landlord's rents would remove, in Howard's view, any immediate conflict of capital with labor and permit the peaceful coexistence of capitalist and socialist industry. The balance between the public and private sectors must shift slowly with the increasing capacity of the citizens for cooperation.

Howard had the patience to begin with imperfect forms because he had the capacity to see his ideal society evolving in time. He realized that a single Garden City of 30,000 was too small to provide the full measure of diversity that a genuine city must have. A Garden City could not, however, increase its size or density; that would spoil its plan. He proposed that it grow by establishing a new sister city beyond the Agricultural Belt. Howard believed that the cities should eventually organize themselves into "town clusters, each town in the cluster being of different design from the others, yet the whole forming one large and well-thought-out plan."[61] A diagram that appeared in *To-morrow* showed six Garden Cities arranged in a circle around a larger Center City. The plan had the cities connected by a circular canal, which provided power, water, and transportation. In the 1902 edition the canal was replaced by a more sober rapid transit system.[62]

The Social City, as Howard called each cluster of towns, represented his most advanced conception of the marriage of town and country; here "each inhabitant of the whole group, though in one sense living in a town of small size, would be in reality living in, and would enjoy all the advantages of, a great and most beautiful city; and yet all the fresh delights of the country . . . would be within a very few minutes' ride or walk."[63] With small communities already established as the basic units in society, these units could be arranged in planned federations to secure the benefits of larger size as well. Rapid communications between the towns meant greater convenience for trade, and, "because the people, in their collective capacity own the land on which this beautiful group of cities is built, the public buildings, the churches, the schools and universities, the libraries, picture galleries, theatres, would be on a scale of magnificence which no city in the world whose land is in pawn to private individuals can afford."[64] Once established, the Social City would become the base for still higher stages of evolution that Howard never ventured to describe.

Howard's reluctance to prescribe every detail or to foresee every contingency is one of the most important aspects of his method. The visionary planner can easily become a despot of the imagination. Working alone, deprived of the checks and balances of other minds, he is tempted to become the *roi soleil* of his realm and to order every detail of life of his ideal society. If Howard's geometric plans resemble a Baroque *Residenzstadt*, Howard himself was singularly free of the pretensions of a Baroque monarch. His plans, as he pointed out, were merely diagrams to be modified when put into practice.

The same may be said for his plans for social organization. In Howard's time the advocates of Socialism and Individualism (both usually capitalized) confronted each other like Matthew Arnold's ignorant armies. Bellamy, as we have seen, believed that the entire economy of the United States could be centrally directed by a few men of "fair ability." Herbert Spencer in his individualist phase held that the use of tax money to support public libraries was a step toward collectivist slavery.[65] Howard did not presume to judge this momentous debate. He made the spatial reorganization of society his fundamental demand because he believed that a new environment would open possibilities for the reconciliation of freedom and order that neither Bellamy nor Spencer could imagine. Howard sought to discover the minimum of organization that would secure the benefits of planning while leaving to individuals the greatest possible control over their own lives. He was a collectivist who hated bureaucratic paternalism and an apostle of organization who realized that planning must stay within self-imposed limits.

Building the Garden City

Howard's theories were now irrevocably tied to what happened on the more than 3,000 acres in Hertfordshire. The necessity of finding large sums of money to develop the new city made Howard increasingly dependent on the support of a few Liberal magnates like Cadbury and Lever. He never succeeded in building the broad coalition of reformist groups he had hoped to assemble – a fact that inevitably modified the tone and substance of his ideas. One source of working-class support that could have improved the balance was conspicuous in its absence: the cooperative movement. Howard looked to the "cooperators" to provide the leadership and experience for the working class to begin its own enterprises. "The true remedy for capitalist oppression where it exists," he wrote, "is not the strike of no work but the strike of true work. . . . If labor leaders spent half the energy in cooperative organization they now waste in cooperative disorganization, the end of our present unjust system would be at hand."[66]

The cooperative movement, moreover, was probably the only working-class organization that had the resources to contribute significantly to the building of the Garden City. The movement had more than two million members organized into 1,600 local societies, which sold £92 million of goods in 1903 and distributed £10 million in profits.[67] The cooperative societies had either built or advanced the money for more than 37,000 houses by 1903, and the movement's factories manufactured more than £10 million of goods annually.[68]

Howard's supporters in the movement hoped that cooperators would be the principal builders of the Garden City. At each of the annual Cooperative Congresses from 1900 to 1909 they argued that the next step toward the cooperative commonwealth was to organize the movement's stores, factories, and homes (which were now scattered over Great Britain) into the new environment that Howard promised.[69] Despite influential support among the national leaders – J. C. Grey, chairman of the Cooperative Wholesale Society, was among the founders of the Manchester branch of the Garden City Association[70] – the congresses refused either to support First Garden City Ltd., or to build their own Garden City. The individual distributive societies were more anxious to preserve their independence than they were to create a new civilization. The cooperative counterbalance to capitalist investment and production at Letchworth never developed.

In the absence of any significant working-class support, the values of Neville and his fellow businessmen dominated First Garden City Ltd. For Howard, the Garden City was an environment in which capitalism could be peacefully superseded. Most of his supporters, however, looked to the Garden City as the place where capitalism could be most easily preserved.

Neville, who assumed the post of chairman of the executive of First Garden City Ltd., proposed to raise funds to begin construction by issuing £300,000 in shares, with the annual dividend not to exceed 5 percent of their par value. Neville believed that if the shares were to be sold, the company must purge itself of any utopian hopes and present itself at all times as a solid business venture and a good investment. "For mere philanthropy the money would not be forthcoming."[71] When Howard in his speeches mentioned the risks involved in starting a new city, Neville sternly reproached him. "I appreciate your reluctance to ask poor people to invest their savings, but there is all the difference in the world between refraining from enticing and deprecating investment."[72]

Faced with a board of prominent businessmen who were used to getting their own way, Howard was in danger of losing control of his own movement. The first test came over the land question. Howard proposed to retain the rise in land values for the community by disposing of all land in thousand-year leases that would provide for reassessment by an impartial committee every four years. If the value had increased over the last assessment, the rent would also be increased.[73] Howard hoped, as we have seen, that the rising income from rents would soon far exceed what was necessary to pay the 5 percent return to the stockholders and that the surplus could be used for community services.

Neville believed, however, that potential residents of Letchworth would be confused by the unfamiliar features of such a lease and would be frightened off by the fear of drastic rent increases. He therefore advocated a standard ninety-nine-year lease at a fixed rent.[74] The community, in other words, would have to wait one hundred years before negotiating a new lease at a higher rent and thus collecting its share of the "unearned increment."

The other businessmen on the board agreed with Neville. Howard, who was still earning his living as a stenographer, was no match for a cocoa millionaire or a soap magnate. He took the defeat in good spirits because he agreed with the businessmen that concern for details must not stand in the way of the speedy completion of the town. The prototype must first exist; it would then inspire others to more perfect efforts.

> The first result [of the building of Letchworth] will be that the number of people who favor the Garden City will be increased a hundredfold; and then a glorious task which an insignificant minority could not compass will be found quite easy by a majority of the nation. A splendid organization will be created and a City will then rise as superior in its beauty and magnificence to our first crude attempt as is the finished canvas of a great artist to the rough and untaught attempts of a schoolboy.[75]

In 1903 the company made perhaps its most important decision: It chose the firm of Parker and Unwin to be the architects of Letchworth. Barry Parker was a young architect from Derbyshire who began his career as a designer of textiles and wallpapers influenced by the arts-and-crafts movement.[76] Raymond Unwin, whose association with the Garden City was the start of a long career in city planning that would make him the leading British authority, was trained as an engineer and came to architecture under the influence of William Morris.[77] Both men were early supporters of Howard; as followers of Morris, they were engaged in a search that paralleled Howard's own. Morris had taught that the artist's efforts to create a beautiful society could not be separated from the activist's attempts to create a just one. "Before there can be a city greatly beautiful," wrote Unwin, "there must be some noble common life to find expression."[78]

But if Parker and Unwin sympathized with Howard's goals, they had no use for his rationalistic, geometric methods of town planning. They gave to the Garden City movement their own vision of the "city greatly beautiful," a vision derived from the medieval village as seen through the eyes of William Morris. They wanted to adapt what they believed were the still valid principles of traditional English town planning to the decentralized society of the future. Where Howard had expressed the architecture of cooperation in the mechanical symmetry of his original plan, Parker and Unwin sought instead what they called "organic unity."

They followed Howard's lead to the extent of clearly separating the town from the countryside that surrounded it. They placed the new city roughly in the middle of the Letchworth estate, setting aside 1,200 acres for the city proper and 2,800 acres for the Agricultural Belt that would surround it. Within the city, however, they rejected Howard's rigidly symmetrical diagrams and instead sought a more subtle "organic" sense of order suggested by the terrain. They took advantage of the positions of the hills, streams, an old Roman road, and even some of the larger trees to define the plan of the town. The "The Crystal Palace" was replaced by a gently curving street of shops. Only the town center remained exactly what Howard intended it to be: a formal arrangement of municipal and cultural buildings.[79]

The contrast between Howard and his two architects was not, however, one simply between Howard's utilitarian bias and Parker and Unwin's aesthetic bent. If anything, Parker and Unwin were more practical than Howard. Industry, instead of forming a uniform periphery to Howard's circle, was grouped into an industrial park adjacent to the power plant and to the railroad. The tracks, in turn, separated industry from the residential area. The plan is effective without calling attention to itself through a calculated prettiness. In their quest for a natural unity Parker and Unwin succeeded – perhaps too well. As Herbert Read has pointed out, it is possible to visit Letchworth and even to live there without being aware that it is a conscious creation.[80]

Parker and Unwin believed that organic unity must extend up from the plan to embrace a common style of architecture. They saw the eclectic architecture of their time – in which a suburban villa tricked out with classical porticoes might be sandwiched between a Gothic extravaganza on the right and Renaissance palazzo on the left – as a horrible symptom of the chaotic individualism of their time. They held that the victory of cooperation in the Garden City could best be expressed in a consistent style derived from traditional village architecture, the brick and stucco, the gables and tile roofs of Hertfordshire. This was not mere antiquarianism, for Parker and Unwin "democratized" traditional architecture. Where other architects had used the vocabulary of picturesque gables and tiled roofs to glorify the suburban castles of the rich, Parker and Unwin employed traditional designs to express the unity of a cooperatively organized community of equals. In the context of their time, their designs for Letchworth stood for cleanliness, simplicity, and the honest use of materials – qualities the arts-and-crafts movement associated with the fourteenth century and hoped to revive in the twentieth. The fourteenth-century village, they believed, was the truest community that England had ever known, and its beauty was the expression of a unique balance of order and uniformity. This balance they hoped to recapture in that revitalized community of the future, the Garden City.

Parker and Unwin's designs thus bore little resemblance to Howard's plan for geometric boulevards and iron-and-steel Crystal Palaces. Nevertheless, both concepts derived from a common search for an architecture of cooperation. Parker and Unwin's plan was a sort of translation of Howard's original diagrams. It was, however, a loose translation that introduced some themes of its own. Unwin's hope that the Garden City would "give life just that order, that crystalline structure it had in feudal times,"[81] sounds a note of nostalgia for vanished stability not heard in Howard. Unwin's aesthetic glorification of the traditional village was also a glorification of the stable social relations he imagined existed there, and an implicit critique of the modern quest for change. For Unwin, the beautiful old English villages had "the appearance of being an organic whole, the home of a community" because they were "the expression of a corporate life in which all the different units were personally in touch with each other, consciously and frankly accepting their relations, and, on the whole, content with them."[82] Like the villagers themselves, "every building honestly confessed just what it was, and so fell into its place."[83] The Garden City, too, would be a community where everyone has his place and is content with it.

Parker and Unwin's concept of the Garden City thus had its reactionary as well as its forward-looking aspects. The two architects lacked Howard's confident faith in industrialization and the nineteenth-century world of rapid social change. For them, the Garden City was a place in which industrialization could be kept in its proper (subordinate) place and the incessant striving of modern times would yield to order and contentment. In their idealization of the English village, Parker and Unwin brought to prominence an element in the Garden City that had hardly existed in Howard: the fear of the great city and its social turmoil, the desire to discard the burdens of progress and return to the simple life. Their plans embodied the new stage in the Garden City movement, the stage in which Howard's influence was counterbalanced by Liberals like Cadbury, who looked back to an imagined paternalistic order. With their mixture of the enlightened and the medieval, Parker and Unwin reflected this split in the movement between an optimistic endorsement of the future and a nostalgic wish to escape from the modern world.

But Parker and Unwin, like the Garden City movement in general, ought to be judged not only on their realized plans but also on their aspirations. Their most revolutionary idea was never put into practice. In 1901, even before the decision to build a Garden City had been undertaken, Unwin proposed that the houses in the new city be organized cooperatively. His plan provided for "quadrangles" of homes in which three sides would be devoted to private apartments and the fourth to a common dining room, recreation room, and nursery. Food and coal would be purchased jointly, and the residents would share the cost of hiring cooks and maids. The quadrangle, he hoped, would become the basic unit of Garden City architecture, giving the city a "greater harmony and unity of effect" than would be possible where the land was carved into separate plots.[84]

Howard himself took up the plan in 1906 – "I believe the time has now come when [cooperation] can be successfully tried as one of the central ideas in domestic life,"[85] he wrote – but even his efforts resulted in only one quadrangle called Homesgarth.[86] Although Unwin modeled the quadrangle on an Oxford college, Homesgarth was too close in conception and design to communitarian experiments to be entirely respectable. Homesgarth, however, was no utopian scheme. "Its first object," Howard said, was "to provide a house of comparative comfort and beauty for the numerous folks of the middle class who have a hard struggle for existence on a mere budget – for those who require domestic help but can very ill afford it."[87] Homesgarth's small scale – only twenty-four families – and careful balance between family privacy and community functions is characteristic of Howard's pragmatic reinterpretation of the utopian tradition. In Howard's view, it was a piece of the new civilization and an important attempt to make cooperation part of the daily life of the Garden City.

Parker and Unwin hoped that even if First Garden City Ltd. would not support their plans for quadrangles, it would still provide funds to build the houses of Letchworth according to their designs. The company, however, was in serious financial difficulty. The original stock issue sold slowly; the directors bought £40,000, and some £60,000 was sold to the public in the first year, but it took three years to reach £150,000.[88] During those three years the company was forced to spend over £600,000 to provide the roads, gasworks, electrical generators, and other utilities the town needed.[89] The company was able to borrow the funds for these necessities, but it was unwilling to go more deeply in debt. Many of the first houses in Letchworth were built by speculative contractors whose designs introduced precisely those eccentricities that Parker and Unwin had wanted to banish from the town. These homes, however, were well suited to the tastes of Letchworth's first residents, many of whom were men and women of independent means and "advanced" opinions. Their enthusiasms included theosophy, vegetarianism, dress reform, and amateur theatricals; Letchworth was soon reputed to have more committees per person than any other town in England.[90] The company, fearing that Letchworth might soon get the reputation as a colony of cranks, then solemnly informed the press that only one resident habitually wore a toga and sandals.[91] When several men broke with convention by refusing to wear hats (which were then considered as necessary to outdoor attire as trousers), the town staged a public debate between the "Hatters" and the "No-Hatters." A company agent who believed that manufacturers would refuse to locate their plants where the norms of society were so openly questioned interrupted the proceedings and roundly denounced the "No-Hatters" as unpatriotic citizens who did not have the interests of Letchworth at heart.[92]

Despite the company's apprehensions, manufacturers did come to Letchworth. Only a few, like the cooperatively run Garden City Press Ltd., were attracted to the city for ideological reasons. Most came for precisely the practical reasons that Howard and especially Neville had foreseen. The rise in business activity in the first decade of the twentieth century created a demand for increased space that was hard to satisfy in London. Letchworth offered low rents, minimal taxes, and ample room to grow. When, for example, the publishing firm of J. W. Dent discovered that its London facilities offered no room for expansion, the publisher established a branch plant at Letchworth. The "Everyman" series of inexpensive classics was printed there.[93] Other enterprises began as the project of an amateur inventor and moved from a Letchworth garage to the industrial park. Light engineering and printing were the principal Garden City industries.[94]

The new factories promised to make Letchworth a self-supporting community. As houses and shops began to line the streets that Parker and Unwin had laid out, the social structure of the new town underwent a rapid change. A census taken of the 1,400 Letchworth residents in 1905 showed that almost all of them were from two groups: middle-class men and women of independent means (and their servants) and the skilled artisans who were building the new town.[95] By 1907 the population had more than doubled, and almost all the new residents were factory workers.[96]

Howard was now faced with the challenge to make good his claim that the Garden City would bring to working people health and living standards they could never have obtained in the old cities. Whatever the interests of his associates, he had not forgotten his belief that the Garden City would provide all the benefits that others were seeking from political and economic revolution. In practice, this challenge focused on housing. Could the Garden City accomplish what no other public or private organization in England had been able to do: construct decent dwellings that even the lowest-paid workers could afford? This meant, of course, building under existing social conditions. Howard had to assume that the tenants' wages would remain low, that interest on capital would continue to be paid, and that no government subsidy could be expected. If the Garden City would create good housing for all its citizens under these circumstances, then Howard's claim that it represented "the peaceful path to real reform" would receive powerful support.

Howard was convinced that planning, architectural ingenuity, and voluntary cooperation could solve the housing question. A cooperative building society, Garden City Tenants Ltd., was established in 1904 to raise capital for workers' housing.[97] As a stopgap measure, Thomas Adams persuaded the editor of *Country Life* to hold that magazine's "cheap cottage" competition at Letchworth. After the exhibition, the model cottages were sold very cheaply indeed to Letchworth workers.[98]

Garden City Tenants Ltd. then turned to Raymond Unwin for the multiunit dwellings the new town needed. Unwin's designs show the Garden City movement at its best – pragmatic, democratic, responsive to the needs of the people it served.[99] Unwin gave the same attention to these projects that other architects devoted to the rich man's villa. He made sure that every cottage got its share of sunlight, that every window and door was properly placed. That institutional bleakness that afflicts British (and not only British) architects when planning for the "lower orders" was completely absent from Unwin's work. Instead, there was a real sense of individual well-being and community solidarity, precisely the "organic unity" that Unwin had proclaimed.

The individual cottages were not left detached, as in the middle-class villas, but joined into rows of three to ten. These rows were then grouped around a central courtyard or field. This plan used far less land per unit than the villas and gave to each family the privacy of a two-story dwelling with its own garden. At the same time, there was substantial open space that could be shared in common. Within each cottage Unwin decided not to attempt to duplicate middle-class layouts, with their separate parlor, living room, dining room, and kitchen; on the small scale of the cottage this would have made the rooms claustrophobic. Moreover, Unwin wanted to design houses that "honestly confessed just what they were," not scaled-down copies of inappropriate models. He appreciated the fact that working-class family life traditionally centered around the hearth, and he therefore designed a combination living room–kitchen to be as comfortable, spacious, and open as possible.

At its best, Unwin's work represents that fruitful balance of individual and community which the Garden City stood for and which housing projects have seldom achieved since. It had, however, one great deficiency. When the costs of the new houses were added up, only skilled workers could afford them. The wages of the unskilled were simply too close to subsistence level for them to be able to pay the rent for any home that Unwin or Howard would call decent. As Howard later admitted, it was the bicycle that saved the situation. Workers who could not find housing in the Garden City bicycled each day from their jobs to apartments in the older towns beyond the Agricultural Belt, where cheap but substandard accommodations could be found.[100] One can hardly blame Unwin and Howard for their failure. If they were unable to build decent workers' housing without a subsidy, neither could anyone else.

These efforts in housing illustrate the real strengths and ultimate limitations of the Garden City idea as a social movement. By 1910 the practicality of Howard's basic concept had been proved. The new town of Letchworth was a clean, healthy, and well-planned environment; it had shown its capacity to attract industry and residents; and the First Garden City Ltd., though still financially pressed, was beginning to reap the rewards of its investment and declare its first dividend. The housing question, however, demonstrated that, despite Howard's hopes, the Garden City could not create its own oasis of social justice in an unjust society. Lower costs, better planning, community ownership of land – none of these could fully compensate for the inequities that were inherent in the social system of Howard's time. The path to real reform lay outside the Garden City.

By 1910, however, Howard was still looking to the future with confidence. He realized that Letchworth had its limitations, but Letchworth was only the first working model, which would surely inspire dozens and then hundreds of improved successors. But in 1910 the First Garden City was still the only Garden City, and no more were in the works. The problem for Howard was, where were the other Garden Cities that would begin to transform England?

The Radiant City

The Radiant City retained the most important principle of the Contemporary City: the juxtaposition of a collective realm of order and administration with an individualistic realm of family life and participation. This juxtaposition became the key to Le Corbusier's attempt to resolve the syndicalist dilemma of authority and participation. Both elements of the doctrine receive intense expression in their respective spheres. Harmony is in the structure of the whole city and in the complete life of its citizens.

The Radiant City was a more daring and difficult synthesis than the Contemporary City. In his effort to realize the contradictory elements of syndicalism, Le Corbusier made the Radiant City at once more authoritarian and more libertarian than its predecessor. Within the sphere of collective life, authority has become absolute. The Contemporary City had lacked any single power to regulate all the separate private corporations that accomplished the essential work of society; Le Corbusier had then believed that the invisible hand of free competition would create the most efficient coordination. The Great Depression robbed him of his faith. He now held that organization must extend beyond the large corporations. They had rationalized their own organizations, but the economy as a whole remained wasteful, anarchic, irrational. The planned allocation of manpower and resources that had taken place within each corporation must now be accomplished for society. In the Radiant City every aspect of productive life is administered from above according to one plan. This plan replaces the marketplace with total administration; experts match society's needs to its productive capacities.

The preordained harmony that Le Corbusier had called for in urban reconstruction would now be imposed on all productive life. The great works of construction would become only one element in the plan. This was a crucial extension of the concept of planning. Ebenezer Howard and Frank Lloyd Wright had believed that once the environment had been designed, the sources of disorder in society would be minimized and individuals could be left to pursue their own initiatives. This belief rested on a faith in a "natural economic order," a faith that Le Corbusier no longer shared. He confronted a world threatened by chaos and collapse. It seemed that only discipline could create the order he sought so ardently. Coordination must become conscious and total. Above all, society needed authority and a plan.

Syndicalism, Le Corbusier believed, would provide a "pyramid of natural hierarchies" on which order and planning could be based. The bottom of this pyramid is the *syndicat*, the group of workers, white-collar employees, and engineers who run their own factory. The workers have the responsibility of choosing their most able colleague to be their manager and to represent them at the regional trade council. Le Corbusier believed that although citizens would usually find it impossible to identify the most able man among a host of politicians, each worker is normally able to choose his natural leader. "Every man is capable of judging the facts of his trade," he observed.[101]

The regional council of plant managers represents the first step in the hierarchy. Each level corresponds to a level of administrative responsibility. The manager runs his factory; the regional leaders administer the plants in their region. The regional council sends its most able members to a national council, which is responsible for the overall control of the trade. The leader of this council meets with fellow leaders to administer the national plan. This highest group is responsible for coordinating the entire production of the country. If, for example, the national plan calls for mass housing, they allot the capital needed for each region and set the goals for production. The order is passed down to the regional council, which assigns tasks to individual factories and contractors. The elected representatives of the *syndicat* return from the regional council with instructions that determine his factory's role in the national productive effort.

This hierarchy of administration has replaced the state. As Saint-Simon had urged, an individual's power corresponds exactly to that person's responsibilities in the structure of production. The administrator issues the orders necessary for fulfilling the required quotas, and these orders provide the direction that society needs. The divisive issues of parliamentary politics cannot arise, for everyone shares a common concern that the resources of society be administered as efficiently as possible. Even the tasks of the national council are administrative rather than political. The members do not apportion wealth and power among competing interests groups. Their task, like that of all the other functionaries, is a "technical" one: they carry out the plan.

"Plans are not political," Le Corbusier wrote.[102] The plan's complex provisions, covering every aspect of production, distribution, and construction, represent a necessary and objective ordering of society. The plan is necessary because the Machine Age requires conscious control. It is objective because the Machine Age imposes essentially the same discipline on all societies. Planning involves the rational mastery of industrial process and the application of that mastery to the specific conditions of each nation. The plan is a "rational and lyric monument" to man's capacity to organize.

The plan is formulated by an elite of experts detached from all social pressure. They work "outside the fevers of mayors' and prefects' offices," away from the "cries of electors and the cries of victims." Their plans are "established serenely, lucidly. They take account only of human truths."[103] In the planner's formulations, "the motive forces of a civilization pass from the subjective realm of consciousness to the objective realm of facts." Plans are "just, long-term, established on the realities of the century, imagined by a creative passion."[104]

This plan for Le Corbusier was more than a collection of statistics and instructions; it was a social work of art. It brought to consciousness the complex yet satisfying harmonies of an orderly, productive world. It was the score for the great industrial orchestra. The plan summed up the unity that underlay the division of labor in society; it expressed the full range of exchange and cooperation that is necessary to an advanced economy.

Le Corbusier used the vocabulary and structures of syndicalism to advance his own vision of a beautifully organized world. His "pyramid of natural hierarchies" was intended to give the human structure of organization the same clarity and order as the great skyscrapers of the business center. The beauty of the organization was the product of the perfect cooperation of everyone in the hierarchy. It was the expression of human solidarity in creating a civilization in the midst of the hostile forces of nature. The natural hierarchy was one means of attaining the sublime.

People at work create a world that is truly human. But that world, once created, is a realm of freedom where people live in accord with nature, not in opposition to it. Like the Contemporary City, the Radiant City identifies the realm of freedom with the residential district. As if in recognition of the need to counterbalance the industrial realm's increased emphasis on organization, Le Corbusier has displaced the towers of administration from the central position they occupied in the earlier plan. The residential district stands in the place of honor in the Radiant City.

It is, moreover, a transformed residential district. Le Corbusier had lost the enthusiasm for capitalism that had led him originally to segregate housing in the Contemporary City according to class – elite in the center, proletariat at the outskirts. Now he was a revolutionary syndicalist, with a new appreciation of workers' rights. When he visited the United States in 1935, he found much to admire in the luxury apartment houses that lined Central Park and Lake Shore Drive, but he added, "My own thinking is directed towards the crowds in the subway who come home at night to dismal dwellings. The millions of beings sacrificed to a life without hope, without rest – without sky, sun, greenery."[105] Housing in the Radiant City is designed for them. The residential district embodies Le Corbusier's new conviction that the world of freedom must be egalitarian. "If the city were to become a human city," he proclaimed, "it would be a city without classes."[106]

No longer does the residential district simply mirror the inequalities in the realm of production. Instead, the relation between the two is more complex, reflecting Le Corbusier's resolve to make the Radiant City a city of organization *and* freedom. The realm of production in the Radiant City is even more tightly organized, its hierarchies of command and subordination even stricter than in the Contemporary City. At the same time, the residential district – the realm of leisure and self-fulfillment – is radically libertarian, its principles of equality and cooperation standing in stark opposition to the hierarchy of the industrial world. The citizen in Le Corbusier's syndicalist society thus experiences both organization and freedom as part of his daily life.

The centers of life in the Radiant City are the great high-rise apartment blocks, which Le Corbusier calls "Unités." These structures, each of which is a neighborhood with 2,700 residents, mark the culmination of the principles of housing that he had been expounding since the Dom-Inos of 1914. Like the Dom-Ino house, the Unité represents the application of mass-production techniques; but where the Dom-Ino represents the principle in its most basic form, the Unité is a masterful expression of scale, complexity, and sophistication. The disappointments of the 1920s and the upheavals of the 1930s had only strengthened Le Corbusier in his faith that a great new age of the machine was about to dawn. In the plans for the Unité he realized that promise of a *collective* beauty that had been his aim in the Dom-Ino design; he achieved a collective grandeur, which the Dom-Ino houses had only hinted at; and finally, he foresaw for all the residents of the Unité a freedom and abundance beyond even that which he had planned for the elite of the Contemporary City. The apartments in the Unité are not assigned on the basis of a worker's position in the industrial hierarchy but according to the size of his family and their needs. In designing these apartments, Le Corbusier remarked that he "thought neither of rich nor of poor but of man."[107] He wanted to get away both from the concept of luxury housing, in which the wasteful consumption of space becomes a sign of status, and from the concept of *Existenzminimum*, the design of workers' housing based on the absolute hygienic minimums. He believed that housing could be made to the "human scale," right in its proportions for everyone, neither cramped nor wasteful. No one would want anything larger nor get anything smaller.

The emphasis in the Unité, however, is not on the individual apartment but on the collective services provided to all the residents. As in the Villa-Apartment Blocks of the Contemporary City, Le Corbusier followed the principle that the cooperative sharing of leisure facilities could give to each family a far more varied and beautiful environment than even the richest individual could afford in a single-family house. These facilities, moreover, take on a clear social function as the reward and recompense for the eight hours of disciplined labor in a factory or office that are required of all citizens in a syndicalist society. The Unité, for example, has a full range of workshops for traditional handicrafts whose techniques can no longer be practiced in industries devoted to mass production. Here are meeting rooms of all sizes for participatory activities that have no place in the hierarchical sphere of production. There are cafes, restaurants, and shops where sociability can be cultivated for its own sake. Most important, in Le Corbusier's own estimation, the Unité provides the opportunity for a full range of physical activities that are severely curtailed during working hours in an industrial society. Within each Unité there is a full-scale gymnasium; on the roof are tennis courts, swimming pools, and even sand beaches. Once again, the high-rise buildings cover only 15 percent of the land, and the open space around them is elaborately landscaped into playing fields, gardens, and parkland.

The most basic services that the Unité provides are those that make possible a new concept of the family. Le Corbusier envisioned a society in which men and women would work full-time as equals. He therefore presumed the end of the family as an economic unit in which women were responsible for domestic services while men worked for wages. In the Unité, cooking, cleaning, and child raising are services provided by society. Each building has its day-care center, nursery and primary school, cooperative laundry, cleaning service, and food store. In the Radiant City the family no longer has an economic function to perform. It exists as an end in itself.

Le Corbusier and Frank Lloyd Wright were both intensely concerned with the preservation of the family in an industrial society, but here as elsewhere they adopted diametrically opposite strategies. Wright wished to revive and strengthen the traditional economic role of the family, to ensure its survival by making it the center both of the society's work and of its leisure. Wright believed in a life in which labor and leisure would be one, whereas Le Corbusier subjected even the family to the stark division between work and play that marks the Radiant City. The family belongs to the realm of play. Indeed, it virtually ceases to exist during the working day. When mother and father leave their apartment in the morning for their jobs, their children accompany them down on the elevator. The parents drop them off at the floor where the school or day-care center is located and pick them up after work. The family reassembles in the afternoon, perhaps round the pool or at the gym, and when the family members return to their apartment they find it already cleaned, the laundry done and returned, the food ordered in the morning already delivered and prepared for serving. Individual families might still choose to cook their own food, do their own laundry, raise vegetables on their balconies, or even raise their own children. In the Radiant City, however, these activities have become leisure-time hobbies like wood-working or weaving, quaint relics of the pre-mechanical age.

The Unité is thus high-rise architecture for a new civilization, and Le Corbusier was careful to emphasize that its design could be truly realized only after society had been revolutionized. He therefore never concerned himself with such problems as muggings in the parks or vandalism in the elevators. In the Radiant City, crime and poverty no longer exist.

But if the Unité looks to the future, its roots are in the nineteenth-century utopian hopes for a perfect cooperative society, the same hopes that inspired Ebenezer Howard's cooperative quadrangles. Peter Serenyi has aptly compared the Unité to that French utopian palace of communal pleasures, the phalanstery of Charles Fourier.[108] An early nineteenth-century rival of Saint-Simon, Fourier envisioned a structure resembling the château of Versailles to house the 1,600 members of his "phalanx" or rural utopian community. "We have no conception of the compound or collective forms of luxury," Fourier complained, and the phalanstery was designed to make up that lack.[109] He believed that in a properly run society all individual desires could find their appropriate gratification. The phalanstery, therefore, contains an elaborate series of lavish public rooms: theaters, libraries, ballrooms, and – Fournier's special pride – the dining rooms where "exquisite food and a piquant selection of dining companions" can always be found.

The phalanstery can be seen as the nineteenth-century anticipation and the Unité as the twentieth-century realization of architecture in the service of collective pleasure. Both designs represent what Le Corbusier termed "the architecture of happiness," architecture created to deliver what he was fond of calling "the essential joys." Fourier, however, could only express his vision in the anachronistic image of the baroque palace. Le Corbusier finds the forms of collective pleasure in the most advanced techniques of mass production. For him, the architecture of happiness is also the architecture for the industrial era.

The comparison of the phalanstery and the Unité suggests, finally, the complexity of Le Corbusier's ideal city. For Fourier was the bitter antagonist of Saint-Simon, whose philosophy is so central to Le Corbusier's social thought. The rivalry of the two nineteenth-century prophets was more than personal. Since their time, French utopian thought has been divided into two distinct traditions. The Saint-Simonian tradition is the dream of society as the perfect industrial hierarchy. Its setting is urban, its thought technological, its goal production, and its highest value organization. Fourier and his followers have envisioned society as the perfect community: rural, small-scale, egalitarian, dedicated to pleasure and self-fulfillment. In the Radiant City, Le Corbusier combines these two traditions into an original synthesis. He places a Fourierist phalanstery in the center of a Saint-Simonian industrial society. Community and organization thus find intense and appropriate expression: both are integral parts of Le Corbusier's ideal city for the Machine Age.

Notes

1   Joseph Conrad, *The Secret Agent* (New York, 1953), p. 11. The quotation is drawn from the Preface, first published in 1921.
2   For statistics of urban growth, see Adna Ferrin Weber, *The Growth of Cities in the Nineteenth Century* (Ithaca, N.Y., 1899).
3   Hsi-Huey Liang, "Lower-class Immigrants in Wilhelmine Berlin," In *The Urbanization of European Society in the Nineteenth Century*, eds. Andrew Lees and Lynn Lees (Lexington, Mass. 1976), p. 223.
4   Le Corbusier, *La ville radieuse* (Boulogne-Seine, 1935), p. 181.
5   For Owen, see J. F. C. Harrison, *Quest for the New Moral World* (New York, 1969).
6   For Fourier, see Jonathan Beecher and Richard Bienvenu, eds., *The Utopian Vision of Charles Fourier* (Boston, 1971).
7   For Haussmann and his influence see David H. Pinkney, *Napoleon III and the Rebuilding of Paris* (Princeton, N.J., 1958); Howard Saalman, *Haussmann: Paris Transformed* (New York, 1971); and Anthony Sutcliffe, *The Autumn of Central Paris* (London, 1970).
8   Peter H. Mann, "Octavia Hill: An Appraisal," *Town Planning Review* 23, no. 3 (Oct. 1953): 223–237.
9   Friedrich Engels, *Zur Wohnungsfrage*, 2d ed. (Leipzig, 1887).
10   See Barbara Miller Lane, *Architecture and Politics in Germany, 1918–1945* (Cambridge, Mass., 1968).
11   Le Corbusier, *Urbanisme* (Paris, 1925), p. 135.
12   Lewis Mumford, "The Garden City Idea and Modern Planning," introductory essay to F. J. Osborn's edition of *Garden Cities of To-morrow* (Cambridge, Mass., 1965), p. 29. Although Osborn's edition bears the title of the 1902 edition, his text restores portions of the 1898 text that were cut in 1902. Osborn's is therefore a "definitive" text and I follow his usage in always referring to Howard's book as *Garden Cities of To-morrow*. All further references will come from Osborn's edition, abbreviated *GCT*.

13   See Donald Canty, ed., *The New City* (New York, 1969) for the details of this recommendation.
14   The New Towns, however, have had their problems. See " 'New Towns' Face Growing Pains," *New York Times*, June 13, 1976. p. 26.
15   F. J. Osborn, Preface to *GCT*, p. 22.
16   Ibid., pp. 22–23.
17   Ebenezer Howard Papers, Hertfordshire County Archives, Hertford, England. Draft of an Unfinished Autobiography, Folio 17.
18   C. C. R., "The Evolution of Ebenezer Howard," *Garden Cities and Town Planning* 2, no. 3 (Mar. 1912): 46.
19   Howard Papers, Folio 17.
20   J. Bruce Wallace, *Towards Fraternal Organization* (London, 1894), p. 19.
21   Ibid., p. 19.
22   Howard Papers, Folio 17.
23   For Bellamy's influence, see Sylvia E. Bowman, *The Year 2000: A Critical Biography of Edward Bellamy* (New York, 1958).
24   E. Howard, "Spiritual Influences Toward Social Progress," *Light*, April 30, 1910, p. 195.
25   E. Howard, "Ebenezer Howard, the Originator of the Garden City Idea," *Garden Cities and Town Planning* 16, no. 6 (July 1926): 133.
26   An account of the Nationalisation of Labour Society can be found in Peter Marshall, "A British Sensation," in Sylvia Bowman, ed., *Edward Bellamy Abroad* (New York, 1962), pp. 86–118.
27   Howard, "Ebenezer Howard, the Originator of the Garden City Idea," p. 133.
28   Edward Bellamy, *Looking Backward* (New York, 1960), p. 127.
29   Peter Kropotkin, *Fields, Factories and Workshops* (London, 1899).
30   Howard Papers, Draft of an Autobiography, Folio 10.
31   *GCT*, p. 131.
32   Howard Papers, Folio 10.
33   *GCT*, p. 47.
34   Ibid., p. 145.
35   Ibid., p. 146.
36   Ibid., p. 48.
37   James Silk Buckingham, *National Evils and Practical Remedies, with the Plan of a Model Town* (London, 1849). Although Howard mentions the utopian city of Buckingham in the text of *GCT* as one of the proposals he combined into the Garden City, he states in a footnote that in fact he had not seen Buckingham's plan until he had "got far on" with his project. *GCT*, p. 119.
38   Howard Papers, Early draft of *GCT*, Folio 3.
39   Ibid.
40   E. Howard, "Spiritual Influences Toward Social Progress," *Light*, April 30, 1910, p. 196. *Hygeia* was published in London in 1876.
41   Benjamin Ward Richardson, *Hygeia, A City of Health* (London, 1876), p. 21.
42   *GCT*, p. 76.
43   Ibid., pp. 50–56 and 71. Placing the churches along Grand Avenue means that no single church occupies the center of town. Howard's religious upbringing was Nonconformist.
44   *GCT*, p. 53.
45   Ibid., p. 54.

46   *GCT*, Diagram #2. The diagram also shows such institutions as "convalescent homes" and the "asylums for blind and deaf" in the green belt. In an earlier version of his plan, Howard wanted the Agricultural Belt to cover 8,000 acres. See his "Summary of E. Howard's proposals for a Home Colony," *The Nationalisation News* 3, no. 29 (Feb. 1893): 20.

47   Howard Papers, Common Sense Socialism, Folio 10.

48   Alfred Marshall, "The Housing of the London Poor," *Contemporary Review* 45, no. 2 (Feb. 1884): 224–231.

49   Howard Papers, Folio 10. Howard recalled meeting Marshall in connection with stenography work he did for parliamentary commissions and discussing the Garden City idea with him. In a note added to *GCT* he claimed that he had not seen Marshall's article when he first formulated his ideas. *GCT*, p. 119.

50   *GCT*, pp. 58–88.

51   Howard Papers. Quoted by Howard in an early draft of *GCT*, Folio 3.

52   *GCT*, pp. 89–111.

53   Ibid., p. 136.

54   "Return of Owners of Land Survey," analyzed in F. M. L. Thompson, *English Landed Society in the Nineteenth Century* (London, 1963), pp. 317–319.

55   Henry George, *Progress and Poverty* (New York, 1911), p. 201.

56   Howard, quoted in W. H. Brown's interview with him. "Ebenezer Howard, A Modern Influence," *Garden Cities and Town Planning* 7, no. 30 (Sept. 1908): 116.

57   *GCT*, p. 131.

58   Ibid., pp. 96–111.

59   Howard Papers, Lecture to a Fabian Society, January 11, 1901, Folio 3.

60   *GCT*, p. 104.

61   Ibid., p. 139.

62   I suspect the population of the Central City was put at 58,000 so that the whole complex would attain a population of exactly 250,000.

63   *GCT*, p. 142.

64   Ibid.

65   Ibid. Spencer held that public libraries in themselves were only "mildly communistic." See his "The New Toryism," *Contemporary Review*, 45, no. 2 (Feb. 1884): 153–167. These of course were Spencer's later views. A younger Spencer in *Social Statics* had called for the nationalization of the land. This permitted Howard to refer to Spencer as one of his influences. *GCT*, pp. 123–125.

66   *GCT*, p. 108.

67   *The Thirty-Sixth Annual Co-operative Congress* (Manchester, 1904), p. 63.

68   Ibid., pp. 65 and 83.

69   See especially Aneurin Williams, "Co-operation in Housing and Town Building," Thirty-ninth Co-operative Congress (Manchester, 1909), pp. 379–397.

70   Minutes of the Manchester Branch of the Garden City Association, April 1, 1902. Now in the possession of the Town and Country Planning Association.

71   Howard Papers, Letter of Neville to Howard, November 13, 1903. Folio 25.

72   Howard Papers, Letter of Neville to Howard, December 14, 1903. Folio 25.

73   Howard Papers, Draft of 1,000-year lease dated "around 1902."

74 The details of Neville's position and the controversy that followed are in Aneurin Williams, "Land Tenure in the Garden City," Appendix A in C. B. Purdom, *The Garden City* (London, 1913).

75 E. Howard, "The Relation of the Ideal to the Practical," *The Garden City*, n.s. 2, no. 13 (Feb. 1907): 267.

76 See Barry Parker and Raymond Unwin, *The Art of Building a Home* (London, 1901), for the best record of the early career and interests of both men.

77 See Walter L. Creese, ed., *The Legacy of Raymond Unwin: A Human Pattern for Planning* (Cambridge, Mass., 1967), especially the editor's introduction.

78 Raymond Unwin, "The Beautiful in Town Building," *The Garden City*, n.s. 2, no. 13 (Feb. 1907): 267.

79 Unwin, *Town Planning in Practice* (London, 1909).

80 Herbert Read, "A Tribute to Ebenezer Howard," *Town and Country Planning* 14, no. 53 (Spring 1946): 14.

81 Raymond Unwin, "On the Building of Houses in the Garden City," Garden City Tract no. 8 (London, 1901), p. 4.

82 Unwin, "Co-operation in Building," in Parker and Unwin, *The Art of Building a Home*, p. 92.

83 Ibid., p. 92.

84 "Co-operation in Building," in Parker and Unwin, *The Art of Building a Home*, pp. 91–108. See also Raymond Unwin, *Cottage Plans and Common Sense*, Fabian Tract no. 109 (London, 1901).

85 E. Howard, "Co-operative Housekeeping," *The Garden City*, n.s. 1, no. 8 (Sept. 1906): 170.

86 Homesgarth was designed not by Unwin but by another architect associated with the Garden City movement, H. Clapham Lander. See his early advocacy of co-ops, "The Advantages of Co-operative Dwellings," Garden City Tract no. 7 (London, 1901).

87 Howard, "Co-operative Housekeeping," p. 171.

88 Aneurin Williams, "Land Tenure in the Garden City," p. 220.

89 First Garden City Ltd., *Prospectus*, 1909.

90 Charles Lee, "From a Letchworth Diary," *Town and Country Planning* 21, no. 113 (Sept. 1953): 434–442.

91 *Daily Mirror* (London), June 17, 1905.

92 Lee, "Letchworth Diary," pp. 439–440.

93 Ernest Rhys, *Everyman Remembers* (London, 1931).

94 C. B. Purdom, *The Building of Satellite Towns* (London, 1949), pp. 214–238.

95 *The Garden City* 1, no. 3 (June 1905): 11.

96 Ibid., n.s. 1, no. 4 (Nov. 1907): 4.

97 Ibid., 1, no. 2 (Feb. 1904): 1.

98 Catalogue of the Cheap Cottage Exhibition at Letchworth (Letchworth, 1905).

99 The best source for Unwin's designs is his "Cottage Planning," in *Where Shall I Live?* (Letchworth, 1907), pp. 103–109.

100 Howard Papers, How the Bicycle Saved the City, Folio 10. Manuscript of an article, probably unpublished, by Howard.

101 Le Corbusier, *La ville radieuse* (Boulogne-Seine, 1935), p. 192.

102 Ibid., title page.

103 Ibid., p. 154.

104 Ibid., p. 153.

105 Le Corbusier, *Quand les cathédrales étaient blanches* (Paris, 1937), pp. 280–281.

106 Le Corbusier, *La ville radieuse*, p. 167.

107 Ibid., p. 146.

108 Peter Serenyi, "Le Corbusier, Fourier, and the Monastery at Ema," cited footnote 15, chapter 21.

109 Charles Fourier, "An Architectural Innovation: The Street Gallery," in Jonathan Beecher and Richard Bienvenu, eds. and trans., *The Utopian Vision of Charles Fourier* (Boston, 1971), p. 243.

3

The Glory, Destruction, and Meaning of the City Beautiful Movement

William H. Wilson

Daniel H. Burnham and the *Plan of Chicago*

Burnham and Bennett's magnificent *Plan of Chicago* (1909) symbolized the maturation of the City Beautiful. Analyses of the plan accept the symbolism and divide its proposals into advanced elements looking forward to contemporary planning and atavistic schemes expressive of a City Beautiful already under attack when the plan appeared.[1]

Critics generally have approved of the plan's attention to the metropolitan region, which Burnham defined as a 60-mile radius from the Loop (Chicago's downtown). They have admired the system of diagonal and circumference roads designed to ease crowding and congestion. They have applauded Burnham's attention to the lakefront, a concern of his virtually from the time of the World's Columbian Exposition. Burnham's bold conception of a continuous green strip from Jackson Park to the north city limits and beyond would banish or suppress the railroad along Lake Michigan and open the vast water sheet to the citizens' recreational

Reprinted by permission from William H. Wilson. !989. *The City Beautiful Movement.* Baltimore and London: The Johns Hopkins University Press, pp 281–305.

and aesthetic enjoyment. Burnham's plans for active recreation areas within the lakefront park strip have worn well with critics, as have his calls for expanded park and boulevard areas and for forest preserves.

The proposed cultural center in lakefront Grant Park, between Lake Michigan and the southern portion of the commercial core, has been less commented upon, but its merits have been recognized despite its dated neoclassical designs. The realization of Burnham's plan for widening Michigan Avenue north of the Chicago River has been hailed because it opened underdeveloped areas to retail-commercial expansion. The critics generally have approved his plans for reorganizing the city's passenger and freight rail traffic and for improving the Chicago River.

Burnham's other proposals, associated with the allegedly narrow social and aesthetic concerns of the City Beautiful, have fared less well. The commentators have been particularly antagonistic toward his grand – or grandiose – civic center at the intersection of Congress and Halsted streets, on the southwestern fringe of the downtown commercial district. Here Burnham fashioned an overpowering centerpiece, a huge city hall with a soaring dome resting upon an elongated drum. Fernand Janin's sketches of the city hall, published with the plan, intended to flatter Burnham's conception but outlined instead a gargantuan parody of an administration building or a capitol. Three analysts of the plan, Carl Condit, Paul Boyer, and Mario Manieri-Elia, have understood the purpose behind the huge building and its vast plaza, which was to inspire the public to civic unity and adoration. But no one expressed the purpose better than Burnham himself, who wrote of the "central administration building, . . . surmounted by a dome of impressive height, to be seen and felt by the people, to whom it should stand as the symbol of civic order and unity. Rising from the plain upon which Chicago rests, its effect may be compared to that of the dome of St. Peter's at Rome."[2]

The other proposed government buildings, the city hall, and their accessories "would combine to unite the square into an harmonious whole." Further, the civic center, "when taken in connection with this plan of Chicago . . . becomes the keystone of the arch." After reviewing the plan's elements of practicality, beauty, and harmony, Burnham returned to "the center of all the varied activities of Chicago," where "will rise the towering dome of the civic center, vivifying and unifying the entire composition."[3]

The civic center had to bear so much heavy symbolic and ceremonial weight and was so obviously costly that there would be doubts about its feasibility. The center conformed in a general way to prevailing civic center theory but was without an existing anchor building such as the Colorado capitol in Denver. It was a mile or so from the northern and eastern areas of downtown and far from the northern expansion of the commercial city that the widening of Michigan Avenue was expected to produce. Burnham himself disclaimed any commitment to specific designs, writing that his were "suggestions of what may be done, for the report does not seek to impose any particular form." Manieri-Elia's reasonable conclusion is that the civic center buildings involved "a kind of ceremony," and "illusionistic" inspiration "persuasive in direct proportion to the improbability of their execution." In order to agree with his fundamental proposition, one need not accept Manieri-Elia's contention that Burnham was boosting real estate in the civic center area. Burnham himself knew very well how little relation to reality his huge hexagonal space could have. In the year of his plan's publication, the city and county broke ground for a new city hall and courthouse well away from his proposed site. There was virtually no possibility of his design becoming more than what it was, an awesome visual idealization of civic harmony.[4]

Commercial buildings of uniform, limited height appear in the Chicago plan, a second source for the criticism of Burnham's supposedly alien, aristocratic, Parisian solution. In the absence of a clarifying statement from Burnham, there are two possible responses to the criticism. One is that Burnham intended his city to adopt height limitations corresponding approximately to the building heights in the perspectives accompanying his plan. Height limitations were hardly unknown in twentieth-century American cities. They dated from the municipally imposed cornice height limits around Boston's famous Copley Square and were inspired by desires for visual harmony, for abundant sunlight and air, which excessively tall buildings would block, and for public safety in case of serious fires or other disasters. Denver had height limitations, though Speer's "Skyscraper Bill" raised them late in 1908. So did Seattle. The Puget Sound city retained its 200-foot limit until 1912, when it permitted the Smith Tower to rise forty-two stories. As Thomas Hines, Burnham's biographer, has pointed out, Beaux-Arts buildings lining the architect's conception of Michigan Avenue were scarcely squat. Uniform ranks of huge, block-long structures rose eighteen stories, although the heights generally tapered off to the north, south, and west.[5]

For all the cohesion and rationality of the uniform facades and heights, and despite ample precedent, it is doubtful whether Burnham intended Chicago to adopt building height limitations. He wrote nothing about height limits, even while he lavished analytical prose upon a civic center practically impossible to build in the shape or on the site projected. Thus, it hardly seems likely that he seriously hoped for the adoption of a height-limit program that he did not bother to defend at all. Had he fought for building height limitations and facade uniformity, he would have added to the already formidable expenses of the plan with the huge costs of demolition, exterior remodeling, and possible purchase of unusable air rights. He would have, additionally, created an aesthetic controversy potentially inimical to his plan's success. Burnham's silence on the subject could be interpreted as indifference to height limits, but if that were so, why did he bother to introduce plate after plate of perspective paintings revealing buildings uniformly clad and corniced?[6]

The more plausible response to Burnham's critics identifies a valid role for his buildings. They served as the matrix for his proposals. Practically superfluous but visually vital, they framed the reconstructed Michigan Avenue and the new railroad stations and deferred without competition to the dominating dome of city hall. They were a pictorial representation of Burnham's hopes for a dynamic cultural and commercial city where mere individualism was subordinated to the harmony of the greater good.

Critics of the *Plan of Chicago* have decried Burnham's brief if trenchant references to the slum problem and his routine solutions, cutting boulevards through dilapidated housing and enforcing sanitation measures. Burnham and other City Beautiful planners were little concerned with housing, it is true. Whether their approach is open to criticism is another matter, to be considered later. For now it may be said that housing details were outside the purview of the comprehensive planning of the era. The planner's task, instead, was to provide the spatial opportunity for good housing at all income levels. Ensuring adequate housing for poor people was a matter for private initiative and for thoroughgoing housing code inspection and enforcement.[7]

Burnham paid little attention to the automobile, an omission costing him additional credibility with the critics. A more charitable approach would suggest how difficult it is to predict the future, especially without any particularly sophisticated tools and substantial data on trends in metropolitan areas. It is one thing to understand the American expectation of democratized technology – Burnham probably had some grasp of it – but quite another to gauge accurately when the inexpensive, durable mass car would arrive. It had not arrived by 1909. To judge beforehand the urban, spatial, social, and economic impact of the mass automobile was a still greater challenge. The planners of the city practical era might better be charged with dereliction. The compilers of *City Planning Progress in the United States: 1917* derided the City Beautiful, as it was fashionable to do, "but barely hinted at the congestion and parking problems the automobile was already causing," problems that only "emerged clearly in the 1920s" with soaring car registrations.[8] It is unreasonable to criticize Burnham for failing to incorporate the car into the city plan when his supposedly scientific successors did not, though the mass car and its developing consequences were right under their noses.

In fact most of the criticism of the *Plan of Chicago*, as well as much of the praise, arises from a misunderstanding of the City Beautiful movement. While the critics correctly acclaim the plan for its sumptuous, evocative craftsmanship and correctly attribute its quality to the extraordinary resources at Burnham's disposal, they do not see it for what it really is – a typical, if grand, City Beautiful plan. Burnham's regional sweep was one proof of his self-assessment as "a door opener"[9] who grasped the implications of tendencies a little in advance of the rest. Many cities grew fabulously after the turn of the century, projecting urban regionalism beyond the era of the big city into the age of the metropolis. Mayor Robert Speer and others in Denver already had under consideration some sort of regional relationship with recreation areas in the Rocky Mountains. Street traffic improvements similar to Burnham's were embedded in Kessler's 1893 Kansas City plan and the 1901 plan for Harrisburg, in various Denver proposals, and in many other plans of the City Beautiful era.

Burnham's lakefront park scheme was as sweeping in its way as his street plans were in theirs, but waterfront improvement ideas reached back at least as far as the senior Olmsted's Charlesbank in Boston, through Manning's River Front Park in Harrisburg, John Olmsted's plans for the Lake Washington boulevard in Seattle, and many more. Burnham's plans for active recreation in the park deferred to a movement whose time had come. His replanning of Chicago's rail traffic extended a City Beautiful tradition in which he and his firm were much involved. Burnham designed the monumental Union Station in Washington in conjunction with the massive rail reorganization in the capital city. He lost the Kansas City station job to Jarvis Hunt but was aware of the great rail relocation in the offing there. His firm's other union station designs testify to the rail transportation activity associated with the City Beautiful.

Nor was the *Plan of Chicago* the swan song of the movement. Continued development under existing comprehensive plans aside, Bogue's *Plan of Seattle* was yet to appear, as was Kessler's Dallas plan. In sum, the *Plan of Chicago* was most extraordinary because of its generous funding by Chicago's business elite, its comprehensiveness, and its evocative paintings and drawings of a sublime City Beautiful.[10]

City Practical Criticisms of the City Beautiful

By the time Burnham's plan appeared, the reaction against the City Beautiful had set in. The attack combined valid criticism with ridicule and misrepresentation, but it was effective. Opponents of the City Beautiful succeeded in stigmatizing it as excessively concerned with monumentality, empty aesthetics, grand effects for the well-to-do, and general impracticality. Most defenders of the City Beautiful offered little resistance to the onslaught and soon joined their attackers' ranks. The city practical carried the battle because it benefited from three interrelated developments: increasing specialization, rising professionalism, and burgeoning bureaucracy.

Specialization developed rapidly in the nineteenth and early twentieth centuries. The National Municipal League dated from 1894, and the

American Society of Landscape Architects from 1899. They joined the revived American Institute of Architects (AIA) and were joined in turn by the National Playground Association of America in 1906. Housing reformers and settlement house workers held conferences and organized the Committee on Congestion of Population. Professional awareness reinforced specialization. The hallmarks of both included university curricula, a growing body of literature, prerequisites for professional standing, and exclusivity. For a time professionals coexisted with enthusiastic laymen in such organizations as the American Park and Outdoor Art Association (APOAA) and the American Civic Association (ACA). But professional organizations and activities increasingly claimed the specialists' time and energy. Although laymen, not professionals, were the primary targets of the City Beautiful bulletins of the American League for Civic Improvement (ALCI) and the ACA, increasingly specialized publications appeared; the Pittsburgh Survey, launched in 1907, the city planning issue of *Charities and the Commons* in 1908, and the appearance of *American City* in 1909 were among several newer entrants in the field of urban problem writing.[11]

The bureaucratization and professionalization of the planning and other functions of city government were equally ominous for the City Beautiful. Beginning in the nineteenth century, municipal engineers deliberately preempted several planning areas, especially those involving sanitation, street grading and surfacing, drainage, and the oversight of improvement construction. The search for discipline, accountability, and professional service in city government moved from "strong mayor" charter proposals, to the city commission form, and to reformers' advocacy of the council-manager system. Simultaneously, the rise of the quasi-independent, specialized commission heralded the increasing bureaucratization of urban government. Most significant for the City Beautiful movement was the establishment of the first city planning commission at Hartford, Connecticut, in 1907. That body forecast a new reality. City governments would assume planning responsibilities and retain professional planners, usurping the catalytic role of the lay activists, who were the backbone of such groups as the ACA.[12]

The planners welcomed the changes because they held out the hope of divorcing professional planning not only from various lay enthusiasms but also from sponsoring elites, who might advance their own ideas with proprietary firmness. As Manning discovered in Harrisburg and John Olmsted learned in Seattle, the experts' continuing supervision of a plan did not ensure harmonious relations with its sponsors. Increasingly, consulting planners worked with city governments directly, with private developers, or with corporate planning groups more remote from electoral politics than earlier organizations such as the Harrisburg League for Municipal Improvements.[13]

All these developments were visible or were just below the horizon when the First National Conference on City Planning convened in Washington, D.C., during May 1909. Benjamin C. Marsh, a New York housing reform enthusiast, organized the conference. Marsh was already on record against the City Beautiful as too concerned with cosmetic display. Parks, civic centers, and other great public works were attractive, he wrote, but the poor only occasionally could afford to "escape from their squalid, confining surroundings to view the architectural perfection and to experience the aesthetic delights of the remote improvements." Marsh mixed practicality with his humanitarianism. He called for zoning, especially limits on factory location, for height limits, efficient transportation, parks and playgrounds in crowded districts, and excess condemnation.[14]

The conference attendees ranged from housing reformers through architects, planners, and engineers, to socially aware businessmen. Politically the group found equilibrium in the moderate left. The sessions reflected Marsh's efforts to condemn the City Beautiful and move planning toward practical humanitarianism as defined by specialists. Robert Anderson Pope, a New York landscape architect, took up the rhetorical cudgels against the City Beautiful movement. The movement's great sin was masking the "true nature" and "proper aim" of city planning, which was "to remedy congestion" of population. Population "congestion" was, not surprisingly, the hobby of Marsh, the guiding spirit of the Committee on Congestion of Population. Pope attacked the City Beautiful for encouraging the assumption that "the first duty of city planning is to beautify." The movement had "made the aesthetic an objective in itself." Pope decried "the expenditure of huge sums for extensive park systems . . . inaccessible improvements . . . made available to but a small portion of the community – the wealthy and leisure classes, who of all society needs these advantages the least." Moreover, "we have rushed to plan showy civic centers of gigantic cost," inspired by "civic vanity, . . . when pressing hard-by, we see the almost unbelievable congestion with its hideous brood of evil: filth, disease, degeneracy, pauperism, and crime. What external adornment can make truly beautiful such a city?"[15]

Other speakers joined Pope in praising European, especially German, cities for improving housing and thereby raising the character and quality of their inhabitants. They asserted, with Pope, that a city planned for social benefit and economic efficiency would be beautiful. Marsh's speeches featured propositions for effective urban improvement: a survey of existing conditions bent on an "ascertaining of the facts," which would discredit "corporate interest"; dissemination of the facts through publicity campaigns; and the creation of powerful planning commissions able to enforce planned change. Marsh called on the federal government to conduct a civic census of American cities in conjunction with a nationwide city planning committee organized along the lines of other national organizations such as the Consumer's League and the Red Cross. At the end of the conference he proposed a "commission on land values in our great cities, similar to the Interstate Commerce Commission," which would determine a "fair profit on the estate," Marsh having already decided to his own satisfaction that "a profit of three or four fold in a few years is . . . unsafe and unnecessary and undemocratic." Marsh could hardly have better expressed the latter-day left-progressive faith in statistics, publicity, and the beneficence of drastic governmental intervention.[16]

Nor could he have more decisively repudiated the City Beautiful belief in the ability of uplifted, enlightened citizens to work through their private destinies harmoniously amid scenes of surpassing public beauty, in a city organized for utility and efficiency. But if any supporter of the City Beautiful believed that Marsh and his fellows represented merely a fad, a passing squall, he was soon disabused. In December 1909 architect Cass Gilbert flayed the City Beautiful at the annual meeting of the AIA. "If I were disposed to delay, interrupt, or confuse the progress of city development I would publish the phrase 'city beautiful' in big head lines in every newspaper," Gilbert declared. "Let us have the city useful, the city practical, the city livable, the city sensible, the city anything but the city beautiful." Gilbert called for "a city that is done, completed, a city sane and sensible that can be lived in comfortably. If it is to be a city beautiful it will be one naturally." Gilbert's tirade was a hit. "The sentiment against the 'city beautiful' term was unanimous." According to one account, the AIA delegates issued a search warrant for "the originator of 'city beautiful'. The culprit had not been discovered at three o'clock this afternoon."[17]

Robinson fell into line. Reporting on the "unanimous and hearty applause" that greeted Gilbert's remarks, he insisted that the people who were "doing most to make cities beautiful, long ago gave up use of the phrase." They now understood the source of urban beauty: the "adaptation to purpose and cooperative harmony of parts." Arnold Brunner echoed Gilbert's and Robinson's themes at the ACA's 1910 convention. "To the average citizen the 'city beautiful' suggests the city impossible," he asserted. Brunner insisted that "boards of aldermen and city treasurers are apt to believe that it means an attempt to tie pink bows on the lamp posts." George B. Ford, a Columbia University planning instructor, took up the cry before the ACA in 1911. The City Beautiful, Ford charged, was too often concerned with "superficialities," with "frills and furbelows," and was "dazzling," but it was a mistake to advance the City Beautiful *"before the problems of living, work and play have been solved."*[18]

At last the leading lay apostle of the City Beautiful capitulated. Although McFarland did "not at all agree with his separation of what he called the aesthetic from the practical," Ford's attack shook the ACA president. The effect of Ford's charges was evident when McFarland stepped forward to address the 1912 convention of the ACA on "Not Only the

City Beautiful." In a speech that surrendered to functionalist aesthetics, he ridiculed laymen who clung to the idea of the City Beautiful as "a tawdry soldier's monument, flanked by a monstrous flagpole, several dismounted cannon . . . and four or five enormous telephone poles." When cities were made clean, practical, and efficient, then they would be beautiful. McFarland looked back to the World's Columbian Exposition, taken in his own time to be the starting point of city planning, but with an eye to its utility. Planners "properly" admired and emulated "that glorious 'White City' that the great Burnham gave to us in 1893," he said. Planners needed to recall, however, that the fair was "both convenient and beautiful, both sanitary and sightly, and therefore truly admirable."[19]

These assaults on the City Beautiful caricatured the movement as being as concerned with the wealthy as it was indifferent to the poor and as obsessed with surface aesthetics as it was disregardful of practicality. It was, furthermore, outrageously expensive, an affront to responsible citizens and public officials. Attacks on the City Beautiful reflected the changing relationships among citizen activists, professional planners, and urban governments. Ideas not professionally or bureaucratically approved could be denounced as allegedly expensive and impractical. Moreover, by 1909 there was some impatience with the optimism of early progressivism, when men of lofty purpose and goodwill would refashion American cities. Perhaps the panic of 1907, the portentous electoral successes of Socialists, and the bureaucratic routinization of reform all made Robinson's and McFarland's hopeful urgings seem a little threadbare.[20]

Nor were the grand city plans all that successful. Some remained partly or wholly unbuilt, unable to confer their presumed psychic and material benefits on the citizenry. "Practically all the planning of cities and 'additions' to cities . . . has been done by Engineers," Olmsted, Jr., wrote in a candid, perceptive letter, "and while most of it has been very badly done their work has simply met the standards and demands of their communities." Landscape architects had planned, usually, better than engineers, with regard for aesthetics and for life's amenities, but their work was "a drop in the bucket" compared with the influence of municipal engineers in the lives of the people. For "real results" in planning "and not just a continuation of the interesting but ineffective talk and theorizing that has been going on for some years now upon this subject, it is essential that able and influential municipal engineers should take a more prominent part in the movement."[21]

Frederick's half-brother John addressed the related issue of taxpayer resistance to expensive grand plans at a time when he yet believed that he would be chosen to help design what became Seattle's Bogue plan. "It is going to be much harder to get the money for expensive schemes here than it was in the case of Cleveland. Grand schemes were devised for St.

Louis, but I haven't heard how the execution is getting on," he wrote to his wife. "I think they wanted $30,000,000 to carry out the St. Louis scheme. . . . It's hard to persuade economical practical voters and taxpayers to spend that much in improving the plan of the city."[22]

Another problem involved the phrase *City Beautiful* itself. By 1909 it had been in service for a decade and was becoming a bit timeworn. It was a protean phrase, comprising activities as disparate as a women's club agitating for improved trash collection and Daniel Burnham superintending the corps of designers at work on the *Plan of Chicago*. Unfortunately, City Beautiful denoted aesthetic concerns, not necessarily an important consideration in housing surveys, recreation, or land-use control. City Beautiful devotees such as Robinson, Kessler, and McFarland could embrace playgrounds, zoning, and improved housing without betraying the movement, but their eclecticism did not deflect the bureaucratic thrust toward utilitarianism.[23]

Finally, the City Beautiful was a victim of its own success. Citizen activists achieved or approximated their goals in Chicago, Denver, Harrisburg, Kansas City, and other places. Utility wires went underground. Graceful street furniture replaced crude utility poles or grotesque drinking fountains. Billboards were tamed by municipal regulation and the self-imposed restrictions of the bill posters.[24] Park, parkway, and boulevard systems expanded while their older segments were developed. Many civic centers were planned, and some were built. Public and semipublic buildings usually improved in design and commodiousness, whether or not they were grouped along civic center malls. All this was expensive, however, and as the years of construction went by, there were fewer fresh victories to inscribe on the banners of the City Beautiful. It became easier for critics to attack the City Beautiful for aesthetic obsessions and to ignore the movement's long-standing concerns in such areas as recreation, traffic and smoke control, and urban efficiency. This city practical critique was a caricature – but it was credible enough to be accepted for years, in the absence of careful studies of the City Beautiful movement. In 1962 an otherwise thoughtful analysis declared the City Beautiful to be "a narrow and pathetically fragile ideal, remote from business, commerce, industry, transportation, poverty, and similar mundane but integral features of urban life."[25] Few critics questioned, then or later, whether the presumably more realistic and more humane city practical could, or did, advance comprehensive planning with greater effectiveness.

The junior Olmsted was one who looked into the pit that the city practical planners were digging for themselves and saw problems almost beyond imagination. Olmsted confessed to the Second National Conference on City Planning his dismay over "the appalling breadth and ramification" of planning and "the play of enormously complex forces which no one clearly understands and few pretend to." Olmsted's solution was to divide the planning task among specialists, from whom a comprehensive plan would somehow emerge. He glossed over the danger of lost or compromised comprehensiveness with the statement that anyone who fashioned *"any smallest element"* of the plan was responsible for the welfare of the entire city. Olmsted's rhetorical resolution of the city practical dilemma was as fatuous as any City Beautiful formulation. John Nolen and other city practical planners, far from abandoning the City Beautiful, appropriated the movement's emphasis on civic consciousness and utility as well as its naturalistic and formal designs. Axial, neoclassical City Beautiful war memorial proposals flourished in the wake of World War I. Mel Scott found that the application of the survey technique or other city practical mechanisms neither eliminated biases or assumptions nor guaranteed a plan's implementation.[26]

Later Attacks on the City Beautiful

Another, later critique censured the movement for its limited achievements. The analysis rests on a number of assumptions. The first assumption is the city practical belief in the impossibility of completing City Beautiful plans. It built on criticisms about unfulfilled plans; these criticisms were made in the early years of the city practical, before greater experience provided a better perspective. The second assumption failed to acknowledge the centrality of politics to the City Beautiful and reduced the movement partly or wholly to civic center design exercises. Then it declared the alleged design movement a failure because so few civic centers were built. Thirdly, the critics asserted a functionalist or "American" aesthetic against the neoclassicism of many City Beautiful designs, assuming that the designs were rejected because they were dated foreign imports false to American needs or ideals. Beyond these three assumptions, the critics believed that the city practical and subsequent planning eras enjoyed a significantly higher rate of implementation than did the City Beautiful. Almost the only positive value of the City Beautiful, in this view, was its success in stimulating public thought and discussion of planning.

This strident criticism dominated in the 1930s and 1940s and persisted much longer. Two examples will impart the flavor. Henry S. Churchill noted in 1945 how "scarcely a single city carried out, except in minor details, any plan that was drawn up. Of the 135 published reports, nearly every one was filed in the City Engineer's office and forgotten." The few exceptional cities "carried out only plans relating to large and spectacular public works," while they avoided "real replanning." To Churchill, the City Beautiful "plan generally meant the paper architectural development of a civic center," one with a domed building, fountains, and marble paving. "Fortunately, little of it came to pass, except in Washington and an occasional place that got out of control, like Harrisburg." James Marston Fitch found "a lot of Baron Haussmann and precious little democracy in these vast geometrics of befountained plazas and intersecting boulevards." For Fitch, their "vastly important role" was "introducing the concept of *planned* reconstruction into the popular mind. However pompous and autocratic the solutions, they were at least admissions that real problems did exist." The movement by and by "involved many well-intentioned souls" who eventually understood "that the problem was much more than one of simple face-lifting."[27]

Unfortunately, the critics of the 1930s and 1940s molded their social and aesthetic biases into a critical framework. It is doubtful whether any City Beautiful plan succeeded or failed because it was judged to be unworkable by city practical standards, included a civic center, or was neoclassical. As for the success rate of City Beautiful plans, comparing City Beautiful successes with later efforts would be a study in itself. In its absence, a present judgment is that the full implementation of comprehensive plans is modest in all eras.

A less biased examination of nationwide City Beautiful planning suggests that a variety of reasons lay behind the limited success of the City Beautiful. The low proportion of plans in the South (an even distribution by states, territories, and possessions should have produced about fifty) indicates that conditions in the region and not the City Beautiful should explain the South's relatively weak planning impulse. Of the 233 planning activity reports in the 1917 compendium *City Planning Progress*, only 34 concerned cities in the states of the Old Confederacy. Of the 34, more than half involved cities in southwestern Texas and in the upper southern states of Virginia, North Carolina, and Tennessee.[28]

Some southern City Beautiful proponents seemed to exhaust themselves in the early stages of the planning struggles. The Woman's Club of Raleigh, North Carolina, hired Robinson in 1912, who submitted a typical Robinsonian effort the next year. The club printed and sold copies of the plan but failed to agitate for concomitant political or administrative reforms. It may have been that Robinson's suggestions were insufficient to gather popular support, but there is no way of knowing, for the Woman's Club conducted no further promotion of the plan, such as newspaper followup stories or reprinted excerpts. Greensboro, North Carolina, hired Robinson in 1917, but he died before completing a plan. The Greensboro movement died with the planner. In Birmingham, Alabama, transplanted Yankees and native southerners worked for civic improvements under the leadership of the chamber of commerce. Warren Manning produced a civic center and park system plan in 1919, the late date indicative of cultural lag. Unfortunately Birmingham's inadequate parks were little improved and expanded, especially in black areas, and "Manning's plans came to naught." Labor spokesmen opposed spending municipal funds on civic improvements until free school textbooks and other services were provided. The Sloss-Sheffield Steel and Iron Company defeated the city's smoke abatement efforts in a series of maneuvers extending over several years. These and other problems frustrated the southern City Beautiful, but they were unrelated to aesthetics.[29]

The areas outside the Deep South, where the greater proportion of City Beautiful plans appeared, were those enjoying the most City Beautiful success. Again, however, design considerations played a negligible or modest role. City Beautiful planning succeeded most often in commercial cities similar to Kansas City, Denver, and Seattle, although manufacturing did not militate against the City Beautiful when it involved light industry and processing. Heavy-industry cities and single-industry towns fared less well, perhaps because they held a higher proportion of laborers likely to be skeptical of sweeping improvement plans. They may have lacked a large, powerful, dedicated middle class. Plans were prepared for eastern cities, but with some exceptions – the reconstruction of politically anomalous Washington, the earlier Boston metropolitan park system, Philadelphia's Fairmount Parkway – much less was done. Sheer size, high land values inhibiting large public works, diversity of interests, and fragmented leadership played negative roles. Smaller cities sometimes fared better, if, like Harrisburg, they were state capitals or for some other reason contained a significant middle class.[30]

New York's City Beautiful failed principally because, as its historian demonstrated, it suffered through a long gestation. When it finally emerged as the *Report of the New York Improvement Commission* in 1907, it was an orphan without adequate media or community support, another reflection of the city's scattered interests and leadership. But its historian condemned the plan, instead, for its "static conception," its failure to "pay enough attention to the vast economic resources of the city and the way in which these resources could be better developed through planning," and its "overemphasis on aesthetic considerations" resulting in "slighted social concerns." All this criticism poured out upon a plan devoted to unifying the city through an expanded park and boulevard system, improved traffic circulation, and revitalized piers, including recreation piers, among many other proposals.[31]

If such ritualistic condemnation of the City Beautiful in the face of its social, economic, and utilitarian concerns does not advance the analysis of failure, what does, beyond naming New York's diversity and fragmentation? Herbert Croly, in his 1907 criticism of the plan, grasped another part of the problem when he cited the stupefyingly high land costs "in the central part of the older city," leading the city fathers to "inevitably adopt the cheapest plan which has any promise of being adequate." But the high costs of a comprehensive plan depended upon New York's size, density, and economic dynamism. New York had long since lost the plasticity allowing for a relatively inexpensive implementation. Charles F. McKim refused to have anything to do with New York planning for that very reason. Although willing to advise Mayor Seth Low of the need for an independent, well-salaried commission to pursue a comprehensive .plan with expert, specialized advice, he would not become personally involved with "any but an ideal proposition, which is not very likely to be made. The difficulties to be overcome here, are, so far as the Borough of Manhattan are [*sic*] concerned, insuperable, and with but a few years of breath left to hope for, there are several ways in which I could put in my time more effectively."[32]

The critics of City Beautiful achievement have one more high card to play: San Francisco. In 1905 Burnham, with Bennett's collaboration, completed his excellent planning report for the bay city elite. On 18 April 1906, the great earthquake and fire destroyed most newly printed copies of the plan while they reduced some 4 square miles of San Francisco to a charred ruin. Within four years the city was rebuilt almost entirely as it had been, without reference to Burnham's plan. The failure allows the plan's most careful interpreter the pleasure of declaring San Francisco to be "better off" without the plan while condemning private property interests for preventing its realization. Many of Judd Kahn's observations about Burnham's plan and the City Beautiful movement in general are intelligent and sympathetic, but his point that the plan required an imperial power lacking in the American system is not well taken. The point is, instead, that existing cities may be replanned through politics, but cities destroyed are almost always reconstructed on the old street pattern, and their damaged areas are rationalized with commercial considerations in mind. Baron Haussmann possessed imperial authority, true, but he worked with an existing city.[33]

Kahn surveyed post-World War II reconstruction and found the "overall pattern" to be "one of continuity" – in other words, rebuilding on the preexisting lines. There were a "number of cities in which street plans were modified and a few in which more extensive changes were accomplished," yet Kahn admitted that "disaster seems more likely to beget substantial continuity in urban form, rather than radical innovation." The post-World War II reconstruction is all the more remarkable when the international growth of planning lore and planning consciousness from Burnham's time is considered. Human beings confront urban destruction with a powerful urge to rebuild. Across time, cultures, and systems of land ownership, existing cities may be more or less replanned and modified. Destroyed cities, including San Francisco, usually are restored.[34]

The civic center problem raises issues similar to those already discussed. Beginning two or three years after the publication of the 1902 plan for Washington, civic center designs were important, if not central, to the City Beautiful. The failure of civic center plans, while not synonymous with an unsuccessful City Beautiful movement, calls into question its methods and goals. For the plans did fail. Joan E. Draper has identified seventy-two civic center plans. Perhaps a tenth of them were begun during the City Beautiful era, and very few after that time. Draper isolated five circumstances affecting a center's fate: "(1) the quality of project leadership; (2) the financial situation of the city and funding methods for the project; (3) the city's legal powers; (4) the degree of cooperation from potential tenants (city, state, federal, and semipublic agencies); and (5) the feasibility of the plan in physical terms." Her induction is sound and, excepting her point 4, could be applied to almost any public improvement project, including the park and boulevard systems identified with the City Beautiful.[35]

A full response to the issue of civic center failure involves two additional considerations. First, cost is an independent variable in the civic center case. Civic centers, apart from the other features of their accompanying plans, were necessarily expensive. Unlike parks, boulevards, street furniture, or other elements of the City Beautiful ensemble, they could not, usually, be gradually acquired. Government functions depended upon the immediate acquisition of adequate land and the timely construction of at least some essential buildings. Necessity and civic center theory both dictated a center near the commercial-retail core, where land was expensive. Neoclassical buildings finished to the standards of the day were costly as well. After World War I, construction costs rose to double and more above those of the City Beautiful era, inhibiting late starts on civic centers during the 1920s.[36]

Second, too many people perceived civic centers to be, in themselves, impractical solutions to problems of poor government organization and inadequate civic idealism. This does not mean that they opposed neoclassical aesthetics. Rather, as in Kansas City and Seattle, they weighed high costs, extreme centralization of government activity, loss of private revenue- and tax-producing property, and the impact on the immediate area of the civic center against the presumed benefits. Not surprisingly, they found the monetary and other costs overwhelming. The realities of civic center politics caution against reading later aesthetic norms, advanced by the architectural and critical avant-garde, into the struggles over realizing the City Beautiful. They also caution against arguing that civic centers and related improvements were meant to increase centralization. City Beautiful advocates saw civic centers as enhancing efficiency, not centralization. They may have subconsciously promoted centralization, but if they did, their unstated agenda left many downtown businessmen unimpressed. Moreover, the street widenings, radial streets, boulevards, and outlying parks associated with the City Beautiful could be interpreted as assisting decentralization.[37]

Design-oriented detractors of the City Beautiful have attacked its architectural handmaiden, neoclassicism. The argument runs essentially as follows: The World's Columbian Exposition imposed a derivative, passé style upon America. Neoclassicism had no proper relation to American aspirations, ideals, or building needs, yet City Beautiful planners adopted neoclassicism from the exposition, just as they did its formality and axiality. The critics expressly or implicitly follow the convictions of the embittered Louis Sullivan, who declared that the Chicago fair foisted neoclassical architecture on the country. Burnham unwittingly lent strength to Sullivan's charge with his assertions that the exposition inspired civic centers.[38]

Despite Burnham's inadvertent support, there is a false ring to Sullivan's charge that the fair clouded the public mind with the neoclassic and throttled the development of native American architecture. Thomas E. Tallmadge challenged Sullivan in 1927, three years after the architect's celebrated autobiography appeared. The challenges have continued and may be summarized as follows. The fair did not end Sullivan's career, nor Frank Lloyd Wright's, nor that of any other advanced architect. Sullivan continued with his designing, and Wright built Prairie-style houses into the twentieth century. Chicago school buildings and Prairie school residences appeared until the eve of World War I. Moreover, Sullivan's Transportation Building at the Chicago fair hardly qualified him to be an architectural seer. Its structure, beneath a mediocre exterior, was less advanced than some others at the exposition. Sullivan himself developed a repugnantly toplofty personality, while Wright reveled in his role of feisty maverick. Neither man conceived of city planning ideas congenial to the local elites who retained planners. Shifts in emphasis of Chicago school architects from commercial to residential design and public infatuation with arts other than architecture also explain the expiration of the Chicago school style.[39]

These challenges may be expanded in several directions. Taking Sullivan first, for all his daring innovation, he was not a high-quality planner. He entertained few notions of the city as ensemble, and the Burnham firm excelled him in interior building design. In his lyrical-to-bombastic *Kindergarten Chats* Sullivan did not ask the capitalist to shut up shop but rather to develop a social conscience in architecture. It is difficult to imagine a building more congenial to private enterprise than the skyscraper, the style of which Sullivan did so much to advance, or an institution more representative than the bank, small examples of which he designed in the declining years of his practice. As for Wright, nothing save his personal lapses stayed his work. He was in full career as America's reigning architectural genius when he died, nearing ninety-two, in 1959. Wright's city plans, when they did come, were unrealistic. No antidote for pressing urban problems, Broadacres instead visualized a suburbanized middle-class utopia held together by ubiquitous automobiles, telephones, and televisions.[40]

So far as the Chicago school goes, its demise has as much to do with its own design sclerosis as with anything else. William H. Jordy remarked on the inability of Chicago architects to develop new wall and window treatments after 1900. Sullivan, though he continued his innovation in detail, achieved his final breakthrough, the Schlesinger, Mayer department store, in 1899. These failures of vision and imagination are as serious as any of those charged against the architects of the City Beautiful. As for the Prairie school, some of its practitioners fed upon City Beautiful ideas. Mark L. Peisch's sensible study notes the positive impact of the Columbian Exposition upon several Chicago architects and how Walter Burley Griffin used City Beautiful devices such as axes, groupings, and waterscapes in his 1913 plan of Canberra.[41]

The Chicago fair and the City Beautiful hardly impeded the rise of the skyscraper. City Beautiful planners usually left commercial-retail cores to their own devices, except for individual building designs and schemes for functional definition and traffic relief. City Beautiful architects created low public buildings more useful to the governments of their day than skyscrapers. When they designed commercial buildings, they sometimes employed neoclassical detailing on the lower floors. Above five or six stories, however, the motif became attenuated or lost in mass and silhouette as the buildings rose. Talbot F. Hamlin's straightforward, popular discussion of the "American style" argued convincingly that the "American" quality of the skyscraper lay in its proportions, not in its ornamental detail. As Lewis Mumford deftly phrased it, tall commercial architecture is for "angels and aviators," not for the terrestrial critic. The City Beautiful influenced the main run of skyscraper design much less than technology, ground rent, labor costs, land-use controls, and tax policy. Sullivan's statement condemning neoclassicism reflects the pain of a picturesque secessionist whose designs and ideas fail to conquer. Nor had the neoclassic conquered. Both styles continued, before and after 1893, borrowing from one another as well as battling. Both helped to prepare the path for the International style and its successors.[42]

More recently the City Beautiful has come under the critical scrutiny of Marxist historians. They argue that the City Beautiful movement, responding to imperialistic impulses and economic cycles, strove to create spatial order and unity in the city. The effort epitomized new governmental efforts to rationalize the urban chaos produced by capitalism and to allow private enterprise to function more efficiently. The movement attempted to impose discipline and control upon the masses through visual and spatial manipulation. It tried to provide a noble idealism and the symbolism of a purified city in neoclassic design. Consultant-planners such as Robinson were bound to fail, or achieve limited success, partly because of their fake aestheticism and altruistic rhetoric. Worse, they could not or would not understand that private enterprise itself was the cause of urban malformations. Therefore, they could only arrange, at best, a somewhat brighter facade behind which capitalism continued its dirty work of exploitation. The limits of the City Beautiful were no more evident than in its failure to deal with housing, for an effective housing program would have challenged exploitative, speculative land values.

Americans, in contrast to Europeans, would not assent to significant land-use controls until planners could demonstrate the capitalist utility of zoning.[43]

A one-paragraph summary cannot do justice to the Marxist analysis, nor can a non-Marxist rebuttal hope to satisfy Marxists. With those caveats entered, the way is open for some observations. First, most of the Marxist critique of the City Beautiful has been advanced by non-Marxists: the relationship to imperialism; the thrust toward utilitarianism, improvement, social control, and civic idealism; and the lack of detailed concern for housing. The critique, in other words, does not necessarily spring from the Marxist beliefs in the depravity of the proletariat. The Marxists themselves, beyond their dialectical conclusions, disagree on such matters as the application of the business cycle to planning and the definition of the City Beautiful movement. A word about housing: Given popular attitudes that place "adequate" housing well down on the list of desirable goods, an ever-expanding definition of adequate housing responding to the rising level of prosperity and to suburbanization, and poor housing in countries having a less potent ideology of private property (or none at all), it does not seem so strange for the City Beautiful movement to place housing beyond the scope of its full treatment. Settlement house workers and others were studying the housing questions without, at the same time, dealing effectively with many of the other problems engaging the City Beautiful planners. It was a sensible division of labor.[44]

The origin and spirit of the City Beautiful idea refute the Marxist belief in beautification as the willing tool of capitalism. The phrase *City Beautiful* had been around at least from the time Frances Hodgson Burnett, in her 1895 formula novel, applied it to the Chicago fair. But the inspiration for its widespread use derived from the lecture series of the Arts and Crafts Exhibition Society in England, published in 1897. Two years later Robinson and *Municipal Affairs* applied its arguments to American cities, and the gathering movement had a slogan. The English lecturers had emphasized two themes: The city, the home of all citizens, should be beautiful; and its beautification involved a substantial restraint on private enterprise. The problem, in their view, was not the inadequacy of individual housing but the pathetic state of humanity's common room, the city. T. J. Cobden-Sanderson declared that "Art must be controlled and directed" toward "the creation of the City Beautiful, the beautiful house of Mankind." Halsey Ricardo spoke for the psychic benefits of a beautiful, polychromatic city. "Strong and brave," he urged, "let us go out to our fight clothed with the distinction that colour can give us, and cheered by the *camaraderie* . . . the day's work done, there is the city beautiful – firm, stable, our home."[45]

The curbs on capitalist activity involved more than those necessary to secure public land and construct various improvements. W. R. Lethaby denounced the "sticky slime of soot" falling from the London sky. Walter Crane attacked advertising posters, "often vulgar, coarse, and debased." Ricardo referred to the struggle "against want and disease, dirt and disorder." Capitalism might survive a cleanup of London soot, strict advertising regulation, and the controls necessary to defeat "want and disease, dirt and disorder." If it survived, it would be as an economic arrangement much modified from the late nineteenth century's. In any case the issue was not the destruction or survival of capitalism. It was the creation of the City Beautiful.[46]

Nor is it correct to claim that the struggle for the City Beautiful involved the more insightful, progressive capitalists versus the retrograde industrial capitalists, who wanted to keep their chimney soot. No such neat vocational divisions existed, as examinations of Kansas City, Harrisburg, and Seattle have demonstrated. Appeals to economic self-interest accompanied improvement campaigns in those cities and others, to be sure. But they rested on a belief in human rationality, a realistic assessment of existing socioeconomic arrangements, and a conviction that the private enterprise system was generally beneficial. They were not born of a blind trust in capitalism or capitalists.

The Survival of the City Beautiful

The ideals of the City Beautiful survived in spite of the critics' best efforts. The phrase *City Beautiful* continued popular for years with laymen, who applied it to a variety of planning and improvement concerns. In 1928 the magazine of the Dallas Chamber of Commerce urged each home-owner to adapt an exterior lighting plan and "develop our residential sections into veritable fairylands after sundown." The use of outdoor lighting would demonstrate how the "quest of the 'City Beautiful' proceeds continuously in America." Two years later the president of the Dallas Chamber told his organization's annual meeting that "the love of beauty prompts and motivates most of our individual desires." Urban beauty in architecture, landscaping, and other arts "differentiates grandeur from mere size" and "leaves its imprint upon the very soul of citizenship." A beautification program would mean "that Dallas might be known throughout the land not only as the 'City of the Hour,' but also as the 'City Beautiful.'" McFarland, inveigh as he might against the use of *City Beautiful*, could not keep the phrase out of circulation.[47]

Critics and planners could censure or ignore the City Beautiful, but they did not rule out urban beautification altogether; nor did most of them completely condemn the movement. Thomas Adams's 1915 statement of city practical planning "factors" would not have caused a quarrel with a City Beautiful advocate. Nelson P. Lewis, a New York engineer and bureaucrat, took a city practical view of planning in 1916 and breathed a sigh of relief over the declining use of *City Beautiful*, but he did not discourage beauty. Indeed, he stressed the need for park development and the intelligent placement of public buildings. The publication in 1922 of Werner Hegemann and Elbert Peets's *The American Vitruvius: An Architects' Handbook of Civic Art* testified to the survival of traditional civic design. The 1922 National Conference on City Planning heard two papers on beautification as an integral part of planning. Two years later Lewis Mumford let fly a scathing criticism of the City Beautiful in his now famous *Sticks and Stones*. But he was far too perceptive to dismiss the movement outright. "The civic center and the parkway represented the better and more constructive side of it", as did railroad stations. In the next decade, when Mumford the critic metamorphosed into Mumford the planner, he proposed many City Beautiful concepts and designs for Honolulu: vistas, formal parks in town and wilder ones in remoter areas, and a comprehensive view of the organic city ranged against the special claims of neighborhoods. The Hubbard and Hubbard's text of 1929 praised contemporary city planning, located its origins in the late nineteenth century, and defused "the bugbear of the 'City Beautiful.'"[48]

Perhaps the most amazing restatement of the City Beautiful ideal was George B. Ford's, delivered to the 1929 National Conference on City Planning. "Yes, most of our towns are colorless and anything but inspiring and so perhaps a wistful longing comes over us to recapture some of the beauty of life," declared a man who led the charge against the City Beautiful. Saying that "the demand for beauty is innate," Ford called for more than making "our towns merely safe, healthy and convenient." He reminded his listeners that beauty "is not a cosmetic" but "is fundamental and basic to the design of any object." He lamented how "our towns, so well planned for safety, health, and efficiency, have failed to inspire our enthusiasm." Ford called for new efforts at tree planting. Of street fixtures and furniture, he says, "We may not be conscious of them, but subconsciously they give us a sense of well-being and satisfaction and a certain unconscious pride in the street." His praise of beauty and of "The City Beautiful" was so fulsome, it is tempting to interpret it as the recantation of a dubious devotion to the city practical. It is evidence, certainly, that City Beautiful positions were defended for a generation after they first came under siege.[49]

In 1943 Harland Bartholomew praised the practicality of City Beautiful plans. "Unfortunately," he wrote, "most of these first comprehensive city plans were considered too visionary or impractical or were misconstrued to be schemes intended chiefly for beautification of the city. Their more fundamental objectives, intended to correct mistakes and bring about a more orderly growth, were seldom appreciated." Bartholomew's appreciation was unusual in a depression and wartime America not so hostile to the City Beautiful as it was forgetful.[50]

In the late 1940s and 1950s professional planners and architectural modernists held the field, but two books forecast a reawakening to the classical heritage. Christopher Tunnard's *The City of Man* (1953) was at once urban and community history, a celebration of the humane environment, a condemnation of modernist self-indulgence, and a recovery of neoclassical civic design. Henry Hope Reed, Jr.'s, paean to the grace, proportion, utility, and humanity of neoclassicism and to City Beautiful planning appeared in 1959. Mainstream architectural historians ridiculed *The Golden City* and its author, but Reed's book foretold a resurgence of neoclassical appreciation.[51]

The ferment of the 1960s focused fresh attention on American cities. A rejuvenated search for the urban past arose from nostalgia, preservationism, fresh scholarship, a yearning for individual and neighborhood stability amid a whirligig of change, dissatisfaction with "modern" commercial and domestic architecture, and disaffection from contemporary city planning. The 1962 protest against the demolition of the magnificent, neoclassical Pennsylvania Station drew attention to the emerging attitudes. Lewis Mumford, who forty years before declared railroad stations to be among the great artifacts of the City Beautiful, walked a picket line in front of the vast building. The protesters failed to halt the great monument's demise, but they helped to spark the preservation movement. Vincent Scully, no uncritical friend of the City Beautiful, was not alone when in 1969 he published second thoughts: "A later generation was to deride [Penn Station's] formal dependence upon the Baths of Caracalla. One is less sure than one used to be that such was a very relevant criticism. . . . It was academic building at its best, rational and ordered according to a pattern of use and a blessed sense of civic excess." Nor were the contributions of landscape architects forgotten, as when in 1964 Leonard K. Eaton published his appreciation of Jens Jensen.[52]

The momentum gathered. Ada Louise Huxtable forcefully criticized contemporary architecture and lovingly evoked Beaux-Arts tradition for New Yorkers and the nation. In 1974 August Heckscher published *Alive in the City: Memoir of an Ex-Commissioner*, a sympathetic appraisal of the New York City parks from his commissioner's perspective. Three years later, in *Open Spaces: The Life of American Cities*, he performed the same service for the rest of the country, praising half-forgotten City Beautiful plans and suggesting how their built features could be recaptured for contemporary use. George E. Condon detailed the beginnings of the revival of Cleveland's mall area, and the Da Capo Press republished Burnham's *Plan of Chicago*. Walter C. Kidney's *The Architecture of Choice* (1974) assayed the substyles of the neoclassical. A preservationist and architecture buff could better comprehend styles through such books as John J.-G. Blumenson's *Identifying American Architecture* (1977). In 1979 the Brooklyn Museum published the sumptuous *The American Renaissance, 1876–1917*, which contained Richard Guy Wilson's thoughtful essay on "Architecture,

Landscape, and City Planning." Historical scholarship on the City Beautiful era and its artifacts, designs, and planning politics continued into the 1980s. Reinforcement of the City Beautiful belief in the psychological and economic value of urban plants came when the first International Symposium on Urban Horticulture, held in 1983, devoted several papers to the subject.[53]

Simultaneously local planning staffs, planning consultants, commissions, city councils, and critics sought to recapture their legacy of urban beauty. In 1956 a Dallas master planning committee compared the Turtle Creek improvement, finished along the lines of Kessler's recommendations, with the ragtag Mill Creek area. Along Turtle, read a photograph underline, "residential values enhanced and stabilized as the direct result of following a Kessler recommendation." On Mill, cheap construction "necessitated installation of a storm sewer at cost of over $4,000,000. . . . Residential decay is prevalent here today." In the 1970s and 1980s other Dallas authors bemoaned the loss of Mill Creek, revived Kessler's idea of a lake in the Trinity River bottoms, and praised Lake Cliff Park in the Oak Cliff section. In Denver in 1971 and again in 1973, the city council imposed building height limitations around the Civic Center area, responding partly to pressure from the private Civic Center Association. The actions were intended to preserve the Rocky Mountain views and prevent skyscraper encroachments on the center. In 1976 the council designated the Civic Center area as a historic district.[54]

Harrisburg's Susquehanna riverfront area has become dowdy with age but still graciously hosts civic celebrations such as Fourth of July fireworks displays. In the early 1960s the Kansas City Board of Park Commissioners published an illustrated historical booklet, *Cowtown 1890 Becomes City Beautiful 1962*, proudly reviving the once ridiculed phrase. Kansas City's public fountains spout and splash, and its Civic Center, built far away from the Union Station during the Boss Pendergast era, is attractively maintained. Seattle's city government has been especially sensitive to its civic areas and to the Olmsted legacy. The city's neighborhood associations have demonstrated a remarkable vitality and success in improving the quality and integrity of their communities. The parks and boulevards continue to be attractive.[55]

The City Beautiful revival continued despite the publication in 1961 of Jane Jacobs's *The Death and Life of Great American Cities*. Her landmark work condemned the professional planners' macroscale mentality and stimulated a neighborhood revival movement already well under way. The book was trenchant and close-grained in argument, but it also contained a condemnation of the City Beautiful movement written from ignorance of its purpose and achievements, as well as special pleading and faulty logic. Fortunately for the survival of City Beautiful artifacts, Jacobs's many adherents read her book selectively.[56]

There is, of course, some validity to the critics' comments, however limited it might be. The City Beautiful movement attempted too much. America's fragmented politics were a formidable barrier to the coordinated physical overhauling of widely varying sizes and types of cities ranged across a continent. Enthusiastic organizing, speech making, and writing were no substitute for determined and intelligent action in each and every city. Too often a published plan and citizen idealism passed for purposefulness.

The movement was too naive and hopeful, socially and architecturally. McFarland's writings are a case in point. "It is well known that environment very greatly influences human beings," the hyperactive, diminutive printer wrote in 1908. That was well enough, but the moralistic McFarland had a corollary to deliver. "The education in ugliness that is constantly proceeding through the special privilege assaults of the billboards is not an education that tends towards the production of good citizens." It is easy to imagine, behind the charming simplicity and directness of McFarland's statements, a chilling assumption of an adroit environmental manipulation that would produce "good citizens." McFarland could not have achieved such a drastic physical reshaping of cities, and anyway, such a reformation almost certainly would not have created McFarland's "good citizens." Later generations inherited McFarland's environmentalism, but they are also the legatees of totalitarianism's horrible brutalities. It is understandable, if nonsensical, for them to read into environmentalist statements an ignorance of the complexity of urban life and an overweening desire for close control of the citizen.[57]

Moreover, the architectonic visions of the movement's civic design phase invited the ridicule and reductionist critiques of the city practical. Changes in architectural taste and in society invite us to depreciate outmoded styles. Nothing else earns a certificate of critical acuity as rapidly and easily as an attack on the architecture of the immediate past from the perspective of the present. It is equally facile and as intellectually slipshod to compare architecture in the mode of the good-natured City Beautiful with that of a repressive totalitarianism.[58]

The Contributions of the City Beautiful

The limitations of the City Beautiful movement and of its critics aside, the movement achieved much. It spoke to yearnings for an ideal community and to the potential for good in all citizens. Therein lies its most important but least remarked contribution. For all its idealistic rhetoric, the movement was imbued with the courage of practicality, for it undertook the most difficult task of all; to accept its urban human material where found, to take the city as it was, and to refashion both into something better. Contrast its realism with the contemporaneous antiurban Garden

City movement, which proposed radical deconcentration and the destruction of the great cities. The Garden City movement and its heirs have thrilled academics with their altruistic systems involving significant restrictions on private ownership and enterprise. The fact is, however, that the Garden Cities and their successors have at best become suburbs with fairly typical suburban dynamics.[59]

The City Beautiful movement was fundamentally an urban political reform movement. It left a legacy of civic activism and flexibility in the urban political structure. The professional planning expert advanced to the fore during the era, but the network of concerned, politically aware laymen was equally important to City Beautiful success. The network survived in the ACA and found outlets in general and specialized periodicals, conventions, and speeches. Women, usually middle-class women, learned how to make their communities aware of problems of sanitation, cleanliness, and public beauty. The physical legacy – tree-shaded boulevards, undulating parks, and graceful neoclassic buildings rich in ornament and craftsmanship – remain to remind later generations of ancestors who built for their own times, to be sure, but who consciously tried to create a future city of order, system, and beauty. We must, therefore, consider not only what City Beautiful planners designed and wrote but also what they did. The City Beautiful mode of civic scale was for a time so pervasive that even the architects of skyscrapers respected it. As Thomas Bender and William R. Taylor have written, the design and detailing of the first five or six stories of the early skyscrapers responded to sidewalk and street viewing.[60]

The movement generated a large and continuing interest in the improvement and preservation of beauty in Washington, D.C. While acknowledging Washington's "undemocratic and arbitrary form of government," McFarland appealed to "the opportunity Washington affords for working out the physical details of city improvement in a broader fashion than is likely to be practicable under the ordinary conditions." McFarland understood Washington's oxymoronic quality. It was politically anomalous and therefore of no practical use to the citizen activist in the midst of a struggle over a bond issue, but its inspirational possibilities were potentially unbounded.[61]

The City Beautiful movement also illuminates some issues of continuity and change in urban America. The City Beautiful assumed, without acknowledgment, much of the Olmstedian rhetoric about the value of urban beautification. City practical planners embraced beauty in the cityscape despite their denunciations of the City Beautiful. The spirit of each era differed one from the other, underlining the simultaneity of continuity and change.[62]

Its development of the comprehensive plan marked the City Beautiful era's great departure from the past. The adjective *comprehensive* has so often modified the noun *plan* as to rob *comprehensive* of all meaning.

Restoring content to *comprehensive* assumes that a truly comprehensive plan is pervasive, reaching into all or almost all parts of the city; that it attempts to deal with a broad range of urban problems; and that, consequently, it is multifunctional.

By such a definition few of the senior Olmsted's plans were comprehensive, although the later ones addressed the issues of recreation, controlled urban growth, and residential area development, among others. They were multifunctional, but they left important central areas untouched. Andrew Green's 1865 plan for Manhattan Island above Fifty-ninth Street was all-embracing but geographically limited. A single-function plan, a sewage disposal system for example, meets only one urban need, albeit an essential one. It cannot be comprehensive, no matter how elegantly designed, no matter what insights into urban structure and form its designer gains while developing it. Nor does deciding where certain buildings or institutions should be scattered about make one "a comprehensive city planner" unless the placing is done with reference to a comprehensive city plan. Partial plans were often intelligently designed, carefully integrated with other activities, and systematically carried out, but none of that makes them comprehensive.[63]

The City Beautiful movement produced the first comprehensive plans based on a theory of the organic city. The park and boulevard systems would provide varied recreational and educational opportunities, help shape cities while they directed their growth, open up new residential developments, divide urban areas into functionally separate subdistricts, and assist in the development of transportation and other utilities. Civic centers adjacent to retail-commercial cores would rationalize and centralize governmental functions, enhance civic pride through inspirational scenes, and build civic patriotism by providing a place of democratic mingling and celebration. The civic center and the park and boulevard system, together with playgrounds, would pervade the city with their positive influences. Later planners would decry the City Beautiful as much as they wished, but they owed it a heavy debt – their own concept of comprehensiveness.

Despite the City Beautiful's contributions, its legacy is not always appreciated or preserved. The realities of urban budget constraints, the pressures of the private automobile, and changes in citizen interest and use combine with public indifference to wreak havoc with some City Beautiful survivals. Harrisburg's boulevard system is a shambles of neglect, obliterated in places by trafficways. Wildwood Park is a ruin, its lake silted, its pathways overgrown and befouled with trash illegally dumped, its meadow the site of a freeway interchange – in all a mockery of McFarland's praise for the reclaimed Harrisburg of the 1910s and 1920s. White Rock Lake Park in Dallas, City and Washington parks in Denver, and Green Lane Park in Seattle attract crowds far beyond their capacity, creating maintenance headaches and, in some cases, heartburn in nearby residents. David Dillon, Dallas's insightful architectural critic, warned of the high-rise buildings, many of indifferent-to-ghastly design, crowding the margins of Turtle Creek. Denver's *Pioneer Monument* stands deserted in a tiny, uninviting triangle reduced to accommodate noisy automobile traffic, its basin empty, its fountain jets turned off. In Kansas City, Jarvis Hunt's grand Union Station, now disused, molders away.[64]

The shabby treatment of some City Beautiful artifacts underscores the reality: However much it may be praised or fondly recalled, the City Beautiful movement is over and cannot be revived in the megalopolitan era. Even sympathetic critics find City Beautiful sumptuousness a little too much. As Joan Draper remarked, when the San Francisco Civic Center was placed on the National Register of Historic Places in 1978, the revived interest in neoclassic design did not lead anyone to propose creating new neoclassical monuments.[65]

Still, a neoclassical revival might not be a bad idea. A look around the later public architecture of Denver's Civic Center area does little to inspire faith in the individuality of architects restrained only by "funding," "the site," and "the problem." The Denver Art Museum appears to be thrown up by a Mesa Verde chieftain to keep his treasures safe from the hordes. Its slabby bulk, too close to the City and County Building, dominates the older structure's tower. The Colorado State Judicial Building stands on two legs at either end of a giant cutout first floor. The four floors above threaten to press down upon the void and bow the building in the middle. It is an unsettling experience either to view this strange white concoction or to walk underneath it, through the cutout. Next to the judicial building is the dark brown Colorado Heritage Center, looking like nothing so much as a wedge of chocolate cake badly cut and indifferently dropped on a plate by a Brobdingnagian hostess. The site and design make the structure practically incapable of expansion, an unfortunate circum-stance in a building dedicated to the perpetual collection and preservation of Colorado's past. Only the 1950s brick-and-glass public library fits comfortably into its corner of the Civic Center and blends well with its surroundings.

It was not just the City Beautiful era in which reach exceeded grasp. So it becomes all the more important to remember what the City Beautiful advocates were reaching for, an ordered society in which digni-fied, cooperative citizens of whatever station or calling moved through scenes suffused with beauty. It was a glorious ideal, incapable of realiz-ation, but eternally beckoning. No one captured the spirit of the ceaseless quest better than Jules Guerin in a painting for the *Plan of Chicago*. In it, the viewer is suspended above Lake Michigan, near the yacht harbor, looking west over the city. It is dusk. A thin band of fading vermilion lingers above the western horizon. The city lights long since should have been turned on, but it is as though the citizens by common agreement have kept them off. There is purpose in their unity. How else could the viewer focus upon the dome of the great city hall, as the sun's last rays light it in glowing gold?

Notes

1   Commentaries on the *Plan of Chicago* include Boyer, *Urban Masses and Moral Order*, Paul Boyer (Cambridge, Mass.: Harvard University Press, 1978) 270–76; Carl W. Condit, *Chicago, 1910–29: Building, Planning, and Urban Technology* (Chicago: University of Chicago Press, 1973), 59–85; Wilbert R. Hasbrouck, "Introduction" to the reprinted *Plan of Chicago* Hasbrouck Chicago: Commercial Club, 1909, v–viii; Hines, *Burnham* (New York: Oxford University Press, 1974), 312–45; Horowitz, *Culture and the City* (Lexington, Ky.: University Press of Kentucky, 1976), 220–25; Mario Manieri-Elia, "Toward an 'Imperial City': Daniel H. Burnham and the City Beautiful Movement," in *The American City: From the Civil War to the New Deal*, Giorgio Ciucci et al (Cambridge: MIT Press, 1979), 89–112; Reps, *Making of Urban America*, Princeton, N.J.: Princeton University Press, 1965), 517–24; Scott, *American City Planning* (Berkeley and LA: University of California Press, 1969) 100–109; and Paul Barrett, *The Automobile and Urban Transit: The Formation of Public Policy in Chicago, 1900–1930* (Philadelphia: Temple University Press, 1983), 73–81.
2   Burnham and Bennett, *Plan of Chicago*, Chicago: Commercial Club, 1909, 116.
3   Ibid., 117, 118.
4   Ibid., 116; and Manieri-Elia, "Toward an 'Imperial City,'" 95. For the city-county building, see Condit, *Chicago, 1910–29*, 178–82; and Joan E. Draper, "Paris by the Lake: Sources of Burnham's Plan of Chicago," in *Chicago Architecture, 1872–1922: Birth of a Metropolis*, ed. John Zukowsky (Munich: Prestel-Verlag, in association with the Art Institute of Chicago, 1987), 107–19.
5   For height limitations in Denver, see Pickering, "Blueprint of Power" Ph.D. diss., University of Denver, 1978, 134–35; and in Seattle, see Neil, "Paris or New York?" *Pacific Quarterly*, 75 (Jan 1984), *Northwest*, 22–23. Hines, *Burnham*, 334–35.
6   Burnham and Bennett, *Plan of Chicago*, plates cxii, cxv, cvxi, cxxi, and cxxii. Chicago: Commercial Club, 1909.
7   Ibid., 108–9.
8   Ford, ed., *City Planning Progress* (Washington D.C., American Institute of Architects, 1917), iii; Scott, *American City Planning*, 167–68, 187.
9   Quoted in Hines, *Burnham*, 369.
10 A list of buildings completed by Burnham's firms is in Hines, *Burnham*, 371–83.
11 Hancock, "John Nolen" (Ph.D. diss. University of Pennsylvania, 1964), 137–42; Newton, *Design on the Land* (Cambridge, Mass.: Belknap Press of Harvard University Press, 1971), 385–87; Peterson, "Origins of the Comprehensive City Planning Ideal" (Ph.D. diss.. Harvard University, 1967), 373–425; and Scott, *American City Planning*, 71–100. For the emergence of city planning professionalism and specialized publications, see Kirschner, *Paradox of Professionalism* (New York: Greenwood Press, 1986), 4–10.

12   Schultz and McShane, "To Engineer the Metropolis" *Journal of American History* 65 (September 1978), 398–402; Clay McShane, "Transforming the Use of Urban Space: A Look at the Revolution in Street Pavements, 1880–1924," *Journal of Urban History* 5 (May 1979): 295–300; and Scott, *American City Planning*, 80–81.

13   For Manning and Harrisburg, see McFarland to Woodruff, 26 Nov. 1915, box 13, McFarland Papers, Pennsylvania State Archives. For expert planners' changing relationships, see Scott, *American City Planning*, 110–269, especially 227–37.

14   Benjamin C. Marsh, "City Planning in Justice to the Working Population," *Charities and the Commons* 19 (1 February 1908): 1514–18.

15   Robert Anderson Pope, "Some of the Needs of City Planning in America," in U.S. Congress, Senate, *City Planning*, including *Program of First National Conference on City Planning, Washington D.C., May 21 and 22, 1909* (Washington, 1910), 75.

16   Ibid., 76–79; John Nolen, "What is Needed in American City Planning," in U.S. Senate, *City Planning*, 74–75; Frederick Law Olmsted, Jr., "The Scope and Results of City Planning in Europe," in ibid., 63–70; Marsh, "A National Constructive Programme for City Planning," in ibid., 61–62; and idem, "Economic Aspects of City Planning," in ibid., 104–5.

17   The report from the delegate of the Washington State Chapter incorporated a newspaper clipping describing Gilbert's speech, WSC Papers, Records, 1894–1910, 173–74. An interpretive biography of Gilbert is Geoffrey Blodgett, "Cass Gilbert, Architect: Conservative at Bay," *Journal of American History* 72 (December 1985): 615–36. Despite Blodgett's title, Gilbert's attack on the City Beautiful identified him with the planning and architectural avant-garde. See also an account of a Gilbert speech in *P–I*, 28 Nov. 1909.

18   [Charles Mulford Robinson], "Notes and Comments: A Protest That Is Timely," *Architectural Record* 27 (February 1910): 202–3; Arnold Brunner, *Washington Star*, 16 Dec. 1910; and George B. Ford, "Digging Deeper into City Planning," *American City* 6 (March 1912): 557–62. See also Robinson's review of Ford's article in "A Broader and Saner City Planning," ibid., 555–56.

19   "The Convention of the American Civic Association," 21 Dec. 1911, box 14, McFarland Papers; and ACA, Department of City Making, *Not Only the City Beautiful*, no. 8, ser. 2 (Washington, D.C., 1913), 3, 10.

20   For McFarland's analysis of his role, see McFarland to John Nolen, 15 Feb. 1909, John Nolen Papers, Collection 2903, Department of Manuscripts and University Archives, Cornell University.

21   Olmsted to Benjamin C. Marsh, 21 Apr. 1909, folder 2921–1, box 183, Olmsted Records, Library of Congress.

22   Olmsted to Olmsted, 12 Dec. 1909, folder 163, box 20A, Olmsted Correspondence. Loeb Library, Graduate School of Design, Harvard University.

23   McFarland's concern for the creation of new slums by failing to provide for the dispossessed from cleared slums is in his letter to Graham Romeyn Taylor, 14 Dec. 1912, box 9, McFarland Papers.

24   For billboards, see Kristin Szylvian Bailey, " 'Fighting Civic Smallpox': The Civic Club of Allegheny County's Campaign for Billboard Regulation,

1896–1917," *Western Pennsylvania Historical Magazine* 70 (January 1987): 3–28; and William H. Wilson, "The Billboard: Bane of the City Beautiful," *Journal of Urban History* 13 (August 1987): 394–425.

25   Roy Lubove, *The Progressives and the Slums: Tenement House Reform in New York City*, 1890–1917 (Pittsburgh: University of Pittsburgh Press, 1962), 220.

26   For "appalling" and "play" quotations, see Olmsted, "Introductory Address on City Planning," in *Proceedings of the Second National Conference on City Planning and the Problems of Congestion* (Boston, 1912), 15, 16; for "any" quotation, "How to Organize a City Planning Campaign," in ibid., 304. For Nolen, see Hancock, "John Nolen," 324–33, 508–16. See also Nolen, *Replanning Small Cities: Six Typical Cities* (New York: B. W. Huebsch, 1912); and idem, *New Ideals in the Planning of Cities, Towns and Villages* (New York: American City Bureau, 1919), 5–7, 10–11, 25–30, 78–83. For war memorials, see the following articles in *American City*: "The Proposed Liberty Memorial Square and Civic Center for Berkeley, California," vol. 20 (May 1919): 428–29; and "Grand Rapids Considering a Memorial Building," ibid.: 429; O. B. McClintock, "Minnesota Proposes a Memorial Hall," vol. 21 (September 1919): 252; and "Civic Centers as War Memorials," vol. 21 (October 1919): 330–34. Scott, *American City Planning*, 120–22.

27   Henry S. Churchill, *The City Is the People* (New York: Harcourt, Brace & World, 1945; reprint, New York: W. W. Norton & Co., 1962), 82, for "scarcely" and "carried" quotations; and 69, for "plan" quotation. James Marston Fitch, *American Building: The Historical Forces That Shaped It*, 2d ed., rev. and enl. (Boston: Houghton Mifflin Co., 1972), 239–40. Fitch's book was first published in 1947.

28   Ford, ed., *City Planning Progress*, v–vi. Most of the plans dated from the City Beautiful era.

29   Huggins, "City Planning in North Carolina" (*North Carolina Historical Review* 46, October 1969), 383–87, 390. Carl V. Harris, *Political Power in Birmingham, 1817–1921* (Knoxville: University of Tennessee Press, 1977), 164–67 (quotation, 166), 229–31.

30   See Ford, ed., *City Planning Progress*, 5–193; and Hancock, "John Nolen," 334–44.

31   Harvey A. Kantor, "The City Beautiful in New York," *New-York Historical Quarterly* 57 (April 1973): 149–67 (quotations, 170, 171). See also Robert A. M. Stern, Gregory Gilmartin, and John Montague Massengale, *New York 1900: Metropolitan Architecture and Urbanism, 1890–1915* (New York: Rizzoli, 1983), 7–143.

32   Herbert Croly, "'Civic Improvements': The Case of New York," *Architectural Record* 21 (May 1907): 350. McKim to Charles Moore, 8 Jan. 1903, Scrapbook: Park Commission Correspondence, Mr. McKim, 1901–1903, Charles Moore Papers, Manuscript Division, Library of Congress.

33   Judd Kahn, *Imperial San Francisco*, 4 ("better off" quotation), and for Kahn's discussion of the influence of property and statement of his belief in the efficacy of centralized government in replanning, see 177–216. See also William Issel and Robert W. Cherny, *San Francisco, 1865–1932: Politics, Power, and Urban Development* (Berkeley and Los Angeles: University of California Press, 1986): 109–16, 170–72. For rebuilding after devastating fires in Chicago, Boston, and Baltimore, see Christine Meisner Rosen, *The Limits of*

Power: Great Fires and the Process of City Growth in America (Cambridge: Cambridge University Press, 1986).

34 Kahn, *Imperial San Francisco*, 200, 201. Other examinations of Burnham's plan are in Hines, *Burnham*, 174–96; and Mellier G. Scott, *The San Francisco Bay Area: A Metropolis in Perspective* (Berkeley and Los Angeles: University of California Press, 1959), 79–121.

35 Draper, *San Francisco Civic Center* (Ann Arbor: University Microfilms, 1979), 12 (quotation, 19). The one-tenth of centers begun is my estimate, not Draper's.

36 For comparative construction costs, see Hines, *Burnham*, 386.

37 For the centralization-decentralization dichotomy, see Samuel P. Hays, "The Changing Political Structure of the City in Industrial America," *Journal of Urban History* 1 (November 1974): 6–38. See also William W. Cutler III, "The Persistent Dualism: Centralization and Decentralization in Philadelphia, 1854–1975," in *The Divided Metropolis: Social and Spatial Dimensions of Philadelphia, 1800–1975*, ed. William W. Cutler III and Howard Gillette (Westport, Conn.: Greenwood Press, 1980), 257, 260, 262, 263.

38 Sullivan, *Autobiography of an Idea* (New York: Dover Publications, 1956), 321–25. The most recent biography of Sullivan is Robert Twombly, *Louis Sullivan: His Life and Work* (New York: Viking Penguin, 1986).

39 Tallmadge, *Architecture in America* (New York: W. W. Norton & Co., 1927), 196–97; David H. Crook, "Louis Sullivan and the Golden Doorway," *Journal of the Society of Architectural Historians* 26 (December 1967): 250–58; Dimitri Tselos, "The Chicago Fair and the Myth of the 'Lost Cause,'" ibid., 259–68; Hines, *Burnham*, 98–100; Burg, *Chicago's White City* (Lexington, Ky.: University Press of Kentucky, 1976), 303–9; and David S. Andrew, *Louis Sullivan and the Polemics of Modern Architecture: The Present Against the Past* (Urbana: University of Illinois Press, 1985), 136–39. For Wright, see Scully, *American Architecture and Urbanism* (New York: Praeger Publishers, 1969), 138; and Thomas S. Hines, "The Paradox of 'Progressive' Architecture: Urban Planning and Public Building in Tom Johnson's Cleveland," *American Quarterly* 25 (October 1973): 445, 447. American architects attacked neoclassicism and the civic center concept at least as early as 1911, but their ideas were neither dominant among their colleagues nor very popular. See Ernest Flagg, "Public Buildings," 42–55; and Irving K. Pond, "Discussion," in *Proceedings of the Third National Conference on City Planning* (Boston, 1911), 74–77.

40 Louis Sullivan, *Kindergarten Chats* (New York: George Wittenborn, 1947). For Sullivan as planner and businessman, see Andrew, *Sullivan*, 75–112, 128–34. Wright's planning ideas are in his *The Living City* (New York: Horizon Press, 1958). Colin Rowe, *The Mathematics of the Ideal Villa and Other Essays* (Cambridge: MIT Press, 1976), contrasts Sullivan's lack of interior planning with Wright's concern for the plan, 96, 98–99. Fishman, *Urban Utopias* (New York: Basic Books, 1977), 122–60.

41 Jordy, *American Buildings: Progressive and Academic Ideals* (Garden City, N.Y.: Doubleday & Co., 1972), 3:63–70, 83–179; Mark L. Peisch, *The Chicago School of Architecture: Early Followers of Sullivan and Wright* (New York: Random House, 1964), 4, 13–15, 18, 32–33, 70, 105–24, 144–45, illus. 28.

42 For discussions of the parallelism of neoclassical and other styles, see

Christopher Tunnard and Henry Hope Reed, *American Skyline: The Growth And Form of Our Cities and Towns* (Boston: Houghton Mifflin Co., 1955), 179–215; and Tunnard, *Modern American City* (New York: VanNostrand Reinhold Co., 1968), 89–92. Talbot F. Hamlin, *The Enjoyment of Architecture* (New York: Charles Scribner's Sons, 1929), 266–97. Lewis Mumford, *Sticks and Stones: A Study of American Architecture and Civilization,* 2d rev. ed. (Boni and Liveright, 1924; reprint, New York: Dover Publications, 1955), 174. For the impact of neoclassicism on federal government construction, see Lois A. Craig et al., *The Federal Presence: Architecture, Politics, and Symbols in United States Government Building* (Cambridge: MIT Press, 1978). A different inter-pretation of the neoclassical impact on commercial architecture is Jack Tager, "Partners in Design: Chicago Architects, Entrepreneurs, and the Evolution of Urban Commercial Architecture," *South Atlantic Quarterly* 76 (Spring 1977): 212–18. For a discussion of "civic horizontalism and corpo-rate verticality," in the New York context, see Thomas Bender and William R. Taylor, "Culture and Architecture: Some Aesthetic Tensions in the Shaping of Modern New York City," in *Visions of the Modern City: Essays in History, Art, Literature,* ed. William Sharpe and Leonard Wallock (Baltimore: Johns Hopkins University Press, 1987), 189–219.

43   Manieri-Elia, "Toward an 'Imperial City,'" 1–121; and Francesco Dal Co, "From Parks to the Region: Progressive Ideology and the Reform of the American City," in Ciucci et al., *American City,* 143–221; M. Christine Boyer, *Dreaming the Rational City: The Myth of American City Planning* (Cambridge: MIT Press, 1983), 3–82, 114–36; Marcuse, "Housing in Early City Planning", 153–76; and Richard E. Foglesong, *Planning the Capitalist City: The Colonial Era to the 1920s* (Princeton: Princeton University Press, 1986), 163–66, 206–10, 216.

44   For imperialism, see Burchard and Bush-Brown, *Architecture of America* (Boston: Little, Brown & Co., 1961), 295. For social control and related issues not cited or discussed elsewhere, see Françoise Choay, *The Modern City: Planning in the Nineteenth Century* (New York: George Braziller, Publisher, 1970), 7–32, 97–110; Stephen Kern *The Culture of Time and Space, 1880–1918* (Cambridge: Harvard University Press, 1983), 39–40, 56, 99–100, 139, 209–10; Weinstein, *Corporate Ideal* (Boston: Beacon Press, 1968), ix–x, 94–96; and Wiebe, *Search for Order* (New York: Hill & Wang, 1967), xiii–xiv, 149. For Marxist disagreements, see Manieri-Elia, "Toward an 'Imperial City,'" 49–52, 91; Boyer, *Dreaming the Rational City,* 5; Dal Co, "From Parks to the Region," 176–78; and Fogelsong, *Planning the Capitalist City,* 89–166. For housing problems, see Boyer, *Dreaming the Rational City,* 100; and Robert B. Fairbanks, "From Better Dwellings to Better Community: Changing Approaches to the Low-Cost Housing Problem, 1890–1925," *Journal of Urban History* 11 (May 1985): 314–34. For settle-ment house workers, see Allen F. Davis, *Spearheads for Reform: The Social Settlements and the Progressive Movement, 1890–1914* (New York: Oxford University Press, 1967), 73–74.

45   For the novel, see Burg, *Chicago's White City,* 290–92. For quotations, see Cobden-Sanderson, "Of Art and Life," in *Art and Life, and the Building and Decoration of Cities: A Series of Lectures by Members of the Arts and Crafts Exhibition Society, Delivered at the Fifth Exhibition of the Society in 1896,* Arts and Crafts

Exhibition Society (London: Rivington, Percival & Co., 1897), 43–44; Halsey Ricardo, "Of Colour in the Architecture of Cities," 259.

46   W. R. Lethaby, "Of Beautiful Cities," in *Art and Life*, 99; Walter Crane, "Of the Decoration of Public Buildings," in ibid., 139; and Ricardo, "Of Colour in the Architecture of Cities," in ibid., 259.

47   "Patriotic Residents of Dallas Can Solve 'City Beautiful' Problem," *Dallas* 7 (December 1923): 22, 23; and Arthur L. Kramer, "Beauty in City Building," ibid. 9 (January 1930): 9, 21. Wilson, "J. Horace McFarland," *Journal of Urban History* 7 (May 1981), 329, 330–31.

48   Thomas Adams, "Some Town Planning Principles Restated," *American City* 12 (March 1915): 213; Nelson P. Lewis, *The Planning of the Modern City: A Review of the Principles Governing City Planning*, 2d ed. rev. (1916; New York: John Wiley & Sons, 1923), 23, 25; Hegemann and Peets, *The American Vitruvius* (New York: Benjamin Blom, 1972), John Nolen, "The Place of the Beautiful in the City Plan: Some Everyday Examples," in *Proceedings of the Fourteenth National Conference on City Planning* (Springfield, Mass., 1922), 133–47; Andrew Wright Crawford, "The Value of Art Commissions in City Planning," in ibid., 148–58. Mumford, in *Sticks and Stones*, criticizes the City Beautiful, 123–51 (quotation, 131). For the Honolulu plan, see Mumford, *City Development: Studies in Disintegration and Renewal* (New York: Harcourt, Brace & Co., 1945), 86–153. Mumford's mentor, Patrick Geddes, criticized "town planning" in the United States but also found much to admire, in *Cities in Evolution: An Introduction to the Town Planning Movement and to the Study of Civics* (1915; reprint, New York: Howard Fertig, 1968), 232–37, 248. Theodora Kimball Hubbard and Henry Vincent Hubbard, *Our Cities To-Day and To-Morrow: A Survey of Planning and Zoning in Progress in the United States* (Cambridge: Harvard University Press, 1929), 5–78, 125, 135, 140, 216–17, 238, 248–51, 263–80 (quotation, 263).

49   George B. Ford, "What Makes 'The City Beautiful'?" in *Planning Problems of Town, City and Region: Papers and Discussions at the Twenty-first National Conference on City Planning* (Philadelphia: Wm. F. Fell Co., 1929), 170, 171, 172–73.

50   Harland Bartholomew and Associates, *Your Dallas of Tomorrow: Master Plan for a Greater Dallas, Report Number One: Character of the City* (Dallas: City Plan Commission, 1943), 31. A biography of Bartholomew and his place in city planning is Norman John Johnston, *Harland Bartholomew: His Comprehensive Plans and Science of Planning* (Ann Arbor: University Microfilms, 1964).

51   Christopher Tunnard, *The City of Man* (New York: Charles Scribner's Sons, 1953); Henry Hope Reed, Jr., *The Golden City* (Garden City, N.Y.: Doubleday & Co., 1959). For comments on Reed, see Burchard and Bush-Brown, *Architecture of America*, 295–96, 451, 490; and Larkin, *Art and Life in America* (New York: Holt, Reinehart & Winston, 1960), 471.

52   For criticisms of planning and planners, see Edward P. Eicher and Marshall Kaplan, *The Community Builders* (Berkeley and Los Angeles: University of California Press, 1967); and Marshall Kaplan, *Urban Planning in the 1960s: A Design for Irrelevancy* (New York: Praeger Publishers, 1973; Cambridge: MIT Press, 1974), especially 85–103. A 1960s planner who had some appreciation for the City Beautiful movement was Edmund K. Faltermayer, *Redoing America: A Nationwide Report on How to Make Our Cities and Suburbs Livable*

(New York: Harper & Row, 1968), 24, 25, 46, 191, 225–26. Lorraine B. Diehl, *The Late, Great Pennsylvania Station* (New York: American Heritage Press, 1985), 18–20, 26–28, 147–48. Scully, *American Architecture and Urbanism*, 142. Leonard K. Eaton, *Landscape Artist in America: The Life and Work of Jens Jensen* (Chicago: University of Chicago Press, 1964).

53   Ada Louise Huxtable, *Kicked a Building Lately?* (New York: Quadrangle Books, 1978), 3–5, 8–12, 217–21, 221–24; August Heckscher, *Alive in the City: Memoir of an Ex-Commissioner* (New York: Charles Scribner's Sons, 1974); idem, *Open Spaces* (see chap. 3, n. 30); George E. Condon, *Cleveland: The Best Kept Secret* (Garden City, N.Y.: Doubleday & Co., 1967), 352–56; Kidney, *The Architecture of Choice* (New York: George Braziller, 1974), John J.-G. Blumenson *Identifying American Architecture: A Pictorial Guide to Styles and Terms, 1600–1945* (Nashville: American Association for State and Local History, 1977); Brooklyn Institute of Arts and Sciences, *The American Renaissance, 1876–1917* (New York: Pantheon Books, 1979) (Wilson's essay is on pages 74–109). Scholarly production, in addition to works already cited, includes two articles by Michael P. McCarthy: "Chicago Businessmen and the Burnham Plan," *Journal of the Illinois State Historical Society* 63 (Autumn 1970): 228–56; and "Politics and the Parks: Chicago Businessmen and the Recreation Movement," ibid. 65 (Summer 1972): 158–72. See also Elizabeth Anne Mack Lyon, "Business Buildings in Atlanta: A Study in Growth and Form" (Ph.D. diss., Emory University, 1971). Joseph L. Arnold, "City Planning in America," in *The Urban Experience: Themes in American History*, ed. Raymond A. Mohl and James F. Richardson (Belmont, Calif.: Wadsworth Publishing Co., 1973), 14–43, as a brief, interpretive review. Joanna Schneider Zangrando, *Monumental Bridge Design in Washington, D.C., as a Reflection of American Culture, 1886 to 1932* (Ann Arbor: University Microfilms, 1974), is detailed and excellent. Among more recent articles are Ralph L. Pearson and Linda Wrigley, "Before Mayor Richard Lee: George Dudley Seymour and the City Planning Movement in New Haven, 1907–1924," *Journal of Urban History* 6 (May 1980): 297–319; John Fahey, "A. L. White, Champion of Urban Beauty," *Pacific Northwest Quarterly* 72 (October 1981): 170–79; and Shirley Leckie, "Brand Whitlock and the City Beautiful Movement in Toledo, Ohio," *Ohio History* 91 (1982): 5–36. On urban horticulture, see David F. Karnosky and Sheryl L. Karnosky, eds., *Improving the Quality of Urban Life with Plants: Proceedings of the June 21–23, 1983, International Symposium on Urban Horticulture*, New York Botanical Garden publication no. 2 (Millbrook, N.Y.: Institute of Urban Horticulture, 1985), especially the following articles: Harold B. Tukey, Jr., "An Overview of Urban Horticulture," 1–6; David R. DeWalle, "Amenities Provided by Urban Plants," 7–14; John F. Dwyer, "The Economic Values of Urban Plants," 15–27; Charles A. Lewis, "Human Dimensions of Horticulture," 35–44; and Rachel Kaplan, "Human Response to Plants and Landscapes," 45–60.

54   Statements not cited in this and subsequent notes are based on my observations. Dallas Master Plan Committee, *A Look At Past Planning for the City of Dallas* (Dallas, 1956), 7–8; Patsy Swank, "Mill Creek," *Vision* 2 (March 1979): 6; Jane Summer, "Getting to the Bottom of Town Lake," *Dallas Life: Sunday Magazine of the Dallas Morning News* 1 (14 November 1982): 10–12,

21–22, 24; and David Dillon, "City Park with a View," *DMN*, 26 Apr. 1984. *Denver Post*, 27 Feb. 1973, 28 Apr. 1976; and *Cervi's Rocky Mountain Journal* 31 (July 1972).

55 Kansas City Board of Park Commissioners, *Cowtown 1890 Becomes City Beautiful 1962: The Story of Kansas City's Parks* (Kansas City, 1962); Urban Design Advisory Board, *Designing a Great City* (Seattle: City Planning Commission, 1965), 3, 6, 7, 28; City Planning Commission, *Framework for Tomorrow: City Planning for Seattle* (Seattle, 1966), 2–4; and Dennis Ryan, "Lay of the Land," *Planning* 49 (March 1983): 18–21. For Seattle organizations, see Barrett A. Lee et al., "Testing the Decline-of-Community Thesis: Neighborhood Organizations in Seattle, 1929 and 1979," *American Journal of Sociology* 89 (March 1984): 1161–88.

56 For Jacobs on the City Beautiful, see her *Death and Life of Great American Cities* (New York: Vintage Books, 1961), 24–25. Jacobs may be correct in her claim that parks do not by themselves raise property values, a subject of much debate, but she loads her argument with a discussion of four small Philadelphia squares obviously unable to control the construction around them, 92–101. Her discussion of a "clay dog"-making beach replaced by a park lawn is poignant but it draws a false analogy between the action of waves and sun on clay deposits and the values of unplanned human activity, 446–47. For one criticism of Jacobs, see Fitch, *American Building*, 298–307. For another criticism of the City Beautiful with little practical effect on the growing interest in the movement, see Robert Goodman, *After the Planners* (New York: Simon & Schuster, 1971), 60, 98–103, 122, 130.

57 McFarland to Editor, *Jersey City Journal*, 21 Mar. 1908, box 15, McFarland Papers.

58 Goodman, *After the Planners*, illustrations on 104, 105.

59 For various problems of the Garden City and "back-to-the-land" movements see Park Dixon Goist, "The City as Organism: Two Recent American Theories of the City" (Ph.D. diss., University of Rochester, 1967), 5; Frederick C. Howe, *The Modern City and Its Problems* (New York: Charles Scribner's Sons, 1915), 6–8; and Merwin Robert Swanson, "The American Country Life Movement, 1900–1940," (Ph.D. diss., University of Minnesota, 1972), 13–17, 25–29, 34–35. For a sympathetic treatment of Ebenezer Howard and the Garden City idea, see Fishman, *Urban Utopias*, 23–88. For the relationship between sanitation and the City Beautiful, see Melosi, *Garbage in the Cities* (College Station: Texas A & M University Press, 1981), 110–13.

60 Bender and Taylor, "Culture and Architecture." For the impact of women on their communities, see Karen J. Blair, *The Clubwoman as Feminist: True Womanhood Redefined, 1868–1914* (New York: Holmes & Meier Publishers, 1980), 93–115, 119.

61 McFarland to Clinton Rogers Woodruff, 31 Dec. 1913, box 12, McFarland Papers. For a sampling of the new extensive material on Washington, see ACA resolution, "Referring to the Improvement of the City of Washington and District of Columbia under Plans of the Commission Appointed by the Senate of the United States" (1904) file 2823, box 135, Olmsted Records; and American Institute of Architects et al., *An Appeal to the Enlightened Sentiment of the People of the United States for the Safeguarding of the Future Development of the Capital of the Nation* (Washington, D.C., 1916). Unfinished

Washington, not historical continuity, was part of an inspiration for a 1960s effort to beautify the city, although a few of the participants in the movement were aware of their predecessors. See Lewis L. Gould, *Lady Bird Johnson and the Environment* (Lawrence: University Press of Kansas, 1988), 37–135.

62   Elements of City Beautiful plans survived in later planning schemes, a phenomenon noted as early as 1927 by Jacob L. Crane, Jr., "Errors to Avoid in City Planning," in *Official Proceedings of the Thirty-third Annual Convention Held at Dallas, Texas, November 14–18, 1927*, American Society for Municipal Improvements (St. Louis, 1928), 98.

63   Dana F. White claims the status of comprehensive planner for the senior Olmsted, and David C. Hammack claims it for Andrew Green and others. See White, "Frederick Law Olmsted, the Place Maker," in *Two Centuries of American Planning*, ed. Daniel Schaffer (London: Mansell, 1988), 87–112; and Hammack, "Comprehensive Planning before the Comprehensive Plan: A New Look at the Nineteenth-Century American City," in ibid., 139–65 (quotation, 156).

64   McFarland to Richard B. Watrous, 27 Sept. 1915, box 11; and to W. C. Reed, 4 Oct. 1921, box 8, McFarland Papers, *DMN*, 9 June 1980. David Dillon, "The Strangling of Turtle Creek," *DMN*, 8 July 1984; idem, and "A Changing Turtle Creek," *DMN*, 5 Aug. 1984. For the Kansas City Union Station, see Roy Kahn, "Tackling 'Impossible' Buildings," *Historic Preservation* 38 (May/June 1986): 42, 44. Although it concerns parks, Patricia O'Donnell's "Historic Preservation as Applied to Urban Parks," in *The Yearbook of Landscape Architecture: Historic Preservation* (New York: Van Nostrand Reinhold Co., 1983), 35, 53, deals effectively with difficult problems of changing uses, design, and restoration.

65   Draper, *San Francisco Civic Center* 59.

4

The Death and Life of Great American Cities

Jane Jacobs

This chapter is an attack on current city planning and rebuilding. It is also, and mostly, an attempt to introduce new principles of city planning and rebuilding, different and even opposite from those now taught in everything from schools of architecture and planning to the Sunday supplements and women's magazines. My attack is not based on quibbles about rebuilding methods or hairsplitting about fashions in design. It is an attack, rather, on the principles and aims that have shaped modern, orthodox city planning and rebuilding.

In setting forth different principles, I shall mainly be writing about common, ordinary things: for instance, what kinds of city streets are safe and what kinds are not; why some city parks are marvelous and others are vice traps and death traps; why some slums stay slums and other slums regenerate themselves even against financial and official opposition; what makes downtowns shift their centers; what, if anything, is a city neighborhood, and what jobs, if any, neighborhoods in great cities do. In short, I shall be writing about how cities work in real life, because this is the only way to learn what principles of planning and what practices in rebuilding can promote social and economic vitality in cities, and what practices and principles will deaden these attributes.

There is a wistful myth that if only we had enough money to spend – the figure is usually put at $100 billion – we could wipe out all our slums in ten years, reverse decay in the great, dull, gray belts that were yesterday's and day-before-yesterday's suburbs, anchor the wandering middle class and its wandering tax money, and perhaps even solve the traffic problem.

But look what we have built with the first several billions: low-income projects that become worse centers of delinquency, vandalism, and general social hopelessness than the slums they were supposed to replace. Middle-income housing projects that are truly marvels of dullness and regimentation, sealed against any buoyancy or vitality of city life. Luxury housing projects that mitigate their inanity, or try to, with a vapid vulgarity. Cultural centers that are unable to support a good bookstore. Civic centers that are avoided by everyone but bums, who have fewer choices of loitering place than others. Commercial centers that are lackluster imitations of standardized suburban chain-store shopping. Promenades that go from no place to nowhere and have no promenaders. Expressways that eviscerate great cities. This is not the rebuilding of cities. This is the sacking of cities.

Under the surface, these accomplishments prove even poorer than their poor pretenses. They seldom aid the city areas around them, as in theory they are supposed to. These amputated areas typically develop galloping gangrene. To house people in this planned fashion, price tags are fastened on the population, and each sorted-out chunk of price-tagged populace lives in growing suspicion and tension against the surrounding city. When two or more such hostile islands are juxtaposed the result is called "a balanced neighborhood." Monopolistic shopping centers and monumental cultural centers cloak, under the public relations hoo-ha, the subtraction of commerce, and of culture too, from the intimate and casual life of cities.

That such wonders may be accomplished, people who get marked with the planners' hex signs are pushed about, expropriated, and uprooted much as if they were the subjects of a conquering power. Thousands upon thousands of small businesses are destroyed, and their proprietors ruined, with hardly a gesture at compensation. Whole communities are torn apart and sown to the winds, with a reaping of cynicism, resentment, and despair that must be heard and seen to be believed. A group of clergymen in Chicago, appalled at the fruits of planned city rebuilding there, asked,

> Could Job have been thinking of Chicago when he wrote:
>
> Here are men that alter their neighbor's landmark . . .
> shoulder the poor aside, conspire to oppress the friendless.
> Reap they the field that is none of theirs, strip they the vine-
> yard wrongfully seized from its owner . . .

A cry goes up from the city streets, where wounded men lie groaning . . .

If so, he was thinking of New York, Philadelphia, Boston, Washington, St. Louis, San Francisco, and a number of other places. The economic rationale of current city rebuilding is a hoax. The economics of city rebuilding do not rest soundly on reasoned investment of public tax subsidies, as urban renewal theory proclaims, but also on vast, involuntary subsidies wrung out of helpless site victims. And the increased tax returns from such sites, accruing to the cities as a result of this "investment," are a mirage, a pitiful gesture against the ever-increasing sums of public money needed to combat disintegration and instability that flow from the cruelly shaken-up city. The means to planned city rebuilding are as deplorable as the ends.

Meantime, all the art and science of city planning are helpless to stem decay – and the spiritlessness that precedes decay – in ever more massive swatches of cities. Nor can this decay be laid, reassuringly, to lack of opportunity to apply the arts of planning. It seems to matter little whether they are applied or not. Consider the Morningside Heights area in New York City. According to planning theory it should not be in trouble at all, for it enjoys a great abundance of parkland, campus, playground, and other open spaces. It has plenty of grass. It occupies high and pleasant ground with magnificent river views. It is a famous educational center with splendid institutions – Columbia University, Union Theological Seminary, the Juilliard School of Music, and half a dozen others of eminent respectability. It is the beneficiary of good hospitals and churches. It has no industries. Its streets are zoned in the main against "incompatible uses" intruding into the preserves for solidly constructed, roomy, middle- and upper-class apartments. Yet by the early 1950s Morningside Heights was becoming a slum so swiftly, the surly kind of slum in which people fear to walk the streets, that the situation posed a crisis for the institutions. They and the planning arms of the city government got together, applied more planning theory, wiped out the most run-down part of the area and built in its stead a middle-income cooperative project complete with shopping center and a public housing project – all interspersed with air, light, sunshine, and landscaping. This was hailed as a great demonstration in city saving.

After that Morningside Heights went downhill even faster.

Nor is this an unfair or irrelevant example. In city after city, precisely the wrong areas, in the light of planning theory, are decaying. Less noticed, but equally significant, in city after city the wrong areas, in the light of planning theory, are refusing to decay.

Cities are an immense laboratory of trial and error, failure and success, in city building and city design. This is the laboratory in which city planning should have been learning and forming and testing its theories.

Instead the practitioners and teachers of this discipline (if such it can be called) have ignored the study of success and failure in real life, have been incurious about the reasons for unexpected success, and are guided instead by principles derived from the behavior and appearance of towns, suburbs, tuberculosis sanatoria, fairs, and imaginary dream cities – from anything but cities themselves.

If it appears that the rebuilt portions of cities and the endless new developments spreading beyond the cities are reducing city and country-side alike to a monotonous, unnourishing gruel, this is not strange. It all comes, first-, second-, third-, or fourth-hand, out of the same intellectual dish of mush, a mush in which the qualities, necessities, advantages and behavior of great cities have been utterly confused with the qualities, necessities, advantages, and behavior of other and more inert types of settlements.

There is nothing economically or socially inevitable about either the decay of old cities or the fresh-minted decadence of the new unurban urbanization. On the contrary, no other aspect of our economy and society has been more purposefully manipulated for a full quarter of a century to achieve precisely what we are getting. Extraordinary govern-mental financial incentives have been required to achieve this degree of monotony, sterility, and vulgarity. Decades of preaching, writing, and exhorting by experts have gone into convincing us and our legislators that mush like this must be good for us, as long as it comes bedded with grass.

Automobiles are often conveniently tagged as the villains responsible for the ills of cities and the disappointments and futilities of city planning. But the destructive effects of automobiles are much less a cause than a symptom of our incompetence at city building. Of course planners, including the highwaymen with fabulous sums of money and enormous powers at their disposal, are at a loss to make automobiles and cities compatible with one another. They do not know what to do with auto-mobiles in cities because they do not know how to plan for workable and vital cities anyhow – with or without automobiles.

The simple needs of automobiles are more easily understood and satis-fied than the complex needs of cities, and a growing number of planners and designers have come to believe that if they can only solve the problems of traffic, they will thereby have solved the major problem of cities. Cities have much more intricate economic and social concerns than automobile traffic. How can you know what to try with traffic until you know how the city itself works and what else it needs to do with its streets? You can't.

It may be that we have become so feckless as a people that we no longer care how things do work but only what kind of quick, easy outer impres-sion they give. If so, there is little hope for our cities or probably for much else in our society. But I do not think this is so.

Specifically, in the case of planning for cities, it is clear that a large number of good and earnest people do care deeply about building and renewing. Despite some corruption, and considerable greed for the other man's vineyard, the intentions going into the messes we make are, on the whole, exemplary. Planners, architects of city design, and those they have led along with them in their beliefs are not consciously disdainful of the importance of knowing how things work. On the contrary, they have gone to great pains to learn what the saints and sages of modern orthodox planning have said about how cities *ought* to work and what *ought* to be good for people and businesses in them. They take this with such devotion that when contradictory reality intrudes, threatening to shatter their dearly won learning, they must shrug reality aside.

Consider, for example, the orthodox planning reaction to a district called the North End in Boston. This is an old, low-rent area merging into the heavy industry of the waterfront, and it is officially considered Boston's worse slum and civic shame. It embodies attributes that all enlightened people know are evil, because so many wise men have said they are evil. Not only is the North End bumped right up against industry, but worse still it has all kinds of working places and commerce mingled in the greatest complexity with its residences. It has the highest concentration of dwelling units, on the land that is used for dwelling units, of any part of Boston, and indeed one of the highest concentrations to be found in any American city. It has little parkland. Children play in the streets. Instead of superblocks, or even decently large blocks, it has very small blocks; in planning parlance it is "badly cut up with wasteful streets." Its buildings are old. Everything conceivable is presumably wrong with the North End. In orthodox planning terms, it is a three-dimensional textbook of "megalopolis" in the last stages of depravity. The North End is thus a recurring assignment for MIT and Harvard planning and architectural students, who now and again pursue, under the guidance of their teachers, the paper exercise of converting it into superblocks and park promenades, wiping away its nonconforming uses, transforming it to an ideal of order and gentility so simple it could be engraved on the head of a pin.

Twenty years ago, when I first happened to see the North End, its buildings – town houses of different kinds and sizes converted to flats, and four- or five-story tenements built to house the flood of immigrants first from Ireland, then from Eastern Europe, and finally from Sicily – were badly overcrowded, and the general effect was of a district taking a terrible physical beating and certainly desperately poor.

When I saw the North End again in 1959, I was amazed at the change. Dozens and dozens of buildings had been rehabilitated. Instead of mattresses against the windows, there were Venetian blinds and glimpses of fresh paint. Many of the small, converted houses now had only one or two families in them instead of the old crowded three or four. Some of the families in the tenements (as I learned later, visiting inside) had uncrowded themselves by throwing two older apartments together, and had equipped these with bathrooms, new kitchens, and the like. I looked down a narrow alley, thinking to find at least here the old, squalid North End, but no: more neatly repointed brickwork, new blinds, and a burst of music as a door opened. Indeed, this was the only city district I have ever seen – or have seen to this day – in which the sides of buildings around parking lots had not been left raw and amputated, but repaired and painted as neatly as if they were intended to be seen. Mingled all among the buildings for living were an incredible number of splendid food stores, as well as such enterprises as upholstery making, metalworking, carpentry, food processing. The streets were alive with children playing, people shopping, people strolling, people talking. Had it not been a cold January day, there would surely have been people sitting.

The general street atmosphere of buoyancy, friendliness, and good health was so infectious that I began asking directions of people just for the fun of getting in on some talk. I had seen a lot of Boston in the past couple of days, most of it sorely distressing, and this struck me, with relief, as the healthiest place in the city. But I could not imagine where the money had come from for the rehabilitation, because it is almost impossible today to get any appreciable mortgage money in districts of American cities that are not either high-rent, or else imitations of suburbs. To find out, I went into a bar and restaurant (where an animated conversation about fishing was in progress) and called a Boston planner I know.

"Why in the world are you down in the North End?" he said. "Money? Why, no money or work has gone into the North End. Nothing's going on down there. Eventually, yes, but not yet. That's a slum!"

"It doesn't seem like a slum to me," I said.

"Why, that's the worst slum in the city. It has 275 dwelling units to the net acre! I hate to admit we have anything like that in Boston, but it's a fact."

"Do you have any other figures on it?" I asked.

"Yes, funny thing. It has among the lowest delinquency, disease, and infant mortality rates in the city. It also has the lowest ratio of rent to income in the city. Boy, are those people getting bargains. Let's see . . . the child population is just above average for the city, on the nose. The death rate is low, 8.8 per thousand, against the average city rate of 11.2. The TB death rate is very low, less than 1 per ten thousand, can't understand it, it's lower even than Brookline's. In the old days the North End used to be the city's worst spot for tuberculosis, but all that has changed. Well, they must be strong people. Of course it's a terrible slum."

"You should have more slums like this," I said. "Don't tell me there are plans to wipe this out. You ought to be down here learning as much as you can from it."

"I know how you feel," he said. "I often go down there myself just to walk around the streets and feel that wonderful, cheerful street life. Say, what you ought to do, you ought to come back and go down in the summer if you think it's fun now. You'd be crazy about it in summer. But of course we have to rebuild it eventually. We've got to get those people off the streets."

Here was a curious thing. My friend's instincts told him the North End was a good place, and his social statistics confirmed it. But everything he had learned as a physical planner about what is good for people and good for city neighborhoods, everything that made him an expert, told him the North End had to be a bad place.

The leading Boston savings banker, "a man way up there in the power structure," to whom my friend referred me for my inquiry about the money, confirmed what I learned, in the meantime, from people in the North End. The money had not come through the grace of the great American banking system, which now knows enough about planning to know a slum as well as the planners do. "No sense in lending money into the North End," the banker said. "It's a slum! It's still getting some immigrants! Furthermore, back in the Depression it had a very large number of foreclosures; bad record." (I had heard about this too, in the meantime, and how families had worked and pooled their resources to buy back some of those foreclosed buildings.)

The largest mortgage loans that had been fed into this district of some 15,000 people in the quarter-century since the Great Depression were for $3,000, the banker told me, "and very, very few of those." There had been some others for $1,000 and for $2,000. The rehabilitation work had been almost entirely financed by business and housing earnings within the district, plowed back in, and by skilled work bartered among residents and relatives of residents.

By this time I knew that this inability to borrow for improvement was a galling worry to North Enders, and that furthermore some North Enders were worried because it seemed impossible to get new building in the area except at a price of seeing themselves and their community wiped out in the fashion of the students' dreams of a city Eden, a fate that they knew was not academic because it had already smashed completely a socially similar – although physically more spacious – nearby district called the West End. They were worried because they were aware also that patch and fix with nothing else could not do forever. "Any chance of loans for new construction in the North End?" I asked the banker.

"No, absolutely not!" he said, sounding impatient at my denseness. "That's a slum!"

Bankers, like planners, have theories about cities on which they act. They have gotten their theories from the same intellectual sources as the planners. Bankers and government administrative officials who guarantee mortgages do not invent planning theories nor, surprisingly, even economic doctrine about cities. They are enlightened nowadays, and they pick up their ideas from idealists, a generation later. Since theoretical city planning has embraced no major new ideas for considerably more than a generation, theoretical planners, financiers, and bureaucrats are all just about even today.

And to put it bluntly, they are all in the same stage of elaborately learned superstition as medical science was early in the last century, when physicians put their faith in bloodletting, to draw out the evil humors that were believed to cause disease. With bloodletting, it took years of learning to know precisely which veins, by what rituals, were to be opened for what symptoms. A superstructure of technical complication was erected in such deadpan detail that the literature still sounds almost plausible. However, because people, even when they are thoroughly enmeshed in descriptions of reality that are at variance with reality, are still seldom devoid of the powers of observation and independent thought, the science of bloodletting, over most of its long sway, appears usually to have been tempered with a certain amount of common sense. Or it was tempered until it reached its highest peaks of technique in, of all places, the young United States. Bloodletting went wild here. It had an enormously influential proponent in Dr Benjamin Rush, still revered as the greatest statesman-physician of our revolutionary and federal periods, and a genius of medical administration. Dr Rush Got Things Done. Among the things he got done, some of them good and useful, were to develop, practice, teach, and spread the custom of bloodletting in cases where prudence or mercy had heretofore restrained its use. He and his students drained the blood of very young children, of consumptives, of the greatly aged, of almost anyone unfortunate enough to be sick in his realms of influence. His extreme practices aroused the alarm and horror of European bloodletting physicians. And yet as late as 1851, a committee appointed by the State Legislature of New York solemnly defended the thoroughgoing use of bloodletting. It scathingly ridiculed and censured a physician, William Turner, who had the temerity to write a pamphlet criticizing Dr Rush's doctrines and calling "the practice of taking blood in diseases contrary to common sense, to general experience, to enlightened reason, and to the manifest laws of the divine Providence." Sick people needed fortifying, not draining, said Dr Turner, and he was squelched.

Medical analogies, applied to social organisms, are apt to be farfetched, and there is no point in mistaking mammalian chemistry for what occurs in a city. But analogies as to what goes on in the brains of earnest and learned men, dealing with complex phenomena they do not understand at all and trying to make do with a pseudoscience, do have a point. As in the pseudoscience of bloodletting, just so in the pseudoscience of city rebuilding and planning, years of learning and a plethora of subtle and complicated dogma have arisen on a foundation of nonsense. The tools of technique have steadily been perfected. Naturally, in time, forceful and able men, admired administrators, having swallowed the initial fallacies and having been provisioned with tools and with public confidence, go on logically to the greatest destructive excesses, which prudence or mercy might previously have forbade. Bloodletting could heal only by accident or insofar as it broke the rules, until the time when it was abandoned in favor of the hard, complex business of assembling, using, and testing, bit by bit, true descriptions of reality drawn not from how it ought to be but from how it is. The pseudoscience of city planning and its companion, the art of city design, have not yet broken with the specious comfort of wishes, familiar superstitions, oversimplifications, and symbols – and have not yet embarked upon the adventure of probing the real world.

So in this chapter we shall start, if only in a small way, adventuring in the real world, ourselves. The way to get at what goes on in the seemingly mysterious and perverse behavior of cities is, I think, to look closely, and with as little previous expectation as is possible, at the most ordinary scenes and events and attempt to see what they mean and whether any threads of principle emerge among them. This is what I try to do in the first part of this book.

One principle emerges so ubiquitously, and in so many and such complex different forms, that I turn my attention to its nature in the second part of this book . . . which becomes the heart of my argument. This ubiquitous principle is the need of cities for a most intricate and close-grained diversity of uses that give each other constant mutual support, both economically and socially. The components of this diversity can differ enormously, but they must supplement each other in certain concrete ways.

I think that unsuccessful city areas are areas that lack this kind of intricate mutual support, and that the science of city planning and the art of city design, in real life for real cities, must become the science and art of catalyzing and nourishing these close-grained working relationships. I think, from the evidence I can find, that there are four primary conditions required for generating useful great city diversity, and that by deliberately inducing these four conditions, planning can induce city vitality (something that the plans of planners alone, and the designs of designers alone, can never achieve). . . .

Cities are fantastically dynamic places, and this is strikingly true of their successful parts, which offer a fertile ground for the plans of thousands of people. . . .

The look of things and the way they work are inextricably bound together, and in no place more so than cities. But people who are interested only in how a city "ought" to look and uninterested in how it works will be disappointed by this book. It is futile to plan a city's appearance, or speculate on how to endow it with a pleasing appearance of order, without knowing what sort of innate, functioning order it has. To seek for the look of things as a primary purpose or as the main drama is apt to make nothing but trouble.

In New York's East Harlem, there is a housing project with a conspicuous rectangular lawn that became an object of hatred to the project tenants. A social worker frequently at the project was astonished by how often the subject of the lawn came up, usually gratuitously as far as she could see, and how much the tenants despised it and urged that it be done away with. When she asked why, the usual answer was, "What good is it?" or "Who wants it?" Finally one day, a tenant more articulate than the others made this pronouncement: "Nobody cared what we wanted when they built this place. They threw our houses down and pushed us here and pushed our friends somewhere else. We don't have a place around here to get a cup of coffee or a newspaper even, or borrow fifty cents. Nobody cared what we need. But the big men come and look at that grass and say, 'Isn't it wonderful! Now the poor have everything!'"

This tenant was saying what moralists have said for thousands of years: Handsome is as handsome does. All that glitters is not gold.

She was saying more: There is a quality even meaner than outright ugliness or disorder, and this meaner quality is the dishonest mask of pretended order, achieved by ignoring or suppressing the real order that is struggling to exist and to be served.

In trying to explain the underlying order of cities, I use a preponderance of examples from New York because that is where I live. But most of my basic ideas come from things I first noticed or was told in other cities. For example, my first inkling about the powerful effects of certain kinds of functional mixtures in the city came from Pittsburgh, my first speculations about street safety from Philadelphia and Baltimore, my first notions about the meanderings of downtown from Boston, my first clues to the unmaking of slums from Chicago. Most of the material for these musings was at my own front door, but perhaps it is easiest to see things first where you don't take them for granted. The basic idea, to try to begin understanding the intricate social and economic order under the seeming disorder of cities, was not my idea at all, but that of William Kirk, head worker of Union Settlement in East Harlem, New York, who, by showing me East Harlem, showed me a way of seeing other neighborhoods, and downtowns too. In every case, I have tried to test out what I saw or heard in one city or neighborhood against others, to find how relevant each city's or each place's lessons might be outside its own special case.

I have concentrated on great cities, and on their inner areas, because this is the problem that has been most consistently evaded in planning theory. I think this may also have somewhat wider usefulness as time passes, because many of the parts of today's cities in the worst, and apparently most baffling, trouble were suburbs or dignified, quiet residential areas not too long ago; eventually many of today's brand-new suburbs or semisuburbs are going to be engulfed in cities and will succeed or fail in that condition depending on whether they can adapt to functioning successfully as city districts. Also, to be frank, I like dense cities best and care about them most.

But I hope no reader will try to transfer my observations into guides as to what goes on in towns, or little cities, or in suburbs that still are suburban. Towns, suburbs and even little cities are totally different organisms from great cities. We are in enough trouble already from trying to understand big cities in terms of the behavior, and the imagined behavior, of towns. To try to understand towns in terms of big cities will only compound confusion.

I hope any reader will constantly and skeptically test what I say against his or her own knowledge of cities and their behavior. If I have been inaccurate in observations or mistaken in inferences and conclusions, I hope these faults will be quickly corrected. The point is, we need desperately to learn and to apply as much knowledge that is true and useful about cities as fast as possible.

I have been making unkind remarks about orthodox city planning theory, and shall make more as occasion arises to do so. By now, these orthodox ideas are part of our folklore. They harm us because we take them for granted. To show how we got them, and how little they are to the point, I shall give a quick outline here of the most influential ideas that have contributed to the verities of orthodox modern city planning and city architectural design.*

The most important thread of influence starts, more or less, with Ebenezer Howard, an English court reporter for whom planning was an avocation. Howard looked at the living conditions of the poor in late-nineteenth-century London and justifiably did not like what he smelled or saw or heard. He not only hated the wrongs and mistakes of the city, he hated the city and thought it an outright evil and an affront to nature that so many people should get themselves into an agglomeration. His prescription for saving the people was to do the city in.

The program he proposed, in 1898, was to halt the growth of London

* Readers who would like a fuller account, and a sympathetic account, which mine is not, should go to the sources, which are very interesting, especially *Garden Cities of To-morrow*, by Ebenezer Howard; *The Culture of Cities*, by Lewis Mumford; *Cities in Evolution*, by Sir Patrick Geddes; *Modern Housing*, by Catherine Bauer; *Toward New Towns for America*, by Clarence Stein; *Nothing Gained by Overcrowding*, by Sir Raymond Unwin; and *The City of Tomorrow and Its Planning*, by Le Corbusier. The best short survey I know of is the group of excerpts under the title "Assumptions and Goals of City Planning," contained in *Land-Use Planning, A Casebook on the Use, Misuse and Re-use of Urban Land*, by Charles M. Haar.

and also repopulate the countryside, where villages were declining, by building a new kind of town – the Garden City, where the city poor might again live close to nature. So that they might earn their livings, industry was to be set up in the Garden City; for while Howard was not planning cities, he was not planning dormitory suburbs either. His aim was the creation of self-sufficient small towns, really very nice towns if you were docile and had no plans of your own and did not mind spending your life among others with no plans of their own. As in all utopias, the right to have plans of any significance belonged only to the planners in charge. The Garden City was to be encircled with a belt of agriculture. Industry was to be in its planned preserves; schools, housing, and greens in planned living preserves; and in the center were to be commercial, club, and cultural places, held in common. The town and green belt, in their totality, were to be permanently controlled by the public authority under which the town was developed, to prevent speculation or supposedly irrational changes in land use and also to do away with temptations to increase its density – in brief, to prevent it from ever becoming a city. The maximum population was to be held to thirty thousand people.

Nathan Glazer has summed up the vision well in *Architectural Forum*: "The image was the English country town – with the manor house and its park replaced by a community center, and with some factories hidden behind a screen of trees, to supply work."

The closest American equivalent would probably be the model company town, with profit sharing, and with the parent-teacher associations in charge of the routine, custodial political life. For Howard was envisioning not simply a new physical environment and social life but a paternalistic political and economic society.

Nevertheless, as Glazer has pointed out, the Garden City was "conceived as an alternative to the city, and as a solution to city problems; this was, and is still, the foundation of its immense power as a planning idea." Howard managed to get two garden cities built, Letchworth and Welwyn, and of course Great Britain and Sweden have, since World War II, built a number of satellite towns based on Garden City principles. In the United States, the suburb of Radburn, New Jersey, and the depression-built, government-sponsored Green Belt towns (actually suburbs) were all incomplete modifications on the idea. But Howard's influence in the literal, or reasonably literal, acceptance of his program was as nothing compared to his influence on conceptions underlying all American city planning today. City planners and designers with no interest in the Garden City as such are still thoroughly governed intellectually by its underlying principles.

Howard set spinning powerful and city-destroying ideas: He conceived that the way to deal with the city's functions was to sort and sift out of the whole certain simple uses, and to arrange each of these in relative self-containment. He focused on the provision of wholesome housing as the central problem, to which everything else was subsidiary; furthermore he defined wholesome housing in terms only of suburban physical qualities and small-town social qualities. He conceived of commerce in terms of routine, standardized supply of goods, and as serving a self-limited market. He conceived of good planning as a series of static acts; in each case the plan must anticipate all that is needed and be protected, after it is built, against any but the most minor subsequent changes. He conceived of planning also as essentially paternalistic, if not authoritarian. He was uninterested in the aspects of the city that could not be abstracted to serve his Utopia. In particular, he simply wrote off the intricate, many faceted, cultural life of the metropolis. He was uninterested in such problems as the way the great cities police themselves, or exchange ideas, or operate politically, or invent new economic arrangements, and he was oblivious to devising ways to strengthen these functions because, after all, he was not designing for this kind of life in any case.

Both in his preoccupations and in his omissions, Howard made sense in his own terms but none in terms of city planning. Yet virtually all modern city planning has been adapted from, and embroidered on, this silly substance.

Howard's influence on American city planning converged on the city from two directions: from town and regional planners on the one hand, and from architects on the other. Along the avenue of planning, Sir Patrick Geddes, a Scots biologist and philosopher, saw the Garden City idea not as a fortuitous way to absorb population growth otherwise destined for a great city but as the starting point of a much grander and more encompassing pattern. He thought of the planning of cities in terms of the planning of whole regions. Under regional planning, garden cities would be rationally distributed throughout large territories, dovetailing into natural resources, balanced against agriculture and woodland, forming one far-flung logical whole.

Howard's and Geddes's ideas were enthusiastically adopted in America during the 1920s, and developed further by a group of extraordinarily effective and dedicated people – among them Lewis Mumford, Clarence Stein, the late Henry Wright, and Catherine Bauer. While they thought of themselves as regional planners, Catherine Bauer has more recently called this group the "Decentrists," and this name is more apt, for the primary result of regional planning, as they saw it, would be to decentralize great cities, thin them out, and disperse their enterprises and populations into smaller, separated cities or, better yet, towns. At the time, it appeared that the American population was both aging and leveling off in numbers, and the problem appeared to be not one of accommodating a rapidly growing population but simply of redistributing a static population.

As with Howard himself, this group's influence was less in getting literal acceptance of its program – that got nowhere – than in influencing city planning and legislation affecting housing and housing finance. Model housing schemes by Stein and Wright, built mainly in suburban settings or at the fringes of cities, together with the writings and the diagrams, sketches, and photographs presented by Mumford and Bauer, demonstrated and popularized ideas such as these, which are now taken for granted in orthodox planning: The street is bad as an environment for humans; houses should be turned away from it and faced inward, toward sheltered greens. Frequent streets are wasteful, of advantage only to real estate speculators who measure value by the front foot. The basic unit of city design is not the street but the block and, more particularly, the superblock. Commerce should be segregated from residences and greens. A neighborhood's demand for goods should be calculated "scientifically," and this much and no more commercial space allocated. The presence of many other people is, at best, a necessary evil, and good city planning must aim for at least an illusion of isolation and suburbany privacy. The Decentrists also pounded in Howard's premises that the planned community must be islanded off as a self-contained unit, that it must resist future change, and that every significant detail must be controlled by the planners from the start and then stuck to. In short, good planning was project planning.

To reinforce and dramatize the necessity for the new order of things, the Decentrists hammered away at the bad old city. They were incurious about successes in great cities. They were interested only in failures. All was failure. A book like Mumford's *The Culture of Cities* was largely a morbid and biased catalog of ills. The great city was Megalopolis, Tyrannopolis, Nekropolis, a monstrosity, a tyranny, a living death. It must go. New York's midtown was "solidified chaos" (Mumford). The shape and appearance of cities was nothing but "a chaotic accident . . . the summation of the haphazard, antagonistic whims of many self-centered, ill-advised individuals" (Stein). The centers of cities amounted to "a foreground of noise, dirt, beggars, souvenirs, and shrill competitive advertising" (Bauer).

How could anything so bad be worth the attempt to understand it? The Decentrists' analyses, the architectural and housing designs that were companions and offshoots of these analyses, the national housing and home financing legislation so directly influenced by the new vision – none of these had anything to do with understanding cities or fostering successful large cities, nor were they intended to. They were reasons and means for jettisoning cities, and the Decentrists were frank about this.

But in the schools of planning and architecture – and in Congress, state legislatures, and city halls too – the Decentrists' ideas were gradually accepted as basic guides for dealing constructively with big cities themselves. This is the most amazing event in the whole sorry tale: that finally people who sincerely wanted to strengthen great cities should adopt recipes frankly devised for undermining their economies and killing them.

The man with the most dramatic idea of how to get all this anticity planning right into the citadels of iniquity themselves was the European architect Le Corbusier. He devised in the 1920s a dream city, which he called the Radiant City, composed not of the low buildings beloved of the Decentrists but instead mainly of skyscrapers within a park. "Suppose we are entering the city by way of the Great Park," Le Corbusier wrote. "Our fast car takes the special elevated motor track between the majestic skyscrapers: as we approach nearer, there is seen the repetition against the sky of the twenty-four skyscrapers; to our left and right on the outskirts of each particular area are the municipal and administrative buildings; and enclosing the space are the museums and university buildings. The whole city is a Park." In Le Corbusier's vertical city the common run of mankind was to be housed at 1,200 inhabitants to the acre, a fantastically high city density indeed, but because of building up so high, 95 percent of the ground could remain open. The skyscrapers would occupy only 5 percent of the ground. The high-income people would be in lower, luxury housing around courts, with 85 percent of their ground left open. Here and there would be restaurants and theaters.

Le Corbusier was planning not only a physical environment. He was planning for a social utopia too. Le Corbusier's utopia was a condition of what he called maximum individual liberty, by which he seems to have meant not liberty to do anything much, but liberty from ordinary responsibility. In his Radiant City nobody, presumably, was going to have to be his brother's keeper any more. Nobody was going to have to struggle with plans of his own. Nobody was going to be tied down.

The Decentrists and other loyal advocates of the Garden City were aghast at Le Corbusier's city of towers in the park, and still are. Their reaction to it was, and remains, much like that of progressive nursery school teachers confronting an utterly institutional orphanage. And yet, ironically, the Radiant City comes directly out of the Garden City. Le Corbusier accepted the Garden City's fundamental image, superficially at least, and worked to make it practical for high densities. He described his creation as the Garden City made attainable. "The garden city is a will-o'-the-wisp," he wrote. "Nature melts under the invasion of roads and houses and the promised seclusion becomes a crowded settlement . . . The solution will be found in the 'vertical garden city.'"

In another sense too, in its relatively easy public reception, Le Corbusier's Radiant City depended upon the Garden City. The Garden City planners and their ever-increasing following among housing reformers, students, and architects were indefatigably popularizing the ideas of the superblock; the project neighborhood; the unchangeable plan; and grass, grass, grass. What is more, they were successfully establishing such attributes as the hallmarks of humane, socially responsible, functional, high-minded planning. Le Corbusier really did not have to justify his vision in either humane or city-functional terms. If the great object of city planning was that Christopher Robin might go hoppety-hoppety on the grass, what was wrong with Le Corbusier? The Decentrists' cries of institutionalization, mechanization, depersonalization seemed to others foolishly sectarian.

Le Corbusier's dream city has had an immense impact on our cities. It was hailed deliriously by architects and has gradually been embodied in scores of projects, ranging from low-income public housing to office-building projects. Aside from making at least the superficial Garden City principles superficially practical in a dense city, Le Corbusier's dream contained other marvels. He attempted to make planning for the auto-mobile an integral part of his scheme, and this was, in the 1920s and early 1930s, a new, exciting idea. He included great arterial roads for express one-way traffic. He cut the number of streets because "cross-roads are an enemy to traffic." He proposed underground streets for heavy vehicles and deliveries, and of course like the Garden City planners he kept the pedestrians off the streets and in the parks. His city was like a wonderful mechanical toy. Furthermore, his conception, as an architectural work, had a dazzling clarity, simplicity, and harmony. It was so orderly, so visible, so easy to understand. It said everything in a flash, like a good advertisement. This vision and its bold symbolism have been all but irre-sistible to planners, housers, designers – and to developers, lenders, and mayors too. It exerts a great pull on "progressive" zoners, who write rules calculated to encourage nonproject builders to reflect, if only a little, the dream. No matter how vulgarized or clumsy the design, how dreary and useless the open space, how dull the close-up view, an imitation of Le Corbusier shouts, "Look what I made!" Like a great, visible ego it tells of someone's achievement. But as to how the city works, it tells, like the Garden City, nothing but lies.

Although the Decentrists, with their devotion to the ideal of a cozy town life, have never made peace with the Le Corbusier vision, most of their disciples have. Virtually all sophisticated city designers today combine the two conceptions in various permutations. The rebuilding technique variously known as "selective removal" or "spot renewal" or "renewal planning" or "planned conservation" – meaning that total clear-ance of a run-down area is avoided – is largely the trick of seeing how many old buildings can be left standing and the area still converted into a passable version of Radiant Garden City. Zoners, highway planners, legislators, land-use planners, and parks and playground planners – none of whom live in an ideological vacuum – constantly use, as fixed points of reference, these two powerful visions and the more sophisticated merged vision. They may wander from the visions, they may compro-mise, they may vulgarize, but these are the points of departure.

We shall look briefly at one other, less important, line of ancestry in orthodox planning. This one begins more or less with the great Columbian Exposition in Chicago in 1893, just about the same time that Howard was formulating his Garden City ideas. The Chicago fair snubbed the exciting modern architecture that had begun to emerge in Chicago and instead dramatized a retrogressive imitation Renaissance style. One heavy, grandiose monument after another was arrayed in the exposition park, like frosted pastries on a tray, in a sort of squat, decorated forecast of Le Corbusier's later repetitive ranks of towers in a park. This orgiastic assemblage of the rich and monumental captured the imagination of both planners and public. It gave impetus to a movement called the City Beautiful, and indeed the planning of the exposition was dominated by the man who became the leading City Beautiful planner, Daniel Burnham of Chicago.

The aim of the City Beautiful was the City Monumental. Great schemes were drawn up for systems of baroque boulevards, which mainly came to nothing. What did come out of the movement was the Center Monumental, modeled on the fair. City after city built its civic center or its cultural center. These buildings were arranged along a boulevard as at Benjamin Franklin Parkway in Philadelphia, or along a mall like the Government Center in Cleveland, or were bordered by park, like the Civic Center at St. Louis, or were interspersed with park, like the Civic Center at San Francisco. However they were arranged, the important point was that the monuments had been sorted out from the rest of the city and assembled into the grandest effect thought possible, the whole being treated as a complete unit, in a separate and well-defined way.

People were proud of them, but the centers were not a success. For one thing, invariably the ordinary city around them ran down instead of being uplifted, and they always acquired an incongruous rim of ratty tattoo parlors and secondhand-clothing stores, or else just nondescript, dispirited decay. For another, people stayed away from them to a remarkable degree. Somehow, when the fair became part of the city, it did not work like the fair.

The architecture of the City Beautiful centers went out of style. But the idea behind the centers was not questioned, and it has never had more force than it does today. The idea of sorting out certain cultural or public functions and decontaminating their relationship with the workaday city dovetailed nicely with the Garden City teachings. The conceptions have harmoniously merged, much as the Garden City and the Radiant City merged, into a sort of Radiant Garden City Beautiful, such as the immense Lincoln Square project for New York, in which a monumental City Beautiful cultural center is one among a series of adjoining Radiant City and Radiant Garden City housing, shopping, and campus centers.

And by analogy, the principles of sorting out – and of bringing order by repression of all plans but the planners – have been easily extended to all manner of city functions, until today a land-use master plan for a big city is largely a matter of proposed placement, often in relation to transportation, of many series of decontaminated sortings.

From beginning to end, from Howard and Burnham to the latest amendment on urban renewal law, the entire concoction is irrelevant to the workings of cities. Unstudied, unrespected, cities have served as sacrificial victims.

5

The Neutral City

Richard Sennett

Nowhere

In the *Canterbury Tales*, Chaucer portrayed a priest who well understood the boundaries of his own faith:

> *And though he hooly were and vertuous,*
> *He was to synful men nat despitous,*
> *Ne of his speche daungerous ne digne,*
> *But in his techung discreet and benygne.*

> *[And yet, though he himself was holy and virtuous,*
> *He was not contemptuous of sinners,*
> *Nor overbearing and proud in his talk,*
> *Rather, he was discreet and kind in his teaching.]*[1]

Chaucer meant to evoke a sense of place when he described the priest's virtues as those of a "good man of the church": They were the virtues of the parish rather than the virtues of the wandering mystic. Yet the Christian impulse to wander was not tamed by promises to bring the journey to an end in a refuge. There were those who remained ever restless in the spiritual quest. This inner turbulence denied them the comforts of the parish; more faith-hungry, their lives in the world were more unbounded, indeterminate. It was from this source of unhappy energy that, eventually, an unlikely logic of space would appear in secular society: the logic of neutral space. Nietzsche's perception of the

Christian discontinuity between inner and outer life would take a new twist: the world would appear not as a veil of tears but as a silent wilderness.

This change in Christian imagery that appeared in the coming of Protestantism connects to a modern way of seeing. It is the way the planner sees who designs neutral, sterile environments. The planner never meant to, of course. Still, it is curious how the designers of parking lots, malls, and public plazas seem to be endowed with a positive genius for sterility, in the use of materials and in details as well as in overall planning. This compulsive neutralizing of the environment is rooted in part in an old unhappiness, the fear of pleasure, which led people to treat their surroundings as neutrally as possible. The modern urbanist is in the grip of a Protestant ethic of space.

It may seem both fitting and odd to take the small band of American Puritans as first instances of this compulsion to neutralize. Odd, because the places in which the Puritans lived would have been instantly recognizable to their contemporaries as traditional European villages re-created in America, a nucleus of houses packed tight around a green. Beyond this traditional village the pastures and fields extended out to the township lines.

While they lasted, these nucleated villages were conceived as spiritual centers, the knot of faithful human beings tied tight in the wilderness. The Salem Village Church Covenant of 1689 states, in part:

> We resolve uprightly to study what is our duty, and to make it our grief, and reckon it our shame, whereinsoever we find our selves to come short in the discharge of it, and for pardon thereof humbly to betake our selves to the Blood of the Everlasting Covenant.
>
> And that we may keep this covenant, and all the branches of it inviolable for ever, being sensible that we can do nothing of our selves, We humbly implore the help and grace of our Mediator may be sufficient for us.[2]

Yet the faithful were to find this tight knot of community to be choking. These pilgrims perhaps dared more than Chaucer's parish priest: they scorned security; the wilderness began to tempt them. In the late seventeenth century, therefore, the traditional village pattern started to give way; once the village nucleus was established, "In land division the settlers abandoned the conservatism which had characterized their street plans. The allotment of wilderness seemed to ridicule humble European field systems."[3] And by the eighteenth century these tight-knit villages had unraveled, as the bulk of the population moved out to live on the land they worked.

The lure of the wilderness had a spiritual meaning as well: The American Puritan imagined himself in need of removal from the Europe in which he was born because of the unhappy warfare within his breast.

His salvation or damnation was predestined by God, who had also, with a twist of the divine knife, made it impossible for the Puritan to know whether he would be saved or damned. A Puritan was obliged, in the words of the American Puritan Cotton Mather, "to preach the unsearchable Riches of Christ." But a Puritan was also human: he was a man who wanted to know his fate, a man in search of evidence.[4] The world's daily sins and temptations were not within his power to control, and he lacked the Catholic relief of absolution for sin. Nothing could be known ultimately, nothing could be absolved – his God was like a sadistic Fortune. Conscience and pain became, therefore, inseparable companions. Perhaps the most graphic expression of this inner conflict was a popular poem of the early seventeenth century by George Goodwin, which reads in part:

> I sing my self; my civil wars within;
> The victories I hourly lose and win;
> The daily duel, the continual strife,
> The war that ends not, till I end my life.[5]

From such misery the Puritan was tempted by the wilderness, by a place of emptiness which made no seductive demands of its own upon him, in order that he try to get his life under control, however forlorn that hope. Cotton Mather's father, Increase Mather, one of the first generation of Puritans to set sail, wrote the following on the title page of his diary:

> Give me a Call
>   To dwell
> Where no foot hath
>   A Path
> There will I spend
>   And End
> My wearied years
>   In tears.[6]

Mundane labels like "the first colonists" or "English adventurers" don't account for the motives that would drive people to make hazardous voyages to a cold, mosquito-infested, rocky landscape to live out their lives. The first settlers were ravaged human beings. They suffered the dual need to "get away from it all" in order to attempt to "get control of their lives." It was an early sign of a duality in modern society: Flight from others occurs for the sake of self-mastery.

In that flight are to be found the seeds of certain of our own attitudes about the physical environment. The churches in the centers of traditional European villages and towns made evident to the eye where to find God. These centers defined a space of recognition. God is legible: he is within, within the sanctuary as within the soul. On the outside there is only exposure, disorder, and cruelty. The Puritan "inside" was illegible, a place of war, conscience at war with itself; this terrible business of "finding oneself" only becomes more confusing if the outside, other people, other confusions intrude. The Spaniard came to the New World as a lord, conversion, and conquest all of a piece; he came as a Catholic. The Puritan came as a refugee; conversion was a duty, conquest a necessity for survival, but neither was his reason for coming. Yet this search for refuge produced a vision of the outside different from the pleasure-filled, violent, bear-baiting outside of the medieval Catholic town. The place the Puritans arrived at had to be treated like a blank canvas for the double compulsion to play itself out, for a man or woman to get more self-control by starting over somewhere else.

Language frequently failed the people embarked on this purifying experiment to conjure what passed within their breasts. The failure of words to reveal the soul was tied to a heightened self-awareness in an immense, alien place. Lacking a language adequate to inner experience, the life of each would be more and more locked within, impossible to declare, perhaps at best intimated by the rendering of an impression. The inner space of medieval Catholicism was physical; it was a space people could share. The inner space of Puritanism was the space of the most radical individualism and was impalpable. The Puritan eye could only see within itself. Outside there was nothing. It exists, this wilderness self, in the space Beckett imagined in *Endgame* or *Waiting for Godot*, an empty space in a time without narrative. If the strange creatures who were American Puritans thus gave the first signs of a certain form of modern sensibility, they also suggested what would be its environmental consequences.

The search for physical sanctuary expressed, as we have seen, a desire to place oneself in the hands of authority. The Protestant imagination of space, on the contrary, expressed a desire for power. Most obviously, a kind of egoistic power. Obsessive inner struggle may imply a deep hostility toward the needs of other people, a resentment of their very presence. Others interfere; to get in control of oneself, nothing "out there" can count. This hostility marks now the way the homeless or mentally disturbed are seen on the streets; they are resented because they, who are obviously needy, are visible. The very sight of their need is an intrusion upon the self. To ward them off, one wants to treat the outside as neutral; then one is alone with oneself at last. But neutrality can organize power in a more systematic way, one that more deeply implicates the eye.

The cultural problems of the city are conventionally taken to be its impersonality, its alienating scale, its coldness. There is more in these charges than is first apparent. *Impersonality, coldness,* and *emptiness* are essential words in the Protestant language of environment; they express a desire to see the outside as null, lacking value. They are words that express a certain interest in seeing; the perception of outer emptiness reinforces the value of turning within. Certainly one does not imagine a shopping-mall designer racked by Cotton Mather's anguish. But that old unhappiness has left its residue as a certain practice of visual denial, as the acceptance of sensory denial in everyday life to be normal. More than normal – reassuring. Nothing as important as the inner struggle to account. Therefore, one can deal with the outside in purely instrumental, manipulative terms, since nothing outside "really" matters. In this modulated form, neutrality becomes an instrument of power. I should like to show how this instrument can be wielded by looking at the modern forms of an ancient urban design.

The Grid

The Egyptian hierograph that the historian Joseph Rykwert believes was one of the original signs for a town is

transcribed as "nywt."[7] This hierograph, a cross within a circle, suggests two of the simplest, most enduring urban images. The circle is a single, unbroken line: It suggests enclosure, a wall or a space like a town square; within this enclosure, life unfolds. The cross is the simplest form of distinct compound lines; it is perhaps the most ancient object of environmental process, as opposed to the circle, which represents the boundary defining environmental size. Crossed lines represent an elemental way of making streets within the boundary, through making grids.

The Babylonians and the ancient Egyptians made cities by planning straight streets to meet at right angles, thus creating regular, repeating blocks of land on which to build. Hippodamus of Miletus is conventionally thought the first city builder to conceive of these grids as expressions of culture; the grid expressed, he believed, the rationality of civilized life. In their military conquests the Romans elaborated the contrast between the rude and formless camps of the barbarians and their own military forts, or *castra*. The Roman camps were laid out as squares or rectangles. The perimeter was at first guarded by soldiers, and then, as the camp grew into a permanent settlement, the four sides were walled. When first established, a *castrum* was divided inside into four parts by two axial streets, the *decumanus* and the *cardo*; at the meeting point of these two principal streets the principal military tents were placed in the early stages of settlement, and later the forum was placed just to the north of the crossing. If the encampment did indeed prosper, the spaces between the perimeter and the center were gradually filled up by repeating the overall idea of axes and centers in miniature. For the Romans, the point of these rules was to create cities on the pattern of Rome itself; wherever in the world a Roman lived, the Roman soldier was at home.

In its origins the grid established a spiritual center. "The rite of the founding of a town touches on one of the great commonplaces of religious experience," Joseph Rykwert writes in his study of the Roman city; the ancient writer Hyginus Gromaticus believed that the priests inaugurating a new Roman town must place the first axis in the cosmos, for "Boundaries are never drawn without reference to the order of the universe, for the *decumani* are set in line with the course of the sun, while the *cardines* follow the axis of the sky."[8]

In the subsequent history of Western urbanism, the grid has been of special use in starting new space or in renovating existing space devastated by catastrophe. All the schemes for rebuilding London after the Great Fire of 1666 – Robert Hooke's, John Evelyn's, and Christopher Wren's – made use of the Roman grid form; these schemes influenced Americans like William Penn in conceiving of making a city from scratch. Nineteenth-century America seems a whole nation of cities created on the principles of the Roman military camp, and the American example of "instant cities" in turn influenced new city building in other parts of the world. No physical design, however, dictates a permanent meaning. Grids, like any design, can become whatever particular societies make them represent. If the Romans saw the grid as an emotionally charged design, the Americans were the first to use it for a different purpose: to deny that complexity and difference existed in the environment. The grid has been used in modern times as a plan that neutralizes the environment. It is a Protestant sign for the neutral city.

The Roman military city was conceived to develop in time within its boundary; it was designed to be filled in. The modern grid was meant to be boundless, to extend block after block after block outward as the city grew. In contriving the grid plan of 1811, which has since determined modern Manhattan above Greenwich Village, the planning commissioners acknowledged, "It may be a subject of merriment, that the Commissioners have provided space for a greater population than is collected at any spot on this side of China."[9] But just as Americans saw the natural world around them as limitless, they saw their own powers of conquest and habitation as subject to no natural or inherent limitation. The conviction that people can infinitely expand the spaces of human settlement is the first way, geographically, of neutralizing the value of any particular space.

The Romans imagined from the sense of a distinct, bounded whole how to generate a center, at the intersection of the *decumanus* and the *cardo*, and then how to create centers for each neighborhood by imitating this crossing of principal axes in each subsection. The Americans tended more and more to eliminate the public center, as in the plans for Chicago devised in 1833 and those for San Francisco in 1849 and 1856, which provided only a handful of small public spaces within thousands of imagined blocks of building. Even when the desire for a center existed, it was difficult to deduce where public places should be, and how they should work, in cities conceived like a map of limitless rectangles of land. The humane civic spaces in colonial Philadelphia created by William Penn and Thomas Holme, or at the opposite pole, the brutal slave-market squares of antebellum Savannah – both workable spaces for organized crowd life – faded as models during the era when vast sums were poured into urban development. The loss of a center is the second geographic way an urban space is neutralized.

The American grids imposed, it is true, a certain intensification of value at the intersections of streets rather than in the middle of blocks; in modern Manhattan, for instance, tall buildings in residential neighbor-hoods are permitted at the corners, whereas the middle of the block is kept low. But even this pattern, when repeated often enough, loses the power of designating the character of specific places and of their relation-ship to the larger city.

Perhaps the most striking grids made in this fashion were in the southern rim of settlement in America, in the cities developed under Spanish rule or influence. On July 3, 1573, Philip II of Spain laid down a set of ordinances for the creation of cities in his New World lands, the "Law of the Indies." The key provision is the decree that towns take form through the planning of their centers, a decree the king expressed simply and rigorously:

> *The plan of the place, with its squares, streets, and building lots is to be outlined by means of measuring by cord and rule, beginning with the main square from which streets are to run to the gates and principal roads and leaving sufficient open space so that even if the town grows it can always spread out in a symmetrical manner.*[10]

Beginning with cities like St. Augustine, Florida, this royal decree was meticulously obeyed, as it was along the entire Spanish rim during the course of nearly three centuries. An early plan for Los Angeles in 1781 would have looked familiar to Philip II or, for that matter, to Julius Caesar. Then, suddenly, with the coming of railroads and massive doses of capital looking for a home, there came a break in towns on the Spanish rim with the principles enunciated in the "Law of the Indies." The square ceased to be a center; it no longer was a reference point in generating new urban space. Town squares became random dots amidst the block after block of building plots, as in a plan for Santa Monica to be part of the "new" Los Angeles in 1875, and then entirely disappeared, as when the "new" Los Angeles on paper became a fact a generation later.

The twentieth century completed both these geographic processes at work in the making of grids, even when development occurred by building a thousand houses along arbitrarily twisting streets, or by digging out lumps of industrial park, office campus, and shopping mall on the edges of highways. In the development of the modern "megalopolis," it has become more reasonable to speak of urban "nodes" than of centers and suburbs. The very fuzziness of the word *node* indicates the loss of a language for naming environmental value: *center* is charged with meanings both historical and visual, while *node* is resolutely bland.

This American pattern is in many ways the extreme toward which other forms of new development tend; the same kind of settlement has occurred in Italy and France, in Israel, in Russia beyond the Urals. In all of these, development lacks a logic of its own limits and of form established within boundaries; the results of amorphous building are places without character. The grid in particular doesn't, as I say, "cause" this blandness; neutrality can take the form of an endless city of regularly intersecting lines or winding housing developments, shopping strips, and clots of offices or factories. But the recent history of the grid reveals how modern neutrality is constituted, as a Protestant language of self and space becomes a modern form of power.

In April 1791, Pierre Charles L'Enfant was courageously engaged in combating Thomas Jefferson's plan to create the new American capital according to a gridiron plan. L'Enfant wrote to President Washington:

> *Such regular plans . . . become at last tiresome and insipid and it [the grid] could never be in its origin but a mean continuance of some cool imagination wanting a sense of the real grand and truly beautiful.*[11]

A capital should reverberate with symbolic power, and L'Enfant imagined the regularities of the grid as empty of such reverberations. The century after L'Enfant was to show, however, that grids would organize power precisely by stripping away the character of a place.

A generation after L'Enfant, the young Alexis de Tocqueville's family were among the band of aristocrats of 1830 who refused to participate in the new regime and made the *émigration intérieure*. He arranged his famous voyage to America as a way out of his own difficulties in taking the regime's oath of loyalty. He saw this new, characterless form of power in the making when making his first visit to New York.

In his time the usual way for a foreigner to journey to New York was to sail into the harbor from the south, a route that afforded the voyager a sudden view of the crowd of masts along the packed wharves, which spread to offices, homes, churches, and schools. This New World scene appeared to be a familiar European one of prosperous mercantile confusion, like Antwerp or the lower reaches of London on the Thames. Tocqueville instead approached New York from the north, through Long Island Sound. His first view of Manhattan was its bucolic upper reaches, still in 1831 pure farmland dotted with a few hamlets. At first what excited him about the view of the city was the sudden eruption of a metropolis in the midst of a nearly pristine natural landscape. He felt the enthusiasm of a European coming here who imagines he can plant himself in this unspoiled landscape just as the city was planted, that America is fresh and simple and Europe is stale and complex. And then, after that fit of youthful enthusiasm passed, New York began to disturb him, as he later wrote to his mother. People seemed not to take where they lived seriously, not to care about the buildings in which they hurried in and out; instead the city was treated simply by its citizens as a complicated instrument of offices and restaurants and shops for the conduct of business. Throughout his American journey Tocqueville was struck by the bland and insubstantial character of American settlement. Houses seemed mere stage sets rather than buildings meant to last; there seemed nothing permanent in the environment. The reason was that these "new men" were too driven to settle, too driven for stone. They wanted nothing to get in their way.

The grid can be understood, in these terms, as a weapon to be used against environmental character – beginning with the character of geography. In cities like Chicago the grids were laid over irregular terrain; the rectangular blocks obliterated the natural environment, spreading out relentlessly no matter that hills, rivers, or forest knolls stood in the way. The natural features that could be leveled or drained were; the insurmountable obstacles that nature put against the grid, the irregular course of rivers or lakes, were ignored by these frontier city planners, as if what could not be harnessed to this mechanical, tyrannical geometry did not exist.

Often, this relentless imposition of a grid required a willful suspension of the logical faculties. In Chicago the grid created immense problems of transport across the river that cuts through the center of the city; the lines of the streets suddenly end at one riverbank only to continue on the other side, as though the river were spanned by innumerable, if invisible, bridges. A visitor to the new town of Cincinnati noticed in 1797 the "inconvenience" of applying the grid to a similar river topography; further, "if they had made one of their principal streets to face the river and the other at the brow of the second bank . . . the whole town would have presented a noble appearance from the river."[12] Cincinnati bore an ancient name but was no Greek city; these urban plans imposed arbitrarily on the land rather established an interactive, sustaining relation to it.

Though it is one of the oldest cities in America, New York's planners treated it during the era of high capitalism as if it, too, were a city on the frontier, a place required to deal with the physical world as an enemy. The planners imposed a grid at one blow in 1811 upon Manhattan from Canal Street, the edge of dense settlement, up to 155th Street, and then in a second stroke in 1870 to the northern tip. They imposed the grid more gradually in Brooklyn east from its old harbor. Settlers on the frontier, whether from fear or simple greed, treated Native Americans as part of the landscape rather than as fellow human beings; on the frontier nothing existed – it was a void to be filled up. Planners could no more see life outside the grid in New York than they could in Illinois. The farms and hamlets dotting nineteenth-century Manhattan were expected to be engulfed rather than incorporated as the grid on paper became building in fact; little adaptation of the plan was made in that process, even when some more flexible arrangement of streets would make better use of a hill or better suit the vagaries of Manhattan's water table. And inexorably, development according to the grid did abolish whatever existing settle-ment was encountered. In this neoclassical age, the nineteenth-century planners could have built as Romans or nearer at hand, like William Penn, laying out squares or establishing rules for where churches, schools, and markets were to go. The land was available, but they were not so minded. Instead, they aggressed against the environment; their victories lay in neutralizing it.

There is a closer connection between neutralizing space and economic development. The New York commissioners declared that "right angled houses are the most cheap to build, and the most convenient to live in."[13] What is unstated here is the belief that uniform units of land are also the easiest to sell. This relationship between the grid city and capitalist economics has been stated at its broadest by Lewis Mumford thus:

> The resurgent capitalism of the seventeenth century treated the individual lot and the block, the street and the avenue, as abstract units for buying and selling, without respect for historic uses, for topographic conditions or for social needs.[14]

In the history of nineteenth-century New York, the matter was in fact more complicated, because the economics of selling land were very different in New York in 1870 than they were in 1811. The city at the beginning of the century was a dense cluster of buildings set in the wilderness. Land sales were of empty space. After the Civil War they were of places that would soon fill up. To sell land profitably required a social reckoning; where people should live, where transport should most effi-ciently be located, where factories should go. Looking at a map that shows only blocks all of the same size answers few of these questions. The grid was rational as an urban design only in an abstract, Cartesian sense. And therefore, as was true of investments in rails and industry, the latter economic history of the grid is as much the story of disastrous investments as of large profits. Those who sought to profit from a neutral environment shared the same necessarily blank consciousness of its char-acter as those, like L'Enfant, who hated it.[15]

The economic history of the grid points to a simple, large truth. Possessing power is quite different from using it to one's own advantage. This large, simple truth is important in understanding the power to neutralize a city. Those who could do so were disturbed in their pursuits by a set of difficulties inherent in the very act of treating the world neutrally. These difficulties the sociologist Max Weber took up in his famous study of the "Protestant ethic." Weber connected self-doubt of the sort the Puritan felt to competition with others; he sought to explain how in winning against others a person wanted to prove something about his own worth. But then, Weber thought, the truly hard-driving competitor is afraid to enjoy what he has gained: he is aggressive in making money and then denies himself its use for comfort, elegance, and amusement. "Christian asceticism," Weber wrote in *The Protestant Ethic and the Spirit of Capitalism*,

> at first fleeing from the world into solitude, had already ruled the world which it had renounced from the monastery and through the Church. But it had, on the whole, left the naturally spontaneous character of daily life in the world untouched. Now it strode into the marketplace of life, slammed the door of the monastery behind it, and undertook to penetrate just that daily routine of life with its methodicalness, to fashion it into a life in the world, but neither of nor for this world.[16]

Christianity, that is, thus took to the streets to find its truths. Perhaps people might make gains in this world that would bear on their life in the next. Just before he wrote *The Protestant Ethic and the Spirit of Capitalism*, Weber traveled to the United States, in the age in which the Vanderbilts had dinners for seventy served by seventy powdered footmen. The luxury-loving capitalists of Weber's day seemed to him an aberration of the species. Instead, he thought, economic drive was much more connected to questions of identity, questions first raised by the Puritans and other Protestant sects. The ghost from the past hovered: who is worthy? This contains the hidden question, Who is worthier? which was answered by the believer and the hard-driving businessman alike: the worthiest person is the least self-indulgent.

The story the Protestant ethic tells is not a happy one. It is a story about value scarcity: there is not enough worth to go around. Moreover, one might go soft and lose control if one stops struggling – and so to prevent this, one treats things and other people as instruments of one's own drives and needs. In themselves they are nothing. Yet the result of this instrumental relation to the world is ever greater confusion about the purposes and the value of what one is doing.

And here is where the grid found its place. It was a space for economic competition, to be played upon like a chessboard. It was a space of neutrality, a neutrality achieved by denying to the environment any value of its own. And, like the Pyrrhic victory earned by the person who competes and wins only to feel he or she has not yet achieved enough, the grid disoriented those who played upon it; they could not establish what was of value in places without centers or boundaries, spaces of endless, mindless geometric division. This was the Protestant ethic of space.

Whenever Americans of the era of high capitalism thought of an alternative to the grid, they thought of bucolic relief, such as a leafy park or a promenade, rather than a more arousing street, square, or center in which to experience the complex life of the city. The nineteenth-century construction of Central Park in New York is perhaps the most bitter example of this alternative, an artfully designed natural void planned for the city's center in the expectation that the cultivated, charming territory already established around it – as bucolic and refreshing a scene as any city dweller could wish for within a few minutes drive from his house – would be razed to the ground by the encroachments of the grid.

Its designers Frederick Law Olmsted and Calvert Vaux wanted themselves to obliterate the simplest reminder that Central Park was located in the midst of a thriving metropolis. This reminder would occur, for instance, in seeing or hearing the traffic crossing it. These Americans therefore built contrary to the makers of the Bois de Boulogne, who made traversing the Bois a pleasure, even for those who had business that required the journey. Olmsted and Vaux hid such people away, literally: They buried the traffic routes in channels below the grade of the park. In their own words, these roads are to

> be sunk so far below the surface. . . . The banks on each side will be walled
> up to the height of about seven feet . . . and a little judicious planting on the
> tops or slopes of the banks above these walls will, in most cases, entirely
> conceal both the roads and the vehicles moving in them, from the view of
> those walking or driving in the park.[17]

These, then, were the dualities of denial: To build you act as though you live in emptiness; to resist the builder's world you act as though you do not live in a city.

Some of this denial of meaning to the built environment has a uniquely American source, derived from the sheer visceral impress of the natural landscape upon all those who traveled in it, Americans and visitors alike. This natural world once was immense, unframed, boundless. The impress of a boundless world comes clear, for instance, in comparing an American painting of wilderness, John Frederick Kensett's *View near West Point on the Hudson* of 1863 with Corot's *Souvenir of Volterra* of 1838, two paintings organized around roughly similar views. What we see in Kensett's painting is limitless space, a view bursting its frame, our eyes going and going and going without obstruction. All the rocks, trees, and people in the painting are deprived of substance because they are absorbed into immensity, whereas in Corot's painting we feel the vivid presence of specific things in a bounded view or, as one critic puts it, "a solid architecture of rocks and even of foliage to measure the deep space."[18] It seemed that only the most arbitrary imposition could tame American vastness: an endless, unbounded grid. This effort of will, however, rebounded: The arbitrary spoiled what it tamed, the grid seemed to render space meaningless – and so sent an eye like Olmsted's searching for a way to recover the value of nature seemingly free of the visible presence of man.

In a classic American text of our Western movement, the novel *The Little House on the Prairie*, the family uproots every time another house becomes visible on the horizon, without anyone in the family being able to explain why another rooftop is an intolerable sight, and yet they all feel threatened, they keep moving. Only without interference from others can the psyche wrestle itself. Later observers who wondered at the relentless push westward of people who could have been richer, and more content, cultivating what they already possessed, were observing the secular, environmental refinement of the Protestant ethic – the inability to believe that whatever is, is sufficient.

This may seem a special story, limited to the nineteenth-century American practices and perceptions geographically. The twentieth century, however, also deploys the grid. It is vertical and more universal; it is the skyscraper. The older geographic modes reappear in this architectural form. More, it is in the building of skyscrapers that the cracks became evident in the edifice of neutralizing power.

In cities of skyscrapers, Hong Kong as much as New York, it is impossible to think of the vertical slices above street level as having an inherent order, like the intersection of *cardo* and *decumanus*; one cannot point to activities that ought particularly to happen on the sixth floors of buildings. Nor can one relate visually sixth floors to twenty-second floors as opposed to twenty-fifth floors in a building. Nor do skyscrapers have the necessary height. The vertical grid lacks definitions of both significant placement and closure.

The tall building sliced into stories depends upon the elevator as a means of internal transport. The elevator has existed since 1846. Originally, it was a platform within a vertical frame, rising or descending by the operator's manipulation of counterweights built within the frame; and that original idea has endured. In 1853 in the Latting Observatory in New York, steam was employed to push and pull on the counterweights; the Dakota Apartments in New York and the Connaught Hotel in London used water-hydraulics instead of metal chains a generation later; the most modern elevators use magnetic calibration to regulate the force exerted on the weights in terms of the mass of people within the elevator, so that speed is always constant. The biggest innovation in this machine was making it safe when it failed to work; this honor fell to Elisha Graves Otis in 1857. His Haughwout building in New York contained an elevator fitted with automatic brakes; in case of loss of energy, the brakes would lock the elevator cab to the guide rails.

Yet as the architectural critic Ada Louise Huxtable has remarked, modern tall buildings have not for the most part explored the possibilities of being tall: "Today architects are looking at some very big buildings in some very small ways. The larger the structure, the less inclination there seems to be to come to grips with the complexities of its condition and the dilemma it creates."[19] The reasons for this have in part to do with commerce, and also in part with visual design. Skyscraper designers have focused their expressive energies on the exterior forms and upon the skin of the tall building at the expense of experimenting with inner volumes.

The elevator was the necessary but not the sufficient condition for the creation of the tall building. What made these buildings feasible was the extensive use of metal framing. The quickness of this kind of construction was first demonstrated in the London Crystal Palace of 1851, where a building larger in volume than Chartres Cathedral was designed by Joseph Paxton in a few weeks and put up in a few months; the cast-iron frame held panels of glass used instead of bricks and tiles for both walls and ceilings. The early skyscraper makers put this technology to vertical use, but not quite confidently. The Monadnock Building in Chicago, for instance, was a metal-framed structure that continued to use masonry bearing walls. The economical use of steel in construction inspired a greater confidence in the frame, as more recently reinforced concrete did, and so freed the wall as a medium for experiment. This freedom gradually engaged the creative attention of the makers of skyscrapers much more than the volumetric possibilities opened up by the elevator. This century has seen experiment in the skins of buildings, and increasing uniformity in the inhabited spaces within the building itself, which consists of repeating open floors served by a central service stack. They are big but simple structures.

From the vantage point of non-Western concepts of space, easy mechanical levitation may in itself seem to destroy the meaning of height. In making the contrast between Japanese and modern Western concepts of "high," the architect Arata Isozaki believes the Western eye fails to see the ethical possibilities of this dimension:

The raised wooden floor is a clean, artificially created surface isolated from the earth, a surface on which people can sit without concern. Unlike the Japanese wooden floor, the upper stories that have not been part of Western homes from early times are not a surface in a completely different phase. Although these upper-story rooms are far removed from the surface of the

earth, shoes are worn in them; and chairs, tables, shelves, beds and so on are
essential because the floor is "unclean."[20]

His image of Western notions of height as agelessly different from the
Japanese is not quite right. The religious height of the medieval city was
sacred because it pointed up to the kingdom of God; it was both physical
and spiritual orientation. Were a medieval builder transported in a time
machine to a modern skyscraper, he would find it profoundly, dis-
turbingly profane, the sanctity of the vertical dimension contaminated
simply by becoming instantly accessible. But the articulations of modern
height are not of unclean values, as the Japanese architect fears, nor of
the worldly clamor of the street brought within a church, as a medieval
builder would. Instead, "up" means "neutral." Skyscraper height lacks
the symbolic value either of the Japanese house or the medieval church.

Gridded space does more than create a blank canvas for development.
It subdues those who must live in the space, but disorienting their ability
to see and to evaluate relationships. In that sense, the planning of neutral
space is an act of dominating and subduing others. But the visual designer
will do so, not with a sense of Machiavellian cunning but in a more self-
conflicted way.

For instance, by the time homes for families were built in vertical grids,
their makers felt that something was wrong. In New York, moreover, the
apartment house aroused echoes from a peculiar past, the use families
made in the nineteenth century of hotels as semipermanent residences.
Such families wandered from hotel to hotel, the children only occasionally allowed to run in the corridors, the families dining in the same large
rooms as commercial travelers and foreigners and unknowable women.
But more generally, planners had come to believe that vertical structures
were inherently neutral, and so "inhumane," forms that provided shelter
in its full meaning. An editorial in the New York *Independent* newspaper
argued in 1902 what was coming to be felt by the Garden City planning
movement in Great Britain and by socialist planners under the sway of
face-to-face community ideals in France and Germany, namely, that
large apartment houses destroy "neighborhood feeling, helpful friend-
ships, church connections and those homely common interests which are
the foundations of civic pride and duty." In New York this view was
codified in the Multiple Dwelling Houses Act of 1911, which treated all
apartment buildings as similar in social function to hotels; the "lack of
fundamentals on which a home was founded" could be perceived, as late
as 1929 in one of the first books on apartment house architecture, to
derive from "a building of six, nine, or fifteen stories, where the plan of
one floor is repeated exactly throughout the entire building; individuality is practically non-existent."[21] A skyscraper is no place for Ruskin's
dream.

The commonsense view of an evil is that when people become

conscious of it they react against it. A more realistic account is that people act out of the evils they discover. They know what they are doing is wrong and yet they move closer and closer to making it happen, in order to see if what they think or perceive is real. Certainly this is true in our time among those who have built vertical grids for families. It was with a fear in their minds of the loss of family values in neutral, impersonal spaces that many architects and planners in the 1930s built the great housing projects that would eventually realize these very fears. In the same way, housing projects meant for the poor, like those along Park Avenue in Harlem in New York, have been designed according to the principles of the unbounded, amorphous grid. Everything is graded flat; there are few trees. Little patches of lawn are protected by metal fences. The Park Avenue projects are relatively free of crime but, according to the complaints of the residents, are a hostile environment for the conduct of family life. That hostility is built into their very functionality; they deny one is living in a place of any value. The massive building of workers' suburbs in Europe has deployed the same visual vocabulary of neutrality. There are, as I say, no devils in this story; the housing project is a reformist dream dating back to nineteenth-century efforts to build healthy homes en masse for workers. Only, the visual vocabulary of building betrays another set of values, one that converts old ideas about unbounded space into new forms of repression.

The very practice of neutrality permits this divorce between intention and act. The Puritan knew a version of this divorce: He lived in the world but not of it. In secular society, power can make use of it: "I wasn't really involved in what I was doing, therefore I wasn't responsible for it; it was not me." The result, for housing planners at least, was that the visual technology of power alienated them, too, from their own work. Weber observed that treating the world neutrally ultimately made the person doing so feel empty as well. This refraction of power is as true of modern architects as it was of early capitalists who sought to take control of the world through detachment.

Neutrality, as a space of social control, seems in this way to explain a great divide between nineteenth-century European planning and those more modern practices that first took shape horizontally in nineteenth-century America and are now more universally, vertically deployed. Baron Haussmann was engaged in remaking Paris during the era in which Central Park was created. Haussmann confronted a congested city a thousand years old whose twisted streets were a breeding ground for, in his mind, the unholy trinity of disease, crime, and revolution. He imagined a traditional means of repression in the face of these dangers. The cutting of straight streets through a congested Paris was to make it easier for people to breathe, for police and, if necessary, troops to move. The new streets of northeastern Paris were to be lined with apartments over elegant shops, in order to attract the bourgeoisie into previously working-class districts; he imagined a kind of internal class colonization of the city. At the same time that he opened the city mass transport to the swift flow of traffic, he also hoped the working classes were to become more locally dependent upon a new urban gentry; the Boulevard Richard Lenoir was built as such a street. Haussmann sought to create a Paris of steady if demanding customers, of concierge-spies, and a thousand little services.

American urbanism during its great flowering has proceeded by another path of power, one that repressed the overt definition of significant space in which domination and dependence were to occur. There is no building form like the Haussmannian apartment house with its service web. Instead, both horizontal and vertical development proceeded among us to a more modern, more abstract operation of extension. In the making of the grid cities "new" Americans proceeded as in their encounters with Native Americans by erasure of the presence of an alien Other rather than by colonization. Instead of establishing the significance of place, control operated through consciousness of place as neutral.

The Spiritual Quest is No Longer a Heroic Struggle

Words like *power* and *control* suggest a solid grip upon the world. In the case of neutralizing control this is wrong. Max Weber sought to evoke the qualities of grid power in his famous image of modern life lived in an "iron cage"; the image makes sense only if it implies that the trainer is shut in the same cage as his beasts. For instance, such consequences of neutrality appear in a short story by Henry James called "The Beast in the Jungle." His tale concerns a man, John Marcher, who is able to live peaceably a life of continuities. But behind this social facade, he apprehends a terrible disaster within himself, poised to destroy him: "Something or other lay in wait for him, amid the twists and turns of the months and the years, like a crouching Beast in the Jungle."[22] By chance, Marcher meets a woman in England, May Bartram, to whom he confided this fear many years before during a visit to Italy. Miss Bartram has remembered his secret and taken it seriously. The two now become friends; his inner dread becomes a bond between them, the promise of a deeper connection between them than that of proper spinster and bachelor. But the beast in the jungle also keeps them apart; since Marcher is haunted, he thinks he must grapple with the beast before he can live. They grow old together thus, intimate at a distance. Miss Bartram falls ill of a blood disease; just before she dies she struggles to tell him what the beast is, but her strength fails.

James intended "The Beast in the Jungle" to be a parable; it was to be of "the man of his time, *the* man, to whom nothing on earth was to have happened."[23] This representative man has failed to live, in living a life of inner anguish: "It wouldn't have been failure to be bankrupt, dishonored, pilloried, hanged; it was failure not to be anything."[24] In mourning he discovers why the seeming inner drama of his life has been no life at all. In the cemetery where he makes regular visits to Miss Bartram's grave, he one day notices a man wrecked with grief over another woman's tomb. At first he is puzzled, and then horror-struck. In observing this woebegone man, Marcher realizes he had "seen *outside* of his life, not learned it within, the way a woman was mourned when she had been loved for herself."[25] He had failed to love Miss Bartram apart from her connection to his secret – and now in the graveyard the beast has sprung. There was a terrible shallowness in his obsession with his inner demons, the beast has bitten his consciousness, his knowledge that he can never regain time delayed. The beast was Marcher's waiting to live.

In one way, this is a parable simply of a modern fear. One has to wait so long to be in a position to be ready, to know what one is doing, to be strong enough to "really live." But James's parable even more suggests something about the consequences of gaining control through acting neutrally.

When no information is conveyed from the neutral exterior of difference, the eye looking inward "sees" not a corresponding emptiness but rather confronts a secret. It is a secret of time that no clock can tell, the secret of what one will become. In the neutral space of the grid, differences are classifications and names that are static in meaning. The interior, by contrast, is the time of process-as-value. Marcher's entire life was such a process he treasured, this secret he carried within that could not be seen, classified, let alone verified. In the world of grid differences, when feelings, desires, or beliefs are stated outside, they become subject to the threat of neutralization. The best defense against the things that one cares about being treated neutrally is never to be too emphatic about them, too exposed.

The self thus remains in process, a process ever stranger to its own needs. The process of intimating, reflecting, hoping, and feeling becomes the search for a catharsis that never comes, an endlessly delayed gratification. All his life Marcher kept faith with his beast, until too much denial turned on him. And at the end, he had become a vacuous man.

In his American travel notes, Tocqueville records how much one place looked like another, how little variation the local economy, climate, and even topography seemed to matter in constructing a town. This homogeneity in building a city Tocqueville had at first explained as the result of unbridled commercial exploitation. In his later years he added a further explanation, resonating to James's story. The famous American "individual," rather than being an adventurer, is in reality most often a man or woman whose circle of reality is drawn no larger than family and friends. The individual has little interest, indeed little energy, outside that circle. The American individual is a passive person, and monotonous space is what a society of passive individuals builds for itself. A bland environment assures people that nothing disturbing or demanding is happening "out there." You build neutrality in order to legitimate withdrawal:

> The reproach I address to the principle of equality is not that it leads men away in the pursuit of forbidden enjoyments, but that it absorbs them wholly in quest of those which are allowed. By these means a kind of virtuous materialism may ultimately be established in the world, which would corrupt, but enervate, the soul and noiselessly unbend its springs of action.[26]

And then the beast springs; in emptiness things come apart.

"Taking control" as we know it in this modern form is thus really about losing control. The duality is evident to the eye now in the bars of New York. There are bars everywhere in the city, bars devoted to heavy drinking and bars that are a mere afterthought, like the bar in the Museum of Modern Art; there are bars in discos, bank buildings, brothels, as well as improvised in housing projects. Spiritual struggle in its form as Protestant ethic denies the outside a reality in itself; denies the value of being present in the world. It is therefore disconcerting to hear "presence" asserted in the bars on the edge of a Harlem project like the one along upper Park Avenue. (There are no places to drink in public within the forest of towers itself.) It is strange because the language of sociability is so broken into fragments. I used to think it was because I was there, but in these Park Avenue bars after a while people forget about a stray, balding, familiar white. These are family bars, cleaning women and janitors drinking beer; more lively places nearby are for people living on the shadows of the underworld. The family bars next to this project seldom have an actual bar; they are just rooms where someone has put bottles on a table. Here it is as though time has stopped; the day hangs in dust roused by the commuter trains shuttling in and out of a tunnel next to the buildings. The bar at night has a television turned on without sound; there is the ebb and flow of police sirens, a fan in summer. This is the space that talk filled, but I came to understand it was enough: The drops of sound made for a consciousness of presence, of living, if barely audible, *here.*

By contrast, a resolutely neutral bar of absence can be found in places of power – for instance, in the bar of the Pierre Hotel on Fifth Avenue just where Central Park begins. The physical contrast between this bar and the room up in Harlem with a table crowded with bottles is so extreme as to be meaningless. The Pierre bar, with its ample tables, flowers, and subdued lights, has always conveyed a peculiar discretion;

people come here who need to do business without being seen to be doing it. This is evident in little details: when people recognize others here, they seldom table-hop; at most there are brief nods of recognition. The drinks at the Pierre are mostly for show. Two men will sit for an hour nursing the glasses in front of them; the waiters are trained not to hover.

It is a nervous bar, with so many people paying careful attention to one another. The Pierre bar is neutral in the way a chessboard is. And yet in this power center, among these men in their quiet, expensive clothes, sunk deep into their leather chairs, the atmosphere seems more charged by fear than entrepreneurial zeal. The men are afraid of giving away too much. *Control* is a meaningless word uptown; here it is a synonym for anxiety. If you don't pay careful attention, things will come apart.

The visitor intent upon seeing men like Marcher in the modern city might do well, though, to avoid either extreme, the bars either of the Harlem housing project or the Pierre Hotel. The signs of his spiritual quest are most likely to be found in certain bars in the afternoon, like the Lion's Head in Greenwich Village, or the little bars at the front of French restaurants in the 1950s, after people have finished lunch. These comprise a scene of truants – a scene of men who should be back at the office but are having a drink instead, not necessarily alcoholic, merely delaying, and of men, and now also of women, who have nowhere particular to go in the afternoon, perhaps unemployed, or engaged in the myriad of jobs in New York – agenting, publicity, graphic design – that do not require the full-time attention of those who aren't at the top.

The bars in which people pass their afternoons in New York are unlike Parisian cafés, the *cafés des amis*. The bartenders don't want these customers; the bowls heaped with salty, thirst-inducing nuts placed on the counters before lunch are withdrawn after it, the bartenders themselves are less responsive to requests for drinks, even though they have more time; some of the truants do drink until they drop, but others are more likely to want to talk, and they expect the men behind the bar, like a captive audience, to listen. In the old working-class bars, Irish in Hell's Kitchen, Polish on the Lower East Side, the windows blacked out and a radio and television blaring at the same time from different stations, afternoons pass in this desultory way, plumbers and carpenters dropping in for a shot and gossip between jobs; on the front stools of the French restaurants, those at leisure are not at rest, their talk is tinged with an undertow of urgency, which is perhaps why the bartenders are uncomfortable having them there, even though people are well, often very carefully, dressed, as if this indeed were the afternoon's appointment.

The urgencies are about something important that is about to happen, a deal shaping up or a love affair, deals that turn out to be a chance remark dropped by a prominent, distant acquaintance and affairs that begin mentally after the first date. Or there are stories about where people grew up, stories that come easily to the speakers because they have been polished through use, one man occasionally interjecting a comment or exclamation to show another he is listening, before he takes up a later point in his own tale. The most curious thing about the stories is how the tellers sit as they talk, usually directly facing the counter in front of them, on which they lean their elbows and behind which the barman bends over his sink polishing a glass, men talking to one another by looking at their reflections in the mirror behind the bar.

Here was "material," I first thought when I entered this sea. And then, after a few years, it was clear there was no writer's "material" here, for these stories seldom made sense. Something was always left out in the account of the important deal that would explain why it might work, or a woman's "problems" would be alluded to, heavily but without specifics, as a man explained why he was alone most nights. The men in the bars lacked craft. And if indeterminate and illogical, these stories were also curiously neutral, the speaker seldom moved by his tale, at least audibly, the voices recounting problems with women or big deals equably, perhaps with the poise that polished repetition does give and also perhaps, like Marcher, driven by the compulsion to tell it once more in order that, by chance, the telling might suddenly reveal the hidden meaning of the tale. In the bars there is a place and a time for each man to recount his fragments as though they are just about to become wholes.

After listening to these year after year, however, I have begun to realize that here, in the stream of bland voices and unfocused words, as the light fades outside the front windows, we are truly within the city's grid. These are emblematic New Yorkers, men and women whose lives are endlessly pregnant with meaning and yet to whom, like Marcher, nothing ever happens. Their lives are afflicted with that peculiar lack of concreteness, that endless becoming, which marks the space of the city.

The cross within the circle is a peculiarly modern as well as ancient Egyptian sign. It represents two ways in which the human subject lives walled in from the world. The circle confines his or her experiences of compassion and mutual regard within the walls of authority; the grid is a geometry of power on which inner life remains shapeless.

Notes

1   Geoffrey Chaucer, *The Canterbury Tales*, ed. and trans. R. M. Lumiansky (New York: Pocket Books, 1971), original p. 357, translation p.10.
2   Reprinted in Charles B. Rice, *Proceedings at the Celebration of the Two Hundredth Anniversary of the First Parish at Salem Village* (Boston, 1874), p. xxv.
3   Anthony N. B. Garvan, *Architecture and Town Planning in Colonial Connecticut* (New Haven: Yale University Press, 1951), p. 52
4   Quoted in Kenneth Silverman, *The Life and Times of Cotton Mather* (New York: Columbia University Press, 1985), p. 24.
5   George Goodwin, "Auto-Machia"; this version, with modern spelling and

without Goodwin's capitalization and italics, is adapted from the original reprinted in Sacvan Bercovitch, *The Puritan Origins of the American Self* (New Haven: Yale University Press, 1975), p. 19.

6   Increase Mather, *A Sermon Concerning Obedience*, in "The Autobiography of Increase Mather," ed. Michael G. Hall, *Proceedings of the American Antiquarian Society* (1961): 352.

7   Joseph Rykwert, *The Idea of a Town: The Anthropology of Urban Form in Rome, Italy and the Ancient World* (Cambridge, Mass.: MIT Press, 1988), p. 192.

8   Ibid., p. 90.

9   "Commissioners' Remarks," quoted in William Bridges, *Map of the City of New York and Island of Manhattan* (New York: n.p., 1811), p. 30.

10   "Royal Ordinances concerning the Laying Out of New Towns," trans. Zelia Nuttall, quoted in John Reps, *The Making of Urban America* (Princeton: Princeton University Press, 1965), p. 29.

11   Pierre Charles L'Enfant, "Note relative to the ground lying on the eastern branch of the river Potomac . . .," undated but necessarily written between April 4, when Washington forwarded Jefferson's ideas to L'Enfant, and April 10, 1791, when Jefferson accepted L'Enfant's control of the planning of the new national capital. Text reproduced in E. L. Kite, *L'Enfant and Washington, 1791–1792* (Baltimore: Johns Hopkins University Press, 1929), pp. 47–48.

12   Francis Baily, *Journal of a Tour in Unsettled Parts of North America in 1796 and 1797* (London: n.p., 1856), p. 226, quoted in Richard Wade, *The Urban Frontier* (Cambridge, Mass.: Harvard University Press, 1959), pp. 24–25.

13   "Commissioners' Remarks," p. 25.

14   Lewis Mumford, *The City in History* (New York: Harcourt Brace Jovanovich, 1961), p. 421.

15   Though notes in this chapter are restricted to giving the sources for quotations, the reader interested in the irrational course that was the actual process of "the logic of capitalism" might want to read Peter Marcuse, "The Grid as City Plan: New York City and Laissez-faire Planning in the Nineteenth Century," *Planning Perspectives* 2 (1987), 287–310.

16   Max Weber, *The Protestant Ethic and the Spirit of Capitalism*, as translated by Martin Green and quoted in Martin Green, *The Von Richthofen Sisters* (New York: Basic Books, 1974), p. 152.

17   Frederick Law Olmsted, "Description of a Plan for the Improvement of the Central Park, 'Greensward,' 1858," in Frederick Law Olmsted, Jr., and Theodora Kimball, *Frederick Law Olmsted* (New York: n.p., 1928), p. 214.

18   John W. McCoubrey, *American Tradition in Painting* (New York: George Braziller, 1963), p. 29.

19   Ada Louise Huxtable, *The Tall Building Artistically Reconsidered* (New York: Pantheon, 1984), p. 9.

20   Arata Isozaki, "Floors and Internal Spaces in Japanese Vernacular Architecture," *Res* 11 (Spring 1986), p. 65.

21   Quotations from John Hancock, "The Apartment House in Urban America," in Anthony D. King, ed., *Building and Society* (London: Routledge and Kegan Paul, 1980), p. 181.

22   Henry James, "The Beast in the Jungle," in Willard Trask, ed., *The Stories of Henry James* (New York: Signet, 1962), p. 417.

23   Ibid., pp. 449–50.
24   Ibid., p. 428.
25   Ibid., p. 449.
26   Alexis de Tocqueville, *Democracy in America*, trans. Edward Reeve (New York: Vintage, 1963), vol. 2, p. 141.

Part II

Planning: Justifications, Critiques, and New Directions

Introduction

The first four readings of this section address the question, What is the justification for planning intervention? We have selected readings that examine the neoclassical, institutional, and Marxist arguments for and against planning. They place planners in the larger political-economic context of the relationship between the private market and government (both local and national). The final two readings then explore the shortcomings of traditional justifications for planning by critiquing the standard planning model. Each author outlines an emerging alternative theoretical model for planning: postmodern planning, and communicative planning.

Richard Klosterman provides a comprehensive overview of the justifications for planning in "Arguments for and Against Planning," originally an article published in 1985. He evaluates political and economic arguments from both traditional and Marxist perspectives. He begins by outlining the standard market failure model, whereby planning steps in to address the periodic shortcomings of the free-market system. This is perhaps the safest ground for planning, since government intervention is justified based on its ability to improve and assist the functioning of an efficient market. Klosterman then examines three other arguments: Planners address the shortcomings of the political system by fully representing the public interest; planners possess unique professional expertise and instrumental rationality; and planners either serve or challenge the capitalist system.

In a brief excerpt from his book *Planning the Capitalist City*, Richard Foglesong provides his own Marxist perspective on the justification for planning. He departs from the market failure model's tidy and benign division of labor between the public and private sector and instead sees a conflicted and contradictory relationship between government and business. The key dynamic to understanding the ambivalent role of planning in capitalist society is the "property contradiction": the contradiction between the social character of land and its private ownership and control. This conflict does not invariably lead to collapse or social upheaval, but it does create political conflict. The private sector naturally resists government intrusion into its affairs, and yet at the same time needs government to socialize the control of land. For example, the private sector needs government to cope with externality problems, to help provide housing for the working poor, and to build and coordinate infrastructure. For Foglesong, this property contradiction is related to a second contradiction: that between capitalism and democracy. Each interest has a separate agenda for land, and the role of planning is to maintain the balance between the two.

In his chapter originally published in 1985 as an article "On Planning the Ideology of Planning," David Harvey also uses Marxist structural analysis to address the question, How do planners handle the conflicts in ideology between serving the poor and helping capital accumulation? Harvey observes a discrepancy between planners' liberal-progressive self-identity and the substance of their actions, a discrepancy that seems more often than not to reinforce the status quo of economic inequality. Like both Foglesong and Fainstein and Fainstein (this volume), Harvey challenges planners' assumptions of political-ideological autonomy by situating the planning profession within the larger state apparatus and the capitalist economy: planners shape the built environment so that it will function efficiently and reproduce the existing social order. However, the role of planners is also more complex; they have a progressive tendency toward righting wrongs, correcting social imbalances, and defending the public interest. If planners can directly address this conflict, they can begin to write a truly progressive ideological agenda for their profession.

Matt Ridley and Bobbi Low address the question of whether the public or private sector is better suited to attain social goals, in this case that of saving the natural environment. Their answer is surprising. In their chapter "Can Selfishness Save the Environment?" they argue that neither the common appeal to voluntary individual sacrifice for the greater common good nor the moral condemnation of Western industrial materialism will be enough to stop environmental degradation. Instead, they see a more sensible approach in using the "human propensity for thinking mainly of short-term self-interest." The authors note the fruitful confluence of economic and biological research – both of which reveal the centrality of the individual – rather than the sociologist's preoccupation with the action of classes. This is not to reject the importance of collective interest but rather to emphasize the challenge of making the individual interest concur with collective interest.

Ridley and Low show that the oft-cited prisoner's dilemma and the tragedy of the commons indicate that simple aggregation of individual interests does not always serve the common good. Common-pool resources invariably lead to some sort of market failure. Yet neither centralized regulation nor the privatization of all natural resources will fully prevent environmental externalities. For Ridley and Low, what works is the control of these resources by small, stable community groups that show a strong concern for the future. Such groups communicate, devise rules, and monitor each other's self-interested use and abuse of natural resources. In the end, one should stop moralistically condemning the selfish orientation of modern urban society as the root of environmental decay and instead use this self-interest to save the environment.

A very different view of planning emerges from the postmodern approach. During the 1980s, many planning theorists were drawn to the emerging ideas of postmodernism, which was novel enough to promote a burst of theoretical creativity and vague enough to tolerate imprecise planning polemics. The appeal was understandable: The modernism-postmodernism divide provided an overall framework in which to critique the whole era of modernist planning. It therefore allowed postmodernist analysts to distance themselves from modernism's monolithic urban obsession with the grid, the box, and the comprehensive plan. Postmodernism's rejection of the master narrative in place of multiple discourses also provided theoretical support for the emerging interest in multiculturalism.

In "Between Modernity and Postmodernity: The ambiguous position of US Planning," originally a 1989 article, Robert Beauregard outlines the postmodern potential for planning. He argues that this transformation is neither smooth nor complete and that planning is currently suspended between modernism and postmodernism. However, planners should not unconditionally embrace postmodernism but instead also redefine and incorporate the strengths of modernist planning. This reorientation should include a focus on the process of physical city building; a mediative role between capital, labor, and the state; and a great push towards democracy.

The last chapter in this section addresses a relatively new theme in planning theory: the centrality of communication in the practice of planning. Patsy Healey argues in "Planning Through Debate: The Communicative Turn in Planning Theory" that planning must simultaneously adapt to two crucial changes: the resurgence of economic evaluation within public policy and the postmodern critique of scientific rationalism. She rejects scientific rationalism, moral idealism, pure relativism, and democratic socialism as all insufficient or inappropriate to address these challenges. As an alternative, she turns to Habermas's intersubjective reasoning. The challenge facing planning is to articulate a common understanding of social problems in a world of multiple, divergent cultures. Planning has the potential to promote democratic debate. Healey illustrates the power of this approach by examining its potential for environmental planning.

6

Arguments for and Against Planning

Richard E. Klosterman

Formal governmental attempts to plan for and direct social change have always been controversial. However, public and academic attention to planning peaked in the "great debate" of the 1930s and 1940s between proponents of government planning such as Karl Mannheim, Rexford Tugwell, and Barbara Wootton and defenders of "free" markets and laissez-faire such as Friedrich Hayek and Ludwig von Mises.[1] By the 1950s the debate had apparently been resolved: the grand issues of the desirability and feasibility of planning had been replaced by more concrete questions concerning particular planning techniques and alternative institutional structures for achieving society's objectives. Planning's status in modern society seemed secure: the only remaining questions appeared to be, Who shall plan, for what purposes, in what conditions, and by what devices?[2]

Recent events in Great Britain, the United States, and other Western societies indicate that planning's status is again being questioned and that the "great debate" had never really ended. National planning efforts have been abandoned in Britain and the United States; and the public agenda in both countries now focuses on deregulation, privatization, urban enterprise zones, and a host of other proposals for severely restricting government's role in economic affairs. Planning is increasingly attacked in the popular press, academic literature, and addresses to Parliament and Congress.[3] Graduate planning enrollments have declined dramatically, and government retrenchment around the world has severely reduced

Reprinted with permission from *Town Planning Review*, Vol. 56, No 1, pp. 5–20, 1985.

job opportunities for professional planners at all levels.[4] At a more fundamental level, practitioners, students, and academics increasingly view
planning as nothing more than a way to make a living, ignoring its potential to serve as a vocation, filling one's professional life with transcending
purpose.[5]

In this environment it seems essential to return to fundamentals and
examine carefully the case for and against planning in a modern industrial context. This article will critically examine four major types of
argument that have been used as two-edged rhetorical swords both to
criticize and defend government planning efforts and to consider the
implications of these arguments for planning in the 1980s and beyond.
The analysis will consider only formal governmental efforts at the local
and regional level to achieve desired goals and solve novel problems in
complex contexts, or what in Britain is called "town and country
planning" and in America "city and regional planning."[6] As a result, the
arguments considered below are not necessarily applicable to national
economic planning or to the planning done by private individuals and
organizations. Also not considered are the legal arguments for planning
in particular constitutional or common-law contexts or arguments such
as Mannheim's,[7] which have had little effect on the contemporary
political debate.

Economic Arguments

Contemporary arguments for abandoning planning, reducing regulation,
and restricting the size of government are generally accompanied by calls
for increased reliance on private entrepreneurship and the competitive
forces of the market. That is, it is often argued, government regulation
and planning are unnecessary and often harmful because they stifle
entrepreneurial initiative, impede innovation, and impose unnecessary
financial and administrative burdens on the economy.

These arguments find their historical roots in the world of Adam Smith,
John Stuart Mill, and others of the classical liberal tradition.[8]
Emphasizing individual freedom, reliance on the "impersonal" forces of
the market, and the rule of law, these authors called for minimal state
interference in society's economic affairs to protect individual liberty and
promote freedom of choice and action. On pragmatic grounds they
argued that competitive markets could be relied upon to coordinate the
actions of individuals, provide incentives to individual action, and supply
those goods and services that society wants, in the quantities it desires,
at the prices it is willing to pay.[9]

Building on these foundations, contemporary neoclassical economists
have demonstrated mathematically that competitive markets are
capable in theory of allocating society's resources in an efficient manner.

That is, given an initial distribution of resources, a market-generated allocation of these resources cannot be redistributed to make some individuals better off without simultaneously making other individuals worse off.[10] However, this Pareto efficient allocation will occur only in perfectly competitive markets that satisfy the following conditions: (1) a large number of buyers and sellers trade identical goods and services; (2) buyers and sellers possess sufficient information for rational market choice; (3) consumer selections are unaffected by the preferences of others; (4) individuals pursue the solitary objective of maximizing profits; and (5) perfect mobility exists for production, labor, and consumption.[11]

The numerous obvious divergences between markets in the real world and economists' competitive market ideal justify a range of government actions fully consistent with private property, individual liberty, and decentralized market choice.[12] The need to increase market competition and promote informed consumer choice in a world of huge multinational firms and mass advertising helps justify restrictions on combinations in restraint of trade and prohibitions on misleading advertising. Indicative planning efforts at a national level in France and elsewhere are likewise justified as providing the information required for rational market choice. The development of municipal information systems and the preparation of long-range economic forecasts are similarly justified as promoting informed market choice with respect to location decisions for which the relevant information is difficult to obtain, experience is limited, and mistakes can be exceptionally costly.[13]

More important, both classical and neoclassical economists recognize that even perfectly competitive markets require government action to correct "market failures" involving (1) public or collective consumption goods; (2) externalities or spill-over effects; (3) prisoners' dilemma conditions; and (4) distributional issues.[14]

Public goods

Public goods are defined by two technical characteristics: (1) "jointed" or "nonrivalrous" consumption such that, once produced, they can be enjoyed simultaneously by more than one person; and (2) "nonexcludability" or "nonappropriability" such that it is difficult (in some cases impossible) to assign well-defined property rights or restrict consumer access.[15] Private goods such as apples, bread, and most "normal" consumer goods exhibit neither characteristic; once produced, they can be consumed by only one individual at a time. It is thus easy to restrict access to these goods and charge a price for their enjoyment. On the other hand, public goods such as open air concerts, television broadcasts, and a healthy and pleasant environment simultaneously benefit more than one individual, because one person's enjoyment does not prohibit another's enjoyment (except for any congestion effects). As a result, controlling access to these goods is either difficult (scramblers must be installed to restrict access to television broadcasts) or impossible (clean air).

Competitive markets can effectively allocate private goods that can be enjoyed only if they are purchased; as a result, the prices individuals are willing to pay for alternative goods accurately reflect their preferences for these goods. For public goods the benefit individuals receive is dependent on the total supply of the good, not on their contribution toward its production. Thus, in making voluntary market contributions to pay for, say, environmental protection, individuals are free to understate their real preferences for environmental quality in the hope that others will continue to pay for its protection – enabling them to be "free riders," enjoying a pleasant environment at no personal expense. Of course, if everyone did this, the money required to protect the environment adequately would no longer be available. Individuals may also under-estimate others' willingness to contribute and "overpay," thereby ending up with more public goods and fewer private goods than they really desire. In either case the aggregated market preferences of individuals do not accurately reflect individual or social preferences for alternative public and private goods – the "invisible hand" fumbles.

Similar arguments can be made for public provision of quasi-public goods such as education, public health programs, transportation facilities, and police and fire protection, which simultaneously benefit particular individuals and provide shared, nonrationable benefits to society as a whole. As a result, public goods can be used to justify over 96 percent of public purchases of goods and services and an almost open-ended range of government activities.[16]

Externalities

Closely related to the concept of public goods are externalities or spill-over effects of production and consumption that are not taken into account in the process of voluntary market exchange.[17] The classic example is a polluting industrial plant that imposes aesthetic and health costs on neighboring firms and individuals not included in its costs of production. Similar spill-over effects are revealed by land developers who can freely ignore the costs of congestion, noise, and loss of privacy that high-intensity development imposes on neighboring landowners. Positive external economies include the increased land values associated with the construction of new transportation links and other large-scale improvements, which adjoining landowners can enjoy without compensation.

As is true for public goods, the divergence between public and private costs and benefits associated with externalities causes even perfectly competitive markets to misallocate society's goods and services. Profit-maximizing firms concerned only with maximizing revenues and controlling costs are encouraged to increase output even though the associated negative external costs vastly outweigh any increases in revenue because the external, social costs are not reflected in their production costs. Neighborhood beautification projects and similar goods with positive external effects similarly tend to be underproduced, because private entrepreneurs cannot appropriate the full economic benefits of their actions. In both situations the "invisible hand" again fails to reflect accurately the needs and desires of society's members.

Prisoner's dilemma conditions

Similar difficulties are revealed in circumstances in which individuals' pursuit of their own self-interest does not lead to an optimal outcome for society or for the individual involved. Consider, for example, the situation faced by landlords in a declining neighborhood who must decide whether to improve their rental property or invest their money elsewhere.[18] If landlords improve their property and others do not, the neighborhood will continue to decline, making the investment financially inadvisable. On the other hand, if the landlords do not improve their property and the others improve theirs, the general improvement of the neighborhood will allow landlords to raise rents without investing any money. As a result, it is in each individual's self-interest to make no improvements; however, if they all refuse to do so, the neighborhood will decline further, making things worse for everyone. An identical inevitable logic leads the competitive market to overutilize "common pool" resources with a limited supply and free access, such as wilderness areas and a healthy environment.[19]

The fundamental problem here, as for public goods and externalities, lies in the interdependence between individual actions and the accompanying disjunction between individual benefits and costs versus social benefits and costs. The only solution in all three cases is government action to deal with the public and external effects that are neglected in the pursuit of individual gain. Solutions for declining neighborhoods include compulsory building codes, public acquisition and improvement of entire neighborhoods, and "enveloping" – public improvements to neighborhood exteriors that will encourage private investments.

Distributional questions

As was pointed out above, economists have demonstrated that, given an initial distribution of resources, perfectly competitive markets will allocate those resources in such a way that no one can benefit without someone else being harmed. However, neither the initial nor the final distribution can be assumed to be in any way optimal. Both are determined largely by inherited wealth, innate talent, and blind luck and can range from states of perfect equality to extremes of tremendous wealth and abject poverty. Economic efficiency alone provides no criterion for judging one state superior in any way to another. As a result, given a societal consensus on the proper allocation of resources, for example, that all babies should receive adequate nutrition and that the elderly should be cared for, government tax collection and income transfer programs are justified to achieve these objectives with minimal market interference.[20]

Implications of the economic arguments

The preceding discussion has identified a range of government functions fully consistent with consumer sovereignty, individual freedom in production and trade, and decentralized market choice. Each of these functions justifies a major area of contemporary planning practice: first, providing the information needed for informed market choice through indicative planning, the development of urban information systems, and the preparation of long-range population, economic, and land-use projections: second, the provision of public goods through transportation, environmental, and economic development planning; third, the control of externalities and resolution of prisoner's dilemma conditions through urban renewal, community development and natural resources planning, and the use of traditional land regulatory devices; and lastly, health, housing, and other forms of social planning to compensate for inequities in the distribution of basic social goods and services. Specific government actions to reduce conflicts between incompatible land uses, coordinate private development and public infrastructure, preserve open space and historic buildings, and examine the long-range impacts of current actions can similarly be justified as needed to correct market failures revealed in the physical development of the city.

It must be recognized, however, that while *necessary* to justify government planning in a market society, these arguments are not *sufficient* to do so. This is true, first, because those activities that are the proper responsibility of government in a market society need not be *planning* matters at all. Government decisions concerning the provision of public goods, the control of externalities, and so on can be made in a number of ways: by professional planners, by elected or appointed public officials, by the proclamations of a divine ruler, or by pure happenstance involving no deliberate decision process at all. If planning is justified by the economic arguments for government alone, it is impossible to differentiate between government planning and government nonplanning – "government" is reduced to an undifferentiated mass.

More fundamentally, the inability of existing markets to allocate society's resources adequately does not necessarily imply that government provision, regulation, or planning are necessary or even advisable. Suitably defined and administered performance standards, building codes, and development requirements may guide the land development process more effectively than traditional master planning and zoning techniques; effluent charges can often control pollution discharges more efficiently than the direct enforcement of effluent standards; and public facilities and services may be provided more equitably by leasing and voucher systems than directly by government. Thus, in these and other areas, the appropriate role for planning may not be the preparation of formal end-state plans but the establishment and maintenance of an appropriate system of quasi-markets.[21]

As a result, the case for planning in a market society cannot be based solely on the theoretical limitations of markets outlined above. Popular dissatisfaction with the free enterprise system is based not on an appreciation of the various theories of market failure but on its inability to provide stable economic growth and an adequate standard of living for all of society's members. Conversely, the informed critiques of planning are made not in ignorance of the theoretical limitations of markets but in the belief that, despite these limitations, markets are still more effective than attempts at centralized coordination by government.[22] As a result, the case for planning in a modern market society cannot be made in the abstract but requires a careful evaluation of planning's effectiveness relative to alternative institutional mechanisms for achieving society's objectives.

Pluralist Arguments

Other arguments for and against planning emerged during the 1960s and 1970s to complement the economic arguments considered above. Accepting the economic arguments for government outlined above, Lindblom, Wildavsky, and other critics of planning suggest that government actions should not be guided by long-range planning or attempts at comprehensive coordination but by increased reliance on existing political bargaining processes.[23] Underlying these arguments is a political analogue to the economists' perfectly competitive market in which competition between formal and informal groups pursuing a range of divergent goals and interests is assumed to place all important issues on the public agenda, guarantee that no group dominates the public arena, maintain political stability and improve individuals' intellectual and deliberative skills. In this model government has no independent role other than establishing and enforcing the rules of the game and ratifying the political adjustments worked out among the competing groups.

Thus, it is assumed, political competition, like market competition, eliminates the need for independent government action, planning, and coordination.[24]

Unfortunately, the pluralist model is subject to the same fundamental limitations that face the economic model of perfect market competition. Just as markets are dominated by gigantic national and mutinational conglomerates, the political arena is dominated by individuals and groups who use their access to government officials and other elites to protect their status, privilege, and wealth and ensure that government acts in their interest. Particularly privileged are corporate and business leaders whose cooperation is essential for government's efforts to maintain full employment and secure stable economic growth. As a result, government officials, particularly at the local level, cannot treat business as only another special interest but must provide incentives to stimulate desired business activity, such as tax rebates and low-interest loans to attract new industry and downtown improvement projects to encourage retail and commercial activity in the central business district. Further supporting business's unique position in the group bargaining process is an unrecognized acceptance of the needs and priorities of business that pervades our political and governmental processes, media, and cultural and educational institutions.[25]

Systematically excluded from the group bargaining process are minority and low-income individuals and groups residing in decaying urban centers and rural hinterlands. Lacking the time, training, resources, leadership, information, or experience required to participate effectively in the political process, these groups have no effective voice in determining the public policies that shape their world. By thus tying individuals' political voice to underlying disparities in political power and resources, current political processes exacerbate existing inequalities in income and wealth and fail to provide adequate information for fully informed policy making.[26]

Group bargaining also fails adequately to provide collective goods and services that provide small benefits to a large number of individuals. In small groups, each member receives a substantial proportion of the gain from a collective good; as a result, it is clearly in their interest to ensure that the good be provided. For large groups, individual benefits are so small and organizational costs so large that it is in no one's immediate interest to provide for the common good. The result is an "exploitation of the great by the small" in which small groups with narrow, well-defined interests – such as doctors and lawyers – can organize more effectively to achieve their objectives than larger groups – such as consumers – who share more broadly defined interests. By turning government power over to the most interested parties and excluding the public from the policy formulation and implementation process, pluralist bargaining systematically neglects the political spill-over effects of government actions and policies on unrepresented groups and individuals.[27]

The limitations of pluralist bargaining, like the limitations of market competition, provide the theoretical justification for a wide range of planning functions. Accepting the critiques of comprehensive planning by Lindblom and others, some authors propose that planning be limited to the "adjunctive" functions of providing information, analyzing alternative public policies, and identifying bases for improved group interaction. The objective here, as for indicative planning, is improving existing decentralized decision processes by providing the information needed for more informed decision making.[28]

The pluralist model is incorporated directly into the advocacy planning approach, which rejects the preparation of value-neutral "unitary" plans representing the overall community interest for the explicit advocacy of "plural plans" representing all of the interests involved in the physical development of the city.[29] Recognizing the inequities of existing political processes, advocate planners have acted primarily as advocates for society's poor and minority members. Particularly noteworthy here are the efforts of the Cleveland Planning Commission to promote "a wider range of choices for those Cleveland residents who have few, if any, choices."[30]

Experience has demonstrated, however, that advocacy planning shares many of the limitations of the pluralist model on which it is based: (1) urban neighborhoods are no more homogeneous and the neighborhood interest no more easy to identify than is true at the community level; (2) group leaders are not representative of the group's membership; (3) it is easier to represent narrowly defined interests and preserve the status quo than to advocate diffuse and widely shared interests or propose new alternatives; and (4) public officials still lack the information required for adequate decision making.[31]

As a result, there remains a fundamental need for public sector planners who can represent the shared interests of the community, coordinate the actions of individuals and groups, and consider the long-range effects of current actions. This does not imply that the shared interests of the community are superior to the private interests of individuals and groups or that the external and long-term effects of action are more important than their direct and immediate impacts. It assumes only that these considerations are particularly important *politically*, because only government can ensure that they will be considered at all.[32] It is on these foundations that the traditional arguments for town and country planning have been made.

Traditional Arguments

The planning profession originated at the turn of the century in response to the widespread dissatisfaction with the results of existing market and political processes reflected in the physical squalor and political corruption of the emerging industrial city. The profession's organizational roots in architecture and landscape architecture were reflected in early views of planning as "do[ing] for the city what . . . architecture does for the home" – improving the built environment to raise amenity levels; increase efficiency in the performance of necessary functions; and promote health, safety, and convenience. The profession's political roots in progressive reform were reflected in arguments for planning as an independent "fourth power" of government promoting the general or public interest over the narrow, conflicting interests of individuals and groups. Others viewed planning as a mechanism for coordinating the impacts of public and private land uses on adjoining property owners and considering the future consequences of present actions in isolation from day-to-day operating responsibilities. Underlying all of these arguments was the belief that the conscious application of professional expertise, instrumental rationality, and scientific methods could more effectively promote economic growth and political stability than the unplanned forces of market and political competition.[33]

Implicit in these traditional arguments for planning are many of the more formal justifications examined above. The arguments for planning as an independent function of government promoting the collective public interest obviously parallel the economic and pluralist arguments for government action to provide public or collective consumption goods. The calls for planning as comprehensive coordination similarly recognize the need for dealing with the external effects of individual and group action. And the arguments for planning that consider the long-range effects of current actions likewise acknowledge the need for more informed public policy making. Noteworthy by its absence is any concern with the distributional effects of government and private actions, which were largely ignored in planners' attempts to promote a collective public interest.[34]

By midcentury, social scientists who had joined the ranks of academic planners began severely to question each of these arguments for public sector planning: Planners' concern with the physical city was viewed as overly restrictive; their perceptions of the urban development process seen as politically naive; their technical solutions found to reflect their Protestant middle-class views of city life; their attempts to promote a collective public interest revealed to serve primarily the needs of civic and business élites; and democratic comprehensive coordination of public and private development proven to be organizationally and politically impossible.[35]

Accompanying these critiques were new conceptions of planning as a value-neutral, rational process of problem identification, goal definition, analysis, implementation, and evaluation. In recent years the rational planning model has come under severe attack as well for failing to recognize the fundamental constraints on private and organizational decision making; the inherently political and ethical nature of planning practice; and the organizational, social, and psychological realities of planning practice. As a result, while the social need for providing collective goods, dealing with externalities, and so on remains, the planning profession currently lacks a widely accepted procedural model for defining planning problems or justifying planning solutions.[36]

Marxist Arguments

The recent emergence of Marxist theories of urban development has added a new dimension to the debate about the desirability and feasibility of planning.[37] From the Marxist perspective, the role of planning in contemporary society can be understood only by recognizing the structure of modern capitalism as it relates to the physical environment. That is, it is argued, the fundamental social and economic institutions of capitalist society systematically promote the interests of those who control society's productive capital over those of the remainder of society. The formal organization of the state is likewise assumed to serve the long-term interests of capital by creating and maintaining conditions conducive to the efficient accumulation of capital in the private sector, subordinating the conflicting short-run interests of the factions of capital to the long-run interests of the capitalist class, and containing civil strife that threatens the capitalist order. These actions are legitimized by a prevailing democratic ideology that portrays the state as a neutral instrument serving the interests of society as a whole.

Marxists argue that fundamental social improvements can result only from the revolutionary activity of labor and the replacement of existing social institutions benefiting capital by new ones serving the interests of society at large. Essential reforms include public ownership of the means of production and centralized planning, which would replace existing market and political decision processes by the comprehensive coordination of investment decisions and democratic procedures for formulating social priorities and restricting individual actions that conflict with the long-term interests of society.[38]

Applying this perspective to urban planning, Marxist scholars have been highly critical of traditional planning practice and theory. The arguments for and against planning examined above are dismissed as mere ideological rationalizations that fail to recognize the material conditions and historical and political forces that allowed planning to emerge and

define its role in society. Accepting the limitations of market and political competition outlined above, Marxists interpret planners' actions in
each sphere as primarily serving the interests of capital at the expense of
the rest of society. Planners' attempts to provide collective goods and
control externalities are assumed to serve the needs of capital by helping
to manage the inevitable contradictions of capitalism revealed in the
physical and social development of the city. Planners' attempts to employ
scientific techniques and professional expertise are seen as helping to
legitimize state action in the interest of capital by casting it in terms of the
public interest, neutral professionalism, and scientific rationality. And
planners' attempts to advance the interests of deprived groups are
dismissed as merely coopting these groups, forestalling the structural
reforms that are ultimately required to bring real improvement to their
positions in society.[39]

While extremely valuable in helping to reveal the underlying nature
of contemporary planning, the Marxist perspective has obvious limitations as a guide to planning practice.[40] A strict Marxist analysis, which
sees all social relations and all government actions as serving the interests of capital, identifies no mechanism for reform other than a radical
transformation of society, which is highly unlikely in the near future: if
needed reforms can result only from the revolutionary action of labor and
all attempts to help the needy merely delay necessary structural changes,
there is no significant role for reform-minded planners who occupy an
ambiguous class position between labor and capital. And rejection of
planners' attempts to apply professional expertise and scientific methods
to public policy making as merely legitimizing and maintaining existing
social and economic relations deprives professional planners of their
main political resource for dealing with other political actors – their
claims to professional expertise.

As a result, as was true for the arguments for and against planning
examined earlier, the Marxist arguments cannot be evaluated in the
abstract but must be examined critically in the light of present economic
and political realities. Thus, while it may be theoretically desirable to
replace existing market and political decision processes, this is highly
unlikely to happen in most Western democracies. The lack of a revolutionary role for planners in traditional Marxist analysis does not mean
that they cannot work effectively for short-term reforms with other
progressive professionals and community-based organizations. And
while contemporary planning may indeed serve the interests of capital,
it need not serve these interests alone and is clearly preferable to exclusive reliance on the fundamentally flawed processes of market and
political competition.

Conclusions and Implications

The preceding discussion has examined a variety of arguments for and against planning in a modern industrial context. Underlying this apparent diversity is an implicit consensus about the need for public sector planning to perform four vital social functions – promoting the common or collective interests of the community, considering the external effects of individual and group action, improving the information base for public and private decision making, and considering the distributional effects of public and private action.

The first need is reflected in the economic arguments for government action to resolve prisoner's dilemma conditions and provide public or collective consumption goods, such as a healthy and pleasant environment, which cannot be provided adequately by even perfectly competitive markets. The second results from the inability of markets to deal with social costs and benefits of production and consumption that are not reflected in market prices or revenues. The third is reflected in the public and private need for improved information on the long-term effects of location decisions necessary for making adequately informed market decisions. And the fourth results from the fact that market competition alone is incapable in principle of resolving distributional questions in a socially acceptable manner.

From the pluralist perspective, planning is required to represent broadly defined interests that are neglected in the competition between organized groups representing narrower interests. And it is required to represent the external effects of political decisions on groups and individuals who are not directly involved in the political bargaining process. Improved information on the short- and long-term consequences of alternative public policies and actions is required to facilitate the group bargaining process. And planners are required to serve as advocates for society's neediest members, who are systematically excluded from the group bargaining process.

The traditional arguments for planning reflect the need for representing the collective interests of the community in the calls for planning as an independent function of government charged with promoting the public interest. The need for considering the external effects of individual action is reflected in the conception of planning as comprehensive coordination. From this perspective, planning is required to provide information on the physical development of the city and the long-range implications of current actions. Distributional questions were regrettably largely ignored in traditional planning's efforts to promote an aggregate public interest.

While largely critical of contemporary planning practice, the Marxist perspective recognizes each of the arguments for planning identified by the other perspectives. The need for representing the collective interests of the community is reflected in the Marxist prescriptions for replacing existing decentralized markets with centralized planning in the interests of society as a whole. The need for considering externalities is reflected in calls for the comprehensive coordination of investment decisions. From the Marxist perspective, traditional forms of planning information primarily serve the interests of capital; thus, to promote fundamental social change planners are called upon to inform the public of the underlying realities of capitalist society. And the need to correct the structural imbalances in power and wealth that shape contemporary society underlies the Marxist call for the radical reformation of society.

While all four perspectives propose that planning is required *in theory* to fulfill these fundamental social requirements, they each recognize in their own way that these theoretical arguments for planning are insufficient. Contemporary economists argue that market competition, properly structured and augmented, can be more efficient and equitable than traditional forms of public sector planning and regulation. Critics such as Lindblom have revealed planners' traditional models of centralized coordination to be impossible in a decentralized democratic society. And the social critics of the 1960s and 1970s and Marxist critics of today have demonstrated convincingly that traditional planning practice, while couched in terms of neutral technical competence and the public interest, has primarily served the interests of society's wealthiest and most powerful members.

An objective evaluation of sixty years' experience with town and country planning in Great Britain and the United States must recognize the tremendous gap between planning's potential and its performance. While there have been several remarkable successes, much of contemporary practice is still limited to the preparation of "boiler plate" plans, the avoidance of political controversy, and the routine administration of overly rigid and conservative regulations.[41] It is thus an open question whether planning, as currently practiced the world over, deserves high levels of public support or whether other professional groups and institutional arrangements can better perform the vital social functions identified above. As a result, the arguments for planning outlined above cannot be taken as a defence of the status quo in planning but must serve as a challenge to the profession to learn from its mistakes and build on new and expanded conceptions of the public interest, information, and political action to realize its ultimate potential.[42]

Acknowledgments

I gratefully acknowledge the valuable comments received from Robert A. Beauregard of Rutgers University, Jay M. Stein of the Georgia Institute of Technology, and the anonymous reviewers of *Town Planning Review*.

Notes

1   See for example, Mannheim, Karl, *Man and Society in an Age of Reconstruction. Studies in Modern Social Structure*. New York, Harcourt, Brace, and World, 1944, pp. 41–75; Tugwell, Rexford G. "Implementing the General Interest", *Public Administration Review*, 1 (1) Autumn 1940, pp. 32–49; Wootton, Barbara, *Freedom Under Planning*, Chapel Hill, University of North Carolina Press, 1945; Hayek, Friedrich A. , *The Road to Serfdom*. Chicago, University of Chicago Press, 1944; and von Mises, Ludwig, *Planning for Freedom and Other Essays*, South Holland, Illinois, Libertarian Press, 1952.

2   Examples here include Schonfield, Andrew, *Modern Capitalism*, New York, Oxford University Press, 1965, and Dahl, Robert A. and Lindblom, Charles E., *Politics, Economics, and Welfare*, New York, Harper and Row, 1953. The quotation is from Dahl and Lindblom, p. 5.

3   For recent critiques of planning see Friedman, Milton and Friedman, Rose, *Free to Choose: A Personal Statement*, New York, Harcourt, Brace and Jovanovich, 1979; Simon, William E., *A Time for Truth*, New York, Reader's Digest Press, 1978; and Wildavsky, Aaron, "If Planning Is Everything, Maybe It's Nothing". *Policy Sciences*, 4 (3) June 1973, pp. 277–295.

4   The dramatically declining enrollments in American planning schools are documented and analyzed by Krueckeberg, Donald A., "Planning and the New Depression in the Social Sciences", *Journal of Planning Education and Research*, 3 (2) Winter 1984, pp. 78–86.

5   Friedmann, John, "Planning as a Vocation," *Plan (Canada)*, 6 (2) April 1966, pp. 99–124 and 7 (3) July 1966, pp. 8–26.

6   A similar definition of planning is proposed by Alexander, Ernest R., "If Planning Isn't Everything, Maybe It's Something", *Town Planning Review*, 52 (2) April 1981, pp. 131–142.

7   Mannheim, op. cit.

8   These writers are "classical" liberals in that their views of government and liberty are fundamentally different from those associated with contemporary liberalism. Classical liberals define liberty in the negative sense in which freedom is determined by the extent to which individuals' actions are *externally* constrained by the actions of others; the wider the sphere of noninterference, the greater an individual's liberty. Thus to increase the (negative) liberty of individuals by decreasing the external interference of the state, classical liberals call for a sharply reduced role for government in the domestic and foreign economy. "Contemporary" liberals, on the other hand, view liberty largely in the positive sense in which individuals are free when no *internal* constraints such as a lack of knowledge, resources, or opportunities restrain their actions. From this perspective, increasing the (positive) liberty of individuals, particularly the most deprived, requires deliberate government action to promote social welfare and reduce the internal constraints on individual action, even though this may restrain the actions (and negative liberty) of some individuals. Compare Friedman, Milton, *Capitalism and Freedom*, Chicago, University of Chicago Press, 1962, pp. 5–6; and Finer, Herman, *Road to Reaction*, Boston, Little, Brown and Co., 1945, pp. 221–228. Contemporary examples of the classical liberal argument include Hayek, op. cit., Friedman and Friedman, op. cit.,

Friedman, op. cit. and Sorensen, Anthony D. and Day, Richard A., "Libertarian Planning", *Town Planning Review*, 52 (4) October 1981, pp. 390–402.

9   Heilbroner, Robert L., *The Worldly Philosophers*, New York, Simon and Schuster, 1969 (3rd edn.), pp. 48–61; Friedman and Friedman, op. cit., pp. 9–27.

10   See, for example, Bator, Francis M., "The Simple Analytics of Welfare Maximization," *American Economic Review*, 47 (1) March 1957, pp. 22–59.

11   Seventeen more restrictive assumptions including perfectly divisible capital and consumer goods and an absence of risk and uncertainty are identified by De V. Graaff, J., *Theoretical Welfare Economics*, London, Cambridge University Press, 1957.

12   For analyses of the many empirical limitations of real markets see Lindblom, Charles E., *Politics and Markets: The World's Politics-Economic Systems*, New York, Basic Books, 1977, pp. 76–89 and 144–157; and Heilbroner, Robert L. and Thurow, Lester C., *The Economic Problem*, Englewood Cliffs, Prentice Hall, 1978 (5th edn.), pp. 201–219.

13   Cohen, Stephen, *Modern Capitalist Planning: The French Model*, Cambridge, Harvard University Press, 1969; Foster, Christopher, "Planning and the Market," in Cowan, Peter (ed.), *The Future of Planning: A Study Sponsored by the Centre for Environmental Studies*, London, Heinemann, 1973, pp. 135–140. Meyerson, Martin, "Building the Middle-range Bridge for Comprehensive Planning," *Journal of the American Institute of Planners*, 22 (1) 1956, pp. 58–64; and Skjei, Stephen S. "Urban Problems and the Theoretical Justification of Urban Planning," *Urban Affairs Quarterly*, 11 (3) March 1976, pp. 323–344.

14   Thus, for example, Adam Smith recognized that government must be responsible for (1) "protecting the society from the violence and invasion of other independent societies"; (2) "establishing an exact administration of justice"; and (3) "erecting and maintaining those public institutions and those public works, which . . . are . . . of such a nature that profit could never repay the expense of an individual or small number of individuals." Smith, Adam, *An Enquiry into the Nature and Causes of the Wealth of Nations* (edited by Edwin Cannon), New York, Modern Library, 1937, pp. 653, 669, and 681; his third category of justified state functions is discussed in pages 681–740. Other government functions recommended by the classical economists include the regulation of public utilities, the establishment of social insurance systems, the enactment of protective labor legislation, and compensatory fiscal and monetary policy. See Robbins, Lionel, *The Theory of Economic Policy in English Classical Political Economy*, London, Macmillan, 1952, esp. pp. 55–61.

15   The literature on public goods is extensive. For excellent reviews see Burkhead, Jesse and Miner, Jerry, *Public Expenditure*, Chicago, Aldine, 1971, and Head, John G., *Public Goods and Public Welfare*, Durham, North Carolina, Duke University Press, 1974, pp. 68–92 and 164–183. In the planning literature see Moore, Terry, "Why Allow Planners to do What They Do? A Justification From Economic Theory", *Journal of the American Institute of Planners*, 44 (4) October 1978, pp. 387–398. The discussion below generally follows that in Bator, Francis M., *The Question of Government Spending: Public Needs and Private Wants*, New York, Collier Books, 1960, pp. 80–102.

16   Bator, op. cit., p. 104; Friedman and Friedman, op. cit., pp. 27–37. Similar arguments can be used to justify government provision of highways, dams, and other "decreasing cost" goods with large initial costs and decreasing marginal costs; see Bator, op. cit., pp. 93–95.

17   The relevant literature here is extensive as well. For excellent reviews see Mishan, E. J., "The Postwar Literature on Externalities: An Interpretive Review", *Journal of Economic Literature*, 9 (1) March 1971, pp. 1–28, and Head, op. cit., pp. 184–213. In the planning literature see Lee, Douglas B. Jr., "Land Use Planning as a Response to Market Failure" in de Neufville, Judith I., (ed.), *The Land Use Planning Debate in the United States*, New York, Pleneum Press, 1981, pp. 153–154.

18   This example is adapted from Davis, Otto A., and Whinston, Andrew B. "The Economics of Urban Renewal", *Law and Contemporary Problems*, 26 (2) Winter 1961, pp. 106–117.

19   See the classic article by Garret Hardin, "The Tragedy of the Commons", *Science*, 162, 13 December 1968, pp. 242–248. For more general discussions see Luce, Duncan and Raiffa, Howard, *Games and Decision: Introduction and Critical Survey*, New York, John Wiley, 1957, pp. 88–154. In the planning literature see Moore, op. cit.,

20   Bator, op. cit., pp. 87–89; Musgrave, Richard S., *The Theory of Public Finance: A Study in Public Economy*, New York, McGraw Hill, pp. 17–22. These points do not, of course, exhaust the economic arguments for and against planning. Thus, while Friedman, op. cit., pp. 7–21, and Hayek, op. cit., pp. 43–118, defend unrestricted markets as necessary to protect individual liberty, Barbara Wootton, op. cit., argues that government planning is fully compatible with the whole range of cultural, civil, political, and economic freedoms. For other economic arguments for planning see Webber, Melvin, "Planning in an Environment of Change, Part Two: Permissive Planning", *Town Planning Review*, 39 (4) January 1969, pp. 282–284; Oxley, op. cit.; and Lee, op. cit. More fundamental "Marxist" critiques of reliance on competitive markets are considered below.

21   See Webber, op. cit., pp. 284–295; Lee, op. cit., pp. 158–164; Friedman, op. cit., pp. 84–107; Moore, op. cit., pp. 393–396; and Foster, op. cit., pp. 153–165.

22   See, for example, Becker, Gary S., "Competition and Democracy", *Journal of Law and Economics*, 1, October 1958, pp. 105–109, and Wolf, Charles Jr., "A Theory of Nonmarket Failure: Framework for Implementation Analysis", *Journal of Law and Economics*, 22 (1) April 1979, pp. 107–140.

23   See, for example, Lindblom, Charles E., "The Science of Muddling Through", *Public Administration Review*, 19 (1) January 1959, pp. 79–88 and Wildavsky, op. cit.

24   Conolly, William E. (ed.), *The Bias of Pluralism*, New York, Atherton, 1969, pp. 3–13.

25   Lindblom, op. cit., pp. 170–233, Elkin, Stephen L., "Market and Politics in Liberal Democracy", *Ethics*, 92 (4) July 1982, pp. 720–732; Miliband, Ralph, *The State in Capitalist Society*, New York, Basic Books, 1969.

26   Gamson, William A., "Stable Underrepresentation in American Society", *American Behavioral Scientist*, 12 (1) November/December 1968, pp. 15–21; Skjei, Stephen S., "Urban Systems Advocacy", *Journal of the American Institute*

of Planners, 38 (1) January 1972, pp. 11–24; also see Dye, Thomas R. and Zeigler, L. Harmon, *The Irony of Democracy: An Uncommon Introduction to American Politics*, North Scituate, Mass., Duxbury Press, 1975 (3rd edn.), pp. 225–284.

27   Olson, Mancur, *The Logic of Collective Action: Public Goods and the Theory of Groups*, Cambridge, Harvard University Press, 1965; Lowi, Theodore J., "The Public Philosophy: Interest-group Liberalism", *American Political Science Review*, 61 (1) March 1967, pp. 5–24. For an extensive discussion of other forms of "nonmarket failure" see Wolf, op. cit.

28   See, for example, Rondinelli, Dennis A., "Adjunctive Planning and Urban Policy Development", *Urban Affairs Quarterly*, 6 (1) September 1971, pp. 13–39; and Skjei, Stephen S., "Urban Problems and the Theoretical Justification of Planning", *Urban Affairs Quarterly*, 11 (3) March 1976, pp. 323–344.

29   Davidoff, Paul, "Advocacy and Pluralism in Planning", *Journal of the American Institute of Planners*, 31 (6) November, 1965, pp. 331–338.

30   Krumholz, Norman, Cogger, Janice and Linner, John, "The Cleveland Policy Planning Report", *Journal of the American Institute of Planners*, 41 (3) September 1975, pp. 298–304. Krumholz, Norman, "A Retrospective View of Equity Planning: Cleveland, 1969–1979," *Journal of the American Planning Association*, 48 (2) Spring 1982, pp. 163–174.

31   Peattie, Lisa R,. "Reflections on Advocacy Planning", *Journal of the American Institute of Planners*, 34 (2) March 1968, pp. 80–88; Skjei, Stephen S., "Urban Systems Advocacy", *Journal of the American Institute of Planners*, 38 (1) January 1972, pp. 11–24; Mazziotti, Donald F., "The Underlying Assumptions of Advocacy Planning: Pluralism and Reform," *Journal of the American Institute of Planners*, 40 (1) January 1974, pp. 38, 40–47.

32   Klosterman Richard E., "A Public Interest Criterion", *Journal of the American Planning Association*, 46 (3) July 1980, p. 330; Barry, Brian, *Political Argument*, New York, Humanities Press, 1965, pp. 234–235.

33   For examples of each argument see (1) Robinson, Charles Mulford, *City Planning*, New York, G. P. Putnams, 1916, pp. 291–303 (the quotation is from p. 291); (2) Howard, John T., "In Defense of Planning Commissions", *Journal of the American Institute of Planners*, 17 (1) Spring 1951, pp. 89–93; and Tugwell, op. cit.; and (3) Bettman, Alfred, *City and Regional Planning Papers* (edited by Arthur C. Comey), Cambridge, Mass., Harvard University Press, pp. 5–30, and Dunham, Allison, "A Legal and Economic Basis for City Planning", *Columbia Law Review*, 58, 1958, pp. 650–671.

34   The earliest example of this concern in the planning literature known to the author is Webber, Melvin M., "Comprehensive Planning and Social Responsibility: Toward an AIP Consensus on the Profession's Role and Purposes", *Journal of the American Institute of Planners*, 29 (4) November 1963, pp. 232–241.

35   For examples of these now-familiar critiques see Gans, Herbert J., "City Planning in America: A Sociological Analysis" in Gans, Herbert J., *People and Plans: Essays on Urban Problems and Solutions*, New York, Basic Books, 1963; Altshuler, Alan A., "The Goals of Comprehensive Planning", *Journal of the American Institute of Planners*, 31 (5) August 1965, pp. 186–195; Bolan, Richard S. "Emerging Views of Planning", *Journal of the American Institute of*

Planners, 33 (4) July 1967, pp. 233–246; and Kravitz, Alan S., "Mandaranism: Planning as Handmaiden to Conservative Politics" in Beyle, Thad L., and Lathrop, George T., (eds.), *Planning and Politics: Uneasy Partnership*, New York, Odyssey Press, 1970.

36   Critiques of the rational planning model have dominated the planning theory literature for the last decade. For reviews of this literature and their implications for contemporary planning practice see DiMento, Joseph F., *The Consistency Doctrine and the Limits of Planning*, Cambridge, Mass., Oelgeschlager, Gunn, and Hain, 1980, pp. 44–117; and Alexander, Ernest R., "After Rationality, What? A Review of Responses to Paradigm Breakdown", *Journal of the American Planning Association*, 50 (1) Winter 1984, pp. 62–69.

37   Examples here include Castells, Manuel, *The Urban Question: A Marxist Approach*, Cambridge, Mass., The MIT Press, 1977; Harvey, David, *Social Justice and the City*, Baltimore, Johns Hopkins University Press, 1973, pp. 195–238; Paris, Chris (ed.), *Critical Readings in Planning Theory*, Oxford, Pergamon, 1982, and the articles cited in footnote 39 below.

38   Harrington, Michael, *Socialism*, New York, Saturday Review Press, 1972, pp. 270–307; Baran, Paul A., *The Longer View: Essays Toward a Critique of Political Economy*, New York, Monthly Review Press, 1969, pp. 144–149. Huberman, Leo and Sweezy, Paul M, *Introduction to Socialism*, New York, Monthly Review Press, 1968, pp. 60–65.

39   See, for example, Fainstein, Norman I. and Fainstein, Susan S., "New Debates in Urban Planning: The Impact of Marxist Theory Within the United States", *International Journal of Urban and Regional Research*, 3 (3) September 1979, pp. 381–403; Beauregard, Robert A., "Planning in an Advanced Capitalist State" in Burchell, Robert W. and Sternlieb, George (eds.), *Planning Theory in the1980s: A Search for New Directions*, New Brunswick, N.J. Center for Urban Policy Research, 1978; Harvey, David, "On Planning the Ideology of Planning" in ibid., Boyer, M. Christine, *Dreaming the Rational City: The Myth of City Planning*, Cambridge, Mass., The MIT Press, 1983.

40   The discussion here draws heavily on that in Fainstein and Fainstein, op. cit.

41   See also Branch, Melville C., "Delusions and Defusions of City Planning in the United States", *Management Science*, 16 (12) August 1970, pp. 714–732, and Branch, Melville C., "Sins of City Planners", *Public Administration Review*, 42 (1) January/February 1982, pp. 1–5.

42   See Alexander, op. cit., pp. 138–140; Klosterman, op. cit.; Forester, John, "Critical Theory and Planning Practice", *Journal of the American Planning Association*, 46 (3) July 1980, pp. 275–286; Clavel, Pierre, Forester, John and Goldsmith, William W. (eds.), *Urban and Regional Planning in an Age of Austerity*, New York, Pergamon, 1980; and Dyckman, John W., "Reflections on Planning Practice in an Age of Reaction", *Journal of Planning Education and Research*, 3 (1) Summer 1983, pp. 5–12.

7

Planning the Capitalist City

Richard E. Foglesong

Capitalism and Urban Planning

David Harvey, a Marxist social geographer, has conceptualized urban
conflict as a conflict over the "production, management and use of the
urban built environment."[1] Harvey uses the term "built environment" to
refer to physical entities such as roads, sewerage networks, parks, railroads, and even private housing – facilities that are collectively owned
and consumed or, as in the case of private housing, whose character and
location the state somehow regulates. These facilities have become
politicized because of conflict arising out of their being collectively
owned and controlled, or because of the "externality effects" of private
decisions concerning their use. At issue is how these facilities should be
produced – whether by the market or by the state, how they should
be managed and by whom; and how they should be used – for what purposes and by what groups, races, classes, and neighborhoods. Following
Harvey, the development of American urban planning is seen as the
result of conflict over the production, management, and use of the urban
built environment.

The development of this analysis depends on the recognition that
capitalism both engenders and constrains demands for state intervention
in the sphere of the built environment. First, let us consider some of the
theories about how capitalism engenders demands for state intervention.

Sources of urban planning

Within the developing Marxist urban literature, there have been a variety of attempts to link urban conflict and demands for state intervention to the reproduction processes of capitalist society. Manuel Castells, one of the leading contributors to this literature, emphasizes the connection between state intervention in the urban development process and the reproduction of *labor power*.[2]

The Problem of Planning

The market system cannot meet the consumption needs of the working class in a manner capable of maintaining capitalism; this, according to Castells, is the reason for the growth of urban planning and state intervention. To the extent that the state picks up the slack and assumes this responsibility, there occurs a transformation of the process of consumption, from individualized consumption through the market to collective consumption organized through the state. This transformation entails not only an expansion of the role of the state, which is seen in the growth of urban planning, but also a politicization of the process of consumption, which Castells sees as the underlying dynamic of urban political conflict.

By contrast, David Harvey and Edmond Preteceille, writing separately, have related state intervention in the urban development process to the inability of the market system to provide for the maintenance and reproduction of the immobilized fixed capital investments (for example, bridges, streets, sewerage networks) used by capital as *means of production*.[3] The task of the state is not only to maintain this system of what Preteceille calls "urban use values" but also to provide for the co-ordination of these use values in space (for example, the coordination of streets and sewer lines), creating what he terms "new, complex use values."[4] François Lamarche, on the other hand, relates the whole question of urban planning and state intervention to the *sphere of circulation* and the need to produce a "spatial organization which facilitates the circulation of capital, commodities, information, etc."[5] In his view capitalism has spawned a particular fraction of capital, termed "property capital," which is responsible for organizing the system of land use and transportation; and urban planning is a complement and extension of the aims and activities of this group. In addition, and somewhat distinct from these attempts to relate urban planning to the reproduction processes of capitalist society, David Harvey has linked urban planning to the problems arising from the *uniqueness of land as a commodity*, namely the fact that land is not transportable, which makes it inherently subject to externality effects.[6]

The theories discussed above demonstrate that there are a variety of problems arising from relying upon the market system to guide urban development. At various times, urban planning in the United States has been a response to each of these problems. Yet these problems have different histories. They have not had equal importance throughout the development of planning. Moreover, not one of these problems is sufficient in itself to explain the logic of development of planning.

Constraints on urban planning

If the problems noted above arise from the workings of the market system, so that capitalism can be said to engender demands for state intervention in response to these problems, the capitalist system also constrains the realization of these demands. The operative constraint in this connection is the institution of private property. It is here that we confront what might be termed the central contradiction of capitalist urbanization: the contradiction between the social character of land and its private ownership and control. Government intervention in the ordering of the urban built environment – that is, urban planning – can be seen as a response to the social character of land, to the fact that land is not only a commodity but also a collective good, a social resource as well as a private right. Indeed, as the Marxist urban literature has sought to demonstrate, the treatment of land as a commodity fails to satisfy the social needs of either capital or labor. Capital has an objective interest in socializing the control of land in order to (1) cope with the externality problems that arise from treating land as a commodity; (2) create the housing and other environmental amenities needed for the reproduction of labor power; (3) provide for the building and maintenance of the bridges, harbors, streets, and transit systems used by capital as means of production; and (4) ensure the spatial coordination of these infrastructure facilities for purposes of efficient circulation. Yet the institution of private property stands as an impediment to attempts to socialize the control of land in order to meet these collective needs. Thus, if urban planning is necessary for the reproduction of the capitalist system on the one hand, it threatens and is restrained by the capitalist system on the other; and it is in terms of this Janus-faced reality that the development of urban planning is to be understood. Moreover, this contradiction is intrinsic to capitalist urbanization, for the impulse to socialize the control of urban space is as much a part of capitalism as is the institution of private property. Each serves to limit the extension of the other; thus, they are in "contradiction."[7] This contradiction, which will be termed the "property contradiction," is one of two that have structured the development of planning.[8]

The "property contradiction"   To state that capitalist urbanization has an inherent contradiction is *not* to predict the inevitable downfall of capitalism (although it does indicate a weakness in the capitalist structure of society that oppositional forces could conceivably exploit). Rather, it is assumed that capitalism is capable of coping with this contradiction, within limits, but that it is a continuing source of tension and a breeding ground of political conflict. Thus, our analytical interest is in the institutional means that have been devised to keep this contradiction from exploding into a system-threatening crisis. In recognizing this contradiction, we therefore gain a better appreciation of the importance, both politically and theoretically, of the institutional forms that urban planning has adopted over the course of its development, and of how (and how well) those institutional forms have responded to the contradiction between the social character of land and its private ownership and control.

In addition, recognizing this contradiction helps us to understand the patterns of alliance formation around planning issues, as well as the role of planners in mediating between different groups and group interests. For if the effort to socialize the control of urban land is potentially a threat to the whole concept of property rights, it is directly and immediately a threat to only one particular group of capitalists, those whom Lamarche terms "property capital." Included are persons who, in his words, "plan and equip space" – real estate developers, construction contractors, and directors of mortgage lending institutions.[9] It is this fraction of capital, in particular, that can be expected to oppose efforts to displace or diminish private control of urban development. Other capitalists, in contrast, may seek an expanded government role in the planning and equipping of space. For example, manufacturing capital may want government to provide worker housing and to coordinate the development of public and private infrastructure (such as utilities and railroads), and commercial capitalists may desire government restrictions on the location of manufacturing establishments. Likewise, nonowner groups have an interest in state intervention that will provide for or regulate the quality of worker housing, build parks, and improve worker transportation, for example. It is possible, therefore, for certain fractions of capital to align with nonowner groups in support of planning interventions that restrict the "rights" of urban landholders. The property contradiction thus manifests itself in the pattern of alliances around planning issues by creating, in intracapitalist class conflict, the possibility of alliances between property-owning and nonproperty-owning groups and allowing planners to function as mediators in organizing these compromises. Inasmuch as the property contradiction is inherent in the capitalist structure of society, existing independent of consiousness and will, recognition of this contradiction enables us to link the politics of planning to the structural ordering of capitalist society.

The "capitalist-democracy contradiction"   The other contradiction affecting the development of urban planning is the "capitalist-democracy contradiction." If the property contradiction is internal to capitalism in that it arises out of the logic of capitalist development, the capitalist-democracy contradiction is an external one, originating between the political and economic structures of a democratic-capitalist society. More specifically, it is a contradiction between the need to socialize the control of urban space to create the conditions for the maintenance of capitalism on the one hand and the danger to capital of truly socializing, that is, democratizing, the control of urban land on the other. For if the market system cannot produce a built environment that is capable of maintaining capitalism, reliance on the institutions of the state, especially a formally democratic state, creates a whole new set of problems, not the least of which is that the more populous body of nonowners will gain too much control over landed property. This latter contradiction is conditioned on the existence of the property contradiction, in that it arises from efforts to use government action to balance or hold in check the property contradiction. Once government intervention is accepted, questions about how to organize that intervention arise: What goals should be pursued? How should they be formulated and by whom? This pattern of the capitalist-democracy contradiction following on the heels of the property contradiction is apparent in the actual history of planning, for while both contradictions have been in evidence throughout the history of planning in America, the property contradiction was a more salient generator of conflict in the earlier, pre-1940 period. The capitalist-democracy contradiction – manifested in the controversy over how to organize the planning process – has been a more potent source of conflict in the history of planning after World War II. It should also be emphasized that the capitalist-democracy contradiction is conditioned on the formally democratic character of the state, out of which the danger of government control of urban development arises. Were it not for the majority-rule criterion and formal equality promised by the state, turning to government to control urban development would not pose such a problem for capital.

Consideration of the capitalist-democracy contradiction leads us back to Offe's analysis of the internal structure of the state. Following Offe's analysis, it can be postulated that capitalism is caught in a search for a decision process, a method of policy making that can produce decisions corresponding with capital's political and economic interests. Politically, this decision process must be capable of insulating state decision making from the claims and considerations of the numerically larger class of noncapitalists, a task made difficult by the formally democratic character of the state. Economically, this decision process must be capable of producing decisions that facilitate the accumulation and circulation of capital (for example, promoting the reproduction of labor power and coordinating the building up of local infrastructure), a function that the market fails to perform and that capitalists do not (necessarily) know how to perform. Both of these problems are captured in the concept of the capitalist-democracy contradiction. The question we are led to ask, then, is, In what ways has the development of urban planning – viewed here as a method of policy formulation – served to suppress or hold in balance the capitalist-democracy contradiction in a manner conducive to the reproduction of capitalism?

Notes

1   "Labor, Capital, and Class Struggle around the Built Environment in Advanced Capitalist Societies," p. 265.

2   *Urban Question*, pp. 460–61. Castells modifies his view in his most recent book, *The City and the Grass Roots*, which appeared after the manuscript of *Planning the Capitalist City* was essentially written. In this new book, Castells seeks to avoid the "excesses of theoretical formalism" that marked some of his earlier work (p. xvii). He also asserts that "although class relationships and class struggle are fundamental in understanding the process of urban conflict, they are by no means the only or even the primary source of urban social change" (p. xviii). My critical evaluation of Castells's earlier work is still valid and useful, however, since it lends emphasis and historical reference to some of Castells's own criticisms. Furthermore, my criticisms apply to a literature and a theoretical orientation that encompasses, as I point out, more than Castells's work.

3   Harvey, "The Political Economy of Urbanization in Advanced Capitalist Societies: The Case of the United States," p. 120; Preteceille, "Urban Planning: The Contradictions of Capitalist Urbanization," pp. 69–76. For Harvey, the need for a built environment usable as a collective means of production is only one of the connections between urban planning and capitalist development; he also recognizes the need for facilities for collective consumption to aid in reproducing labor power. See, e.g., his "Labor, Capital, and Class Struggle Around the Built Environment."

4   Preteceille, "Urban Planning," p. 70.

5   "Property Development and the Economic Foundations of the Urban Question," p. 86.

6   *Social Justice*, chapter 5.

7   For a discussion of this use of *contradiction*, see Godelier, "Structure and Contradiction in *Capital*," pp. 334–68.

8   Cf. Michael Dear and Allen Scott's assertion that the "urban question" (a reference to the work of Castells) is "structured around the particular and indissoluble geographical and land-contingent phenomena that come into existence as capitalist social and property relations are mediated through the dimension of urban space." They also write that planning is "a historically-specific and socially-necessary response to the self-disorganizing tendencies of *privatized* capitalist social and property relations as these appear in urban space" ("Towards a Framework for Analysis," pp. 6, 13). Cf. also, in the same volume, Shoukry Roweis's statement that "[u]rban planning in capitalism,

both in theory and in practice, and whether intentionally or unknowingly, attempts to grapple with a basic question: how can *collective action* (pertinent to decisions concerning the social utilization of urban land) be made possible under capitalism?" ("Urban Planning in Early and Late Capitalist Societies," p. 170). These two theoretical analyses relate urban planning under capitalism to the problem of "collective control" – how to organize socially necessary forms of collective consumption and control in a society based upon private ownership – but they do not take note of the contradiction between capital's need for collective control in its own interest and the limits imposed by the internal structure of the *state*. This is the issue raised by Offe and which I capture in my concept of the "capitalist-democracy contradiction" (below).

9   "Property Development," pp. 90–93.

Further Reading

Castells, Manuel. *The Urban Question.* Cambridge: MIT Press, 1977.

Dear, Michael, and Scott, Allen J., "Towards a Framework for Analysis." In *Urbanization and Urban Planning in Capitalist Society,* edited by Michael Dear and Allen J. Scott, pp. 3–18. London: Methuen, 1981.

Godelier, Maurice. "Structure and Contradiction in *Capital*." In *Ideology and Social Science,* edited by Robin Blackburn, pp. 334–68. New York: Vintage Books, 1973.

Harvey, David. "Labor, Capital, and Class Struggle around the Built Environment in Advanced Capitalist Societies," *Politics & Society* 6 (1976): 265–95.

—— "The Political Economy of Urbanization in Advanced Capitalist Societies: The Case of the United States." In *The Social Economy of Cities.* Urban Affairs Annual, edited by Gary Grappert and Harold M. Rose, no. 9, pp. 119–63. Beverly Hills: Russell Sage, 1975.

—— *Social Justice and the City.* Baltimore: John Hopkins University Press, 1973.

Lamarche, François. "Property Development and the Economic Foundations of the Urban Question." In *Urban Sociology: Critical Essays,* edited by Chris Pickvance, pp. 85–118. London: Tavistock Press, 1976.

Offe, Claus. "The Abolition of Market Control and the Problem of Legitimacy (I)." *Kapitalistate,* no. 1 (1973): 109–16.

Preteceille, Edmond. "Urban Planning: The Contradictions of Capitalist Urbanization." *Antipode* 8 (March 1976): 69–76.

Roweis, Shoukry. "Urban Planning in Early and Late Capitalist Societies." In *Urbanization and Urban Planning in Capitalist Society,* edited by Michael Dear and Allen Scott, pp. 159–78. London: Methuen, 1981.

8

On Planning the Ideology of Planning

David Harvey

It is a truism to say that we all plan. But planning as a profession has a much more restricted domain. Fight as they might for some other rationale for their existence, professional planners find themselves confined, for the most part, to the task of defining and attempting to achieve a "successful" ordering of the built environment. In the ultimate instance the planner is concerned with the "proper" location, the appropriate mix of activities in space of all the diverse elements that make up the totality of physical structures – the houses, roads, factories, offices, water and sewage disposal facilities, hospitals, schools, and the like – that constitute the built environment. From time to time the spatial ordering of the built environment is treated as an end sufficient unto itself, and some form of environmental determinism takes hold. At other times this ordering is seen as a reflection rather than a determinant of social relations, and planning is seen as a process rather than as a plan – and so the planner heaves himself away from the drawing board to attend meetings with bankers, community groups, land developers, and the like, in the hope that a timely intervention here or a preventive measure there may achieve a "better" overall result. But "better" assumes some purpose, which is easy enough to specify in general but more difficult to particularize about. As a physical resource complex created out of human labor and ingenuity, the built environment must primarily function to be useful for production, circulation,

Reprinted by permission from David Harvey, 1985. *The Urbanization of Capital*. Baltimore: Johns Hopkins University Press, pp 165–84.

exchange, and consumption. It is the job of the planner to ensure its proper management and maintenance. But this immediately poses the question, useful or better for what and to whom?

Planning and the Reproduction of the Social Order

It would be easy to jump from these initial questions straight away into some pluralistic model of society in which the planner acts either as an arbitrator or as a corrective weight in the conflicts amongst a diversity of interest groups, each of which strives to get a piece of the pie. Such a jump leaves out a crucial step. Society works, after all, on the basic principle that the most important activity is that which contributes to its own reproduction. We do not have to enquire far to find out what this activity entails. Consider, for example, the various conceptions of the city as "workshops of industrial civilization," as "nerve centers for the economic, social, cultural and political life" of society, as centers for innovation, exchange, and communication, and as living environments for people.[1] All of these – and more – are common enough conceptions. And if we accept one or all of them, then the role of the planner can simply be defined as ensuring that the built environment comprises those necessary physical infrastructures that serve the processes we have in mind. If the "workshop" dissolves into a chaos of disorganization, if the "nerve center" loses its coherence, if innovation is stymied, if communication and exchange processes become garbled, if the living conditions become intolerable, then the reproduction of the social order is in doubt.

We can push this argument farther. We live, after all, in a society that, for want of a better phrase, is founded on capitalist principles of private property and market exchange, a society that presupposes certain basic social relationships with respect to production, distribution, and consumption, which themselves must be reproduced if the social order is to survive. And so we arrive at what may appear a rather cosmic question: What is the role of the urban-regional planner in the context of these overall processes of social reproduction? Critical analysis should reveal the answers. Yet it is a measure of the failings of contemporary social science (from which the planning literature draws much of its inspiration) that we have to approach answers with circumspection as well as tact should we dare to depart from the traditional canons as to what may or may not be said. For this reason I shall begin with a brief digression in order to open up new vistas for discussion.

When we consider the economic system, most of us feel at home with analyses based on the categories of land, labor, and capital as "factors" of production. We recognize that social reproduction depends upon the perpetual combination of these elements and that growth requires the recombination of these factors into new configurations that are in some sense more productive. These categories, we often admit, are rather too abstract, and from time to time we break them down to take account of the fact that neither land nor labor is homogeneous and that capital can take productive (physical) or liquid (money) form. Nevertheless, we seem prepared to accept a high level of abstraction, without too much questioning as to the validity or efficacy of the concepts employed. Yet most of us blanch when faced with a sociological description of society that appeals to the concept of class relations between landlords, laborers, and capitalists. If we write in such terms, we will likely be dismissed as too simplistic or as engaging in levels of abstraction that make no sense. At worst, such concepts will be regarded as offensive and ideological compared to the supposedly nonideological concepts of land, labor, and capital. Why and on what ground – philosophical, practical, or otherwise – was it decided that one form of abstraction made sense and was appropriate, while the other was out of order? Does it not make reasonable sense to connect our sociological thinking with our economics, albeit in a rather simplistic and primitive way? Does it make sense even to tell the inner-city tenant that the rent paid to the landlord is not really a payment to that man who drives a big car and lives in the suburbs but a payment to a scarce factor of production? The "scientization" of social science seems to have been accomplished by masking real social relationships – by representing the social relations between people and groups of people as relations between things. The reification implied by this tactic is plain enough to see, and the dangers of reification are well known. Yet we seem to be at ease with the reifications and to accept them uncritically, even though the possibility exists that in so doing we destroy our capacity to understand, manage, control, and alter the social order in ways favorable to our individual or collective purposes. In this chapter, therefore, I seek to place the planner in the context of a sociological description of society that sees class relations as fundamental.

Class Relations and the Built Environment

In any society the actual class relations that exist are bound to be complex and fluid. This is particularly true in a society such as ours. The class categories we use are not regarded as immutable. And in the same way that we can disaggregate land, labor, and capital as factors of production, so we can produce a finer mesh of categories to describe the class structure. We know that land and property ownership comprises residual feudal institutions (the church, for example), large property companies, part-time landlords, homeowners, and so on. We know also that the interests of rentier "money capitalists" may diverge substantially from the interests of producers in industry and agriculture and that the laboring class is not homogeneous because of the stratifications and differentials generated according to the hierarchical division of labor and various wage rates. But in a short chapter of this sort I must perforce stick to the simplest categories that help us to understand the planner's role within the social structure. So let us proceed with the simplest conception we can devise and consider, in turn, how each class or fraction of a class relates to the built environment, which is the primary concern of the planner.

1   The class of laborers is made up of all of those individuals who sell a commodity – labor power – on the market in return for a wage or salary. The consumption requirements of labor – which are in practice highly differentiated – will in part be met by work within the household and in part be procured by exchanges of wages earned against commodities produced. The commodity requirements of labor depend upon the balance between domestic economy products and market purchases as well as upon the environmental, historical, and cultural considerations that fix the standard of living of labor. Labor looks to the built environment as a means of consumption and as a means for its own reproduction and, perhaps, expansion. Labor is sensitive to both the cost and the spatial disposition (access) of the various items in the built environment – housing, educational and recreational facilities, services of all kinds, and so on – that facilitate survival and reproduction at a given standard of living.

2   We can define capitalists as all those who engage in entrepreneurial functions of any kind with the intent of obtaining a profit. As a class, capitalists are primarily concerned with accumulation, and their activities form, in our kind of society, the primary engine for economic development and growth. Capital "in general" – which I use as a handy term for the capitalist class as a whole – looks to the built environment for two reasons. First, the built environment functions as a set of use values for enhancing the production and accumulation of capital. The physical infrastructures form a kind of fixed capital – much of which is collectively provided and used – which can be used as a means of production, of exchange, or of circulation. Second, the production of the built environment forms a substantial market for commodities (such as structural steel) and services (such as legal and administrative services) and therefore contributes to the total effective demand for the products that capitalists themselves produce. On occasion the built environment can become a kind of "dumping ground" for surplus money capital or idle productive capacity (sometimes by design, as in the public works programs of the 1930s), with the result that there are periodic bouts of overproduction and subsequent devaluation of the assets embedded in the built environment itself. The "wavelike" pattern of investment in the built environment is a very noticeable feature in the economic history of capitalist societies.[2]

3   A particular faction of capital seeks a rate of return on its capital by constructing new elements in the built environment. This faction – the construction interest – engages in a particular kind of commodity production under rather peculiar conditions. Much of what happens in the way of construction activity

has to be understood in terms of the technical, economic, and political organization of the construction interest.

4   We can define landlords as those who, by virtue of their ownership of land and property, can extract a rent (actual or imputed) for the use of the resources they control. In societies dominated by feudal residuals, the landlord interest may be quite distinct from that of capital; but in the United States, ownership in land and property became a very important form of investment from the eighteenth century onward. Under these conditions the "land and property interest" is simply reduced to a faction of capital (usually the money capitalists and the rentiers) investing in the appropriation of rent. This brings us to consider the important role of property companies, developers, banks, and other financial intermediaries (insurance companies, pension funds, savings and loan associations, etc.) in the land and property market. And I should also add that "homeownership" does not quite mean what it says, because most homeowners actually share equity with a financial institution and do not possess title to the property. In the United States, therefore, we have to think of the land and property interest primarily as a faction of capital investing in rental appropriation.

I shall assume for purposes of analytic convenience that a clear distinction exists between these classes and factions and that each pursues its own interests single-mindedly. In a capitalist society, of course, the whole structure of social relations is founded on the domination of capitalists over laborers. To put it this way is simply to acknowledge that the capitalists make the investment decisions, create the jobs and commodities, and function as the catalytic agents in capitalist growth. We cannot hold, on the one hand, that America was created by the efforts of private entrepreneurs and deny, on the other, that capital dominates labor. Labor is not passive, of course, but its actions are defensive and at best confined to gaining a reasonable share of the national product. But if labor controlled the investment decisions, then we would not be justified any longer in describing our society as capitalist. Our interest here is not so much to focus on this primary antagonism but to examine the myriad secondary forms of conflict that can spin off from it to weave a complex web of arguments over the production and use of the built environment. Appropriators (landlords and property owners) may be in conflict with construction interests, capitalists may be dissatisfied with the activities of both factions, and labor may be at odds with all of the others. And if the transport system or the sewage system does not work, then both labor and capital will be equally put out. Let us consider two examples that, in spite of their hypothetical nature, illustrate the complex alliances that can form and shed some light on the kinds of problems urban planners typically face.

I start with the proposition that the price of existing resources in the built environment – and, hence, the rate of rental appropriation – is highly sensitive to the costs and rate of new construction. Suppose the construction interests are badly organized, in a slump, or unable to gain easy access to cheap land and that the rate of new construction is low and the costs high. Under these conditions, those seeking the appropriation of rent possess the power to increase their rate of return by raising rental on, say, housing. Labor may resist; tenant organizations may spring up and seek to control the rate of rental appropriation and to keep the cost of living down. If they succeed, tenant organizations may even drive the rate of return on existing resources downward to the point where investment withdraws entirely (perhaps producing abandonment). If labor lacks organization and power in the community but is well organized and powerful in the workplace, a rising rate of appropriation may result in the pursuit of higher wages, which, if granted, may lower the rate of profit and accumulation. A rational response of the capitalist class under these conditions is to seek an alliance with labor to curb excessive rental appropriations, to free land for new construction, and to see to it that cheap (perhaps even subsidized) housing is built for the laboring class. We can see this sort of coalition in action when large corporate interests in suburban locations join with civil rights groups in trying to break suburban zoning restrictions that exclude low-wage populations from the suburbs. An exploration of this dimension of conflict can tell us much about the structure of contemporary urban problems.

The second case I shall consider arises out of the general dynamic of capitalist accumulation, which from time to time generates chronic overproduction, surplus real productive capacity, and idle money capital desperately in need of productive outlets. In such a situation, money is easily come by to produce long-term investments in the built environment, and a vast investment wave flows into the production of the built environment, which serves as a vent for surplus capital – such was the boom experienced from 1970 to 1973. But at some point the existence of overproduction becomes plain to see – be it office space in Manhattan or housing in Detroit – and the property boom collapses in a wave of bankruptcies and "refinancings" (consider, for example, the fall of the secondary banks associated with the London property market in 1973 and the dismal performance of the Real Estate Investment Trusts in the United States, which has $11 billion in assets, half of them currently earning no rate of return at all). What becomes evident in this case is that excessive investment brings in its wake disinvestment and devaluation of capital for at least some segment of the landed interest. The construction interest is also faced with an extremely difficult pattern of booms and slumps, which militates against the creation of a viable long-term organization for the coherent production of the built environment. If labor sinks part of its equity into the property market, then it, too, may find its savings devalued by such processes; and through community organization and political action, it may seek to protect itself as well as it can. In this case also, we can discern a structure to our urban problems that is explicable in terms of the conflicting requirements of the various classes and factions as they face up to the problems created by the use of the built environment as a vent for surplus capital in a period of over-accumulation.

These dimensions of conflict are cut across, however, by a completely different set of considerations, which arise out of the fact that the built environment is composed of assets that are typically both long-lived and fixed in space. This means that we are dealing with commodities that must be produced and used under conditions of "natural monopoly" in space. It also happens that, since the built environment is to be conceived of as a complex composite commodity, the individual elements have strong "externality" effects on other elements. We thus find that competition for use of resources is monopolistic competition in space – that capitalists can compete with capitalists for advantageously positioned resources, that laborers can compete with laborers for survival chances, access, and the like, and that land and property owners seek to influence the positioning of new elements in the built environment (particularly transport facilities) so as to gain indirect benefits. The basic structure of class and factional conflicts is therefore modified, and in some instances totally transformed, into a structure of geographical conflict that pits laborers in the suburbs against laborers in the city, capitalists in the industrial Northeast against capitalists in the Sun Belt, and so on.

The distinctive role and tasks of the planner have to be understood against the background of the strong currents of both interclass and factional conflict on the one hand and the geographical competition that natural monopolies in space inevitably generate on the other.

The Production, Maintenance, and Management of the Built Environment

The built environment must incorporate the necessary use values to facilitate social reproduction and growth. Its overall efficiency and rationality can be tested and measured in terms of how well it functions in relationship to these tasks. The sophisticated model builders within the planning fraternity have long sought to translate this conception into a search for some idealized *optimum optimorum* for the city or for regional structure. Such a search can be entertaining and can generate insights into certain typical characteristics of urban structure, but as an enterprise it is utopian, idealized, and fruitless. A more down-to-earth analysis suggests that the indications of failure of the built environment to provide the necessary use values are not too hard to spot. The evidence of crisis and of failure to reproduce effectively or to grow at a steady rate of accumulation is a clear indicator of a lack of balance that requires some kind of corrective action.

Unfortunately, *crisis* is a much overused word. Anybody who wants anything in this society is forced to shout "crisis" as loudly as possible in order to get anything done. For the underprivileged and the poor, the crisis is permanent and endemic. I shall take a narrower view and define a crisis as a particular conjuncture in which the reproduction of capitalist society is in jeopardy. The main signals are falling rates of profit; soaring unemployment and inflation; idle productive capacity and idle money capital lacking profitable employment; and financial, institutional, and political chaos and civil strife. And we can identify three wellsprings out of which crises in capitalist society typically flow. First, an imbalanced outcome of the struggle between the classes or factions of classes may permit one class or faction to acquire excessive power and so destabilize the system (well-organized workers can force the wage rate up and the accumulation rate down; finance capital may dominate all other factions of capital and engage in uncontrolled speculative binges, and so forth). Second, accumulation pushes growth beyond the capacity of the sustaining natural resource base at the same time as technological innovation slackens. Third, a tendency toward overaccumulation and overproduction is omnipresent in capitalist societies because individual entrepreneurs, pursuing their own individual self-interest, collectively push the dynamic of aggregative accumulation away from a balanced growth path.

The particular role of the built environment in all of this is complex in its details but simple in principle. Failure to invest in those elements in the built environment that contribute to accumulation is no different in principle than the failure of entrepreneurs to invest and reinvest in fixed capital equipment. The problem with the built environment is that much of it functions as collective fixed capital (transport, sewage, and disposal systems, etc.). Some way has to be found, therefore, to ensure a flow of investment into the built environment and to ensure that individual investment decisions are coordinated in both time and space so that the aggregative needs of capitalist producers are met. By the same token, failure to invest in the means of consumption for labor may raise the wage rate, generate civil strife, or (in the worst kind of eventuality) physically diminish the supply of labor. In both cases, failure to invest in the right quantities, at the right times, and in the right places can be a progenitor of a crisis of accumulation and growth. Overinvestment in the built environment is, in contrast, simply a devaluation of capital that nobody, surely, welcomes. And so we arrive at the general conception of the *potential* for a harmonious, balanced investment process in the built environment. Any departure from this path will entail either underinvestment (and a constraint upon accumulation) or overinvestment (and the devaluation of capital). The problem is to find some way to ensure that such a potentiality for balanced growth is realized under the conditions of a capitalist investment process.

The built environment is long-lived; fixed in space; and a complex, composite commodity, the individual elements of which may be produced, maintained, managed, and owned by quite diverse interests. Plainly, there is a problem of coordination, because mistakes are very difficult to recoup and individual producers may not always act to produce the proper mix of elements in space. The time stream of benefits to be derived also poses some peculiar problems. The physical landscape created at one point in time may be suited to the needs of society at that point but become antagonistic later as the dynamics of accumulation and societal growth alter the use value requirements of both capital and labor. Tensions may then arise because the long-lived use values embedded in the built environment cannot easily be altered on a grand scale – witness the problems endemic to many of the older industrial and commercial cities in the industrial Northeast of the United States at the present time.

Investment in the built environment can be coordinated with general social requirements in one way, or in a mix of three:

1   Allocations can be arrived at through market mechanisms. Elements that can be privately appropriated under the legal relations of private property – houses, factories, offices, stores, warehouses, etc. – can be rented and traded. This sets up the price signals that, under pure competitive bidding, will allocate land and plant to the best-paying uses. The price signals also make it possible to calculate a rate of return on new investments, which usually generates a flow of new investment to wherever the rate of return is above that to be had, given similar risks, in other sectors of the capital market. But the innumerable externality effects and the importance of "public goods" items that cannot be privately appropriated – streets, sidewalks, and so on – generate frequent market failures and imperfections so that in no country is investment in the built environment left entirely to competitive market mechanisms.

2   Allocations may be arrived at under the auspices of some hegemonic controlling interest – a land or developer monopoly, controlling financial interests, and the like.[3] This is not an irrational move, because a large-scale enterprise coordinating investments of many different types can "internalize the externalities" and thereby make more rational decisions from the investor standpoint – the land-grant railroads provide an excellent historical example of such monopolistic control, while Rouse's Columbia provides a contemporary example. The trouble with monopolization and hegemonic control is that the pricing system becomes artificial (and this can lead to misallocations), while there is nothing to ensure that monopoly power is not abused.

3   State intervention is an omnipresent feature in the production, maintenance, and management of the built environment.[4] The transport system – prime example of a "natural monopoly" in space – has always posed the problem of private gain versus public social benefit, private property rights versus

aggregative social needs. The abuse of monopoly power (which it is all too easy to accumulate in spatial terms) has ever brought forth state regulation as a response. The pervasive externality effects have in all countries led to state regulation of the spatial order to reduce the risks that attach to long-term investment decisions. And the "public goods" elements in the built environment – the streets, sidewalks, sewer and drainage systems, and so on – which cannot feasibly be privately appropriated have always been created by direct investment on the part of the agencies of the state. The theme of "public improvement" has been writ large in the history of all American cities.

The exact mix of private market, monopolistic control, and state intervention and provision has varied with time as well as from place to place. Which mix is chosen or, more likely, arrived at by a complex historical process is not that important. What is important is that it should ensure the creation of a built environment that serves the purpose of social reproduction and that it should do so in such a manner that crises are avoided as far as is possible.

Urban Planning as Part of the Instrumentalities of State

The proper conception of the role of the state in capitalist society is controversial.[5] I shall simply take the view that state institutions and the processes whereby state powers are exercised must be so fashioned that they too contribute, insofar as they can, to the reproduction and growth of the social system. Under this conception we can derive certain basic functions of the capitalist state. It should

1   help to stabilize an otherwise rather erratic economic and social system by acting as a "crisis manager";

2   strive to create the conditions for "balanced growth" and a smooth process of accumulation;

3   contain civil strife and factional struggles by repression (police power), cooptation (buying off politically or economically), or integration (trying to harmonize the demands of warring classes or factions).

The state can effectively perform all of these functions only if it succeeds in internalizing within its processes the conflicting interests of classes, factions, diverse geographical groupings, and so on. A state that is entirely controlled by one and only one faction, that can operate only repressively and never through integration or cooptation, will likely be unstable and will likely survive only under conditions that are, in any case, chronically unstable. The social democratic state is one that can internalize diverse conflicting interests and that, by means of the checks and balances it contains, can prevent any one faction or class from seizing direct control of all of the instrumentalities of government and putting them to its own direct use. Yet the social democratic state is still a capitalist state in the sense that it is a capitalist social order that it is helping to reproduce. If the instrumentalities of state power are turned against the existing social order, then we see a crisis of the state, the outcome of which will determine whether the social order changes or whether the organization of the state reverts to its basic role of serving societal reproduction.

The urban planner occupies just one niche within the total complex of the instrumentalities of state power. The internalization of conflicting interests and needs within the state typically puts one branch of the bureaucracy at loggerheads with another, one level or branch of government against another, and even different departments at odds with one another within the same bureaucracy. In what follows, however, I shall lay aside these diverse cross-currents of conflict and seek to abstract some sense of the real limitations placed upon the urban planner by virtue of his or her role and thereby come to identify more clearly the nature of the role itself. To hasten the argument along, I shall simply suggest that the planner's task is to contribute to the processes of social reproduction and that in so doing the planner is equipped with powers vis-à-vis the production, maintenance, and management of the built environment that permit him or her to intervene in order to stabilize, to create the conditions for "balanced growth," to contain civil strife and factional struggles by repression, cooptation, or integration. And to fulfill these goals successfully, the planning process as a whole (in which the planner fulfills only one set of tasks) must be relatively open. This conception may appear unduly simplistic, but a down-to-earth analysis of what planners actually do, as opposed to what they or the mandarins of the planning fraternity think they do, suggests that the conception is not far from the mark. And the history of those who seek to depart radically from this fairly circumscribed path suggests that they either encounter frustration or else give up the role of planner entirely.[6]

The Planner's Knowledge and Implied World View

In order to perform the necessary task effectively, the planner needs to acquire an understanding of how the built environment works in relationship to social reproduction and how the various facets of competitive, monopolistic, and state production of the built environment relate to one another in the context of often conflicting class and factional

requirements. Planners are therefore taught to appreciate how everything relates to everything else in an urban system, to think in terms of
costs and benefits (although they may not necessarily resort to techniques of cost-benefit analysis), and to have some sympathetic
understanding of the problems that face the private producers of the built
environment, the landlord interest, the urban poor, the managers of
financial institutions, the downtown business interests, and so on. The
accumulation of planning knowledge arises through incremental understandings of what would be the "best" configuration of investment (both
spatial and in terms of quantitative balance) to facilitate social reproduction. But the most important shifts in understanding come in the course
of those crises in which something obviously must be done because social
reproduction is in jeopardy.

The planner requires something else as well as a basic understanding
of how the system works from a purely technical standpoint. In resort-
ing to tools of repression, cooptation, and integration, the planner
requires justification and legitimation, a set of powerful arguments with
which to confront warring factional interests and class antagonisms. In
striving to affect reconciliation, the planner must perforce resort to the
idea of the potentiality for harmonious balance in society. And it is on
this fundamental notion of social harmony that the ideology of planning
is built. The planner seeks to intervene to restore "balance," but the
"balance" implied is that which is necessary to reduce civil strife and to
maintain the requisite conditions for the steady accumulation of capital.
From time to time, of course, planners may be captured (by corruption,
political patronage, or even radical arguments) by one class/faction or
another and thereby lose the capacity to act as stabilizers and harmoniz-
ers – but such a condition, though endemic, is inherently unstable, and
the inevitable reform movement will most probably sweep it away when
it is no longer consistent with the requirements of the social order. The
role of the planner, then, ultimately derives its justification and legitimacy from intervening to restore that balance that perpetuates the
existing social order. And the planner fashions an ideology appropriate
to the role.

This does not necessarily mean that the planner is a mere defender of
the status quo. The dynamics of accumulation and of societal growth are
such as to create endemic tensions between the built environment as is
and as it should be, while the evils that stem from the abuse of spatial
monopoly can quickly become widespread and dangerous for social
reproduction. Part of the planner's task is to spot both present and future
dangers and to head off, if possible, an incipient crisis of the built environment. In fact, the whole tradition of planning is progressive in the sense
that the planner's commitment to the ideology of social harmony – unless
it is perverted or corrupted in some way – always puts the planner in the
role of "righter of wrongs," "corrector of imbalances," and "defender of

the public interest." The limits of this progressive stance are clearly set, however, by the fact that the definitions of the public interest, of imbalance, and of inequity are set according to the requirements for the reproduction of the social order, which is, whether we like the term or not, a distinctively capitalist social order.

The planner's knowledge of the world cannot be separated from this necessary ideological commitment. Existing and planned orderings of the built environment are evaluated against some notion of a "rational" socio-spatial ordering. But it is the capitalistic definition of rationality to which we appeal (Godelier 1972). The principle of rationality is an ideal – the central core of a pervasive ideology – which itself depends upon the notion of harmonious processes of social reproduction under capitalism. The limits of the planner's understanding of the world are set by this underlying ideological commitment. In the reverse direction, the planner's knowledge is used ideologically, as both legitimation and justification for certain forms of action. Political struggles and arguments may, under the planner's influence, be reduced to technical arguments for which a "rational" solution can easily be found. Those who do not accept such a solution are then open to attack as "unreasonable" and "irrational." In this manner both the real understanding of the world and the prevailing ideology fuse into a world view. I do not mean to imply that all planners subscribe to the same world view – they manifestly do not, and it would be dysfunctional were they to do so. Some planners are very technocratic and seek to translate all political issues into technical problems, while other planners take a much more political stance. But whatever their position, the fusion of technical understandings with a necessary ideology produces a complex mix within the planning fraternity of capacity to understand and to intervene in a realistic and advantageous way and capacity to repress, coopt, and integrate in a way that appears justifiable and legitimate.

Civil Strife, Crisis of Accumulation, and Shifts in the Planner's World View

The planner's world view, defined as the necessary knowledge for appropriate intervention and the necessary ideology to justify and legitimate action, has altered with changing circumstances. But knowledge and ideology do not change overnight. The concepts, categories, relationships, and images through which we interpret the world are, so to speak, the fixed capital of our intellectual world and are no more easily transformed than the physical infrastructures of the city itself. It usually takes a crisis, a rush of ideas pouring forth under the pressure of events, radically to change the planner's world view, and even then radical change comes but slowly. And while the fundamentals of ideology – the notion of social harmony – may stay intact, the meanings attached must change according to whatever it is that is out of balance. The history of capitalistic societies these last two hundred years suggests, however, that certain problems are endemic, and simply will not go away no matter how hard we try. Consequently we find that the shifting world view of the planner exhibits an accumulation of technical understandings combined with a mere swaying from side to side in ideological stance from which the planner appears to learn little or nothing. Let me illustrate.

The capitalist growth process has been punctuated, at quite regular intervals, by phases of acute social tension and civil strife. These phases are not historical accidents but can be traced back to the fundamental characteristics of capitalist societies and the growth processes entailed. I have not space to elaborate on this theme here, but it is important to note that the organization of work under capitalism is predicated on a separation between "working" and "living," on control of work by the capitalist and alienated labor for the employee, and on a dynamic relation between the wage rate and the rate of profit, which is founded on the social necessity for a surplus of labor that may vary quantitatively according to time and place. Generally speaking, it is the concentration of low-wage populations and unemployment in either time or space that sets the stage for civil strife.

The response is some mixture of repression, cooptation, and integration. The urban planner's role in all of this is to define policies that facilitate social control and that serve to reestablish social harmony through cooptation and integration. Consider, for example, the spatial distribution of the population, particularly of the unemployed and low-wage earners. The revolutions of 1848, the Paris Commune of 1871, the urban violence that accompanied the great railroad strikes of 1877 in the United States, and Chicago's celebrated "Haymarket affair" of 1886 demonstrated the revolutionary dangers associated with high concentrations of what Charles Loring Brace (1889) called, in the 1870s, the "dangerous classes" of society. The problem could be dealt with by a policy of dispersal, which meant that ways had to be found to permit the poor and the unemployed to escape their chronic entrapment in space. The urban working class had to be dispersed and subjected to what reformers on both sides of the Atlantic called "the moral influence" of the suburbs (Tarr 1973). Suburbanization facilitated by cheap communication was seen as part of the solution. The urban planners and reformers of the time pressed hard for policies of dispersal via mass transit facilities such as those provided under the Cheap Trains Act of 1882 in Britain and the streetcars in the United States, while the search for cheap housing and means to promote social stability through working-class homeownership began in earnest. In much the same way, planners in the 1960s responded to the urban riots by seeking ways to disperse the ghetto by improved transport relations, promoting home-ownership, and opening up housing opportunities in the suburbs (although this time round, the Victorian rhetoric of "moral influence" was replaced by the more "rational" appeal of "social stability"). In the process, the laboring classes undoubtedly gain in real living standards while the planner acts as advocate for the poor and the underprivileged, raises the cry of social justice and equity, expresses moral outrage at the conditions of life of the urban poor, and reaches for ways to restore social harmony.

The alternative to dispersal is what we now call "gilding the ghetto," and this, too, is a well-tried tactic in the struggle to control civil strife in urban areas. As early as 1812, the Reverend Thomas Chalmers raised the specter of a tide of revolutionary violence sweeping Britain as working-class populations steadily concentrated in large urban areas. Chalmers saw "the principle of community" as the main bulwark of defense against this revolutionary tide – a principle that sought to establish harmony between the classes around the basic institutions of community. The principle also entailed a commitment to community improvement, the attempt to instill some sense of civic or community pride capable of trans-gressing class boundaries. The church was then the most important institution, but we now think of other instrumentalities also – political inclusion, citizen participation, and community commitment to edu-cational, recreational, and other services as well as the sense of pride in neighborhood that inevitably means a "better" quality of built environ-ment. From Chalmers through Octavia Hill and Jane Addams, to Model Cities and citizen participation, we have a continuous thread of an argument that suggests social stability can be restored in periods of social unrest by an active pursuit of "the principle of community" and all that this means in the way of community betterment and social improvement – and again, the planner typically acts as advocate, as catalyst in promot-ing the spirit of community improvement.

One dimension of this idea of "improvement" is that of environmen-tal quality. Olmsted was perhaps the first fully to recognize that the efficiency of labor might be enhanced by providing a compensatory sense of harmony with nature in the living place, although it is important to recognize that Olmsted was building on a rather older tradition.[7] At issue here is the relation to nature in a most fundamental sense. Industrial capitalism, armed with the factory system, organized a work process that transformed the relation between worker and nature into a travesty of its older artisan self. Reduced to a thing, a commodity, a mere "factor" of production, the worker became alienated from the product of work, the process of production, and ultimately from pure nature itself, partic-ularly in the industrial city, where, as Dickens (1961) puts it, "Nature was as strongly bricked out as killing airs and gases were bricked in." The romantic reaction against the new industrial order ultimately led in the practice of urban design and planning to the attempt to counter in the sphere of consumption for what had been lost in the sphere of production. The attempt to "bring nature back into the living environments" within the city has been a consistent theme in planning since Olmsted's time. Yet it is, in the final analysis, an attempt based on what Raymond Williams (1973) calls "an effective and imposing mystification," for there is something in the relation to nature in the work process that can never be compensated for in the consumption sphere. The planner, armed with concepts of ecological balance and the notion of harmony with nature, acts once more as advocate and brings real gains. But the real solutions to these problems lie elsewhere, in the work process itself.

Civil strife and social discontent provide only one set of problems that the planner must address. The dynamic of accumulation, with its periodic crises of overaccumulation, poses an entirely different set. The crises are not accidental. They are to be viewed, rather, as major periods of "rationalization," of "shake-outs and shake-downs" that restore balance to an economic system temporarily gone mad. The fact that crises perform this rationalizing function is no comfort to those caught in their midst. And at such conjunctures planners must either simply administer the budget cuts and plan the shrinkage according to the strict requirements of an externally imposed fiscal logic of the sort recently applied to New York or seek to head a movement for a forced rationalization of the urban system. The pursuit of the City Beautiful is replaced by the search for the city efficient; the cry of social justice is replaced by the slogan "efficiency in government"; and those planners armed with a ruthless cost-benefit calculus, a rational and technocratic commitment to efficiency for efficiency's sake, come into their own.

"Rationalization" means, of course, doing whatever must be done to reestablish the conditions for a positive rate of accumulation. When economic growth goes negative – as it did, for example, in 1893, in the early 1930s, or in 1970 and 1974, then the reproduction of the social order is plainly in doubt. The task at such conjunctures is to find out what is wrong and to right it. The physical infrastructure of the city may be congested, inefficient, and too costly to use for purposes of production and exchange. Such barriers (which were obvious to all in the Progressive Era, for example) must be removed, and if the planner does not willingly help to do so, then the escalating competition between jurisdictions for "development" at times of general decline will force the planner into action if he or she values the tax base (this kind of competitive pressure often leads communities to subsidize profits). If the problem lies in the consumption sphere – underconsumption or erratic movements in aggregate personal behaviors – then the state may seek to manage consumption either by fiscal devices or through collectivization. The management of collective consumption by means of the built environment at such points becomes a crucial part of the planner's task.[8] If the problem lies in lack or excess of investment in the built environment, then the planner must perforce set to work to stimulate investment or to manage and rationalize devaluation with techniques of "planned shrinkage," urban renewal, and even the production of "planning blight" (which amounts to nothing more than earmarking certain areas for devaluation).

I list these various possibilities because it is not always self-evident what must be done in the heat of a crisis of accumulation. At such conjunctures our knowledge of the system and how it works is crucial for action, unless we are to be led dangerously near the precipice of cataclysmic depression. And it is exactly at such points that the world view of the planner, restricted as it is by an ideological commitment, appears most defective, while the ideological stance of the planner may have to shift under the pressure of events from advocacy for the urban poor to one dedicated to business rationality and efficiency in government.

But ideologies, I have argued, do not change that easily, nor does our knowledge of the world. And so we find, at each of the major turning points in our history, a *crisis of ideology*.[9] Past commitments must obviously be abandoned because they hinder our power to understand and most certainly lose their power to legitimate and justify (imagine trying to justify what happened to New York City's budget in the mid-1970s by appealing to concepts of social justice). And as the pillars of the planner's world view slowly crumble, so the search begins for a new scaffolding for the future. At such a juncture, it becomes necessary to plan the ideology of planning.

Planning the Ideology of Planning

By the mid-1970s it became clear that the planning inspirations of the 1960s had faded and that our main task was to define new horizons for planning into the 1980s – new technologies, new instrumentalities, new goals . . . new everything, in fact, *except* a new ideology. Yet if my analysis is correct, the real task was to plan the ideology of planning to fit the new economic realities rather than to meet the social unrest and civil strife of the 1960s.

Since many of those who inspired us in the 1960s are still active, it is useful to ask what, if anything, went wrong. The crucial problem of the 1960s was civil strife and in particular the concentrated form of it associated with the urban riots in central city areas. That strife had to be contained by repression, cooptation, and integration. In this the planner, armed with diverse ideologies and a variety of world views, played a crucial role. The dissidents were encouraged to go through "channels," to adhere to "procedures laid down," and somewhere down that path the planner lay in wait with a seemingly sophisticated technology and an intricate understanding of the world, through which political questions could be translated into technical questions that the mass of the population found hard to understand. But discontent cannot so easily be controlled, and so the other string to the planner's bow was to find ways to disperse the urban poor, to divide and control them and to ameliorate their conditions of life (Piven and Cloward 1971; Cloward and Piven 1974). The management of this process fell very much within the domain of urban planning, and it generated conflicting ideological stances and world views within the planning profession itself. At first sight (and indeed at the time) it seemed as if planning theory was fragmented in the 1960s as different segments of the planning fraternity moved according to their position or inclination to one or the other pole of the ideological spectrum. With the benefit of hindsight, we can see that this process was nothing more than the internalization within the planning apparatus of conflicting social pressures and positions. And this internalization and the oppositions that it provoked proved functional, no matter what individuals thought or did. The technocrats helped to define the outer bounds of what could be done at the same time as they sought for new instrumentalities to accomplish dispersal and to establish social control. The advocates for the urban poor and the instrumentalities that they devised provided the channels for cooptation and integration at the same time as they pushed the system to provide whatever could be provided, being careful to stop short at the boundaries that the technocrats and "fiscal conservatives" helped to define. Those who pushed advocacy too far were either forced out or deserted planning altogether and became activists and political organizers.

Judged in terms of their own ideological rhetoric, the pursuers of social justice failed, much as they did in the Progressive Era, to accomplish what they set out to do, although the position of the "dangerous classes" in society undoubtedly improved somewhat in the late 1960s. But judged in relation to the reduction of civil strife, the reestablishment of social control, and the "saving" of the capitalist social order, the planning techniques and ideologies of the 1960s were highly successful. Those who inspired us in the 1960s can congratulate themselves on a job well done.

But conditions changed quite radically in 1969–70. Stagflation emerged as the most serious problem, and the negative growth rate of 1970 indicated that the fundamental processes of accumulation were in deep trouble. A loose monetary policy – the most potent tool in the management of the "political business cycle" – saw us through the election of 1972. But the boom was speculative and heavily dependent upon a massive overinvestment in the land, property, and construction sectors that easy money typically encourages. By the end of 1973 it was plain that the built environment could absorb no more in the way of surplus capital, and the rapid decline in property and construction, together with financial instability, triggered the subsequent depression.

Unemployment doubled, real wages began to move downward under the impact of severe "labor-disciplining" policies, social programs began to be savagely cut, and all of the gains made after a decade of struggle in the 1960s by the poor and underprivileged were rolled back almost within the space of a year. The underlying logic of capitalist accumulation asserted itself in the form of a crisis in which real wages diminished in order that inflation be stabilized and appropriate conditions for accumulation be reestablished.

The pressure from this underlying logic was felt in all spheres. Local budgets had to shift toward fiscal conservatism and had to alter priorities from social programs to programs to stimulate and encourage development (often by subsidies and tax benefits). Planners talked grimly of the "hard, tough decisions" that lay ahead. Those who sought social justice as an end in itself in the 1960s gradually shifted their ground as they began to argue that social justice could best be achieved by ensuring efficiency in government. Those who sought ecological balance and conservation in its own right in the 1960s began to appeal to principles of rational and efficient management of our resources. The technocrats began the search for ways to define more rational patterns of investment in the built environment, to calculate costs and benefits more finely than ever. The gospel of efficiency came to reign supreme.

All of this presupposes the capacity to accomplish a transformation of ideological balance within the planning fraternity – a transformation that turns out to be almost identical to that which was successfully accomplished during the Progressive Era. It can, of course, be done. But it takes effort and fairly sophisticated argument to do it. And the transformation is made that much easier because the fundamentals of ideology remain intact. The commitment to the ideology of harmony within the capitalist social order remains the still point upon which the gyrations of planning ideology turn.

But if we step aside and reflect awhile upon the tortuous twists and turns in our history, a shadow of doubt might cross our minds. Perhaps the most imposing and effective mystification of all lies in the presupposition of harmony at the still point of the turning capitalist world. Perhaps there lies at the fulcrum of capitalist history not harmony but a social relation of domination of capital over labor. And if we pursue this possibility, we might come to understand why the planner seems doomed to a life of perpetual frustration, why the high-sounding ideals of planning theory are so frequently translated into grubby practices on the ground, how the shifts in world view and in ideological stance are social products rather than freely chosen. And we might even come to see that it is the commitment to an alien ideology that chains our thought and understanding in order to legitimate a social practice that preserves, in a deep sense, the domination of capital over labor. Should we reach *that* conclusion, then we would surely witness a markedly different reconstruction of the planner's world view than we are currently seeing. We might even begin to plan the reconstruction of society, instead of merely planning the ideology of planning.

Notes

1   These various conceptions of the city can be found in, for example, L. Mumford (1961); J. Jacobs (1969); L. Wirth (1964); National Resources Committee (of the United States) (1937); and R. Meier (1962).
2   Economic cycles and in particular those associated with investment in the various components of the built environment are discussed in B. Thomas (1973); M. Abramovitz (1964); S. Kuznets (1961); and E. Mandel (1975).
3   Some idea of the extent of hegemonic control exercised by finance capital over the land and property market can be gained from L. Downie (1974); G. Barker, J. Penney, and W. Seccombe (1973); and P. Ambrose and R. Colenutt (1975).
4   The French urbanists have worked on this aspect most carefully as in M. Castells and F. Godard (1973) and C. G. Pickvance (1976). See also the various essays in *Antipode* 7, no. 4 – a special issue entitled *The Political Economy of Urbanism* – and D. Harvey (1975).
5   See, for example, E. Altvater (1973, 1:96–108 and 3:76–83); R. Miliband (1968); N. Poulantzas (1973); and J. O'Connor (1973).
6   A good example of how planners might move down such a path is written up in R. Goodman (1971).
7   See, for example, T. Bender (1975) and R. A. Walker (1976).
8   Again, the French urbanists have discussed this idea at length in, for example, E. Preteceille (1975) and M. Castells (1975).
9   There is an important connection between crises in ideology and legitimation – see, for example, J. Habermas (1975); for a history of shifting ideology in urban development, see R. A. Walker (1976).

References

Works by Marx

The poverty of philosophy. International Publishers, New York, 1963.
The eighteenth brumaire of Louis Bonaparte. International Publishers, New York, 1963.
Wages, price and profit. Foreign Languages Press, Peking, 1965.
Capital. 3 vols. International Publishers, New York, 1967.
Critique of Hegel's philosophy of right. Ed. J. O'Malley, Cambridge University Press, London, 1970.
Theories of surplus value. 3 vols. Lawrence and Wishart, London, pts. 1 and 2, 1969; pt. 3, 1972.

Grundrisse. Ed. M. Nicolaus. Penguin Publishers, Harmondsworth, Middlesex, 1973.

The results of the immediate process of production. Appendix to *Capital*, vol. 1. Ed. E. Mandel. Penguin Publishers, Harmondsworth, Middlesex, 1976.

Works by Marx and Engels

Manifesto of the Communist Party. Progress Publishers, Moscow, 1952.
Selected correspondence. Progress Publishers, Moscow, 1955.
The German ideology. Ed. C. J. Arthur. International Publishers, New York, 1970.
On colonialism. International Publishers, New York, 1972.
Ireland and the Irish question. Prepared by L. I. Goldman and V. E. Kumina. International Publishers, New York, 1972.

Other Works Cited

Abramovitz, M. 1964. *Evidences of long swings in aggregate construction since the Civil War*. New York.

Altvater, E. 1973. Notes on some problems of state interventionism. *Kapitalistate* 1:96–108.

Ambrose, P., and R. Colenutt. 1975. *The property machine*. Harmondsworth, Middlesex.

Barker, G., J. Penney, and W. Seccombe. 1973. *Highrise and superprofits*. Kitchener, Ontario.

Bender, T. 1975. *Toward an urban vision: Ideas and institutions in nineteenth-century America*. Lexington, Ky.

Castells, M. 1975. Collective consumption and urban contradictions in advanced capitalist societies. In *Patterns of advanced societies*, ed. L. Lindberg. New York.

Castells, M., and F. Godard. 1973. *Monopolville: L'enterprise, l'état, l'urbain*. The Hague.

Cloward, R., and F. Piven. 1974. *The politics of turmoil*. New York.

Downie, L. 1974. *Mortgage on America*. New York.

Godelier, M. [1966] 1972. *Rationality and irrationality in economics*. Trans. B. Pearce. London.

Goodman, R. 1971. *After the planners*. New York.

Habermas, J. [1973] 1975. *Legitimation crisis*. Trans. T. McCarthy. Boston.

Harvey, D. 1975. The political economy of urbanization in the advanced capitalist societies – the case of the United States. In *The social economy of cities*, ed. G. Gappert and H. Rose. Annual Review of Urban Affairs no. 9. Beverly Hills.

Harvey, D. 1982. *The limits to capital*. Oxford.

Jacobs, J. 1969. *The economy of cities*. New York.

Kuznets, S. 1961. *Capital in the American economy: Its formation and financing*. Princeton.

Mandel, E. [1972] 1975. *Late capitalism*. Trans. J. de Brés. London.

Miliband, R. 1968. *The state in capitalist society*. London.

Mumford, L. 1961. *The city in history*. New York.

O'Connor, J. 1973. *The fiscal crisis of the state*. New York.

Pickvance, C., ed. 1976. *Urban sociology: Critical essays*. London.

Piven, F., and R. Cloward. 1971. *Regulating the poor*. New York.

Poulantzas, N. [1968] 1973. *Political power and social classes*. Trans. and ed. T. O'Hagen. London.

Preteceille, E. 1975. *Equipements collectifs, structures urbaines, et consommation sociale.* Paris.

Tarr, J. 1973. From city to suburb: The "moral" influence of transportation technology. In *American Urban History*, ed. A. Callow. New York.

Thomas, B. 1972. *Migration and economic growth: A study of Great Britain and the Atlantic economy.* 2d ed., rev. London.

Walker, R. A. 1976. The suburban solution, Ph.D. diss., Department of Geography and Environmental Engineering, Johns Hopkins University, Baltimore.

Wirth, L. 1964. *On cities and social life.* Ed. A. J. Reiss, Jr. Chicago.

9

Can Selfishness Save the Environment?

Matt Ridley and Bobbi S. Low

John Hildebrand, who has lived in the Artesian Valley, near Fowler, Kansas, since he was two years old, remembers why the valley has the name it does. "There were hundreds of natural springs in this valley. If you drilled a well for your house, the natural water pressure was enough to go through your hot-water system and out the shower head." There were marshes in Fowler in the 1920s, where cattle sank to their bellies in mud. And the early settlers went boating down Crooked Creek, in the shade of the cottonwoods, as far as Meade, twelve miles away.

Today the creek is dry, the bogs and the springs have gone, and the inhabitants of Fowler must dig deeper and deeper wells to bring up water. The reason is plain enough: Seen from the air, the surrounding land is pockmarked with giant discs of green – quarter-section pivot-irrigation systems water rich crops of corn, steadily depleting the underlying aquifer. Everybody in Fowler knows what is happening, but it is in nobody's interest to cut down on individual consumption of water. That would just leave more for somebody else.

Five thousand miles to the east, near the Spanish city of Valencia, the waters of the River Turia are shared by some 15,000 farmers in an arrangement that dates back at least 550 years and probably longer. All farmers, when their turn comes, take as much water as they need from the distributory canal and waste none. They are discouraged from cheating – watering out of turn – merely by the watchful eyes of their neighbors above and below them on the canal. If they have a grievance,

---

they can take it to the Tribunal de las Aguas, which meets on Thursday mornings outside the Apostles' door of the Cathedral of Valencia. Records dating back to the 1400s suggest that cheating is rare. The *huerta* of Valencia is a profitable region, growing at least two crops a year.

Two irrigation systems: one sustainable, equitable, and long-lived, the other a doomed free-for-all. Two case histories cited by political scientists who struggle to understand the persistent human failure to solve "common pool resource problems." Two models for how the planet Earth might be managed in an age of global warming. The atmosphere is just like the aquifer beneath Fowler or the waters of the Turia: limited and shared. The only way we can be sure not to abuse it is by self-restraint. And yet nobody knows how best to persuade the human race to exercise self-restraint.

At the center of all environmentalism lies a problem: whether to appeal to the heart or to the head – whether to urge people to make sacrifices on behalf of the planet or to accept that they will not, and instead rig the economic choices so that they find it rational to be environmentalist. It is a problem that most activists in the environmental movement barely pause to recognize. Good environmental practice is compatible with growth, they insist, so it is rational as well as moral. Yet if this were so, good environmental practice would pay for itself, and there would be no need to pass laws to deter polluters or regulate emissions. A country or a firm that cut corners on pollution control would have no cost advantage over its rivals.

Those who do recognize this problem often conclude that their appeals should not be made to self-interest but rather should be couched in terms of sacrifice, selflessness, or, increasingly, moral shame.

We believe they are wrong. Our evidence comes from a surprising convergence of ideas in two disciplines that are normally on very different tracks: economics and biology. It is a convergence of which most economists and biologists are still ignorant, but a few have begun to notice. "I can talk to evolutionary biologists," says Paul Romer, an economist at the University of California at Berkeley and the Canadian Institute for Advanced Research in Toronto, "because, like me, they think individuals are important. Sociologists still talk more of the action of classes rather than individuals." Gary Becker, who won the Nobel Prize in economics last year, has been reading biological treatises for years; Paul Samuelson, who won it more than twenty years ago, has published several papers recently applying economic principles to biological problems. And biologists such as John Maynard Smith and William Hamilton have been raiding economics for an equally long time. Not that all economists and biologists agree – that would be impossible. But there are emerging orthodoxies in both disciplines that are strikingly parallel.

The last time that biology and economics were engaged was in the

Social Darwinism of Herbert Spencer and Francis Galton. The precedent is not encouraging. The economists used the biologists' idea of survival of the fittest to justify everything from inequalities of wealth to racism and eugenics. So most academics are likely to be rightly wary of what comes from the new entente. But they need not fear. This obsession is not with struggle but with cooperation.

For the Good of the World?

Biologists and economists agree that cooperation cannot be taken for granted. People and animals will cooperate only if they as individuals are given reasons to do so. For economists that means economic incentives; for biologists it means the pursuit of short-term goals that were once the means to reproduction. Both think that people are generally not willing to pay for the long-term good of society or the planet. To save the environment, therefore, we will have to find a way to reward individuals for good behavior and punish them for bad. Exhorting them to self-sacrifice for the sake of "humanity" or "the earth" will not be enough.

This is utterly at odds with conventional wisdom. "Building an environmentally sustainable future depends on restructuring the global economy, major shifts in human reproductive behavior, and dramatic changes in values and lifestyles," wrote Lester Brown, of the Worldwatch Institute, in his *State of the World* for 1992, typifying the way environmentalists see economics. If people are shortsighted, an alien value system, not human nature, is to blame.

Consider the environmental summit at Rio de Janeiro last year. Behind its debates and agreements lay two entirely unexamined assumptions: that governments could deliver their peoples, and that the problem was getting people to see the global forest beyond their local trees. In other words, politicians and lobbyists assume that a combination of international treaties and better information can save the world. Many biologists and economists meanwhile assert that even a fully informed public, whose governments have agreed on all sorts of treaties, will still head blindly for the cliff of oblivion.

Three decades ago there was little dissonance between academic thinking and the environmentalists' faith in the collective good. Biologists frequently explained animal behavior in terms of the "good of the species," and some economists were happy to believe in the Great Society, prepared to pay according to its means for the sake of the general welfare of the less fortunate. But both disciplines have undergone radical reformations since then. Evolutionary biology has been transformed by the "selfish gene" notion, popularized by Richard Dawkins of Oxford University, which essentially asserts that animals, including man, act altruistically only when it brings some benefit to copies of their own genes. This happens under two circumstances: when the altruist and the beneficiary are close relatives, such as bees in a hive, and when the altruist is in a position to have the favor returned at a later date. This new view holds that there simply are no cases of cooperation in the animal kingdom except these. It took root with an eye-opening book called *Adaptation and Natural Selection* (1966), by George Williams, a professor of biological sciences at the State University of New York at Stony Brook. Williams's message was that evolution pits individuals against each other far more than it pits species or groups against each other.

By coincidence (Williams says he was unaware of economic theory at the time), the year before had seen the publication of a book that was to have a similar impact on economics. Mancur Olson's *Logic of Collective Action* set out to challenge the notion that individuals would try to further their collective interest rather than their short-term individual interests. Since then economics has hewed ever more closely to the idea that societies are sums of their individuals, each acting in rational self-interest, and policies that assume otherwise are doomed. This is why it is so hard to make a communist ideal work, or even to get the American electorate to vote for any of the sacrifices necessary to achieve deficit reduction.

And yet the environmental lobby posits a view of the human species in which individual self-interest is not the mainspring of human conduct. It proposes policies that assume that when properly informed of the long-term collective consequences of their actions, people will accept the need for rules that impose restraint. One of the two philosophies must be wrong. Which?

We are going to argue that the environmental movement has set itself an unnecessary obstacle by largely ignoring the fact that human beings are motivated by self-interest rather than collective interests. But that does not mean that the collective interest is unobtainable: Examples from biology and economics show that there are all sorts of ways to make the individual interest concordant with the collective – so long as we recognize the need to.

The environmentalists are otherwise in danger of making the same mistakes that Marxists made, but our point is not political. For some reason, it is thought conservative to believe that human nature is inherently incapable of ignoring individual incentives for the greater good and liberal to believe the opposite. But in practice liberals often believe just as strongly as conservatives in individual incentives that are not monetary. The threat of prison, or even corporate shame, can be incentives to polluters. The real divide comes between those who believe it is necessary to impose such incentives and those who hope to persuade merely by force of argument.

Wherever environmentalism has succeeded, it has done so by changing individual incentives, not by exhortation, moral reprimand, or appeals to our better natures. If somebody wants to dump a toxic chemical or smuggle an endangered species, it is the thought of prison or a fine that deters him. If a state wants to avoid enforcing the federal Clean Air Act of 1990, it is the thought of eventually being "bumped up" to a more stringent nonattainment category of the act that haunts state officials. Given that this is the case, environmental policy should be a matter of seeking the most enforceable, least bureaucratic, cheapest, most effective incentives. Why should these always be sanctions? Why not some prizes, too? Nations, states, local jurisdictions, and even firms could contribute to financial rewards for the "greenest" of their fellow bodies.

Playing Games with Life

The new convergence of biology and economics has been helped by a common methodology – game theory. John Maynard Smith, a professor of biology at the University of Sussex in Britain, was the first effectively to apply the economist's habit of playing a "game" with competing strategies to evolutionary enigmas, the only difference being that the economics games reward winners with money, whereas evolutionary games reward winners with the chance to survive and breed. One game in particular has proved especially informative in both disciplines: the prisoner's dilemma.

A dramatized version of the game runs as follows: Two guilty accomplices are held in separate cells and interrogated by the police. Each is faced with a dilemma. If they both confess (or "defect"), they will both go to jail for three years. If they both stay silent (or "cooperate"), they will both go to jail for a year on a lesser charge that the police can prove. But if one confesses and the other does not, the defector will walk free on a plea bargain, while the cooperator, who stayed silent, will get a five-year sentence.

Assuming that they have not discussed the dilemma before they were arrested, can each trust his accomplice to stay silent? If not, he should defect and reduce his sentence from five to three years. But even if he can rely on his partner to cooperate, he is still better off if he defects, because that reduces his sentence from three years to none at all. So each will reason that the right thing to do is to defect, which results in three years for each of them. In the language of game theorists, individually rational strategies result in a collectively irrational outcome.

Biologists were interested in the prisoner's dilemma as a model for the evolution of cooperation. Under what conditions, they wanted to know, would it pay an animal to evolve a strategy based on cooperation rather than defection? They discovered that the bleak message of the prisoner's dilemma need not obtain if the game is only one in a long series – played by students, researchers, or computers, for points rather than years in jail. Under these circumstances the best strategy is to cooperate on the first trial and then do whatever the other guy did last time. This strategy became known as tit-for-tat. The threat of retaliation makes defection much less likely to pay. Robert Axelrod, a political scientist, and William Hamilton, a biologist, both at the University of Michigan, discovered by public tournament that there seems to be no strategy that beats tit-for-tat. Tit-for-two-tats – that is, cooperate even if the other defects once, but not if he defects twice – comes close to beating it, but of hundreds of strategies that have been tried, none works better. Field biologists have been finding tit-for-tat at work throughout the animal kingdom ever since. A female vampire bat, for example, will regurgitate blood for another, unrelated, female bat that has failed to find a meal during the night – but not if the donee has refused to be similarly generous in the past.

Such cases have contributed to a growing conviction among biologists that reciprocity is the basis of social life in animals like primates and dolphins, too. Male dolphins call in their debts when collecting allies to help them abduct females from other groups. Baboons and chimpanzees remember past favors when coming to one another's aid in fights. And human beings? Kim Hill and Hillard Kaplan of the University of New Mexico have discovered that among the Ache people of Paraguay, successful hunters share spare meat with those who have helped them in the past or might help them in the future.

The implication of these studies is that where cooperation among individuals does evolve, surmounting the prisoner's dilemma, it does so through tit-for-tat. A cautious exchange of favors enables trust to be built upon a scaffolding of individual reward. The conclusion of biology, in other words, is a hopeful one. Cooperation can emerge naturally. The collective interest can be served by the pursuit of selfish interests.

The Tragedy of the Commons

Economists are interested in the prisoner's dilemma as a paradoxical case in which individually rational behavior leads to collectively irrational results – both accomplices spend three years in jail when they could have spent only one. This makes it a model of a "commons" problem, the archetype of which is the history of medieval English common land. In 1968 the ecologist Garrett Hardin wrote an article in *Science* magazine that explained "the tragedy of the commons" – why common land tended to suffer from overgrazing, and why every sea fishery suffers from over-fishing. It is because the benefits that each extra cow (or netful of fish) brings are reaped by its owner, but the costs of the extra strain it puts on the grass (or on fish stocks) are shared among all the users of what is held in common. In economic jargon, the costs are externalized. Individually rational behavior deteriorates into collective ruin.

The ozone hole and the greenhouse effect are classic tragedies of the commons in the making: Each time you burn a gallon of gas to drive into town, you reap the benefit of it, but the environmental cost is shared with all five billion other members of the human race. You are a "free rider." Being rational, you drive; the atmosphere's capacity to absorb carbon dioxide is "overgrazed," and the globe warms. Even if individuals will benefit in the long run from the prevention of global warming, in the short run such prevention will cost them dear. As Michael McGinnis and Elinor Ostrom of Indiana University at Bloomington put it in a recent paper, global warming is a "classic dilemma of collective action: a large group of potential beneficiaries facing diffuse and uncertain gains is much harder to organize for collective action than clearly defined groups who are being asked to suffer easily understandable costs."

Hardin recognized two ways to avoid overexploiting commons. One is to privatize them, so that the owner has both costs and benefits. Now he has every incentive not to overgraze. The other is to regulate them by having an outside agency with the force of law behind it – a government, in short – restrict the number of cattle.

At the time Hardin published his article, the latter solution was very popular. Governments throughout the world reacted to the mere existence of a commons problem by grabbing powers of regulation. Most egregiously, in the Indian subcontinent communally exploited forests and grasslands were nationalized and put under the charge of centralized bureaucracies far away. This might have worked if governments were competent and incorruptible, and had bottomless resources to police their charges. But it made problems worse, because the forest was no longer the possession of the local village even collectively. So the grazing, poaching, and logging intensified – the cost had been externalized not just to the rest of the village but to the entire country.

The whole structure of pollution regulation in the United States represents a centralized solution to a commons problem. Bureaucrats decide, in response to pressure from lobbyists, exactly what levels of pollution to allow, usually give no credit for any reductions below the threshold, and even specify the technologies to be used (the "best available technology" policy). This creates perverse incentives for polluters, because it makes pollution free up to the threshold, and so there is no encouragement to reduce pollution further. Howard Klee, the director of regulatory affairs at Amoco Corporation, gives a dramatic account of how topsy-turvy this world of "command and control" can become. "If your company does voluntary control of pollution rather than waiting for regulation, it is punished by putting itself at a comparative disadvantage. The guy who does nothing until forced to by law is rewarded." Amoco and the Environmental Protection Agency did a thorough study of one refinery in Yorktown, Virginia, to discover what pollutants came out from it and how dangerous each was. Their conclusion was startling. Some of the things that Amoco and other refiners were required to do by EPA regulations were less effective than alternatives; meanwhile, pollution from many sources that government does not regulate could have been decreased. The study group concluded that for one-fourth of the amount that it currently spends on pollution control, Amoco could achieve the same effect in protection of health and the environment – just by spending money where it made a difference, rather than where government dictated.

A more general way, favored by free-market economists, of putting the same point is that regulatory regimes set the value of cleanliness at zero: if a company wishes to produce any pollutant, at present it can do so free, as long as it produces less than the legal limit. If, instead, it had to buy a quota from the government, it would have an incentive to drive emissions as low as possible to keep costs down, and the government would have a source of revenue to spend on environmental protection. The 1990 Clean Air Act set up a market in tradable pollution permits for sulfur dioxide emission, which is a form of privatization.

The Pitfalls of Privatization

Because privatizing a common resource can internalize the costs of damaging it, economists increasingly call for privatization as the solution to commons problems. After all, the original commons – common grazing land in England – were gradually "enclosed" by thorn hedges and divided among private owners. Though the reasons are complex, among them undoubtedly was the accountability of the private landowner. As Sir Anthony Fitzherbert put it in *The Boke of Husbandrie* (1534): "And thoughe a man be but a farmer, and shall have his farm XX [20] yeres, it is lesse coste to hym, and more profyte to quyckeset [fence with thorns], dyche and hedge, than to have his cattell goo before the herdeman [on common land]." The hawthorn hedge did for England what barbed wire did for the prairies – it privatized a common.

It would be possible to define private property rights in clean air. Paul Romer of Berkeley points out that the atmosphere is not like the light from a lighthouse, freely shared by all users. One person cannot use a given chunk of air for seeing through – or comfortably breathing – after another person has filled it with pollution, any more than two people in succession can kill the same whale. What stands in the way of privatizing whales or the atmosphere is that enforcement of a market would require as large a bureaucracy as if the whole thing had been centralized in the first place.

The privatization route has other drawbacks. The enclosure movement itself sparked at least three serious rebellions against the established order by self-employed yeomen dispossessed when commons were divided. It would be much the same today. Were whale-killing rights to be auctioned to the highest bidder, protectors (who would want to buy rights in order to let them go unused) would likely be unable to match the buying power of the whalers. If U.S. citizens were to be sold shares in their national parks, those who would rather operate strip mines or charge access might be prepared to pay a premium for the shares, whereas those who would keep the parks pristine and allow visitors free access might not.

Moreover, there is no guarantee that rationality would call for a private owner of an environmental public good to preserve it or use it sustainably. Twenty years ago Colin Clark, a mathematician at the University of British Columbia, wrote an article in *Science* pointing out that under certain circumstances it might make economic sense to exterminate whales. What he meant was that because interest rates could allow money to grow faster than whales reproduce, even somebody who had a certain monopoly over the world's whales and could therefore forget about free riders should not, for reasons of economic self-interest, take a sustainable yield of the animals. It would be more profitable to kill them all, bank the proceeds, sell the equipment, and live off the interest.

So until recently the economists had emerged from their study of the prisoner's dilemma more pessimistic than the biologists. Cooperation, they concluded, could not be imposed by a central bureaucracy, nor would it emerge from the allocation of private property rights. The destructive free-for-all of Fowler, Kansas, not the cooperative harmony of Valencia's *huerta*, was the inevitable fate of common-pool resources.

The Middle Way

In the past few years, however, there has been a glint of hope amid the gloom. And it bears an uncanny similarity to tit-for-tat, in that it rewards cooperators with cooperation and punishes defectors with defection – a strategy animals often use. Elinor Ostrom and her colleagues at Indiana University have made a special study of commons problems that were solved, including the Valencia irrigation system, and she finds that the connective thread is neither privatization nor centralization. She believes that local people can and do get together to solve their difficulties, as long as the community is small, stable, and communicating and has a strong concern for the future. Among the examples she cites is a Turkish inshore fishery at Alanya. In the 1970s the local fishermen fell into the usual trap of heavy fishing, conflict, and potential depletion. But they then developed an ingenious and complicated set of rules, allocating by lot each known fishing location to a licensed fisher in a pattern that rotates through the season. Enforcement is done by the fishermen themselves, though the government recognizes the system in law.

Valencia is much the same. Individuals know each other and can quickly identify cheaters. Just as in tit-for-tat, because the game is played again and again, any cheater risks ostracism and sanction in the next round. So a small, stable community that interacts repeatedly can find a way to pursue the collective interest – by altering the individual calculation.

"There's a presumption out there that users always overexploit a common resource," Ostrom says, "and therefore governments always have to step in and set things right. But the many cases of well-governed and -managed irrigation systems, fisheries, and forests show this to be an inadequate starting point. A faraway government could never have found the resources to design systems like Alanya." Ostrom is critical of the unthinking application of oversimplified game-theory models because, she says, economists and biologists alike frequently begin to believe that people who have depended on a given economic or bio-logical resource for centuries are incapable of communicating, devising rules, and monitoring one another. She admits that cooperation is more likely in small groups that have common interests and the autonomy to create and enforce their own rules.

Some biologists go further and argue that even quite big groups can cooperate. Egbert Leigh, of the Smithsonian Tropical Research Institute, points out that commons problems go deep into the genetics of animals and plants. To run a human body, 75,000 different genes must "agree" to cooperate and suppress free riders (free-riding genes, known as out-law genes, are increasingly recognized as a major force in evolution). Mostly they do, but why? Leigh found the answer in Adam Smith, who argued, in Leigh's words, that "if individuals had sufficient common interest in their group's good, they would combine to suppress the activ-ities of members acting contrary to the group's welfare." Leigh calls this idea a "parliament of genes," though it is crucial to it that all members of such a parliament would suffer if cooperation broke down – as the members of real national parliaments do not when they impose local solutions.

What Changed Du Pont's Mind?

For all these reasons, cooperation ought not to be a problem in Fowler, Kansas – a community in which everybody knows everybody else and shares the immediate consequences of a tragedy of the commons. Professor Kenneth Oye, the director of the Center for International

Studies at the Massachusetts Institute of Technology, first heard about Fowler's sinking water table when his wife attended a family reunion there.

Oye's interest was further piqued when he subsequently heard rumors that the state had put a freeze on the drilling of new wells in the Fowler area: Such a move might be the beginning of a solution to the water depletion, but it was also a classic barrier to the entry of new competitors in an industry. Oye had been reflecting on the case of Du Pont and chlorofluorocarbons (CFCs), wondering why a corporation would willingly abandon a profitable business by agreeing to phase out the chemicals that seem to damage the ozone layer. Du Pont's decision stands out as an unusually altruistic gesture amid the selfish strivings of big business. Without it the Montreal protocol on ozone-destroying chemicals, a prototype for international agreements on the environment, might not have come about. Why had Du Pont made that decision? Conventional wisdom, and Du Pont's own assertions, credit improved scientific understanding and environmental pressure groups. Lobbyists had raised public consciousness about the ozone layer so high that Du Pont's executives quickly realized that the loss of public goodwill could cost them more than the products were worth. This seems to challenge the logic of tit-for-tat. It suggests that appeals to the wider good can be effective where appeals to self-interest cannot.

Oye speculates that this explanation was incomplete, and that the company's executives may have been swayed in favor of a ban on CFCs by the realization that the CFC technology was mature and vulnerable. Du Pont was in danger of losing market share to its rivals. A ban beginning ten years hence would at least make it worth no potential rival's while to join in; Du Pont could keep its market share for longer and meanwhile stand a chance of gaining a dominant market share of the chemicals to replace CFCs. Again self-interest was part of the motive for environmental change. If consciousness raising really changes corporate minds, why did the utility industry fight the Clean Air Act of 1990 every step of the way? The case of Du Pont is not, after all, an exception to the rule that self-interest is paramount.

The Intangible Carrots

Besides, environmentalists cannot really believe that mere consciousness raising is enough or they would not lobby so hard in favor of enforceable laws. About the only cases in which they can claim to have achieved very much through moral suasion are the campaigns against furs and ivory. There can be little doubt that the world's leopards breathe easier because of the success of campaigns in recent decades against the wearing of furs. There was no need to bribe rich socialites to wear fake furs – they were easily shamed into it. But then shame can often be as effective an incentive as money.

Certainly the environmental movement believes in the power of shame, but it also believes in appealing to people's better natures. Yet the evidence is thin that normative pressures work for necessities. Furs are luxuries; and recycling works better with financial incentives or legal sanctions attached. Even a small refund can dramatically increase the amount of material that is recycled in household waste. In one Michigan study recycling rates were less than 10 percent for nonrefundable glass, metal, and plastic and more than 90 per cent for refundable objects. Charities have long known that people are more likely to make donations if they are rewarded with even just a tag or a lapel pin. Tit-for-tat.

The issue of normative pressure versus material incentive comes into sharp focus in the ivory debate. Western environmentalists and East African governments argue that the only hope for saving the elephant is to extinguish the demand for ivory by stifling supply and raising environmental consciousness. Many economists and southern African governments argue otherwise: that local people need incentives if they are to tolerate and protect elephants, incentives that must come from a regulated market for ivory enabling sustained production. Which is right depends on two things: whether it is possible to extinguish the demand for ivory in time to save the elephants, and whether the profits from legal ivory trading can buy sufficient enforcement to prevent poaching at home.

Even if it proved possible to make ivory so shameful a purchase that demand died, this would be no precedent for dealing with global warming. By giving up ivory, people are losing nothing. By giving up carbon dioxide, people are losing part of their standard of living.

Yet again and again in recent years environmentalists have persisted in introducing an element of mysticism and morality into the greenhouse debate, from Bill McKibben's nostalgia about a nature untouched by man in *The End of Nature* to James Lovelock's invention of the Gaia hypothesis. Others have often claimed that a mystical and moral approach works in Asia, so why not here? The reverence for nature that characterizes the Buddhist, Jain, and Hindu religions stands in marked contrast to the more exploitative attitudes of Islam and Christianity. Crossing the border from India to Pakistan, one is made aware of the difference: The peacocks and monkeys that swarm, tame and confident, over every Indian temple and shrine are suddenly scarce and scared in the Muslim country.

In surveying people's attitudes around the Kosi Tappu wildlife reserve in southeastern Nepal, Joel Heinen of the University of Michigan discovered that Brahmin Hindus and Buddhists respect the aims of conservation programs much more than Muslims and low-caste Hindus. Nonetheless, religious reverence did not stand in the way of the overexploitation of nature. Heinen told us, "Sixty-five percent of the households in my survey expressed negative attitudes about the reserve, because the reserve took away many rights of local citizens." Nepal's and India's forests, grasslands, and rivers have suffered tragedies of the commons as severe as any country's. The eastern religious harmony with nature is largely lip service.

The Golden Age that Never Was

In recent years those who believe that the narrow view of selfish rationalism expressed by economists and biologists is a characteristically Western concept have tended to stress not Buddhist peoples but preindustrial peoples living close to nature. Indeed, so common is the view that all environmental problems stem from man's recent and hubristic attempt to establish dominion over nature, rather than living in harmony with it, that this has attained the status of a cliché, uttered by politicians as diverse as Pope John Paul II and Albert Gore. It is a compulsory part of the preface in most environmental books.

If the cliché is true, then the biologists and economists are largely wrong. Individuals can change their attitudes and counteract selfish ambitions. If the cliché is false, then it is the intangible incentive of shame, not the appeal to collective interest, that changes people's minds.

Evidence bearing on this matter comes from archeologists and anthropologists. They are gradually reaching the conclusion that preindustrial people were just as often capable of environmental mismanagement as modern people, and that the legend of an age of environmental harmony – before we "lost touch with nature" – is a myth. Examples are now legion. The giant birds of Madagascar and New Zealand were almost certainly wiped out by man. In 2,000 years the Polynesians converted Easter Island, in the eastern Pacific, from a lush forest that provided wood for fishing canoes into a treeless, infertile grassland where famine, warfare, and cannibalism were rife. Some archeologists believe that the Mayan empire reduced the Yucatán peninsula to meager scrub, and so fatally wounded itself. The Anasazi Indians apparently deforested a vast area.

History abounds with evidence that limitations of technology or demand, rather than a culture of self-restraint, are what has kept tribal people from overgrazing their commons. The Indians of Canada had the technology to exterminate the beaver long before white men arrived; at that point they changed their behavior not because they lost some ancient reverence for their prey but because for the first time they had an insatiable market for beaver pelts. The Hudson's Bay Company would trade a brass kettle or twenty steel fishhooks for every pelt.

Cause for Hope

We conclude that the cynicism of the economist and the biologist about man's selfish, shortsighted nature seems justified. The optimism of the environmental movement about changing that nature does not. Unless we can find a way to tip individual incentives in favor of saving the atmosphere, we will fail. Even in the preindustrial state or with the backing of a compassionate, vegetarian religion, humanity proves incapable of overriding individual greed for the good of large, diverse groups. So must we assume that we are powerless to avert the tragedy of the aerial commons, the greenhouse effect?

Fortunately not. Tit-for-tat can come to the rescue. If the principles it represents are embodied in the treaties and legislation that are being written to avert global warming, then there need be no problem in producing an effective, enforceable, and acceptable series of laws.

Care will have to be taken that free-rider countries don't become a problem. As Robert Keohane of Harvard University's Center for International Affairs has stressed, the commons problem is mirrored at the international level. Countries may agree to treaties and then try to free-ride their way past them. Just as in the case of local commons, there seem to be two solutions: to privatize the issue and leave it to competition between sovereign states (that is, war), or to centralize it and enforce obedience (that is, world government). But Keohane's work on international environmental regimes to control such things as acid rain, oil pollution, and overfishing came to much the same conclusion as Ostrom's: a middle way exists. Trade sanctions, blackmail, bribes, and even shame can be used between sovereign governments to create incentives for cooperation as long as violations can be easily detected. The implicit threat of trade sanctions for CFC manufacture is "a classic piece of tit-for-tat," Paul Romer observes.

Local governments within the nation can play tit-for-tat as well. The U.S. government is practiced at this art: it often threatens to deprive states of highway construction funds, for example, to encourage them to pass laws. States can play the same game with counties, or cities, or firms, and so on down to the level of the individual, taking care at each stage to rig the incentives so that obedience is cheaper than disobedience. Any action that raises the cost of being a free rider, or raises the reward of being a cooperator, will work. Let the United States drag its feet over the Rio conventions if it wants, but let it feel the sting of some sanction for doing so. Let people drive gas-guzzlers if they wish, but tax them until it hurts. Let companies lobby against antipollution laws, but pass laws that make obeying them worthwhile. Make it rational for individuals to act "green."

If this sounds unrealistic, remember what many environmental lobbyists are calling for. "A fundamental restructuring of many elements of society," Lester Brown proposes, "a whole new economic order." "Modern society will find no solution to the ecological problem unless it takes a serious look at its lifestyle," the Pope has said. These are hardly realistic aims.

We are merely asking governments to be more cynical about human nature. Instead of being shocked that people take such a narrow view of their interests, use the fact. Instead of trying to change human nature, go with the grain of it. For in refusing to put group good ahead of individual advantage, people are being both rational and consistent with their evolutionary past.

10

Between Modernity and Postmodernity: The Ambiguous Position of U.S. Planning

Robert A. Beauregard

Introduction

From the early decades of the twentieth century through the 1960s, state planning in the United States of America was able to maintain the integrity of its modernist project.[1] In that project, planners strove to (1) bring reason and democracy to bear on capitalist urbanization, (2) guide state decision making with technical rather than political rationality, (3) produce a coordinated and functional urban form organized around collective goals, and (4) use economic growth to create a middle-class society. Planners took on the challenge of an industrial capitalism forged in the nineteenth century and shaped a response to the turmoil of modernization. They did so shrouded in modernism, the "*cultural* precipitates of this socio-historical period" (Schulte-Sasse 1987, page 6).

By the 1980s, the modernist planning project was under attack. Some even talked about a crisis of state planning (Friedman 1987) emanating from a series of profound changes involving urban restructuring, state

Reprinted with permission from *Environment and Planning D: Society and Space*, Vol. 7, 1989, pp 381–95. Pion Limited, London.

politics, and cultural practices; each related to new activities and sensibilities often subsumed under a postmodern rubric. The landscape of postmodernity with its hypermobile capital, concentrations of advanced services, juxtaposition of vast wealth and extreme poverty, downscaled and customized production complexes, and deconcentrated central cities (Cooke 1988) poses novel and difficult problems for modernist planners. Moreover, the cultural practices of postmodernists undermine earlier commitments to a middle-class society, a disciplined urban form, the efficacy of rationalism, and political neutrality. U.S. planning thus finds itself suspended between modernity and postmodernity, with its practitioners and theorists astride an ever-widening chasm.

In this chapter my objectives are threefold. My first is to examine the historical roots of state planning, highlighting its modernist elements. My second is to argue that the deconstruction of modernist planning represents a clash between new (postmodern) and old (modern) forms of urban political economies and of social thought. Last, I will offer suggestions as to how planning practitioners and theorists might respond critically to a postmodern capital restructuring and cultural transformation, heeding its calls to be flexible and open but not abandoning the modernist quest for a democratic and reformist planning and a commitment to the city.

Historical Backdrop

The roots of U.S. state planning lie in the late nineteenth and early twentieth centuries and within local responses to the modern city: its physical degradation, functional chaos, and the miseries suffered by the working class (Gans 1968; McKelvey, 1963; Scott 1969; Sharpe and Wallock 1987). Although the planning of the built environment in the United States can be traced to the seventeenth-century European colonists (Foglesong 1986), the impetus for the institutionalization of planning grew out of social problems related to massive immigration, large-scale manufacturing, and the lack of controls over the built environment.

Planning took shape as part of a reform movement at the turn of the century, centered on the middle class and comprising diverse elements (Hofstadter 1955). One element was focused on the built environment and was mainly concerned with population congestion and public health. Reformers championed local legislation that would improve working-class slums by regulating the quality of the built environment through building and housing codes and instituted efforts to develop model, working-class housing (Fairbanks 1988). Public attention also turned to the provision of sanitation facilities and the imposition of public health regulations that would prevent the spatial diffusion of disease (Peterson

1983). These concerns intersected at the regulation of "nuisances" (for example, fire-prone laundries) that might create hazards and spread disease in residential areas.

Another group of reformers contributed to the establishment of state planning. Often referred to as "planners" rather than "housers," they concerned themselves, more broadly, with the emerging form of the industrial city and its chaotic juxtaposition of land uses (Boyer 1983). Joined with civic boosters, the planners supported rapid urban growth through the ordering of the built environment. Their actions were based on the notion that organized and physically coherent cities grounded in good functional and aesthetic principles are better than those that are not. This notion was inspired by an awareness of the anarchic qualities of capitalist urban development. Planners grasped early on that different capitalists pursue different spatial investment strategies in an uncoordinated fashion, thus creating an intracapitalist competition alongside a capital–labor struggle for control over the built environment. If the industrial city was to be an efficient mechanism for capital accumulation, and if labor was to be allowed respite from the ever-expanding oppression of the factory system and be given protection from unrestrained property capital (Walker 1978), someone had to bring order to its fragmented form.

The early planners thus undertook various "master planning" schemes that would arrange land-using activities in ways that achieved functional and aesthetic objectives. The Chicago World's Fair of 1893 set forth one model of downtown design that could be used to situate public buildings (for example, library, post office, city hall) and capitalist infrastructure (for instance, railroad stations, office structures) around public spaces. The aesthetic was unabashedly "classical " – linear, holistic, and heroic – and the functional concerns unequivocally supportive of the production and circulation of capital and the emergence of a new pact between capital and the state. In this way, the emerging political economy of industrial capitalism would be manifested in a planned built environment, with the additional benefit of utilizing such a scheme to eradicate slums. Expanded and subdued, that paradigm became the "master plan," a document taking into account the functional and economic determinants of urban activities and their proper aesthetic and spatial interrelationships.

Through the early decades of the twentieth century, this mode of planning practice held sway with only minor variations. Restrictive legislation on housing was partially displaced by a call for public housing, the 1920s witnessed greater emphasis on highway and subdivision planning, and zoning as a local regulatory device began to displace the master plan. After World War II, housing, zoning, and transportation planning flourished. Urban renewal was added to the practice of planners, itself helping to revive, though only temporarily, the master planning tradition. During its spurt of growth in the 1960s, planning practice diversified into a multitude of specialities: environmental, manpower, social planning, health planning, transportation, energy planning, and regional planning along with the traditional land use and housing (Beauregard 1986). Being a planner no longer meant regulating the spatial arrangements of land uses and providing housing. A variety of social planners challenged the increasingly specialized physical planners. As a result, planning practice underwent centrifugal disintegration. The common object of interest – the city – that had initially attracted "progressive" reformers was lost.

Theory and pedagogy

The history of practice, however, is only a partial history of planning. One must also pay attention to education and theory. University-based education for planners appeared in the late 1920s and remained relatively vocational until after World War II. At that time, planning education began to fracture into two camps: practitioners with professional degrees and theorists ordained as doctors of philosophy. Moreover, education became not only an occupational gateway but also a strong link between the practice and theory of planning, and between the actions of planners and the ideology that encased them.

Theoretically, planning has always been difficult to define; it can be said to have had only briefly a dominant paradigm and has remained on the fringes of critical social theory (Dear 1986; Friedmann 1987).[2] The planning extolled by the reformers of the Progressive Era was based on a mixture of common sense, emerging middle-class values of civic responsibility and organization, and selective elements of sociology and economics, all flavored with a strong sense of "classical" order related both to architecture and to the city. The central focus for reformers of housing and sanitation was the consequences for health of the slums, with theoretical understanding only partially advised by a rudimentary theory of disease. Those concerned with the city as a whole, people like Frederick Law Olmsted, organized their thinking mainly around organic analogies (Olmsted 1916), though many times the factory mentality induced the metaphor of the city as machine. During the interwar years (1918 to 1939), planning theory incorporated the Chicago school of sociology and human ecology to explain urban form and urban problems (Bailey 1975). Early planning theory was about the city and the built environment, and merged with practice; there were no "planning theorists," only reformers or practitioners with ideas about how the city should be structured.

After World War II, however, theory evolved as a specialization within planning (Beauregard 1987; Cooke 1983). The impetus was the Program in Education and Research in Planning at the University of Chicago (Sarbib, 1983). It was founded in 1947 with the goal of training

Ph.D. students and thereby establishing planning as a legitimate academic discipline rather than solely as a profession. One result was to move planning education away from a "studio" model based upon learning by doing, the utilization of paradigmatic examples, and postgraduate apprenticeship under a "master planner." The replacement was the pedagogical model of the lecture and seminar; knowledge was fragmented into subdisciplines, and students learnt through texts rather than direct problem solving. Once graduated, only a dose of on-the-job training was needed.

The second result was to sever professional training from academic training by creating a career path for teachers of planning that did not necessarily intersect with planning practice. This allowed for the emergence of planning theorists who erected the intellectual base for planning practice but did not themselves act as practitioners. Dual career paths, however, undermined the contribution to practice; theorists looked for validation within academia rather than without. The combination of an academic pedagogical model, severance from practice, and creation of alternative career paths was fertile ground for the emergence of abstract theorizing distanced from the performative demands of practitioners.

Nonetheless, a dominant theoretical paradigm emerged in the 1950s and 1960s to define the contribution of planning (Beauregard 1984): a comprehensive, rational model of problem solving and decision making to guide state intervention. Theorists of this model believed that they had found the intellectual core of planning: a set of procedures that would generate conceptual problems for theorists, serve as a joint object for theory and practice, and guide practitioners in their daily endeavors. This view proved to be erroneous; while early postwar theorists articulated this "essence" of planning, the modernist project on which such an essence was based was being eroded.

The Modernist Project of Planning

The initial thrusts of the modernist project of planning were to diminish the excesses of industrial capitalism while mediating the intramural frictions among capitalists that had resulted in a city inefficiently organized for production and reproduction. Planners were to do this from within local and, less so, state governments. Their planning project was modernist because it engaged the city of industrial capitalism and became institutionalized as a form of state intervention. Underlying these concrete manifestations are procedural assumptions and substantive commitments that sealed the fate of planning as a modernist project.

Procedural assumptions

In the modernist planning project, reality that can be controlled and perfected is assumed. The world is viewed as malleable, and it is malleable because its internal logic can be uncovered and subsequently manipulated. Thus, modernist planners rejected the alienation that is often viewed as part of modernization (Schulte-Sasse 1987) yet adopted a viewpoint, also modernist, that overcomes alienation through a belief in the efficacy of human action and the importance of commitment (Kraushaar 1988; Orwell 1953). Modernist planners believe in a future in which social problems are tamed and humanity liberated from the constraints of scarcity and greed (Hutcheon 1987; Jencks 1985). Social control is wielded in order to drive society forward along a path of progress; planning is part of the modern "struggle to make ourselves at home in a constantly changing world" (Berman 1988: 6).

Planners' involvement in this modernist struggle was not as people of action. Rather, their contribution was utilitarian understanding. Knowledge in planning would precede and shape the actions taken by investors, households, and governments. In effect, planning would liberate through enlightenment (Albertsen 1988; Friedmann 1987). Knowledge and reason would free people from fatalism and ideologies, allowing the logic intrinsic to an industrial society to be uncovered and exploited. Modernist planners thus situated themselves clearly within both a European rationalism and an American pragmatism (Hofstadter 1958; Scott and Shore 1979). To this extent, knowledge in planning had to be evaluated on a performative criterion, based as it was within a scientific mode of legitimation (Lyotard 1984). As such, planners were somewhat anti-intellectual; impatient with abstract theorizing and thus with social theory. Nevertheless, the aim of modernist planners was to act as experts who could utilize the laws of development to provide societal guidance.

Fostering the faith of modernist planners in the liberating and progressive potential of knowledge was their corresponding belief in their ability to maintain a critical distance (Bernstein 1987; Jameson 1984b). Planners laid claim to a scientific and objective logic that transcended the interests of capital, labor, and the state. This logic allowed modernist planners to disengage themselves from the interests of any particular group, avoid accusations of self-interest, and identify actions in the public interest, that is, actions that benefit society as an organic whole. Such an ideology served modernist planners in two ways: First, they could position themselves within the state without having to be labeled "political," and second, they could assert a mediative role between capital and labor.

Last, both the practice and theory of modernist planning revolves around the use of master narratives (Jameson 1984b). For practice, the narrative synthesizes developmental processes and the built environment into a coherent urban form that fulfills the functional necessities of the city. The text is the master plan. For theory, it involves the formulation of a dominant paradigm – comprehensive rationalism – that focuses the normal science of theorists. The "planning process" is its plot (Beauregard 1984). In essence, modernist planners believe in totalizing what planners call "comprehensive" solutions that have a unitary logic.

Substantive commitments

Such bowing to modernization is reflected in the substantive orientation of planning to the city and the state. As already mentioned, the modernist project is based upon a belief in the "synthetic" city; that is, the city of singular form invariant over time. This holistic and ahistoric perspective is derived from a revealed internal logic of how a city (under capitalism) functions. The task for planners is to take the fragments produced by the contradictions and struggles of capitalism and integrate them into a unique and orderly whole. As with modern art, "the unity of [planners'] work was assembled from fragments and juxtapositions" (Gitlin 1988: 35). This in turn enabled modernist planners to claim a privileged position in the realm of specialists; planners were to transcend specializations and provide the contextual integration for numerous experts involved in the reform of the industrial city.

The holism that modernist planners propounded was dependent both on the economic dynamics of the industrial city and on the parallel rise of a middle class. The "spatial paradigm" of modernist planning (Cooke 1988) was focused on the production of standard commodities for large markets, the importance of transportation infrastructure for the circulation of commodities, and the location of investment in proximity to labor. As well as disciplining the city for capital accumulation (Boyer 1983) and assuring an adequate supply of labor for the factories, however, planners had to meet the demands of a new administrative work force and an emerging professional stratum desirous of urban amenities (such as parks) and residential areas isolated from manufacturing districts. The contradiction between demands made on the work force by industrialists and the consumption demands of an emerging professional and managerial elite were reconciled in the minds of planners by a belief in the *embourgeoisement* of the working class. As capitalism was tamed, the city organized, and prosperity diffused socially and spatially, the lower classes would rise to affluence and take on the values and behaviors of the middle class (Gans 1968).

The expansion of the middle class also validated the belief that society was not riven by contradictions, and thus the city could be organized physically for "public" purposes. Invidious class distinctions were being erased by economic growth; thus the city could be viewed as the physical container for the workings of a conflict-free society (Hayden 1984).

Modernization, and thus progress, meant that the good life diffused across all groups, natives and immigrants alike.

Moreover, modernization was possible because the state had progressive tendencies to be reformist and serve the long-run needs of all groups. From the "progressive" perspective, the state could be an instrumentality representative of the interests of all its citizens as disclosed by the expertise of planners. In this way, modernist planners skirt the ideological issue of the compatibility of planning and democracy (Aptheker 1967; Hayek 1944). Instead, they rest easy on the democratic pretensions of the state and their privileged insights into the public interest.

Intrinsic to this perspective is a need for functional equilibrium. The singular, organic, and totalizing view taken of the city leaves little leeway for chaos and indeterminacy.[3] For the great majority of planners involved with the "city functional," the efficient organization of the city was the preferred social interest (Hall 1989). Reason replaced greed, and a nonpartisan logic displaced self-regarding behavior. The public interest would be revealed through a scientific understanding of the organic logic of society.

In terms of its interest in growth and quest for efficiency, the logic of planning overlapped with that of capital, but it denied capital's way of achieving them. The ideology of planning was more attuned to political reform embedded within the state, thus reinforcing the substantive commitment to a state that is external to the economy, a further manifestation of the adherence to the idea of keeping a critical distance. Without this understanding, planners could not view themselves as interceding without bias in the workings of capitalism, nor could they be reformers and governmental employees. Modernist planners thus adopted the separation of the political from the economic – the capitalist trenches (Katznelson 1981) – that channels oppositional movements and enables the capitalist state to be viewed as an arena for reform.

In sum, the modernist project is derived from beliefs about knowledge and society and is inextricably linked to the rise of capitalism, the formation of the middle class, the emergence of a scientific mode of legitimation, the concept of an orderly and spatially integrated city that meets the needs of society, and the fostering of the interventionist state. Technical rationality is viewed as a valid and superior means of making public decisions, and information gathered scientifically is regarded as enlightening, captivating, and convincing. The democratic state contains an inherent tendency to foster and support reform, whereas its planners maintain a critical distance from specialized interests. Such beliefs repeat and mimic beliefs about enlightenment that are associated with the rise of capitalist democracies and with the modernist quest for control and liberation.

Modernist Planning Besieged

Modernist planning began to come apart in the 1970s and 1980s (Dear 1986). Novel political forms, economic relations, and restructured cities posed new difficulties for the premises that underlie practice. The critical distance that modernist planners attempted to maintain was radically altered, and the emancipatory potential of planning was virtually abandoned. Numerous commentators began to ask, "Who controls planning?" In turn, the theoretical quest for a master narrative that could be applied both to the city and to planning thought was brought to an end by eclecticism and a reluctance to embrace social theory. Such changes reflect the realities of a post-Fordist political economy and postmodern cultural sensibilities.[4]

Practice

There are numerous versions of the most recent round of capital restructuring (Beauregard 1989; Bluestone and Harrison 1982; Bradbury 1985; Castells 1985; Chase-Dunn 1984; Fainstein and Fainstein 1989; Harrison and Bluestone 1988; Peet 1987; Soja et al. 1983). One dominant interpretation is that Fordist means, techniques, and social relations of production have been superseded by post-Fordist and postmodern forms: high-technology products and processes, an expanded emphasis on the financial circuit of capital, more flexible procedures in the workplace, and a defensive and weakened labor force (Albertsen 1988; Cooke 1988). The state has become more ideologically conservative and more subservient to the needs and demands of capital, turning away from the simultaneous pursuit of both economic growth and welfare. Although the needs and demands of capital are (still) achieved through state assistance, the state has turned away from the simultaneous pursuit of welfare and economic growth (Kantor 1988; Smith 1988). Local politics, moreover, increasingly pivots around economic development and jobs (Stone and Sanders 1987). New spatial forms also have appeared (Conzen 1988; Cooke 1988): a postmodern city to join the postmodern political economy of flexible accumulation and the globalization of capital (Harvey 1987; Soja 1986).

Whether one accepts this or another version of "late capitalism," contemporary restructuring of capital has made the practice of modernist planning more precarious. On the one hand, planners are increasingly vulnerable to property and industrial capital through the state's deepening involvement in capital accumulation. Thus, planners are less able to maintain a desired critical distance. Economic development is so highly valued by elected officials that planners, even if they were not to share this ideology of growth, would find it difficult, if not impossible, to oppose the state's complicity. The result has been a peculiar form of nonplanning in which planners participate in individual projects, often attempting to temper the most egregious negative externalities, while failing to place these projects into any broader framework of urban development, a basic tenet of modernist planning (Fainstein and Fainstein 1987; Goldberger 1989).

The totalizing vision and the reformist tendencies of modernist planning have been undermined. Comprehensive planning that articulates the organic integrity of the city has become politically untenable. Such planning requires a balancing of interests and a taming of the excesses of capital, thereby hindering economic expansion. Planners, however, are less and less able to maintain even the facade of being concerned with those outside the "loop" of economic prosperity. No longer is the idea to improve society. The new strategy is to flee the problems of society by creating wider and wider circles of growth (Logan and Molotch 1987). Economic development, not reform, is the political aim of the 1980s, and it sacrifices regulation and the welfare state to the lure of new investment and jobs.

Under modernist planning, reform and growth were viewed as compatible even if they were not pursued equally. This distinguished planners from property developers. Now, the two groups have formed public–private partnerships. Even the schools train students in real estate development, the cutting edge of planning education. Planning has become entrepreneurial, and planners have become deal makers rather than regulators (Fainstein 1988). The critical distance cherished by modernist planners is eroding.

In turn, the proponents of policies to promote local growth attempt, often unsuccessfully, to conduct their business outside the realm of public scrutiny and debate. Private–public partnerships and public authorities isolate development politics from democratic politics (Friedland et al. 1978). Decisions about subsidies to private property, industrial investment, and public infrastructure are cast as technical decisions, and thereby depoliticized and confined to the deliberations of experts. Yet because planners still talk about the public interest and the negative consequences of development, if not reform, they are also kept to the fringes of the discussion. Development politics are for development-oriented individuals trained in business schools and housed in quasi-public economic development agencies.

More than the politics of the modernist project have been undermined by the recent capital restructuring. The form and dynamics of the city have changed to such an extent that the principles of modernist planning are less credible (Cooke 1988; Simonsen 1988; Soja 1986; Zukin 1988). First, whereas modernist planners had assumed that local actions were determinative of local conditions, thus partially justifying local planning, that fiction has been severely compromised. The heightened spatial mobility of capital has made large-scale property development and industrial investment into affairs of regional, national, and even international proportions. Locational determinants of investment are increasingly ephemeral. State subsidies are ubiquitous, and the quality-of-life factors that attract "advanced service" industries and educated labor are hardly confined to a few global cities.

In addition, and in order to attract capital investment, civic boosters and economic development officials attempt to commodify the "particularities of place" through public spectacles and festival marketplaces (Harvey 1987). To the extent that communities rely on cultural conditions and social amenities to generate growth, they are even more vulnerable to the influence of capital over consumption and "lifestyles." Accumulation and consumption have become more flexible and less place-bound (Harvey 1987), and planners lack the legal capacity and political weight to reshape the investment and employment prerogatives of capital.

Second, planners' grasp of a functional and unitary notion of urban development is even less justifiable. The expanding urban economies of "Progressive Era" cities and of metropolitan economies of the postwar period seemed to offer opportunities to maximize the interests of all classes, but the increasing fragmentation of capital and labor in the postmodern era and the failure of growth to eliminate or even ameliorate tenacious inequalities of class, race, and gender make ludicrous any assumption of unitary planning. The emergence of the modern city neither brought forth a society whose many groups participated equally in affluence nor erased the manifestation of past injustices. Rather, the postmodern city is layered with historical forms and struggled over by fractions of capital and labor, each of which is dependent upon economic activities that are industrial and postindustrial, formal and informal, primary and secondary (Davis 1987; Soja 1986). Under such conditions, it is difficult to maintain a modernist commitment to a conflict-free public interest.

National attempts to obliterate class distinctions through prosperity and collective consumption and the local attempts to provide events (for example, multiethnic affairs) that celebrate yet minimize differences have not led to the *embourgeoisement* of the working class. Neighborhoods of "displaced" blue-collar workers in marginalized households, recent immigrants from Asia and Latin America, and the extremely wealthy coexist in numerous cities. Even more compelling is the continued existence and expansion of the black "underclass" and the poverty and unemployment experienced by white and nonwhite working-class households alike (Wilson 1987). The fringes of black, Hispanic, and other immigrant areas, moreover, are increasingly the sites of racial confrontations.

Last, the lessening of state controls and the deepening obeisance to capital investment have exacerbated the negative consequences of rapid economic growth and have even intensified the "seesaw" effect of uneven development (Smith 1984). Fueled by the hypermobility of capital, cities like Houston have experienced prosperity but not without wide-ranging social and environmental costs (Feagin 1988). Such conditions thwart movement to an ideal city. Instead, the city functions as a locus of unending struggle around the distribution of the costs and benefits of growth and decline. The implications for modernist planning are profound. Without a conflict-free society and the possibility of a single textual response, the modernist planning project is cut adrift.

In essence, the master narrative of modernist planning is incompatible with a spatially problematic and flexible urban form whose articulations are intrinsically confrontational and whose purposes are more and more the ephemeral ones of consumption. Subsequently, a modernist striving for orderliness, functional integration, and social homogeneity is unlikely to succeed, as is the desire on the part of planners to maintain a critical distance and apply technical rationalism. Broadly cast, modernist planners are in the grip of a postmodern helplessness (Gitlin 1988).

Theory

Theoretically, planning remains in a modernist mode. The literature on planning theory is devoid of attempts to view planning theory through the lens of the postmodern cultural critique. Rather, this theoretical investigation has been initiated by urban geographers, mainly Michael Dear, Phillip Cooke, David Harvey, Edward W. Soja, and Edward Relph. This does not mean that planning theory has remained unaffected. The turmoil attendant to modernist planning practice reverberates into academe as planning theorists reflect upon the nature of planning practice and consider how to educate students. Moreover, the work of the above-mentioned urban geographers has begun to diffuse into the literature on planning theory, posing a postmodern challenge to planning theorists as they look toward the social sciences for theoretical guidance.

The postmodernist cultural critique is a complex one. It includes a turn to historical allusion and spatial understandings, the abandonment of critical distance for ironic commentary, the embracing of multiple discourses and the rejection of totalizing ones, a skepticism toward master narratives and general social theories, a disinterest in the performativity of knowledge, the rejection of notions of progress and enlightenment, and a tendency toward political acquiescence (Bernstein 1987; Cooke 1988; Dear 1986; Gregory 1987; Jameson 1984a; Jencks 1985; Lyotard 1984; Relph 1987; Soja 1989). Each aspect challenges modernist planning theory.

To begin, the postmodern interest in space and time would seem, at first glance, to be supportive of modernist planning. Planners have made location central to their work and have always had a strong need to relate past trends to future possibilities. The postmodern debate is filled with commentary on the new hyperspaces of capitalism (Jameson 1984a), with the more empirical literature extolling the uniqueness of localities. At the same time, postmodernism involves a turn to the past, particularly in terms of urban design and architectural styles.

Excluding neo-Marxist political economy, modernist planning has been dominated by procedural theories; that is, generic, paradigmatic theories meant to be applicable regardless of context, thus leaving space and time unattended. Moreoever, the space and time of postmodernism are not the space and time of modernist planning. Planning theorists and practitioners cling to relativist and physically inert notions of space and a linear sense of time. The postmodern challenge is to conceive of space and time dialectically, socially, and historically; and to integrate such conceptions into a critical social theory. In turn, even though planning in the United States has been a local project, focusing mainly on communities, planning theorists have rejected materialist perspectives for idealistic ones and thus have difficulty relating to postmodern locality studies. Rather, too little attention is given to spatial scales and the interaction of the structural and the particular.

This theoretical stance indicates the way in which modernist planning theorists have interpreted the notion of maintaining a critical distance. With few exceptions (Davidoff 1965; Goodman 1971), they rejected the role of social critic. Despite the need for a radical critique of U.S. society, and the potential to do so when subsidized and protected by an academic position, theorists did not challenge the prevailing orthodoxy concerning the domestic benefits of economic growth. Rather, most retreated from political involvement, content to accept the "end of ideology" and thus to abandon a modernist commitment to reform. Prior to the 1960s, then, criticism centered on planning theories, specifically the comprehensive rational model. Modernist planning theorists turned away from the realities of planning practice and engaged in internal academic debates. Any commitment to being "public" was cast aside (Jacoby 1987). The critics within planning who emerged in the 1960s to debunk the conservative politics and middle-class bias of planning made explicit connections between the racism and inequality of U.S. society and planning, but they did not venture outside the profession to share their criticism with a wider public.

For theorists, the modernist commitment to a master narrative became at once easier and more difficult as academic forces increasingly distanced them from practitioners and isolated them from public debates. Practice no longer constrained their thoughts with pragmatic, political economic realities. As a body, planning theorists became highly eclectic, pursuing theoretical projects for their own sake. Collectively, they lost the object, the city, that had given planning its legitimacy. Their new objects – the planning process, policy making, decision making, and so on – were only tangentially the objects of practitioners; they were procedurally relevant, but not substantively so.

This postmodern fragmentation of planning theory would have been acceptable if it had paralleled a corresponding adoption of an integrative framework that critiqued society and advanced planning practice. Theorists did look toward economic, management science, and mathematics for a synthesis. However, the modernist disciplinary blinders that come with these bodies of knowledge only narrowed the theoretical perspectives of planners. The great nineteenth-century theories of Charles Darwin, Emile Durkheim, Sigmund Freud, and Max Weber, for example, have not been plumbed for their views on society and relevance for planning. References to twentieth-century grand theorists such as Michel Foucault, Claude Lévi-Strauss, Ferdinand Braudel, and even Lewis Mumford are just as rare.

Planning theorists operating with a leftist or neo-Marxist perspective have been more sensitive to integrative social theories and to broad and significant transformations under way in society. Friedmann (1987) is certainly attuned to deep intellectual currents, Forester (1989) has made major advances in planning theory by building on the ideas of Habermas, and Boyer's history of U.S. planning (1983) owes much to the structuralism of Foucault. The neo-Marxists (for example, Fainstein and Fainstein 1979; Harvey 1978) have prepared a powerful critique of the function of planning under capitalism but offer little guidance in practical affairs. Hayden's feminist analysis (1984) and Clavel's (1986) investigation of progressive planning have been successful in linking social theory to planning practice. Neither, however, has crystallized planning thought or attracted many adherents.

Planning theorists, with the above exceptions, have thus avoided the task of making sense of the post-Fordist economy and the postmodern city. They are silent about spatiality and treat planning ahistorically, despite a recent surge of interest in planning history. While other disciplines look outward (Dear 1988; Soja 1989), most planning theorists turn inward to planning pedagogy rather than to the social context of practice.

The postmodern cultural and literary theories that speak of the demise of the master narrative, the bankruptcy of positivism, and the political deficiencies of technical expertise are of little moment amongst planning theorists. A tinge of anti-intellectualism characterizes planning theory as a whole, at least if one interprets this as an unfamiliarity with and avoidance of current intellectual debates and the foundations of modern social thought. Planning theorists tend to carry on a dialogue among themselves, reflecting in their insularity the ambiguous and the peripheral social position of planning in the United States. The little enlightenment that is generated is thus confined to theorists rather than extended to practitioners and citizens. This further distances theorists from society and makes a clear political statement.

The postmodern debate, nonetheless, is not simply an issue of theoretical possibilities and cultural practices but also a political agenda, muddled though it is, that has implications for planning theory (Smith 1987). On the one hand, political and economic reform are not high on that agenda, and political acquiescence seems to extend from the celebration of multiple discourses. Such political inclinations coincide well with the directions taken by most modernist planning theorists, who have abandoned any critical role and turned to academic debates. To the extent that planning education, however, trains its students to think in terms of dampening the excesses of capitalism, improving society, and understanding the political role of the expert, a tension exists between modernist and postmodernist political sensibilities. On the other hand, the postmodern debate does offer a useful antidote to planners' belief in the *embourgeoisement* of the working class and the conflict-free homogeneity of social interests.

Overall, then, the modernist planning project has disintegrated but not disappeared. Practice has lost its "neutral" mediative position, forsaken its clear object of the city, abandoned its critical distance, and further suppressed reformist and democratic tendencies. Yet practitioners still cling to a modernist sensibility and search for ways to impose expertise on democracy and to integrate their many specialities around a grand vision such as the master plan. Theory, on the other hand, has undergone centrifugal disintegration without a corresponding refocusing of knowledge around social theories and a broadening of the planning debate. Neither does one find a theoretical commitment to more than a pragmatic political agenda. From this perspective, planning seems suspended between modernity and postmodernity, with practitioners and theorists having few clues as to how to (re)establish themselves on solid ground.[5]

Toward City-Centered and Democratic Planning

Though the modernist project of planning is under attack, and seemingly less and less viable as a response to contemporary social conditions and intellectual tendencies, one should not propose too hastily that planners should resolve the confusion by unconditionally adopting postmodernist alternatives. The modernist project needs to be reconstructed in a way that takes into account its strengths – the focus on the city, the commitment to reform, the mediative role within the state – and eradicates its weaknesses – the outmoded view of the city, the lack of democracy, an illiberal attitude toward narratives, and an insensitivity to the diversity of communities. Three modest suggestions are offered as a way to this reconstruction (see Beauregard 1990).

First, practitioners and theorists must rededicate themselves to the built environment as the object of action and inquiry. At present, the physical city exists within planning as a series of unconnected fragments rather than as a practical and theoretical synthesis of planning action and thought. The built environment is a source of capital accumulation, a place of consumption and reproduction, and a terrain of profound struggle. Moreover, the physical city is the object of practice and theory that historically enabled state planning to be established. To abandon it is to abandon the meaning of urban planning in the United States as well as the source of its legitimacy as a state activity.

Nonetheless, the "modernist" city of the unitary plan and the city of property capital have to be rejected. Instead, planners need to recognize the emergence of a post-Fordist city of dynamics and forms heretofore unaddressed. At the center of that perspective must be an object of integrative potential, substantive moment, and theoretical extension. One such object is the city-building process and its product, the built environment (Beauregard 1988). Such a focus can reintegrate the various specialties of planning around an object of historical significance and long-term legitimacy. It can provide substantive problems for grounding planning in the practicalities of everyday life and historical trends. Moreoever, by understanding the way in which building a city is linked to political, economic, and cultural phenomena, planners can extend their reach (both practically and theoretically) and establish the basis for a critique of capitalist ideology and the politics of growth.

Second, planners need to take a mediative position between capital, labor, and the state. Although contradictory and certainly difficult to realize, such a position can be used to enhance political debate around the processes and outcomes of urban development. The idea is for planners to abandon political neutrality for a new "progressivism" linked simultaneously to the imperatives of the state and the needs of labor. Planning needs to be a countervailing power to capital, and it can do so under present conditions only by establishing a base within the community and by exploiting its institutional position within the state. Reaching out to the public with numerous opportunities for involvement in planning deliberations will enable planners to wield more influence within state channels (Benveniste 1977). Instead of hiding behind the cloak of expertise or remaining distant from controversy, planners must participate. The development of a constituency for planning is a prerequisite and a positive outcome; the enhancement of democracy would be its most important contribution.[6]

Practitioners and theorists, then, must open planning to a variety of constituencies. The United States is a multiplicity of communities and cultures. Theorists can support this by giving greater attention to broad social theories that offer explanations of current capital restructuring, critiquing existing epistemologies, and advancing new techniques and knowledge bases for thinking about practicing planning. Such theories must address more directly the conflicts within society and its social and cultural heterogeneity. In these ways, the modernist project of planning can be partially reconstructed while its links to postmodernism are enhanced. In order to establish a state planning concerned with the humanity of the city, a clear practical and theoretical discourse must be combined with political conviction and a respect for democracy.

Acknowledgments

I extend my thanks to Michael Dear, Susan S. Fainstein, and an anonymous referee, each of whom provided extremely useful critiques of earlier drafts.

Notes

1   Throughout the text, state planning is synonymous with planning under-taken by the various levels of government in the United States. When state planning refers to planning by the state-level government in contrast to the federal or local levels, the context will make the distinction clear. I use state in a similar fashion.
2   To this extent, I disagree with Soja (1989: 55, footnote 10, emphasis added) who claims that "the anglophonic tradition of planning education through-out the twentieth century has been one of the most important places for the preservation of practical geographical analysis, *critical social theory*, and the geographical imagination."
3   Pluralist political theorists in the postwar period, of course, interpreted this ostensible cacophony of voices as simply the workings of democracy.
4   For a similar argument concerning human geography, see Dear (1988) and Soja (1989).
5   This is also to say that postmodernism is not "modernism at its end" (Lyotard 1984); there is as much continuity as discontinuity. On this point, see Soja (1989) and the essays in the fourth 1987 issue of *Environment and Planning D: Society and Space* (EPD 1987).
6   Such a mediative position is politically vulnerable. That is no reason, though, to avoid it. Moreover, I do recognize the pedagogical issues here of how to train planning students to be socially and politically conscious (and critical), technically astute, and employable.

References

Albertsen N, 1988, "Postmodernism, post-Fordism, and critical social theory" *Environment and Planning D: Society and Space* 6 339–365
Aptheker H, 1967 *The Nature of Democracy, Freedom and Revolution* (International Publishers, New York)
Bailey J, 1975 *Social Theory for Planning* (Routledge and Kegan Paul, Andover, Hants)
Beauregard R A, 1984, "Making planning theory: a retrospective" *Urban Geography* 5 255–261

Beauregard R A, 1986, "Planning practice" *Urban Geography* 7 172–178

Beauregard R A, 1987, "The object of planning" *Urban Geography* 8 367–373

Beauregard R A, 1988, "The city as built environment", paper presented at the International Sociological Association Research Committee on the Sociology of Urban and Regional Development Conference, "Trends and Challenges of Urban Restructuring", Rio de Janeiro; copy available from author

Beauregard R A, 1989, "Space, time, and economic restructuring", in *Economic Restructuring and Political Response* Ed. R A Beauregard (Sage, Beverly Hills, CA) pp 209–240

Beauregard R A, 1990, "Bringing the city back in" *Journal of the American Planning Association* 56

Benveniste G, 1977, *The Politics of Expertise* second edition (Boyd and Fraser, San Francisco, CA)

Berman M, 1988, *All that is Solid Melts into Air* (Penguin Books, New York)

Bernstein C, 1987, "Centering the postmodern" *Socialist Review* 17 45–56

Bluestone B, Harrison B, 1982 *The Deindustrialization of America* (Basic Books, New York)

Boyer M C, 1983 *Dreaming the Rational City* (MIT Press, Cambridge, MA)

Bradbury J H, 1985, "Regional and industrial restructuring processes in the new international division of labor" *Progress in Human Geography* 9 38–63

Castells M, 1985 *High Technology, Space, and Society* (Sage, Beverly Hills, CA)

Chase-Dunn C K, 1984, "The world-system since 1950: what has really changed?", in *Labor in the Capitalist World-Economy* Ed. C Bergquist (Sage, Beverly Hills, CA) pp 75–104

Clavel P, 1986 *The Progressive City* (Rutgers University Press, New Brunswick, NJ)

Conzen M P, 1988, "American cities in profound transition", in *The Making of Urban Amercia* Ed. R A Mohl (Scholarly Resources, Wilmington, DE) pp 277–289

Cooke P, 1983 *Theories of Planning and Spatial Development* (Century Hutchison, London)

Cooke P, 1988, "Modernity, postmodernity and the city" *Theory, Culture and Society* 5 475–492

Davidoff P, 1965, "Advocacy and pluralism in planning" *Journal of the American Institute of Planners* 31 596–615

Davis M, 1987, "Chinatown, part two?: the 'internationalization' of downtown Los Angeles" *New Left Review* 164 65–86

Dear M, 1986, "Postmodernism and planning" *Environment and Planning D: Society and Space* 4 367–384

Dear M, 1988, "The postmodern challenge: reconstructing human geography" *Transactions of the Institute of British Geographers* 13 262–274

EPD, 1987, "Reconsidering social theory: a debate" *Environment and Planning D: Society and Space* 5 367–434

Fainstein N I, Fainstein S S, 1979, "New debates in urban planning: the impact of Marxist theory" *International Journal of Urban and Regional Research* 3 381–401

Fainstein N I, Fainstein S S, 1987, "Economic restructuring and the politics of land use planning in New York City" *Journal of the American Planning Association* 53 237–248

Fainstein S S, 1988, "Urban transformation and economic development policy", paper presented at the annual meeting of the Association of Collegiate Schools of Planning, Buffalo, NY; copy available from author

Fainstein S S, Fainstein N I, 1989, "Technology, the new international division of labor, and location", in *Economic Restructuring and Political Response* Ed. R A Beauregard (Sage, Beverly Hills, CA) pp 17–39

Fairbanks R, 1988 *Making Better Citizens* (University of Illinois Press, Champaign, IL)

Feagin J R, 1988 *Free Enterprise City* (Rutgers University Press, New Brunswick, NJ)

Foglesong R, 1986 *Planning the Capitalist City* (Princeton University Press, Princeton, NJ)

Forester J, 1989 *Planning in the Face of Power* (University of California Press, Berkeley, CA)

Friedland R, Piven F F, Alford R, 1978, "Political conflict, urban structure, and the fiscal crisis", in *Comparing Urban Policies* Ed. D Ashford (Sage, Beverly Hills, CA) pp 175–225

Friedmann J, 1987 *Planning in the Public Domain* (Princeton University Press, Princeton, NJ)

Gans H (Ed.), 1968, "City planning in America: a sociological analysis", in *Essays on Urban Problems and Solutions: People and Plans* (Basic Books, New York) pp 50–70

Gitlin T, 1988, "Hip-deep in post-modernism" *The New York Times* 6 December, pages 1, 35, and 36

Goldberger P, 1989, "When developers change the rules during the game" *The New York Times* 19 March, pages 36 and 38

Goodman R, 1971 *After the Planners* (Touchstone Books, New York)

Gregory D, 1987, "Postmodernism and the politics of social theory" *Environment and Planning D: Society and Space* 5 245–248

Hall P, 1989, "The turbulent eighth decade: challenges to American city planning" *Journal of the American Planning Association* 55 275–282

Harrison B, Bluestone B, 1988 *The Great U-turn* (Basic Books, New York)

Harvey D, 1978, "On planning the ideology of planning", in *Planning Theory in the 1980s* Eds R W Burchell, G Sternlieb (Center for Urban Policy Research, Rutgers University, New Brunswick NJ) pp 213–234

Harvey D, 1987, "Flexible accumulation through urbanization: reflections on 'postmodernism' in the American city" *Antipode* 19 260–286

Hayden D, 1984 *Redesigning the American Dream* (W W Norton, New York)

Hayek F, 1944 *The Road to Serfdom* (University of Chicago Press, Chicago, IL)

Hofstadter R, 1955 *The Age of Reform* (Vintage Books, New York)

Hofstadter R, 1958 *Social Darwinism in American Thought* (Beacon Press, Boston, MA)

Hutcheon L, 1987, "The politics of postmodernism: parody and history" *Cultural Critique* 5 179–207

Jacoby R, 1987 *The Last Intellectuals* (Farrar, Straus and Giroux, New York)

Jameson F, 1984a, "Postmodernism, or the cultural logic of late capitalism" *New Left Review* 146 53–92

Jameson F, 1984b, "Foreword", in *The Postmodern Condition* J F Lyotard (University of Minnesota Press, Minneapolis, MN) pp vii–xxi

Jencks C, 1985 *Modern Movements in Architecture* (Viking Press, New York)

Kantor P, 1988 *The Dependent City* (Scott Foresman, Glenview, IL)

Katznelson I, 1981 *City Trenches* (University of Chicago Press, Chicago, IL)

Kraushaar R, 1988, "Outside the whale: progressive planning and the dilemmas of radical reform" *Journal of the American Planning Association* 54 91–100

Logan J R, Molotch H L, 1987 *Urban Fortunes* (University of California Press, Berkeley, CA)

Lyotard J F, 1984 *The Postmodern Condition* (University of Minnesota Press, Minneapolis, MN)

McKelvey B, 1963 *The Urbanization of America, 1860–1915* (Rutgers University Press, New Brunswick, NJ)

Olmsted F L, 1916, "Introduction", in *City Planning* Ed. J Nolen (D Appleton, New York)

Orwell G, 1953, "Inside the whale", in *A Collection of Essays by George Orwell* (Harcourt Brace Jovanovich, New York) pp 210–252

Peet R, 1987 *International Capitalism and Industrial Restructuring* (Allen and Unwin, Winchester, MA)

Peterson J A, 1983, "The impact of sanitary reform upon American urban planning, 1840–1890", in *Introduction to Planning History in the United States* Ed. D A Krueckeberg (Center for Urban Policy Research, Rutgers University, New Brunswick, NJ) pp 13–39

Relph E, 1987 *The Modern Urban Landscape* (The Johns Hopkins University Press, Baltimore, MD)

Sarbib J L, 1983, "The University of Chicago program in planning" *Journal of Planning Education and Research* 2 77–81

Schulte-Sasse J, 1987, "Modernity and modernism, postmodernity and post-modernism: framing the issue" *Cultural Critique* 5 5–22

Scott M, 1969 *American City Planning* (University of California Press, Berkeley, CA)

Scott R A, Shore A R, 1979 *Why Sociology Does Not Apply* (Elsevier, New York)

Sharpe W, Wallock L, 1987, "From 'great town' to 'non-place urban realm': reading the modern city", in *Visions of the Modern City* Eds W Sharpe, L Wallock (The Johns Hopkins University Press, Baltimore, MD) pp 1–50

Simonsen K, 1988, "Planning on 'postmodern' conditions", paper presented at the International Sociological Association Research Committee on the Sociology of Urban and Regional Development Conference, "Trends and Challenges of Urban Restructuring", Rio de Janeiro; copy available from author

Smith M P, 1988 *City, State, and Market* (Basil Blackwell, New York)

Smith N, 1984 *Uneven Development* (Basil Blackwell, Oxford)

Smith N, 1987 "Rascal concepts, minimalizing discourse, and the politics of geography" *Environment and Planning D: Society and Space* 5 377–383

Soja E W, 1986, "Taking Los Angeles apart: some fragments of a critical human geography" *Environment and Planning D: Society and Space* 4 255–272

Soja E W, 1989 *Postmodern Geographies* (Verso, London)

Soja E W, Morales R, Wolff G, 1983, "Urban restructuring: an analysis of social and spatial change in Los Angeles" *Economic Geography* 59 195–230

Stone C N, Sanders H T, 1987 *The Politics of Urban Development* (University Press of Kansas, Lawrence, KN)

Walker R A, 1978, "The transformation of urban structure in the nineteenth century and the beginnings of suburbanization", in *Urbanization and Conflict in Market Societies* Ed. K R Cox (Maaroufa Press, Chicago, IL) pp 165–205

Wilson W J, 1987 *The Truly Disadvantaged* (University of Chicago Press, Chicago, IL)

Zukin S, 1988, "The postmodern debate over urban form" *Theory, Culture and Society* 5 431–446

11

Planning Through Debate:[1] The Communicative Turn in Planning Theory[2]

Patsy Healey

This chapter is about what "planning" can be taken to mean in contemporary democratic societies. Its context is the dilemma faced by all those committed to planning as a democratic enterprise, aimed to promote social justice and environmental sustainability. The dilemma is that the technical and administrative machineries advocated and created to pursue these goals in the past have been based on what we now see as a narrow scientific rationalism. These machineries have further compromised the development of a democratic attitude and have failed to achieve the goals promoted. So how can we now support a renewal of the enterprise of planning? If we can, what are its forms and principles?

The chapter is written specifically for those planners in Britain, in planning schools and in planning practice, who have shared a particular experience of the 1970s and 1980s. The 1970s provided us with a soft social and environmental commitment and a hard political critique of the enterprise of planning. In this critique, planning was a site of struggle

Reprinted from *Town Planning Review*, Vol. 63, No. 2, 1992. (Note: a shorter version of this article also appeared in Frank Fischer and John Forester, eds, *The Argumentative Turn in Policy Analysis and Planning*. Durham, N.C.: Duke University Press, 1993)

between class forces for control of the management of the urban environment. By the 1980s, this critique had itself dissolved into a search for a less one-dimensional view of conflict and cleavage in society and a more nuanced appreciation of the diversity of the experience of urban life and environment. This search for a democratic pluralism[3] took place, however, against the harsh backcloth of the Thatcherite hegemonic agenda. This set out to destroy not merely democratic socialist thought and practices but the very enterprise of urban management and planning that was the object of the democratic socialist critique.

The Thatcherite project has now been brought to a remarkably sudden halt as a political idea, though many of the practices it instituted remain.[4] Citizen responsiveness and environmental sustainability, as vague political principles, are now widely asserted, as in the general idea of environmental planning and the specific principle of a plan-led regulatory land-use planning system. But what kind of a planning can be compatible with our contemporary understandings of a democratic attitude? And how can the concept of planning survive the contemporary philosophical challenges to materialism, modernism, and rationalism, these central pillars of the traditions of "modernity" that dominated Western thought from the middle of last century until late into the present one?[5] How can there be a "planning" without "unifying" conceptions of systems and structures, based on scientific knowledge, from which to articulate hypotheses as to key relationships and appropriate interventions? How can decisions be arrived at without systematic "rational" procedures for knowledgeable and collective "deciding and acting"?

Throughout the past decade, signs of alternative conceptions of planning purposes and practices have been increasingly identified and debated in planning theory. One route to imagining alternatives has focused on substantive issues, moving from material analyses of options for local economies exposed to global capitalism to concerns with culture, consciousness, community, and "placeness."[6] Another has taken a "process" route, exploring the communicative dimensions of collectively debating and deciding on matters of collective concern.[7]

The problem with the substantive route is its *a priori* assumptions of what is "good/bad," "right/wrong." Local economic development is presented as often "good," national economic intervention as oppressive, "bad." By what knowledge and reasoning has this been arrived at? If such principles are embodied in our plans, will we not have fallen yet again into the trap of imposing the reasoning of one group of people on another? Does the process route offer a way out of this dilemma of relativism, which treats every position as merely someone's opinion, and hence the dominance of a position pursued through planning strategies and their implementation as nothing more than the outcome of a power game?

This chapter argues that it can. The argument is explored first by a brief

review of the idea of planning and its challenges. The chapter then identifies five directions for the management of the urban environment that
seem to be prefigured in present discussions. Of these, it is argued that
the conception of planning as a communicative enterprise holds most
promise for a democratic form of planning in the contemporary context.
The article concludes with some implications for the systems and practices of environmental planning.

Throughout, the contextual "locus" of the article is environmental
planning in Britain, although this merely allows the purposes and practices for planning to be developed in a specific context. More generally,
the challenge for planning in the contemporary era lies at the heart of
our efforts to reinterpret a progressive meaning for democracy in Western
societies.[8]

The Idea of Planning and its Challenges

As with so much of Western culture, the contemporary idea of planning
is rooted in the enlightenment tradition of "modernity."[9] This freed individuals from the intellectual tyranny of religious faith and from the
political tyranny of despots. Such free individuals, in democratic association, could, it was believed then and since, combine in one way or
another to manage their collective affairs. By the application of scientific
knowledge and reason to human affairs, it would be possible to build a
better world, in which the sum of human happiness and welfare would
be increased. For all our consciousness of the errors of democratic
management in the past two centuries, it is difficult not to recognize the
vast achievements that this intellectual and political enlightenment has
brought.

This modern idea of planning, as Friedmann has described in his
authoritative account of its intellectual origins,[10] is centrally linked to
concepts of democracy and progress. It centers on the challenge of finding
ways in which citizens, through acting together, can manage their collective concerns with respect to the sharing of space and time.

In this century, Mannheim's advocacy of a form of planning that
harnessed systematized social scientific knowledge and techniques to the
management of collective affairs in a democratic society proved inspirational for the influential Chicago school of rational decision making.[11] A
procedural view evolved that presented planning as a progressive force
for economic and social development in a world where democracy and
capitalism were seen to coexist in comfortable consensus.[12] It challenged
populist "clientelism" (as in Chicago in the late 1950s)[13] as much as
idealist totalitarianism.

But as with any progressive force, procedures developed with a progressive democratic intention may be subverted for other purposes. In the

early 1970s, this subversion was identified with the power of capitalist forces to dominate everyone's life opportunities. Environmental planning, it was argued, put the needs of capital (through regional economic development and the implicit opportunities for land and property markets created by planning regimes) before citizens and the environment.[14]

However, a more fundamental challenge to the Mannheimian notion of planning was gathering force, through the critique of scientific reason itself. German critical theorists and French "deconstructionists" elaborated ideas that challenged reason's dominance of human affairs. Reason, understood as logic coupled with scientifically constructed empirical knowledge, was unveiled as having achieved hegemonic power over other ways of being and knowing, crowding out moral and aesthetic discourses. Further, rationalizing power dominated the very institutions set up in the name of democratic action, the bureaucratic agencies of the state. Following Foucault's analysis, planning could be associated with the dominatory power of systematic reason pursued through state bureaucracies.[15] Evidence for this seemed to be everywhere, from the disaster of high-rise tower blocks for the poor to the dominance of economic criteria justifying road projects and the functional categorization of activity zones, which worked for large industrial companies and those working in them but not for women (with their necessarily complex lifestyle), the elderly and disabled, and many ethnic groups forced to discover ways of existing on the edge of established economic practices.

This "challenge to systematized reason" and, with it, to the planning enterprise, strikes at the heart of the enlightenment project, or as we now understand it, the project of "modernity." The challenge is now labeled as postmodernist, drawing on a terminology first developed in art and architectural critique.[16] But whereas postmodernism in architecture is primarily a critique of a particular paradigm and style *within* Western art and architecture, philosophical postmodernism challenges the foundations of two hundred years of Western thought.

The postmodern challenge to Western thought is both progressive and regressive in its potential, as was the idea of systematized reason. It is also highly diverse, with different lines of development. Only some of these claim to *replace* the "project of modernity" with that of postmodernity. Others, following the position of the economic geographer Harvey and the critical theorist Habermas, seek new ways of reconstituting the "incomplete" project of modernity. Some of the strands of postmodernist debate leave space for a form of planning, that is, for collective activity. Others dismiss planning as, variously, impossible, irrelevant, or oppressive.

Moore Milroy, reviewing the development of the postmodernist debate in planning thought, identifies four "broad characteristics" to the challenge postmodernism presents to modernism.

> *It is* deconstructive *in the sense of questioning and establishing a sceptical distance from conventional beliefs and, more actively, trying both to ascertain who derives value from upholding their authority and to displace them;* antifoundationalist *in the sense of dispensing with universals as bases of truth;* nondualistic *in the sense of refusing the separation between subjectivity and objectivity along with the array of dualisms it engenders including the splits between truth and opinion, fact and value; and* encouraging of plurality and differences.[17]

This double challenge, to the tendency for progressive values to be destroyed by the very systems created to promote them and to the systems of technocratic rationalist thought that have underpinned so much of Western and Eastern bloc thinking about planning, seems so powerful as to be fatal to the idea of planning. Is there any way out? It is argued here not only that there is, via the development of communicative forms of planning, but also, following Harvey and Habermas, that some directions of the postmodern challenge to planning need to be actively resisted in their turn as regressive and undemocratic. Current debate suggests several routes for invention of a new planning. Five such routes or directions are outlined here. These directions are not necessarily exclusive. Their presentation in the planning literature varies in its coherence. They are offered as a sketch of possibilities, through which to foreground the promise of a communicative form of planning in promoting and realizing a progressive democratic attitude.

Directions for a New Planning

The five directions discussed are

1   A retreat to the bastions of scientific rationalism as expressed through neoclassical economics. Planning is reformulated to provide a framework of rules to ensure that collectively experienced impacts are addressed through the price mechanism.

2   An idealism based on fundamental moral or aesthetic principle. Planning purposes and practices would be directed to realizing this principle.

3   A relativism in which self-conscious individuals assert their own principle and mutually adjust when they get in each other's way. Planning has little purpose in this route except as deconstructive technique, to reveal "dominatory" systems in order to remove them.

4   Enlarged conceptions of democratic socialism beyond economic struggles over material conditions, to incorporate other loci of "cleavage," such as gender and race, and allow more space for cultural issues (moral and aesthetic). This

refocuses the purposes and practices of planning around a reformulated substantive agenda.

5   A communicative conception of rationality, to replace that of the self-conscious autonomous subject using principles of logic and scientifically formulated empirical knowledge to guide actions. This new conception of reasoning is arrived at by an intersubjective effort at mutual understanding. This refocuses the practices of planning to enable purposes to be communicatively discovered.

The principle of price

This conception ignores most of the debates and challenges just discussed and continues the rationalist project. In conformity with the post-Enlightenment tradition, individuals are constituted as autonomous subjects confronting the object world. They allocate their resources according to their subjectively perceived wants and their material opportunities. Public policy facilitates this allocatory process by authoritative structures (rules) based on market information about supply, demand, and the blockages to market exchange. Environmental planning comes into play to conserve assets that are not readily traded in the marketplace (national parks, wildlife reserves, historic buildings, agricultural land) and to ensure that the actions of individuals do not impose excessive costs on neighbors, communities, and environments. As far as possible, such a planning should proceed by pricing strategies that require everyone to internalize these external costs. Only when this is difficult to enforce or where positive conservation is required should regulatory intervention be used. David Pearce's approach to environmental economics provides a clear example of how "environmental sustainability" objectives could be achieved in this paradigm.[18]

Though hesitantly and inconsistently, it is this route that was followed by the British government in the 1980s.[19] Some planning theorists have been developing its dimensions in the planning field.[20] It has been a dominant tradition for some years in the United States and is now being vigorously developed in Britain in ideas for traffic management and an "impact fee" approach to planning gain. But as environmental debates clearly illustrate, it proceeds ignorant of any doubts about the supreme power of scientific rationalism and assumes that most aesthetic and moral issues can be converted into priceable preferences.[21]

It is not hard to see the dominatory force of scientific rationalism at work here. This is not to argue that such an approach is *never* appropriate, merely that it is but one possibility among many. We may criticize its practitioners for their failure to grasp that it "lives together" with other ways of making policy issues manageable, and we may criticize governments and knowledge production institutions for prioritizing it above others. If postmodernism has any progressive meaning, it must mean that this direction for planning turns away from, rather than toward, the challenge of "making sense together while living differently."

Idealist fundamentalism

Several strands of contemporary postmodern critique focus on unmasking the corrupting power of scientific rationalism at the heart of our thought, to reveal deeper unifying principles that hold our world together.[22] From this perspective individuals are constituted not as autonomous subjects responsible for their own actions but as bearers and interpreters of a metaphysical principle. This principle becomes the locus of moral and aesthetic order, and its contemplation fosters a reflective "interiorization" of experience rather than "acting in the world."[23] The preoccupation is with existence, with *being*, rather than a collective "exteriorized" enterprise of *becoming* something different and better *in* the world. While such a fundamentalism has progressive force in releasing and legitimating people's search for a moral basis for their lives, it also contains within it a dominatory potential. Examples of this can be seen in the adoption of religious codes in public spheres (for example, the British 1988 Education Act's requirement for a "daily corporate act of worship of an essentially Christian nature") or proposals for environmental actions irrespective of their economic and social consequences justified in terms of scientifically and aesthetically constructed notions of ecological apocalypse. Planning in this context becomes either an irrelevance to the contemplative interior life or an expression of the metaphysical principle (as in, for example, Chinese *fung schiu* or Islamic principles for environmental planning derived from the Koran). In essence, this direction merely replaces one unidimensional hegemony (rationalism) with another (a particularly moral principle). It is hard to see how such an approach can advance the project of progressive democratic pluralism.

Aesthetic relativism

Others elevate experience and the aesthetic mode to the central dimension of human life. This focuses on the self-conscious autonomous individual, existing *being*, to be extricated from the oppression of functional systems based on scientific rationalism. Within this conception, there is no unifying metaphysical source to be contemplatively revealed once the reasoning dominance has been unmasked. Instead, all interpretations are valid. The unifier of humanity is merely the experiential capacity. This leads to a celebration and enjoyment of differences,[24] but experienced individually rather than collectively. No criteria seem to be available for distinguishing one person's interpretations and actions from another's since to distinguish would involve recourse to reason or idealist beliefs. All have equivalent standing; all have validity through interior reflection. The much-criticized outcome is a potentially regressive idealist nihilism. The dominatory potential within this strand of postmodernism is of enraged anarchistic violence between individuals and groups struggling to stake out the territory within which their purposes and practices can prevail. The Western media's portrayal of interethnic and factional strife in the former USSR and Yugoslavia provides examples of what this could mean. If planning has any role at all in this direction, it is to stake out and defend boundaries and at the same time to foster the celebration of difference. But without a discursive reasoning capacity, it is difficult to see what practices could constitute such a planning. To argue this is not to reject the importance of aesthetic and emotional experience in forming our understandings and values. It is the *prioritizing* of a particular dimension of experience and understanding (in this case the aesthetic) above all others that compromises the project of progressive democratic pluralism. The progressive challenge is instead to find ways of acknowledging different ways of experiencing and understanding, while seeking to "make sense together."

Extending modernity's tolerance

Another route has been to develop the socialist project beyond a preoccupation with material conditions and economic classes. This project, whether in Marxian or democratic humanist forms, aims to develop a society in which the conditions of material existence are adequate for all, and in which everyone has the opportunity to work in conditions where we are justly rewarded and respected for the work we do and in which we have real control over the economic and political conditions of the societies in which we live. Marxist analysis conceived of individuals as self-conscious and reflective. But people's perceptions and worth were seen as constituted by the material conditions of the societies in which we live, and specifically by the mode of production. Through scientific historical analysis, people could become aware of this and through collective action change the conditions of our existence. Planning thus became the means for redesigning less oppressive societies than those dominated by feudal, capitalist, and colonial power.

But scientific materialism as the basis for the socialist project in retrospect engendered a domination by state bureaucrats pursuing scientific management principles in the name of working-class power (in Eastern European countries, often in highly corrupt forms). Moral principles and aesthetic consensus were interpreted within a set of scientific "laws" about economic class interests. By the 1970s in Britain and elsewhere, many socialist thinkers were identifying similar tendencies within the welfare state machinery of Western capitalist economies.[25] Critiques developed that first highlighted power-distributing cleavages other than economic class, notably those of gender and race, and, second, sought to break out of a "totalizing" scientific rationalism. The new socialism of the 1980s in Britain has been concerned with developing a pluralist understanding of people's needs, values, and ways of experiencing oppression. Appreciating diversity and recognizing differences are key elements in this conception, requiring collective action to be informed by principles of tolerance and respect. There is not one route to progress but many, not one form of reasoning but many. The socialist project thus comes to focus on both restructuring the control of economies and the flow of the fruits of material effort, while at the same time discovering ways of "living together differently but respectfully."[26] Planning retains its traditional importance in socialist thought, but the planning enterprise is refocused to recognize diverse forms of disadvantage.

The frame of reference of these efforts remains a struggle for opportunities for the disadvantaged against a systematically understood capitalist world order. This provides a frame of reasoning that interprets and selects among the various claims for attention that a pluralist socialism can generate.[27] But where does this frame of reasoning come from, and what gives it its authority? Is it merely providing a slightly more sensitive development of the notion of class interests? And does this really accommodate the claims and arguments of the different ethnic communities in Britain, or the anger of those oppressed by racial and gender prejudice? These "voices" may argue that the pluralist socialist project of "living together but differently" dominates them by failing to *listen* to their different ways of *experiencing*. It requires acceptance of a belief in the analyses propounded, in a particular interpretation of what "living together" and "difference" mean. The planning frameworks developed within this route thus cannot escape the critique of scientific rationalism. In other words, the pluralist socialist project is still founded on systematized rationality and scientific understanding of social structure in its conception of "living together" and "difference."

Communicative rationality

It is here that Habermas's search for a reformulation of modernity's concept of reason offers a way forward. Habermas argues that, far from giving up on reason as an informing principle for contemporary societies, we should shift perspective from an individualized, subject-object conception of reason to reasoning formed within intersubjective communication. Such reasoning is required where "living together but differently" in shared space and time drives us to search for ways of finding agreement on how to "act in the world" to address our collective concerns. Habermas's communicative rationality has parallels within conceptions of practical reasoning, implying an expansion from the notion of reason as pure logic and scientific empiricism to encompass all the ways we come to understand and know things and to use that knowledge in acting. Habermas argues that without some conception of reasoning, we have no way out of fundamentalism and nihilism. For him, the notion of the self-conscious autonomous individual, refining his or her knowledge against principles of logic and science, can be replaced by a notion of reason as intersubjective mutual understanding arrived at by particular people in particular times and places, that is, historically situated. Both subject and object are constituted through this process. Knowledge claims, upon which action possibilities are proposed, are validated in this conception of reasoning through discursively establishing principles of validity, rather than through appeal to logic or science, although both may well be considered as possibilities within the communicative context.[28]

In this way, knowledge for action, principles of action, and ways of acting are actively constituted by the members of an intercommunicating community, situated in the particularities of time and place. Further, the reasoning employed can escape from confines of rational-scientific principles to include varying systems of morality and culturally specific traditions of expressive aesthetic experience. "Right" and "good" actions are those we can come to agree on, in particular times and places, across our diverse differences in material conditions and wants, moral perspectives, and expressive cultures and inclinations. We do not need recourse to common fundamental ideals or principles of "the good social organization" to guide us. Planning and its contents, in this conception are a way of acting that we can *choose*, after *debate*.

Habermas's conception of communicative action has been criticized in the context of the present discussion on two grounds. First, by holding on to reason, it retains the very source of modernity's dominatory potential. Second, Habermas would like to believe that consensual positions can be arrived at, whereas contemporary social relations reveal deep cleavages of class, race, gender, and culture, which can be resolved only through power struggle between conflicting forces.[29]

Habermas justifies his retention of reasoning as a legitimate guiding principle for collective affairs on the grounds that, where collective "acting in the world" is our concern, we need to engage in argumentation and debate. We need a reasoning capacity for these purposes. We cannot just engage in aesthetic presentation or moral faith if at some point we are faced both with "making sense together" and "working out" how to act together. This does not mean that the language of morality or aesthetics is excluded from our reasoning. Habermas argues that our intersubjective practical reasoning draws on the store of knowledge and understandings of technique, morality, and aesthetics. In this way, our collective reasoning is informed by, situated within, the various "lifeworlds" from which we come to engage in our collective enterprises.[30] Our intersubjective arguments may involve "telling stories" as well as "doing analyses."[31] Thus, the narrative mode should accompany and intersect with experiential expression and the analytical mode. But in the end, the purpose of our efforts is not these (doing analysis, telling stories, rhetoric) but *doing something*, namely, "acting in the world." For this, we need to discuss what we could and should do, why, and how. There is an interesting parallel here with Walzer's notion of principles of justice for different spheres of social activity.[32]

But does not this process of collective argumentation merely lead to a new and potentially dominatory consensus, as the agreement freely arrived at through argument in one period imposes itself on the different differentiations of the next? Habermas proposes to counteract this possibility through criteria to sustain a dynamic critique within the reasoning process. Claims should be assessed in terms of their comprehensibility, integrity, legitimacy, and truth.[33] Forester has since developed these as heuristic questions for planners to use in critiquing themselves and others as they search for a progressive power-challenging planning.[34]

The mutual understandings and agreements reached for one purpose at one time are thus revisable as the flow of communicative action proceeds. Habermas himself would clearly like to see stable consensuses emerge, societies built around principles of mutual understanding. Several planning theorists have also proposed the development of a communicative "metalanguage" or a "metadiscourse" for planning discussion.[35] Such an enterprise parallels the search noted above by the "New Left" in Britain for forms of a democratically pluralist participation.

But a metalanguage, however full of internal principles of critique, unavoidably contains dominatory potential. It could all too easily settle into assumptions of understanding and agreement detached from those whose ways of being, knowing, and valuing are supposed to be reflected in the agreement. To be liberating rather than dominating, intercommunicative reasoning for the purposes of "acting in the world" must accept that the differences between which we must communicate are not just differences in economic and social position, or in specific wants and needs, but in *systems of meaning*. We see things differently because words, phrases, expressions, objects, are interpreted differently according to our frame of reference. It is this point, long understood in anthropology[36] and emphasized in phenomenology, that underpins the strength of the relativist position. It is here that the present author would part company with Habermas, in order to recognize the inherent localized specificity and untranslatability of the systems of meaning. We may shift our ideas, learn from each other, adapt to each other, "act in the world" together. Systems of meaning or frames of reference shift and evolve in response to such encounters. But it can never be possible to construct a stable consensus around "how we see things," merely a temporary accommodation of different, and differently adapting, perceptions.

The critics of modernity argue that the system of meaning proposed by scientific rationalism has dominated and crowded out all other systems of meaning. If communicative action is to transcend this dominatory threat, its concern should rather be to develop understandings and practices of *interdiscursive* communication, of translation rather than superimposition. For, as Geertz argues, no one system of meaning can ever fully understand enough.[37] It can merely search for ways of opening windows on what it means to see things differently.

Developed in this way, this direction is for a new form of planning through interdiscursive communication, a way of "living together differently through struggling to make sense together." Its openness, its exteriorizing quality, its internal capacity for critique should counteract any potential to turn mutual understanding arrived at at one historical moment into a repressive cultural regime at the next. It offers the hope that "progress," a "project of becoming," is still possible. It is this direction that, in the present author's view, holds an important promise and challenge for planning and, more generally, for democracy, as Forester argues.[38]

Planning as a Communicative Enterprise

Environmental planning has been understood in this chapter as a process for collectively, and interactively, addressing and working out how to act, in respect of shared concerns about how far and how to "manage" environmental change. Mannheim argued that scientific rationalism provided the central resource for this enterprise.[39] The collapse of the unidimensional domination of scientific rationalism has now demolished this route to invention for planning. Apart from the vestigial endeavors of a politically dominant economics, any recourse to scientific knowledge or rational procedures must now be contained within some other conception of what makes for democratic "acting in the world." Habermas offers an alternative that retains the notion of the liberating and democratic potential of reasoning, but broadened to encompass not merely rational-technical forms of reasoning but moral appreciation and aesthetic experience. This wider understanding of what we know and how we know it, rooted as much in "practical sense"[40] as in formalized knowledge, is brought into collective "deciding and acting" through intersubjective communication rather than the self-reflective consciousness of autonomous individuals. The effort of constructing mutual understanding as the locus of reasoning activity replaces the subject-centered "philosophy of consciousness" that, Habermas argues, has dominated Western conceptions of reason since the Enlightenment.[41] Through it, the specificities of time and place; of culture, society, and personality; of "habitus," as Bourdieu puts it,[42] are expressed, and constituted. For Habermas, a conscious intersubjective understanding of collective communicative work is a force to sustain an internally critical democratic effort, resisting the potential domination of "one-dimensional" principles, whether scientific, moral, or aesthetic.

What can planning mean in this context of postrationalist, intercommunicative, reasoned, many-dimensional "thinking about and acting" in the world? What purposes and practices should it have? A communicative approach to knowledge production – knowledge of conditions, of cause and effect, moral values, and aesthetic worlds – maintains that knowledge is not preformulated but is specifically created anew in our communication through exchanging perceptions and understanding and through drawing on the stock of life experience and previously consolidated cultural and moral knowledge available to participants. We cannot, therefore, predefine a set of tasks that planning must address, since these must be specifically discovered, learnt about, and understood through intercommunicative processes.

Nevertheless, ongoing processes of debate about environmental matters have created a thought-world, a contemporary "common sense" within which, however fluid and in need of critique it may be, the elements of a substantive agenda are evident. The contemporary rediscovery of environmental planning is fueled by a widespread and interdiscursive concern with managing economic development, enriching our cultural life, avoiding polarizing, and segregating tendencies in lifestyles and life opportunities, and undertaking all these within an attitude to the natural environment that is both respecting and sustaining of long-term ecological balances. The general purposes of environmental planning situated in this context are to balance these connecting, but often contradictory, aims. But what constitutes the "balance" in particular times and places cannot be known in advance. "Standardized" approaches to "balancing," which have a long history in planning thought and practice, encapsulated in substantive "blueprint" plans, merely "dominate" the situations they land upon.

This shifts attention from the substantive purposes of environmental planning to the practices by which purposes are established, actions identified, and followed through. What does a communicative rationality suggest as appropriate when addressing environmental management issues in contemporary Western democracies, and how could their conversion into a "process" blueprint be avoided?

The outlines of appropriate practices for an intercommunicative planning are beginning to emerge through the work of a range of planning theorists during the 1980s. This work has been influenced not only by Habermas but by other and often conflicting contributors to the postmodern and antirationalist debate, notably Foucault and Bourdieu, and by an increasing number of "ethnographic" studies of planning practice.[43] An attempt is made here to summarize this new planning direction through ten propositions:

1   Planning is an interactive and interpretive process, focusing "deciding and acting" within a range of specialized allocative and authoritative systems but drawing on the multidimensionality of "lifeworlds" or "practical sense," rather than a single formalized dimension (for example, urban morphology or scientific rationalism).[44] Formal techniques of analysis and design in planning processes are but one form of discourse. Planning processes should be enriched by discussion of moral dilemmas and aesthetic experience, using a range of presentational forms, from telling stories to aesthetic illustrations of experiences. Statistical analysis coexists in such processes with poems and moral fables.[45] A prototype example here might be some of the new initiatives in Britain in working to help tenants and residents improve the quality of their living environment.

2   Such interaction assumes the preexistence of individuals engaged with others in diverse, fluid, and overlapping "discourse communities," each with its own meaning systems and, hence, knowledge forms and ways of reasoning and valuing. Such communities may be nearer or farther from each other in relation to access to each other's languages, but no common language or fully common understanding can be arrived at. Communicative action thus focuses on searching for achievable levels of mutual understanding for the purposes in hand, while retaining awareness of that which is not understood (that is, we may not understand why someone says no, but we should recognize the negation as valid; that we know there is a reason but it cannot [yet] be understood by us.)[46]

3   Such interaction involves respectful discussion within and between discursive communities, respect implying recognizing, valuing, listening, and searching for translative possibilities between different discourse communities.[47] A prototype example here might be the public participation exercise undertaken on Sheffield City Centre's Local Plan.[48]

4   It involves invention not only through programs of action but in the construction of the arenas within which these programs are formulated and conflicts identified and mediated. Such a planning thus needs to be reflective about its own processes.[49] The Sheffield City Centre Local Plan exercise is one example among several in Britain that illustrate this sensitive attention to arenas within which planning work gets done.

5   Within the argumentation of these communicative processes, all dimensions of knowing, understanding, appreciating, experiencing, and judging may be brought into play. The struggle of engaging in interdiscursive communicative action is to grasp these and find ways of reasoning among the competing claims for action they generate, without dismissing or devaluing any one until it has been explored. Nothing is "inadmissible" except the claim that some things are "off agenda" and cannot be discussed. All claims merit the reply, "We acknowledge you feel this is of value. Can you help us understand why? Can we work out how it affects what we thought we were trying to do? Are there any reasons why the claim cannot receive collective support?"[50]

6   A reflexive and critical capacity should be kept alive in the processes of

argumentation, using the Habermasian claims of comprehensibility, integrity, legitimacy, and truth. But the critical intent should not be directed at the discourses of the different participative communities (not, "We are right and you are wrong"; "we are good and you are bad") but at the discourse around specific actions being *invented* through the communicative process (for example, "Watch out, this metaphor we are using blocks out the ideas our other colleagues are proposing"; or "This line of thinking will be dismissed as illegitimate by central government. Do we really think it is illegitimate? Are we really going to challenge their power? OK, so how?"[51] A sensitive illustration of this was the discussion around developing the women's agenda for the Greater London Development Plan as described by Allen.[52]

7   This inbuilt critique, a morality for interaction, serves the project of democratic pluralism by according "voice," "ear," and "respect" to all those with an interest in the issues at stake. This is no easy matter, as interest overlaps and conflict, with the conflicts experienced within each one of us magnified in the interdiscursive arena. The important point is that morality and the dilemmas are addressed interdiscursively, forming thereby both the processes and arenas of debate.

8   The literature on negotiation counsels us that apparently fixed preferences may be altered when individuals and groups are encouraged to articulate their interests together.[53] Interaction is thus not simply a form of exchange, or bargaining around predefined interests. It involves mutually reconstructing what constitutes the interests of the various participants – a process of mutual learning through mutually searching to understand.[54]

9   It is not only innovative but has the potential to change, to transform material conditions and established power relations through the continuous effort to "critique" and "demystify"; through increasing understanding among participants and hence highlighting oppressions and "dominatory" forces; and through creating well-grounded arguments for alternative analyses and perceptions, through actively *constructing* new understandings. Ultimately, the transformative potential of communicative action lies in the power embodied in "the better argument,"[55] in the power of ideas, metaphors, images, stories. This echoes Bourdieu's point that how we talk about things helps to bring them about.[56] In this way, diverse people, with experience of different societal conditions and cultural communities, are encouraged to recognize each other's presence and negotiate their shared concerns. Through such processes of argumentation, we may come to agree, or accept a process of agreeing, on what should be done, without necessarily arriving at a unified view of our respective lifeworlds. The critical criteria built into such a process of argument encourages openness and "transparency," but without simplification. If collective concerns are ambivalent and ambiguous, such a communicative process should allow acknowledgment that this is so, perhaps unavoidably so. So the dilemmas and creative potentials of ambiguity enrich the interdiscursive effort, rather than being washed out in the attempt to construct a one-dimensional language.[57]

10   The purpose of such an intercommunicative planning is to help to "start out" and "go along" in mutually agreeable ways based on an effort at interdiscursive understanding, drawing on, critiquing, and reconstructing the understandings we bring to discussion. The inbuilt criteria of critique, if kept alive, should prevent such "starting agreements" and "traveling pacts" consolidating into a unified code and language that could then limit our further capacities at invention. We may be able to agree on what to do next, on how to "start out," and "travel along" for a while. We cannot know where this will take us. But we can act with hope and ambition to achieve future possibilities. Neither the "comprehensive plan" nor "goal-directed" programs have more than a temporary existence in such a conception of communicative and potentially transformative environment planning.[58]

Systems and Practices for Environmental Planning

How can this conception of communicative practices for constructing and critiquing understanding among diverse discursive communities assist in the development of systems for environmental planning, of local realizations of these, and of the specific contents of local planning systems? The very concept of a system immediately conjures up notions of dominatory practices that impose themselves on our actions. Yet with respect to our mutual environmental concerns, a key purpose of communicative action is to work out what rules or codes of conduct we can agree we need to allow us to "live together but differently" in shared environments.

Planning systems consist of formal rules to guide the conduct, the resource allocation, and management activities of individuals and businesses. But they are more than a set of rules. The rules derive from conceptions of situations (contexts), problems experienced in these situations, ways of addressing these problems and ways of changing situations. It is where planning effort is deliberately focused on *changing* situations that we can speak of a planning with transformative intent.[59]

"Urban design" or "physical blueprint" approaches to environmental planning focused on "transforming towns." Ideas of urban existence were consolidated into principles of urban structure and form, and from these to rules to govern proposals for development projects. Debates were confined to principles of urban form, conducted primarily within a narrow expert group (architects, engineers) legitimated by paternalist notions of "planning *for* people." It was supported by a narrow architectural engineering discourse about the relative merits of different urban forms, drawing on aesthetic and moral principles. The "dominatory" consequences of this for our towns and cities are notorious. This was essentially a continuation of a pre-Enlightenment tradition of city planning carried forward into the context of nineteenth- and twentieth-century industrialization and urbanization.

The Mannheimian conception of planning as the "rational mastery of the irrational"[60] provided a more appropriate realization of a "modern" conception of planning. Translated through the Chicago school, this became the rational comprehensive process model of planning that has since been so influential in planning practice. This focused on the processes through which goals were formulated and strategies for achieving them devised. Here, rule generation operates on two levels – the methodological rules for arriving at a plan or program, and the criteria necessary for realizing that program. Both were designed to be recursive, with feedback loops via monitoring procedures intended to sustain an internal critique of planning principles. Planning effort was focused on comprehensive understanding of urban and environmental systems and the "invention" of sets of objectives and guidance principles for the comprehensive management of these systems. Rules to govern change in systems were expressed as performance criteria, linked back to objectives. The vocabulary of this approach is still influential in plan-making practice in Britain, in the way strategy is identified and expressed and rules for development control articulated. In this rationalist conception, citizens contribute to the process, but only by "feeding in" their rationalized goals, rather than debating the understandings through which they come to have their goals. The concerns of politicians and citizens are in effect translated, converted into the technical scientific language of policy analysts and urban and regional science. The metaphors of this language focused around images of process forms, of strategy and programmatic action. The dominatory potential of the rational procedural model lies in the claims to comprehensiveness of what was primarily a narrow, econ-omistic, and functionalist conception of the dimensions of lifeworlds. The critical capacity of the monitoring feedback loops merely shifted priori-ties within the discourse. It did not provide a mechanism for critiquing the discourse itself.

Pluralist conceptions of interest mediation, of the kind first proposed by Davidoff,[61] but later widely developed, seemed to reflect more clearly the reality of environmental planning politics. The practice of environ-mental planning has been described by many in Britain, including the present author, as one within which environmental perceptions and interests were asserted and mediated.[62] The strategies, rules, and the way rules were used were the product of bargaining processes among conflict-ing interests. But as Forester argues, this treats each interest as a source of power, bargaining with others to create a calculus that expresses the power relations among the participants. Its language is that of prevalent political power games. It is not underpinned by any effort at "learning about" the interests and perceptions of the participants and, with that knowledge, revising what each participant thinks about each other's and their own interests. Only if this could happen could a creative, inventive form of environmental planning develop, rather than merely a power-broking planning.[63]

The focus of an intersubjective communicative argumentation is exactly at this point. It starts by recognizing the potential diversity of ways in which concerned citizens (citizens with an interest in issues) come to be concerned. Citizens may share a concern but arrive at these through different cultural, societal, and personal experiences. "Understanding each other" must therefore be accepted as a challenging task that is unlikely to be more than partially achieved. The language of interdiscursive communication, as already discussed, uses multiple modes, moving between analysis, moral fables, and "poems."

The struggle within such interdiscursive communication is to maintain a capacity for critique. This requires the development of a critical, interactively reflexive habit. Of course, the dynamics of the ongoing flow of relations means that people cannot pause to reflect collectively at every instant. What it means is that "taking breath" and "sorting things out" should become a normal part of the practical endeavor of planning work. The Habermasian criteria help here, but reflection is also required as to the arenas of the communicative effort itself. Are there other concerned people who should be involved? Are there other ways of understanding these issues, discursive practices, that we should include? How should the position we have reached be expressed to maximize its relevance to all of us, allowing us to move on but yet minimize the potential that what we have agreed will live on beyond our need for it and come to dominate us?[64] Through these processes of active discursive critique, ideas for action may be invented, and necessary codes of conduct for the collective management of shared concerns may be identified and agreed upon.

This conception of a planning invented through reflective processes of intersubjective communication within which are absorbed internal criteria of critique is suggestive of ways in which existing processes of plan-making, conflict resolution and implementation programs might be transformed. Specifically, the active presence of a planning in this form will be reflected in the language and metaphor used within the various arenas constituted for environmental planning work. It would reflect efforts at honesty and openness, without losing a recognition of the layers and range of meanings present among those concerned with the issue in hand. It would acknowledge with respect the limited scope for mutual understanding between diverse discourse communities, while struggling to enlarge that understanding. It would accept other limits – to power, to empirical knowledge, to the resolvability of moral dilemmas – but seek to enable the world-of-action to start out or move on toward something better, without having to specify precisely a goal. Rather than Lindblomian marginal adjustments to the present,[65] its language would be *future seeking*, but not, like its physical blueprint and goal-directed predecessors, *future defining*. Its images and metaphors would draw on both the experiential and abstract knowledge and understanding of those involved, recognizing the interweaving of rational-technical, moral, and aesthetic dimensions in our lives. It would seek to reason between conflicting claims and conflicting ways of validating claims. It would not force one dimension of knowledge to dominate over another. It would be courageous, challenging power relations through critique and the presentation of alternative arguments. It would reflect the internal critical monitoring practices of participants. It is thus by the *tone* of its practices that it would be identified.

The Dialectics of a New Planning

To those seeking specific substantive solutions to particular problems, the planning outlined here may seem too leisurely. With environmental disasters near at hand, can we afford to take the time to invent answers? To those seeking knowledgeable actions, this planning may seem too unfocused and diffuse. What happens if mystical perceptions of aesthetic reification crowd out the useful empirical and theoretical knowledge we have about cause and effect? To those conscious of the scale of inequalities in power relations, it may seem idealistic and innocent. Does it not merely cocoon us into a naive belief in the power of democratic discussions, while the forces of global capitalism ever more cleverly conceal the ways they oppress us?

To these doubts there are two replies. One is that to engage in any other strategy is to generate once again forms of planning that have inherent within them an antidemocratic dominatory potential. Each is one-dimensional, drawing on the power of design, of moral imperative, of scientific reasoning or, unmasked, as a direct power struggle, drawing on the possibility of replacing one dominant power source with another. The second is that the practices involved are not so far from our experience. Prefigurative examples can be found in Britain in some of the work of the New Left for example, in the Greater London Council (GLC), particularly in dealing with women's issues[66] and, recently, in a few of the new efforts in plan making in Britain resulting from requirements to prepare Urban Development Plans and District Development Plans.[67] More generally, some branches of the environmental and feminist movements have been moving in this direction. Further prefigurative potentials can even be recognized in contemporary management theory's emphasis on group culture formation and empowerment, rather than management through hierarchical authoritarian structures.[68] At a broader level, the struggle for democracy in Eastern Europe and China has highlighted awareness in Western societies as to what democracy might mean. It is in Britain perhaps that this awareness has most progressive potential, since a critical eye finds so few guarantees of democracy in our political and legal systems.

"Inventing democracy" is thus, for British people, an issue that is moving increasingly sharply into focus. It is a time, as noted at the start of this chapter, for the invention of democratic processes. The field of environmental concerns is one of the critical arenas within which such invention is being demanded and tested.[69]

However, there are many democracies that might be invented. Learning and listening, respectful argumentation, are not enough. We need to develop skills in translation, in constructive critique, in collective invention, and respectful action to be able to realize the potential of a planning understood as collectively and intersubjectively addressing and working out how to act in respect of common concerns about urban and regional environments. We need to rework the store of techniques and practices evolved within the planning field to identify their potential *within* a new communicative, dialogue-based, form of planning. This chapter has drawn on the work of a number of planning academics searching within the lifeworld of planning practice for a better understanding of these skills. What is being invented, in planning practice and planning theory, is a new form of planning, a respectful argumentative form of *planning through debate*, appropriate to our recognition of the failure of modernity's conception of "pure reason," yet searching, as Habermas does, for a continuation of the Enlightenment project of democratic progress through reasoned intersubjective argument among free citizens.

Yet as the planning community explores the hopefulness of this new approach, it is important to remember the experience of past efforts at "democratic making." Habermas offers the theory of communicative action as an intersubjective project of emancipation from fundamentalism, totalitarianism, and nihilism through deliberate efforts in mutual understanding through argument. But this can only succeed for more than a historical moment so long as the processes of internal critique are kept constantly alive; if what Habermas calls "the lifeworld" is constantly brought into the collective thinking about "acting in the world" in respect of common affairs; and if the communicative effort of mutual understanding is sustained as a critical as well as a creative process. Either we succeed in keeping a critical dialectic alive within communicative action, or we remain caught within the dialectic of totalizing systems. As the opposition of capitalism versus communism collapses, perhaps there is a hope that, through dynamically critical communicative processes, the democratic project of "making sense together while living differently" can develop as a progressive force.

Notes and References

1   Debate is used here in preference to "argumentation," as a more collaborative and positive word. Others see debate as involving opposition between two sides. It will become clear that this is not what I associate with the word.

2   This article is a very substantial development of ideas initially sketched in Healey, P., "Planning through Debate" (Paper given to *Planning Theory Conference*, Oxford, April 1990). A shorter version will appear in Fischer, F. and Forester, J. (eds.), *The Argumentative Turn in Policy Analysis and Planning*, Durham, NC, Duke University Press. My thanks to my sister Bridget, who allowed me to write this and read Habermas while on holiday. My thanks to Huw Thomas, John Forester, Seymour Mandelbaum, Jean Hillier, Jack Ellerby, Michael Benfield, Beth Moore Milroy, Gavin Kitching, Judith Allen, Michael Synnott, and Nilton Torres for their critical attention to an earlier draft.

3   See, for example, Rustin, M., *For a Pluralist Socialism*, London, Verso, 1985.

4   See Thorneley, A., *Urban Planning under Thatcherism*, London, Routledge, 1991 for a discussion of its impact in the planning field.

5   For discussions of the meaning of *modernity* and *postmodernity* in relation to planning, see Friedmann, J., *Planning in the Public Domain*, Princeton, NJ, Princeton University Press, 1987; Moore Milroy, B., "Into Postmodern Weightlessness" *Journal of Planning Education and Research*, 10 (3) 1991, pp. 181–87, and other articles in this issue of the *Journal*; and Goodchild, B., "Planning and the Modern/Postmodern Debate", *Town Planning Review*, 61 (2) 1990, pp. 119–37.

6   This is evident particularly in discussion on locality, place and local economic development. See, for example, Cooke, P. N. *Back to the Future*, London, Unwin Hyman, 1990; Massey, D., "The Political Place of Locality Studies", *Environment and Planning* A, 23 (2) 1991, pp. 267–81.

7   See Forester, J., *Planning in the Face of Power*, Berkeley, CA, University of California Press, 1989, Throgmorton, J., "Planning and Analysis as Persuasive Storytelling: The Case of Electric Power Rate-Making in the Chicago Area" (paper presented to the ACSP Congress, Austin, Texas, November 1990.

8   "Democracy" is, of course, used in contemporary debate in a wide and confused range of meanings (Williams, R., *Keywords* [2nd ed], London, Fontana, 1988). By a "progressive meaning," I align myself with the position adopted by British authors such as Held, D., *Models of Democracy*, Oxford, Polity Press, 1987, who argue for a notion of democracy based on the principle of autonomy in both political and economic spheres, in a system which promotes "discussion, debate and competition among many divergent views" (p. 280). Within this conception, open debate, access to power centres, and general political participation are key requirements for democratic public life (p. 284). It is principles such as these that have helped to fuel the *Charter* 88 constitutional movement in Britain.

9   See note 6, and also Bernstein, R. J. (ed.), *Habermas and Modernity*, Cambridge, Polity Press, 1981; Berman, M., *All That's Solid Melts to Air*, London, Verso, 1983; Harvey, D., *The Condition of Postmodernity*, Oxford, Blackwell, 1989.

10   See Friedmann, J., op. cit., N5.

11   Mannheim, K., *Man and Society in an Age of Reason*, London, Routledge, 1960; Friedmann, J., *Retracking America*, New York, Anchor, 1973; Friedmann, J., op. cit., N5; and Faludi, A., *Critical Rationalism and Planning Methodology*, London, Pion, 1986.

12   See discussion in Friedmann, J., op. cit., N11.

13   See Meyerson, M. and Banfield, E., *Politics, Planning and the Public Interest*, New York, Free Press, 1955.

14   This position was most forcefully articulated in Castells, M., *The Urban Question*, London, Edward Arnold, 1977. See also Ambrose, P. and Colenutt, B., *The Property Machine*, Harmondsworth, Penguin, 1973; and Scott, A., and Roweis, S. T., "Urban Planning in Theory and Practice", *Environment and Planning* A. 9, 1977, pp. 1097–1119.

15   See Habermas, J. *The Philosophical Discourse of Modernity*, Cambridge, Polity Press, 1987 for a helpful debate on the work of Adorno, Marcuse, Foucault and Derrida.

16   See note 9 above.

17   Moore Milroy, B., op. cit., N5.

18   Pearce, D., Markandya, A. and Barbier, E. B. *Blueprint for a Green Economy*. London, Earthscan, 1989.

19   See Thornley, op. cit., N4.

20   See Sorensen, A. "Towards a Market Theory of Planning", *The Planner*, 69 (3) 1983; pp. 78–80.

21   For good critiques of this "direction" with respect to environmental issues, see Hajer, M. "Bias in Environmental Discourse: an Analysis of the Acid Rain Controversy in Great Britain" in Fischer, F., and Forester, J. (eds.), *The Argumentative Turn in Policy and Planning*, Durham, N.C. Duke University Press (forthcoming); and Grove White, R., "Land, the Law and Environment", *Journal of Law and Society* (forthcoming).

22   See the discussion of Nietzsche's Dionysian Search and Heidegger's justification of Nazism in Habermas, J., op. cit., N15, and Moore Milroy's discussion of the fundamentalism in some "postmodern" thought (Moore Milroy, op. cit., N5).

23   See discussion in Sennett, R., *The Conscience of the Eye: The Design and Social Life of Cities*, London, Faber & Faber, 1990; and Habermas, J., op. cit., N15.

24   See Habermas's discussion of Derrida and difference in Habermas, J., op. cit., N15.

25   See Cockburn, C., *The Local State*, London, Pluto, 1977.

26   See Rustin, M., op. cit., N3 and Massey, D., op. cit., N6. Interestingly, this thinking parallels some ideas developed by Mel Webber on "persuasive planning" for pluralist, democratic societies in the 1970s, which aimed to foster debate and encompass difference (Webber, M., "A Difference Paradigm for Planning" in Burchell, R. W. and Sternlieb, G., *Planning Theory in the 1980s*, Rutgers, NJ, Center for Urban Policy Research, 1978.

27   See Rustin, M., op. cit., N3.

28   See Habermas, J., op. cit., N15.

29   See Moore Milroy, B., "Critical Capacity and Planning Theory", *Planning Theory Newsletter*, Winter 1990; pp. 12–18; and Sennett, R., op. cit., N23.

30   Habermas, J, op. cit., N15.

31   See Innes, J., *Knowledge and Public Policy: The Search for Meaningful Indicators*, New Brunswick, Transaction Publishers, 1990; Mandelbaum, S. "Telling Stories", *Journal of Planning Education and Research*, 10 (3) 1991, pp. 209–14; and Forester, J., "The Politics of Storytelling in Planning Practice" (Paper to the ACSP Congress, Austin, Texas, November 1990), for an appreciation of the role of "storytelling" in policy analysis.

32   Walzer, M., *Spheres of Justice: A Defence of Pluralism and Equality*, Oxford, Blackwell, 1983.

33   Habermas, J., *The Theory of Communicative Action Vol. 1: Reason and the Rationalisation of Society*, London, Heinemann, Polity Press, 1984.

34   Forester, J., op. cit., N7.

35   See, for example, Hillier, J., "Deconstructing the Discourse of Planning" and Throgmorton, J., "Impeaching Research: Planning as a Persuasive and Constitutive Discourse" (both Papers presented to the ACSP/AESOP Congress, Oxford, July 1991).

36   See Geertz, C., *Local Knowledge: Further Essays in Interpretive Anthropology*, New York, Basic Books, 1983; and Bourdieu, P., *In Other Words: Essays Towards a Reflexive Sociology*, Oxford, Polity Press, 1990.

37   See Geertz, C., op. cit., N36.

38   Forester, J., "Envisioning the Politics of Public Sector Dispute Resolution" in Silbey, S. and Sarat, A. (eds.). *Studies in Law, Politics and Society*, Vol. 12, Greenwich, CT. JAI Press, 1992, pp. 83–122.

39   See a recent reassessment of Mannheim's thinking by van Houten, D., "Planning Rationality and Relativism", *Environment and Planning B: Planning and Design*, 16 (2) 1989, pp. 201–14.

40   See Bourdieu, P., op. cit., N36.

41   See Habermas, J., op. cit., N15, pp. 196–297.

42   Bourdieu, P., op. cit., N36.

43   See Forester, J., op. cit., N7, Throgmorton, J., op. cit., N7, and also Hoch, C., "Conflict at Large: A National Survey of Planners and Political Conflict", *Journal of Planning Education and Research* , 8 (1) 1988, pp. 25–34; Hendler, S., "Spending Time with Planners: Their Conflicts and their Stress" (Paper presented to the ACSP Congress, Austin, Texas, November, 1990).

44   See Innes, J., op. cit., N31, and Healey, P., "A Day's Work", *Journal of the American Planning Association*, 58 (1) 1992, pp. 9–20.

45   See Mandelbaum, S., op. cit., N31, and Forester J., op. cit. 31.

46   This goes beyond Habermas's argument into the ideas offered by "ethnographic" scholars such as Bourdieu and Geertz.

47   The emphasis on respect is powerfully expressed in John Forester's work. Geertz (op. cit., N36) highlights the challenge of translation.

48   Alty, R., and Darke, R., "A City Centre for People: Involving the Community in Planning for Sheffield's Central Area", *Planning Practice and Research*, 3, 1987, pp. 7–12.

49   See Forester, J., "Anticipating Implementation: Normative Practices in Planning and Policy Analysis" in Fischer, F., and Forester, J., (eds.), *Confronting Values in Policy Analysis: The Politics of Criteria*, California, Sage, 1987; and, at a more organizational level, Bryson, J., and Crosby, B., "The Design and Use of Strategic Planning Arenas", *Planning Outlook*, 32 (1) 1989, pp. 5–13.

50   The importance of this listening and learning attitude is emphasized in Forester, J., op. cit., N7. See also Throgmorton, J., op. cit., N35, and Healey, P., op. cit., N44.

51   See Throgmorton, J., op. cit., N35, and Tait, A. and Wolfe, J., "Discourse Analysis and City Plans", *Journal of Planning Education and Research*, 10 (3) 1991, pp. 195–200 for the critical "deconstructive" analysis of planning texts.

52   Allen, J., "Smoke Over the Winter Palace: The Politics of Resistance and London's Community Areas" (Paper presented to the Second International *Planning Theory in Practice* Conference, Torino, Italy, September 1986).

53   I am indebted to Seymour Mandelbaum for the phrasing of this sentence.

54   See Forester, J., op. cit., N38.

55   As Habermas, J., op. cit., N15, claims.

56   Bourdieu, P., op. cit., N36 is referring to Marx's idea of class.

57   See Forester's discussion of Nussbaum's work (Forester, J., op. cit., N31).

58   I am indebted to correspondence about the qualities of a democratic plan with John Forester for my thinking here, as well as the ideas of Sennett, R., op. cit., N23, on designing with the grain of diversity.

59   Following the usage of Friedmann, J., op. cit., N15, "transformative" here refers to changing the context deliberately as well as acting within the context.

60   Mannheim, K., op. cit., N11.

61   Davidoff, P., "Advocacy and Pluralism in Planning", *Journal of the American Institute of Planning*, 31, November 1965, pp. 331–38.

62   Healey, P., McNamara, P. F., Elson, M. J. and Doak, A. J., *Land Use Planning and the Mediation of Urban Change*, Cambridge, Cambridge University Press, 1988; Brindley, T., Rydin, Y. and Stoker, G., *Remaking Planning*, London, Hutchinson, 1989; Blowers, A. *The Limits of Power: the Politics of Local Planning Policy*, Oxford, Pergamon, 1980.

63   See Forester, J., op. cit., N38.

64   I have developed ideas on the constitution of *process forms* in Healey, P., "Policy Processes in Planning", *Policy and Politics* 18 (1) 1990, pp. 91–103.

65   Lindblom, C. E. *The Intelligence of Democracy*, New York, Free Press, 1965.

66   See Allen, J., op. cit., N52.

67   See Healey, P., "The Communicative Work of Development Plans", *Environment and Planning B: Planning and Design*, forthcoming.

68   See Handy, C., *Understanding Organisation* (3rd ed), Harmondsworth, Penguin, 1985.

69   Grove White, R., op. cit., N21 makes this point very cogently.

Part III

Planning Types

Introduction

This section of readings reviews the dominant approaches to planning: comprehensive, incremental, advocacy, and the more recent strategic and equity planning. It is useful to begin with comprehensive planning and then see the four other approaches as responses to comprehensiveness. Incrementalism challenges the viability of large-scale, complex decision making and offers the much more modest approach of comparisons of limited policy changes. Advocacy planning questions the existence of a single, consensual public interest and instead calls for the promotion of the particular interests of the disadvantaged. Strategic planning rejects trying to serve overly broad, vague social goals and proposes planning that takes constraints into account. Equity planning challenges the ability of traditional planning to get at the roots of poverty and inequality and makes redistribution its principal goal. Both incremental planning and strategic planning share a frustration with the unwieldiness and inefficiency of comprehensive planning, whereas both advocacy planning and equity planning presume that comprehensive planning does not go far enough to deal with the unfairness of cities.

Susan and Norman Fainstein summarize these various planning approaches in their article "City Planning and Political Values: An Updated View." Significantly, they argue that planning theorists have too often debated these concepts in a political vacuum, assuming too much autonomy of planners to choose the best concept based on their intrinsic merits. Instead, Fainstein and Fainstein place these competing planning concepts in the larger context of the American political system. By linking the question of how best to plan (discussed in this section) with the question of what gives planners the power and legitimacy in society to plan (discussed in Part II), they position planners as part of the larger governmental bureaucracy and state power rather than as independent, technocratic professionals directly serving the public interest. This political perspective helps the Fainsteins answer a nagging question of planning theory: Why has America rejected most planning – even traditional, technocratic planning, which does not constitute a threat to the status quo? The answer lies in the dominance of the nineteenth-century liberal tradition. This engenders a deference to market mechanisms and incrementalism in which planners serve as arbiters rather than as proactive shapers of the built environment.

An early and highly influential attack on the foundations of comprehensive planning was Charles Lindblom's 1959 article, "The Science of Muddling Through."* If comprehensive planning was to be the unifying paradigm for the emerging postwar field of planning, this consensus did not last long. Lindblom argued that the comprehensive model required a level of data and analytical complexity that was simply beyond the grasp and ability of planners. In fact, the actual practice of planners is rarely comprehensive; by default they fall back on a more modest, incremental approach. Lindblom argues that planners should abandon the comprehensive model and explicitly define their efforts as incremental planning using "successive limited comparisons" to achieve realistic, short-term goals.

Incremental planning itself has been criticized for being too timid and conservative, both reinforcing the status quo and neglecting the power of revolutionary social change. It also shares the shortcoming of inductive thinking by assuming that short-term stimulus and response can replace the need for vision and theory. Nevertheless, the incrementalist stance has been a powerful and enduring counterargument to traditional master planning, and its ascendancy reflects a fundamental transformation of planning thought. Where formerly it was grounded in the comprehensiveness of architecture and urban design, it is increasingly oriented to the marginal analysis of economic policy and pragmatic politics.

If incremental planning challenged comprehensive planning's reliance on massive information and complex analysis to serve the public interest, advocacy planning attacked the fundamental notion of whether there even is a single, common "public interest." Paul Davidoff, in his classic and still definitive 1965 article , "Advocacy and Pluralism in Planning," argues that unitary planning perpetuates a monopoly over planning power and discourages participation. If planning is to be inclusive, it must not pretend that a single agency can represent the interests of a divergent and conflicted society. Instead, planning should promote equitable pluralism by *advocating* (Latin; "to give voice") the interests of the disenfranchised. Traditional planning creates at least two barriers to effective pluralism. First, planning commissions are undemocratic and poorly suited to represent the competing interests of a pluralist society. Second, traditional city planning too narrowly addresses issues of physical

---

* Though Lindblom later revisited this issue in his 1979 article, "Still Muddling, Not Yet Through" (*Public Administration Review*, vol. 39, pp. 517–526) the newer article was overly complex and itself muddled. The original remains the clearest statement of the argument.

planning, separating the physical from the social and thereby neglecting social conflict and inequality in the city. In this light Davidoff's call for a shift from land-use to social-economic planning reflects a more general effort to shift the identity of the planner from the objective technocrat of the conservative 1950s to the engaged, social advocate of the contentious 1960s.

Later, many planners turned to strategic planning as a new model, which they borrowed from the corporate and military worlds. Its appeal to planners lay in its streamlined, efficient focus on specific tasks, rather than the often vague and broad goals of comprehensive planning. It represented a way to privatize the style of public planning without privatizing public ownership. Yet it was also in part an abandonment of the laudable comprehensive planning goal of serving a broad public interest.

Jerome Kaufman and Harvey Jacobs assess the rise and merit of this planning approach in their 1987 article, "A Public Planning Perspective on Strategic Planning." Significantly, they address the question of whether strategic planning can work for a whole community rather than its traditional client of a specific public corporation or single city agency. They also interview practicing planners to find out how much they actually use strategic planning. Most important, Kaufman and Jacobs challenge the overly simplistic historicism that sees strategic planning as a fundamentally different alternative to current planning practice. They conclude that many of the basic features of strategic planning – action-oriented, environmental scanning; participation; assessment of community strengths and weaknesses – have actually long been incorporated into mainstream planning. Much of the rhetoric about strategic planning's novelty arose from an outdated straw man argument that planning still adheres to a strict, naive version of comprehensive planning. In this light, Kaufman and Jacobs view strategic planning as "old wine in new bottles."

Yet the post–Great Society era was not simply a retreat from comprehensive to strategic planning. A second group put forth the alternative of equity planning, which sought to return planning to a more progressive path of both promoting the larger public interest and directly addressing urban inequalities. Equity planning followed the tradition of Davidoff's advocacy planning in both perceiving the roots of socioeconomic disparity in the nature of urban development and arguing that planners have an explicit responsibility to help the disadvantaged. Equity planning can be seen as a less combative form of advocacy planning; it is a "kinder and gentler" form of advocacy planning that suits the conciliatory, pragmatic 1980s better than the activist, sometimes revolutionary-minded 1960s. Equity planning thus asserts a greater faith in finding a common ground of public interest and working within the system of public sector planning.

Norman Krumholz, the name most associated with equity planning, recounts his experiences as Cleveland's planning director in "A Retrospective View of Equity Planning: Cleveland, 1969–79," originally published in 1982. Especially impressive was the effort to promote redistribution in a declining manufacturing city; in the 1980s the usual expectation was that planning efforts for social redistribution would take place in thriving cities like Boston and San Francisco, which could "afford" such programs as inclusionary zoning and linkages of office construction to the creation of affordable housing. Though Krumholz notes that his efforts were only partly successful, he does persuasively argue that the path towards equity planning is a long one, requiring persistent commitment, clear goals, and less caution among planners.

12

City Planning and Political Values: An Updated View[1]

Susan S. Fainstein and Norman Fainstein

Contemporary planning theorists have virtually all accepted the argument that planning decisions are unavoidably political. Nevertheless, analyses of planning, while increasingly grounded in contemporary social thought, have largely ignored the classical literature of political theory. The intent of this chapter is to make explicit the links between current discussions of planning and long traditions of political thought. An examination of the political thought that underlies different approaches to planning can reveal the political value and interests embodied in planning procedures and allow planning processes to be related to political culture. The exercise therefore serves two purposes: First, it shows the implications of each type of planning in terms of political benefits; that is, it makes clear which social groups each form favors. Second, it points toward an explanation of why planning has largely been shunned within the American polity.

We define planning here as future-oriented, public decision making directed toward attaining specific goals; for the purposes of our discussion, we exclude planning carried out by private bodies. Although a plan once enacted constitutes a politically determined public policy, it differs from other kinds of political decisions in that it is based on formal rationality and is explicit about ends and means. This specificity is in sharp contrast to many other public decisions, which are left purposefully vague and ambiguous so as to mitigate controversy. While a decision need not be labeled a plan in order to fit our definition, political decisions directed at long-term goals are rarely made except under the auspices of a planning group.

It is possible to set up a typology of planning approaches on the basis of who determines the plan's goals and who determines its means. While one can conceive of a number of different bases for typologies of planning, that of policy determination is politically the most important. For once planning is viewed as a political process, and once a typology is established that is based upon the location of authoritative decision making, it becomes possible to equate each planning type with a particular model of decision making in political theory.

The Planning Typology

The categories that follow are derived from the points of view presented in discussions of planning and are not necessarily either exhaustive or mutually exclusive. Like the political doctrines to which they will be related, they contain internal contradictions and elements in common with one another. Thus, the planning typology that we are establishing is empirical rather than strictly logical. But as we shall attempt to show later, the differences among the types make a great deal of sense within the history of political thought.

The four kinds of planning we discuss are (1) traditional, (2) democratic, (3) equity, and (4) incremental (although we shall attempt to demonstrate that incrementalism, while often presented as a *de facto* planning model, is not truly planning). We trace these four planning approaches to technocratic, democratic, socialist, and liberal political theory respectively, although our discussion of socialism shows that equity planning is a hybrid form incorporating elements of both democratic and socialist thought.

Traditional planning

In this type of planning, the planner prescribes both the goals of the plan and the means of attaining them (Gans 1993: chapter 8). The justification for the elitism involved in such an approach is that there is a right and wrong way to develop a city. Planners, by virtue of their expertise and experience, know the correct path, can exercise unbiased judgment, and can be trusted to use their technical knowledge to discover the public interest.

The principal objective of traditional planners is the orderly development of the urban environment, and the proximate goals of the plan are derived from standards that supposedly measure desirable physical arrangements. Thus, for example, the amount of land to be devoted to parks is calculated on the basis of a fixed ratio between green space and population density. The use of general standards permits the designation of planning objectives without consulting groups within the general population. Thomas A. Reiner (1967: 232) summarizes the traditional outlook as follows:

> An appealing and plausible idea attracts planners the world over: we are scientists, or at least capable of becoming such. As scientists, or technicians, we work with facts to arrive at truth, using methods and language appropriate to our tasks, and our ways of handling problems are not subject to outsiders' criticism.

The conception of scientific planning assumes that planners' special qualifications free them from class or special-interest biases when they are formulating the contents of the plan. Like the entire movement for municipal reform, of which the planning movement formed part, planning advocates assumed that efficiency and orderly administration in government were general public goals that did not serve particular social interests. Gans (1993: 128), however, correctly points out that planners have generally advocated policies that fit the predispositions of the upper classes but not those of the rest of the population.

> The ends underlying the planners' physical approach reflected their Protestant upper- and middle-class view of city life. As a result, the master plan tried to eliminate as "blighting influences" many of the facilities, land uses, and institutions of working-class, low-income, and ethnic groups. . . . The plans called for many parks and playgrounds, but left out the movie house, the neighborhood tavern, and the local club room; they proposed museums and churches, but no hot-dog stands and nightclubs; they planned for industrial parks, but not loft industry; for parking garages, but not automobile repair stations.

The much-criticized replacement of Boston's West End (see Fried 1967; Gans 1967) by a group of neatly arranged, high-rise apartments for upper-income residents marked the apogee of the movement to upgrade the urban environment through the imposition of physical orderliness. The different kinds of order that observers such as Gans found in the West End were not apparent to the planners, whose criteria for demarcating slums rated the number of "standard" dwelling units present in an area.

Critics of the claims of scientific analysis supposedly embodied in planning contend that the vocabulary of planners primarily functioned to deflect opposition, masking the interests served by the urban system:

> *Does it make sense even, to tell the inner-city tenant that the rent paid to the landlord is not really a payment to that man who drives a big car and lives in the suburbs but a payment to a scarce factor of production? The "scientization" of social science seems to have been accomplished by masking real social relationships – by representing the social relations between people and groups of people as relations between things. (Harvey 1985: 167; see also Fischer 1990, 1991)*

Even the one element within the planning movement that did concern itself with the plight of the poor incorporated upper-class assumptions. The advocates of urban playgrounds and public housing were attempting to improve the welfare of slum dwellers and showed considerable concern with the lot of the disadvantaged. Their overall goal of an orderly physical environment for both rich and poor, however, reflected a class bias against the seeming disorderliness of the lower classes, a belief that along with physical neatness went desirable patterns of social behavior, and an unwarranted hope that social problems resulting from insufficient income could be remedied through physical improvements.

Democratic planning

During the 1960s, critics of traditional planning accused planners of imposing their vision of an idealized bourgeois world on a resistant population. They called for the transformation of planning from a top-down to a participatory process. For example, Gans, in discussing planning for the public library, argued that "the planning of its facilities ought to be determined by whatever goal or goals the community considers important . . ." (Gans, 1968: 102–3). According to David R. Godschalk (1967: 972), "What is needed is a *modus operandi* which brings governmental planners face-to-face with citizens in a continuous cooperative venture. Such a venture could not only educate and involve the community in planning, but could also educate and involve the planners in their community."

Godschalk's stress on the importance of constant communication between planners and the public continues to the present in the works of such influential planning theorists as John Friedmann and John Forester. Friedmann (1987: 327) calls for a "struggle . . . for a recovery of the political community on which our Western ideas of democratic governance are based." He discusses the role of radical planners in achieving this social transformation, stipulating that they must be open to the knowledge possessed by those "in the front line of action – households, local communities, social movements" (Friedmann 1987: 394). Similarly, Forester (1989: 155) exhorts planners to develop a set of community relations strategies, for example, cultivating community networks, alerting less organized interests of significant issues, assuring that community-based groups are adequately informed and engage in critical analysis of policies affecting them, exercising skills in conflict management and group relations, and compensating for political and economic pressures.

Democratic planners rely on the public as the ultimate authority in the formulation of plans and take a populist view that differentiates between special interests and the public interest. Most writers in this tradition generally side with the underdog, thereby privileging economically or politically disadvantaged groups in their analysis. To this extent their arguments merge with those of equity planners (discussed below), and there is a tendency in theory – although not in practice – to favor those least well off, often at the expense of those in the middle. Inherently, however, democratic theory cannot assume that the interests of any group should be preferred; therefore, there is confusion over which clienteles should be involved in the formulation of plans. As Gans (1968: 103) puts it in his discussion of the public library, "The question is, which users should be planned for?"

While the problem is not insurmountable in the planning of a library, where different branches can accommodate different users, it becomes much more difficult in cases where there are fewer possibilities of serving a plurality of interests simultaneously. For example, should urban redevelopment planning involve only present or also potential future occupants of the site? Should it involve business and other groups that may not occupy the site but may nonetheless have an important stake in opportunities presented by revitalization? Should zoning regulations and housing programs be aimed at perpetuating the character of a district as it is, or should they respond to the desires of outsiders who might wish to move into the district? Is the issue different when the outsiders are low-income people seeking to enter a higher-income area than when they are high-income households gentrifying a low-income one? The democratic planner must contend with the problem of conflicting interests and must judge the legitimacy of the representatives of various clienteles. By accepting the right of community actors to participate in the planning process, democratic planners find themselves forced to make political judgments that the insulated, traditional planner never had to confront. Yet in making these judgments, they evade admitting that they are advancing the particular values or interests of some segment of society; rather, they claim to be acting in the public interest or, by pressing for the interests of typically excluded groups, creating the necessary condition for genuine democracy. Although, according to the democratic planning ideal, the public chooses both ends and means, in practice the planner shapes the alternatives that will be considered by determining the composition of the planning group.

Equity planning

Equity and democratic planning are overlapping types, but while democratic planning emphasizes the participatory process, the thrust of equity planning is on the substance of programs. The issue thus shifts from who governs to who gets what. Planners begin with the overarching goal of increasing equality; who determines the means and intermediate goals depends on the situation.

The concept of equity planning contains an explicit recognition of a multitude of conflicting social interests, some of which may become irreconcilable. From this viewpoint all public programs create winners and losers, and all too often the typical losers are those who already are suffering from social and economic disadvantages. Rather than attempting to plan for society as a whole, the equity planner would "promote a wider range of choices for those . . . residents who have few" (Krumholz and Forester 1990: 48). Equity planners, rather than engaging in cost-benefit analyses that determine whether a policy is beneficial in the aggregate, examine the distribution of costs and benefits.

The terms *equity* and *advocacy planning* are now used more or less interchangeably.[2] As originally defined by Paul Davidoff, however, advocacy planning referred to the defense of excluded interests. While the advocate planner could theoretically work for any social group, the term has generally been interpreted to mean "advocate for the poor." Advocacy planning, in this first formulation, was a more limited concept than equity planning, since it did not present a model of a planner working for a public body. Rather, Davidoff based his model on the legal system and developed a scenario in which the planner was responsible to his or her client and unabashedly sought to express only the client's interests (Davidoff 1967).[3] Advocacy planning, as limited to this approach, was an extension of what Lindblom calls partisan mutual adjustment (see below). It depended on a pluralist bargaining system in which previously excluded groups were given equal standing with other interests that had always been able to purchase the services of professional planners. Advocate planners were simply consultants who acted on behalf of groups that could afford their services only if offered *pro bono* or financed by outside sources like foundations or government programs.

The concept of advocacy planning, however, has evolved to include planners inside as well as outside government. The planner's activities, paralleling changes in the profession in general, have become more or less fixed and less tied to plan preparation: "This kind of advocacy is more entrepreneurial than legal – more open in its framework of assumptions, more creative in its solutions, much broader in the kinds of understanding it tries to synthesize, more interactive and responsive" (Marris 1994). In this new formulation, there is no distinction between advocacy and equity planning.

Equity planning differs fundamentally from traditional planning, in that particular planning specifics need not be justified as being in the general public interest (although equity planners argue that their overall objective of achieving redistributional goals is in the public interest and, if they occupy a public office, would certainly try to look nonpartisan). Unlike traditional planners, equity planners enlist the participation of the public or client group in determining substantive goals and explicitly accept planning as a political rather than a strictly scientific endeavor. Traditional planning was part of the old movement for municipal reform; equity planning is part of the new movement for urban change that calls for greater representation of disadvantaged groups in the governmental process and for the decentralization of governmental policy making. Equity planners are not always democrats, since they will favor redistributional goals even in the absence of a supportive public. Nevertheless, as noted above, equity and democratic planning overlap, arising as they do from the same impulse toward social equality. Democratic planners, however, are ambivalent on the subject of whether each citizen is to be counted equally and whether popular majorities should rule. Since the democratic planner's ethic is a procedural one of allowing all voices to be heard, he or she runs into serious difficulty if the popular will conflicts with the interests of deprived groups. Equity planners, even when holding office, have a particular responsibility to advance the interests of the poor and racial or ethnic minorities, even when opposed by popular majorities. Formulation of those interests ideally includes involvement of the people on whose behalf planning is being done, but ongoing participation is not a necessary condition, for the aim is equity, not consultation.

Incremental planning

In incremental planning, policy makers come to a decision by weighing the marginal advantages of a limited number of alternatives. Rather than working in terms of long-range objectives, they move ahead through successive approximations:

> Decision makers typically consider, among all the alternative policies that they might be imagined to consider, only those relatively few alternatives that represent small or incremental changes from existing policies. In this sense ... decision making is incremental. In short, policy makers and analysts take as their starting point not the whole race of hypothetical possibilities, but only the here and now in which we live, and then move on to consider how alterations might be made at the margin. (Lindblom 1965: 144)

Planning is not done by a single agency: "That society requires conscious control and manipulation is one assertion; that an 'organizing center' is required is quite another" (Lindblom 1965: 5). Like Davidoff, Lindblom recognizes a multitude of interests. But where the advocate planner sees irremediable conflict, the incrementalist sees an ultimate harmony (see Lindblom 1965: 4).

In terms of our definition of planning, incrementalism is not really planning at all. Policy outcomes are not arrived at through formal rationality, and there is no specifying of ends and means. But Lindblom claims that the mechanism of "partisan mutual adjustment" – the working out of different claims through compromise, adherence to procedural rules, and the market process – results in rational decision making: "The concern of this study has been . . . with partisan mutual adjustment as a method for calculated, reasonable, rational intelligent, wise, policy making" (Lindblom 1965: 294). Even though ends and means are not formulated, decision makers work out ways to reach socially desirable goals:

> Behind the incremental and disjointed tactics we have just summarized is a concept of problem solving as a strategy. In this view public problems are too complex to be well understood, too complex to be mastered. One develops a strategy to cope with problems, not to solve them. (Lindblom 1965: 148).

Therefore, while incrementalism embodies the opposite of planning in its methods, it produces the fruits of planning in its results. Like an economic system of numerous buyers and sellers, a political system of atomized decision makers working at cross-purposes can rely on the invisible hand to produce orderly progress toward social goals – in fact, to produce the very goals themselves.

Lindblom (1965: 223) attempts to show that seemingly *ad hoc* methods of arriving at public policies result in a hidden rationality. The ultimate decision-making power does not lie with a single group, and it is not desirable that any one social interest should prevail. Political interaction causes the clash of interests to be resolved in a Pareto optimum, so that no group can benefit further without some other group losing out. Lindblom assumes that such an optimum, which implies the preservation of the existing arrangement of social power, is desirable.[4]

Four Types of Political Theory

Planners have mainly been satisfied to contain within narrow bounds their debate over who should make planning decisions. To a large extent, they have attempted to justify their arguments by evaluating the merits of the policies each type of planning is likely to produce rather than looking at the fundamental questions of social power and legitimacy that each type raises. The principal exceptions to this assertion are provided by Marxist and poststructuralist planning theorists, who are very concerned with these fundamental questions but who, for the most part, have not provided prescriptive theories of planning within capitalist societies (see Fainstein and Fainstein 1979).[5] As Peter Hall (1988: 239) says of the Marxists: "[Their] logic is strangely quietist; it suggests that the planner retreats from planning altogether into the academic ivory tower." Similarly, poststructuralists tend to be critical rather than proactive, espousing strategies for resistance rather than formulating roles for planners (see Beauregard, 1991).

Political theorists offer insights into appropriate behavior for planners, since, like most planning theorists, they endeavor to find models of decision making that will produce desirable social outcomes. They differ from other social theorists because they go beyond simply analyzing social relations to address practical questions of governance. Within the tangle of political thought in the modern, Western world – that is, in the period since Locke – we can identify four major types of political theory that correspond to our typology of planning theories. Even though this typology of political theories is not exhaustive,[6] it offers a framework by which we can judge the strengths and weaknesses of the planning theories and evaluate the fit between the planning theories and American political traditions.

Technocratic theory and traditional planning

Technocratic thinking is a product of the industrial era. It represents an effort to come to grips with the central social problems created by the Industrial Revolution – the miserable condition of the lower classes and the breakdown in the old structure of authority that previously maintained order. Like the conservatives, the technocrats desire to restore the order of the preindustrial world, but unlike the conservatives they accept modernization, welcoming technology as the cure for the ills of mankind. Their motto is "order and progress." Their most significant thinkers are Comte, Saint-Simon, and, to a lesser extent, Owen and Fourier.[7]

The technocrats stand in opposition to the social anarchy they see created by capitalism. In their eyes, capitalism dissolved the bonds of the *ancien régime*, replacing community with the marketplace, and the paternalism of the old elite with the laissez-faire of the new. But rather than intending a return to the days before industrialization – an impossibility – they wish to harness the power of technology to create a new society and thereby to ameliorate the condition of the lower classes, as well as the threat they pose to social order. The technocrats desire to unleash the power of reason and science, to transpose the old, theological religion into a modern, positivist one. Through rational planning, the power of the state will be employed to regulate the economy and advance the lower classes, as well as to ensure the position of the productive ones. All of this will be possible only when the scientific and industrial classes control the state and do away with politics in the name of science and reason.

In the words of Comte (n.d.: 781):

> Since the abolition of personal servitude, the lowest class has never been really incorporated with the social system; the power of capital . . . has become exorbitant in daily transactions, however just is its influence through its generality and superior responsibility. . . . This philosophy will show that industrial relations, instead of being left to a dangerous empiricism and an oppressive antagonism [between the classes], must be systematized according to moral laws. The duty [of the upper classes] to the lower classes will not consist in almsgiving. The obligation will be to procure for all suitable education and employment – the only condition that the lower classes can justly demand.

The Saint-Simonians, who echo Comte's faith in science and concern for the condition of the lower classes, also stress the positive quality of power as a tool in remolding society.

> The most direct method of improving the moral and physical welfare of the majority of the population is to give priority in State expenditures to ensuring work for all fit men, to secure their physical existence. We must add to this the measures necessary to ensure that the national wealth is administered by men most fitted for it, and most concerned in its administration, that is to say, the most important industrialists. (Saint-Simon 1964 edn: 77)

The technocrats visualize a hierarchical society in which the lower orders are secure and happy, but strictly subordinate to the managerial-scientific elite. In this respect, as in others, technocratic theory, while more detailed and explicit than discussions of traditional planning, presents a picture of society that is quite compatible with traditional planning ideas and useful in baring their hidden foundation. Underlying traditional planning is the technocratic faith in progress through science and rationality tied to the constructive use of power in the form of the plan. The technocrats make explicit the planner's belief that there is indeed some unitary public interest that experts of goodwill can identify and maximise. Like traditional planners, they seek to replace politics with scientific administration.

According to the technocrats, social change must be engineered from the top, by social strata that command the economy, and in the public interest, indeed in the interest of the lower classes; for they see a harmony of interests between themselves and the masses. Here again, technocratic theory makes explicit an assumption of traditional planning: that social change for the benefit of all society must be initiated paternalistically by the upper classes. Because all classes benefit from increasing productivity and public order, the interests of the upper classes become identical with the public interest. If the natural rulers fail to play their roles, sometimes even resist change, it is only because they remain as yet insufficiently enlightened.

Traditional planners, much more limited in their expectations than the technocrats, did manage to see some of their programs carried out. Parks were built, building codes passed and sometimes enforced, transit lines planned and constructed, slums razed; land-use zoning became a commonplace. Social change was initiated from the top in the name of the public good, sometimes in the interest of the lower classes, and with the ultimate necessity of legislative sanction.

Nevertheless, traditional planning suffered from the basic weaknesses of technocratic thought within the United States. It was always limited in its scope by the unwillingness of the upper strata to support reform (see Foglesong 1986). In fact, traditional planners have long been perplexed by the all-too-common refusal of the holders of political and economic power to recognize the importance of rational planning as a means for the improvement of life (see Fainstein and Fainstein 1985). Equally significant, in a culture permeated by a majoritarian populist ideology, technocratic elitism provoked widespread suspicion of its progenitors and its aims. From the time of the defeat of Alexander Hamilton's national bank to the present, Americans have rejected dominance by small groups claiming special expertise. Thus, the role of traditional planning was limited by well-founded distrust of decision makers insulated from accountability, generalized hostility to abstract ideas, and the refusal of most of the upper class to engage in long-range planning.

Democratic theory and democratic planning

Democratic planning stands squarely within the mainstream of democratic thought. The following argument relies mainly on the work of Alexis de Tocqueville as exemplifying democratic political thought; other democratic theorists diverge considerably in their arguments concerning appropriate democratic forms, the protection of minority and individual rights, the role of intermediate groups, and the scope of governmental action.

Democratic theory begins with the sanctity of the individual and the primacy of his or her interests. Not only does all sovereignty emanate from the people, they are also the only source of public values: "Everyone is the best and sole judge of his own private interests" (see Tocqueville 1957 edn: 67). Everyone is equal and has an equal right to advance his or her cause. There is no interest in society that cannot be

related to that of its members. Thus, the democrats start with equal individuals and their desires – rather than the social origin or intrinsic merit
of these desires – and goes on to equate the public interest with the
interests of the public, or at least with those of the majority.

Having accepted individual sovereignty as a basic axiom, the democrats then go on to deal with the problem of government, of how public
power is to be distributed. Some form of differentiation between the
government and the citizenry becomes immediately necessary – unless,
of course, the size of the polity is severely limited.[8] Even though some
form of representation is necessary, democratic thinkers seek to maintain
as much political power in the hands of the citizenry as is feasible. The
rule of the majority becomes the instrument by which citizens control the
government. For "the very essence of democratic government consists in
the absolute sovereignty of the majority" (Tocqueville 1957 edn: 264).
The governors must be forced to remain the delegates of the governed.
Unless they do – and they will only if power remains within the hands of
the citizenry – government cannot be expected to advance the interests
of the majority. Government by representatives freed from the control of
the majority, by an independent aristocracy of wealth (or even merit), is
likely to act in its own interests, which are necessarily at odds with those
of the sovereign people.

> *Democratic laws generally tend to promote the welfare of the greatest possible*
> *number; for they emanate from the majority of the citizens, who are subject*
> *to error, but [who] cannot have an interest opposed to their own advantage.*
> *The laws of an aristocracy tend, on the contrary, to concentrate wealth and*
> *power in the hands of the minority; because an aristocracy, by its very*
> *nature, constitutes a minority (Tocqueville 1957 edn: 247).*

> *Under aristocratic governments public men are swayed by the interest of*
> *their order, which, if it is sometimes confused with the interests of the*
> *majority, is very frequently distinct from them (Tocqueville 1957 edn: 249).*

Democratic planning requires the planner to act as delegate of the citizenry. But this is not to say that the democratic planner must be a passive
figure blindly following instructions. Rather, the democratic planner, like
the democratic governor, both responds to constituents and attempts to
educate them, to show them alternatives and the relation between particular policies and their interests. Indeed, the reason that citizens must
participate in government and retain power in their hands is not only to
prevent governmental outcomes contrary to their interests but also so
that they themselves may grow, learn from participation, and become
even more knowledgeable and better able to govern themselves.

There are three major criticisms of democratic theory, which apply
equally to democratic planning. First, democratic policy makers are

immediately confronted with the short-term relative ignorance and self-ishness of the citizenry, and the fact that "education through participation" is a slow process for which public policy cannot wait. In real life, participating citizens may not readily accept the planner's under-standing of how means are related to goals, or of how particular policies may be derived from their interests. In addition, people are frequently unwilling to make long-run decisions, that is, to plan, when doing so necessitates the deferment of immediate gratification. As a result, democ-racies are less likely to plan than technocracies. Most worrisome is the problem Rousseau confronted when he established a dichotomy between the general will and the will of all: Instead of acting as citizens seeking to determine the well-being of the community in which they participate (that is, acting in accordance with the general will), people will typically act in their narrow self-interest (that is, in conformity with the will of all).[9] The perennial planning problems captured by the term "NIMBYism" ("not in my backyard") point to the difficulty of getting democratic agree-ment on necessary but costly policies.

Second, it is difficult for democratic theory to explain why citizens should bother to participate in public policy making or planning at all, for a rational calculus of the costs and benefits of participation often makes apathy quite compatible with the private interests of individuals (see Olsen 1968, and his followers in the resource mobilization school of theory[10]). Given the minimal impact of the individual, the cost of one person's time and effort outweigh any real benefits that could accrue to him or her personally. So most citizens are apathetic most of the time, and the democratic planner has only a small minority with whom to plan. Democratic planning in these circumstances either becomes impossible or requires planners to take upon themselves the task of divining the will of the majority, in which case the planning process can hardly be called democratic.[11]

The final criticism of democratic theory suggests that the rule of the majority leads to social mediocrity and even to fascist authoritarianism. Tocqueville regarded democracy as a threat to elevated taste; in a classic statement of the problem (1957 edn: 262) he stated:

> *Do you wish to give a certain elevation to the human mind and teach it to regard the things of this world with genuine feelings, to inspire men with a scorn of mere temporal advantages? Is it your object to refine the habits, embellish the manners, and cultivate the arts, to promote the love of poetry, beauty and glory? If you believe such to be the principal object of society, avoid the government of the democracy, for it would not lead you with certainty to the goal.*

Although Tocqueville's formulation now sounds dated and insuffer-ably elitist, contemporary critics of mass culture mount a similar attack, although their claim, somewhat confusingly, is that the vulgarized forms of urbanity embodied in Disneyland and "theme-parked" urban spaces are inherently antidemocratic. Thus, when Michael Sorkin, an architectural critic, argues against synthetic spaces in the name of democracy, he is echoing Tocqueville's aristocratic claim concerning "genuine" feeling:

> *The theme park presents its happy regulated vision of pleasure – all those artfully hoodwinking forms – as a substitute for the democratic public realm, and it does so appealingly by stripping troubled urbanity of its sting, of the presence of the poor, of crime, of dirt, or work. (Sorkin 1992: xv)*

The argument here is essentially that people are fooled into accepting the ersatz as real. Rather than blaming democracy for the failures of mass taste to recognize the genuine, Sorkin castigates those who pander to it. But the subtext of his argument parallels Tocqueville's: The people are easily misled into accepting the tawdry over the genuine.

Even more serious, however, is the concern that mass participation is conducive to the triumph of demagoguery as unscrupulous leaders play on the fears and aspirations of the public (see Ortega y Gasset 1932). The danger of mass mobilization behind authoritarian nationalist movements has been glaringly evident in the twentieth century. Even at the level of city and community we see, in widespread resistance to school integration or housing for the homeless, the pitting of incensed majorities against weak minorities. Within liberal-democratic systems the protection of minority rights and civil liberties is intended to guard against immoderate majorities. Clearly, however, the threat of democracy out of control is inherent to this method of governance rather than aberrational.

Socialist theory and equity planning

Since the first formulations of socialist theory in the nineteenth century, socialists have divided according to whether or not they believed in peaceful reform as a means of achieving significant social change. The aspects of the theory of socialism that we will develop here are concerned entirely with obtaining power and benefits for the poor within an existing democratic capitalist society, as opposed either to socialist revolution or the operation of a purely socialist government. We are thus developing a reformist rather than a Marxist model of socialism, since Marxist socialism precludes the possibility of achieving equity under capitalism.

Socialism begins with a conflict analysis of society. It highlights the divergence of interests among different social strata and emphasizes the extent to which the upper strata maintain control of a disproportionate share of social resources through their use of power. Socialism sees the interests of individuals as determined by the objective, material circumstances of their lives – that is, by their class situation. Since the advantages gained by the capital-owning class are at the expense of the working class, the conflict of interests is real and unavoidable. This situation will continue so long as the capitalist class controls the conditions under which the remainder of society labors.

From the argument that interests are class-based, it follows that what is generally called "the public interest" must not be such at all. Rather, it is merely a reflection of the values and programs of the politically and economically dominant groups. Only these groups are in a position to define what is particularly beneficial to them as being also generally beneficial to the whole society. This view was stated most strongly by Marx and Engels (1947 edn: 39): "The ideas of the ruling class are in every epoch the ruling ideas: i.e., the class which is the ruling material force of society, is at the same time its ruling intellectual force." Even in varieties with a more flexible diagnosis of the range of possibility within capitalist society, socialist thought assumes the prevalence of a dominant ideology favoring capital.

The socialist emphasis on material, rather than simply legal or political, equality also characterizes the argument for equity planning. For equity planners, as for socialists, the general good of society is embodied in the welfare of its most numerous class; and the fundamental value by which to judge a society is equality. Both groups throw in their lot with those at the bottom of the social order and realize that doing so places them in conflict with the particular interests of the upper strata. Equity planning likewise shares the socialist drive to demystify state policies that benefit capital while claiming to be in the public interest. Thus, downtown renewal, which is supposed to promote economic development and jobs for the working class, is revealed as providing subsidies to developers and corporations while displacing low-income people and failing to improve their employment situation.

Despite their class analysis of society, however, equity planners believe in the potential of democratic government. Thus, although recognizing conflict as unavoidable, Krumholz also expresses his faith "that equity in the social, economic, and political relationships among people is a requisite condition for a just and lasting society" (Krumholz and Forester 1990: 51). He considers that his logic will lead authoritative decision makers to support "people less favored by present conditions" (Krumholz and Forester 1990: 49), even though they lack power and may even be fewer in number than their opponents. The final outcome will be based on "ultimate consensus" (Krumholz and Forester 1990: 50).

Equity planning assumes an ultimately benevolent state. Although the advocacy strand within it posits endemic social conflict, even Davidoff, in his seminal article on advocacy planning, takes it for granted that a neutral judge – presumably a public official – will rule in favor of disadvantaged groups who have adequate spokespersons for their cause. Hence, while Davidoff begins with a conflict perspective and does not explicitly deal with the role of the state, he, like Krumholz, accepts an autonomous role for public policy and a state sector that does not simply act in the narrow interests of officials dependent on capitalist largesse.

Equity planning combines the socialist's belief in equality with the democrat's faith in government by the people. Consequently, its philosophical home is within democratic socialism, which extends the concept of democracy to include social as well as political rights. As the British political philosopher, T. H. Marshall (1965: 103) stated, "Social rights imply an absolute right to a certain standard of civilization which is conditional only on the discharge of the general duties of [democratic] citizenship." Within this framework the democratic state, rather than being overwhelmed by the power of property holders, can force powerful social interests to give up their privileges to promote the good of others.

In contrast, for Marx and Engels and their followers, real social change never takes place from the top. It does not result from the persuasive power of reasonable argument directed toward those who control our government and economy, for the upper classes are willing to redistribute their power or wealth only when under duress from those beneath them. Social change, in fact, can be initiated only by a social force arising from the collective action of an exploited class; it cannot be produced by public officials acting in accordance with a philosophical position.

Marxist socialism, however, while internally logical, offers little guidance for planners. Within its constraints even reformist planners have no choice but to uphold the status quo (Harvey 1985: chapter 7). Planners searching for a role that allows them to assist those with fewest choices may share much of the Marxist critique of contemporary society, but they almost necessarily must abandon the Marxist remedy of total social restructuring if they are going to take action short of revolution.

On the other hand, the democratic socialist stance, while offering a direction for altruistic policy makers, does not provide a strong defense against critics on either the left or the right. On the left, adversaries can demonstrate that the space for state-sponsored reformism is quite narrow. Because capital is free to flee those places that seriously limit capitalist autonomy – in other words, those that have a "poor business climate" – it holds the upper hand in restricting attempts at redistribution. On the right, critics contend that well-meaning radicals oppose policies that benefit hardworking, middle-class taxpayers to favor unproductive social parasites. In response to both these attacks, democratic socialists are left arguing a moral position that, unlike Marxism, neither makes claims to historical inevitability nor, as does belief in the invisible hand of the market, purports to produce efficiency or reward individual merit. Recently, Norman Krumholz explained that he remained committed to equity planning "because it is right."[12] Ultimately, the argument for democratic socialism depends on this justification as well.

Liberal theory and incrementalism

Incremental decision making is the form of planning logically implied by liberal political theory. Lindblom's model is nothing more than the particular application of the general premises of liberal thought, as formulated by Locke in the seventeenth century and developed by Bentham, Spencer, and a number of other thinkers in the nineteenth century. Liberalism begins with an atomistic conception of human society, seeing human beings as rational actors who are the best judges of their own private interests. The public interest is accepted as real but is regarded as resulting from the interplay of a multiplicity of private interests within the confines of the political marketplace.

The obligation of liberal government is first and foremost to guarantee the rule of law, to defend agreed-upon procedures; as Locke put it, to act as an impartial judge or umpire. Liberalism in pure form gives government no other function than this role of umpire and thus no mandate to address social inequality. There is, however, another strand of liberal thought, often called "positive liberalism," which developed during the early part of the twentieth century. It does give to government the additional function of trying to advance its own conception of the public interest. In this activist version of the liberal state, government aids private interests that are ill-treated in the marketplace. Positive liberalism weds the technocratic conception of constructive governmental action to the mainstream of liberal thought; in its most radical identity, positive liberalism begins to merge with democratic socialism.

Nevertheless, liberalism in all its forms emphasizes the prime importance of a diffusion of power within society. Freedom is the most important social value, and efficiency is the outcome of its exercise. Neither the technocrat's elite, the democrat's majority, nor the socialist's deprived class should have absolute power. No group or institution should have so much power that it can corner the political market. The most proactive liberal conception of government still sees it as being only *primus inter pares*. The largest role played by the governmental decision maker is to add another input to the market of alternative policies – a government may create plans and attempt to implement them, but it can never be assured of their being carried out.

Thus, the general direction in which society is to move, or the way in which political benefits are to be distributed, is not decided explicitly at all. Rather, it is the result of a large number of decisions, some of which may be made by government. Overall social policy is not made deliberately but results from a mechanism that acts like an invisible hand, producing outcomes that are ultimately rational.

Incrementalism, like classic liberalism, is based on a procedural value of maximizing individual freedom. Consequently, it benefits primarily those social groups already most privileged under present conditions. These are the strata that command the greatest share of power resources (see Dahl 1961: esp. 94 for use of the term), enabling them to take a disproportionate amount of social rewards. The most acceptable form of governmental activity for these groups is that which ensures their present position – hence, the acceptability of zoning ordinances and the like. Because they have favored government as an arbiter rather than positive actor, they have rallied behind the values of efficiency and economy in municipal government rather than behind those of welfare and innovation.

Incrementalism thus shares the weaknesses of liberalism. In a society where not just wealth but also power is unequal, those who are worst off materially also have the least ability to change the system. Moreover, the very pluralism of interests makes any transformative change extraordinarily difficult, even if the great majority would benefit from it. Thus, for example, efforts at environmental preservation and conservation of energy resources founder as a result of a process of incremental decision making that strictly limits the scope of change.

Significance of the Typology

Our discussion of the relationship between planning types and political theories shows the concepts of planning to be not just analogous to certain strains in modern political thought but actually fragments of these political formulations. The fuller articulation of the planning types in terms of value assumptions and justifications of social power permits us to understand why America has largely rejected the programs of city planners – apart from certain exceptions, in the area of parks, zoning, and urban renewal.

For a variety of historical and cultural reasons, the United States has been dominated by the liberal tradition.[13] This tradition values individualism, accepts the primacy of private interests, and prefers minimal government. Thus, the very notion of planning, which assumes an overriding and ascertainable public interest that can be realized through the positive actions of government, is antithetical to general American political values. As Lindblom correctly argues, most decision making in this country follows his description of partisan mutual adjustment. Policy is determined incrementally; it is arrived at through the clash and compromise of opposing views within the political marketplace. But this incrementalism itself marks the absence of planning.

Incrementalism and partisan mutual adjustment maximize liberal values: They restrict the role of government to that of umpire in the political marketplace, thus guaranteeing the enforcement of procedural rules but remaining oblivious to outcomes, to which groups win and which lose in the process of politics. At a maximum, government becomes another actor in the political process, offering its own solutions to social problems, with the proviso that its solutions must compete with those offered by private decision makers.

The American political tradition is, of course, democratic as well as liberal. Why, then, has there been an absence of democratic planning in the United States? For, to the extent that we have had planning, it has not involved widespread participation. In the United States "positive" government has been associated with the centralization of power. Reasons are both inherent in any effort at democratic planning and also specific to the U.S. system of fragmented democracy.

Unlike democratic planning, traditional planning has been inhibited neither by a lack of institutional mechanisms nor by the absence of supportive social conditions. Like Europe, the United States has a powerful scientific-industrial class. But this group in America has largely rejected technocratic thought in favor of liberalism. Thus, planning has been much more powerful in Europe, where the capitalist elite has consciously visualized itself as an aristocracy of talent, attempting to supplant the old aristocracy of birth. The technocratic idea has been embodied in the European planned city, the mixed public-private corporation, the whole *dirigiste* tendency of the modern western European economies.

American business leaders have tended to see themselves as individual entrepreneurs rather than as members of an aristocratic class. They have supported laissez-faire instead of *dirigisme*. It is extremely significant that the great successes of traditional planning in the United States have occurred in those cases where business interests have participated in "public-private partnerships" to improve the central city. In these instances planning was carried on in the name of the general good, but its direct beneficiaries were downtown business interests and upper-middle-class residents (Squires 1989). It was assumed that everyone would benefit from the economic expansion that supposedly would result from the construction of new office buildings and retail centers, even though most of the people who received specific advantages in terms of governmental subsidies were already well off.

The relative absence of equity planning, like the limited extent of traditional planning, can be attributed largely to American political values. There are two prerequisites for socialist planning: The first is the political organization of those seeking redistribution; the second is the existence of a political spectrum broad enough to permit the presentation of a radical ideology by advocates for the poor. Except perhaps for a brief period during the 1930s, these conditions did not exist in the United States at all until the 1960s. Low-income people accepted the individualist bias of the general political culture. The middle-class sympathizers who constituted the intellectual leadership of European socialist movements were unable to escape from the dominant American liberal ideology. Thus, they stumbled into technocratic reformism rather than socialist radicalism. It was only the rise of black militancy, based on the premise that the interests of lower-class blacks are fundamentally opposed to those of middle-class white Americans, that led to a new consciousness on the part of a segment of the lower class. This change in the consciousness of the lower class, combined with the movement toward the left among young American intellectuals during the 1960s and 1970s, laid the foundation for the development of equity planning.

Until the present time, social change in America has largely been unplanned. While the poor may have benefited from increasing material prosperity, they have not been the special beneficiaries of change, and the improvement of their lot – to the extent that it has taken place – has been largely accidental. The planners who intend to ameliorate the conditions of the deprived must recognize that redistribution of social goods will not take place without social conflict. As advocates for the poor, they must admit, at least to themselves, that they are supporting the particular interests of a particular social group. Realistic planners must give up the delusions that they can serve the whole public equally well and that there is an indissoluble social good, which they are particularly well circumstanced to ascertain. They must, in short, reject many of the technocratic biases underlying the professional rhetoric of planning and construct a new rationale for themselves.

Notes

1   This is a substantially revised version of the article, "City Planning and Political Values," originally published in the *Urban Affairs Quarterly*, 6 (March 1971), pp. 341–62. At the time the original article was published, planning theory as a distinct realm of analysis barely existed. This situation, as well as the preoccupations of planning theorists, has changed dramatically in the intervening quarter century. This revision seeks to take into account this transformation.

2   See the articles in the recent forum on advocacy planning in Checkoway (1994).

3   Krumholz and Forester (1990: 250, n.6) quote Charles Hoch to this effect: "I would argue that you [Krumholz and his staff] were not really advocate planners, that is, identifying with a client and representing their interests in a partisan manner."

4   Any redistribution of social power would require some other group to suffer a loss equal to the benefit received by the gaining group.

5   For Marxist critiques of planning, see Dear and Scott (1981), especially the

chapter by S. T. Roweis; Castells (1977); Harvey (1985: chapter 7). For post-structuralist examinations, see Boyer (1983); Beauregard (1991); Liggett and Perry (forthcoming).

6   It is important to recognize that we are discussing secular systems of thought that, within the discourse of Weberian sociology, would be defined as modern. We have seen a resurgence of political conflict in the world that has been defined by religious principles and inherited identities that are not part of this "modern" debate. Indeed, our focus may seem a bit of hand waving designed to cover up a rather glaring omission, for there is no mention in our typology of truly conservative thought – that, for example, associated with Edmund Burke in England or with Bonald and de Maistre in France.

   We have purposely ignored conservative thought for two reasons. The first is that conservative thinking stands antithetical to the whole idea of rational policy making. If we took the time to discuss it, it would only be to dismiss it. Second, there is in America a total absence of conservative thinking, of the conservative desire to maintain a feudal past. What genuine conservatism exists is combined with praise of industrialism and thus fits under our classification of technocratic thought. What is sometimes called conservatism in the United States is nothing more than liberalism at its extreme – the liberalism of Spencer and the Social Darwinists; as such, we treat it in our section on liberalism.

7   The reader may note that the last three names are usually associated with the category "utopian socialism." The use of this term is, we feel, misleading and almost entirely a result of the fact that Marx made the label stick. Louis Hartz calls them "feudal socialists," which is a better choice of words, since it makes any simplistic association of their names with socialism more difficult. By choosing to emphasize Comte and the elements in the thought of the others most closely related to his theories, we have even further loosened the connection between technocratic and socialist thought.

8   Rousseau imposes precisely such a limitation when he describes his own democracy.

9   Rousseau, in the *Social Contract*, distinguishes between the citizen as a member of the community and unsocialized natural man, who is not evil but who does not have the benefits of civilization. Through his theory of democracy he attempts to make the constraints of civilization legitimate. In a democratic society citizens themselves determine the laws that will limit their freedom rather than having constraints imposed upon them. When each citizen makes a decision in conformity with the collective good, the resulting choice embodies the general will. When decisions are made only on the basis of narrow self-interest, the consequence is the will of all. (Rousseau 1950 edn; see Hartz 1990: chapter 5).

10   Olsen develops his argument within the paradigm of neoclassical economics; like all neoclassical economic models, his places the individual prior to the community and defines rationality as the maximization of individual self-interest.

11   Altshuler (1965) describes the difficulties encountered by Minneapolis's planners when they sought to involve citizens in formulating the goals for downtown redevelopment. At the stage of general goal setting, few people

could foresee the implications of decisions for themselves. But by the time the planning process got down to specifics, the framework had already gelled. In my own recent work on Minneapolis (Fainstein et al. 1993), which has examined the neighborhood planning process, I have found that in most neighborhoods, relatively few people participate and that in particular, the low-income, renter population does not become involved.

12   Forum on Equity Planning, Cleveland State University, May 14, 1994.
13   For extensive arguments in support of this interpretation, see Hartz (1955), Boorstein (1953), and Lipset (1963).

References

Altshuler, A. A. 1965. *The City Planning Process*. Ithaca: Cornell University Press.
Beauregard, R. A. 1991. "Without a net: modernist planning and the postmodern abyss." *Journal of Planning Education and Research*, 10 (Summer 1991): 189–94.
Boorstin, D. J. 1953. *The Genius of American Politics*. Chicago: University of Chicago Press.
Boyer, M. C. 1983. *Dreaming the Rational City*. Cambridge, MA: MIT Press.
Castells, M. 1977. *The Urban Question*. Cambridge, MA: MIT Press.
Checkoway, B. (ed.) 1994 "Paul Davidoff and advocacy planning in retrospect." *Journal of the American Planning Association*, 60 (Spring 1994): 139–61.
Comte, A. n.d. *The Positive Philosophy of Auguste Comte*. Trans. H. Martineau. New York: Peter Eckler.
Dahl, R. 1961. *Who Governs?* New Haven: Yale University Press.
Davidoff, P. 1965. "Advocacy and pluralism in planning." *Journal of the American Institute of Planners*, 31 (December): 544–555.
Dear, M., and A. J. Scott (eds). 1981. *Urban Planning and Urbanization in Capitalist Society*. London: Methuen.
Fainstein, S. S., and N. I. Fainstein. 1985. "Is state planning necessary for capital?" *International Journal of Urban and Regional Research*, 9(4) (December): 485–507.
—— 1979. "New Debates in urban planning: the impact of Marxist theory within the United States." *International Journal of Urban and Regional Research*, 3(3) (September): 381–403.
Fainstein, S. S., with N. J. Glickman, C. Gravon, and C. Hirst. 1993. *An Interim Evaluation of the Minneapolis Neighborhood Revitalization Program*. New Brunswick, NJ: Center for Urban Policy Research.
Fischer, F. 1991. "Risk assessment and environmental crisis: toward an integration of science and participation," *Industrial Crisis Quarterly*, 5: 113–32.
—— 1990. *Technocracy and the Politics of Expertise*. Newbury Park, CA: Sage.
Foglesong, R. E. 1986. *Planning the Capitalist City*. Princeton: Princeton University Press.
Forester, J. 1989. *Planning the Face of Power*. Berkeley, CA: University of California Press.
Fried, M. 1967. "Grieving for a lost home." Pp. 359–379 in J. Q. Wilson, ed., *Urban Renewal*. Cambridge, MA: MIT Press.
Friedmann, J. 1987. *Planning in the Public Domain*. Princeton: Princeton University Press.

Gans, H. 1993. *People, Plans, and Policies*. New York: Columbia University Press.

Gans, Herbert. 1968. *People and Plans*. New York: Basic Books.

—— 1967a. "The failure of urban renewal." Pp. 540–542 in J. Q. Wilson, ed., *Urban Renewal*. Cambridge, MA: MIT

Godschalk, D. R. 1967. "The circle of urban participation." Pp. 971–978 in H. W. Eldridge, ed., *Taming Megalopolis*, vol. 2. New York: Anchor.

Hall, P. 1988. *Cities of Tomorrow*. Oxford: Blackwell.

Hartz, L. 1990. *The Necessity of Choice*. Edited, compiled, and prepared by Paul Roazen. New Brunswick, NJ: Transaction.

—— 1955. *The Liberal Tradition in America*. New York: Harcourt, Brace & World.

Harvey, D. 1985. *The Urbanization of Capital*. Baltimore: Johns Hopkins University Press.

Krumholz, N., and J. Forester. 1990. *Making Equity Planning Work*. Philadelphia: Temple University Press.

Lasswell, H. Edn. 1958. *Politics: Who Gets What, When, How*. New York: Meridian.

Liggett, H., and D. Perry. Forthcoming. *Spatial Practices*. Newbury Park, CA: Sage.

Lindblom, C. 1965. *The Intelligence of Democracy*. New York: Free Press.

Lipset, S. M. 1963. *The First New Nation*. New York: Basic Books.

Marris, P. 1994. "Advocacy planning as a bridge between the professional and the political." *Journal of the American Planning Association*, 60 (Spring): 143–6.

Marshall, T. H. 1965. *Class, Citizenship, and Social Development*. New York: Anchor.

Marx, K., and F. Engels. 1947 edn. *The German Ideology*. New York: International. (Originally published in 1846).

Olson, Mancur. 1968. *The Logic of Collective Action*. New York: Schocken.

Ortega y Gasset, José. 1932. *The Revolt of the Masses*. New York: Norton.

Reiner, T. A. 1967. "The planner as value technician: two classes of Utopian constructs and their impact on planning." Pp. 232–247 in H. W. Eldridge, ed., *Taming Megalopolis*, vol. 1. New York: Anchor.

Rousseau, J. J. 1950 edn. *The Social Contract and Discourses*. New York: E. P. Dutton.

Saint-Simon, H. de 1964 edn. "On social organization." Pp. 76–80 in F. Markham (ed. and trans.), *Henri de Saint-Simon: Social Organization, the Science of Man and Other Writings*. New York: Harper. (Originally published in 1825.)

Sorkin, M. (ed.) 1992. *Variations on a Theme Park*. New York: Hill and Wang.

Squires, Gregory, (ed.) 1989. *Unequal Partnerships*. New Brunswick, NJ: Rutgers University Press.

Tocqueville, A. de. 1957 edn. *Democracy in America*. New York: Vintage. (Originally published circa 1848.)

13

The Science of "Muddling Through"

Charles E. Lindblom

Suppose an administrator is given responsibility for formulating policy with respect to inflation. He might start by trying to list all related values in order of importance, for example, full employment, reasonable business profit, protection of small savings, prevention of a stock market crash. Then all possible policy outcomes could be rated as more or less efficient in attaining a maximum of these values. This would of course require a prodigious inquiry into values held by members of society and an equally prodigious set of calculations on how much of each value is equal to how much of each other value. He could then proceed to outline all possible policy alternatives. In a third step he would undertake systematic comparison of his multitude of alternatives to determine which attains the greatest amount of values.

In comparing policies he would take advantage of any theory available that generalized about classes of policies. In considering inflation, for example, he would compare all policies in the light of the theory of prices. Since no alternatives are beyond his investigation, he would consider strict central control and the abolition of all prices and markets on the one hand and elimination of all public controls with reliance completely on the free market on the other, both in the light of whatever theoretical generalizations he could find on such hypothetical economies.

Finally, he would try to make the choice that would in fact maximize his values.

An alternative line of attack would be to set as his principal objective, either explicitly or without conscious thought, the relatively simple goal of keeping prices level. This objective might be compromised or complicated by only a few other goals such as full employment. He would in fact disregard most other social values as beyond his present interest and he would for the moment not even attempt to rank the few values that he regarded as immediately relevant. Were he pressed he would quickly admit that he was ignoring many related values and many possible important consequences of his policies.

As a second step, he would outline those relatively few policy alternatives that occurred to him. He would then compare them. In comparing his limited number of alternatives, most of them familiar from past controversies, he would not ordinarily find a body of theory precise enough to carry him through a comparison of their respective consequences. Instead he would rely heavily on the record of past experience with small policy steps to predict the consequences of similar steps extended into the future.

Moreover, he would find that the policy alternatives combined objectives or values in different ways. For example, one policy might offer price level stability at the cost of some risk of unemployment; another might offer less price stability but also less risk of unemployment. Hence, the next step in his approach – the final selection – would combine into one the choice among values and the choice among instruments for reaching values. It would not, as in the first method of policy making approximate a more mechanical process of choosing the means that best satisfied goals that were previously clarified and ranked. Because practitioners of the second approach expect to achieve their goals only partially, they would expect to repeat endlessly the sequence just described as conditions and aspirations changed and as accuracy of prediction improved.

By Root or by Branch

For complex problems the first of these two approaches is of course impossible. Although such an approach can be described, it cannot be practiced except for relatively simple problems and even then only in a somewhat modified form. It assumes intellectual capacities and sources of information that people simply do not possess, and it is even more absurd as an approach to policy when the time and money that can be allocated to a policy problem is limited, as is always the case. Of particular importance to public administration is the fact that public agencies are in effect usually instructed not to practice the first method. That is to say, their prescribed functions and constraints – the politically or legally possible – restrict their attention to relatively few values and relatively few alternative policies among the countless alternatives that might be imagined. It is the second method that is practiced.

Curiously, however, the literatures of decision making, policy formulation, planning and public administration formalize the first approach rather than the second, leaving public administrators who handle complex decisions in the position of practicing what few preach. For emphasis I run some risk of overstatement. True enough the literature is well aware of limits on human capacities and of the inevitability that policies will be approached in some such style as the second. But attempts to formalize rational policy formulation – to lay out explicitly the necessary steps in the process – usually describe the first approach and not the second.[1]

The common tendency to describe policy formulation even for complex problems as though it followed the first approach has been strengthened by the attention given to, and successes enjoyed by, operations research, statistical decision theory, and systems analysis. The hallmarks of these procedures, typical of the first approach, are clarity of objective, explicitness of evaluation, a high degree of comprehensiveness of overview, and – wherever possible – quantification of values for mathematical analysis. But these advanced procedures remain largely the appropriate techniques of relatively small-scale problem solving, where the total number of variables to be considered is small and value problems restricted. Charles Hitch, head of the Economics Division of RAND Corporation, one of the leading centers for application of these techniques has written:

> I would make the empirical generalization from my experience at RAND and elsewhere that operations research is the art of sub-optimizing, i.e., of solving some lower-level problems, and that difficulties increase and our special competence diminishes by an order of magnitude with every level of decision making we attempt to ascend. The sort of simple explicit model which operations researchers are so proficient in using can certainly reflect most of the significant factors influencing traffic control on the George Washington Bridge, but the proportion of the relevant reality which we can represent by any such model or models in studying, say, a major foreign-policy decision, appears to be almost trivial.[2]

Accordingly I propose in this chapter to clarify and formalize the second method, much neglected in the literature. This might be described as the method of *successive limited comparisons*, I will contrast it with the first approach which might be called the rational-comprehensive method.[3] More impressionistically and briefly – and therefore generally used in this chapter – they could be characterized as the branch method and root method, the former continually building out from the current situation step by step and by small degrees; the later starting from fundamentals anew each time, building on the past only as experience is embodied in a theory, and always prepared to start completely from the ground up.

Let us put the characteristics of the two methods side by side in simplest terms.

Table 13.1   Comparison of comprehensive versus incremental approaches

Rational-Comprehensive (Root)	Successive Limited Comparisons (Branch)
1a Clarification of values or objectives distinct from and usually prerequisite to empirical analysis of alternative policies.	1b Selection of value goals and empirical analysis of the needed action are not distinct from one another but are closely intertwined.
2a Policy formulation is therefore approached through means-end analysis: First the ends are isolated, then the means to achieve them are sought.	2b Since means and ends are not distinct, means-end analysis is often inappropriate or limited.
3a The test of a "good" policy is that it can be shown to be the most appropriate means to desired ends.	3b The test of a "good" policy is typically that various analysts find themselves directly agreeing on a policy (without their agreeing that it is the most appropriate means to an agreed objective).
4a Analysis is comprehensive: every important relevant factor is taken into account.	4b Analysis is drastically limited: i) Important possible outcomes are neglected. ii) Important alternative potential policies are neglected. iii) Important affected values are neglected.
5a Theory is often heavily relied upon.	5b A succession of comparisons greatly reduces or eliminates reliance on theory.

Assuming that the root method is familiar and understandable, we proceed directly to clarification of its alternative by contrast. In explaining the second we shall be describing how most administrators do in fact approach complex questions, for the root method, the "best" way as a blueprint or model, is in fact not workable for complex policy questions, and administrators are forced to use the method of successive limited comparisons.

Intertwining Evaluation and Empirical Analysis (1b)

The quickest way to understand how values are handled in the method of successive limited comparisons is to see how the root method often breaks down in *its* handling of values or objectives. The idea that values should be clarified, and in advance of the examination of alternative policies, is appealing. But what happens when we attempt it for complex social problems? The first difficulty is that on many critical values or objectives, citizens disagree, congressmen disagree, and public administrators disagree. Even where a fairly specific objective is prescribed for the administrator there remains considerable room for disagreement on subobjectives. Consider, for example the conflict with respect to locating public housing, described in Meyerson and Banfield's study of the Chicago Housing Authority[4] – disagreement that occurred despite the clear objective of providing a certain number of public housing units in the city. Similarly conflicting are objectives in highway location, traffic control, minimum wage administration, development of tourist facilities in national parks, or insect control.

Administrators cannot escape these conflicts by ascertaining the majority's preference, for preferences have not been registered on most issues; indeed, there often *are* no preferences in the absence of public discussion sufficient to bring an issue to the attention of the electorate. Furthermore, there is a question of whether intensity of feeling should be considered as well as the number of persons preferring each alternative. By the impossibility of doing otherwise administrators often are reduced to deciding policy without clarifying objectives first.

Even when an administrator resolves to follow his own values as a criterion for decisions he often will not know how to rank them when they conflict with one another, as they usually do. Suppose, for example, that an administrator must relocate tenants living in tenements scheduled for destruction. One objective is to empty the buildings fairly promptly, another is to find suitable accommodation for persons displaced, another is to avoid friction with residents in other areas in which a large influx would be unwelcome, another is to deal with all concerned through persuasion if possible and so on.

How does one state even to himself the relative importance of these partially conflicting values? A simple ranking of them is not enough; one needs ideally to know how much of one value is worth sacrificing for some of another value. The answer is that typically the administrator chooses – and must choose – directly among policies in which these values are combined in different ways. He cannot first clarify his values and then choose among policies.

A more subtle third point underlies both the first two. Social objectives do not always have the same relative values. One objective may be highly prized in one circumstance, another in another circumstance. If, for example, an administrator values highly both the dispatch with which his agency can carry through its projects *and* good public relations, it matters little which of the two possibly conflicting values he favors in some abstract or general sense. Policy questions arise in forms that put to administrators such a question as: given the degree to which we are or are not already achieving the values of dispatch and the values of good public relations, is it worth sacrificing a little speed for a happier clientele, or is it better to risk offending the clientele so that we can get on with our work? The answer to such a question varies with circumstances.

The value problem is as the example shows always a problem of adjustments at a margin. But there is no practicable way to state marginal objectives or values except in terms of particular policies. That one value is preferred to another in one decision situation does not mean that it will be preferred in another decision situation in which it can be had only at great sacrifice of another value. Attempts to rank or order values in general and abstract terms so that they do not shift from decision to decision end up by ignoring the relevant marginal preferences. The significance of this third point thus goes very far. Even if all administrators had at hand an agreed set of values, objectives, and constraints, and an agreed ranking of these values, objectives, and constraints, their marginal values in actual choice situations would be impossible to formulate.

Unable consequently to formulate the relevant values first and then choose among policies to achieve them, administrators must choose directly among alternative policies that offer different marginal combinations of values. Somewhat paradoxically the only practicable way to disclose one's relevant marginal values even to oneself is to describe the policy one chooses to achieve them. Except roughly and vaguely, I know of no way to describe – or even to understand – what my relative evaluations are for say, freedom and security, speed and accuracy in governmental decisions, or low taxes and better schools than to describe my preferences among specific policy choices that might be made between the alternatives in each of the pairs.

In summary two aspects of the process by which values are actually handled can be distinguished. The first is clear: evaluation and empirical analysis are intertwined; that is, one chooses among values and among policies at one and the same time. Put a little more elaborately one simultaneously chooses a policy to attain certain objectives and chooses the objectives themselves. The second aspect is related but distinct: the administrator focuses his attention on marginal or incremental values. Whether he is aware of it or not he does not find general formulations of objectives very helpful and in fact makes specific marginal or incremental comparisons. Two policies X and Y confront him. Both promise the same degree of attainment of objectives *a, b, c, d,* and *e.* But X promises him somewhat more of *f* than does Y, while Y promises him somewhat more of *g* than does X. In choosing between them, he is in fact offered the alternative of a marginal or incremental amount of *f* at the expense of a marginal or incremental amount of *g.* The only values that are relevant to his choice are these increments by which the two policies differ; and when he finally chooses between the two marginal values he does so by making a choice between policies.[5]

As to whether the attempt to clarify objectives in advance of policy selection is more or less rational than the close intertwining of marginal evaluation and empirical analysis, the principal difference established is that for complex problems the first is impossible and irrelevant, and the second is both possible and relevant. The second is possible because the administrator need not try to analyze any values except the values by which alternative policies differ and need not be concerned with them except as they differ marginally. His need for information on values or objectives is drastically reduced as compared with the root method; and his capacity for grasping, comprehending, and relating values to one another is not strained beyond the breaking point.

Relations Between Means and Ends (2b)

Decision making is ordinarily formalized as a means-ends relationship: Means are conceived to be evaluated and chosen in the light of ends finally selected independently of and prior to the choice of means. This is the means-ends relationship of the root method. But it follows from all that has just been said that such a means-ends relationship is possible only to the extent that values are agreed upon, are reconcilable and are stable at the margin. Typically, therefore, such a means-ends relationship is absent from the branch method, where means and ends are simultaneously chosen.

Yet any departure from the means-ends relationship of the root method will strike some readers as inconceivable. For it will appear to them that only in such a relationship is it possible to determine whether one policy choice is better or worse than another. How can an administrator know whether he has made a wise or foolish decision if he is without prior values or objectives by which to judge his decisions? The answer to this question calls up the third distinctive difference between root and branch methods: how to decide the best policy.

The Test of "Good" Policy (3b)

In the root method a decision is "correct," "good," or "rational" if it can be shown to attain some specified objective, where the objective can be specified without simply describing the decision itself. Where objectives are defined only through the marginal or incremental approach to values described above, it is still sometimes possible to test whether a policy does in fact attain the desired objectives; but a precise statement of the objectives takes the form of a description of the policy chosen or some alternative to it. To show that a policy is mistaken one cannot offer an abstract argument that important objectives are not achieved; one must instead argue that another policy is to be preferred.

So far the departure from customary ways of looking at problem solving is not troublesome for many administrators will be quick to agree that the most effective discussion of the correctness of policy does take the form of comparison with other policies that might have been chosen. But what of the situation in which administrators cannot agree on values or objectives, either abstractly or in marginal terms? What then is the test of "good" policy? For the root method, there is no test. Agreement on objectives failing, there is no standard of "correctness". For the method of successive limited comparisons, the test is agreement on policy itself, which remains possible even when agreement on values is not.

It has been suggested that continuing agreement in Congress on the desirability of extending old age insurance stems from liberal desires to strengthen the welfare programs of the federal government and from conservative desires to reduce union demands for private pension plans. If so, this is an excellent demonstration of the ease with which individuals of different ideologies often can agree on concrete policy. Labor mediators report a similar phenomenon: the contestants cannot agree on criteria for settling their disputes but can agree on specific proposals. Similarly, when one administrator's objective turns out to be another's means, they often can agree on policy.

Agreement on policy thus becomes the only practicable test of the policy's correctness. And for one administrator to seek to win the other over to agreement on ends as well would accomplish nothing and create quite unnecessary controversy.

If agreement directly on policy as a test for "best" policy seems a poor substitute for testing the policy against its objectives, it ought to be remembered that objectives themselves have no ultimate validity other than they are agreed upon. Hence agreement is the test of "best" policy in both methods. But where the root method requires agreement on what elements in the decision constitute objectives and on which of these objectives should be sought, the branch method falls back on agreement wherever it can be found.

In an important sense, therefore, it is not irrational for an administrator to defend a policy as good without being able to specify what it is good for.

Noncomprehensive Analysis (4b)

Ideally, rational-comprehensive analysis leaves out nothing important. But it is impossible to take everything important into consideration unless "important" is so narrowly defined that analysis is in fact quite limited. Limits on human intellectual capacities and on available information set definite limits to man's capacity to be comprehensive. In actual fact, therefore no one can practice the rational-comprehensive method for really complex problems, and every administrator faced with a sufficiently complex problem must find ways drastically to simplify.

An administrator assisting in the formulation of agricultural economic policy cannot in the first place be competent on all possible policies. He cannot even comprehend one policy entirely. In planning a soil bank program, he cannot successfully anticipate the impact of higher or lower farm income on, say, urbanization – the possible consequent loosening of family ties, possible consequent eventual need for revisions in social security and further implications for tax problems arising out of new federal responsibilities for social security and municipal responsibilities for urban services. Nor, to follow another line of repercussions, can he work through the soil bank program's effects on prices for agricultural products in foreign markets and consequent implications for foreign relations, including those arising out of economic rivalry between the United States and the USSR.

In the method of successive limited comparisons, simplification is systematically achieved in two principal ways. First, it is achieved through limitation of policy comparisons to those policies that differ in relatively small degree from policies presently in effect. Such a limitation immediately reduces the number of alternatives to be investigated and also drastically simplifies the character of the investigation of each. For it is not necessary to undertake fundamental inquiry into an alternative and its consequences; it is necessary only to study those respects in which the proposed alternative and its consequences differ from the status quo. The empirical comparison of marginal differences among alternative policies that differ only marginally is, of course, a counterpart to the incremental or marginal comparison of values discussed above.[6]

Relevance as well as realism

It is a matter of common observation that in Western democracies public administrators and policy analysts in general do largely limit their analyses to incremental or marginal differences in policies that are chosen to differ only incrementally. They do not do so, however, solely because they desperately need some way to simplify their problems; they also do so in order to be relevant. Democracies change their policies almost entirely through incremental adjustments. Policy does not move in leaps and bounds.

The incremental character of political change in the United States has often been remarked. The two major political parties agree on fundamentals; they offer alternative policies to the voters only on relatively small points of difference. Both parties favor full employment but they define it somewhat differently; both favor the development of water power resources but in slightly different ways; and both favor unemployment compensation but not the same level of benefits. Similarly, shifts of policy within a party take place largely through a series of relatively small changes, as can be seen in their only gradual acceptance of the idea of governmental responsibility for support of the unemployed, a change in party positions beginning in the early 1930s and culminating in a sense in the Employment Act of 1946.

Party behavior is in turn rooted in public attitudes and political theorists cannot conceive of democracy's surviving in the United States in the absence of fundamental agreement on potentially disruptive issues, with consequent limitation of policy debates to relatively small differences in policy.

Since the policies ignored by the administrator are politically impossible and so irrelevant, the simplification of analysis achieved by concentrating on policies that differ only incrementally, is not a capricious kind of simplification. In addition, it can be argued that given the limits on knowledge within which policy makers are confined, simplifying by limiting the focus to small variations from present policy makes the most of available knowledge. Because policies being considered are like present and past policies, the administrator can obtain information and claim some insight. Nonincremental policy proposals are therefore typically not only politically irrelevant but also unpredictable in their consequences.

The second method of simplification of analysis is the practice of ignoring important possible consequences of possible policies, as well as the values attached to the neglected consequences. If this appears to disclose a shocking shortcoming of successive limited comparisons, it can be replied that, even if the exclusions are random, policies may nevertheless be more intelligently formulated than through futile attempts to achieve a comprehensiveness beyond human capacity. Actually, however the exclusions, seeming arbitrary or random from one point of view, need be neither.

Achieving a degree of comprehensiveness

Suppose that each value neglected by one policy-making agency were a major concern of at least one other agency. In that case, a helpful division of labor would be achieved and no agency need find its task beyond its capacities. The shortcomings of such a system would be that one agency might destroy a value either before another agency could be activated to safeguard it or in spite of another agency's efforts. But the possibility that important values may be lost is present in any form of organization, even where agencies attempt to comprehend in planning more than is humanly possible.

The virtue of such a hypothetical division of labor is that every important interest or value has its watchdog. And these watchdogs can protect the interests in their jurisdiction in two quite different ways: first by redressing damages done by other agencies; and second, by anticipating and heading off injury before it occurs.

In a society like that of the United States in which individuals are free to combine to pursue almost any possible common interest they might have and in which government agencies are sensitive to the pressures of these groups, the system described is approximated. Almost every interest has its watchdog. Without claiming that every interest has a sufficiently powerful watchdog, it can be argued that our system often can assure a more comprehensive regard for the values of the whole society than any attempt at intellectual comprehensiveness.

In the United States, for example, no part of government attempts a comprehensive overview of policy on income distribution. A policy nevertheless evolves and one responding to a wide variety of interests. A process of mutual adjustment among farm groups, labor unions, municipalities and school boards, tax authorities, and government agencies with responsibilities in the fields of housing, health, highways, national parks, fire and police accomplishes a distribution of income in which particular income problems neglected at one point in the decision processes become central at another point.

Mutual adjustment is more pervasive than the explicit forms it takes in negotiation between groups; it persists through the mutual impacts of groups upon each other even where they are not in communication. For all the imperfections and latent dangers in this ubiquitous process of mutual adjustment it will often accomplish an adaptation of policies to a wider range of interests than could be done by one group centrally.

Note, too, how the incremental pattern of policy making fits with the multiple pressure pattern. For when decisions are only incremental – closely related to known policies, it is easier for one group to anticipate the kind of moves another might make and easier too for it to make correction for injury already accomplished.[7]

Even partisanship and narrowness, to use pejorative terms, will sometimes be assets to rational decision making for they can doubly ensure that what one agency neglects, another will not; they specialize personnel to distinct points of view. The claim is valid that effective rational coordination of the federal administration, if possible to achieve at all, would require an agreed set of values[8] – if "rational" is defined as the practice of the root method of decision making. But a high degree of administrative coordination occurs as each agency adjusts its policies to the concerns of the other agencies in the process of fragmented decision making I have just described.

For all the apparent shortcomings of the incremental approach to policy alternatives, with its arbitrary exclusion coupled with fragmentation when compared to the root method, the branch method often looks far superior. In the root method, the inevitable exclusion of factors is accidental, unsystematic, and not defensible by any argument so far developed, while in the branch method the exclusions are deliberate, systematic, and defensible. Ideally, of course, the root method does not exclude; in practice it must.

Nor does the branch method necessarily neglect long-run considerations and objectives. It is clear that important values must be omitted in considering policy, and sometimes the only way long-run objectives can be given adequate attention is through the neglect of short-run considerations. But the values omitted can be either long-run or short-run.

Succession of Comparisons (5b)

The final distinctive element in the branch method is that the comparisons, together with the policy choice, proceed in a chronological series. Policy is not made once and for all; it is made and remade endlessly. Policy making is a process of successive approximation to some desired objectives in which what is desired itself continues to change under reconsideration.

Making policy is at best a very rough process. Neither social scientists nor politicians nor public administrators yet know enough about the social world to avoid repeated error in predicting the consequences of policy moves. Wise policy makers consequently expect that their policies will achieve only part of what they hope and at the same time will produce unanticipated consequences they would have preferred to avoid. If they proceed through a *succession* of incremental changes, they avoid serious lasting mistakes in several ways.

In the first place past sequences of policy steps have given them knowledge about the probable consequences of further similar steps. Second, they need not attempt big jumps toward their goals that would require predictions beyond their or anyone else's knowledge, because they never expect their policy to be a final resolution of a problem. Their decision is only one step, one that if successful can quickly be followed by another. Third, they are in effect able to test their previous predictions as they move on to each further step. Lastly they can often remedy a past error fairly quickly – more quickly than if policy proceeded through more distinct steps widely spaced in time.

Compare this comparative analysis of incremental changes with the aspiration to employ theory in the root method. People cannot think without classifying, without subsuming one experience under a more general category of experiences. The attempt to push categorization as far as possible and to find general propositions that can be applied to specific situations is what I refer to with the word "theory". Where root analysis often leans heavily on theory in this sense, the branch method does not.

The assumption of root analysts is that theory is the most systematic and economical way to bring relevant knowledge to bear on a specific problem. Granting the assumption, an unhappy fact is that we do not have adequate theory to apply to problems in any policy area, although theory is more adequate in some areas – monetary policy, for example – than in others. Comparative analysis as in the branch method, is sometimes a systematic alternative to theory.

Suppose an administrator must choose among a small group of policies that differ only incrementally from each other and from present policy. He or she might aspire to "understand" each of the alternatives – for example, to know all the consequences of each aspect of each policy. If so the administrator would indeed require theory. In fact, however, he or she would usually decide that *for policy-making purposes*, it was essential to know, as explained above, only the consequences of each of those aspects of the policies in which they differed from one another. For this much more modest aspiration, the administrator requires no theory (although it might be helpful, if available), for the individual can proceed to isolate probable differences by examining the differences in consequences associated with past differences in policies, a feasible program because he or she can draw on observations from a long sequence of incremental changes.

For example, without a more comprehensive social theory about juvenile delinquency than scholars have yet produced, one cannot possibly understand the ways in which a variety of public policies – say on education, housing, recreation, employment, race relations, and policing – might encourage or discourage delinquency. And one needs such an understanding to undertake the comprehensive overview of the problem prescribed in the models of the root method. If, however, one merely wants to mobilize knowledge sufficient to assist in a choice among a small group of similar policies – alternative policies on juvenile court procedures, for example – one can do so by comparative analysis of the results of similar past policy moves.

Theorists and Practitioners

This difference explains – in some cases at least – why administrators often feel that outside experts or academic problem solvers are sometimes not helpful and in turn often urge more theory on them. And it explains why administrators often feel more confident when "flying by the seat of their pants" than when following the advice of theorists. Theorists often ask administrators to go the long way round to the solution of their problems, in effect ask them to follow the best canons of the scientific method when the administrators know that the best available theory will work less well than more modest incremental comparisons. Theorists do not realize that administrators are often in fact practicing a systematic method. It would be foolish to push this explanation too far, for sometimes practical decision makers are pursuing neither a theoretical approach nor successive comparisons, nor any other systematic method.

It may be worth emphasizing that theory is sometimes of extremely limited helpfulness in policy making for at least two rather different reasons. It is greedy for facts; it can be constructed only through a great collection of observations. And it is typically insufficiently precise for application to a policy process that moves through small changes. In contrast, the comparative method both economizes on the need for facts and directs the analyst's attention to just those facts that are relevant to the fine choices faced by the decision maker.

With respect to precision of theory, economic theory serves as an example. It predicts that an economy without money or prices would in certain specified ways misallocate resources, but this finding pertains to an alternative far removed from the kind of policies on which administrators need help. On the other hand, it is not precise enough to predict the consequences of policies restricting business mergers and this is the kind of issue on which the administrators need help. Only in relatively restricted areas does economic theory achieve sufficient precision to go far in resolving policy questions; its helpfulness in policy making is always so limited that it requires supplementation through comparative analysis.

Successive Comparison as a System

Successive limited comparison is, then, indeed a method or system; it is not a failure of method for which administrators ought to apologize. None the less, its imperfections, which have not been explored in this chapter are many. For example, the method is without a built-in safe-guard for all relevant values and it also may lead the decision maker to overlook excellent policies for no other reason than that they are not suggested by the chain of successive policy steps leading up to the present. Hence it ought to be said that under this method, as well as under some of the most sophisticated variants of the root method – operations research for example – policies will continue to be as foolish as they are wise.

Why then bother to describe the method in all the above detail? Because it is in fact a common method of policy formulation and is, for complex problems, the principal reliance of administrators as well as of other policy analysts.[9] And because it will be superior to any other decision-making method available for complex problems in many circumstances, certainly superior to a futile attempt at superhuman comprehensiveness. The reaction of the public administrator to the expo-sition of method doubtless will be less a discovery of a new method than a better acquaintance with an old. But by becoming more conscious of their practice of this method, administrators might practice it with more skill and know when to extend or constrict its use. (That they sometimes practice it effectively and sometimes not may explain the extremes of opinion on "muddling through," which is both praised as a highly sophis-ticated form of problem solving and denounced as no method at all. For I suspect that insofar as there is a system in what is known as "muddling through," this method is it.)

One of the noteworthy incidental consequences of clarification of the method is the light it throws on the suspicion an administrator sometimes entertains that a consultant or adviser is not speaking relevantly and responsibly when in fact by all ordinary objective evidence the person is. The trouble lies in the fact that most of us approach policy problems within a framework given by our view of a chain of successive policy choices made up to the present. One's thinking about appropriate policies with respect, say, to urban traffic control is greatly influenced by one's knowledge of the incremental steps taken up to the present. An administrator enjoys an intimate knowledge of his past sequences that "outsiders" do not share, and his thinking and that of the outsider will consequently be different in ways that may puzzle both. Both may appear to be talking intelligently, yet each may find the other unsatisfactory. The relevance of the policy chain of succession is even more clear when an American tries to discuss, say, antitrust policy with a Swiss, for the chains of policy in the two countries are strikingly different, and the two individuals consequently have organized their knowledge in quite different ways.

If this phenomenon is a barrier to communication, an understanding of it promises an enrichment of intellectual interaction in policy formu-lation. Once the source of difference is understood, it will sometimes be stimulating for an administrator to seek out a policy analyst whose recent experience is with a policy chain different from his own.

This raises again a question only briefly discussed above on the merits of like-mindedness among government administrators. While much of organization theory argues the virtues of common values and agreed organizational objectives, for complex problems in which the root method is inapplicable, agencies will want among their own personnel two types of diversification: administrators whose thinking is organized by reference to policy chains other than those familiar to most members of the organization and, even more commonly, administrators whose professional or personal values or interests create diversity of view (perhaps coming from different specialties, social classes, geographical areas) so that even within a single agency, decision making can be fragmented and parts of the agency can serve as watchdogs for other parts.

Notes

1   James G. March and Herbert A. Simon similarly characterize the literature. They also take some important steps, as have Simon's recent articles, to describe a less heroic model of policy making. See *Organizations* (John Wiley and Sons, 1958), p. 137.

2   "Operations Research and National Planning – A Dissent." 5 *Operations Research* 718 (October 1957). Hitch's dissent is from particular points made in the article to which his paper is a reply; his claim that operations research is for low-level problems is widely accepted.

For examples of the kind of problems to which operations research is applied see C. W. Churchman, R. L. Ackoff and E. L. Arnoff, *Introduction to Operations Research* (John Wiley and Sons, 1957); and J. F. McCloskey and J. M. Coppinger (eds.) *Operations Research for Management*, Vol II (The Johns Hopkins Press, 1956).

3   I am assuming that administrators often make policy and advise in the making of policy and am treating decision making and policy making as synonymous for purposes of this chapter.

4   Martin Meyerson and Edward C. Banfield, *Politics, Planning and the Public Interest* (The Free Press, 1955).

5   The line of argument is, of course, an extension of the theory of market choice, especially the theory of consumer choice, to public policy choices.

6   A more precise definition of incremental policies and a discussion of whether a change that appears "small" to one observer might be seen differently by another is to be found in my "Policy Analysis," 48 *American Economic Review* 298 (June, 1958).

7   The link between the practice of the method of successive limited comparisons and mutual adjustment of interests in a highly fragmented decision-making process adds a new facet to pluralist theories of government and administration.

8   Herbert Simon, Donald W. Smithburg and Victor A. Thompson, *Public Administration* (Alfred A. Knopf, 1950). p. 434.

9   Elsewhere I have explored this same method of policy formulation as practiced by academic analysts of policy ("Policy Analysis," 48 *American Economic Review* 298 [June, 1958]). Although it has been here presented as a method for public administrators, it is no less necessary to analysts more removed from immediate policy questions, despite their tendencies to describe their own analytical efforts as though they were the rational-comprehensive method with an especially heavy use of theory. Similarly, this same method is inevitably resorted to in personal problem solving, where means and ends are sometimes impossible to separate, where aspirations or objectives undergo constant development, and where drastic simplification of the complexity of the real world is urgent if problems are to be solved in the time that can be given to them. To an economist accustomed to dealing with the marginal or incremental concept in market processes, the central idea in the method is that both evaluation and empirical analysis are incremental.

14

Advocacy and Pluralism in Planning

Paul Davidoff

The present can become an epoch in which the dreams of the past for an enlightened and just democracy are turned into a reality. The massing of voices protesting racial discrimination have roused this nation to the need to rectify racial and other social injustices. The adoption by Congress of a host of welfare measures and the Supreme Court's specification of the meaning of equal protection by law both reveal the response to protest and open the way for the vast changes still required.

The just demand for political and social equality on the part of the African American and the impoverished requires the public to establish the bases for a society affording equal opportunity to all citizens. The compelling need for intelligent planning, for specification of new social goals and the means for achieving them, is manifest. The society of the future will be an urban one, and city planners will help to give it shape and content.

The prospect for future planning is that of a practice openly inviting political and social values to be examined and debated. Acceptance of this position means rejection of prescriptions for planning that would have the planner act solely as a technician. It has been argued that technical studies to enlarge the information available to decision makers must take precedence over statements of goals and ideals:

We have suggested that, at least in part, the city planner is better advised to start from research into the functional aspects of cities than from his own

Reprinted by permission of the *Journal of the American Institute of Planners* Vol. 31, No. 4, 1965.

estimation of the values which he is attempting to maximize. This suggestion springs from a conviction that at this juncture the implications of many planning decisions are poorly understood, and that no certain means are at hand by which values can be measured, ranked, and translated into the design of a metropolitan system.[1]

While acknowledging the need for humility and openness in the adoption of social goals, this statement amounts to an attempt to eliminate, or sharply reduce, the unique contribution planning can make: understanding the functional aspects of the city and recommending appropriate future action to improve the urban condition.

Another argument that attempts to reduce the importance of attitudes and values in planning and other policy sciences is that the major public questions are themselves matters of choice between technical methods of solution. Dahl and Lindblom put forth this position at the beginning of their important textbook, *Politics, Economics, and Welfare.*[2]

In economic organization and reform, the "great issues" are no longer the great issues, if they ever were. It has become increasingly difficult for thoughtful men to find meaningful alternatives posed in the traditional choices between socialism and capitalism, planning and the free market, regulation and laissez faire, for they find their actual choices neither so simple nor so grand. Not so simple, because economic organization poses knotty problems that can only be solved by painstaking attention to technical details – how else, for example, can inflation be controlled? Nor so grand, because, at least in the Western world, most people neither can nor wish to experiment with the whole pattern of socio-economic organization to attain goals more easily won. If for example, taxation will serve the purpose, why "abolish the wages system" to ameliorate income inequality?

These words were written in the early 1950s and express the spirit of that decade more than that of the 1960s. They suggest that the major battles have been fought. But the "great issues" in economic organization, those revolving around the central issue of the nature of distributive justice, have yet to be settled. The world is still in turmoil over the way in which the resources of nations are to be distributed. The justice of the present social allocation of wealth, knowledge, skill, and other social goods is clearly in debate. Solutions to questions about the share of wealth and other social commodities that should go to different classes cannot be technically derived; they must arise from social attitudes.

Appropriate planning action cannot be prescribed from a position of value neutrality, for prescriptions are based on desired objectives. One conclusion drawn from this assertion is that "values are inescapable elements of any rational decision-making process"[3] and that values held by the planner should be made clear. The implications of that conclusion for planning have been described elsewhere and will not be considered in this chapter.[4] Here I will say that the planner should do more than explicate the values underlying his prescriptions for courses of action; he should affirm them; he should be an advocate for what he deems proper.

Determinations of what serves the public interest, in a society containing many diverse interest groups, are almost always of a highly contentious nature. In performing its role of prescribing courses of action leading to future desired states, the planning profession must engage itself thoroughly and openly in the contention surrounding political determination. Moreover, planners should be able to engage in the political process as advocates of the interests both of government and of such other groups, organizations, or individuals who are concerned with proposing policies for the future development of the community.

The recommendation that city planners represent and plead the plans of many interest groups is founded upon the need to establish an effective urban democracy, one in which citizens may be able to play an active role in the process of deciding public policy. Appropriate policy in a democracy is determined through a process of political debate. The right course of action is always a matter of choice, never of fact. In a bureaucratic age great care must be taken that choices remain in the area of public view and participation.

Urban politics, in an era of increasing government activity in planning and welfare, must balance the demands for ever-increasing central bureaucratic control against the demands for increased concern for the unique requirements of local, specialized interests. The welfare of all and the welfare of minorities are both deserving of support: Planning must be so structured and so practiced as to account for this unavoidable bifurcation of the public interest.

The idealized political process in a democracy serves the search for truth in much the same manner as due process in law. Fair notice and hearings, production of supporting evidence, cross-examination, reasoned decision are all means employed to arrive at relative truth: a just decision. Due process and two (or more) party political contention both rely heavily upon strong advocacy by a professional. The advocate represents an individual, group, or organization. He affirms their position in language understandable to his client and to the decision makers he seeks to convince.

If the planning process is to encourage democratic urban government, then it must operate so as to include rather than exclude citizens from participating in the process. "Inclusion" means not only permitting citizens to be heard. It also means allowing them to become well informed about the underlying reasons for planning proposals, and to respond to these in the technical language of professional planners.

A practice that has discouraged full participation by citizens in plan making in the past has been based on what might be called the "unitary plan." This is the idea that only one agency in a community should prepare a comprehensive plan; that agency is the city planning commission or department. Why is it that no other organization within a community prepares a plan? Why is only one agency concerned with establishing both general and specific goals for community development, and with proposing the strategies and costs required to effect the goals? Why are there not plural plans?

If the social, economic, and political ramifications of a plan are politically contentious, then why is it that those in opposition to the agency plan do not prepare one of their own? It is interesting to observe that "rational" theories of planning have called for consideration of alternative courses of action by planning agencies. As a matter of rationality, it has been argued that all of the alternative choices open as means to the ends sought be examined.[5] But those, including myself, who have recommended agency consideration of alternatives have placed upon the agency planner the burden of inventing "a few representative alternatives."[6] The agency planner has been given the duty of constructing a model of the political spectrum and charged with sorting out what he conceives to be worthy alternatives. This duty has placed too great a burden on the agency planner and has failed to provide for the formulation of alternatives by the interest groups who will eventually be affected by the completed plans.

Whereas in a large part of our national and local political practice contention is viewed as healthy, in city planning, where a large proportion of the professionals are public employees, contentious criticism has not always been viewed as legitimate. Further, where only government prepares plans and no minority plans are developed, pressure is often applied to bring all professionals to work for the ends espoused by a public agency. For example, last year a federal official complained to a meeting of planning professors that the academic planners were not giving enough support to federal programs. He assumed that every planner should be on the side of the federal renewal program. Of course government administrators will seek to gain the support of professionals outside government, but such support should not be expected as a matter of loyalty. In a democratic system opposition to a public agency should be just as normal and appropriate as support. The agency, despite the fact that it is concerned with planning, may be serving undesired ends.

In presenting a plea for plural planning I do not mean to minimize the importance of the obligation of the public planning agency. It must decide upon appropriate future courses of action for the community. But being isolated as the only plan maker in the community, public agencies as well as the public itself may have suffered from incomplete and shallow analysis of potential directions. Lively political dispute aided by plural plans could do much to improve the level of rationality in the process of preparing the public plan.

The advocacy of alternative plans by interest groups outside government would stimulate city planning in a number of ways. First, it would serve as a means of better informing the public of the alternative choices open, *alternatives strongly supported by their proponents*. In current practice those few agencies that have portrayed alternatives have not been equally enthusiastic about each.[7] A standard reaction to rationalists' prescription for consideration of alternative courses of action has been, "It can't be done; how can you expect planners to present alternatives of which they don't approve?" The appropriate answer to that question has been that planners, like lawyers, may have a professional obligation to defend positions they oppose. However, in a system of plural planning, the public agency would be relieved of at least some of the burden of presenting alternatives. In plural planning the alternatives would be presented by interest groups differing with the public agency's plan. Such alternatives would represent the deep-seated convictions of their proponents and not just the mental exercises of rational planners seeking to portray the range of choice.

A second way in which advocacy and plural planning would improve planning practice would be in forcing the public agency to compete with other planning groups to win political support. In the absence of opposition or alternative plans presented by interest groups, the public agencies have had little incentive to improve the quality of their work or the rate of production of plans. The political consumer has been offered a yes/no ballot in regard to the comprehensive plan; either the public agency's plan was to be adopted, or no plan would be adopted.

A third improvement in planning practice that might follow from plural planning would be to force those who have been critical of "establishment" plans to produce superior plans, rather than only to carry out the very essential obligation of criticizing plans deemed improper.

The Planner as Advocate

Where plural planning is practiced, advocacy becomes the means of professional support for competing claims about how the community should develop. Pluralism in support of political contention describes the process; advocacy describes the role performed by the professional in the process. Where unitary planning prevails, advocacy is not of paramount importance, for there is little or no competition for the plan prepared by the public agency. The concept of advocacy as taken from legal practice implies the opposition of at least two contending viewpoints in an adversary proceeding.

The legal advocate must plead for his own and his client's sense of legal propriety or justice. The planner as advocate would plead for his own and his client's view of the good society. The advocate planner would be more than a provider of information, an analyst of current trends, a simulator of future conditions, and a detailer of means. In addition to carrying out these necessary parts of planning, he would be a *proponent* of specific substantive solutions.

The advocate planner would be responsible to his client and would seek to express his client's views. This does not mean that the planner could not seek to persuade his client. In some situations persuasion might not be necessary, for the planner would have sought out an employer with whom he shared common views about desired social conditions and the means toward them. In fact one of the benefits of advocate planning is the possibility it creates for a planner to find employment with agencies holding values close to his own. Today the agency planner may be dismayed by the positions affirmed by his agency, but there may be no alternative employer.

The advocate planner would be above all a planner, responsible to his or her client for preparing plans and for all of the other elements comprising the planning process. Whether working for the public agency or for some private organization, the planner would have to prepare plans that take account of the arguments made in other plans. Thus, the advocate's plan might have some of the characteristics of a legal brief. It would be a document presenting the facts and reasons for supporting one set of proposals, and facts and reasons indicating the inferiority of counter proposals. The adversary nature of plural planning might, then, have the beneficial effect of upsetting the tradition of writing plan proposals in terminology that makes them appear self-evident.

A troublesome issue in contemporary planning is that of finding techniques for evaluating alternative plans. Technical devices such as cost-benefit analyses by themselves are of little assistance without the use of means for appraising the values underlying plans. Advocate planning, by making the values underlying plans more apparent, and definitions of social costs and benefits more explicit, should greatly assist the process of plan evaluation. Further, it would become clear (as it is not at present) that there are no neutral grounds for evaluating a plan; there are as many evaluative systems as there are value systems.

The adversary nature of plural planning might also have a good effect on the uses of information and research in planning. One of the tasks of the advocate planner in discussing the plans prepared in opposition would be to point out the nature of the bias underlying information presented in other plans. In this way, as critic of opposition plans, the planner would be performing a task similar to the legal technique of cross-examination. While painful to the planner whose bias is exposed (and no planner can be entirely free of bias) the net effect of confrontation between advocates of alternative plans would be more careful and precise research.

Not all the work of an advocate planner would be of an adversary nature. Much of it would be educational. The advocate would have the job of informing other groups, including public agencies, of the conditions, problems, and outlook of the group he or she represented. Another major educational job would be that of informing clients of their rights under planning and renewal laws, about the general operations of city government, and of particular programs likely to affect them.

The advocate planner would devote much attention to helping the client organization to clarify its ideas and to give expression to them. In order to make clients more powerful politically the advocate might also become engaged in expanding the size and scope of his or her client organization. But the advocate's most important function would be to carry out the planning process for the organization and to argue persuasively in favor of its planning proposals.

Advocacy in planning has already begun to emerge as planning and renewal affect the lives of more and more people. The critics of urban renewal[8] have forced response from the renewal agencies, and the ongoing debate[9] has stimulated needed self-evaluation by public agencies. Much work along the lines of advocate planning has already taken place, but little of it by professional planners. More often the work has been conducted by trained community organizers or by student groups. In at least one instance, however, a planner's professional aid led to the development of an alternative renewal approach, one that will result in the dislocation of far fewer families than originally contemplated.[10]

Pluralism and advocacy are means for stimulating consideration of future conditions by all groups in society. But there is one social group that at present is particularly in need of the assistance of planners. This group includes organizations representing low-income families. At a time when concern for the condition of the poor finds institutionalization in community action programs it would be appropriate for planners concerned with such groups to find means to plan with them. The plans prepared for these groups would seek to combat poverty and would propose programs affording new and better opportunities to the members of the organization and to families similarly situated.[11]

The difficulty in providing adequate planning assistance to organizations representing low-income families may in part be overcome by funds allocated to local antipoverty councils. But these councils are not the only representatives of the poor; other organizations exist and seek help. How can this type of assistance be financed? This question will be examined below, when attention is turned to the means for institutionalizing plural planning.

The Structure of Planning

Planning by special interest groups

The local planning process typically includes one or more "citizens'" organizations concerned with the nature of planning in the community. The Workable Program requirement for "citizen participation"[12] has enforced this tradition and brought it to most large communities. The difficulty with current citizen participation programs is that citizens are more often *reacting* to agency programs than *proposing* their concepts of appropriate goals and future action.

The fact that citizens' organizations have not played a positive role in formulating plans is to some extent a result of both the enlarged role in society played by government bureaucracies and the historic weakness of municipal party politics. There is something very shameful to our society in the necessity to have organized "citizen participation." Such participation should be the norm in an enlightened democracy. The formalization of citizen participation as a required practice in localities is similar in many respects to totalitarian shows of loyalty to the state by citizen parades.

Will a private group interested in preparing a recommendation for community development be required to carry out its own survey and analysis of the community? The answer would depend upon the quality of the work prepared by the public agency, work that should be public information. In some instances the public agency may not have surveyed or analyzed aspects the private group thinks important; or the public agency's work may reveal strong biases unacceptable to the private group. In any event, the production of a useful plan proposal will require much information concerning the present and predicted conditions in the community. There will be some costs associated with gathering that information, even if it is taken from the public agency. The major cost involved in the preparation of a plan by a private agency would probably be the employment of one or more professional planners.

What organizations might be expected to engage in the plural planning process? The first type that comes to mind are the political parties; but this is clearly an aspirational thought. There is very little evidence that local political organizations have the interest, ability, or concern to establish well-developed programs for their communities. Not all the fault, though, should be placed upon the professional politicians, for the registered members of political parties have not demanded very much, if anything, from them as agents.

Despite the unreality of the wish, the desirability for active participation in the process of planning by the political parties is strong. In an ideal situation local parties would establish political platforms, which would contain master plans for community growth, and both the majority and minority parties in the legislative branch of government would use such plans as one basis for appraising individual legislative proposals. Further, the local administration would use its planning agency to carry out the plans it proposed to the electorate. This dream will not turn to reality for a long time. In the interim other interest groups must be sought to fill the gap caused by the present inability of political organizations.

The second set of organizations that might be interested in preparing plans for community development are those that represent special interest groups having established views in regard to proper public policy. Such organizations as chambers of commerce, real estate boards, labor organizations, pro- and anti-civil rights groups, and anti-poverty councils come to mind. Groups of this nature have often played parts in the development of community plans, but only in a very few instances have they proposed their own plans.

It must be recognized that there is strong reason operating against commitment to a plan by these organizations. In fact it is the same reason that in part limits both the interests of politicians and the potential for planning in our society. The expressed commitment to a particular plan may make it difficult for groups to find means for accommodating their various interests. In other terms, it may be simpler for professionals, politicians, or lobbyists to make deals if they have not laid their cards on the table.

There is a third set of organizations that might be looked to as proponents of plans and to whom the foregoing comments might not apply. These are the ad hoc protest associations that may form in opposition to some proposed policy. An example of such a group is a neighborhood association formed to combat a renewal plan, a zoning change, or the proposed location of a public facility. Such organizations may seek to develop alternative plans, plans that would, if effected, better serve their interests.

From the point of view of effective and rational planning, it might be desirable to commence plural planning at the level of citywide organizations, but a more realistic view is that it will start at the neighborhood level. Certain advantages of this outcome should be noted. Mention was made earlier of tension in government between centralizing and decentralizing forces. The contention aroused by conflict between the central planning agency and the neighborhood organization may indeed be healthy, leading to clearer definition of welfare policies and their relation to the rights of individuals or minority groups.

Who will pay for plural planning? Some organizations have the resources to sponsor the development of a plan. Many groups lack the means. The plight of the relatively indigent association seeking to propose a plan might be analogous to that of the indigent client in search of legal aid. If the idea of plural planning makes sense, then support may be found from foundations or from government. In the beginning it is more likely that some foundation might be willing to experiment with plural planning as a means of making city planning more effective and more democratic. Or the federal government might see plural planning, if carried out by local anti-poverty councils, as a strong means of generating local interest in community affairs.

Federal sponsorship of plural planning might be seen as a more effective tool for stimulating involvement of citizens in the future of their community than are the present types of citizen participation programs. Federal support could be expected only if plural planning were seen not as a means of combating renewal plans but as an incentive to local renewal agencies to prepare better plans.

The public planning agency

A major drawback to effective democratic planning practice is the continuation of that nonresponsible vestigial institution, the planning commission. If it is agreed that the establishment of both general policies and implementation policies are questions affecting the public interest and that public interest questions should be decided in accord with established democratic practices for decision making, then it is indeed difficult to find convincing reasons for continuing to permit independent commissions to make planning decisions. At an earlier stage in planning, the strong arguments of John T. Howard[13] and others in support of commissions may have been persuasive. But it is now more than a decade since Howard made his defense against Robert Walker's position favoring planning as a staff function under the mayor. With the increasing effect planning decisions have upon the lives of citizens, the Walker proposal assumes great urgency.[14]

Aside from important questions regarding the propriety of allowing independent agencies far removed from public control to determine public policy, the failure to place planning decision choices in the hands of elected officials has weakened the ability of professional planners to have their proposals effected. Separating planning from local politics has made it difficult for independent commissions to garner influential political support. The commissions are not responsible directly to the electorate, and the electorate in turn is at best often indifferent to the planning commission.

During the last decade, in many cities power to alter community development has slipped out of the hands of city planning commissions, assuming they ever held it, and has been transferred to development coordinators. This has weakened the professional planner. Perhaps planners unknowingly contributed to this by their refusal to take concerted action in opposition to the perpetuation of commissions.

Planning commissions are products of the conservative reform movement of the early part of this century. The movement was essentially anti-populist and pro-aristocracy. Politics was viewed as dirty business. The commissions are relics of a not-too-distant past when it was believed that if men of goodwill discussed a problem thoroughly, certainly the right solution would be forthcoming. We know today, and perhaps it was always known, that there are no right solutions. Proper policy is that which the decision-making unit declares to be proper.

Planning commissions are responsible to no constituency. The members of the commissions, except for their chairperson, are seldom known to the public. In general the individual members fail to expose their personal views about policy and prefer to immerse them in group decision. If the members wrote concurring and dissenting opinions, then at least the commissions might stimulate thought about planning issues. It is difficult to comprehend why this aristocratic and undemocratic form of decision making should be continued. The public planning function should be carried out in the executive or legislative office and perhaps in both. There has been some question about which of these branches of government would provide the best home, but there is much reason to believe that both branches would be made more cognizant of planning issues if they were each informed by their own planning staffs. To carry this division further, it would probably be advisable to establish minority and majority planning staffs in the legislative branch.

At the root of my last suggestion is the belief that there is or should be a Republican and Democratic way of viewing city development; that there should be conservative and liberal plans, plans to support the private market and plans to support greater government control. There are many possible roads for a community to travel, and many plans should show them. Explication is required of many alternative futures presented by those sympathetic to the construction of each such future. As indicated earlier, such alternatives are not presented to the public now. Those few reports that do include alternative futures do not speak in terms of interest to the average citizen. They are filled with professional jargon and present sham alternatives. These plans have expressed technical land-use alternatives rather than social, economic, or political value alternatives. Both the traditional unitary plans and the new ones that present technical alternatives have limited the public's exposure to the future states that might be achieved. Instead of arousing healthy political contention as diverse comprehensive plans might, these plans have deflated interest.

The independent planning commission and unitary plan practice certainly should not coexist. Separately, they dull the possibility for enlightened political debate; in combination they have made it yet more difficult. But when still another hoary concept of city planning is added to them, such debate becomes practically impossible. This third of a trinity of worn-out notions is that city planning should focus only upon the physical aspects of city development.

An Inclusive Definition of the Scope of Planning

The view that equates physical planning with city planning is myopic. It may have had some historical justification, but it is clearly out of place at a time when it is necessary to integrate knowledge and techniques in order to wrestle effectively with the myriad of problems afflicting urban populations.

The city planning profession's historical concern with the physical environment has warped its ability to see physical structures and land as servants to those who use them.[15] Physical relations and conditions have no meaning or quality apart from the way they serve their users. But this is forgotten every time a physical condition is described as good or bad without relation to a specified group of users. High density, low density, green belts, mixed uses, cluster developments, centralized or decentralized business centers are per se neither good nor bad. They describe physical relations or conditions but take on value only when seen in terms of their social, economic, psychological, physiological, or aesthetic effects upon different users.

The profession's experience with renewal over the past decade has shown the high costs of exclusive concern with physical conditions. It has been found that the allocation of funds for removal of physical blight may not necessarily improve the overall physical condition of a community and may engender such harsh social repercussions as to severely damage both social and economic institutions. Another example of the deficiencies of the physical bias is the assumption of city planners that they could deal with the capital budget as if the physical attributes of a facility could be understood apart from the philosophy and practice of the service conducted within the physical structure. This assumption is open to question. The size, shape, and location of a facility greatly interact with the purpose of the activity the facility houses. Clear examples of this can be seen in public education and in the provision of low-cost housing. The racial and other socioeconomic consequences of "physical decisions" such as location of schools and housing projects have been immense, but city planners, while acknowledging the existence of such consequences, have not sought or trained themselves to understand socioeconomic problems, their causes or solutions.

The city planning profession's limited scope has tended to bias strongly many of its recommendations toward perpetuation of existing social and economic practices. Here I am not opposing the outcomes, but the way in which they are developed. Relative ignorance of social and economic methods of analysis have caused planners to propose solutions in the absence of sufficient knowledge of the costs and benefits of proposals upon different sections of the population.

Large expenditures have been made on planning studies of regional transportation needs, for example, but these studies have been conducted in a manner suggesting that different social and economic classes of the population did not have different needs and different abilities to meet them. In the field of housing, to take another example, planners have been hesitant to question the consequences of locating public housing in slum areas. In the field of industrial development, planners have seldom examined the types of jobs the community needed; it has been assumed that one job was about as useful as another. But this may not be the case when a significant sector of the population finds it difficult to get employment.

"Who gets what, when, where, why, and how" are the basic political questions that need to be raised about every allocation of public resources. The questions cannot be answered adequately if land-use criteria are the sole or major standards for judgment.

The need to see an element of city development, land use, in broad perspective applies equally well to every other element, such as health, welfare, and recreation. The governing of a city requires an adequate plan for its future. Such a plan loses guiding force and rational basis to the degree that it deals with less than the whole that is of concern to the public.

The implications of the foregoing comments for the practice of city planning are these. First, state planning enabling legislation should be amended to permit planning departments to study and to prepare plans related to any area of public concern. Second, planning education must be redirected so as to provide channels of specialization in different parts of public planning and a core focused upon the planning process. Third, the professional planning association should enlarge its scope so as not to exclude city planners not specializing in physical planning.

A year ago at the American Institute of Planners (AIP) convention it was suggested that the AIP constitution be amended to permit city planning to enlarge its scope to all matters of public concern.[16] Members of the Institute in agreement with this proposal should seek to develop support for it at both the chapter and national level. The constitution at present states that the institute's "particular sphere of activity shall be the planning of the unified development of urban communities and their environs and of states, regions and the nation *as expressed through determination of the comprehensive arrangement of land and land occupancy and regulation thereof.*"[17]

It is time that the AIP delete the words in my italics from its constitution. The planner limited to such concerns is not a city planner, but a land planner or a physical planner. A city is its people; their practices; and their political, social, cultural and economic institutions as well as other things. The city planner must comprehend and deal with all these factors.

The new city planners will be concerned with physical planning, economic planning, and social planning. The scope of their work will be no wider than that presently demanded of a mayor or a city council member. Thus, we cannot argue against an enlarged planning function on the grounds that it is too large to handle. The mayor needs assistance, in particular the assistance of a planner, trained to examine needs and aspirations in terms of both short- and long-term perspectives. In observing the early stages of development of Community Action Programs, it is apparent that our cities are in desperate need of the type of assistance trained planners could offer. Our cities require for their social and economic programs the type of long-range thought and information that have been brought forward in the realm of physical planning. Potential resources must be examined and priorities set.

What I have just proposed does not imply the termination of physical planning, but it does mean that physical planning be seen as part of city planning. Uninhibited by limitations on their work, city planners will be able to add their expertise to the task of coordinating the operating and capital budgets and to the job of relating effects of each city program upon the others and upon the social, political, and economic resources of the community.

An expanded scope reaching all matters of public concern will not only make planning a more effective administrative tool of local government, it will also bring planning practice closer to the issues of real concern to the citizens. A system of plural city planning probably has a much greater chance of operational success where the focus is on live social and economic questions instead of rather esoteric issues relating to physical norms.

The Education of Planners

Widening the scope of planning to include all areas of concern to government would suggest that city planners must possess a broader knowledge of the structure and forces affecting urban development. In general this would be true. But at present many city planners are specialists in only one or more of the functions of city government. Broadening the scope of planning would require some additional planners who specialize in one or more of the services entailed by the new focus.

A prime purpose of city planning is the coordination of many separate functions. This coordination calls for planners with general knowledge of the many elements comprising the urban community. Educating a planner to perform the coordinator's role is a difficult job, one not well satisfied by the present tradition of two years of graduate study. Training urban planners with the skills called for in this article may require both longer graduate study and development of a liberal arts undergraduate program affording an opportunity for holistic understanding of both urban conditions and techniques for analyzing and solving urban problems.

The practice of plural planning requires educating planners who would be able to engage as professional advocates in the contentious work of forming social policy. The person able to do this would be one deeply committed both to the process of planning and to particular substantive ideas. Recognizing that ideological commitments will separate planners, there is tremendous need to train professionals who are competent to express their social objectives.

The great advances in analytic skills, demonstrated in the recent May issue of this journal dedicated to techniques of simulating urban growth processes, portend a time when planners and the public will be better able to predict the consequences of proposed courses of action. But these advances will be of little social advantage if the proposals themselves do not have substance. The contemporary thoughts of planners about the nature of individuals in society are often mundane, unexciting or gimmicky. When asked to point out to students the planners who have a developed sense of history and philosophy concerning the place of individuals in the urban world, one is hard put to come up with a name. Sometimes Goodman or Mumford might be mentioned. But planners seldom go deeper than acknowledging the goodness of green space and the soundness of proximity of linked activities. We cope with the problems of the alienated citizen with a recommendation for reducing the time of the journey to work.

Conclusion

The urban community is a system composed of interrelated elements, but little is known about how the elements do, will, or should interrelate. The type of knowledge required by the new comprehensive city planner demands that the planning profession comprise groups of people well versed in contemporary philosophy, social work, law, the social sciences, and civic design. Not every planner must be knowledgeable in all these areas, but each planner must have a deep understanding of one or more of these areas and must be able to give persuasive expression to this understanding.

As members of a profession charged with making urban life more beautiful, exciting, creative, and just, we have had little to say. Our task is to train a future generation of planners to go well beyond us in its ability to prescribe the future urban life.

Acknowledgments

I wish to thank Melvin H. Webber for his insightful criticism and Linda Davidoff for her many helpful suggestions and for her analysis of advocate planning. Special acknowledgment is made of the penetrating and brilliant social insights offered by the eminent legal scholar and practitioner, Michael Brodie, of the Philadelphia Bar.

Notes

1   Britton Harris, "Plan or Projection," *Journal of the American Institute of Planners*, XXVI (November 1960) 265–272.

2   Robert Dahl and Charles Lindblom, *Politics, Economics, and Welfare* (New York: Harper and Brothers, 1953) p. 3.

3   Paul Davidoff and Thomas Reiner, "A Choice Theory of Planning," *Journal of the American Institute of Planners*, XXVIII (May 1962) 103–115.

4   Ibid.

5   See for example, Martin Meyerson and Edward Banfield, *Politics, Planning and the Public Interest* (Glencoe: The Free Press 1955) p. 314 ff. The authors state "By a *rational* decision, we mean one made in the following manner: 1. the decision-maker considers all of the alternatives (courses of action) open to him; . . . 2. he identifies and evaluates all of the consequences which would follow from the adoption of each alternative; . . . 3. he selects that alternative the probable consequences of which would be preferable in terms of his most valued ends."

6   Davidoff and Reiner, op. cit.

7   National Capital Planning Commission. *The Nation's Capital: a Policies Plan for the Year 2000* (Washington D.C.: The Commission, 1961).

8   The most important critical studies are Jane Jacobs, *The Life and Death of Great American Cities* (New York: Random House 1961); Martin Anderson, *The Federal Bulldozer* (Cambridge: M.I.T. Press 1964); Herbert J. Gans, "The Human Implications of Current Redevelopment and Relocation Planning," *Journal of the American Institute of Planners*, XXV (February 1959) 15–26.

9   A recent example of heated debate appears in the following set of articles: Herbert J. Gans, "The Failure of Urban Renewal," *Commentary* 39 (April 1965) p. 29; George Raymond, "Controversy," *Commentary* 40 (July 1965) p. 72; and Herbert J. Gans, "Controversy," *Commentary* 40 (July 1965) p. 77.

10 Walter Thabit, *An Alternate Plan for Cooper Square* (New York: Walter Thabit, July 1961).

11 The first conscious effort to employ the advocacy method was carried out by a graduate student of city planning as an independent research project. The author acted as both a participant and an observer of a local housing organization. See Linda Davidoff, "The Bluffs: Advocate Planning," *Comment*, Dept. of City Planning, University of Pennsylvania (Spring 1965) p. 59.

12 See Section 101(c) of the United States Housing Act of 1949, as amended.

13   John T. Howard, "In Defense of Planning Commissions," *Journal of the American Institute of Planners*, XVII (Spring 1951).

14   Robert Walker, *The Planning Function in Urban Government*; Second Edition (Chicago: University of Chicago Press 1950). Walker drew the following conclusions from his examination of planning and planning commissions. "Another conclusion to be drawn from the existing composition of city planning boards is that they are not representative of the population as a whole." p. 153. "In summary the writer is of the opinion that the claim that planning commissions are more objective than elected officials must be rejected." p. 155. "From his observations the writer feels justified in saying that very seldom does a majority of any commission have any well-rounded understanding of the purposes and ramifications of planning." p. 157. "In summary, then, it was found that the average commission member does not comprehend planning nor is he particularly interested even in the range of customary physical planning." p. 158. "Looking at the planning commission at the present time, however, one is forced to conclude that despite some examples of successful operations, the unpaid board is not proving satisfactory as a planning agency," p. 165. ". . . (it) is believed that the most fruitful line of development for the future would be replacement of these commissions by a department or bureau attached to the office of mayor or city manager. This department might be headed by a board or by a single director, but the members or the director would in any case hold office at the pleasure of the executive on the same basis as other department heads." p. 177.

15   An excellent and complete study of the bias resulting from reliance upon physical or land-use criteria appears in David Farbman, *A Description, Analysis and Critique of the Master Plan*, an unpublished mimeographed study prepared for the Univ. of Pennsylvania's Institute for Urban Studies, 1959–1960. After studying more than one hundred master plans Farbman wrote:

> "As a result of the predominantly physical orientation of the planning profession many planners have fallen victims to a malaise which I suggest calling the 'Physical Bias.' This bias is not the physical orientation of the planner itself but is the result of it . . .
>
> "The physical bias is an attitude on the part of the planner which leads him to conceive of the principles and techniques of *his profession* as the key factors in determining the particular recommendations to be embodied in his plans . . .
>
> "The physically biased planner plans on the assumption (conviction) that the physical problems of a city can be solved within the framework of physical desiderata: in other words, that physical problems can be adequately stated, solved and remedied according to physical criteria and expertise. The physical bias produces both an inability and an unwillingness on the part of the planner to 'get behind' the physical recommendations of the plan, to isolate, examine or to discuss more basic criteria . . ."
>
> ". . . There is room, then, in plan thinking for physical principles, i.e., theories of structural inter-relationships of the physical city; but this is

only part of the story, for the structural impacts of the plan are only a part of the total impact. This total impact must be conceived as a web of physical, economic and social causes and effects," pp. 22–26.

16   Paul Davidoff. "The Role of the City Planner in Social Planning," *Proceedings of the 1964 Annual Conference*, American Institute of Planners (Washington, DC: The Institute, 1964) 125–131.
17   Constitution of AIP, Article II "Purposes," in *AIP Handbook & Roster – 1965*, p. 8.

15

A Public Planning
Perspective on
Strategic Planning

Jerome L. Kaufman
and Harvey M. Jacobs

Twenty-five years ago, at a planning conference session on the newly minted Community Renewal Program – in which many in the room spoke enthusiastically about the potential of this new program – a skeptic got up and stated bluntly: "The Community Renewal Program is just the latest fad to hit town. Sooner or later it, too, will fade away into oblivion." Whether or not the corporate strategic planning approach to planning in the public sector will prove to have been another passing fad remains to be seen. But there is no doubt that it is the center of a lot of attention.

In the past five years a rash of articles have called on state and local governments to use the strategic planning approach developed in the corporate world (Olsen and Eadie 1982; Eadie 1983; Boyle 1983; Sorkin, Ferris, and Hudak 1984; Toft 1984; Denhardt 1985; Bryson, Van de Ven, and Roering 1986; Eadie and Steinbacher 1985; Tomazinis 1985). During the same period, strategic plans based on the corporate model have been undertaken for an increasing number of governmental jurisdictions: cities such as San Francisco, San Luis Obispo, and Pasadena, California;

Reprinted by permission of the *Journal of the American Planning Association* Vol. 53, No. 1, 1987.

Philadelphia, Pennsylvania; Albany, New York; Memphis, Tennessee; and Windsor, Connecticut; counties such as Hennepin in Minnesota, Dade in Florida, Prince Georges in Maryland, and Prince William in Virginia; and states such as California, Ohio, and Wisconsin. The number of conferences on how to do strategic planning in the public sector is also on the rise. Even the Reagan administration has become a strong supporter of the strategic planning approach for communities. A key section in the administration's 1982 National Urban Policy Report, "Strategies for Cities," reads as if it were taken from a textbook on corporate strategic planning, with its liberal use of terms such as "strategic approach," "external factors," "threats and opportunities," "internal strengths and weaknesses," "comparative advantages," "strategic issues," and the like. The emergence of corporate strategic planning in public planning parallels the rise of economic development in the late 1970s as a focus of local planning. But corporate strategic planning is not limited to economic development planning. It can be and has been applied to transportation, health, environmental, and other functional planning areas. Likewise, it can be and has been applied to planning at the regional and state levels as well as at the city level.

Proponents of corporate strategic planning claim that numerous benefits will accrue to communities that follow it. The authors of the *Strategic Planning Guide* funded by the U.S. Department of Housing and Urban Development (Sorkin, Ferris, and Hudak 1984), for example, contend that the approach can result in getting important things accomplished, educating the public, building consensus, developing a shared vision that extends past the next election, positioning a community to seize opportunities, shedding new light on important issues, identifying the most effective uses of resources, and providing a mechanism for public-private cooperation. Some academics contend that "when done well, strategic planning offers one approach to the revitalization and redirection of governments and the public service" (Bryson, Van de Ven, and Roering 1986).

But there is another side of corporate strategic planning that directly challenges the public planning profession. Some proponents of the approach explicitly or implicitly fault traditional public planning for not having done the job, accusing it of falling short of the mark. They see the corporate strategic planning approach as better suited than more traditional public planning to helping communities cope with changes induced by a dwindling resource base. Given the criticism of traditional public planning approaches and the growing popularity of the corporate strategic planning approach, the field of urban and regional planning may well face crises of both relevance and professional identity.

It is the purpose of this chapter to examine strategic planning from a public planning perspective, stressing the application of this approach to communitywide planning, the traditional focus of public planning. This is distinct from the application of strategic planning to organizations, which might focus on how the city as a public corporation or a single city agency can accomplish its missions more effectively. We first define the corporate strategic planning approach examined in this article. Then we examine the approach in terms of its similarities to and differences from other public planning approaches, based on a review of literature familiar to most public planners. We supplement the literature review with an exploratory study of fifteen public sector planners who work in communities where corporate strategic planning is under way, in order to assess practitioners' perspectives on how this approach is similar to and different from other public planning approaches. We close with speculations on how public sector planners might view the advent of strategic planning.

A Definition

Strategic planning originated about twenty years ago in the private sector. Its roots are tied to the need of rapidly changing and growing corporations to plan effectively for and manage their futures when the future itself appeared increasingly uncertain. By the end of the 1960s, Steiner (1969) estimated, three-quarters of the large industrial corporations in the United States had formal strategic planning in place. By the mid-1980s more than half of the publicly traded companies were using some form of strategic planning (Denhardt 1985).

As it developed, strategic planning began taking a variety of paths. Taylor (1984) identifies five main styles of corporate strategic planning that have emerged in recent years: central control, framework for innovation, strategic management, political planning, and futures research. Bryson, Freeman, and Roering (1986) also distinguish among five models of strategic planning: the Harvard policy, portfolio, industrial economics, stakeholder, and decision process models.

The central features of public sector strategic planning are captured in the acronym *SWOT*, a derivative of the Harvard policy model. In general, a community assesses its *s*trengths, *w*eaknesses, *o*pportunities, and *t*hreats as a basis for devising action strategies to achieve goals and objectives in certain key issue areas. Recognizing that variations are possible in the sequencing of, time spent in, and analytic depth devoted to each phase of the strategic planning process, Sorkin, Ferris, and Hudak (1984) identify the following as the basic steps in strategic planning at the community level:

1   Scan the environment.
2   Select key issues.
3   Set mission statements or broad goals.

4   Undertake external and internal analyses.

5   Develop goals, objectives, and strategies with respect to each issue.

6   Develop an implementation plan to carry out strategic actions.

7   Monitor, update, and scan.

In this conception of corporate strategic planning, opportunities and threats are assessed in step 1 and used as the basis for action in steps 2 and 3. Strengths and weaknesses are developed most pointedly in step 4, but they also serve as the basis for refining decisions in steps 2 and 3 and formulating strategies in steps 5 and 6. Strengths, weaknesses, opportunities, and threats are used together in step 7 to evaluate a plan and determine its continued viability.

For our purpose, we use the above conception as the definition of strategic planning as it is applied in the public sector. Our concern is with the application of strategic planning to communitywide planning, the traditional domain of public planners. Eadie and Steinbacher (1985) and Bryson, Freeman, and Roering (1986) note that strategic planning can be, and has been, applied to both communitywide and line agency planning. The approach outlined above applies broadly to both. The strong history of strategic planning, however, is as a management tool for organizations. It is the proposed application of strategic planning to communitywide issues that is new and raises issues of theory and method for public planners.

The View from the Planning Literature

Consider the following scene: Two rooms adjoin each other with a door between them. In one room people are busily at work developing and refining the strategic planning model for use by private corporations. In the other room, a similar intensity of activity goes on as people work at developing and refining planning process models for use in the public sector. No movement, however, takes place between occupants of the two adjoining rooms. The door between the rooms is shut tightly.

This metaphor is intended to describe what we believe went on from the 1960s to the early 1980s in the respective spheres of corporate strategic planning and public planning. People were hard at work in both spheres, but little or no interaction took place between them. We doubt that more than a handful of corporate strategic planners ever read the articles and books that were cornerstones of reading lists in graduate planning theory courses – for example, Altshuler (1965), Davidoff and Reiner (1962), Etzioni (1967), Meyerson (1956), and Friedmann (1973). Likewise, readings on the corporate strategic planning approach probably were never assigned to students who took planning theory courses before 1980 – for instance, the works of Drucker (1954), Chandler (1962), Ansoff (1965), Steiner (1969), and Steiner and Miner (1977).

But in the 1980s the door between the two rooms has opened, and some of the occupants are moving between them. Some planning academics are walking into the corporate strategic planning room, looking around, and coming to the conclusion that the corporate strategic planning model has applicability for public planning (Bryson, Van de Ven, and Roering 1986; Lang 1986; Tomazinis 1985). Likewise, some proponents of the corporate strategic planning approach (Eadie 1983; Sorkin, Ferris, and Hudak 1984; Toft 1984, Denhardt 1985) are strolling into the public planning room, gazing around, and arriving at a similar conclusion – that the corporate strategic planning approach can be of benefit to communities that public planners traditionally have served.

Some proponents of strategic planning point to significant differences between this approach and the conventional public planning approach. A few are taking some healthy whacks at public planning for its shortcomings. One, for example, says city and regional planning has lost "its flexibility to change dramatically the subject matter of its concerns, the process of its explorations, and the tools of its inquiries" (Tomazinis 1985: 14). Another is even more sweeping and caustic in his criticism: "The history of public planning is replete with tales of overexpectation, underestimation of costs, and disillusionment . . . [It] has proved increasingly less useful" (Eadie 1983: 447–48).

Rather than focus on the harsher criticisms of public planning, we want to look more carefully at the distinctions that proponents of strategic planning draw between that approach and public planning. We want to assess whether these distinctions are real or imagined and, if they are real, whether they are only differences of emphasis or raise truly new points. We will draw on an analysis of the public planning literature with which most graduates of planning schools are familiar.

What, then, are the main distinctions that proponents of the corporate strategic planning approach see between it and conventional public planning?

- Corporate strategic planning is oriented more toward action, results, and implementation.
- It promotes broader and more diverse participation in the planning process.
- It places more emphasis on understanding the community in its external context, determining the opportunities and threats to a community via an environmental scan.
- It embraces competitive behavior on the part of communities.
- It emphasizes assessing a community's strengths and weaknesses in the context of opportunities and threats.

We believe proponents of corporate strategic planning are essentially correct in contending that their approach differs significantly from conventional planning in those ways, if by "public planning" they mean long-range comprehensive or master planning. And there is reason to believe that that is the conception many strategic planning proponents hold of public planning (Eadie and Steinbacher 1985; Denhardt 1985; Toft 1984; Eadie 1983; Sorkin, Ferris, and Hudak 1984).

But that conception of public planning has been the subject of long-standing critiques in the planning literature – critiques that have been widely recognized. Several strong strands in the planning literature have moved beyond the notion that public planning should be long-range comprehensive or master planning. Strategic planning proponents may be fixing on a model of public planning that planning authors no longer acknowledge as representative of contemporary planning thought or professional practice. In fact, we contend that most of the principal distinctions that strategic planning proponents draw between their approach and public planning are, as evidenced by contemporary planning literature, much less pronounced or do not exist.

Action and Results Orientation

A major claimed distinction between corporate strategic planning and public planning is that the former is more oriented toward action and results, in other words more relevant for decision making. Yet the call for more decision-relevant planning information and analysis has been the basis of the first important set of critiques of comprehensive planning that began in the 1950s and continue into the present. Walker (1950) raised questions about the organizational position of planners and the independent planning commission and called for a more direct link with decision making and decision makers. Beginning with their groundbreaking study of planning practice (Meyerson and Banfield 1955), Meyerson (1956), Banfield (1959), and then others (for example, Altshuler 1965; Bolan 1967) began to argue that, even if comprehensive planning was a good idea in theory, it was largely unattainable in the real world of politics and policy.

In his well-known critique, Lindblom (1959) argued that comprehensive planning was an impossible undertaking. It required more intelligence and information than was ever available. Banfield (1959) argued further that in many cases organizations neither wanted to nor could engage in rational comprehensive planning. As a result, these authors and others (for example, Meyerson 1956; Bolan 1971; Benveniste 1972; Catanese 1974) began to articulate models of more decision-relevant planning that were also more limited in scope, shorter-range in time frame, and more sensitive to the decision environment in which planners operate. One of these authors (Meyerson 1956) specifically warned planners that their role could be usurped if they did not move in these directions.

On this one point, then, we contend that planners have long had their attention drawn to the need for being oriented more toward action and results and have been presented with various ways of achieving those ends. The abundance of applied policy analysis techniques in planning curricular, the actual philosophical shift of certain planning schools in that direction, and the support of planners for middle-range, action-oriented programs like the Community Renewal and Model Cities programs suggest that practitioners and academics have gotten the message. We believe that the need for policy relevancy has been widely recognized and is, with perhaps only recent dissension (for example, Isserman 1985; Kreditor 1985), the mainstream of opinion about the appropriate role of planning.

Participation

A second claimed distinction of corporate strategic planning is that it broadens the basis of participation in planning. Denhardt (1985) is an example of a strategic planning proponent who suggests that the constituency for planning is too narrow. Again, as in the above discussion, Denhardt (1985), Eadie (1983), and others seem unaware of the many calls from planning academics for broadening participation in planning (Burke 1968; Friedmann 1973; Rosener 1978) and planning practitioners (AICP Code of Ethics 1981).[1] Advocate and progressive planners, in particular, stress the need to bring people into the planning process who, by design or practice, have not participated (Davidoff 1965; Arnstein 1969; Goodman 1971; Clavel 1983). Like proponents of corporate strategic planning, all these authors argue that diverse participation will lead to more insightful and responsive planning.

So, as with the issue of policy relevancy, the call by strategic planning proponents for more participation in planning is not, in and of itself, a new call to the public planning profession. For more than twenty years we have conducted vigorous debates on and experiments in participation in planning. What is emphasized more by some strategic planning proponents is the suggestion that we might need greater participation from selected segments of the private business community, although the call for public-private partnership is not absent from the planning literature (Catanese 1974; Branch 1983).

Environmental Scanning

An important contribution that corporate strategic planning has to offer public planning is the idea of scanning the environment. According to Denhardt (1985: 175), under strategic planning "the organization is not assumed to exist in a vacuum, but rather both the organization's objectives and steps to achieve those objectives are seen in the context of the resources and constraints presented by the organization's environment." This environmental sensitivity allows the organization to do smarter, more focused planning and improves its ability to understand the relative risks associated with alternative courses of action. The environmental scan encourages an organization to look beyond itself in space and time.

This basis for planning fits well with the interest in futures studies in general and the work of Naisbitt (1982) in particular. The world is understood to comprise limited resources and certain unchangeable circumstances that need to be accepted and creatively used. Within the context of an environmental scan, an organization then assesses its strengths and weaknesses. That is, strengths and weaknesses are determined relative to opportunities and threats, which are themselves given and essentially unchangeable.

Although the emphasis on environmental scanning is both well developed and, from our perspective, well deserved, it also is not entirely new, though it is perhaps less well accepted within the planning community. As far back as the 1920s and 1930s Lewis Mumford, Benton MacKaye, and their associates in the Regional Planning Association of America wrote plans and developed planning theory that explicitly called for planning within broad social-economic-technological contexts (Stein 1926; MacKaye 1928; Mumford 1938). Under the Roosevelt administration, the work of the National Resource Planning Board, especially in its early years, similarly reflected the importance to planning of broad trend analysis (National Resources Board 1934a; 1934b; National Resources Committee 1937; Clawson 1981).

More recently, planners from many different subfields have stressed the importance of understanding and planning for an organization within a broad context. Environmental planners base much of the justification for their practice on the relation of local activities to broader environmental systems and activities (for example, McHarg 1969). Planning for air pollution, water pollution, groundwater contamination, farmland preservation, wildlife habitat, and forest management, for example, requires planners to examine resource use and economics regionally, nationally, and even internationally. Likewise, in the field of economic development, planners have available ample literature that stresses the importance of planning for plant location within an understanding of intra- and international changes in population, economics, and technological investment (Perry and Watkins 1977; Bluestone and Harrison

1982). Similarly, in social planning, the definition of key problem areas and target populations for service delivery is commonly based on analysis of broad demographic and economic trends. Etzioni (1967) has formulated an approach to planning in general that stresses what corporate strategic planning proponents call environmental scanning. As noted earlier, Etzioni's work is a source common to graduate planning theory courses, and thus environmental scanning is an idea to which public planners have been long exposed.

Competitive Behavior

Another feature of corporate strategic planning is how it encourages a community to embrace competitive behavior. Its proponents are quite explicit in this regard. For example, Toft argues that "what is called for in most situations . . . is competitive strategy. A successful community must view itself as a competitive product." In the 1980s "governments and community organizations . . . must be proactive given a more erratic and uncertain environment where there will be winners and losers" (Toft 1984, 6, 7).

That cities, counties, states, and regions are in a competitive position with each other is no news to planners. It is the basis of much of the frustration in planning; to wit, communities searching for an ever-increasing tax base, the related inability to rein in municipal boundaries, the difficulties in managing regional environmental resources, and the companion proposals these frustrations have engendered: tax sharing, councils of governments, and regional and state land-use planning reform (Williams 1970; Long 1977; Scott 1975). Practising planners have long acknowledged the competition of a city with surrounding suburban communities (Catanese and Farmer 1978; Krumholz 1982). Recently, planners have become more acutely aware of interregional and even international competition for jobs and industrial plant location (Perry and Watkins 1977; Bluestone and Harrison 1982).

What is different about corporate strategic planning is not its recognition of competition but its perspective on that competition. The traditional perspective on competition in public planning is to view it as damaging to the economic and social health of a community. Planners and planning theory strove to seek out and foster cooperative, shared solutions. Under strategic planning, competition is seen as inevitable. Communities therefore are exhorted to identify their competitive niche and exploit it or suffer the consequences.

Community Strengths and Weaknesses

The final distinctive feature claimed for corporate strategic planning is the community's critical appraisal of strengths and weaknesses relative to the environmental scan of opportunities and threats and within the parameters of the other features discussed above – action orientation, public involvement process, and competitive perspective on intergovernmental relations. This, too, we conclude, is not an entirely new idea for the planning community, though the exact terms used to describe the exercise and the emphasis accorded this phase of planning may be different under corporate strategic planning.

According to proponents of strategic planning, traditional public planning (that is, long-range comprehensive or master planning) too often perceives the world around and within as one-dimensional. That is, goals, objectives, and policies that are developed and stated in a plan too often seem to cover all topics of possible concern to the locality and to assume that the planning policy, and administrative units of the government have equal capacity and incentive to act on the plan's recommendations. In contrast, strategic planning is supposed to encourage an honest assessment of a community's capacity to act, seeking to maximize strengths and minimize weaknesses in the context of opportunities and threats. As with the points discussed above, however, this perspective is not entirely new to planning theory or practice, though it may not be as well developed, for reasons that point up one of the main differences in public and private planning.

The discussion of strengths and weaknesses borrows directly from the economic literature on competitive advantage. In fact, it can be seen as nothing more than a shifting of the competitive advantage idea from the market to the organizational and community sector. At the community level, Tiebout's (1956) formulation of local expenditures and the public choice school of economics has kept the issues of competitive advantage and strengths and weaknesses before the planning community for a long time. Practitioners such as Krumholz (1982; Krumholz, Cogger, and Linner 1975) have shown how planners with particular ethical orientations can pointedly address the strengths and weaknesses of current city planning processes and move an organization toward maximizing its strengths. Likewise, certain traditional and well-regarded plans, such as New York City's (1969), explicitly address the weaknesses of certain city agencies and activities. Other plans we are aware of, such as Chicago's (1966), had similar sections in early drafts that were later edited out to reduce organizational friction and to help generate diverse support for the plans. At one level identifying strengths and weaknesses, especially the latter, has been a politically unwise and difficult undertaking. But it is not an idea to which planners have been unaccustomed.

Thus, when we examine the planning literature, we find that the components of corporate strategic planning that proponents say are fundamentally different are not really all that different. Many of the implied and explicit criticisms are directed at the comprehensive, long-range, or master planning model. Most of these criticisms are long-standing within the theory and practice of public sector planning. Planners have been told of the need to be more "policy relevant", to involve more and different types of people in the planning process, and to do their planning within a realistic assessment of the systems and networks of which they are part. Planners also are aware both of competition and of the idea of identifying and acting on strengths and weaknesses.

What, then, is different about strategic planning from the point of view of the planning literature? We note two differences. The first is the framework of corporate strategic planning, which brings all the above points together. It may be true that the literature has drawn planners' attention to most or all of the points that proponents claim are distinctive about strategic planning. The strategic approach is distinctive, however, in pulling all those elements together into a coherent planning structure. Continuing to highlight the importance of individual elements and stressing their interrelationship may help planners to do better planning.

The second difference is the ideological and programmatic usefulness of corporate strategic planning. By introducing a model of planning that is seen to come out of the private sector, the practice of planning – which nowadays is under attack in some quarters – may be seen as more legitimate. Corporate strategic planning thus may be shifting the debate in public sector planning from *whether* to do it to *how* to do it. In these times, that would be a significant shift.

The View from the Planning Trenches

Strategic planning applied to the public sector is a relatively recent development. The preceding analysis of literature indicates that key features of the strategic planning approach, which proponents claim are distinct from the conventional public planning approach, are well ensconced in planning theory and recognized in some of the writings on planning practice. But the exhortations of academics are not necessarily guideposts that all practitioners follow. As we know, the gap between what planning theorists say and what planning practitioners do can be wide (Krueckeberg 1971; Kaufman 1974).

For that reason we decided to examine how planning practitioners view strategic planning as it has been applied at the communitywide level. We wanted to get firsthand information about how planners steeped in the public planning tradition felt about a planning approach that, although nurtured in the corporate world, is being implanted in the public sector vineyard. Do planners see important differences between strategic planning efforts and the approaches followed in public planning? If so, what are these differences? What are planners' attitudes toward community-based strategic planning ventures – enthusiasm? acceptance? skepticism? hostility?

To answer these questions, we conducted telephone interviews with fifteen public planners about their views of strategic planning efforts under way at the communitywide level. Each planner interviewed worked either in a community where a strategic planning program was under way or in one where such a program had been completed recently.[2] These planners represented communities for which strategic planning was far enough along to allow for an informed interview. Therefore, they could give opinions about the contrast, if any, of the strategic planning process with other, more traditional planning approaches. It was important to the validity of the study that each planner had held his or her position long enough before the introduction of strategic planning to discuss its differences from and similarities to other forms of public planning in the community. The interview group was small, reflecting the newness of corporate strategic planning. Given the size of the group, we want to stress the exploratory nature of these interviews and to offer these data as the basis for more extensive research in the future.

In a recent paper, Tomazinis (1985: 14) said, "Strategic planning has the potential to revitalize public planning . . . by invigorating the planning agencies, revitalizing the interest in planning of top elected officials, and helping cities and regions rediscover and redefine their crucial problems." We read this positive statement about strategic planning to the group of planners as the opening to our telephone interview, asking whether and why they agreed or disagreed with it.

In general, these planners were divided in their opinion about strategic planning. A few were quite positive about its value. Others were mildly supportive, seeing some benefits but also having some reservations. And some were downright skeptical.

One enthusiast, for example, stated that he unequivocally agreed with the Tomazinis statement. Another supporter saw strategic planning as an opportunity to put planning on a more vigorous footing. Still another commented that the strategic planning program in his community definitely had value in revitalizing elected officials' interest in planning.

Skeptics responded differently to the Tomazinis statement. One said planning in his community was already vigorous, top elected officials already had a strong interest in planning, and crucial problems were being addressed continually by his agency; strategic planning therefore was not really needed. Another said strategic planning "was just an advertising gimmick to sell the old stuff in a new way." Other skeptics saw it as trendy. As one put it, "Nowadays it's the way to get federal bucks for planning. You have to use the right buzz words to get a share of the dwindling dollars."

Going beneath these surface reactions, we sensed that a planner's attitude toward strategic planning was conditioned principally by two factors: the planner's educational background and the perceived status of the planning function in the community where the planner worked.

We observed that planners with degrees from planning schools were generally less sanguine about strategic planning than those with degrees in fields other than planning. As one planner with a graduate planning degree said, "I don't see the strategic planning process as significantly different from what I learned in planning school." Another planning school graduate put it this way: "Strategic planning is like pouring old wine into new bottles."

In contrast, a supporter of strategic planning who had a degree in economic geography justified his support by criticizing the planning done in his agency as producing "too many plans that are just damn inventories." He went on to say, "Just as one of Congress's problems is that it has too many lawyers, one of the problems with planning agencies is that they have too many planners." Likewise, an economist who has worked as a planner for many years suggested that "comprehensive plans that planners prepare tend to be too illusionary. The interconnectedness of goals, objectives, and policies is not always clear. Strategic planning avoids these pitfalls."

A cross-cutting factor affecting planners' attitudes toward strategic planning was the perceived status of the planning function in the community. Where public planning was perceived to be more vigorous, respected, and involved in community issues, planners viewed strategic planning as unnecessary or redundant. Where the public planning function was perceived to be weak, strategic planning efforts took on a rosier complexion in the planner's view.

The following comments about strategic planning were made by planners who saw their planning programs as strong and healthy:

In our community, we have an ongoing and lively discussion of issues. Interest in public affairs is high. I don't think we need a strategic planning approach.

An aggressive planning department like ours is already doing the things that strategic planning proponents are saying strategic planning does. I don't think the strategic planning done by the Chamber of Commerce has much value. It's regarded as a business advocacy plan. It has neither been adopted nor has it had much influence on public policy.

In our agency, which has lots of professionals who are broadly educated and policy-sensitive, strategic planning is not needed.

This last planner, however, acknowledged that in a community where the planning function is weak, "strategic planning might help to invigorate the planning agency." Likewise, one planner, who admitted he worked for an agency that was not well regarded, saw definite advantages to the strategic planning approach: "It pushes us to be more focused on issues, and it increases our chances of getting things implemented." Another who worked in a community where planning was not considered strong liked the strategic planning approach because it emphasized community strengths as well as weaknesses. He claimed it had led to the realization that "we have some good things going for us in our community, counteracting the tendency to knock ourselves too much."

Whether they were favorable or unfavorable toward strategic planning, the planners we interviewed agreed that it was *not* fundamentally different from good traditional public planning.

Some skeptics offered these contentions:

Strategic planning doesn't strike me as much different than the kind of middle-range, policy-sensitive planning we do now in our community.

We do essentially the same things in our planning program that proponents of corporate strategic planning claim that approach accomplishes.

Strategic planning doesn't represent much of a change from what we already do. For the last ten years in our agency we've been taking a strategic approach, looking at strengths and weaknesses of our city, focusing on crucial issues, developing action strategies. Strategic planning is not a new direction.

Even strong supporters of strategic planning saw no fundamental differences:

Intuitively we were doing strategic planning before. But we didn't have a model that we could specifically cite, like strategic planning, to give a name to what we were doing.

Although we're doing strategic planning for economic development, the approach is not new; the basis of it isn't any different from what you expect from good comprehensive planning.

Although in agreement that the two planning approaches are not fundamentally different, both the supporters and the skeptics of corporate strategic planning cited differences in emphasis between the two approaches. Both groups seemed to agree that the strategic planning approach tended to be shorter-range in focus and targeted on more realistic and feasible proposals. In addition, they were in agreement that strategic planning efforts at the local level emphasized the need to market communities attractively, package action proposals in ways designed to excite the public and policy makers, and highlight the community's competitive advantages – all ideas consistent with the private sector origins of the model. Differences of opinion did surface, however, between the supporters and the skeptics. Whereas supporters tended to assess strategic planning efforts as more analytically rigorous, involving a broader cross-section of the community in planning, and achieving more implementation success, skeptics – as befitted their label – disagreed with those contentions.

Differences of opinion were sharpest over the limitations of the corporate strategic planning approach. Although supporters acknowledged that strategic planning had some weaknesses (for example, it can be very time-consuming, it's difficult to maintain the interest level of top decision makers in the process, and it can be a costly undertaking), their criticisms were decidedly tamer than those of the skeptics. The latter were especially blunt in their contentions that strategic planning programs were too narrowly based, reflected too much of a business community agenda, had much less influence on policy decisions than its advocates claimed, and seriously underestimated the problem of implementing priority actions in the decentralized, pluralistic decision-making system of the public sector. Given their contention that their planning agencies were already active both in identifying crucial community issues and in thinking and acting strategically long before strategic planning came on the scene, one senses that planners who hold strong reservations about strategic planning see little value in it. Quite clearly, their views are not shared by all the planners we interviewed. As we said, a few were quite enthusiastic about the strategic planning efforts under way in their communities, and more who were lukewarm were still positive about some features of the approach.

Conclusion

It is the purpose of this chapter to examine, from a public planning perspective, the adaptation of the corporate strategic planning model to communitywide planning. We have examined five points that proponents of corporate strategic planning put forth as distinguishing it from traditional public planning. We argue that the implied or explicit critique of so-called traditional planning is, at base, a critique of comprehensive, long-range, or master planning; that this is only one mode of planning; and that it is a mode that has long sustained criticism for the very points highlighted by proponents of corporate strategic planning. From the planning literature, we find that the critiques and suggestions embodied in strategic planning are long-standing, well developed, and well known.

We note, though, that corporate strategic planning is distinctive in bringing these points together into a coherent planning process model.

In addition, we conducted telephone interviews with fifteen planners around the United States whose communities have engaged in strategic planning. We found them divided in their assessment of the approach. A few were quite supportive, some had mixed feelings, and still others were decidedly skeptical. All, however, found that strategic planning was not significantly different from good comprehensive planning; it was different in emphasis, they said, but not in kind.

We are aware of the limitations of the methods used to arrive at the above and subsequent conclusions. Our examination of planning literature, founded in the survey by Klosterman (1981), represents the material we believe is central to debate and development in planning theory. Others whose assessment of the literature is different may find our argument less compelling. In terms of the interviews with practicing planners, the size of the study population was small and necessarily nonrandom. As such our data are exploratory. A more verifiable assessment of what practicing public planners think about strategic planning efforts at the local level would require a larger group of interviewees and a more rigorous interview structure. Nevertheless, we believe that the phone interviews provide an accurate snapshot of how selected public planners with exposure to strategic planning view it today. Further, these data provide a basis for developing hypotheses about planners' perceptions of corporate strategic planning and its application in current planning practice.[3]

In the way of general conclusions, we offer the following thoughts. First, recent introspection about corporate strategic planning (Kiechel 1982; *Business Week* 1984; Hayes 1985) reflects an emerging skepticism toward its application to the management of corporations. Bryson, Van de Ven, and Roering (1986) and Eadie (1983), proponents of corporate strategic planning, show a growing sensitivity to the complexities of transferring this approach to the public sector.

Second, we stress that, at least in the short term, strategic planning will remain an issue in the public sector. Especially in the area of economic development, strategic planning has become an important technique to develop a program of action based on a public-private partnership. As noted earlier, in certain ways we believe that is good for public planning. In a time of fiscal constraint and possible crisis, strategic planning is redefining the nature of the public planning debate. It may be that corporate strategic planning will help turn the discussion from *whether* to do planning to *how* to do planning.

This suggests our third set of thoughts. The public planning community can look at the advent and popularity of corporate-style strategic planning in any of three ways: as a threat, as an opportunity, or as another fad. As a threat, strategic planning seems poised to replace the way public planners have done planning and even the planners themselves (see, for example, Denhardt 1985: 175). Even if planners embrace strategic planning, however, it is possible that, although they may become more integrated into decision making, the planning they do may be little different from the management-type planning undertaken by public administrators. Success with strategic planning thus might be bittersweet. Seen in that light, strategic planning is something to be either avoided or fought against so as to preserve the place and style of existing public planning. How successful this posture would be is unclear, especially given the strong support that corporate strategic planning receives from influential members of the private sector and political communities.

On the other hand, strategic planning seems to offer significant opportunities for public planners. If we are correct in our assessment of the components of strategic planning and its relation to existing planning theory, planners already should be well exposed to its concepts and techniques. Even its jargon is becoming familiar to planners. In this case, public planners should be well positioned to play significant roles in strategic planning programs at the community level. They can stress their skills in facilitation, communication, analysis of secondary data, and forecasting. If strategic planning in the future follows the examples of the recent past, substantial amounts of money will be available for such programs. If they look at strategic planning as an opportunity, public planners could be central to deciding how and for what those funds get used. Otherwise, the torch for planning will be carried by other professionals and groups.

Finally, corporate-style strategic planning may be just another passing fad. Like planning-programming-budgeting systems, it may be bursting onto the scene with a great deal of fanfare, only to slip into relative obscurity later (So 1984). That is an unknown now, and we attempt no prediction. Instead, we close by noting that, since it is unknown, planners would do well to treat the advent of strategic planning seriously and to view it, in the parlance of the approach, as an opportunity rather than as a threat.

Ultimately, public planners will need to wait for more data before making definitive judgements about corporate strategic planning. More strategic plans need to be prepared, and existing strategic plans need to be acted on. Only then will it be known if strategic planning can bring about more effective public planning.

Acknowledgments

We would like to thank the practitioners, academic colleagues, and students who commented on drafts of this material. We give special acknowledgment to our colleagues at the University of Wisconsin-Madison, Stephen M. Born and

Rosalind J. Greenstein, as well as *JAPA* coeditor Raymond J. Burby, guest editors John M. Bryson and Robert C. Einsweiler, and the anonymous reviewers.

Notes

1   The American Institute of Certified Planners Code of Ethics (1981) states clearly that planners "must strive to give citizens the opportunity to have meaningful impact on plans and programs." Participation is defined as "broad enough to include people who lack formal organization or influence."

2   Interviews were conducted with top-level planners in San Francisco; the Philadelphia area; the Minneapolis–St. Paul area; Dade County, Florida; Fort Collins, Colorado; Pittsburgh; Madison, Wisconsin; Memphis, Tennessee; Oxford, Ohio; and Albany, New York. For the purposes of this article, the names, titles, and positions of the interviewees are omitted.

3   A broad range of research questions could be pursued with regard to applications of corporate strategic planning in the public sector. For instance, why is strategic planning used in some communities but not in others? Is it a function of leadership, organization, business influence? Who benefits from strategic planning efforts, and how are those benefits realized? Do strategic planning efforts strengthen the planning function? Do strategic planning programs that involve widespread public participation reflect broader consensus or more watered-down compromise? Is the idea of regionalism advanced or weakened when communities follow a strategic planning approach that emphasizes competition?

References

Altshuler, Alan A. 1965. *The city planning process: A political analysis.* Ithaca, N.Y.: Cornell University Press.

American Institute of Certified Planners. 1981. Code of ethics and professional conduct. Washington: AICP.

Ansoff, Igor. 1965. *Corporate strategy: An analytic approach to business policy for growth and expansion.* New York: McGraw-Hill.

Arnstein, Sherry R. 1969. A ladder of citizen participation. *Journal of the American Institute of Planners* 35, 4: 216–224.

Arthur Anderson & Co. n.d. *Guide to public-sector strategic planning.* Chicago: Arthur Anderson & Co.

Banfield, Edward C. 1959. Ends and means in planning. *International Social Science Journal* 11, 3: 361–68.

Benveniste, Guy. 1972. *The politics of expertise.* Berkeley, Calif.: Glendessary Press.

Bluestone, Barry, and Bennett Harrison. 1982. *The deindustrialization of America.* New York: Basic Books.

Bolan, Richard. 1967. Emerging views of planning. *Journal of the American Institute of Planners* 33, 4: 234–246.

———.1971. The social relations of the planner. *Journal of the American Institute of Planners* 37, 6: 386–395.

Boyle, M. Ross. 1983. The strategic planning process: Assessing a community's economic assets. *Economic Development Commentary* 7, 2: 3–7.

Branch, Melville C. 1983. *Comprehensive planning: General theory and principles.* Pacific Palisades, Calif.: Palisades Publishers.

Bryson, John M., Andrew H. Van de Ven, and William D. Roering. 1986. Strategic planning and the revitalization of the public service. In *Toward a New Public Service* edited by Robert C. Denhardt and Edward Jennings. Columbia, Mo.: University of Missouri Press. In press.

Bryson, John M., R. Edward Freeman, and William D. Roering. 1986. Strategic planning in the public sector: Approaches and future directions. In *Strategic Approaches to Planning Practice*, edited by Barry Checkoway. Lexington, Mass.: Lexington Books. Forthcoming.

Burke, Edmund C. 1968. Citizen participation strategies. *Journal of the American Institute of Planners* 34, 5: 287–294.

Business Week. 1984. The new breed of strategic planner. *Business Week* September 17: 62–68.

Catanese, Anthony James. 1974. *Planners and local politics: Impossible dreams.* Beverly Hills, Calif.: Sage Publications.

———, and W. Paul Farmer, eds. 1978. *Personality, politics, and planning.* Beverly Hills, Calif.: Sage Publications.

Chandler, Alfred. 1962. *Strategy and structure.* Boston: MIT Press.

Chicago Department of Development and Planning. 1966. *The comprehensive plan of Chicago.* Chicago: CDDP.

Clavel, Pierre. 1983. *Opposition planning in Wales and Appalachia.* Philadelphia: Temple University Press.

Clawson, Marion. 1981. *New Deal planning.* Baltimore: Johns Hopkins University Press.

Davidoff, Paul. 1965. Advocacy and pluralism in planning. *Journal of the American Institute of Planners* 31, 4: 331–38.

———, and Thomas Reiner. 1962. A choice theory of planning. *Journal of the American Institute of Planners* 28, 2: 103–115.

Denhardt, Robert B. 1985. Strategic planning in state and local government. *State and Local Government Review* 17, 1: 174–79.

Drucker, Peter. 1954. *The practice of management.* New York: Harper and Row.

Eadie, Douglas C. 1983. Putting a powerful tool to practical use: The application of strategic planning in the public sector. *Public Administration Review* 43, 5: 447–452.

———, and Roberta Steinbacher. 1985. Strategic agenda management: A marriage of organizational development and strategic planning. *Public Administration Review* 45, 3: 424–430.

Etzioni, Amitai. 1967. Mixed scanning: A 'third' approach to decision-making. *Public Administration Review* 27, 5: 385–392.

Friedmann, John. 1973. *Retracking America: A theory of transactive planning.* New York: Anchor Press/Doubleday.

Goodman, Robert. 1971. *After the planners.* New York: Simon and Schuster.

Hayes, Robert H. 1985. Strategic planning – Forward in reverse? *Harvard Business Review* 63, 6: 111–19.

Isserman, Andrew M. 1985. Dare to plan: An essay on the role of the future in planning practice and education. *Town Planning Review* 56, 4: 483–491.

Kaufman, Jerome L. 1974. Contemporary planning practice: State of the art. In *Planning in America: Learning from Turbulence*, edited by D. Godschalk. Washington: American Institute of Planners.

Kiechel, Walter. 1982. Corporate strategists under fire. *Fortune* 106, 13: 34–39.

Klosterman, Richard E. 1981. Contemporary planning theory education: Results of a course survey. *Journal of Planning Education and Research* 1, 1: 1–11.

Kreditor, Alan. 1985. Dilemmas in planning education: Dichotomies between visionary and utilitarian. Paper presented at the annual meeting of the Association of Collegiate Schools of Planning, Atlanta, Georgia. November.

Krueckeberg, Don. 1971. Variations in behavior of planning agencies. *Administrative Science Quarterly* 16, 2: 192–202.

Krumholz, Norman. 1982. A retrospective view of equity planning: Cleveland 1969–1979. *Journal of the American Planning Association* 48, 2: 163–174.

——,Janice M. Cogger, and John H. Linner. 1975. The Cleveland policy planning report. *Journal of the American Institute of Planners* 41, 5: 298–304.

Lang, Reg. 1986. Achieving integration in resource planning. In *Integrated Approaches to Resource Planning and Management*, edited by Reg Lang. Calgary, Alberta: University of Calgary Press. In press.

Lindblom, Charles E. 1959. The science of muddling through. *Public Administration Review* 19, 2: 79–88.

Long, Norton E. 1977. How to help cities become independent. In *How Cities Can Grow Old Gracefully*, prepared for the Subcommittee on the City, Committee on Banking, Finance, and Urban Affairs, U.S. House of Representatives. Washington: U.S. Government Printing Office.

MacKaye, Benton. 1928. *The new exploration: A philosophy of regional planning.* New York: Harcourt, Brace and Co.

McHarg, Ian. 1969. *Design with nature.* Garden City, N.Y.: Doubleday and Co.

Mumford, Lewis. 1938. *The culture of cities.* New York: Harcourt Brace Jovanovich.

Meyerson, Martin. 1956. Building the middle-range bridge for comprehensive planning. *Journal of the American Institute of Planners* 22, 2: 58–64.

——,and Edward Banfield. 1955. *Politics, planning and the public interest.* New York: Free Press.

Naisbitt, John. 1982. *Megatrends.* New York: Warner Books.

National Resources Board. 1934a. *Report of the land planning committee.* Washington: U.S. Government Printing Office.

—— 1934b, *Report of the National Resources Board.* Washington: U.S. Government Printing Office.

National Resources Committee. 1937. *Our cities: Their role in the national economy.* Washington: U.S. Government Printing Office.

New York City Planning Commission. 1969. *Plan for New York City: Critical issues.* New York: NYCPC.

Olsen, John B., and Douglas C. Eadie. 1982. *The game plan: Governance with foresight.* Washington: Council of State Planning Agencies.

Perry, David C., and Alfred J. Watkins, eds. 1977. *The rise of the sunbelt cities.* Urban Affairs Annual Reviews, vol. 14. Beverly Hills, Calif.: Sage.

Rosener, Judy. 1978. Matching method to purpose: The challenges of planning citizen-participation activities. In *Citizen Participation in America*, edited by Stuart Langdon. Lexington, Mass.: Lexington Books.

Scott, Mel. 1969. *American city planning since 1890*. Berkeley: University of California Press.

Scott, Randall W., ed. 1975. *The management and control of growth*. Vol. 1–3. Washington: Urban Land Institute.

So, Frank S. 1984. Strategic planning: Reinventing the wheel? *Planning* 50, 2: 16–21.

Sorkin Donna L., Nancy B. Ferris, and James Hudak. 1984. *Strategies for cities and counties: A strategic planning guide*. Washington: Public Technology, Inc.

Stein, Clarence. 1926. *Report of the New York State Commission of Housing and Regional Planning*. Albany, N.Y.: New York State Legislature.

Steiner, George A. 1969. *Top management planning*. London: Macmillan.

——,and J. B. Miner. 1977. *Management policy and strategy: Text, readings, and cases*. New York: Macmillan.

Taylor, Bernard. 1984. Strategic planning – Which style do you need? *Long Range Planning* 17, 3: 51–62.

Tiebout, Charles M. 1956. A pure theory of local expenditures. *Journal of Political Economy* 64, 5: 416–424.

Toft, Graham S. 1984. Strategic planning for economic and municipal development. *Resources in Review* 6, 6: 6–11.

Tomazinis, Anthony R. 1985. The logic and rationale of strategic planning. Paper presented at the annual meeting of the Association of Collegiate Schools of Planning, Atlanta. November.

Walker, Robert. 1950. *The planning function in urban government*. Chicago: University of Chicago Press.

Williams, Norman Jr. 1970. The three systems of land use control. *Rutgers Law Review* 25, 1: 80–101.

16

A Retrospective View of Equity Planning: Cleveland, 1969–1979

Norman Krumholz

In 1969, I came to Cleveland, Ohio, as director of the Cleveland City Planning Commission to serve under Carl B. Stokes, the first black mayor of any American city with over 500,000 people. It is hard for me to express how deeply I felt about the importance of this assignment. I had always been involved in liberal issues; I had hoped for a racially integrated society, and was strongly sympathetic to the civil rights movement. I was deeply devoted to our country but did not believe that America as a nation had solved all its problems or achieved all its objectives. Stokes's election had been of huge importance to large segments of the black and liberal communities, and I jumped at the chance to work in his administration. I served under Stokes for two years. Later, I continued my work under Republican Ralph J. Perk for six years and resigned in the waning days of Dennis J. Kucinich's two-year term. During the ten years, my staff and I served in turn a liberal black Democrat, a conservative white ethnic Republican, and a self-styled urban populist. I also watched (and some say helped) Cleveland become the first American city since the Great Depression to default on its fiscal obligations. The purpose of this reading is to describe and evaluate that experience, and to update some of the case studies and findings discussed in an earlier *APA Journal* article (Krumholz 1975; Gans 1975; Piven 1975; Long 1975; Davidoff 1975).

Reprinted by permission of the *Journal of the American Planning Association* Vol. 48, No. 4, 1982.

Regardless of who was mayor, the staff of the Cleveland City Planning Commission consistently operated in a way that was activist and interventionist in style and redistributive in objective. Our overriding goal, articulated in the *Cleveland Policy Planning Report* published in 1975, was "to provide a wider range of choices for those Cleveland residents who have few if any choices" (Cleveland City Planning Commission 1975). The approach has been called "advocacy" or "equity" planning by many in the planning profession; it has also been called "cut-back planning" by Professor Herbert Gans and "opportunity planning" by Anthony Downs. It has received considerable scholarly attention, perhaps as a polar example of the application of local planning efforts to issues of social equity.

Why would this particular group of city planners act in a way that was highly visible and frequently politically risky? My thoughts on the strategy and tactics of operating a planning department developed jointly with several outstanding coworkers (initially Ernest R. Bonner, Janice M. Cogger, John H. Linner, and Douglas G. Wright) in the following four related lines: (1) the urgent reality of conditions in Cleveland, (2) the inherent unfairness and exploitative nature of our urban development process, (3) the inability of local politics to address these problems, and (4) our conception of the ethics of professional planning practice.

Conditions in Cleveland

Consider Cleveland's problems – the city's population had fallen rapidly. It dropped 39,000 in the 1950s: 125,000 in the 1960s; and 180,000 in the 1970s. Over that period, the proportion of blacks in the city's population rose from 16 to 44 percent; and in Cleveland, the poor were more often than not black, the black were more often than not poor.[1]

A rising share of the city's population was economically dependent, and its income was falling in relative terms. About 20 percent of Cleveland's families received Aid to Families with Dependent Children, and one-sixth had incomes below $2,000 a year.[2] More affluent families had been departing for decades; in the 1960s the city lost 25 percent of its families with incomes over the median for the Standard Metropolitan Statistical Area.[3]

The city had a high and rising crime rate. Crime was seen as the number-one problem by 73 percent of all residents (Cleveland City Planning Commission 1972). In 1975, the rate of violent crimes against persons was 1,730 per 100,000. That was 16 percent over the 1970 rate and 164 percent over the 1965 rate (Cleveland Police Department 1974).

The city had a declining assessed value base – it fell 5 percent from 1969 to 1974, while the Consumer Price Index rose 34.5 percent. Local general fund operating revenues declined 37 percent in constant dollars during that same period.[4]

These depressing central city phenomena were not shared by the Cleveland region. In 1973, per capita income in the region, excluding the city, was $6,750 or 14 percent above the national average. In the city, per capita income was $3,160 or 37 percent less than the U.S. average.

The region continued to expand its employment base with almost 25,000 new jobs added to the regional economy between 1972 and 1976. Between 1958 and 1977 the region gained 210,000 jobs; the city lost 130,000 jobs over the same period.[5]

The Cleveland region's unemployment rate (5.9 percent in 1977) was usually lower than the U.S. average (7.0 percent in 1977). However, the city suffered higher unemployment rates than the U.S. average (11.5 percent in 1977), and among young blacks the unemployment rate (38.8 percent in 1977) represented a tragic waste of enormous proportions.[6]

Not surprisingly, the fiscal and economic disparities between central city and region were wider in Cleveland than in almost any other place in the U.S. Unemployment, poverty, crime, inadequate education, rotting housing, and the other elements of the urban crisis were concentrated in the city, and particularly in the city's low income neighborhoods.

Exploitative development process

Perceiving these city-suburban disparities, we were profoundly disturbed – even outraged. We saw them not as the result of simple coincidence or of market forces, but partially as the result of an urban development process that inherently exploited the poor – especially the minority poor. The same customs and institutional arrangements that produced safe neighborhoods, satisfactory schools, and viable public institutions for the middle class also concentrated the poor into neighborhoods where the very business of day-to-day living was extremely difficult. The minority poor were excluded from many suburbs, not by market forces but by zoning codes that maintained unreasonably large building parcels, by restrictive covenants on the sale of land, by building and housing codes that ensured ever-rising home prices, by informal customs, and by legal cooperation agreements that sharply limited the location of new public housing to the central city and its worst neighborhoods. We felt that these arrangements were not the result of any deliberate malevolent conspiracy but that they were exploitative and contrary to American notions of justice and fairness and so should be resisted by city planners and others.

Inadequacy of local politics

Why didn't the local political structure deal with these problems? Because, we thought, the problems were based at their roots on poverty and racial prejudice and were national in origin. Unless there was broad

concern over these issues expressed in national legislation and enforcement, there was very little that local politics could or would do.

There was also the relative lack of influence of Cleveland's resident
population. Influence, like wealth, was unevenly distributed in the population. When goals conflicted, groups with wealth and influence were
likely to win every time, although it was hard to see how such winning
contributed either to democracy or to the public good. The result was that
public facilities rotted without attention in low-income neighborhoods
while public and philanthropic resources were lavished on public spaces
and old buildings downtown. Within the context of this contending but
unequal power and influence, placing priority attention on the needs of
the poor would tend to provide them with countervailing power and, like
universal suffrage and majority rule, would help strengthen democracy.

Professional ethics

Finally, the planners recognized that this was an ethical issue, not just for
us as individuals but for the profession of city planning. The Code of
Ethics of the American Institute of Planners did, in a way, justify our
actions, and we quoted it in our work:

> A planner shall seek to expand choice and opportunity for all persons, recog-
> nizing a special responsibility to plan for the needs of disadvantaged groups
> and persons, and shall urge the alteration of policies, institutions and deci-
> sions which militate against such objectives.

With these views as a guide, we deemphasized many of our concerns
with zoning, land use, and urban design. We altered the planner's traditional posture as an apolitical technician serving a unitary public interest.
Instead, we devoted ourselves to "providing more choices to those who
have few, if any choices."

As a result, our work did not map out an ideal future in terms of land
use, public facilities, and transportation routes. Rather it was made up of
studies, proposals, and recommendations that seemed likely to resolve or
ameliorate the worst problems of Cleveland and its residents. In some
respects our work could be criticized as having been "short term"; in other
respects, it was most visionary since it was seeking a society fundamentally different from the present, a society in which justice and equity were
at least as important as efficiency.

Our equity activities in Cleveland covered almost ten years. After my
departure in 1979, all the staff members I hired left the planning agency
for other positions at city hall, and many left the city entirely. New leadership was introduced to the planning commission, which now appears
to view its planning responsibilities in a more traditional vein. For the

present, at least, the equity planning experiment in Cleveland is over. How much difference did it make?

To try to answer that question, I will try to assess the impact of our work on some of the major issues in which we were involved, on the mayors we served, on other practicing city planning professionals, and on the teaching of city planning.

The CTS-RTA Negotiations

Our greatest success had to do with the negotiations that led in 1975 to the transfer of the Cleveland Transit System (CTS) to the Greater Cleveland Regional Transit Authority (RTA).

Transportation problems are usually defined in terms of rush hour congestion, automobile access, or the need for more off-street parking. However, our goal led us to define Cleveland's most significant transportation problem in a different way: the need to improve the mobility of Cleveland's transit-dependent population, those families who lacked automobiles and who depended entirely on public transit.

As we saw it, Cleveland was part of an automotive society that provided unprecedented mobility for those who had been able to take advantage of it. In the course of choosing this automotive civilization, however, we had chosen to ignore the problems created for those without access to an automobile. As cars proliferated and new development was scattered at low densities across the region, ridership on transit declined, service was cut, and fares increased. For the transit-dependent rider, most of whom were poor, elderly, or physically handicapped, there were fewer and fewer destinations that could be reached at ever-higher fares after longer waiting periods.

This might be a trivial problem except that the transit-dependent population made up a sizable portion of Cleveland's population. About one-third of all Cleveland families had no car; among families over age sixty-five or earning less than $6,000 a year, about one-half had no car.

It seemed clear to us that Cleveland's highest transportation priority should be to ensure a decent level of mobility to those transit-dependent persons who were prevented by extreme poverty or a combination of low income and physical disability (including old age) from moving around our metropolitan area.

We first became involved in the transit issue through the Cleveland area's Five-County Transit Study, which began in 1970. The city-owned CTS, at the time the largest system in the world to be operating exclusively from fare-box revenues, was rapidly approaching financial disaster. The five-county planning process was seen locally as providing the impetus and framework for a regional transit system.

We represented Mayor Stokes and later Mayor Perk on the transit study's executive committee. In that capacity, we argued that expanded mobility for the transit-dependent population should be acknowledged as the study's highest priority objective; that staff and consultants should be selected who were sensitive to the needs of the transit-dependent population; and that adequate funding should be provided for the transit-dependent element of the study. We won on each of these points, but they were fleeting victories. The project's staff quickly identified its interests in terms of responding to and even anticipating political pressures, and a wide gap developed between the goals stated in the study and the final recommendations.

The study's final recommendations placed major emphasis on the expenditure of more than $1 billion for expanded rail facilities. Based upon a careful review of the analysis supporting this recommendation, my staff and I concluded that such a rail system was likely to provide few benefits to anyone except those involved in its management, construction, and financing. Moreover, it threatened to draw resources away from those service improvements offering the greatest potential benefits to the transit-dependent. In the eighteen-month interim between the publication of the study's "Ten Year Transit Development Program" report and the initiation of negotiations over formation of a regional transit authority, we worked to discredit the rail expansion plan at the local, regional, and federal levels.

By the end of 1974, CTS was in crisis, and Cleveland decision makers began the serious business of forming the RTA. With our four years of experience and prepared position papers, we soon began to function as the administration spokesperson.

The negotiations centered on one issue – what the city would receive in return for transferring CTS to a new regional authority. Initially, the city's political leaders simply demanded a majority of the appointments to the RTA board. We felt that this was insufficient and were convinced that the city should be bargaining for fare reductions and service improvements for the city's transit-dependent population. We took elements of the Five-County Transit Study, translated them into terms that local decision makers could understand, and presented them to the mayor and city council. When the city's political leaders realized that abstract concepts such as "route-spacing guides," "loading coefficients," and "service headways" meant tangible improvements for their constituents, they shifted the focus of their demands.

Throughout these negotiations, James B. Davis, the city's law director, and I argued for fare and service guarantees while our opposition county officials, suburban mayors, representatives of the business community, and the city's own CTS management argued for "flexibility" for the RTA. It was clear that when the transit operators and downtown boosters spoke in term of "flexibility" for the RTA, the billion-dollar plus rail expansion plan was on their minds. Thus, while our opposition fought to keep the guarantees to the city as meaningless as possible, the planners, aided by the law director and a young council member named Dennis J. Kucinich, fought to ensure that the RTA would be legally committed to reducing fares and improving service for Cleveland residents.

During the protracted negotiations, we were forced to make a number of concessions, but when agreement was finally reached, it was clear that we had made substantial progress toward ensuring that the RTA would be responsive to the needs of the transit-dependent population. In the final agreement the city was guaranteed the following:

1   A twenty-five-cent fare would be maintained for at least three years.
2   Senior citizens and the handicapped would ride free during nonpeak periods (twenty hours daily) and pay only half fare during the four peak hours.
3   Service frequencies and route coverage within the city would be improved.
4   The RTA would be prohibited from spending funds on planning or developing a downtown subway or elevated system for at least five years.
5   Community Responsive Transit (CRT), a door-to-door, dial-a-ride service would be initiated.

The best service and fare guarantees we could get were only three and five years long. They have now expired, and the RTA's management has begun the dreary cycle of raising fares and cutting services while programming and making heavy expenditures on maintaining and expanding Cleveland's rail system.

The RTA's capital expenditures in its first six years were indicative of the system's priorities. Of its first $120 million capital improvement program, $100 million was spent upgrading the entire Shaker Rapid line, a line that carries less than 4 percent of the system's ridership, albeit the most wealthy, influential, and vocal 4 percent. Fifty-one percent of Shaker Rapid riders have two or more cars; only 8 percent have none. So much for the emphasis on the transit-dependent rider! The RTA is also planning a $50-million extension of one of the Shaker lines as well as a $5-billion, four-mile downtown subway. The agency has budgeted $694 million for various rail improvements in its 1982–1987 planning, and has spent over $234 million, or 72 percent, of all capital grants received from 1975 to 1981 on rail. Meanwhile, over 87 percent of the RTA's ridership takes the bus.

However, the CRT program we pressed on the RTA over management's objections has been under way for five years. CRT now has an organized constituency that understands, uses, and supports the service, so CRT will probably continue, even though it is programmed at only about 2 percent of the system's $117-million annual budget. Similarly, the sharply discounted fares for the elderly and handicapped were left untouched by the two RTA fare hikes in 1981. So some elements of our package will outlast the guarantees we were able to negotiate. Even if they all expired on schedule the three to five years of service and fare benefits were more than our transit-dependent clients would have gotten had we not been ready with clear objectives and the will to fight for them.

Tower City

A second major issue in which we were involved had to do with public subsidies to a private downtown development.

In the winter of 1974, a local real estate developer approached the city with plans to construct a major downtown commercial complex called Tower City. The developer claimed that the total value of planned construction would reach $350 million. The media, the business community, and the city's political leadership hailed the proposal as a bold step toward revitalizing downtown Cleveland.

The planning commission staff reviewed the legislation and found several disturbing aspects. The city was asked both to waive rights it held to the development site and to agree to repair some railroad bridges on the site. Our probing revealed that other entities, not the city, were responsible for the bridge repairs, and that the estimated costs of the repairs were open-ended and could exceed $15 million. Further, it appeared that the developer would request property tax abatement for twenty years.

We concluded that the city had little to gain from Tower City. The bridge repairs would be expensive, and our responsibility for them was unclear; the city might be forced to give away any new property tax revenue; the promise of new income tax revenue was not bright, since our studies showed the market for downtown office space was not growing but simply shifting from one location to another; and the developer was not offering any permanent new jobs for the city's unemployed.

We were not opposed to new development per se. We realized new development might keep firms in downtown that otherwise might have left the city completely; that development provides short-term construction jobs; and that it adds to the tax base (unless new tax revenues are abated). We wanted new development that was of benefit to the city and its people.

Following the staff's recommendation, the planning commission refused to approve the legislation unless several amendments were made in which the developer would guarantee a number of new jobs to city residents, agree to forgo tax abatement, and pay full property taxes on the project. These conditions were not acceptable to the developer.

Very quickly our position came under fire from the city council and the newspapers. We were accused of obstructing progress and being antidevelopment. Our rebuttal that the health and vitality of a city did not depend on the construction of new office buildings and hotels in downtown but rather on how well the city helped provide jobs, opportunities, and services to its residents did not convince anyone.

Attacks on the planners grew stronger and more personal throughout the city council committee hearings. Council President George Forbes, then, as now, the ringmaster of city hall, called the commission "a bunch of baboons" and on television demanded my resignation. Eventually, council overrode the planning commission's disapproval 32–1 and passed the legislation.

On this particular issue we lost badly, but we succeeded in placing some important issues on the public agenda. We pointed out that the money to subsidize this project would come at the expense of high-priority capital improvements in the city's working-class and poor neighborhoods. We asked to what extent the city should go to underwrite the risk of private development. Also, we tried to make clear that the city's scarce resources should be applied to facilitating private development only if that development provided permanent, productive jobs for the city's people and net increases in tax revenues for the city's coffers. In short, we proposed the doctrine that the city spend its money and power in businesslike ways.

Tower City has not been built for reasons unrelated to our opposition, but the idea that the city should expect some return on any public investments it makes in support of private development now seems to be understood. Our position, which was an isolated one at the time, may have been part of a chain of events that later led the Ohio Public Interest Campaign and the Commission on Catholic Community Action to vigorously oppose tax abatements. For whatever reason, no property tax abatements have been granted to any development in Cleveland since 1977, although downtown continues to enjoy a boom in new construction.

Public Versus Private Power

Perhaps the most important issue in which we were involved is still to be resolved, the issue of public versus private electric power. Cleveland is served by two electrical systems: The Cleveland Electric Illuminating Company (CEI), an investor-owned regional utility company that serves about 80 percent of the accounts in Cleveland, and the city's own Municipal Electric Light Plant (Muny Light). In 1971, a series of power blackouts caused us to examine Muny Light's physical needs as a routine part of our preparation of the city's annual capital improvement program. As the analysis unfolded, however, it became apparent that the issue was more complex than Muny's need for a few pipes and boilers.

The planners found that CEI has been interested in purchasing Muny for decades, presumably to eliminate competition. We also found that, apparently to injure Muny's competitive position, CEI has steadfastly refused to allow Muny to tie in to other power sources. Therein lay Muny's problem. Nearly all electric power companies have tie-ins to other power systems so that they can continue service should their own facilities need repair or fail. Because it had no such tie-in, Muny was plagued with power failures. This led to numerous complaints about Muny's service, and several council members proposed to sell the facility to CEI.

We concluded that this might solve the blackout problem, but it would also mean that Muny's customers would experience an immediate rate hike and that the city would no longer have an effective brake on future rate increases. Thus, the issue appeared to have serious economic implications for the city's poor. Because electricity is a relatively fixed item of household consumption, any change in rates would have a definite effect upon the real incomes of city residents. Moreover, a significant change in rates might influence the location of firms within the Cleveland region and, thus, the access of city residents to jobs.

After the planners analyzed the fiscal and legal aspects of this question and the history of CEI's apparent long-term attempt to subvert and destroy Muny, they proposed something quite different from the sale of Muny to CEI. We proposed that Muny Light use state law to condemn and purchase CEI's transmission and generating capacity in the city. This would expand the small municipal power system into a citywide network, eliminate blackouts, and also provide electricity at a much lower cost to city residents.

Needless to say, this proposal was greeted with derision by the news media and did not result in the condemnation of CEI. However, it may have helped to forestall the sale of Muny Light and to prevent rate increases. It also served to remind local decision makers of the rationale for Muny Light's establishment. Beyond this, our study may have played a role in the events that followed.

In 1975, under Mayor Ralph Perk, the city filed a $327-million antitrust suit against CEI and four allied power companies for anticompetitive practices. A year later, the U.S. Justice Department filed a brief in support of the city, and the Atomic Safety and Licensing Board of the U.S. Nuclear Regulatory Commission (NRC) handed down a decision that elaborated on the planners' findings of four years earlier, which confirmed that CEI had a history of acting "individually and collectively to eliminate one or more electric entities and to preclude competition."

In the years that followed, Mayor Perk reversed his long-standing support for Muny and proposed to sell the system to CEI. One of the terms of the sale provided that the city would drop its antitrust suit. However, the sale was never consummated; Dennis Kucinich used the issue as a rallying point in his 1977 drive to the mayor's office and killed it. The present administration of Mayor George V. Voinovich has pursued the suit vigorously, and it is now before the federal court.

Did the work of Cleveland's city planners in publishing their 1972 report, in making depositions in the city's suit, and in publicizing the CEI-Muny Light issue have anything to do with Muny's present affection in the hearts of the city's leadership? Perhaps, but for most of us, it is enough to know that we used our skills in data gathering and analysis for the useful purpose of exposing CEI's stratagems in trying to destroy a municipal asset.

Other Issues

Having recounted three of the most significant issues in which we were involved, I would like to make a few additional points about the less heroic activities of the planning staff.

First, most planning issues that came before the staff lacked high drama and visibility and had little to do with "providing more choices for those who have few." However, we did this work diligently, no matter how routine, and it served to maintain and elaborate the planning agency's reputation for competence.

Second, although the three issues described above in detail involve conflicting values or political views, many of the issues in which my staff and I were involved were successfully concluded through the building of a broad consensus, not through conflict.

In one such issue, we headed a committee that successfully drafted and saw passed a new state law shortening and simplifying the foreclosure procedure for tax-delinquent and abandoned property. The new law has also allowed the city to land-bank these foreclosed parcels as trustee for the other two taxing bodies, Cuyahoga County and the Cleveland Board of Education. The development of this issue over a three-year period represents a virtually perfect textbook model of effective planning practice in which the planners identify a local problem; study its cause; recommend a likely solution to the planning commission, the mayor, and council; develop broad support across the state for the proposed solution; seek and get foundation help to draft a new state law; and lobby the law through the general assembly and governor's office. We even wrote an article and a book about the case (Olson and Lachman 1976)! Such activities can hardly be undertaken, let alone brought to a successful conclusion, without the building of broad, supportive coalitions.

Similar consensus building was essential to our efforts in other issues. In 1977, the city's once elegant lakefront parks were virtually open dumps, and Mayor Perk realized both his political vulnerability on the issue and his inability, because of fiscal inadequacies, to reverse the downward trend. He established and asked me to chair a Mayor's Task

Force on Lakefront Development, which within a year established a new state park in Cleveland, using as the core of the park the lakefront parks the city could no longer afford to maintain. In agreeing to set up this park, the Ohio Department of Natural Resources reversed its historic policy of building state parks only in rural areas. Agreement on this issue required political consensus among the mayor and city council, the governor's office, and the general assembly, as well as support from local foundations, the media, and "good government" groups.

Did our reputation as advocates willing to accept conflict in certain situations hinder our efforts to establish cooperative coalitions in other situations? Not so far as we could tell. I believe we were regarded by the other players as competent professionals who might frequently disagree with their views, but who were willing to join others (and anxious for others to join us) when our objectives coincided.

Professionalism, quiet agreement, close communication, and shared confidence were essential as the city planners attempted to improve city services by providing advice and technical assistance to other operating departments. In one such successful example, members of the planning staff worked within the city's Waste Collection and Disposal Division for five years in order to help improve its management capacity. During that time, the planners helped reorganize collection routes, recommended manpower reassignments, and helped direct the division's capital expenditures toward cost-saving equipment. In the process, the division was able to save several million dollars a year. When we were invited to begin working with the division it had no internal planning capabilities whatever. The division knew it was in trouble, but it didn't know how to address its problems analytically. Our work was quiet, completely behind the scenes, and long-term. The division's willingness to accept our advice was based on the trust that our advice was worthy, that we would stay with them over the long pull, and that we would take some of the political heat as they sought to implement our recommendations. By the time we ended our work with them, the division's commissioner (a former garbage collector) was a frequent speaker at national solid waste conferences, where he would talk of picking up garbage "heuristically."

It should be noted that many of our studies and proposals had little discernible impact on the issues we addressed. We drilled a lot of dry holes. For example, one of our first large-scale planning efforts was a 1970 proposal for a new town on some 850 acres of city-owned, largely vacant land seven miles from downtown Cleveland in a nearby unincorporated township. The proposal was innovative and detailed and interested the HUD new town desk, the Office of Economic Opportunity, and the Harvard Graduate School of Education. However, the city council was not very interested, and the people in surrounding municipalities were actively hostile. When Ralph Perk replaced Stokes as mayor in

1971, the new town idea was axed, and the land remains undeveloped to this day.

A similar fate awaited our proposal to decontrol the city council's grip over entry into the taxi business and the setting of taxi fares. We made the proposal so that the city's poor – who use taxis to a disproportionate degree – could take advantage of the lower fares, better service, and job opportunities that deregulation seemed to offer. To no avail; we could find no one with the necessary political power willing to adopt and pursue the idea.

Impact on the Mayors

What was the impact of our work on the mayors we served: Stokes, Perk, and Kucinich?

Stokes enjoyed our studies and analyses of various issues, and he supported most of them. He also appreciated the stream of speeches and articles that flowed from his planners and which he used for a variety of local and national purposes. In company with many other mayors, Stokes was not particularly interested in the day-to-day administrative responsibilities of his office. He provided broad policy direction. Within these broad guidelines, his directors had wide latitude to establish their own policies and programs. If and when they got into trouble, the mayor usually stood by them.

This relatively loose structure gave us great freedom to innovate. As part of our work in the first year we helped block the Clark Freeway (I-290), which would have displaced 1,400 families on the city's east side; proposed a much less damaging alternative route for the highway; published our new town proposal; set in motion the events that would decertify the Northeast Ohio Areawide Coordinating Agency (the regional planning group) and ultimately quadruple city representation on its board; and proposed a "fair share" plan for public housing in Cuyahoga County. Stokes supported all these efforts. They fit well with his objectives and strengthened the links between the mayor and his constituency. Yet in the larger sense we did not have much impact on the mayor's program, and he gave us little public recognition either at the time or in his political autobiography *Promises of Power* (Stokes 1973).

Stokes's major objectives had to do with building black political power locally and nationally, reforming the police department, and trying to keep the city fiscally solvent in the face of a hostile council. Although his planners had important things to say on each of these issues, we were not the key players. Most of us would agree, however, that recognition by the mayor was considerably less important than the unique experience of working in the Stokes administration.

Ralph Perk, who succeeded Stokes as mayor in 1971, seemed at first to offer his planners no entry into policy making. None of us had met the new mayor prior to his election, and we were concerned with many of the conservative views he articulated in the campaign. To our surprise, he was as supportive of most of our proposals as Stokes had been, and against the background of a mayor less charismatic and less liberal than Stokes, our own role as advocates became more prominent.

Perk had built a successful political career as a city council member, county auditor, and mayor by articulating the grievances of his largely ethnic, Democratic, and working-class constituency rather than by being a loyal Republican party functionary. His appointments and his city politics tended to be bipartisan. With some important exceptions, Perk's appointments reflected more concern for patronage than professionalism or technical capacity. His planners, well trained and seasoned, quickly shouldered into a number of issues with analytical policy papers and bargaining positions that set out how the interests of city residents (and Perk's own political fortunes) might be affected by this or that choice.

As mayor, Perk ran a casual and unstructured operation, presenting an ideal opportunity for planners with specific objectives in mind to become involved in significant matters ordinarily outside their traditional responsibilities. Ironically, although Perk's personal political philosophy was far to the political right of our views, he supported us in important work, and we helped each other achieve our most significant successes. In a way, as "house liberals" and advocates for Cleveland's have-nots, we may have played a supportive role for Perk in neutralizing opposition to his administration from minority groups.

Later in his administration, Perk began to see himself as a potential governor or U.S. senator, with a broader constituency and funding needs than those represented only by his city supporters. As Mayor Perk moved away from his city base in search of this broader constituency, our influence with the mayor's office waned.

Dennis J. Kucinich, who took office as mayor in November 1977, was a close student of Cleveland's city planning operation. He had a strong sense of the planning staff's political philosophy and technical ability, since he had asked for our help on a number of issues during his six years in Cleveland City Council. Kucinich was one of the first council members to provide consistent support for our position in the RTA transit negotiation. We looked forward to a close association and assumed that we would be heavily and continually involved in policy making at the mayoral level. For a period of ten months, Kucinich even gave me increased responsibility as head of his Community Development Department, the agency that spends Cleveland's $35-million plus block grant.

Regrettably, our relationship with the mayor began to deteriorate almost immediately. We agreed on virtually all policy issues: saving

Muny Light, ending tax giveaways, and the need to concentrate the resources of the community on its residents and neighborhoods. We also agreed on the ultimate heresy: that elected officials should have more to say about running Cleveland than the leadership of the city's law firms, banks, or utility companies. However, the mayor and his key lieutenants insisted on an approach that was confrontational in style and unnecessarily brutal, one that many feared would be destructive to the objectives we all sought and to the mayor's very ability to govern. Attempts to point out quietly effective ways to accomplish a given objective were rejected in favor of the bugle call, a fusillade of pejoratives, and a frontal assault. It gave the mayor more trouble than he needed.

After his first tumultuous year in office, during which he came into conflict with virtually every formal institution in Cleveland (mostly justified in my view) and survived a bitter recall election by 236 votes, Kucinich came into conflict with his own political base. He began by demanding loyalty and political support from Cleveland's neighborhood organizations as the price of city support for their projects. The groups, which were issue-oriented and had built their bases on protest tactics and strict political independence, refused to comply. Then, at an annual meeting of neighborhood organizations, his lieutenants threw down the gauntlet – either the groups would accept his decisions and requests without complaint, or they would be entirely cut off by city hall. Before the meeting was over, chairs were flying through the air, several people were wrestling for control of the microphone, and the stage was set for the open political warfare with the neighborhoods that was to sweep Kucinich out of city hall a year later.

Impact on Practicing Planners

How did our work in Cleveland affect the work of other practicing city planners? Probably not to any great degree, so far as I could tell. Our model, after all, asked city planners to be what few public administrators are: activist, risk-taking in style, and redistributive in objective. As I got around to other cities, I began to perceive that most planners were not so inclined. Despite an ideological mystique, which stresses a liberal point of view and selfless service to a broad public interest, planning practice actually is cautious and conservative.

Most planners, I began to think, were ordinary bureaucrats seeking a secure career, some status, and regular increases in salary. They rarely took unpopular public positions, since these might prejudice their chances to achieve these modest objectives. The average planner came out of a middle-class background and was not likely to be upset by social conditions or matters bearing on who-gets-what issues in society to the point where substantial, radical change would seem a legitimate objective. Many planners absorbed the values and philosophy of business, which has helped their status, income, and security.

One of the goals of city planning was comprehensiveness, but most planners were more at home with incremental decisions. They would agree that they were properly involved in locating and laying out a subdivision of low-income housing, but they would rarely seek to explore possible changes in the distribution of income and power that might lessen the need for such housing. Many planning agencies devoted themselves to operating within the narrowest limits of their charters, even if much of their work was repetitive or completely inapplicable. Tried and true techniques might not provide powerful insights into an issue, but at least they were safe. For all these reasons it was not surprising that the Cleveland model has little known application by practicing planning professionals in other cities.

At the same time, practicing planners in other cities will have to note that our brand of equity planning in Cleveland did not lead to disaster, in spite of the fact that it generated conflict from time to time with powerful individuals and institutions having a vested interest in the status quo. Our experience may suggest to other planners that in the right setting an advocacy planning agency not only can survive, it can grow and prosper.

Impact on Teaching of Planning

If our work had little impact on practicing planners, it apparently affected the teaching of planning to some degree. Almost all of the five hundred copies of the *Cleveland Policy Planning Report* that we originally printed were sent to professors of city planning at various universities around the country. It seems likely that our materials were used in seminars on planning administration to present an alternative model of real agency operations. Over the years, various members of the staff and I were invited to talk to dozens of city planning classes in many universities about our program in Cleveland. I also received a good deal of supportive mail on our approach from planning students. Perhaps in this respect our impact on the planners who will be practicing in the future is wider than we can know.

Conclusion

What else do our activities suggest that might be of interest or use to planners or the general public? There are some lessons.

1   Advocacy or equity planning is a way of addressing poverty and racial

segregation, the root causes of crisis in many American cities. Unless there is a concentrated attack on these problems, it is difficult to see how many cities can overcome the drift toward the status of being a "sandbox" (where the kids are parked while the rest of us proceed with the important matters at hand) or an "Indian reservation" (an island of dependency). The activities of traditional planning agencies may succeed in slightly altering the physical environment, but they are largely irrelevant to the needs of the people in cities such as Cleveland where the problems are largely economic, social and political.

2   As a profession, planning has been too timid. This criticism is pointed less toward the rank-and-file staff of most agencies than at their directors. They are the individuals confronted with the challenge and opportunity to create an activist role for their organizations, and they have the freedom to do so because there is much "slack" in local government and because planning practice is not uniform by law or tradition. Beyond the narrow powers and responsibilities mandated to planners by their city charters, the scope and content of the planning function in most cities waits to be defined by the planners themselves, by their planning commissions, and by their mayors. However, mayors and planning commissioners will rarely provide leadership, especially toward equity objectives. This means that the planners themselves must seize the initiative and define their own roles relative to the real needs of the city and its people. This course of action involves some political risks, but as our experience in Cleveland indicates, the risks are manageable. As an imperialist for the planning profession, I believe that planners can do much more than they are now doing. We will never know how much more we can do until we try.

3   The essential step toward developing an activist role lies in the adoption of a clearly defined goal. Without such a goal, planners have had difficulty answering the question of how best to allocate limited agency resources. Our goal in Cleveland of providing more choices for those who have few provided us with a convenient framework for day-to-day practice and a direction for broader, longer-range studies.

4   Pursuit of equity objectives requires that planners focus on the decision-making process, and focus on it not with rhetoric but with hard, relevant information. In the decision-making process those who have better information and know what outcomes they want to achieve have a great advantage over the other participants. The presentation of policies and programs to mayors, council members, and key political and business figures requires basic critical skills and abilities. Among these are the ability to deal with voluminous statistical information, familiarity with public and private financial procedures and techniques, a working knowledge of law, an appreciation of the workings of bureaucracies, and the ability to write and express ideas simply and clearly. Frequently, the successful advocacy of a desirable program or legislative change will rely entirely on the quality of staff work and the ability to present verbal or written recommendations clearly and quickly, remembering always that most politicians do not read much and have short attention spans. The only legitimate power the planner can count on in such matters is the power of information, analysis, and insight, but that

power is considerable when harnessed to an authentic conceptualization of the public need.

5   To be an effective part of the decision-making process, planners must participate in an issue for a relatively long period of time. The transit case evolved over a period of five years, our help to the solid waste division lasted five years, the land-banking issue developed over three years, and the issue of public versus private power has been in the mill for ten years and is still unresolved. To influence the outcomes of such issues, planners must be seen by the other participants as serious long-term players who are ready to give the participation necessary to help shape outcomes.

6   Planners who are interested in affecting outcomes must take their recommendations beyond their planning commission. This is difficult for many planners to understand, because they feel that the commission is their boss. Ordinarily, a planner will take a study and findings to the commission, present his or her recommendations as persuasively as possible and stop. The planner stops because the presentation to the commission appears to represent the end of planning legitimacy; the dangers of politics lie beyond. However, planning commissioners rarely decide the important issues; politicians, business leaders, and important bureaucrats decide them. If a planner's work is to be used, it must be taken beyond the commission into the political arena, and the planner must take risks while arguing on many fronts for the implementation of the study's recommendations.

This should not be construed as an argument for the abolition of the planning commission. The commission provides its staff with some protection against the vagaries of politics. It is possible that Mayor Perk, who removed almost all of Stokes's directors on taking office, would have removed Stokes's planners as well except for the buffering presence of the planning commission. The commission also provides a regular, institutionalized forum, which its staff can use to place issues, opinions, and analyses on the public agenda.

7   A planning agency that offers its staff an activist, user-oriented, problem-solving program will never lack for outstanding recruits. In my ten years in Cleveland, the planning agency hired more than thirty planners from all over the country. These recruits were not interested in coming to Cleveland for its sunshine, surf, or other amenities; they came to work seriously on problems related to poverty, unemployment, neighborhood development, and racial discrimination. Most of these young planners left after a few years in Cleveland for more attractive jobs, but several have remained in Cleveland city hall and now occupy important posts in other city departments where they continue contributing their high-quality work. In some respects, I think my most significant accomplishment may have been bringing these dedicated people into Cleveland government.

8   Finally, planners must have hope that change in the direction of more equity is possible and that their work may contribute to that change. This observation is not based on some misguided notion of intrinsic moral or political power of the planner. On the contrary, the planning agency is a weak platform from which to call for reform. Nevertheless, if planners consistently place before their political superiors analyses, policies, and recommendations that lead to greater equity, and if they are willing publicly to join in the fight

for the adoption of these recommendations, some of them will be adopted when the time is ripe. It is this process, conducted with verve, imagination, and above all with persistence, that offers the planner challenging and rewarding work and a better life for others.

Notes

1   See United States Department of Commerce, Census of Population for 1950, 1960, 1970, 1980.
2   These figures are from the ADC caseload figures and from the Cleveland Federation of Community Planning.
3   See United States Censuses of Population and Housing for 1960 and 1970.
4   Figures from the reports of the Cuyahoga County Auditor.
5   Figures from the United States Department of Labor, Bureau of Labor Statistics, *Employment and Earnings* (1977), and the Ohio Bureau of Employment Services.
6   Figures from the Ohio Bureau of Employment Services and the Cleveland Department of Human Resources and Economic Development.

References

Cleveland City Planning Commission. 1975. *Cleveland Policy Planning Report*. Cleveland: the Commission.

Cleveland City Planning Commission. 1972. *Two percent household survey; results of all questions*. Cleveland: the Commission.

Cleveland Police Department 1974. *Census tract distribution of uniform crime report offenses*. Cleveland: the Department.

Davidoff, Paul. 1975. Working toward redistributive justice. *Journal of the American Institute of Planners* 41, 5: 317–318.

Gans, Herbert J. 1975. Planning for declining and poor cities. *Journal of the American Institute of Planners* 41, 5: 305–307.

Krumholz, Norman, et al. 1975. The Cleveland policy planning report. *Journal of the American Institute of Planners* 41, 5: 298–304.

Long, Norton E. 1975. Another view of responsible planning. *Journal of the American Institute of Planners* 41, 5: 311–316.

Olson, S., and Lachman, M. L. 1976. *Tax delinquency in the inner city*. Toronto: D. C. Heath and Company.

Piven, Frances Fox. 1975. Planning and class interests. *Journal of the American Institute of Planners* 41, 5: 308–310.

Stokes, Carl B. 1973. *Promise of Power*. New York: Simon and Schuster.

Part IV

Planning in Action: Successes, Failures, and Strategies

Introduction

The case studies presented in the fourth section illustrate the opportunities and constraints to planners in the United States and Great Britain. One emerging theme is that the practice of planning often uses a different logic and strategy from that of the "rational model" of planning. In "What Local Economic Developers Actually Do: Location Quotients Versus Press Releases," John Levy argues that the primary work of economic developers is selling rather than traditional planning. His survey of economic development directors reveals that agencies spend most of their time in public relations, advertising, outreach to existing firms, and the like, and devote far less time to "rational model" activities such as planning, research, and project development. This sales work is effective in land markets with imperfect information; it also serves as self-promoting advertising for the economic development agency and director. Indeed, Levy argues that this local promotion is not necessarily a case of zero-sum smokestack chasing among communities but may actually make an overall positive contribution by improving the dissemination of information relevant to location decisions. The resulting challenge to planning theory is to incorporate into community planning models the dominance of this sales role and the need for high-visibility activities with political payoffs.

The most instructive case studies of planning are not always the successful ones. This perspective is illustrated by Peter Hall's 1980 study, *Great Planning Disasters*, which examined problematic large-scale planning projects such as the Concorde aircraft, London's plans for a third airport, and the San Francisco BART system. We include here his case on the planning of London's motorways. For Hall, it is a classic case of a "negative planning disaster": of 350 miles of roadway planned in 1961, only 40 miles were built, with many routes leading nowhere and rights of way often abandoned. The failure grew from faulty forecasting of future traffic, a blindness to secondary impacts, a neglect of public transportation, the institutional structure of the Greater London Council (GLC), and a misconceived appropriation of American transportation planning. The eventual abandonment of these plans by the early 1970s represented the loss of much planning effort and resources. However, one might also counterargue that this planning failure was actually a public success in the name of thriftiness, a growing environmental awareness, and commonsense. In the end, the effective opposition to London's motorways reflected not only a transformation of the highway's image from efficient infrastructure to destructive intrusion but also a more general transformation of planning from a top-down, technocratic, big-project mode to a more flexible system that reacted to changing community concerns.

Planning has also evolved into new forms that defy the simple division of labor between government and business. Quasi-autonomous public authorities have emerged as complex hybrids that combine the practices and motivations of both the public and private sector and stretch the traditional definition of planning. Americans, traditionally seen as hostile to centralized, regional planning, demonstrate a surprising tolerance for massive, regional-scale infrastructure planning in this guise of self-sufficient, technocratic management. Jameson Doig offers a rich account of such an institution in "Coalition Building by a Regional Agency: Austin Tobin and the Port of New York Authority." Doig traces the rise of the Port Authority from its creation in 1921 through the early postwar period as it struggled to gain control of the emerging airport sector in addition to the marine terminals. Central to the story is Austin Tobin, who, after being appointed director of the authority in 1942, aggressively redefined and expanded the role and autonomy of this public-private hybrid. He successfully retained the tax-exempt status of bonds, pushed for self-sustaining projects, maintained a political balance between the New Jersey and New York coalitions in the authority, and fought off the challenges of Robert Moses. The case illustrates the enviable planning power available to public authorities that have a monopoly on revenue-rich infrastructure while being largely shielded from democratic pressures.

17

What Local Economic Developers Actually Do: Location Quotients versus Press Releases

John M. Levy

The activities of local economic developers fall into two general categories: "rational model" activities (after the planner's rational model) and
sales activities. In the rational model a problem is defined, facts are
gathered and analyzed, goals are chosen, courses of action are selected,
programs are implemented, and the results are analyzed for future
guidance (Banfield 1973). Thus, a rational model approach to local
economic development might begin with defining the economic problem
to be addressed. The problem might be seen, for example, as poor labor
market conditions. or as the deterioration of the downtown area, or as
tax base inadequacy.[1] If labor market conditions are the problem, the
issue might be specified in terms of unemployment or underemploy-
ment, low wage rates in the local economy generally, low wage rates in
certain occupations, or problems with seasonal fluctuations or cyclical
instability. After the problem has been defined, facts would be gathered
and analyzed, goals (for example, so many jobs of certain types) would
be selected, and detailed strategies for achieving these goals would be

Reprinted by permission of the *Journal of the American Planning Association* Vol. 56, No. 2,
1990.

developed. Strategies might include infrastructure development schemes, subsidization policy, marketing programs, and the like. The choice of both goals and strategies would be informed by calculations of costs as well as benefits, both monetary and nonmonetary.

Thus, rational model activities include studies of labor markets and tax bases, studies of traffic and environmental impacts and the effects of employment growth on housing markets, financial feasibility analysis, cost-revenue studies, and industry studies for targeting purposes. Rational model activities, of course, also include land use, transportation, and capital facilities planning. A successful economic development program is likely to promote population growth whether or not this is a desired effect. Thus, one could argue that virtually all the usual elements of comprehensive planning have some relevance to a rational model approach to economic development planning.

The foregoing description implies a full-blown rational model approach. The more limited approaches, such as those that Malizia (1985) characterizes as "contingency" and "strategic" planning, would also fall on the rational side of the rational model/sales dichotomy. In fact, Malizia notes that these more limited approaches may serve as elements in a more comprehensive approach.

Sales activities ("marketing" would be an equally good term) are those activities that do not alter the physical, financial, or demographic realities of the community but rather inform and persuade firms and investors. They include calls on firms, speeches to rotary clubs, public relations, advertising, writing and dissemination of brochures, attendance at trade shows and other events, and "networking."

Though rational model and sales activities are conceptually separable, they are related. The "selling" that the economic developer does is generally highly factual and therefore makes use of at least some of the same data that would be necessary for a rational model planning approach. Then, too, techniques associated with the rational model might be used in designing sales and marketing strategies.

In most of the scholarly literature on local economic development, the emphasis is on rational model activities. If one had no acquaintance with the field other than through the scholarly literature, one would be likely to perceive local economic development as a rather systematic process akin to municipal planning. Bendavid-Val (1980), Friedman and Darragh (1988), Malizia (1985), and Moriarty and Cowen (1980) all treat local economic development in this manner. For the local economic development practitioner, however, the rational model activities definitely are secondary to sales activities. The process, as its practitioners report it, is far closer to sales than it is to planning.

This article examines survey data from the directors of local economic development agencies to determine how their agencies actually allocate effort and what activities they find to be most and least effective. It then offers speculations on why practitioners give more attention to sales activities than to planning activities and why there seems to be a certain cognitive dissonance between practitioner's behavior and the majority of scholarly literature.

A Survey of Economic Development Agencies

The survey was a mail questionnaire sent to the directors of 320 economic development agencies in February 1989. The agencies were randomly selected from the 1989 Economic Development Directory in the October 1988 issue of *Area Development*, the most widely read practitioner-orientated publication in the local economic development field. The survey excluded chambers of commerce, consulting firms, profit-making development organizations, and specialized agencies like port authorities and foreign trade zones, on the grounds that they generally do not perform a complete range of development functions.

Slightly more than half of the respondents were from governmental agencies, and the remainder were from quasi-public agencies.[2] Replies were received from 121 agency directors (37 percent). Of these replies, 112 (34 percent of the survey group) were usable and coded.[3] The mean full-time staff size of the responding agencies, exclusive of the director, was 6.2. Of the 107 respondents who answered the question on staff size, 52 indicated a staff size of 3 or less and 55 a staff size of 4 or more. Seventeen of the 107 respondents to the staff-size question indicated a full-time staff of more than 10.

The statistical results reported in this article should be regarded as indicative rather than definitive. The sampling frame, the Area Development Directory, may not be perfectly representative of the field, in that larger and better-known agencies have a greater probability of being included. Then, too, a number of the questions asked were open-ended. Therefore, tabulating them required some grouping and interpretation. Despite these limitations, the results are sufficiently strong and the responses to different questions sufficiently consistent to seem worthy of dissemination.

How Developers View their Activities

Selling activities clearly predominate over rational model activities. Most economic developers describe the selling side of their jobs as the most important, the most time-consuming, and the most productive part of their work. Tables 17.1 through 17.5 show their responses in greater detail.

TABLE 17.1 Economic developers' opinions of the most important function of their agency

Function	Percentage of responses
Publicizing the area and providing information (S)	65
Providing sites (R)	23
Financing (R)	23
Joint ventures (R)	2
Obtaining grants (R)	6
Other	11

Notes: The question was "What would you say is the most important function of your agency?" and the choices were those shown in the table. The numbers add to more than 100 percent because approximately one-fifth of the respondents checked more than one item.

(S) denotes "sales" activity. (R) denotes "rational model" activity.

TABLE 17.2 The single activity on which economic development agencies spend most of their time

Activity	Percentage of respondents
Public relations, advertising, provision of data, and response to inquiries (S)	42
Outreach to existing firms (S)	32
Planning and research (R)	8
Site and project development and operations (R)	6
Financing (R)	6
Applications for grants (R)	4
Other	6

Notes: This table and table 17.3 are derived from the same question. Respondents were asked to use their own words to indicate, in descending order, the five items on which their agencies spend the most time. The responses were then grouped by the author. This table indicates the percentage of respondents who listed each of the above activities as the number-one time consumer. In the small number of cases where "administration" was listed as number one, the number-two item was substituted. This adjustment was made on the grounds that all agencies must spend time on administration and that it is, in effect, overhead to be spread across all specific activities.

(S) denotes "sales" activity. (R) denotes "rational model" activity.

As table 17.1 indicates, economic development directors view the sales activity – "publicizing the area and providing information" – as the single most important function that their agencies perform. In fact, the number of responses showing the sales function as the most important one is virtually equal to the total of all other responses combined.

As table 17.2 demonstrates, economic development agency directors also rank sales activities (represented by "public relations, advertising, provision of data, and response to inquiries") as the single biggest consumer of agency time. The second item in the table, "outreach to existing firms," combines large elements of sales and public relations with a certain amount of ombudsman activity, such as soothing relations between firms and government. In the rational model/sales dichotomy, outreach clearly falls on the sales side. The other items in the table fall into the rational model category. Table 17.3 shows the percentage of respondents who listed the activities shown in table 17.2 among the top five time-consumers. Again, the preponderance of sales, as opposed to rational model responses is evident. The combined 170 percent for the first two items (sales) in the table substantially exceeds the combined 143 percent for the other five activities (rational model).

TABLE 17.3   Percentages of respondents naming various activities among the top five consumers of time

Activity	Percentages of respondents
Public relations, advertising, provision of data, and response to inquiries (S)	80
Outreach to existing firms (S)	70
Planning and research (R)	59
Applications for grants (R)	30
Site and project development and operation (R)	14
Financing (R)	11
Other	29

Notes: This table is derived in the same manner and from the same data as table 17.2.
   (S) denotes "sales" activity. (R) denotes "rational model" activity.

Table 17.4 indicates those activities that the directors of economic development agencies find the most and least useful. The responses are essentially consistent with the data in the previous tables. Note the large number of replies for the first two items in the "most productive" column.

TABLE 17.4   The most and least productive activities of economic development agencies

Activity	Percentage of responses	
	Most productive	Least productive
Advertising, public relations, providing data, responding to inquiries (S)	26	10
Outreach to firms now in the jurisdiction (S)	26	2
Deal making, financing, and assisting new businesses (R)	9	1
Research and planning (R)	8	1
Networking (S)	6	1
Site and project development (R)	5	0
Grant applications and compliance and reporting to higher levels of government (R)	3	15
Events and meetings (S)	2	14
Promoting tourism and convention business (S)	2	1
Dealing with politics (O)	0	8
Outside prospecting and overseas marketing (S)	1	3
Other	11	12

Notes: Respondents replied in their own words to the questions, "Over the last several years what do you think was the most (least) productive use of your professional time?" The replies were grouped by me. The terms used in grouping are as close as possible to the language used by the respondents. Several respondents indicated more than one most or least productive activity, and many respondents replied to the "most productive" question but left the "least productive" question blank. Thus, the two column totals are not the same. The "other" category includes a miscellany of replies that were obviously unique or that could not be readily coupled to a final activity – for example, "attending seminars" or "installing a computer system." (S) denotes "sales" activity. (R) denotes "rational model" activity. (O) denotes an organizational necessity that does not fit the rational model/sales dichotomy.

Several items that drew predominantly "least productive" responses are worth discussing. One item, grant applications, was grouped with "compliance and reporting to higher levels of government" because so much compliance and reporting is connected with the receipt of grant monies. Roughly half of the respondents in the negative category indicated the application process itself as least productive, and the remainder listed the postgrant-reporting and compliance procedures as least productive. In answering this question, one economic development director cited "working on grant applications which did not have a chance of being funded but [which we] needed to do for political reasons." A number of respondents who indicated "events and meetings" as least productive noted that they spend much time at events they know will be unproductive because it is politically necessary. The response to "dealing with politics" is self-explanatory.

Targeting firms for recruitment purposes might be regarded as a prototypical rational model activity. Data on place characteristics can be matched against industry requirements and industrial sectors then targeted with a high degree of specificity. This seems to be the sensible way to maximize the effect of the selling effort. The conceptual tools for doing it – for example, location theory and financial analysis – are available. However, as table 17.5 indicates, the amount of targeting performed by most economic development agencies is modest. Although one director responded to the targeting question with "four digit SIC code and specific company parameters," answers like "manufacturers in the Northeast and upper Midwest" were more common. Most economic development directors who know their own areas should be able to reach the two-digit SIC code almost intuitively. Yet only 10 percent of the

TABLE 17.5   Degree of sectoral targeting specificity

Level of specificity	Percentage of respondents
No targeting	22
Targeting at the 1-digit SIC level	25
Targeting at the 2-digit SIC level	34
Targeting at the 3- or 4-digit SIC level	10
Indicated targeting but supplied no specifics	8

Notes: This table is based on replies to the questions, "Do you actively recruit firms? (yes) (no), If yes, do you target particular types of firms or particular industries? Please specify." The characterizations in the table are based on the Standard Industrial Classification (SIC) code, but since respondents replied in their own terms rather than SIC terms some interpretation was necessary. A reply like "corporate headquarters," "manufacturing," or "light manufacturing" would be recorded as 1-digit SIC level. A reply like "metalworking industries" or "food processing" would be recorded as 2-digit SIC level. Any response more specific like "medical instruments" would be listed in the 3- or 4-digit SIC category. Totals do not add to 100 because of rounding.

respondents went beyond the two-digit level.[4] Only two respondents mentioned having had professional studies done to select targeting categories. In response to the question, "Do you target?" a few respondents indicated that they did not target but intended to or thought they should. One director responded, "Technically yes, practically no."

The Focus on Sales

The survey included four related questions regarding the rational model/sales dichotomy. These can be summarized as follows:

1   What do you think is your agency's most important function? (Table 17.1)
2   On what activities does your agency spend most time? (Tables 17.2 and 17.3)
3   What activities are most and least productive for your agency? (Table 17.4)
4   How specifically do you target for recruiting purposes? (Table 17.5)

The responses to all four questions showed a consistent emphasis on the sales activities rather than the rational model activities. This response is not what most of the literature would lead us to expect. Consequently, for the remainder of this article we turn to the questions of whether the sales emphasis makes sense from a local perspective and whether or not it is useful when viewed from a national perspective.

Does emphasizing sales make sense?

One goal of the economic developer, though not the only one, is to achieve concrete results. To understand why the sales emphasis is likely to be more effective than a rational model emphasis, consider the economists' concept of the "perfect market." One requirement for the perfect market is that both buyers and sellers have complete information (Hirshleifer 1980). In this regard the market for commercial and industrial sites and structures is very far from perfect. Consider, for example, a task like "Find the best county within overnight trucking distance of Philadelphia in which to locate a widget-making plant of 500,000 square feet." The amount of data on taxes, wage rates, utility costs, construction costs, land availability and cost, shipping costs, environmental and land-use regulations, cost of living, housing costs and availability, amenities, and quality-of-life considerations that would be needed for each of several hundred counties would be formidable indeed. Narrowing the task to the municipal or site level would increase the data requirements still further. In a world of imperfect information, it is no wonder that public relations, promotion, advertising, sales, and related activities can become extremely important.

As the survey results indicate, local economic developers do find the offering of grants and financial incentives productive, but not nearly so useful as the sales aspect of their work. This should not be surprising. Most studies of location decisions do not show tax concessions and other financial incentives to be major factors. This is true of both recent studies (Hack 1988; Tosh et al. 1988; Wolkoff 1985) and older studies (Hellman et al. 1976; Reigeluth and Wolman 1979; Schmenner 1982; Vaughn 1980). To a considerable extent, similar incentives are offered by a wide range of localities. For example, in response to another question on financial programs in the survey, respondents by a large margin listed industrial revenue bonds (IRBs) as the most useful financial incentive.[5] In the 1980s IRBs were available in forty-seven out of fifty states (Richardson 1981). Although the details of their issuance varied somewhat from state to state, the basic process was necessarily similar. This is because all agencies that issued IRBs did so pursuant to the same provisions in the IRS code.

It is thus hard for the economic developer to be a winner through incentives, though it is possible to be a loser by failing to offer them when most of one's rivals do. In fact, much local economic development activity may be defensive. A community may maintain a program simply to stay even and to protect what it has from the depredations of other communities' economic developers. There might well be some mutual savings to be had from "disarmament," but the institutions for arranging it do not exist.

The emphasis on the sales role serves the economic developer in another important purpose that, to my knowledge, has been generally ignored in the literature. Namely, it helps the economic developer to keep his or her job. Economic development is not usually regarded as an absolutely essential community function in the sense that, say, police or fire protection is. Further, the educational and experiential qualifications for doing economic development are not usually defined with great specificity. It may be a statutory requirement that the commissioner of public works have a professional engineer's license and that the commissioner of planning have a planning degree, but it is not likely that there will be a comparable requirement for the director of economic development.[6] For these reasons, the field is characterized by high turnover. Thus, an economic developer who wants to maintain a hold on his or her position must participate in high-visibility activities. If a new firm opens a plant in town, the economic developer needs to be prominently associated with that event. If a firm is about to leave town, the economic developer must be seen as having fought a determined battle to prevent this unhappy event. For how else do the director and his or her staff justify their lines in the municipal budget? If the body politic does not know what the economic developer is doing, he or she may not be doing it much longer – no matter how good the developer may be.

Another reason high-visibility activity is advantageous to the local economic developer is that it is useful to the administration that pays the developer's salary. In a political climate in which government does not always enjoy high repute among the citizens and in which many politicians campaign for office by running against government, maintaining an economic development operation enables government to present itself in a very attractive light. The image of government allying itself with business to bring its citizens lower taxes and more jobs is quite a change from government's normal, ogrelike roles of taxing and regulating. However, this political gain can be had only if the operation is highly visible. In my experience as an economic development agency director in the late 1970s, this handshake with government is well understood by many in the economic development profession.

Is emphasizing sales useful?

Having argued that the pattern of behavior shown in the tables makes sense, we turn to the question of whether it is useful. Certainly, at the municipal level successful economic development efforts are useful. They deliver gains both to capital and to labor. Often, but not inevitably, they reduce property tax rates (McGuire 1987).

At the national level, it is not quite so evident that all this activity is useful. At first glance, the combat over who gets what firm might be considered a zero-sum game. Assume that community X, through its more competent development program, induces Acme Widget to locate there instead of in community Y, as it would otherwise have done. Is it not possible that the gain for X minus the loss for Y nets out to zero? Is it possible, in fact, that, when the costs of running the winning and the losing program are added in, the process becomes a negative sum game?

Orthodox economic theory suggests, however, that all this combat may actually perform a useful function when viewed at macroeconomic level. The net effect of all the advertisements, brochures, data sheets, press releases, talks to rotary clubs, calls on firms, liaison activity between firms and local governments and the like is to disseminate massive amounts of information relevant to location decisions. To the extent that this information improves the market, and to the extent that improved markets allocate resources more efficiently, a useful function is being performed. If, in a $5-trillion economy, we spend a few billion on a process that promotes better decision making, we may well be getting our money's worth.

In fact, one can argue that improving the market is the main, perhaps even the only, contribution that local economic development efforts make to national economic performance. It is true that the variety of financing incentives and tax expenditures provided in connection with local economic development efforts constitute a subsidy to capital formation and may thus accelerate the growth of GNP. However, it is hard to believe that an equal stimulus to capital formation could not be achieved at far lower cost by changes in the federal tax code. Some authors deny that local economic development efforts are at all connected with national economic performance (Kirby 1985). Others, on the basis of commonly accepted principles of economics, have asserted for a number of years that the effect of subsidization is to distort business decision making and thus to produce a net loss. Goffman, (1962) has observed, "What a subsidy does, then, is to make it profitable for a company to locate in a less than optimal location."

Whether there are net equity gains from the sum of all local economic development activity is an open question. It is unlikely that more needy places generally outcompete less needy places for new industry. Two observers have recently suggested that, in fact, more affluent communities make more efficient use of their expenditures on economic development than do poorer municipalities (Rubin and Rubin 1987). Whether even the giving of subsidies, taken by itself, has the net effect of promoting equity is far from certain. At the federal level, grant sources like the Urban Development Action Grant Program and Economic Development Administration programs are guided at least in part by such considerations as poverty and unemployment rates. However, it would be naive to believe that need considerations are the only, or necessarily even the major consideration in determining the winners in the competition for grants (Gatons and Brintall 1984; Gist and Hill 1981, 1985). The very large tax expenditure in the form of IRB financing is not needs-based (Richardson 1981).[7] At the state and local level, both wealthy and poor jurisdictions can use more jobs and a larger tax base, and so both offer them. It would be amazing if there were not a great many canceling effects.

Consider a group of firms competing with one another in the national "widget" market. Firm A has been subsidized by the EDA. It competes with firm B, which has been subsidized with a UDAG grant. They both compete with firm C, which is located in an affluent suburb that is ineligible for both EDA and UDAG monies. However, firm C's capital costs were lowered by means of an IRB. These firms all compete with firm D, which received a state investment tax credit to encourage it to move from a less affluent to a more affluent state. Another competitor, firm E, does not benefit from any state or federal program or tax expenditure. However, it receives a substantial municipal property tax abatement. And so on. When one contemplates the multiplicity of grant programs and tax expenditures, as well as the large number of firms benefiting from one or more of them, it is evident that estimating the net effect would be a formidable task indeed. Thus, paradoxically, it may well be that the part of the local development process that lies more or less outside the rational model framework delivers the major, or possibly the only, aggregate benefit.

If the sales side of economic development looms so large to the practitioner, why is it so often slighted in the literature? One possible explanation is that, until recently, the field of economics generally has not taken much interest in advertising (or related activities like public relations). It is often regarded as overhead or as a phenomenon that exists only because of market imperfections. The fact that advertising makes nonrational as well as rational appeals may make it fit rather awkwardly into a discipline that takes as an axiom the existence of a rational "economic man." This situation is beginning to change in the scholarly literature (Nichols 1985). However, the fact that advertising is still not well integrated into the field can be verified by looking up the subject in any mainstream introductory text and noting that it is either covered very lightly or not mentioned at all.

Many scholars who have written about local economic development come from a planning or economics background. Thus, they tend to focus on the planning and economic aspects of the field – its rational model side – rather than on its selling side. Perhaps, more generally, scholars, being committed to systematic rationality, naturally tend to focus on the rationalistic and the quantifiable.

An Approach for Planners

It would be the subject of another chapter or perhaps a book, to convert these findings regarding practitioner behavior into detailed proposals for local economic development policy. However, some general comments are appropriate. Local economic development efforts, as reported by practitioners, are a relatively untargeted intermunicipal sales or marketing competition. As such, their connections with specific municipal planning goals will generally be tenuous. The fact that programs tend to have a sales rather than planning basis explains why so few programs are terminated. Were programs based on a rational model planning effort, one would occasionally observe a community saying, in effect, "We've reached our goal, let's stop." The dominance of the sales perspective may also explain why one sees economic development pursued when it cannot be justified in rational model terms. The affluent suburb that has low unemployment rates, labor shortages in some categories, low vacancy rates, tight controls on residential construction, and sky-high housing prices, but still assiduously pursues its own economic development is a case in point. So far as housing is concerned, this is not a new observation. Almost two decades ago Wilbur Thompson (1973) stated, "It is irresponsible to promote local industrial expansion without coupling this action to a low income housing policy which picks up the pieces. But we do it all the time." There is no reason to believe that his words are any less apropos today than in 1973.

The results of the game may be given an overall shape by the structure and requirements of state and national funding. But most practitioners do not regard such funding as a major element in the game. Then, too, as already noted, there is a very large potential for randomization due to the canceling effects among the myriad of grant and tax expenditure programs offered by various levels of government. For these reasons the shaping effect of federal and state programs is likely to be quite small.

It would certainly be desirable if we could integrate local economic development programs into the community planning process. When successful, the economic developer's efforts change the community. Obviously, it would be better for this to be done by design than by accident. But as responses to the questionnaires indicated, we are very far from that point. And it must be admitted that the mechanisms by which economic developers' efforts could be closely tied into the overall process of community planning and development are not evident.

Vigorous intermunicipal economic competition is here to stay. It would remain even if every cent of federal and state subsidy for local economic development were withdrawn. One task for the planner is to try to integrate local economic development efforts into a larger planning framework – not as is done in much of the literature but in the reality of municipal growth and development.

The academician who wishes to increase the usefulness of his or her contribution to the practice of economic development at the local level, or to make useful suggestions regarding state or national policy directed to local economic development, must recognize the dominance of the sales side of the process in the practitioner's work. Efforts to tie local economic development efforts into the broad context of community planning must be fitted into a setting in which sales is likely to remain the dominant mode. Such an approach is likely to be more effective than one that ignores sales activity or relegates it to a secondary role. It is also important to recognize the heavily political nature of the process and to concede that high-visibility activities with political payoff will inevitably have a prominent place.

Acknowledgments

I would like to express my appreciation for very useful comments on survey technique by my colleague Patricia K. Edwards. I would also like to thank another colleague, Timothy Fluck, for numerous useful and perceptive comments on both the substance and the structure of this paper.

Notes

1   Tax base considerations have not generally been counted directly in federal criteria for funding economic development. In my suburban experience they are, nonetheless, the most common motivation. This makes sense in

that, if the jurisdiction is small relative to the metropolitan labor market, it cannot hope to capture most of the employment gains from new activity. However, it can capture the property tax gains.

2　"Public" means here an agency that is part of the structure of government and whose staff are government employees. "Quasi-governmental" means a public benefit corporation set up by and perhaps partially funded by government, but not part of the structure of government, and not staffed by government employees. There were no statistically significant differences in response between the two groups and therefore they were not disaggregated.

3　Several replies were rejected because they were from chambers of commerce, consultants, or agencies so new that they were unable to answer the questions.

4　In the Standard Industrial Classification (SIC) system the broadest categories of economic activity (manufacturing, trade, etc.) are one-digit codes. Each of these categories is then disaggregated. Within manufacturing there are twenty two-digit codes. For example, chemicals and allied products are SIC code 28; industrial inorganic chemicals are SIC code 281. Within that category, alkalies and chlorine are SIC code 2812, industrial gases are SIC code 2813, and so forth. The system is described in detail in *Standard Industrial Classification Manual* (U.S. Department of Commerce, 1987, and earlier editions).

5　Respondents were asked to classify a variety of federal and state programs on a three-part scale: most useful, somewhat useful, and least useful or no experience. IRBs received a 73 percent "most useful" response. The next largest "most useful" programs were revolving loan funds at 48 percent and interest rate reductions at 44 percent.

6　The American Economic Development Council gives a Certified Industrial Developer (CID) certificate, but it is generally not required as a condition of employment or responsibility, nor is it universally known in the field.

7　Perhaps these comments on EDA, UDAG, and IRBs should be cast in the past tense. The UDAG Program operated in fiscal 1989 entirely on "recaptured" funds, and at this writing further appropriations are not expected. EDA's budget for 1989 was about $200 million, or less than half of what it was in the 1970s. The Reagan administration repeatedly tried to eliminate the agency entirely and, at this writing, the Bush administration appears likely to pursue the same course. Industrial revenue bonds are likewise on the way out at this writing. The Tax Reform Act of 1986 eliminated IRBs for most uses other than manufacturing. Their use for manufacturing is scheduled to be terminated December 31, 1989. Only use for a limited range of public purposes such as sewage treatment will be permitted after 1989. But even before the 1989 phaseout, IRB effectiveness had been reduced simply by the reductions in marginal tax rates under the various Reagan administration tax bills.

References

Banfield, Edward C. 1973. Ends and Means in Planning. In *A Reader in Planning Theory*, edited by Andreas Faludi. New York: Pergamon.

Bendavid-Val, Avrom. 1980. *Local Economic Development Planning: From Goals to Projects*. PAS Report no. 353. Washington, D.C.: American Planning Association.

Friedman, Stephan B., and Alexander J. Darragh. 1988. Economic Development. In *The Practice of Local Government Planning*, 2d ed. Washington, D.C.: International City Management Association.

Gatons, Paul K., and Michael Brintall. 1984. Competitive Grants: The UDAG Approach. In *Urban Economic Development*. Vol. 27, *Urban Affairs Annual Reviews*, edited by Richard D. Bingham and John P. Blair. Beverly Hills, CA: Sage.

Gist, John R., and J. Carter Hill. 1981. The Economics of Choice in the Allocation of Federal Grants: An Empirical Test. *Public Choice* 36, 1: 63–73.

———.1984. Political and Economic Influences in the Bureaucratic Allocation of Federal Funds: The Case of Urban Development Action Grants. *Journal of Urban Economics* 16, 2: 158–72.

Goffman, Irving. 1982. Local Subsidies for Industry: Comment. *Southern Economic Journal* 29, 2: 112–14.

Hack, Gordon D. 1988. Location Trends: 1958–1988. *Area Development*, October: 12.

Hellman, Daryll A., Gregory H. Wassall, and Laurance H. Falk. 1976. *State Financial Incentives to Industry*. Lexington, MA: Lexington Books, D. C. Heath.

Hirshleifer, Jack. 1980. *Price Theory and Applications*, 2d ed. Englewood Cliffs, NJ: Prentice-Hall.

Kirby, Andrew. 1985. Nine Fallacies of Local Economic Change. *Urban Affairs Quarterly* 21, 2: 207–220.

Malizia, Emil E. 1985. *Local Economic Development: A Guide to Practice*. New York: Praeger.

McGuire, Therese J. 1987. The Effect of New Firm Locations on Property Taxes. *Journal of Urban Economics* 22, 2: 223–29.

Moriarty, Barry M., and David J. Cowen. *Industrial Location and Community Development*. Chapel Hill: University of North Carolina Press.

Nichols, L. M. 1985. Advertising and Economic Welfare. *American Economic Review* 75, 1: 213–18.

Reigeluth. George A., and Harold Wolman. 1979. *The Determinants and Implications of Communities' Changing Competitive Advantage: A Review of Literature*. Working Paper no. 1264–03. Washington, D.C.: Urban Institute.

Richardson, Pearl. 1981. *Small Issue Industrial Revenue Bonds*. Washington, D.C.: Congressional Budget Office.

Rubin, Irene S., and Herbert J Rubin. 1987. Economic Development Incentives: The Poor (Cities) Pay More. *Urban Affairs Quarterly* 23, 1: 15–36.

Schmenner, Roger W. 1982. *Making Business Location Decisions*. Englewood Cliffs, NJ: Prentice-Hall.

Thompson, Wilbur. Problems Which Sprout in the Shadow of No Growth. *AIA Journal*, December, 1973.

Tosh, Dennis E., Troy A. Festervard, and James R. Lumpkin. 1988. Industrial Site

Selection Criteria: Are Economic Developers, Manufacturers and Industrial Real Estate Brokers Operating on the Same Wavelength. *Economic Development Review* 6, 3: 62–67.

Vaughn, Roger J. 1980. How Effective Are They. *Commentary*, National Council for Urban Economic Development. January 8: 12–18.

Wolkoff, Michael J. 1985. Chasing a Dream: The Use of Tax Abatements to Spur Urban Economic Development. *Urban Studies* 22, 4: 305–315.

18

London's Motorways

Peter Hall

As with London's third airport, so with its motorway system: The most important point about it is that it does not exist. Or, strictly, only small fragments of it exist – some 40 miles, out of 350 once planned. These fragments terminate arbitrarily at junctions that lead nowhere. The rest is abandoned, and for the most part even the lines of the motorways are no longer safeguarded by the planners. London's motorways compete with its third airport for the title of the most costly civil engineering project ever planned in this country; and both were aborted. They represent classic cases of negative planning disasters. How so much effort and resources came to be invested in their planning, how such a firm political commitment came to be overturned, form a central case study in the pathology of planning.

The core of the story occupies only thirteen years: from the decision to start a major traffic survey and plan for London in 1961 to the abandonment of the motorway plan by the incoming Labour administration of the Greater London Council in 1973. But to understand its full dimensions it is necessary to go back to the time of Patrick Abercrombie's great wartime plans for London in 1943–4 and also, since Abercrombie too drew on previous ideas, some way before that.

The Abercrombie Plan and its Antecedents

Engineers and planners had been grappling with the problem of London traffic at least since the start of the automotive era.[1] Already in 1905, a royal commission on London traffic had devoted eight bulky volumes to the subject and had proposed an ambitious system of new arterial highways boldly slicing through London's built-up fabric. Already, too, in 1910, the London Traffic Branch of the Board of Trade had produced a massive plan for new arterial highways just outside the then built-up area, which would relieve existing overloaded radial roads and would provide a new North Circular Road skirting the northern suburbs. And though the royal commission's proposals disappeared for the most part into obscurity, the vast majority of the planned roads of 1910 were actually built between the two world wars. They provide the familiar infrastructure of bypasses in suburban Greater London, and they were ironically completed by the opening of Westway from the White City to Paddington in 1970. The irony lay not merely in that the road had been sixty years in gestation; it lay more in the fact that the resulting outcry led directly to the abandonment of London's motorway plans three years later.

These new roads of the 1920s and 1930s, however, had two grievous limitations. First, they were built for the most part without any adequate planning of the associated land uses. They were all-purpose roads, with frequent side access; soon, speculative builders ran ribbon developments all along them. Some visionary souls called for a system of *Autobahnen* on the German model, but a royal commission of 1930 ridiculed the idea that Britain would ever need such a system of "Motor-Ways." Second, they failed to penetrate into the built-up area of 1918. Thus, while access in the interwar suburbs was at least improved, in inner London it got worse, if anything, as traffic grew. William Robson, writing in 1939 on the government and misgovernment of London, could point out that in its whole history since its creation in 1888, the London County Council – responsible for this inner area – had completed just one major new road in central London, Kingsway; and that had been largely planned some years before by its Victorian predecessor, the Metropolitan Board of Works.

As congestion worsened with the growth of private motoring, the government stirred itself to act. In conjunction with the local authorities of the conurbation, it commissioned an eminent engineer, Sir Charles Bressey, and an equally eminent architect, Sir Edwin Lutyens, to prepare a regional highway plan. Published in 1937, this plan proposed an ambitious series of new boulevards, including an embryonic inner circular route round the City and West End, and a major east–west route linked to it formed by the extensions of Eastern and Western avenues (this last proposal picked up from the 1910 report and eventually to be implemented by the disastrous Westway project of 1970).[2] It was, however, an exception. For the Bressey plan was for the most part never implemented; only a few short stretches can be identified in the road plan of Greater London in the late 1970s. Its importance lay more in the fact that it was the immediate precursor to the Abercrombie plans.

Patrick Abercrombie, first holder of the chair of planning at the University of Liverpool and then at University College London, was by common consent the most distinguished town planner in Britain in the late 1930s. He played a leading role in the work of the Royal Commission on the Distribution of the Industrial Population, the so-called Barlow Commission, which reported in 1940 with a then revolutionary proposal that after the war the government should seek to curb industrial growth in London as a means of controlling its physical growth. It was logical that the London County Council should ask him to join its own Chief architect, J. H. Forshaw, in preparing a plan for inner London, and that the government should then ask him to produce a regional plan for the whole area of the conurbation and beyond. Together these two plans of 1943–4 represent the culmination of Abercrombie's planning concepts, and nowhere more than in their treatment of traffic.

In understanding them it is first important to realize that they were based on no detailed surveys. In the middle of gasoline-rationed World War II, that would have been both impossible and irrelevant. But in any case, the modern techniques of transportation planners, with their jargon words – generation and attraction, desire lines, trip distribution and assignment, and modal split – simply did not then exist; they were an American invention of the mid-1950s. Abercrombie was content to work with such limited evidence as he had, from prewar annual Metropolitan Police surveys of traffic flows along the main roads. But in any case, his interest and concern lay in far more than simply improving traffic flow – though that was certainly an important objective for him.

Abercrombie planned in fact to achieve several objectives simultaneously and thus to gain the best of all possible worlds for everyone. First, of course, he wanted to improve traffic flow and to reduce or eliminate congestion. This could be achieved only by a new system of free-flowing roads. Second, he wanted to reduce the danger and the environmental intrusion that traffic represented whenever it penetrated into living or working areas. This concern Abercrombie shared with his contemporary, the Scotland Yard assistant commissioner for traffic, Sir Alker Tripp; and his solution – precincts barred to through traffic – was borrowed from Tripp. Third, he wanted to use road planning, together with open-space planning and the removal of extraneous industry from residential areas, to define new, more homogeneous areas for living or working. Thus, the precincts would also be areas of social cohesion; they would be living communities or neighborhoods. Bringing these elements together, Abercrombie achieved a remarkable synthesis: a concept of a city replanned on organic principles, with cells and arteries, in which each part performed its proper function as a member of the whole urban body. This city would function effectively on three different dimensions: functionally, in terms of efficient movement; communally, in terms of

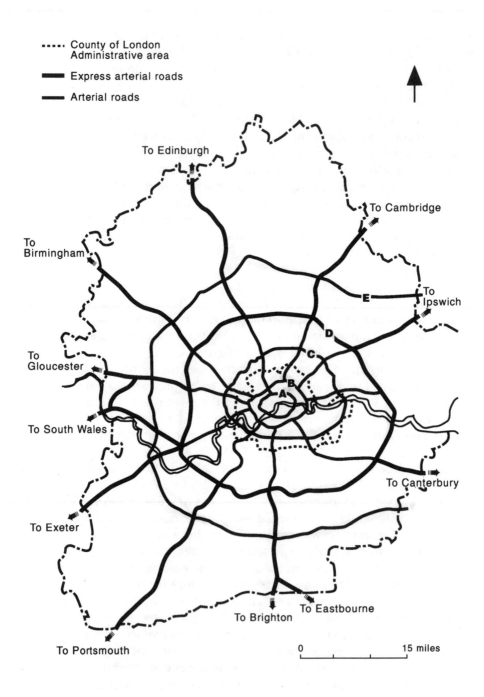

Figure 18.1 Abercrombie's roads plan, 1944

social cohesion and identity; and monumentally, in terms of a strong sense of place.[3]

More particularly, Abercrombie saw the need for a hierarchy of roads both to move traffic effectively and to perform the vital job of reinforcing the organic structure of the city. The topmost level of the hierarchy would be a new system of arterial roads built for through traffic on motorway principles, with limited access and segregation from other traffic. A second level would consist of subarterial roads adapted from the existing system, serving as distributors from the arterials and also separating residential and other areas. A third level would consist of the strictly local roads in these precincts, which would connect with the subarterials at controlled junctions.

The arterials, moreover, would take a particular form. For Abercrombie wanted them to perform not only a traffic function but also a vital planning function in giving coherence and identity to the structure of London, a structure he felt had been up to then latent, because the road system needed to define it had been lacking. This must now be remedied. The logical system to provide the structure would be a system of rings and radials, a plan that Abercrombie had advocated for other places and at other times.[4] In this system the innermost ring, designated by Abercrombie the A ring, would serve as an inner bypass immediately round the central area of the West End; it had antecedents in the Bressey plan. The next ring, the B ring, would run about four miles from the center, serving to drain the congested inner residential and industrial districts. The next, the C ring, consisted of the recently completed North Circular Road plus a completely new equivalent south of the Thames. This would serve as a bypass for Victorian London as a whole. The next, the D ring, would serve as an outer drain for the suburban areas, near or at the limits of the built-up area. And finally, the E ring was the partly built orbital highway around London, which would henceforth run as a parkway through the green belt that would forever limit London's physical sprawl. Connecting these to form a rich spider's web, radial roads, for the most part new arterials, would provide a coherent system of high-speed routes and would also help complete the vital process of defining the main organic elements in the planned geography of London.[5]

[handwritten margin note: E Ring: Prevent sprawl]

Incorporating other equally large notions – the green belt itself, the ring of new towns around it, the belt of expanded towns beyond that, and the planned migrations that would take more than a million Londoners to new homes outside – Abercrombie's vision was a grand one. The wartime government accepted it in principle; postwar governments produced the necessary legislation to help implement it. The green belt was established and maintained; the new towns were built. But, despite continuing support in principle, the roads became a casualty of the plan. Shortages of money in the decade after the end of the war in 1945, followed by a concentration of road-building funds on interurban motorways from the mid-1950s onwards, left all too little for London. And by the late 1950s, with car ownership rising rapidly in London as elsewhere, traffic congestion came to be seen as a major problem requiring solution. Restraint and control must provide part of the answer, and the first parking meters, introduced experimentally in Soho in 1958, were quickly followed by a rash of controlled zones, one-way streets, clearways and other restrictions. But, beyond that, there was a developing consensus that the problem could not entirely be contained.

The Birth of the London Traffic Survey

Spectacular rush hour traffic jams, on a scale never before witnessed by Londoners, thus gave rise to a growing demand for positive action in the form of new roads for London, a demand that was channeled by powerful pressure groups such as the British Road Federation and the Roads Campaign Council. At the same time there was much concern about the inadequacies of London's administrative machinery, particularly for the control and planning of transport, but also more generally. The Greater London conurbation, as officially recognized by the census takers for statistical purposes and by the Home Office as the concern of the Metropolitan Police, was then administered by over one hundred different local authorities, including six county councils in whole or in part, three county boroughs, the City of London, twenty-eight metropolitan boroughs, forty-one municipal boroughs, twenty-nine district councils, and a variety of ad hoc bodies. The resulting divisions of responsibility, for measures ranging from one-way streets to road-building, caused delay and muddle. Finally the Ministry of Transport, under its energetic Conservative minister Ernest Marples, was driven to wrest many of the necessary powers over traffic management from the London County Council and the boroughs. But the longer-term planning problems were still unresolved.

In 1957 the government, already conscious of these problems, appointed a Royal Commission into Local Government in Greater London – the Herbert Commission. Its report, published in 1960, was scathing about the procrastination and inefficiency of London government in handling the traffic problem. And there is no doubt that its proposed new structure – with a Greater London Council and a new streamlined system of London boroughs – was largely a response to the perceived need for a single strategic planning authority both for transport planning and for associated land-use planning. The Ministry of Housing and Local Government's evidence, for instance, had defined traffic congestion as London's key problem.[6] Bitterly fought by the Labour opposition in Parliament, the resulting London Government Bill was passed into law in 1963. It set 1 April, 1965, as the date for the assumption of power by the Greater London Council and the thirty-two new boroughs.

Meanwhile, however, the Ministry of Transport under the ever impatient Ernest Marples had moved on its own. Anticipating the 1963 act, or perhaps guarding against its possible nonpassage, at the end of 1961 it had already agreed with the old London County Council jointly to set up a London Traffic Survey. Consultants, consisting of a leading British firm of civil engineers and an American organization, would introduce into Britain the new techniques (and also the jargon) of scientific transportation planning. The early 1960s was a period of intense, almost religious fervour for new technology and the fruits it would bring. And within that paradigm, the new breed of transportation planner fitted perfectly, offering a vision of computerized infallibility that would point the way to a totally motorized, totally mobile future. By 1962, the consultants were ready to conduct the huge sample household surveys, which for the first time would present a comprehensive picture of the way Londoners lived, worked, played and moved about. From this survey would come the models that would provide the predictions of Londoners' future travel needs.

Only one more element was needed to provide the psychological impetus; and once again, with uncanny political flair, Ernest Marples provided it. Shortly after setting up the London Traffic Survey, he appointed a Ministry of Housing and Local Government inspector, Colin Buchanan, to undertake a general study of traffic and planning in towns. Buchanan, then known to the general public only through his handling of an important inquiry into the future of Piccadilly Circus, was picked as the only man who seemed to know anything about the vital relationships between traffic and environmental nuisance. When the report appeared in November 1963, it was an immediate popular bombshell. Buchanan became a household name overnight, and his central planning precept – that environmental quality standards must limit accessibility by car, but that accessibility could be increased by spending money – became almost an article of faith.[7]

In his detailed proposals Buchanan, as he freely admitted, drew heavily on the ideas of Alker Tripp twenty years before. His environmental areas were essentially Tripp's precincts, and his hierarchical road system was also essentially Tripp's. The important point was that, in a political sense, he changed the popular consciousness of the traffic problem. No longer was it seen merely as one of congestion; just like his mentor Abercrombie, Buchanan argued that it was as much a matter of good planning and good environmental standards. The critical point is this: though in theory the Buchanan principles could justify either little spending on roads or a great deal, according to society's preferences for accessibility, in practice, once the standards for environment were set, to buy the existing level of access would cost a great deal indeed. So, as became evident in the years that followed, the Buchanan creed was in practice a demand for massive increase in spending on urban roads. Marples, who was a passionate and effective advocate in his own cause, had once again picked the right person at the right time.

LTS: The Technical Planning Process

At this time, therefore, and throughout the mid-1960s, there was massive political commitment toward heavy expenditure on urban roads. Public opinion, so far as it could be gauged through the filter of the media, was heavily in favor. London newspapers protested at the creeping thrombosis that threatened their city and enthusiastically applauded the plans for new highways.[8] Their readers in some cases were even persuaded to join in with ideas of their own. The importance of this was that, in a benign political climate, the technical experts were left to get on with the job.

They did so speedily. The London Traffic Survey, as it was originally known, conducted its basic household and other surveys in 1962 and published the results in 1964. This picture of London's movement patterns formed Volume 1 of the original survey; it became Phase 1 of the London Transportation Study, as the survey later came to be known. Covering an area slightly larger than both the then conurbation and the differently defined Greater London Council area of 1965, it included some 8,800,000 people (over 17 per cent of the total population of Great Britain) with nearly 4,800,000 jobs. Each normal weekday, Londoners made some 11,300,000 trips (these were "basic trips," sometimes using two or more kinds of transport), of which 90 percent started or ended at the home, and within which nearly 5,400,000 were trips to and from work. Perhaps most significantly, though in 1962 only 38 percent of households owned cars, close on 6,300,000 trips a day were made in cars as against just under 6,500,000 by bus and train. The average person in a household made 1.33 trips a day. But while a person in a noncar-owning household would make only 0.93 trips, a person in a car-owning household would make an average of 1.87 trips. Thus, the survey could already argue, as car ownership continued its apparently inexorable climb, the impact on traffic would be dramatic.

Precisely how dramatic, Volume 2 of the survey showed in 1966. And here, for the first time, technical questions of forecasting became critical. The consultants' method, inherited from countless similar American studies, was to concentrate on road travel and, above all, travel by car. Walking trips were ignored in the original 1962 survey, and subsequently; now, travel by public transport was relegated to a subsidiary category, and the main efforts were devoted to forecasting the rise in car use. It was assumed that as car ownership rose, people would behave roughly as they had been observed to behave in 1962. Thus, trip generation rates for car-owning and noncar-owning households were obtained from the 1962 survey and applied to the forecasts of rising car ownership. Then the trips were distributed between traffic-planning zones. Lastly, they were assigned to networks on the logical assumption that they would follow the quickest path, in terms of time, from starting point to finishing point.

The critical point about this method is contained in a sentence in the summary report on the whole study published in 1969: "The pattern of travel was calculated using a trip distribution model calibrated from 1962 conditions and using speeds for the primary roads that might reasonably be expected in uncongested conditions and speeds on secondary roads similar to those observed in 1962."[9] In other words, though traffic grew, congestion was expected to be no worse – a clearly unrealistic assumption. For as critics have often pointed out, traffic in towns follows a kind of Parkinson's Law: it tends to expand to fill the space available. During peak hours, and during other times in some areas, traffic congestion will deter some drivers; they will either use public transport or abandon the journey. But if new roads are built these drivers may bring their cars out, so that new traffic is (in the jargon) generated. There is thus a circular element in traffic forecasting: to some degree, though of course not entirely, the traffic will depend on the roads plan.

'if you build it they will come'

In 1966 the experts took an extremely crude approach to this problem, though the fact is tucked away in an appendix to their report.[10] First, they used the computer to forecast total trip generations and attractions, that is, separate forecasts of trips made at each end of the main journey. They were sufficiently close to satisfy the planners that their method was basically sound. But the results were well below what they had expected from their experience in American cities. So then they developed an alternative set of figures, euphemistically called "control totals." They were in truth no more than guesses of how they thought Londoners would behave if they had an adequate road system, such as Americans had. Thus, trips to stores or to visit friends were simply inflated by an arbitrary factor of 25 percent. And the result – a total of 16,693,000 trips a day in the year 1981, as against 15,367,000 by the original method – was solemnly presented as the figure that would result if London had a new highway system.[11]

From that point they went on to distribute the resulting traffic and then to assign it to a network, using their well-developed computer models. For this purpose they had to have a theoretical network, and in fact they chose two. One, the 1981 B network, simply consisted of bits and pieces of new road, to which the GLC and the Ministry of Transport were firmly committed. There was a complete ring around Greater London near the edge, which was Abercrombie's D ring. But inward from this there were just fragments of national motorways like the M1 and M4 and M23, plus a new East Cross Route through the Blackwall Tunnel that the old LCC had planned as part of its reconstruction of the East End. The other, the 1981 A network, was now presented as a first sketch of London's new motorways. It derived heavily from the Abercrombie Plan, as a number of commentators have pointed out,[12] for it reproduced the familiar Abercrombie spider's web of rings and radials, the only substantial difference being the omission of the innermost A ring, which the government had abandoned in the 1950s on the grounds of cost. Instead of Abercrombie's five rings, there were now three inside London (later named Ringways 1, 2 and 3) plus another, the ministry's planned Orbital Road, in the green belt outside it, and thus outside the plan.

The genesis of this plan was interesting. For it had developed very rapidly after the creation of the GLC'S new Highways and Transportation Department under its energetic chief engineer Peter Stott. One critical element – the so-called Motorway Box, later Ringway 1, following roughly the line of Abercrombie's B ring some four miles from the centre – had already been unveiled by the GLC on its first day of authority, 1 April, 1965. The rest soon followed. What happened then was that the new authority committed itself immediately in principle to an old set of plans, which had lain in the drawers but were now exhumed.[13] But as Hart later pointed out, they were now represented purely as a technical solution to a narrow traffic problem, not as a central element in the grand design for London that Abercrombie had conceived.[14]

Even at a technical level, however, some of the results were odd. The 1981 A network contained an integrated system of 444 miles of high-class roads of motorway or near-motorway standard. The 1981 B network contained some 260 miles of this system, but nearly all of it was in the outer suburbs, so that there was no coherent system nearer the center.[15] Yet the effect on total traffic generation was only to reduce travel from 16,700,000 to 15,900,000 trips a day, or by 5 percent.[16] The flows on parts of the network were equally odd. On the West Cross Route of Ringway 1 between the Cromwell Road and the river Thames, for instance, the forecast 1981 flow was 339,000 vehicles a day – well in excess of anything ever recorded in Los Angeles or elsewhere, and probably requiring a capacity of some fourteen lanes of traffic.

The traffic planners were very conscious of these problems themselves. In Phase 3, the final stage of their study, they sought to make a much more refined analysis that took them, as they confessed, into difficult research frontier territory.[17] They tested a much greater variety of networks, ranging from a minimal one to a very elaborate one; and they specifically looked at the effect of restraining traffic wherever, on any particular one of these networks, the capacity was too limited to allow traffic to flow freely. They started with new calculations of trip generations and attractions in 1981, and they started by assuming that the quality of the road system would not affect the results. The results are the Phase 3 "No traffic restraint" figures in table 18.1. As compared with the Phase 2 figures, they show slightly fewer trips than the "maximum" figures of Phase 2 (corresponding to the 1981 A network) but substantially more than the "minimum" ones (corresponding to the 1981 B network). Then, however, they incorporated a constraints procedure into their computer models. Where parts of the assumed road network clogged up, some drivers were assumed to be persuadable to transfer to public transport, or abandon the trip. The results now emerged very differently for the two networks, as the figures in the two right-hand columns of Table 18.1 show. The "assumed" network (roughly the same as the "maximum" network of Phase 2, and described now as Plan 3) produced slightly fewer trips than before, because even it could not cope with all the forecast demand. (Only an even bigger network, described as Plan 9, could achieve that.) But the "minimum" network, carried over from Phase 2 and now christened Plan 1 now choked off a very large amount of traffic. Car trips were now reduced by well over 3 million; nearly another 1 million transferred to public transport, and the net result was a reduction of over 2 million personal trips per day.[18]

This was a substantial difference. It meant that if only the minimal network were built, the increase in personal trips over the nineteen-year period would be some 23 percent; if the Plan 3 network were constructed, it could be as much as 41 percent. But compared with the heady forecasts of Phase 2, both these are somewhat more sober. For Phase 2 had forecast an increase in trips by private transport of no less than 118 percent if the 1981 A network were built, as against only 90 percent for the assumed network in Phase 3. Perhaps most significant, though the Phase 2 forecasts assume an increase in the percentage of private trips from 46 to 70, the Phase 3 forecast for the assumed network calculates an increase to only 62 percent. The minimal network has only 50 percent, a very bare increase on the 1962 figure. This was very important; for the GLC used it to argue that, without the bigger network, the level of restraint on private car travel would be intolerable.

The other critical point is that in any case the assumed network, or something very like it, had already been committed by the Greater London Council as a result of the Phase 2 studies. This had occurred in 1966, and in November 1967, two years before publication of Phase 3, the Council had already announced its plan for three rings and radials at a cost then estimated at £860 million.[19] The plan was thus accepted before full knowledge was available from the studies on which it was supposed to be based, though in the event these provided some degree of justification.

Just how great a degree emerged from the economic evaluation made by the Greater London Council at the end of Phase 3. By this point the practical options had been reduced to three: first, the "minimal" (Plan 1)

Table 18.1 London Transportation Study: Forecasts of 1981 Trips, Phases 2 And 3*

	Phase 1 1962	Phase 2 1981 No Restraint		Phase 3 1981 No Restraint		Phase 3 1981 Restraint	
	Actual	Min.	Max.	Min.	Assumed	Min.	Assumed
Internal car-driver	4.12	8.18	8.98	8.09	8.15	5.20	7.35
Other internal private	1.49	2.98	3.30	2.95	2.99	2.34	3.30
Total internal private	5.61	11.16	12.28	11.04	11.14	7.54	10.65
Internal public	5.72	4.71	4.41	5.46	5.39	6.59	5.71
Unreported public	0.82	0.82	0.82	0.82	0.82	0.82	0.82
Total public	5.54	5.53	5.23	6.28	6.21	7.41	6.53
Total	12.15	16.69	17.51	17.32	17.35	14.95	17.18

*Table 18.1 was difficult to produce because the figures are not strictly comparable. First, by Phase 3 the planners found that they had earlier lost some public transport trips, estimated at 820,000 a day; these are separately shown. Second, the key Phase 3 figures exclude car passengers; these have to be factored indirectly to produce the comparison.
Source Greater London Council, *London Traffic Survey* (London, 1966), 85; Greater London Council, *Movement in London* (London, 1969), 74.

150-mile network costing £451 million; second, the "assumed" (Plan 3) 347-mile network costing £1,841 million; third, the "ultimate" or maximal (Plan 9) 413-mile network costing £2,276,000,000. (All these three sets of costs are based on 1966 prices and include associated parking costs. The actual motorway land and construction costs are for Plan 1, £372 million for Plan 3, £1,658 million; and for Plan 9, £2,063 million.)[20] The GLC economists calculated a so-called one-year rate of return for the year 1981, which was a much simpler and also less satisfactory measure than the discounted flow of benefits generally used in evaluating road schemes. It indicated that Plan 3 after restraint gave an 8.8 percent rate of return when compared with Plan 1, while Plan 9 gave an 8.7 percent rate also as compared with Plan 1. Plan 3 was therefore preferred.

This calculation was the source of fierce controversy in the subsequent public inquiry into the Greater London Development Plan. For one thing, though the costs included the associated costs of parking, they excluded expenditure on the associated secondary network, which the GLC had always calculated, on a rule-of-thumb basis, as 50 percent of the costs of the primary highway system.[21] For another, it was a one-year rate of return. Third, the consultants who made it warned that the results had to be treated with great caution.[22] Finally, it appeared to be a distinctly poor rate of return compared with the norm generally used by the Treasury for judging such investments, which would be at least 10 percent. Critics therefore argued with some justification that in comparison with other major public projects, including other roads, there was a weak case for the Plan 3 network.

Also tested in Phase 3 were two alternative public transportation packages. But these were literally bundles of proposals culled from London Transport and British Rail, without any notion of forming a coherent network. Throughout the three phases of the study, indeed, public transportation played a strictly subsidiary role; it was clearly very much at the back of the transportation planners' minds. For this there were at least three good reasons. The first was that the whole study had arisen as a political response to problems of road traffic. The second was that the techniques inherited from the American studies were simply not well adapted to the needs of an agglomeration where public transportation played such an important role. And the third, quite simply, was that the Greater London Council was not particularly interested because until the 1969 Transport (London) Act it had no direct responsibility for public transportation at all. Even after that act came into force in 1970, it meant only that the GLC acquired general policy control over London Transport. The relationship with British Rail was still very tenuous, and it fell a good deal short of the arrangements then being developed in the provincial conurbations, where the Passenger Transport Authorities could arrange to take over British Rail suburban services. Whatever the reason, this lack

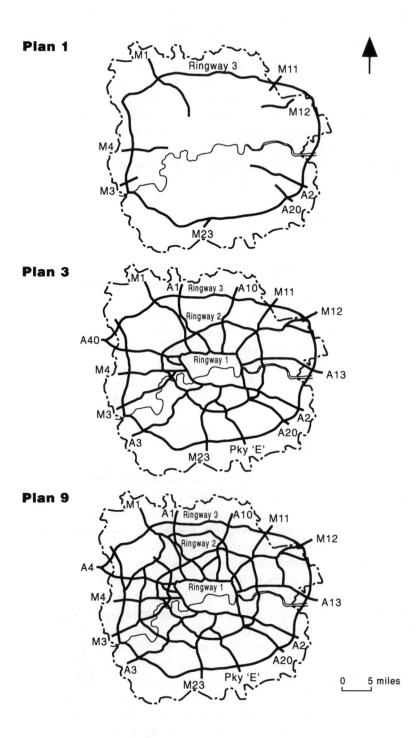

Figure 18.2 The three options in the GLC transportation plan

of interest in public transportation was to prove one of the major sources of criticism in the great public debate that followed.

The GLDP Inquiry: The Roads Plan and its Critics

By this time, the results of the Transportation Study had been incorporated into the Greater London Development Plan, the production of which was indeed one of the GLC's main statutory responsibilities under the London Government Act. It was published in 1969, and the summary results of the study were set out in the volume *Movement in London*.[23] A year later, the public inquiry into the plan opened before a panel headed by Sir Frank Layfield, the notable expert on planning law. It was to rival Roskill on the third London airport as the most protracted planning inquiry in British history.

In its opening evidence, the GLC put the case for the roads in the most forceful terms. Without them, it argued, the result would be "...a continuation of the present conflicts between roads and the environment but over a wider area and of a more intense character in many places ... Overall one must conclude that the London that would be created if there were no investment in roads would be one that would not meet the social and economic objectives of the GLDP."[24] The main problem, it went on, would be that a policy of no investment would require levels of restraint over traffic that would be neither technically feasible nor socially desirable. Restraint might be possible in and near the center and at peak hours, but it would not be acceptable over wide areas where people lived – and yet this might be necessary if the roads were not there. The major need, it stressed, was to provide new capacity to satisfy the very large increases in demand for orbital journeys.[25] Two years later, in a modified statement, it repeated its belief: "The transport strategy in its entirety must be implemented or else the general strategy for improving the quality of life in London will suffer and the value of the total public and private investment in general renewal and development be diminished."[26]

But a large number of influential people disagreed. The panel's discussion of strategic transport issues took sixty-three days and involved 460 Proofs of Evidence and support documents; on local transport issues, it took sixty-seven days and read 560 documents.[27] Indeed, of the 28,392 objections to the plan, some three-quarters dealt with transport and especially with roads. A great number of individual local residents' groups, directly concerned at the impact of the plans on their areas, made both collective and individual representations. But the job of collating and synthesizing them into a coherent set of objections was performed by two related groups: the London Motorway Action Group and the London Amenity and Transport Association.[28] This evidence was principally the work of two experts, J. Michael Thomson and Stephen Plowden, who each published books with cogent criticisms of the plan.[29] From all this mass of evidence, certain dominant lines of counterargument emerged.

The most important was that the American-style approach to transport planning, which the GLC had inherited, was fundamentally misconceived. It concentrated on providing for future increases in demand for the use of roads, instead of first seeking to identify and cure weaknesses in the quality of existing transportation services, above all in public transportation. It provided for new journeys, mainly of an optional social character, rather than easing present-day journeys to work. Thus it paid all too little systematic attention to the speed and reliability of public transportation, the comfort of the ride, and the length and conditions of transfers or waits for services, and it almost ignored the problems of carless families, who by 1981 would still constitute 45 percent of all households in inner London.[30] It assumed that public transportation should in general pay its way, while providing new road space without any such criterion. And its mathematical predictions ignored the need first to set policy objectives for the whole system.[31]

Second, and associatedly, the plan ignored its own impact on travel preferences and patterns. The new motorways, it was argued, would actually generate substantial amounts of traffic that otherwise would not be there: between 70 and 100 percent more, according to Thomson's estimates.[32] (The corresponding GLC prediction, which can be read from table 18.1, was 41 percent.) This generated traffic would inevitably use secondary and local roads on its way to and from motorways, thus making conditions there worse rather than better. And the diversion of trips from public transportation into cars would almost inevitably intensify the vicious circle, already long observed in London, whereby fewer passengers meant poorer service, which in turn meant fewer passengers.

Third and in any event, the critics argued, the plan greatly exaggerated the likely amount of long-distance travel. This was because it projected the travel habits of 1962 car owners, who were mainly middle class, onto future car owners, who would be mainly working class.[33] The new owners, it was argued, had more limited social frameworks and were far more likely to make short local trips in their own areas – journeys that would seldom require the use of the motorway network. Thus, the network was partly irrelevant, and insofar as it was relevant, it was likely to be deleterious.

Fourth, it was said, the plan ignored the considerable indirect costs that the motorways would impose, including accidents to the extra traffic and environmental intrusion. It was alleged that one million people would live within the 200-yard strip that formed the noise shadow of the new roads, 250,000 of them within the shadow of Ringway 1.

Lastly, because of these and other factors, it was argued that the

system had no economic justification. Thomson in 1969 had already calculated that though Ringway 3 gave an adequate return on investment
of 14.9 percent, the corresponding rate on Ringway 1 was as low as 5.3
percent, well below any Treasury yardstick for public investment.[34]
Later, at the inquiry, the objectors argued that when proper account was
taken of factors like depreciation, tax benefits, and unperceived congestion costs, the benefits from Plan 3 as against Plan 1 were reduced from
£125 million (the GLC'S figure) to a mere £19 million; indeed, if (as
seemed likely) the traffic predictions were too high, the balance might
actually be negative.[35]

The objectors did recognize that without the motorways congestion
would be fairly widespread and restraint on the use of the private car
would be needed. On these points, at least, they were in agreement with
the GLC. But they were in total disagreement on two points. The first was
that in their view the result of the motorways would be on balance even
worse; they saw a system that "generates large quantities of additional
traffic, fails to make much impact on congestion in Inner London and the
major suburban centres, and brings relatively modest benefits to road
users."[36] The second was that a general policy of restraint could be effective: It was argued that central London had already shown what could be
done without extensive new road construction.[37] The level of restraint
need not be onerous; it would be needed only in peak hours and would
amount to a modest charge (for instance, on parking) of 20–35p in inner
London.

Thirdly, the objectors made a critical relationship (which the GLDP had
not) between transport planning policies and land-use planning policies.
(It was a criticism of other witnesses at the inquiry that the plan had failed
to evaluate alternative distributions of living and working.) Land-use
planning, in the view of people like Thomson and Plowden and their
colleague Mayer Hillman, should seek to provide a maximum range of
facilities within easy walking distance, without the need for car travel –
and in inner London this should be particularly easy to achieve.

It amounted to a formidable case, based on a fundamentally different
philosophy from the one that had animated the whole transport-
planning process since 1961. And perhaps, though technical argument
about forecasts and evaluations were important, in the last resort the
argument was really about what kinds of policies would improve
the quality of life for the average Londoner. On this there could be no
real reconciliation, for the outlooks were too different.

Faced with this clash, the panel finally steered a judicious middle
course and thus, perhaps, tried to reconcile the irreconcilable. Its report
specifically rejected the extreme courses of meeting the full demand for
road space, and of extreme restraint and regulation: "Since the cost of the
first extreme would be prohibitive, and the effect of the second crippling,
the policy choice lies in practice somewhere between the two."[38] It

argued instead that planning should be developed within a comprehensive and balanced framework, which should include restraint on the use of the private car and on the routing of commercial vehicles; improvement in the quality of public transportation; and improvement in environmental quality. Within that framework, the objective should be to provide as little new road space as was strictly necessary.[39]

However, the panel agreed with the GLC on the critical argument that there were limits, political as well as economic, to the possibilities of traffic restraint. Probably, it concluded, the GLC had somewhat underestimated the public tolerance for restraint and the public response to better public transport. Nevertheless, some demands would need to be met. The panel concluded that the minimal network was smaller than the GLC's Plan 3, but larger than the objectors' preference (which was in essence close to Plan 1). They recommended that instead of four ringways (three of them within the GLC area, one, the Orbital, outside) there should be only two. Ringways 3 and 4 should be combined into one, while Ringway 2 should be omitted (though the North Circular Road, which was already there, would clearly remain and could be upgraded). Most contentiously of all, therefore, the panel recommended that Ringway 1 should remain part of the plan and that many of the main radial routes should be carried through, at motorway standard, to meet it.

The justification for this had to lie partly in economic evaluation. But this was literally impossible, because the GLC had evaluated so few options. The panel recorded a general agreement between the GLC and its critics that the return on Ringway 1 was low: only some 5.1 percent. This compared with a Treasury norm of 10 percent and a Department of the Environment rule of 15 percent for interurban roads. Lacking any evidence to prove or disprove its case, the panel ventured that as part of a reduced system, the rate on Ringway 1 would be higher than this. But the case for Ringway 1 lay in more than the traffic benefits: It was, the panel argued, an essential element in relieving inner London of heavy commercial traffic, and hence in improving the quality of environment there. This was the case the objectors had strenuously denied. But, the panel countered, it made sense so long as road construction took place within a framework of traffic constraint.[40]

The reduced network would still be considerable – and expensive. It would include some 300 to 350 miles of high-speed road and would cost £2,165 million at 1972 prices, excluding the costs of rehousing (which would be formidable, since the housing take was estimated at 16,600). Additionally there would be a substantial bill for the improvement of the secondary road system, where the panel wanted to see the GLC produce a completely new plan.[41]

The 1973 Election: Politics Intervene

The government's reply was remarkably prompt. Simultaneously with the publication of the panel's report in February 1973, the secretary of state for the environment (Geoffrey Rippon) issued a statement. The government did this, the statement said, because it thought that ". . . early decisions of principle will serve to allay public uncertainty and curtail planning blight."[42]

In general the government simply accepted the panel's main recommendations. Ringway 1 would remain in the plan, though its phasing would be further discussed. The government reserved its views about a possible modification to the line in south-east London. Ringway 2, south of the river, would be struck out. On Ringway 3 the government reserved its position until it could see how far the Orbital Road would cope with all the traffic. The government could also not be drawn on the panel's recommendation that the whole network should be completed within twenty years; it would merely try to build as fast as resources allowed. Lastly, the government accepted the panel's recommendation for a new plan for the secondary roads, but wished the proposals in the existing plan to remain as the basis for the highest-priority schemes until new proposals were worked out.

Government responses to independent reports are seldom as prompt as this, least of all to plans needing so much money. But there was by now a pressing political case for haste. Already at the 1970 GLC election, some of the key critics of the motorways plans had organized a campaign under the banner of the Homes Before Roads party. They won as many as 100,000 votes but no seats; so they subsequently changed their tactics. They argued that the Labour party should publicly declare its opposition to the plans on the grounds that they were unnecessary, uneconomic, and inevitable in their incidence of costs and benefits. After much internal debate, in June 1972 Labour embraced the antiroads program in its campaign for the 1973 GLC elections. The Layfield Panel report thus appeared only two months before the polls, at a time when the existing Conservative administration was fighting for its life – and for the life of the motorway proposals.

For by now there has been a remarkable shift of popular opinion, as D. A. Hart chronicles.[43] As late as the 1970 election, both major parties still officially supported the plans, though both were already backpedaling. The success of the Homes Before Roads campaign was undoubtedly a warning sign to the politicians. By 1971 David Wilcox, planning correspondent of the *Evening Standard*, could describe "ringway bashing" as a "favourite sport." Most of the press, together with leading academics, the Town and Country Planning Association and the Royal Institute of British Architects, were by now on balance antimotorway. The well-reported objections at the public inquiry further weakened the GLC case.

By September 1972 even the Conservative party was clearly weakening when it produced a cut-price plan that combined sections of Ringways 1 and 2. For the political momentum was clearly now with the antimotorway campaigners. In April 1973 Labour regained power at County Hall; on the very morning of the victory, they announced that the motorway plans were abandoned and the safeguarding removed. Hart comments: "Exactly 30 years after the publication of Abercrombie's *County of London Plan* (1943) and 10 years after the publication of Buchanan's *Traffic in Towns* (1963) the concept of urban order which both documents supported and in a sense which the Primary Road Network symbolized was effectively abandoned."[44] Labour's victory at County Hall was soon afterwards paralleled across the river. Under the new secretary of state for the environment, Anthony Crosland, the government reaction to the Layfield Report was sharply reversed. The official argument was that times had changed:

> Since the Inquiry, public concern over the reconciliation of the needs of road traffic and the environmental consequences of large scale road building has grown, and the costs of any extensive motorway network have become altogether unacceptable. The present Council have indeed rejected most of the proposals for new primary roads that were contained in the plan submitted, including the inner ringways.[45]

So the government followed the GLC's lead. Ringway 1, apart from those few sections already built or in construction, was deleted, as was Ringway 2, south of the Thames. Only the outer orbital motorway, for the most part outside the GLC boundaries, was committed.

Yet, the statement went on, there was a continuing need for orbital movement along the general corridors once marked by Ringway 1 and Ringway 3. The government would discuss with the GLC how to deal with this. Any plan would have to make the best use of existing roads, but some new construction might be needed. What was left on the map instead of the abandoned roads, therefore, was a curious set of numbered points to be connected up by imaginary lines – rather like the children's games that produce a magic drawing. In this case the fairy picture showed the ringways. Perhaps this was a private joke of Crosland or his advisers. Whatever the case, it seemed to be lost on most people.

That was the position in 1975. In 1979, with a Conservative government in Westminster and a Conservative administration in County Hall, the position is again more fluid. The London Conservatives have made it clear that they want to spend a lot of money on roads again. Though they officially deny that the ringways are to reappear, part of Ringway 1 (the West Cross Route from Shepherds Bush to the river) is in their plan, as is improvement of the North Circular Road and its extension southwards from Wanstead to a new Thames crossing at Barking-Thamesmead.

Indeed the proposals are quite consistent with the modified Conservative plan of September 1973, and in June 1974 the government and GLC agreed on a package for East London. But already before the London elections there had been a shift in thinking within the London Labour party; for the industrial decline of east and south London is producing a new set of local pressures actually in favour of major road building again. Meanwhile, much of Greater London seems to have settled into the state of generalized congestion that the planners had forecast. And in a strange way, perhaps Londoners have simply got used to it.

Analysis of a Negative Disaster

In order to understand better the balance of forces that produced the extraordinary reversal of policy in London in 1973, it is useful to make the three-part analysis created by John Grant in his study of transportation planning in three English provincial cities.[46] He found that there were three key groups of actors: the politicians, the community groups and the professionals. The same three key groups certainly can be identified in London, though perhaps a fourth, the opinion makers and shapers, might profitably be distinguished from the general complex of community activists.

The technicians are perhaps easiest to understand. They are concerned with career maintenance and advancement, which leads them to support interventionist policies based on large injections of public funds. In the case of transport planning, the general history and the traditional organization further strengthened and also focused this tendency. The highway engineers in the Ministry of Transport and in the Greater London Council had a specific training and a specific professional competence. Their general philosophy was based on concepts of efficiency in moving people or goods. Flows of either of these commodities should be accommodated by providing channels of the requisite capacity. The notion that there were alternative ways of handling the problem, or other policy considerations, was injected only slowly and painfully. Organizational divisions had much to do with this, for the GLC's remit down to 1970 was effectively restricted to roads, and during this period generous specific grants were available for road building but not for investment in public transportation. Only after the 1967 Transport Act was this changed, and by that time the London Transportation Study was largely fixed.

All this was no doubt exacerbated by the fact that, for the most part, the GLC's new Department of Highways and Transportation – the name itself is significant – had been set up apparently to perform a particular task: to plan and provide a large increase in highway capacity. It should have been no surprise that the professionals were passionately attached to their task. Later, when Transportation was merged with Planning, many saw the move as a takeover by Transportation rather than the reverse. As Hart points out, the central philosophical concept of traditional British planning – that of organic order in a city, in which the transportation system provides just one element – was weakening during the 1960s. The comprehensive mode of planning, represented by this view, was being replaced by a narrower functional concept, in which professionals attacked well-defined problems. And perhaps the most important of these, as it was seen at the time, was the problem of traffic growth.

It was the historical function of the community groups, and in particular their expert spokesmen and related publicists, to point out that in fact the problem was quite ill defined. They attacked the road plans by seeking to show that the engineers had seen only one small aspect of a multifaceted problem. It was perhaps significant that this antiestablishment group of transport planners was composed not of engineers but of economists and other social scientists. They expressed a view then becoming common, through the influence of the social sciences on the planning schools: that the first essential was to understand and order the problems to be solved.

The reaction of these groups, especially at the grassroots level, was partly an instinctive, emotional one. When the GLC opened Westway in 1970, instead of satisfaction the informed popular reaction was one of environmental outrage at the intrusive elevated structure. The same reaction was happening in cities all over the world, following the first recorded motorway abandonment, that of the Embarcadero Freeway in San Francisco, in 1966. It happened to correspond with a general reaction at the time against massive large-scale development in cities – a reaction expressed in London by the controversies over Piccadilly Circus and Covent Garden. While the catchphrase of the early 1960s was "comprehensive development," that of the early 1970s was "small-scale rehabilitation." In this new world, motorways had no obvious place.

Partly, therefore, the community reaction was an automatic, dialectical one. Some, who might once have supported the idea of motorway planning at an abstract strategic level, suddenly found that the result threatened their home or their neighborhood. Others reacted, more generally, to what they saw with their own eyes or on television. For most people, a reaction against motorways, or anything else, first requires something to react against. In many American cities and in some British ones (Birmingham, Leeds) this happened only after a good part of the network was actually built. But in London, perhaps because of its middle-class activists and the associated media people, it happened remarkably quickly.

Once it did, the critical question concerns the political route the community activists and their allies chose to follow. During the Layfield inquiry from 1970 to 1972, they chose primarily to follow the route of intervention in the process of technical inquiry. Through highly expert and critical objections to the GLC professionals' forecasts and evaluations, they sought to defeat the professionals on their own territory. In the event, the Layfield Panel compromised on the basis of judgment rather than of strict technical argument, and in doing so, it effectively rejected much of the objectors' case. But by then, they had increasingly switched to an alternative route, through takeover of a critical group of politicians. In this way they won. The technical-professional planning process was simply overcome by the political planning process.

Perhaps this was inevitable. Faced with arguments that were finally as much about basic values as about techniques of forecasting, the Layfield Panel steered its middle course. But faced with increasing political pressure from a passionate minority, equally the politicians reacted in a political way. In a democratic society there was probably little else they could do. In London, as in most British cities, local elections are marked by political apathy; a minority turn out to vote. When to this fact is allied the fact that most constituencies tend to be stable politically and only a handful are key marginal ones, the leverage exerted by a small turnover in those key places can be considerable. The most controversial of the motorways, Ringway 1, ran through these key constituencies at the border of working-class and middle-class inner London, the classic territory in which the outcome of an urban election will be decided. And so, in 1973, it was.

There was more than pure political opportunism in all this. The Conservatives, at both central and local government levels, tend to have been more unequivocally committed to road building than Labour, for reasons that are intuitively obvious: greater support of (and by) industrial interests, greater support of (and by) middle-class car owners, plus a general commitment to private forms of transport. Conversely, Labour politicians are more likely to see road building as an expensive sport that does relatively little for their working-class constituents, who need better public transportation instead. This might suggest that the anomalous fact was the strong Labour support for the roads policy from 1965, when they were actually responsible for initiating it, until the 1973 reversal. Perhaps so. But road building for the old LCC politicians was seen as an essential element in the comprehensive reconstruction of blitzed and blighted areas, especially in the East End, where their constituencies were. Indeed the East Cross Route of Ringway 1, the only section to be completed, was planned entirely by the old LCC as part of this process, without notable opposition. It was only when the plans threatened middle-class London that they ran into trouble, and it was to capture these areas that Labour reversed its policies.

Cynics might say that the outcome changed very little. What the voters and the media forgot was that by an accident – possibly a deliberate one

– of the 1963 London Government Act, most of the planned motorways were not a GLC responsibility but remained a central government one. The only unambiguous GLC motorway was Ringway 1, which had been inherited from the old LCC. And in its 1975 statement on the GLDP, the government kept most of its options open. In any case, public expenditure cuts in the mid-1970s meant that there was clearly no money to afford the full motorway program, so it made sense to concentrate government spending on the outer Orbital Road, which significantly became top national priority, plus reconstruction of the North Circular Road.

In the last resort, though, the history does teach more than this. There was a profound shift of mood among thinking people, in London and other cities, both about the problem and about its solution. One generation, the Abercrombie-Buchanan one, had taken its stand on a planning concept of urban order: Hart's cohesive planning mode. A slightly later generation had narrowed this to a technical problem assessment and a resulting technical solution based on heavy investment: Hart's factored mode. But both these were similar in the important respect that they were hard planning solutions, demanding investment for major urban surgery. And both were in turn faced by a radically alternative planning mode: a demand for a more flexible system in which policies were progressively shaped by changing opinion and above all community concern. Here, in Hart's diffused mode it was difficult to make large-scale changes; the planning process has a repetitive, often time-consuming character.[47] This is perhaps the most profound change to affect British planning for more than a generation; its impact was felt far more widely than on London's ringways alone. It was felt, for instance, on the third airport scheme.

The strange irony is that all the proponents still claim that their chief concern is with the quality of life of the archetypal average Londoner. Their visions of what make up the good life are very different, and to some extent they represent a *Zeitgeist*. The good future life of the early 1960s consisted in ceaseless mobility in search of an ever-widening range of choice in jobs, education, entertainment and social life. The good future life of the early 1970s was seen in almost the reverse kind of life: in a small, place-bounded, face-to-face community. Truly these interpretations recall Blake's alternative visions of the Deity:

> The vision of Christ that thou dost see
> Is my vision's greatest enemy.
> Thine has a great hook nose like thine,
> Mine has a snub nose like to mine.

And almost without doubt, before long a new *Zeitgeist* will produce a new vision – or the revival of an old one.

Notes

1   Greater London Council, *London Road Plans* 1900–1970.
2   Ibid., pp. 19–23.
3   Hart, pp. 59–63.
4   G. Dix, 'Little Plans and Noble Diagrams', p. 332.
5   Hart, pp. 66–78.
6   Ibid., p. 36.
7   GB Ministry of Transport, *Traffic in Towns*.
8   Hart, p. 112.
9   Greater London Council, *Movement in London*, p. 39.
10 Greater London Council, *London Traffic Survey*, Vol. II, p. 184.
11 Ibid., pp. 48–9, 184.
12 Greater London Council, *London Road Plans*; Hart.
13 Hart, p. 136.
14 Ibid., p. 116.
15 Greater London Council, *London Traffic Survey*, Vol. II, p. 145.
16 Ibid., p. 85.
17 Greater London Council, *Movement in London*, p. 53.
18 Ibid., pp. 53–5, 68, 74.
19 Greater London Council, *London Road Plans*, p. 45.
20 Greater London Council, *Movement in London*, p. 66.
21 Greater London Council, *Greater London Development Plan. Public Inquiry, Stage 1. Transport.*
22 Freeman Fox, Wilbur Smith and Associates, *London Transportation Study, Phase III.*
23 Greater London Council, *Movement in London*.
24 Greater London Council, *GLDP*, Stage 1, p. 59.
25 Ibid., p. 104.
26 Greater London Council, *Greater London Development Plan: Statement Revisions*, p. 29.
27 GB Department of the Environment, *Greater London Development Plan: Report of the Panel of Inquiry*, Vol. 1: *Report*, p. 268.
28 London Motorway Action Group and London Amenity and Transport Association, *Transport Strategy in London*.
29 J. M. Thomson, *Motorways in London*; S. Plowden, *Towns Against Traffic*.
30 Plowden, *Towns Against Traffic*, p. 116.
31 Thomson, *Motorways in London*, pp. 160–3.
32 Ibid., p. 165.
33 Plowden, pp. 112–13.
34 Thomson, p. 151.
35 London Motorway Action Group, *Transport Strategy*, pp. 90–1.
36 Thomson, p. 125.
37 London Motorway Action Group, *Transport Strategy*, pp. 65–6.
38 GB Department of the Environment, *GLDP: Report*, Vol. 1, p. 257.
39 Ibid., p. 285.
40 Ibid., pp. 442–4.
41 Ibid., pp. 451–7.

42　GB Department of the Environment, *Greater London Development Plan: Statement by the Rt. Hon. Geoffrey Rippon, QC, MP*, p. 10.

43　Hart, pp. 159–60.

44　Ibid., p. 175.

45　GB Department of the Environment, *Greater London Development Plan: Statement by the Rt. Hon. Anthony Crosland, MP*, p. 6.

46　Grant.

47　Hart, pp. 183–94.

References

Dix, G., 'Little Plans and Noble Diagrams', *Town Planning Review*, 49 (1978), pp. 329–52.

Freeman, Fox, Wilbur, Smith and Associates, *London Transportation Study, Phase III*, 4 Vols. (London: The Associates, Mimeo 1968).

Grant, J., *The Politics of Urban Transport Planning* (London: Earth Resources Research 1977).

—— *Greater London Development Plan: Report of the Panel of Inquiry*, Vol. 1 (London: HMSO 1973).

—— *Greater London Development Plan: Statement by the Rt. Hon. Geoffrey Rippon, QC, MP* (London: HMSO 1973).

—— *Greater London Development Plan: Statement by the Rt. Hon. Anthony Crosland, MP* (London: HMSO 1975).

GB Ministry of Transport, *Traffic in Towns* (London: HMSO 1963).

Greater London Council, *London Traffic Survey*, Vol. II (London: The Council 1966).

—— *Movement in London* (London: The Council 1969).

—— *London Road Plans 1900–70*, Greater London Research, Research Report No. 11 (London: Greater London Research and Development Unit 1970).

—— *Greater London Development Plan: Public Inquiry. Statement Evidence*, Stage 1, Transport (London: The Council 1970).

—— *Greater London Development Plan: Statement Revisions* (London: The Council 1972).

Hart, D.A., *Strategic Planning in London: The Rise and Fall of the Primary Road Network* (Oxford: Pergamon 1976).

London Motorway Action Group and London Amenity and Transport Association, *Transport Strategy in London* (London: The Group 1971).

Plowden, S., *Towns Against Traffic* (London: André Deutsch 1972).

Thomson, J. M., *Motorways in London* (London: Duckworth 1969).

19

Coalition-building by a Regional Agency: Austin Tobin and the Port of New York Authority

Jameson W. Doig

During the three decades between the late 1930s and the late 1960s, a team of career officials at the Port of New York Authority used the resources and flexibility available at this bistate agency to build political coalitions that would support their efforts to redirect their own agency and to reshape broader public policies. They led the fight against the FDR-Morgenthau plan to strip tax exemption from municipal bonds; they battled Robert Moses and elected officials in New York City and Newark in order to gain control of the region's major airports and important marine terminals along the New Jersey shore; they cooperated with city officials to construct massive truck terminals in Newark and Manhattan and to build the world's largest bus terminal in mid-Manhattan – also over Moses' opposition. Working jointly with Moses and state highway officials, they added new bridges and major highways to the region's

Reprinted by permission from Clarence Stone and Heywood Sanders, eds, *Politics of Urban Development*. Lawrence: University of Kansas Press, pp. 73–104. Copyright © 1987.

arterial system. During these years they also experimented with a major containerport, built the World Trade Center, and reluctantly took control of an important rail link that connects Newark, Jersey City, Hoboken, and Manhattan. And they led the successful effort to gather the airport operators across the country into a national alliance whose goal was to develop and operate air terminals without taxpayer subsidies.

The efforts of this band of career officials – Austin Tobin, Daniel Goldberg, Walter Hedden, Lee Jaffe, and their colleagues – illustrate the advantages that independent public authorities can have in shaping public policy, especially in the fields of physical development and construction. And they suggest some analytic and political strategies that can be used by public officials more generally.

Their leader in these three decades and more was Austin J. Tobin, who had joined the Port Authority in 1927, when Calvin Coolidge was in the White House and the authority had no bridges or marine terminals or, indeed, any operating facilities at all. Rising through the ranks in the Law Department, Tobin was chosen in 1942 as the agency's executive director, and his days and nights thereafter were occupied almost entirely with the programs and the needs of the port agency. He was, from this perspective, an exemplar of the career civil service tradition.

However, if that tradition implies neutral competence in the service of goals and policies decided elsewhere (by elected leaders and by the electorate), then perhaps he was not the ideal civil servant. For Austin Tobin enjoyed the exercise of power too much, looked forward too eagerly to the challenge of battling vigorous opponents, and had too clear a vision of how his agency could shape the future of the New York metropolis to sit in careerist harness, awaiting orders. He was, in brief, too entrepreneurial to be neutral.

The press often treated Austin Tobin as though he were the Robert Moses of the Port Authority; the reality is much more complex. For unlike Moses and some other government entrepreneurs, Tobin was a team builder, not a solo acrobat. He attracted to the Port Authority men and women of high potential and often of quality already proven, and he encouraged them to stretch their own mental and entrepreneurial wings. They experimented with new techniques in engineering, planning, and other fields; they challenged legal constraints and often won; and a dozen or more became leaders in their own professional associations – in regional planning, public administration, engineering, law, marine development, aviation, and other fields. Moreover, Tobin recognized that he was uncomfortable in talking with the press and in the give-and-take of political bargaining, and he reached out for practitioners who could employ these black arts with skill and thus shore up his individual weaknesses, turning them into institutional strengths.

While Tobin was the clear leader during his decades at the Port Authority helm – far more than *primus inter pares* – to understand fully the evolution of the agency during these years would require that we explore the activities, successes, and failures of this large entrepreneurial team. It was an association of complex individuals, whose personal styles and values sometimes generated sparks of conflict and longer battles, resolved at times by reassigning responsibilities or quiet resignation. If Tobin was directing a team of stylish horses, it was on occasion a quite unruly team!

This chapter, which is drawn from a longer study of Tobin and the authority, first outlines the origins and early activities of the Port Authority, and then describes the strategies employed by Tobin and his colleagues to gather and use political influence in several policy arenas: the conflict in the late 1930s on the FDR-Morgenthau proposal to abolish tax exemption for municipal bonds; the development of airports and marine terminals in the New York region after World War II; and the creation of the national alliance of airport operators.

The Joining of Region and Opportunity

Keen instruments, strung to a vast precision
Bind town to town and dream to ticking dream.

– Hart Crane, *The Bridge*

When Hart Crane began his epic poem on the Brooklyn Bridge, in the 1920s, the New York area had just taken its third major step in four decades to challenge localism in outlook and politics with the banner of "regionalism." Historically, the cities and towns clustered about Manhattan had been deeply divided – torn into parts first by wide rivers and bays and then by the state line, which separated the densely populated New York communities and their eastern suburbs from New Jersey's wary and often jealous cluster of smaller towns – Hoboken, Jersey City, Newark, and dozens more. The first of the three major steps to join what God and early politics had put asunder was the Brooklyn Bridge. Completed in 1883, it leaped over the wide East River and brought the growing population centers of Brooklyn and Long Island into easy congress with Manhattan's thriving employment districts.

The second step was a matter of political rather than engineering design. In the 1890s, a campaign to combine the independent city of Brooklyn with Manhattan and nearby territories was carried forward in earnest. And though many Brooklynites opposed the merger, and some Manhattan politicos were uncertain too, the state legislature finally adopted a new charter in 1897, which consolidated Brooklyn, Manhattan, the Bronx, and rural Queens and Staten Island into a "Greater" New York on the first day of January 1898.

The third step, also political but more tentative in the joining of

regional forces, brings us to Austin Tobin and our story. In the early twentieth century, commercial activity in the bistate New York region
expanded rapidly and each state sought to increase its share. For some
political and business leaders in northern New Jersey, economic growth
and vitality seemed much more likely if marine and rail traffic could be
attracted from Manhattan and Brooklyn to their own shores, and both
public criticism and legal action were directed toward that end. New York
interests challenged the New Jersey effort and sought to maintain the
competitive position of the eastern side of the harbor. But some of its
spokesmen also emphasized the need for cooperative bistate action to
reduce acute congestion in the harbor and at major terminal points and
to enhance the economic vitality of the entire region in meeting challenges from other East Coast ports.[1]

The intellectual leader in developing the case for bistate cooperation
was Julius Henry Cohen, an imaginative lawyer who was familiar with
the Port of London Authority (created in 1908) and who urged that a
bistate port authority be created to undertake the necessary regional
effort. This proposal, first put forward in 1918, generated extensive opposition, particularly from local politicians in New York City and Jersey City
– who feared a loss of local sovereignty and who were unhappy that a
new agency might be created which would not be easily controlled for
patronage and partisan purposes. As a result of the opponents' efforts, the
strong regulatory and planning powers envisioned by commissions that
were studying the bistate issue were omitted from the final proposal.
However, with wide support from business and civic groups on both sides
of the Hudson River, bills creating the Port of New York Authority as an
interstate compact agency were passed in Trenton and Albany early in
1921, and the compact was then approved by Congress.

On 30 April, 1921, the Port Authority came into being. It was governed
by a Board of Commissioners – half appointed by the governor of each
state for six-year terms – and its mandate was extremely broad: established by the two states as their joint agency to ensure "faithful
cooperation in the future planning and development of the port of New
York," the authority was empowered to construct or purchase, and to
operate, "any terminal or transportation facility" within the Port District,
which extended – across three hundred cities and towns – for twenty-
five miles into each state. However, it was given no power to raise
revenues by taxation or to pledge the credit of the two states; the Port
Authority would have to rely on grants from other agencies and devise a
program that otherwise would be financially self supporting.[2]

For those who favored the creation of the authority, a major hope was
that the agency could devise and implement a plan to reduce the congestion and cost of freight handling by rail and water in the port area. The
Port Authority's staff devoted several years to this effort during the early
1920s, but the private railroad lines refused to cooperate, blocking any

improvement in rail facilities. The authority then turned to studies of vehicular bridges that might aid freight and passenger movement in the region, and by 1926 it had obtained approval from both states to construct three bridges between New Jersey and Staten Island, as well as a vast span across the Hudson River.

The Port Authority's potential and the opportunities for challenging work there attracted Austin Tobin to the bistate agency. Born in Brooklyn in 1903, Tobin attended Holy Cross College, where he graduated near the top of his class. Returning to his hometown in 1925, he enrolled at Fordham Law School, taking classes in the evening while casting about for what he should do next.[3] In 1926, a friend of Tobin's was hired by the Port Authority's Law Department, and he urged Tobin to apply too. The authority's general counsel was Julius Henry Cohen, who by now had a national reputation for his innovative approach to important legal and substantive problems.[4] The prospect of working with Cohen, together with the authority's expanding general program, attracted Tobin, who applied and joined the agency as a law clerk in February 1927. A year later, law degree in hand, he was promoted to assistant attorney in Cohen's office.

Within a few years, however, the Port Authority and Austin Tobin appeared to be on divergent trajectories – the authority slipping slowly downward, Tobin spreading his wings, moving up.

For the Port Authority, the decade of the 1930s opened with great achievement and much promise. By 1932, the agency had built an inland freight terminal in Manhattan, it had completed three bridges between New Jersey and Staten Island, and its great George Washington Bridge – the longest suspension bridge in the world – now spanned the Hudson River. Through adroit maneuvering, the authority had also taken control of the Holland Tunnel and its lucrative toll revenues. With its own financial security strengthened and vehicular traffic expanding, the agency then obtained legislative approval to construct a new vehicular crossing – the Lincoln Tunnel beneath the Hudson River.[5]

Under the impact of the depression, however, automotive traffic declined drastically, yielding barely enough revenue during the mid 1930s to pay debt service on the outstanding bonds. A mood of caution soon permeated the board and the senior staff. Led by Chairman Frank Ferguson, a conservative banker from Jersey City, the authority sought no new duties and behaved as though its main goal was "to retire debt in all haste."[6]

In the Port Authority's Law Department, however, the atmosphere was one not of prudent investment and caution but of lively challenge and legal inventiveness.[7] The intellectual leader was Julius Henry Cohen, and Tobin was one of Cohen's small band of assistants; in Tobin's efforts during these years we see many of the characteristic traits that shaped his later career and the Port Authority's direction for decades to follow.

In 1928 the agency identified a site in lower Manhattan for its inland freight terminal. Condemnation procedures were required in order to obtain portions of the site, and in 1930 Cohen turned that task over to Tobin, who was named to the new post of real estate attorney. When the authority announced that it was planning to erect an office building on top of the freight terminal in order to generate revenue on the terminal site, private interests sued. Tobin met with Cohen and suggested that "since this case is related to our real estate concerns, I assume you want me to take it." Cohen agreed, Tobin took the lead in preparing the brief, and Cohen then argued the case, which the Port Authority won in the lower court in 1934.[8]

While this case was in the courts, the Internal Revenue Service initiated a series of actions, arguing that salaries paid to employees of the Port Authority (and similar agencies) were subject to federal income taxes. Since Tobin was already involved in (real estate) tax litigation, he again approached Cohen with the suggestion that since this was "another tax case," he should take it on too. Again Cohen assented.

Toward a National Alliance

By 1935 Tobin was in charge of all tax litigation for the Port Authority and was anxious to shed the "backwater" image of a "real estate lawyer."[9] Cohen accepted his argument that a change of title was appropriate, and Tobin was promoted to assistant general counsel. In the same year, he recruited Daniel Goldberg, who was fresh out of Columbia Law School and at the age of twenty still too young to take the bar examination, to join the Port Authority's staff. Because the issue of tax exemption for salaries affected many municipal and state agencies, Tobin and Goldberg then contacted attorneys general in several states, as well as other public authorities, and obtained supporting briefs; indeed, Tobin and Goldberg drafted the briefs submitted by New York State and by the American Association of Port Authorities.

The Port Authority and its allies won the initial court round but finally lost the salary cases in the United States Supreme Court in 1938 and 1939.[10] Franklin D. Roosevelt and Henry Morgenthau, Jr., then took the next step, as expected: they challenged the tax-exempt status of bonds issued by state and local governments and their agencies. In 1938 the administration's allies in Congress created a special Senate committee to consider legislation that would strip tax exemption from these securities; a detailed Department of Justice study supporting the Morgenthau position was provided to the committee; and hearings were scheduled for early 1939. FDR and his advisers were known to be strongly in favor of such legislation; they argued that tax exemption of income from the bonds gave undue benefits to investors, many of whom were wealthy individuals. A "short and simple statute," as Roosevelt put it, would solve the problem.[11]

Tobin then went to Cohen and to general manager John Ramsey with the suggestion that the Port Authority, building on the alliance developed in the salary fight, take the lead in opposing the administration's proposal. That proposal, he argued, was particularly threatening to the Port Authority's ability to sell bonds and carry forward its program, and he urged that the authority use its own greater flexibility in allocating staff and funds in order to underwrite and direct the campaign.[12]

Cohen, Ramsey, and the commissioners accepted Tobin's analysis, and Tobin and Goldberg then turned to the attorneys general of New Jersey and New York State, who agreed to send telegrams to the attorneys general across the country, calling for a meeting on the tax-exemption issue. At that meeting, Tobin and Goldberg spoke, pointing out that federal taxation of state and municipal bonds would increase financing costs by 25 percent or more and that this would require higher state and local taxes and might drive some cities into bankruptcy. The assembled officials agreed to join together in a Conference on State Defense in order to resist the "inevitable onslaught" from the federal government. Tobin was named secretary and was asked to develop a plan of action.

During the later half of 1938, Tobin and his aides devised a strategy and, with the endorsement of the conference's titular leaders, carried it out. They traveled across the country, visiting state capitals and city finance offices, urging that letters and telegrams opposing the Treasury's plan be sent to members of Congress. They located experts who were willing to testify against the administration's plan, and they helped prepare the needed testimony. They sent out frequent reports to their allies, discussing substantive issues and political developments. ("It was Tobin's idea and a great tool – to keep all the people around the country informed and to unify their efforts," recalled one member of the team.) Tobin was the editor, and "he made sure Cohen, Ramsey and the Commissioners saw copies," noted another person who was active in the campaign.

Tobin had tremendous energy, and his enthusiasm infected the staff in New York and their allies across the country. "We put in 100-hour weeks," an associate recalled. "He worked as hard as anyone, and he gave us opportunities to try out our own ideas; and he gave credit when one of us made a useful contribution," another remarked. "Austin inspired great loyalty. We loved to work for him."

Until this fight, Tobin had had almost no contact with people in the financial world. But now Tobin and his aides met with top bankers in New York and other leaders in finance; and they in turn got to know Austin Tobin and his remarkable organizing ability.

At the Special Senate Committee hearings in early 1939, Tobin orchestrated the opposition to the administration's plan, and he and his associates helped prepare the testimony presented by state and local officials, investment bankers, scholars, and civic associations. Then they turned to the House Committee, which was scheduled to hold hearings that summer. They believed that the ten Republicans on the House Committee were opposed to the proposal, but there were fifteen Democrats who, if not "educated," might be expected to support FDR. So they identified the congressional districts of these fifteen, divided them into two groups, and Tobin and Goldberg took off on their own campaign swings. With them they carried information on the tax rate and debt of each city and town in each district; they met with the mayor and the city council ("or the city manager, or whoever would talk with us"), and they explained the impact that the administration's bill would have on the town's debt. And they got results: resolutions from cities and towns across the country landed on the doorsteps of the Democratic committee members. By the fall of 1939, neither the House nor the Senate had much appetite for the proposal, and though the Special Senate Committee voted for the bill by a bare majority, lobbying by the Conference on State Defense continued, and when the bill reached the Senate floor in 1940, it was defeated. This was a "bitter defeat for the Administration," one participant later recalled.

But Morgenthau and Treasury were only temporarily subdued; having lost in Congress, they soon turned to the courts. In March 1941, the Internal Revenue Service (IRS) targeted several individuals who held tax-exempt bonds issued by public authorities and began proceedings to collect income taxes on the interest from the bonds; one of the individuals was Alexander Shamberg, a longtime commissioner of the Port of New York Authority. So Tobin and his colleagues went back to work, devoting much of 1941 to preparing the briefs and organizing the effort to counter the IRS position in the courts.[13]

This was an exciting time in the Law Department, especially in Austin Tobin's division. Julius Henry Cohen was nearly seventy, suffering from health problems, and not very active; but he gave plenty of leeway to his colleagues. Tobin and his aides were fully engaged during these years, handling real estate issues arising from the freight terminal and the Lincoln Tunnel project, while battling the Roosevelt administration on the tax issue. The main problem facing Tobin and his associates was that they were joined to a large organization that seemed to be going nowhere.[14]

An Entrepreneurial Team Takes Control

By early 1942, the Port Authority had been operating under tight financial constraints for ten years, and with World War II now under way, gasoline rationing would soon be in force. Traffic would probably decline again, and more staff members of the authority might have to be laid off. John Ramsey, the agency's top staff member, was reluctant to "tackle a whole new round of problems": he was eligible to retire, and he decided that it was time to leave.

But who should replace him? One group of commissioners, led by Chairman Frank Ferguson, favored Billings Wilson, then assistant general manager, who could be counted on to exert strong managerial control – reducing expenses while maintaining the bridges and tunnels in good repair. Overall policy would be set by banker Ferguson and his colleagues, with excess revenues being used to pay off the bonds.

To another group of commissioners, Ramsey's departure offered an opportunity to break free from the cautious approach of the previous decade. What was needed was an executive team that would look ahead to the economic opportunities facing the New York region once the war was over, identify projects that the Port Authority might undertake to aid the region's economic growth, and then devise strategies to gain public support for the agency's plans. This faction was led by Howard Cullman, a wealthy New York commissioner who had worked closely with Alfred E. Smith when Smith was governor of the state; Cullman had welcomed appointment to the Port Authority Board in 1927 as a way to help keep the New York region a vital commercial center. Cullman was energetic and a risk taker, and he found the cautious approach of Ferguson and his allies uncongenial.[15] As Tobin took on the legal issues confronting the bistate agency, Cullman got to know him, and he liked the young man's style, his enthusiasm, and his capacity to develop a dedicated staff, as well as Tobin's ability to carry out complex strategies in the political arena.

In a series of meetings during the spring of 1942, Tobin emerged as the choice of a majority of the commissioners, and on 1 July he took office as executive director of the Port Authority – a position he would occupy for nearly thirty years.

Tobin had already demonstrated – in his work on the tax exempt bond issue – the talent and the inclination to identify new goals and to marshall support inside and beyond the Authority. Soon after becoming the executive director, he applied these qualities in new and complex directions – in identifying larger missions for the Port Authority, in developing and nourishing external constituencies in support of the new goals and programs, in creating internal constituencies for the new initiatives (while neutralizing opposition), and so in acting as an "entrepreneurial" leader.[16]

Although Austin Tobin appeared in these ways to reach beyond the tradition of a "neutral" career official, it would be incorrect to view Tobin and his Port Authority colleagues simply as freewheeling entrepreneurs, indifferent to the shackles of legislative control and the sentiments of the general public, going their own way much as did the railroad barons of

the nineteenth century. No major program initiatives could be undertaken by the Port Authority without legislative support; indeed, the
legislatures of two states – New Jersey and New York – had to vote their
approval. And the influence of the two governors was potentially overwhelming: they could block any new program by failing to sign legislative
bills; moreover, every month they received the minutes of actions taken
by the Port Authority's commissioners, and each governor held the
power to veto any and all items in those monthly minutes.[17]

Within the domain of the Port Authority, too, Tobin operated under
substantial constraints, for the authority's policies were formally determined not by the executive director but by the Board of Commissioners
– twelve individuals appointed by the governors, six from each state who
relied upon Tobin and his staff for "day-to-day management of the organization."[18]

These factual characterizations do not, however, adequately capture
the reality, which is more interesting and more complex. For years on
end, the legislatures of both states and the two governors carefully delin-
eated functions and policies for the Port Authority – but they did so, with
few exceptions, in response to the authority's own carefully developed
proposals. During the 1940s and 1950s, Tobin and his staff devised
impressive plans for improving transportation and terminal facilities in
the New York region and took them to business leaders, local officials,
and the press for discussion and – quite often – for applause. The Port
Authority's own commissioners were also informed, at an early stage; a
few of them made suggestions that modified the proposals in modest
ways, and many of the commissioners used their own enthusiasm and
persuasive energy to convince their colleagues in the business world to
support these plans. Governors and other key officials in Trenton and
Albany were consulted too.

And then these plans, crafted with imagination and skill, honed and
modified in negotiations with influential leaders and groups, were laid
upon the legislative desks – with a promise that the Port Authority would
cover all costs. For once World War II had ended, the traffic across Austin
Tobin's bridges and through his tunnels, later joined by the revenue from
airports and marine terminals, generated enough income that the Port of
New York Authority could pay out of its own pocket for every new
project its officials proposed. Perhaps it was not surprising, then, that
throughout these years state officials were generally willing to approve
the Port Authority's plans, which arrived with wide public and press
support, which would not cost a penny in state taxes, and which might,
if approved and carried out, reflect credit on governors and legislators too.
Even if some of these officials might prefer that these funds be employed
in other ways – for other transportation programs or even for hospitals
or education – those choices were not presented, and essentially were not
available. And so the projects favored by Tobin and his aides went

forward. Not all of them through thirty years of plans and proposals, but many, large and small.[19]

New Goals and Well-Crafted Constraints

There was also a cat in a willow basket, from the partly-opened lid of which she gazed with half-closed eyes, and affectionately surveyed the small birds around.
— Thomas Hardy, *Far from the Madding Crowd*

Until he was chosen to be executive director, in the spring of 1942, Tobin had been absorbed in matters of law and politics. He had devoted little attention to the transportation and economic development problems facing the New York region or to the possible role of the Port Authority in meeting those challenges. During the summer and fall of 1942, Tobin spent long hours reading about these issues and opportunities, and he gathered around him staff members who could help him devise strategies to meet the region's needs. Walter Hedden, the agency's top planner, was especially crucial; now promoted to head the new Department of Port Development, Hedden worked closely with Tobin in developing plans for the postwar era.

By June 1943, Tobin and Hedden had completed a preliminary study of the port's problems and had identified a number of activities that the Port Authority might undertake to help maintain the region's position as "the gateway for world commerce." Included on the list were several projects that had been proposed by Hedden and others in earlier staff reports – truck terminals, produce centers, and a large bus terminal in Manhattan. Tobin and Hedden also suggested other and larger tasks – the Port Authority might take over the dilapidated piers in New York City and along the New Jersey waterfront, reconstruct them, and operate a series of marine terminals; and perhaps it should take on a central role in the development of air transport in the bistate region.[20] Tobin appreciated the marine terminals and the airports for their potential; perhaps he even hungered a bit for them; but like Thomas Hardy's cat, he would need to be patient, making plans while awaiting the right time to pounce.

Tobin then went to the board to obtain funds for detailed studies in each project area. Chairman Ferguson and two of his conservative allies objected to Tobin's plans, and a few other members of the twelve-person board supported Ferguson, though reluctantly, in deference to his long service (since 1934) as chairman of the Port Authority. The board majority stood with Tobin, but during the next year the board's enthusiasm was at times only lukewarm.

Then, at the end of 1944, one of Ferguson's strongest supporters on the board died, and the term of another expired, and their successors turned away from the chairman. At their February 1945 meeting, the commissioners replaced Ferguson with Howard Cullman and named Joseph Byrne of New Jersey vice chairman. Both were enthusiastic advocates of vigorous Port Authority efforts to reach out in new directions, and both were strong supporters of Austin Tobin. At last the board was essentially unified behind Tobin's leadership and ready to support an aggressive Port Authority role in grappling with the region's problems. It was a state of harmony that would last for more than two decades, until the battles of Tobin's final years.

Airports and marine terminals: strategies for action

Even before the board had ousted Ferguson from the chairmanship, Tobin and his aides had begun the analytical and public relations efforts that would permit them to take control of the region's major airports and a large chunk of its marine facilities as well. These strategies, begun in 1943 and extending into the 1950s, were pursued with the following guidelines as central.

1   *The "self-supporting" criterion.* The Port Authority would undertake construction projects, rehabilitation programs, and other activities only if the new facilities would, in the long run, generate enough income to meet their total costs. Having no direct access to tax revenues – and very limited access to federal and state grants – the authority's leaders were unwilling to commit their funds and energies to any project that seemed likely to become a permanent drain on the agency's revenues. Therefore, careful studies of consumer demand and other market factors, and of construction methods and costs, were essential. The possibility of federal aid or other outside funding that could reduce the total to be funded through the authority's bridge-and-tunnel revenues should also be actively explored.

2   *The need for "regional balance."* The creation of the Port Authority in 1921 had been possible because business and political leaders had tentatively agreed to replace conflict with cooperation in seeking economic growth for the New York region; but suspicion between officials of the two states had not been abolished by waving the Port Authority wand. Tobin and his associates realized that proposals to aid commercial vitality in New York must be balanced with projects to aid the cities of New Jersey, whose elected officials were always ready to denounce the agency for charging their citizens fifty cents per car to journey to Manhattan.

3   *The passive stance of the Port Authority.* The agency's leaders believed that its political and public relations position would be weakened if they took the initiative by announcing a range of programs the agency was ready to undertake; for that initiative would encourage the fears of those who viewed the Port Authority as a sort of octopus, reaching out to claim

new domains and to squeeze the life from municipal government. Therefore, Tobin and his aides preferred to have suggestions for authority action emanate from others – from business associations, civic and planning groups, mayors and governors – permitting the Authority to respond to such requests. If a project involved action to take over an existing municipal activity, it was especially crucial to have the initiative come from other groups in the region.

The Port Authority would then gather the best experts, study the proposal, and report the experts' conclusions. Whether any action should then be taken to require the port agency to go forward with a project would be the responsibility of the elected officials at the two state capitals.

4 *The need to deflect political pressure for reducing bridge-and-tunnel tolls.* Before the war, there had been recurrent efforts to require the Port Authority to reduce the fifty-cent charge on its bridges and tunnels.[21] With the probable increase in postwar traffic, the authority's toll revenue would rise, and pressure to reduce the fifty-cent rate might become intolerable. However, such action would siphon off the surplus funds needed if the port agency was to reach into new fields. Therefore, it was important to develop a portfolio of useful projects and to ensure that influential business and civic groups were ready and willing to press for action to carry out such projects. Then any campaign for toll reduction could be challenged, and perhaps defeated, because of the trade-offs involved: If the tolls were reduced, less money would be available to carry out projects that were "urgently needed" to enhance the economic vitality of the region.

These four guidelines represented a complex mix of real constraints and public relations strategies. They tended to be ingrained in all authority staff members whose activities in the 1930s involved both analytical studies and political negotiation; thus, the previous experience of Tobin and some of his assistants was invaluable. But many of the authority's projects in the postwar world would require learning how to operate in new terrain – where technological uncertainty was greater and where a tradition of municipal control made Port Authority initiatives more difficult politically.

Using the confidential 1943 report as a basic inventory of possible Port authority activities, Tobin marshalled and deployed the agency's resources for action. A complex array of analytical studies, behind-the-scenes negotiations, and public battles then followed, as the Port Authority moved to build two massive truck terminals and a gigantic bus terminal; to take over the marine terminals at Newark and Hoboken, with a solid try for New York City's piers – an effort that failed; and to wrest the most glamorous transportation projects of the postwar era – the airports – from Newark's political legions, from New York City's mayors, and from Moses' own competing agency. The effort to extend the Port Authority's reach in these several directions occupied the first ten years of Tobin's thirty-year reign in office. To illustrate these entrepreneurial patterns, we focus below on the Tobin initiatives that involved the most complex strategies – those that brought the Newark and New York City airports and Newark's seaport into the Port Authority's fond embrace.[22]

During the fall and winter of 1943–4, Hedden and Tobin created a small staff to analyze the prospects for growth in air transport in the postwar era, the costs of developing more airport facilities across the bistate region, and the income that could be expected from airline leases and terminal concessions to offset these costs. They also met with federal officials to urge that federal aid be provided for airport development. Similar studies and negotiations were carried out by Tobin's staff in the seaport area. By early 1945 it seemed clear that if given the opportunity, the authority would be able to modernize and operate major airports and selected marine terminals in the New York region on a break-even basis.

Here, however, a major challenge faced Tobin and his associates: the attitude of the regional press, local governmental officials, and the general public. For years, the Port Authority had faced hostile editorials from the suburban New Jersey press and criticism from citizens and politicians on both sides of the Hudson. A major complaint was the authority's "exorbitant" bridge-and-tunnel tolls; and some people were suspicious of its wealth, unhappy about neighborhood disruption caused by its construction efforts, and fearful that its leaders were mainly interested in helping Manhattan maintain its economic dominance over the hinterland. Any plans to expand the agency's activities would generate unease, and proposals to add marine terminals and airports might encounter vitriolic opposition – particularly if the Port Authority reached out toward Newark's and New York City's airports and seaports, which generated municipal pride and a modicum of patronage jobs for the party faithful.

Tobin recognized that a skillful public relations strategy would be needed to gain public support and to blunt municipal opposition, and he obtained the board's approval to hire a specialist to lead that operation. The goal would be to develop close ties with reporters, editorial writers, and civic and business leaders across the bistate region – so that the region's opinion leaders would come to understand the importance of airport and seaport development to the region's economy and the advantages that the Port Authority could bring if it were invited to take on these challenging tasks.

To help gather allies to the Port Authority's cause, Tobin hired Lee K. Jaffe, who was named director of public relations in 1944. Tobin and Jaffe "hit it off immediately," as a close observer recalled, and she was soon included in policy meetings with Tobin, Hedden, chief engineer John Evans, and the agency's airport planner, James Buckley. Building on a decade of experience as a reporter and governmental press officer in Washington and New York, Jaffe established close working relationships with editorial writers and reporters on all of the region's daily newspapers, kept them constantly informed of new studies and human interest stories in the Port Authority's domain, and suggested ways of making a story newsworthy.[23] By late 1944 and 1945, stories and editorials on the authority's concerns about air and marine transport were appearing with increasing frequency, laying the groundwork for editorial and public support for the authority to take a central role in postwar air and seaport operations.

In addition to a careful economic analysis and a skillful public relations program, Tobin's strategy involved a crucial third element – developing close relationships with experts engaged in surveys of the airport and seaport issues and in studies of broader development needs in the New York area. By 1944–5, Hedden and his aides were working with the Regional Plan Association and with the U.S. Department of Commerce and other federal agencies in developing a plan for airports in the region. Most important, with the assistance of Joseph Byrne, his board's vice chairman and a leading citizen of Newark, Tobin had made contact with planner Harland Bartholomew who had been engaged in 1943 by Newark's business leaders to study that aging city's development needs. Early in their studies Bartholomew and his associates concluded that the expansion of Newark's airport and the revitalization of its decaying marine terminal would be vital steps in aiding the city's postwar economy, but that the city government lacked the managerial talent and the political capacity needed to convert these two havens of patronage into engines of economic growth. Confidential meetings between these planners and authority staff members led to an informal understanding – that the Port Authority stood ready to study a possible takeover of the Newark airport and seaport *if* Bartholomew were to take the lead in recommending Port Authority operation as desirable.

And so he did. In October 1945, the Bartholomew report was made public, and its conclusions were spread prominently across the front pages of the region's newspapers: in view of the Port Authority's large staff with "long experience in all forms of transportation" and its tradition of using "good business practices," the authority should be asked to lease and operate Newark's airport and marine terminal. In addition, Bartholomew set forth an argument that would frame the airport issue in a way consistent with Tobin's long-range goals: seaport and marine terminal development throughout the New York region should be part of an "integrated" system, the report concluded, and the "greatest usefulness" of Newark and other air and sea terminals would be attained only when they were all combined in a coordinated regional system.[24]

The Newark planning board, composed of civic and business leaders in the city soon endorsed the Bartholomew proposal and urged the Port Authority to meet with Newark's elected officials to explore the possible takeover of the airport and marine facilities. Tobin moved cautiously, however, for he knew that interstate rivalry was ingrained in the hearts and minds of some Newark officials.[25] The Port Authority could properly allocate the staff time and funds needed for a definitive survey only in response to an official request from the city, Tobin said; then it would be "our statutory duty" to comply. The city fathers then reluctantly asked – and the port agency quickly agreed – to go forward with a study.

Now the Port Authority could turn to larger game – New York City's two airports and those who guarded their gates, New York's mayor and its other majordomo, Robert Moses.[26] During his twelve years as mayor, Fiorello H. LaGuardia had fought successfully to displace Newark as the region's primary air traffic center, and in 1944 and 1945 he had pressed for large appropriations to improve LaGuardia Airport and to develop Idlewild – now Kennedy – Airport as the Northeast's greatest air terminal. In January 1946, however, the "Little Flower" was succeeded by William O'Dwyer. The new mayor preferred to husband New York's capital funds for schools, streets, and other urgent needs, and he endorsed an alternative suggested by Moses – the creation of a new City Airport Authority to develop and run the two air terminals. And when a citizens' group proposed Port Authority operation as better, O'Dwyer attacked that view. The mayor said he was "astonished" by the proposal, for it would involve "an abject surrender of the city planning powers" to an agency subject to control by the two governors – thus giving New Jersey's governor the ability to "determine whether Newark instead of Idlewild" would be the region's international air center.[27]

In order to counter the Moses-O'Dwyer plan, the issue would have to be redefined for the business and political leaders of the region. Prompted by the authority's leaders the major daily newspapers began to carry stories that framed the issue of air transport in a larger perspective – as a long-term investment program, requiring millions of dollars before the air terminals could be self-supporting; as a complex package of engineering and administrative challenges, which could best be carried out by an organization with a highly qualified technical staff and a proven track record; and as a regional problem, which could best be resolved through coordinated planning and action, not through narrow competitive actions by individual cities. The Port Authority's commissioners took the lead in preaching the regional gospel, and their speeches against "the barriers of provincialism" were picked up and amplified by friendly reporters and editors.[28]

A bite out of Robert Moses

These energetic efforts did not halt Robert Moses, who, with O'Dwyer's support in hand, strode to Albany to urge that state legislation creating his City Airport Authority be enacted forthwith. By early April 1946 both houses of the legislature had voted for his bill, Governor Dewey had signed it, and three commissioners selected by Moses and the mayor were sworn in and stood poised to take control of LaGuardia and Idlewild airports.

To block Moses' strategy, Tobin would now need to devise alliances with several crucial groups – the airline executives; the investment banking community, whose members would have to purchase the new authority's bonds before the Moses enterprise could sign contracts and move ahead with expansion plans; and influential business and political leaders, whose support for Port Authority operation might permit the bistate agency to gain control of the two New York fields before the City Authority could develop its own plans.

The airlines were readily brought into the Port Authority camp. Their leaders were already wary of the City Airport Authority, for they knew that agency could turn LaGuardia and Idlewild into first-rank postwar airports only if it could tap a large pool of funds. O'Dwyer had already made it clear that city tax revenues could not be counted upon; and the other readily available source – so Moses had argued publicly – would be sharply increased fees, levied by the City Airport Authority on the airlines themselves. In contrast the Port Authority could draw on growing bridge-and-tunnel revenues to build the airfields and terminals the major airlines would need as traffic increased. The airline executives supported the Port Authority cause through informal contacts with business and governmental leaders, and by commenting publicly on that agency's abilities and vision. Invited to view the authority's developing plans at Newark, for example, airline officials expressed "great surprise and gratification" at the Port Authority's ideas for that airport.[29]

Members of the investment community also had their doubts about the City Airport Authority's ability to repay any bonds it attempted to float. In the spring of 1946, Moses urged the City Authority's commissioners to issue $60 million in bonds to finance the development of Idlewild Airport, but financial experts who were friendly to the Port Authority informally contacted O'Dwyer to warn him that the City Authority's solution to the airport problem would probably not work.

Meanwhile, Tobin and Hedden pressed ahead toward completion of the Newark studies. Stories soon reached the press that linked the Port Authority's plans to "25,000 new jobs" in the Newark area and on 30 July Tobin announced a $55-million program for Newark Airport that would "provide one of the greatest airports in the world."[30] In New York, sentiment began to turn away from the Moses-O'Dwyer Airport Authority; and among the city's business leaders, pressure for O'Dwyer to ask the Port Authority to study New York's air terminal needs intensified.

Moses denounced the idea, but he was soon outmaneuvered. Cullman and Tobin had already begun to hold informal meetings with Harry F. Guggenheim, who chaired the City Airport Authority, and in late July he resigned, urging the mayor to "get the airports out of politics" and to turn them over to the Port Authority. Then a leading investment banker, Eugene Black, who had worked closely with Tobin on the fight for tax-exempt bonds, called O'Dwyer and paved the way for a meeting at which the mayor, Tobin, and Cullman explored how the Port Authority might best proceed. On 2 August, 1946, O'Dwyer abandoned Moses' plan and asked the Port Authority to study the takeover of the New York airports, in order to "relieve the city of a tremendous burden of future airport financing."[31]

Tobin and his aides quickly responded and in December the Port Authority announced a $191-million proposal to rehabilitate and expand New York's two airports. Moses' creation, still alive though headless, said it could do the job for less than half the total. For the financial analysts and editorial writers in the region, the choice was easy: the Port Authority had outlined a far more ambitious program, which seemed more likely to meet the needs – or at least the hopes – of the city's business community; and the port agency had great financial resources and staff expertise, especially compared with the untried, unfunded City Airport Authority. Moreover, the Port Authority's extensive efforts to persuade the region's opinion leaders to think in regional rather than narrower terms now paid dividends, as commentators noted that airports are "a regional business" and therefore desirable meat for the Port agency's bistate jaws.[32]

Moses then abandoned his City Airport Authority, but he did not abandon all hope. In early March he persuaded O'Dwyer that the city government should keep the airports and run them with a "bare bones" investment strategy. Again, the Port Authority's legions swung into action: Tobin and Jaffe explained the options in meetings with the editorial writers and commentators, who then attacked O'Dwyer for relying on a "makeshift, patch-and-ragtag program" and urged that the Port Authority do the job. A close friend of Tobin's in the banking community met with O'Dwyer to emphasize the dangers of adding the airport burden to the city's existing debt obligations. And Tobin offered to modify the original Port Authority proposal, providing the city with three-fourths of any net profit at the airports, rather than the 50-50 split that had been proposed initially. On 17 April, 1947, the Port Authority and the city agreed that the bistate agency would develop the city's airports under a fifty-year lease. What the mayor had denounced a year earlier as "abject surrender of the city's planning powers" was now an accomplished fact.[33]

Tasty morsels across the bay

In Newark, meanwhile, the Port Authority's July 1946 plan had met with enthusiastic support among local business leaders and New Jersey editorial writers, but the proposal was vigorously attacked by Newark's elected officials. After several months of negotiation, Tobin was doubtful that the city commissioners would soon agree to Port Authority operation of the local airport and marine terminal. In October, looking back over his agency's long experience, he reminded the Port Authority's commissioners that perseverance, not quick victory, was a hallmark of Port Authority tradition: "The history of every . . . project is one of protracted effort, of temporary set-backs, of opposition that at the time seemed immovable."[34]

Two months later, however, with the proposal for the New York airfields nearly completed, Tobin and his allies began to tighten the noose around the necks of the reluctant Newark city commissioners. The Newark Planning Board's chief consultant, Harland Bartholomew, returned to the city to urge that its air and marine terminals be transferred to the Port Authority in order to save Newark's taxpayers from the burden of $47 million in capital improvements needed at the two facilities. Tobin and his New Jersey commissioners met with Alfred Driscoll, who had been elected governor of the state in November 1946; and in January, Driscoll announced his support for Port Authority operation of the two terminals. Working in harmony, the *Newark News* and Port Authority leaders urged Newark's city fathers to act and warned them that the Port Authority's large plans for Idlewild and LaGuardia airports would soon outstrip other air terminals, which would then be little more than "whistle stops on a suburban line."[35]

Still the city's elected officials hesitated, and early in the fall, Tobin and the New Jersey board members again asked Governor Driscoll to lend a helping hand. Driscoll then reminded the Newark commissioners that they would need his support for state programs to help Newark and other older cities; and in four days of intensive discussions with local leaders, he pressed them to accept the Port Authority's offer.[36]

The combined forces of local, regional, and state pressures overcame the attractions of municipal independence and patronage, and the city fathers finally succumbed. On 22 October, 1947, Newark and the bistate agency signed an agreement leasing the city's airport and marine facilities to the Port Authority for fifty years. Now air transport services on both sides of the Hudson could be planned and developed on a "truly regional basis," Tobin commented to his board. Moreover, Tobin noted, in adding Port Newark, the authority had also taken an important step toward the "unification of pier and waterfront activities" throughout the region.[37]

Across the Country Once Again

As it turned out, the conflicts leading to Port Authority takeover of the region's major air terminals were only the first of several battles that would occupy Tobin and his aides in this new field; and the next conflict came directly on the heels of the 1947 victory. During the initial Port

Authority studies in 1946–7 Tobin had been assured by his staff and outside experts that LaGuardia and Idlewild airports could in time become self-supporting operations, under the leases that the airlines had signed with Mayor LaGuardia. Tobin's assurance that those contracts need not be renegotiated was welcome news to the airline presidents, who knew that Robert Moses wanted to tear up the leases and squeeze more money out of their metallic hides. As a result, the airlines actively supported Tobin's campaign against the Moses stratagems and aided Tobin in the Newark battle as well.

By early 1948, Tobin realized that he had received bad advice. The New York air terminals could not become self-supporting unless the LaGuardia leases were sharply revised to produce more revenue. The airlines objected to any changes, and a long battle ensued, punctuated by Governor Thomas E. Dewey's active intervention to achieve a tentative agreement in 1949; final negotiations were not completed until 1953. Meanwhile, indignant at the intransigence of Juan Trippe, Eddie Rickenbacker, and the other airline executives, Tobin launched a campaign built on his experience in the bond fight of the 1930s; and this brings us to the final case in this chapter.[38]

Until 1948, municipal airports across the United States were operated much as some sports stadiums are today – as "loss leaders" whose operation was subsidized by tax dollars, with the tax burden justified because of the jobs generated at and near the airport, and, because of the advantages of "municipal prestige" and business vitality that allegedly flowed from having an airport and providing local air service to other cities. Most city airports were operated by line departments (marine and aviation, or recreation, typically), whose leaders had little professional or continuing interest in the economics of airport service and who rarely exchanged information on airport costs, services, or possible innovations.

This system served the short-run interests of the major U.S. airlines quite well. The landing charges and other airport service costs (levied by the airports on the airlines) were kept low – about 10 percent of actual costs and about one-fifth of comparable charges at European airports. The major five or six U.S. carriers (Pan Am, Eastern, American, etc.) maintained informal contact with one another as they pressed municipal airports for long-term, low-cost leases; and if a city balked and asked that an airline pay higher rates, the airline would threaten to bypass the city in setting its major route pattern, and that threat was usually enough to quiet the upstart. Moreover, the airport operators were not organized, so that the airlines could readily pick them off one by one in demanding low charges for airport use.

In the longer run, however, the fact that the airports were losing money meant that they could modernize and expand only when the city government was willing to allocate funds to that city department instead of to schools or roads. As air travel expanded after World War II, the airlines were faced – especially in busy air centers like New York, Chicago, and San Francisco – with small, outmoded quarters and with reluctant municipal owners. The ability of the airlines to achieve higher levels of service and profit was, in effect, being undermined by their traditional tendency to measure "success" in airport rates by how low the rates were – that is, by how much the airlines could shift their costs to the city exchequer and other tax sources. In time, certainly, the system would have to be changed; but through the 1940s and early 1950s, the airline policy makers focused on the short-term goal of minimizing charges, even though that undermined their own preferred long-term goals of airport expansion and efficient management of the air terminals.

Enter the Port of New York Authority. Having announced that the airports would be made self-supporting, Tobin and his aides bent every effort in 1946 and 1947 to find ways to ensure that, in a few years, the airports would at least break even financially. Creative efforts were used to add revenue via stores, restaurants and other concessions. But by early 1948 it had become clear that the "LaGuardia leases" would provide far too little return in relation to costs and that higher charges would be needed if a "break-even" operation of the airports were to be achieved. When the airlines resisted renegotiating the leases Tobin did two things: He fought them tooth and nail to break the local leases; and he sent his chief aviation aide, James Buckley, around the country to explain to the operators of the other large airports what the facts of airline charges and strategies were.

Tobin and Buckley then took the initiative (in 1948) in establishing an organization of airport executives – the Airport Operators Council (AOC) – which provided a way for the municipal operators to exchange information and bring counterpressure on the airlines. Within two or three years devising strategy and exchanging information through the AOC, the municipal agencies had recruited skilled executives and negotiators and had achieved the upper hand in setting the charges that the airlines paid for airport use. Led by the Port Authority's newly hired real estate expert, Robert Curtiss, the AOC also helped the airport officials to redesign airport facilities so that substantial income would flow in from concessions. The net result at the large airports has been to reverse the outflow of tax dollars to subsidize airports and, instead, at many airports, to generate a net income.

The long-term result is that this more "entrepreneurial" approach to airport management has permitted airports to modernize and expand more rapidly than would have been possible under the old "tax drain" approach and that airlines have, in terms of their own profitability, benefited. In the context of this study of the Port of New York Authority, the argument is that one of the major ways in which Tobin and his aides have had an impact on the American economic system has been their leader-

ship, through the AOC, in altering the attitudes and relationships that
have shaped the development of airport services and the air transport
system nationally.

Leadership, Coalitions, and Their Impact

> [For] officials at every level . . . a keen appreciation of the real components
> of their organization is the beginning of wisdom. These components will be
> found to stretch far beyond the government payroll.[39]

Austin Tobin and his colleagues found it easy to think and to act in these
expansive terms. Reaching far beyond their own agency, they gathered
sympathetic attention and then support, developed alliances with private
interests and other public officials and waged battle – for programs that
would strengthen their agency and their own capacity to function and
that would, as they viewed it, strengthen the economy of the New York
region and perhaps aid the vitality of American society more generally.

In *City Limits*, Paul Peterson argues that the transportation and other
development-oriented programs of public authorities and city agencies
are examples of "consensual politics," in which "conflict within the city
tends to be minimal, decision-making processes tend to be closed . . .
[and] local support is broad and continuous." Indeed, Peterson singles
out the activities of Tobin's Port Authority and Robert Moses' agencies,
especially as they operated before the 1960s, as exemplars of his theme
– that there is "no place" in this policy arena for "contentious group
conflict."[40]

As the early pages of this chapter indicate, consensual politics is what
the Port of New York Authority often preferred and sometimes was able
to obtain. But the charm of Tobin's rhetoric, which Peterson quotes in
his text, seems to have diverted that careful observer from a conflict-filled
reality.[41] In the airport and seaport cases in this chapter and in other
initiatives during these postwar decades, Tobin and his associates were
compelled to battle jealous local governmental officials, private corporations, and local residents who viewed the authority's proposals as
dangerous to their own political and economic advantages. So the agency
found it essential to enter the political arena and to devise and nourish
coalitions that could overwhelm these opponents. Sometimes, too, the
opposing coalition was stronger still, and the Port Authority lost.[42]

As Clarence Stone argues in the opening chapter of *The Politics of Urban
Development*, these patterns are found in cities and regions across the
country. Economic development proposals and programs often generate
sharp conflict, rather than widespread agreement on what policies will
best benefit the entire city. Certainly the pattern of alliances in the airport
and Newark seaport cases supports Stone's position. It is worth noting,

however, that in some cases described in this chapter, each city (and there are dozens of cities and towns involved) *does* speak with a single voice. When faced with a strong external threat, a city – like a nation – is more likely to adopt a unified position; and in the cases of the fight for tax-exempt bonds and the problem of airline leases, the cities could use the perception of a common enemy to facilitate cooperation with others in the same plight.

Moreover, these alliances were built on long-term advantages, and the coalitions have survived. The Airport Operators Council continues to be a central clearinghouse for information on airport fees, terminal design, airport security, and other issues. The Conference on State Defense, which was active throughout the 1940s against Treasury Department efforts to reduce or eliminate tax exemption for municipal bonds, was revived in the 1950s; and subsequently, its members have pursued the same protective goals into the 1980s through joint action of several related organizations, in which Port Authority staff members have central roles.[43]

In contrast, the coalition that supported the Port Authority's takeover of the air and sea terminals was a temporary alliance of business leaders in Newark and New York, of newspaper editors and civic associations, together with the airline executives and a few elected officials, which dissolved in 1947, once the Port Authority's goals had been achieved. Or perhaps that misstates the central point: Better phrased, one might say, "The alliance is ended; long live the alliance." The particular coalition that Tobin constructed to attack the bastions of Newark, New York City, and Emperor Moses ended once the airports and Newark's seaport had been won. But those victories did not suspend Norton Long's "iron law of alliance-building": No government agency will endure and thrive if it does not continually reach out for broader support in its relevant communities. As the Port Authority pressed forward with new plans and projects in subsequent years, it called again and again on these allies of the 1940s, adding and dropping particular groups as their interests coincided or were likely to collide. And during periods of quiescence, Tobin and his staff maintained continual, friendly contact with those whose active support would often be needed in future battles – business leaders in Newark and New York, the editorial boards of the *New York Times* and several other daily newspapers, the leaders of the Regional Plan Association and other influential civic groups, the two governors and their staffs, and key legislative leaders in Albany and Trenton. In time, even Robert Moses was neutralized and added to that friendly coterie.[44]

The Port Authority's successes were not, of course, an unmixed blessing. To gain control of New York City's airports and Newark's airport and marine facilities was to remove important areas of policy choice from the direct responsibility of local citizens and their elected officials. These outcomes may be defended on the grounds of increased efficiency and benefit to the local and regional economy, but the trade-off is a loss in terms of democratic politics.[45]

However, in the other two cases considered in this chapter – the fight over tax-exempt bonds and the creation of AOC – the ledger seems more clearly favorable. While there are certainly trade-offs that could be examined, the outcome in both might be claimed as a victory for local political vitality and economic strength, as well as providing clear benefits to the Port Authority.

If one asks, "Under what conditions are coalitions likely to be formed?" the cases discussed in this chapter suggest the wide variety of motivations and organizing efforts that would need to be described in order fully to answer this question. Looked at another way, however, these cases have important elements in common, suggesting a few generalizations that might hold across a wide range of situations.

To note the dissimilarities first: The Conference on State Defense arose as a *defensive* response to a threat from the national government – a court suit and a congressional bill, in the late 1930s, that would have ended tax exemption for municipal bonds. The second case, involving an alliance that supported the transfer of the region's major airports and Newark's marine terminals to the Port Authority, was essentially an *offensive* coalition, bent on changing the traditional pattern of policy making for these important facilities of commerce and local pride. The third, focused on the creation of a national association of local airport operators, was motivated by *both dangers and opportunities*. The local operators were municipal agencies and authorities, which met continuing operating deficits through grants and other subsidies paid for largely by the local taxpayer. That source was becoming restive, and city mayors resisted airport managers' pleas when schools, highways, and hospitals were competing for the same monies. The opportunity was that these airfield managers could expand their airport enterprises and become municipal heroes, if they could pool their political power and use business strategies in order to exact larger fees from the airlines and to build rental income through the creation of thriving restaurants and other concessions in each terminal.

Those elements are dissimilar; but others are not. In all three cases, one individual and his close associates played a central role. The coalitions formed *not* because of unplanned collisions and conjunctions of need, nor because several "similarly situated" people met to explore important issues confronting them and then concluded, through reasoned examination, that they would all benefit through allied action. Instead, the personal drive and needs and vision of one man were crucial; and his analysis and strategies for action described a sort of "rational model of coalition-building." Austin Tobin identified goals that were important to him personally and strategies to achieve those goals – to break free from the "backwater image" of a "real estate lawyer" by challenging FDR's taxation scheme; to make the work of the Port Authority more interesting, and his own job more challenging, by wresting airports and marine terminals from the mayors of New York and Newark and from Robert Moses; to make the airports pay their own way and to give the Eddie Rickenbackers of the world a well-deserved punch in the snout, by challenging the airlines' monopoly strategy with countervailing political and economic power. Tobin then inventoried the obstacles to be overcome in order to achieve his preferred goals and identified the strategies needed to surmount those obstacles. Among those strategies were the creation of alliances with other groups and institutions that might benefit if the objectives of Tobin and the Port Authority were achieved. To Tobin and his aides, therefore, the "mobilization of resources" to achieve their goals entailed – in these three cases and in essentially all others during the Port Authority's history – not only the allocation of staff time and money and the preparation of technical plans to guide and support their efforts but also, as a central element, the building of external coalitions of support.[46]

Tobin's ability to construct alliances and act successfully in these and other cases was not, certainly, entirely of his own making. Even exceptional leaders depend on opportunities provided to them by external factors and by the special strengths of their own organizations; and they are also constrained by traditions, economic trends, and technological forces that they can only marginally affect. Thus, the capacity of Tobin and his Port Authority to behave as "rational actors" was greatly facilitated by certain advantages that his agency shared with other semi-independent public authorities, but with few other governments in the New York region. Most of the agency's income was gathered via tolls and rents at its own facilities, which meant that its officials could target funds for study, alliance building, and other action without waiting for approval from legislative appropriations committees or executive budget officers. Policy making was lodged in a board of twelve commissioners, appointed for overlapping six-year terms, which provided some insulation from elected officials and some advantage, too, in attracting high-quality staff members interested in working on complex long-term projects, who could be confident that the authority would be able to sustain a focus on a program through several years despite the vagaries of politics.

Moreover, several of the agency's early projects were visible, highly regarded structures: the George Washington Bridge, the longest single span crossing in the world; the Bayonne Bridge, which won prizes for its design; and the less glamorous but crucially important Holland and Lincoln tunnels. So the Port Authority had, by the late 1930s, earned a reputation among business leaders and the general public as an agency that "got things done", and that reputation provided a basis for access to decision makers in the region and for obtaining cooperation from others around the country who were helpful in the three cases described in this chapter and in others in later decades.[47]

Even with these advantages, Tobin and his aides probably could not have wrested the airports and the marine terminals from Newark and New York City if their city governments had not suffered from great weaknesses – a tradition of patronage and poor management at their seaports, and legal limitations on municipal debt that constrained their ability to float bonds for capital improvements.

Had these factors been otherwise Tobin's successes during the 1930s and 1940s might have been modest indeed. However, once presented with interesting opportunities, as Herbert Kaufman comments, Tobin "seized every one of them with a sure hand."[48] And when he grasped these opportunities, Tobin carried the issue forward in ways that offer lessons for local public officials and for governmental executives generally. He and his aides identified potential sources of political support in the business community and in civic associations, at the state capital, and in other cities. They gathered detailed information on the specific advantages that would flow to their potential allies from adopting the Port Authority's preferred approach and on the drawbacks of other alternatives. They employed experts to analyze development options, markets, and revenue flows and to provide the valuable stamp of objective approval for their plans. They worked closely with local reporters and editors and, through newspaper articles and editorials, made a complex and confusing world of regional growth and political choices much clearer – and more favorable to their own designs.[49] And so they helped the New York region prosper, though at some cost to local control, and built broader networks that could help other cities. And the Port Authority prospered too – its leaders gathering political experience and reputation, which in the 1950s and beyond would permit them to build further coalitions and add still other projects – new marine terminals, bus and rail programs, highway projects, and large office buildings – to the vast Port Authority diadem.

Acknowledgments

This chapter is drawn from a study of leadership strategies, innovation, and accountability at the Port of New York Authority during the years 1932 to 1972. Financial support has been provided by the Lavanburg, Sloan, and Daniel and Florence Guggenheim Foundations. The author acknowledges with thanks the assistance of the following individuals who were directly involved in some of the events or who were closely associated with the officials whose work is described in this chapter: Harland Bartholomew, Charles Breitel, Joseph Byrne, Jr., Stacy Tobin Carmichael, Mortimer Edelstein, John Fitzgerald, Roger Gilman, Daniel Goldberg, Sidney Goldstein, Lee Jaffe, Doris Landre, Edward Olcott,

Harvey Sherman, Austin Tobin, Jr., Rosaleen Skehan Tobin, Robert Tuttle, Robert Wagner, Sr., and John Wiley. Helpful comments on drafts of this paper were also provided by Erwin Bard, Fred Greenstein, Erwin Hargrove, Pendleton Herring, Herbert Kaufman, Duane Lockard, Alpheus Mason, Richard Stillman, Clarence Stone, and Martha Weinberg. In gathering and organizing the materials, the assistance of Bevin Carmichael and Julianne Bauer is gratefully acknowledged.

Some of the materials in this chapter are taken from a longer essay published by the Johns Hopkins University Press in *Innovation: A Biographical Perspective on Entrepreneurs in Government*, edited by Jameson W. Doig and Erwin C. Hargrove.

Notes

1   The political and legal conflicts during these years are described in Erwin W. Bard, *The Port of New York Authority* (New York: Columbia University Press 1942) chap. 1.

2   The quotations are from the interstate compact, reprinted on pp. 329–39, ibid.

3   For additional information on Tobin's early years and his developing social and political values see the chapter on Tobin in *Leadership and Innovation*, ed. Jameson W. Doig and Erwin C. Hargrove (Baltimore, Md.: Johns Hopkins University Press, 1987).

4   In addition to devising the interstate-compact strategy which led to the creation of the Port of New York Authority, Cohen had done path-breaking work on the arbitration of commercial disputes.

5   The Holland Tunnel connected Canal Street, in lower Manhattan, to Jersey City; and the George Washington Bridge ran from 178th Street to Fort Lee, New Jersey. When completed, the Lincoln Tunnel would join midtown Manhattan at Fortieth Street and Weehawken on the Jersey side. For additional discussion of these developments see Michael N. Danielson and Jameson W. Doig, *New York: The Politics of Urban and Regional Development* (Berkeley: University of California Press, 1982) chap. 6; and Bard, *Port of New York Authority*, chap. 7.

6   Bard, *Port of New York Authority*, p. 266.

7   The unusual character of the Port Authority as a governmental agency generated much controversy and required much legal nimbleness. The authority was the first agency in the United States to be constructed as a semi-independent "authority" and also the "first instrumentality with continuing administrative functions to be created by an interstate compact, thus serving as the agent of more than one sovereign" (Joseph Lesser, "Great Legal Cases Which Have Shaped the Port Authority." *Port Authority Review* 7 (1969): 5; Bard, *Port of New York Authority*, p. 280). Consequently its staff was continually confronted with complex problems of legal drafting, and many of its actions generated court suits by those who argued that the agency was exceeding its appropriate, but not yet clearly defined, powers.

8   *Bush Terminal Co.* v. *City of New York and Port of New York Authority*, Sup. Ct., N.Y. Co., 1934. The suit alleged that a mixed terminal and office building

exceeded the authority's statutory powers and that any such facility should pay full real estate taxes, rather than a lower amount, which the authority would normally pay in lieu of taxes.

9   The discussion of Tobin's attitudes and actions during the 1930s is based on interviews with those who worked closely with him in the Law Department during these years.

10 *Helvering* v. *Gerhardt*, 304 U.S. 405, 1938; *Graves* v. *N.Y. ex. rel. O'Keefe*, 306 U.S. 466, 1939.

11 "President Seeks Tax Immunity End . . ." *New York Times*, 18 Jan. 1939. Discussion of the bond issue is based on the author's interviews no. 22, 42, 51, and 201; J. H. Cohen, *They Builded Better Than They Knew* (New York: Julian Messner Inc., 1946), pp. 317–28, 357–58; Bard, *Port of New York Authority*, pp. 276–77.

12 Because of budgetary restrictions set by legislative committees and central budget offices, it was difficult for state agencies and local officials to shift funds and personnel in the middle of a budgetary year; the Port Authority could reallocate funds and shift duties readily, as long as the Board of Commissioners approved.

13 See Brief for Petitioner, in *Commissioner of Internal Revenue* v. *Shamberg's Estate*, 144 F. 2d 998, 2d Cir., 1944. The Treasury Department also tried again in 1941 and 1942 to obtain congressional action, but without success. See, e.g., "States Will Fight Federal Tax Plan," *New York Times*, 10 Jan. 1942.

14 As Erwin Bard concluded in his definitive study of the authority's first two decades: "Its policy has become totally receptive rather than aggressive." The agency sat passively, Bard concluded, "on dead center" (*Port of New York Authority*, pp. 320, 327).

15 "Howard liked new things," an associate recalled, "and he loved to bring new things into being" (interview 68). See also the extended review of his activities in "Howard S. Cullman, 80, of Port Authority, Dies," *New York Times*, 30 June 1972.

16 As these comments suggest, "entrepreneurial leadership" – as the term is used in this essay – involves both the identification of new possibilities *and* sustained efforts to implement the new designs. This perspective is used in a comparative study of governmental leadership that is being conducted by a group of researchers with grants from the Alfred Sloan and the Lavanburg foundations; for further discussion of the concept see chapter one in Doig and Hargrove, *Leadership and Innovation*.

17 As Tobin commented some years later: "Very few authorities are so completely subject to review by the elected representatives of the people. This is a complete answer to the alleged autonomy of the Port Authority" (statement at the joint public hearing of New York State Assembly Committee and New Jersey Legislative Commission, 5 Mar. 1971, p. 36).

18 Austin Tobin, "Management Structure and Operating Policies in Public Authorities: The Port of New York Authority" (1963 speech), p 3.

19 To use an analogy suggested by one close observer of the Port Authority's activities at the state capitals, the Port Authority chef would appear before an assembled throng of hungry legislators, one of whom calls out, "What is on the menu today?" "Excellent bluefish, sir!" responds chef Tobin. "OK, but I think I'd like beef," the legislator replies. "Ah, but the bluefish is

excellent, and it's free. And there isn't anything else on the menu today,"
the chef explains. "We'll take bluefish!" the legislators cry in unison.

20 The quotation and other information in this paragraph are taken from the
Tobin-Hedden report on the "port planning program," dated June 1943. I
am indebted to Edward S. Olcott, who held Hedden's post in recent years
for locating the document.

21 These included the George Washington Bridge and the Lincoln and Holland
tunnels between New Jersey and Manhattan, plus three bridges between
New Jersey and Staten Island (Bayonne, Goethals and Outerbridge).

22 Other activities of Tobin's years as executive director (1942–72) are
described in the chapter on Tobin in Doig and Hargrove, *Leadership and
Innovation*, and in a separate paper on the final decade, J. W. Doig, "In
Treacherous Waters" (mimeographed, 1986).

23 "She always had the facts," recalled one of the region's best veteran
reporters, "and if you needed more, she would get them and call you right
back . . . She was head and shoulders above anyone else in the public-rela-
tions field."

24 Quotations in the text are from Bartholomew's draft report, October 1945.
The report also noted that the Port Authority, in contrast with the Newark
city government, was in a financial position to underwrite large construction projects; this statement was based on the authority's own projections
of postwar traffic on the bridges and tunnels.

25 Tobin had received a forceful reminder of Newark's concerns only a few
months earlier, when the possibility of Port Authority operation of its
airport and seaport had been suggested publicly by Vice Chairman Byrne.
Newark Commissioner John A. Brady had attacked the proposal as "municipal suicide" which would cause Newark's destiny as a great air and marine
terminal center to "vanish into the stratosphere." He also criticized the
authority's "powerful, arrogant administrative staff" for its tendency to treat
Newark as a "service station for Manhattan" (see "Brady Attacks Port
Proposal," *Newark News*, 30 Apr. 1945).

26 The discussion below draws upon Herbert Kaufman's detailed case study
"Gotham in the Air Age," in *Public Administration and Policy Development*, ed.
Harold Stein (New York: Harcourt, Brace, 1952), pp. 143–97; and Port
Authority documents. Robert Caro's massive study of Moses includes only
a few lines on this important Moses venture and defeat (*The Power Broker:
Robert Moses and the Fall of New York* [New York: Knopf, 1974], pp. 763,
766–67).

27 Quoted in *New York Times*, 9 Feb. 1946.

28 See, e.g., "Regional Air Plan to Solve New York – Newark Issue?" *Christian
Science Monitor*, 3 Jan. 1946, "Area Airport Authorities Seen Needed in U.S.,"
New York Herald Tribune, 13 Jan. 1946; "City Airports and State Lines," *New
York Herald Tribune*, 13 May 1946.

29 See "Airlines Fear Moses Authority," *New York Post*, 6 Feb. 1946; "Air
Lanes," *Newark News*, 18 Mar. 1946.

30 See, e.g., "25,000 in Port Jobs Predicted." *Newark News*, 27 July 1946;
"Newark Airport Projected to Rival Idlewild," *New York Herald Tribune*, 25
July, 1946. Tobin announced at the same time an $11-million plan for Port

Newark (see Port of New York Authority, *Development of Newark Airport and Seaport*, July 1946).

31   See "Airport Proposal Derided by Moses," *New York Times*, 25 July 1946; "O' Dwyer Invites Port Authority to Run City Airports," *New York Herald Tribune*, 3 Aug. 1946, Kaufman, "Gotham in the Air Age," pp. 171ff.

32   E.g., Leslie Gould, "Port Authority Offers Better Airport Deal," *New York Journal American*, 14 Feb. 1947.

33   The negotiations are summarized in Kaufman, "Gotham in the Air Age," p. 190. The "makeshift" quotation in the text is from Allan Keller, "City Air Leadership Periled." *New York World-Telegram*, 20 Mar. 1947.

34   Weekly Report to the Commissioners, 4 Oct. 1946. By 1946, only Chairman Cullman had served as long as Tobin (both having joined the agency in 1927), and eight of the twelve members had served less than five years each.

35   The comment is from a speech by Cullman, which is quoted in "Time for Decision," an editorial in the *Newark News*, 19 May 1947; see also editorials in the *Newark News*, 23 Jan. and 28 Mar. 1947.

36   See "The Wider View" (editorial), *Newark News*, 12 Oct. 1947; Driscoll's letter to the mayor of Newark, reprinted in the Weekly Report, 18 Oct. 1947; and Tobin's summary of the governor's efforts, in the Weekly Report, 25 Oct. 1947.

37   The quotations are taken from Tobin's Weekly Report to the Commissioners, 25 Oct. 1947.

38   The information in this section is drawn mainly from interviews with those active on "both sides" of the controversy in the 1940s and 1950s, together with documents in Port Authority files. For useful published information see Joseph L. Nicholson, *Air Transportation Management* (New York: Wiley, 1951), chap. 6; Frederick L. Bird, *A Study of the Port of New York Authority* (New York: Dun & Bradstreet, 1949), chaps. 12–14; John R. Wiley, *Airport Administration* (Westport Conn.: Eno Foundation, 1981), chaps. 7 and 8; *Airport System Development* (Washington, D.C.: U.S. Office of Technology Assessment, 1984), chaps. 6 and 7.

39   Norton Long, "Power and Administration," *Public Administration Review* 9 (Autumn 1949): 259.

40   Paul E. Peterson, *City Limits* (Chicago: University of Chicago Press, 1981), pp. 132–34.

41   "An authority is designed," explains Tobin, "to put revenue producing public facilities on their own feet . . . ; to free them from political interference," and to permit them to use "the administrative standards of a well-managed private corporation" in carrying out their duties (quoted in Peterson, *City Limits*, p. 134).

42   E.g, in the 1940s and 1950s the Port Authority's proposal to take over the Hoboken piers was blocked for several years because of local opposition; its plan to rehabilitate and operate New York City's piers was defeated; its proposal for a Manhattan bus terminal was held up for several years because of opposition from Robert Moses and the Greyhound Bus Company, and its plan for a large jetport in New Jersey was permanently blocked through the efforts of local residents and others. One important source of resistance in these cases was the perception of the Port Authority as an "outside" agency, reaching for valuable local property; there were other important factors,

too, which made it difficult for the Port Authority to employ the "consensual" political mode.

43 The Airport Operators Council is now the AOCI (International). The AOCI, the American Association of Port Authorities, and the Municipal Finance Officers Association (MFOA) are the main members of the alliance that has defended tax exemption during recent congressional deliberations; a Port Authority official chairs the relevant MFOA committee. Of course the ability of each city to speak with a single voice on these issues has been aided by the fact there are few citizens within any of the cities who perceive their financial or other interests as being harmed by the policies advocated by the Port Authority and the other members of these coalitions.

44 See the chapter on Tobin in Doig and Hargrove, *Leadership and Innovation*, for a summary of these patterns during the 1950s and 1960s.

45 For further discussion see Annmarie H. Walsh, *The Public's Business* (Cambridge, Mass.: MIT Press, 1978), esp. chap. 12, and Jameson W. Doig, "Answering the Grand Inquisitor." More generally, see Theodore J. Lowi, *The End of Liberalism*, 2d ed. (New York: Norton, 1979), pp. 177ff., Clarence N. Stone, "Efficiency Versus Social Learning," *Policy Studies Review* 4 (Feb. 1985): 484–96; Michael Walzer, *Radical Principles* (New York: Basic Books, 1980).

46 For further discussion of the conditions under which coalitions are likely to form see the analysis of business-government relationships in Dallas, in the chapter by Stephen L. Elkin, as well as James Q. Wilson, *Political Organizations* (New York: Basic Books, 1973), pp. 267–72, 275–77, 317ff.; and Barbara Hinckley, *Coalitions and Politics* (New York: Harcourt Brace Jovanovich, 1981), chap. 4.

47 On these general and specific advantages see J. W. Doig, "'If I See a Murderous Fellow Sharpening a Knife Cleverly . . .': The Wilsonian Dichotomy and the Public Authority Tradition," *Public Administration Review* 43 (1983): 292–304.

48 Letter from Kaufman to Doig, 14 Sept. 1984.

49 In their discussions with newspaper editors, in their speeches, and in their public reports, the creation and nourishment of political symbols was a central strategy. Like David Lilienthal's "Grassroots Democracy," the themes of "nonpolitical administration" and projects created "without cost to the taxpayer" were a significant part of the armor and the lance used by Austin Tobin and his agency, as they fended off politicians seeking favors and critics seeking assistance for programs that would not be financially self-supported.

Part V

A Discussion on Gender

Introduction

Gender has emerged as a powerful and transformative theme in urban planning in recent years. The forces behind an emerging feminist planning theory are numerous, among them the larger feminist movement, the entry of women into the labor force in large numbers, the growth in the number of women planners and professors, parallels between the civil rights movement and the feminist movement, and links with intellectual movements such as postmodernism and multiculturalism. The feminist perspective addresses many issues of urban life: the differing uses of urban space by men and women; the threats to personal safety of women in cities; structural discrimination against women in economic development; the transportation needs of women beyond the traditional "journey to work"; and the impacts of traditional suburban housing on antiquated nuclear family structures.

Feminist Perspective issues

The readings in this section address the specific issue of how emerging feminist ideas are changing planning theory. In particular, these readings examine how basic epistemological and methodological issues in planning theory should change to address previous shortcomings in traditional theories. They all originally appeared in a 1992 symposium published by the Italian English-language journal, *Planning Theory Newsletter*.

Marsha Ritzdorf, in "Feminist Thoughts on the Theory and Practice of Planning," provides an overview of the rising feminist interest in planning and criticizes planning theory as a particularly male bastion. She addresses the implicit and explicit set of values and attitudes found in planning theory about the role of women. She also notes how the feminist perspective merges the boundaries between the personal and the political, and between domestic work and wage work. It rejects the rational model of planning in favor of a model that recognizes different voices and thus draws upon both postmodernism and multiculturalism. Process, flexibility, communication, and negotiation take precedence over rigid planning principles and theory divorced from practice.

In "Knowing Women/Planning Theory," Helen Liggett argues that feminist theory, like advocacy planning before it, offers a foundation to redefine the planning discipline. She discusses three areas of possible change. The first is to give equal value to the work of women, both in the general work force and in the field of planning. The second is to recognize women's experience as an important element in making plans, for example, the differing transportation and community needs of women. The third is to recognize the importance of reproduction. The goal is to challenge the kind of planning logic that once excluded women and to explore whether there can be differences without hierarchy and exclusion.

In "Planning in a Different Voice," Susan Fainstein addresses both the power and the shortcomings of feminist planning theorists focusing on difference. Though the subjectivist politics of difference offer much promise, Fainstein warns that an uncritical acceptance of this postmodernist perspective runs the risk of losing the original progressive values of feminist planning. Specifically, feminist planners should not reject rationality, for this Enlightenment thinking has been the basis for progressive social transformation in the Western world.

Beth Moore Milroy also addresses this troublesome issue in "Some Thoughts About Difference and Pluralism." She examines exactly what is meant by this concept of "difference" and how it should be taken into account in planning practice. Milroy distinguishes between two possible origins of difference, juridical and existential. The first difference is the inequality that arises from social arrangements. The second difference arises from more fundamental sexual origins, experiences, and symbols.

In "Feminist and Planning Theories: The Epistemological Connection," John Friedmann considers the issue of power – and women's subjugation to men – as the central concern of feminist practice. He discusses two feminist contributions of importance for planning theory, especially for Friedmann's radical approach planning. The first is the question of gender differences in moral judgments, contrasting the social relationships of caring and solidarity versus the ethics of individual, competitive justice. The second is the emerging feminist methodology that emphasizes difference, consciousness raising, challenges to traditional objectivity, and the emancipatory power of practice.

In "Feminist Theory and Planning Theory: The Epistemological Linkages," Leonie Sandercock and Ann Forsyth outline a feminist epistemology for planning that departs from objective, scientific ways of knowing. They emphasize the oral tradition of storytelling, its companion activity of listening, intuitive knowing, innovative forms of symbolic communication, and "learning by doing." Feminist planning theory should therefore not only be critical but also autobiographical and emancipatory. However, their postmodern awareness of other cultures and identities prevents Sandercock and Forsyth from an absolute embrace of this epistemology. They argue that there is no single unitary theory of planning and conclude that "planners must, finally, learn to live with unstable paradigms."

20

Feminist Thoughts on the Theory and Practice of Planning

Marsha Ritzdorf

High on the list of popular non fiction books during 1990 was Professor Deborah Tannen's *You Just Don't Understand: Men and Women in Conversation*. Tannen, a sociolinguist, decided to enter the dialogue on gender and language "because the risk of ignoring differences is greater than the danger of naming them. Sweeping something big under the rug doesn't make it go away; it trips you up and sends you sprawling when you venture across the room" (1990; 16).

When theory is put forth in general categorical language as "gender blind," it denies that the analysis is most often based on the experience of white, middle-class and upper-class men in Western societies (Forsyth 1990). While gender is not the only possible category of analysis (certainly class and race are highly significant), it is a category that has been virtually invisible in planning theory and practice.

As Okin sums up in her book on women in Western political thought, "it is by no means a simple matter to integrate the female half of the human race into a tradition of political theory which has defined them and intra-familial relationships as outside the scope of the political." (Okin in Nelson 1989: 286). At the heart of all feminist work is a unifying idea: that gender is a significant aspect of the cultural, social, political, and economic construction of reality. Feminist thought rejects the facile

Reprinted by permission from *Planning Theory* 7/8, 1992.

explanation that theory can be or is "neutral," and thus rejects the suppression of differences.

Whether or not gender is explicitly mentioned in a theoretical construct, there is an implicit, if not explicit, set of values and attitudes about the role of women that frame the analysis. Three root assumptions are central to feminist work. While all three might not be present in an individual piece of work, at least one of the following will frame the inquiry: (1) the position that women are exploited, oppressed or devalued by society; (2) an interest on the part of the feminist thinker in changing the conditions of women's lives; and (3) the assertion that traditional, still dominant theory, research, and practice ignore or justify inappropriate and/or exploitative treatment of women (adapted from Aker et al. 1983)

Most feminist inquiry thus rejects current male-centered epistemological points of view. Feminist theory rejects the pretense of value-free research in favor of consciously valued thought, arguing that the supposedly value-free, neutral science model is actually male-defined (Hess and Ferree 1987). In addition, many feminists assert that the best research ideas are those that bridge the gap between theory and practice (Hesse and Ferree 1987), acknowledge that personal experience and grounded research are valuable theory-building and research tools, and do not attempt to achieve a neutral stance for the researcher toward the research.

Value-free Research? [handwritten marginal note]

Planning Theory and Feminist Planning

Planning theory, as pointed out by Sandercock and Forsyth (1990) remains a male bastion. "Of all the fields within planning that of theory remains arguably the most male dominated, the least influenced by an awareness of the importance of gender" (Sandercock and Forsyth 1990: 3). Still, planning theorists, like feminist theorists, do not agree on any one theory. Instead, competing theoretical perspectives are under discussion, and it is fair to say that their differential meaning to and impact upon men and women have not been explored in the literature. Sandercock and Forsyth nonetheless suggest that there are diverse intersections where the analysis of gender is relevant: "the economic status of women, how women are located in and move through space, the connection between capitalist production and patriarchal relationships and between 'public' and 'domestic' life, how women know about the world and about what is good and what forms of communication women are most comfortable with or most threatened by and more" (1990: 4).

In the 1970s and 1980s, literature about women and planning flourished. This literature primarily focused on policy and practice. Gerda

Wekerle's (1980) edited volume *New Space for Women* was instrumental in defining women and environments research. A special edition of *Signs* (the premier feminist journal) devoted to women and the city appeared the same year. These collections addressed women's activities in the urban environment. The pieces acknowledged that women have different daily life activities and patterns than men and therefore make different use of the environment and encounter different problems than do their male counterparts. The authors asserted that understanding and responding to these differences are important in developing the community. Their analyses of urban and suburban structures and the policy-making process from a feminist perspective took into account the totality of people's lives and the ways in which men and women are treated and situated differently in political, social, economic, and physical space.

Writing about feminist advocacy theory in 1986, Jacqueline Leavitt asserted: "Planners assume a value set that is inherently and historically masculine . . . the overriding goals and objectives are more likely to be shaped by men than women politicians, male corporate heads rather than female" (187). However, in addition to the growing body of literature, demographic changes during these two decades made it almost impossible for planning practitioners to continue to ignore the differences between men and women's lives in the community. A recent census report indicates that 49 percent of mothers of one-year-old babies are currently working outside their homes, and it is estimated that 80 percent of mothers of children under the age of eighteen will be in the work force by the year 2000.

A growing body of feminist planning academicians see to it that these issues are discussed in the literature and at conferences. While much of their work contains important theoretical statements that are widely quoted in other feminists' research, their papers are rarely presented on theory panels at the conferences or cited in traditional planning theorists' work.

Contemporary planning theory, according to Beauregard, is anchored in values and perspectives that emphasize a "belief in the transferability of knowledge across time, space and social groups" and "an authoritarian stance that assumes an Archimedean position from which to speak" (Beauregard 1990: 2). This means that it is strongly committed to functional rationality as the basis of human action and to the use of abstract "principles and rights as the criteria for decision making" (Beauregard 1990: 2). Only a small number of planning theorists are questioning the notion of objectivity, neutrality, and the maintenance of a critical distance. It is little wonder that most feminist planners have steered clear of theory as their primary field of discourse in planning education.

Feminist political theorists debate the scope and meaning of citizenship and the nature of political action for women in contemporary society.

Writing about the meaning of feminist citizenship, Jones (1988) suggests that the following themes are important to understanding women's citizenship: Expanding the Meaning of Political Action, Personal Commitment and Connection, and the Search for New Forms of Organization. Since planning is inherently political, planning theory and practice need to attend to this debate as well. The boundaries between the personal and the political are merged for women. Women are generally interested in expanding the range, intensity, and modes of action in planning. They are interested in holistic approaches to problems and cooperative problem solving and see issues impacting their bodies, their families, and their neighborhoods as both political and personal.

Women will often use language that is familial to discuss public actions. Words like "nurturing" appear often in their discussions. In addition, the issues they feel are important are, for most men, far removed from their primary concerns in the public policy arena. The language and issues of family life are significant to the majority of women. Reproductive and domestic activities are inextricably bound up with traditional economic production in their assessments of policy and their analysis of needed change.

While the above is true for most women whether or not they are feminists in their orientation, female planners and planning scholars have to make a conscious choice about their "identity". A female planner who chooses to approach planning from a feminist perspective must be ready to be labeled and have her professional credibility, intelligence or research methodology questioned by hostile, or at best indifferent, colleagues. After all, if one admits they have a perspective, they are denying the myth of neutral, technological rationality on which many planners depend for their identity. "In the planning profession, to be a feminist or interested in women's issues is to reject explicitly much of the professional socialization of one's training," (Leavitt 1986: 185).

While Leavitt was referring to planning practitioners, the same pressures to conform exist in academia. For feminist thought truly to impact planning theory will require an acceptance, at a minimum, of the notions of pluralistic thought and personal connection. It will mean a rejection of the rational model in favor of a model acknowledging that there are different ways of "knowing" the world and constructing answers to problems. It means a model based on flexibility rather than immutable principles of the "right" and "wrong" decision. Certainly, the new emphasis on negotiation and mediation as essential tools of the practitioner's trade are indications that flexibility is becoming more important in planning decision making.

Through their life experiences women have learned that the end result of an action always reflects the personal experiences of those involved in the decision making. A simple example of this is the lack of attention to rape and personal safety in environmental design and planning, where most practitioners are men. For women, a poorly lit street, an ill-designed or poorly placed parking lot, even too much landscaping, can be a life-or-death issue.

Women are highly sensitive to the misuse of power and arbitrary claims of rational or correct behavior or answers. Process is extremely important. More and more frequently, the importance of process is acknowledged in many contemporary planning theorists' work. I doubt, however, that by process these theorists are thinking about the totality of life experiences that the planner or theorist brings to her or his work.

Planning theory is grounded in many of the principles that feminist theorists reject outright, making it difficult to find a common ground. In addition to the feminist acceptance of a relationship between research subject and object, feminist theorists question the existence of universally applicable principles and do not regard rationality as the basis of most human action. They are generally uninterested in knowledge only for its own sake and want to see how it will be applicable to real problems. Beth Moore Milroy and Caroline Andrew (1988: 177) comment:

> The debate about theorizing in the research community at large reminds us to think about why we do research in the social sciences in the first place. Is it purely to acquire knowledge for its own sake? Or is it to change and improve something? Feminist researchers who are acutely aware of the pervasive androcentricity that has influenced the shape of urban environments cannot be disinterested inquirers removed from the prospect of creating a non-sexist environment. For that half of humankind which feels isolated from the social science explanations of its own experience, it would be shooting itself in the foot to settle simply for understanding. Acknowledging purposefulness in the research experience, in both researcher and researched, creates a dialectic between understanding and changing.

For feminists, theory and practice will always be integrated activities. For planning theory to be meaningful in a changing world "acknowledged purposefulness" needs to be the benchmark of discourse.

Acknowledgments

I wish to thank John Forester and Ann Forsyth who gave generously of their time to discuss feminist theory and planning theory with me while I was in residence at Cornell University during fall semester, 1990. This material is excerpted from a longer article in *Planning Ethics*, Sue Hendler, editor, from Center for Urban Policy Research (New Brunswick, NJ), 1985.

References

Andrew, C., Moore Milroy, B. (eds.) (1988), *Life Spaces: Gender, Household and Employment*, Vancouver, Canada, University of British Columbia Press.

Acker, J., Barry, K., Essveld, J. (1983), "Objectivity and Truth: Problems in Doing Feminist Research", *Women's Studies International Forum*, 6, 423–435.

Beauregard, R.A. (1990), "Raising the Questions: The Meeting of Feminist Theory and Planning Theory", unpublished memorandum.

Forsyth, A. (1990), Correspondence and conversations with the author.

Forester, J. (1990), Correspondence and conversations with the author.

Hess, B.B., Ferree, M.M. (1987), *Analyzing Gender: Handbook of Social Science Research*, Newbury Park, CA, Sage.

Jones, K.B. (1988), "Citizenship in a Women Friendly Polity", *Signs*, 15, 781–812.

Leavitt, J. (1986), "Feminist Advocacy Planning in the 1980s", *Strategic Perspectives in Planning Practice*, in Barry Checkoway, ed., Lexington, MA, Lexington Books.

Okin, S.M. (1979), *Women in Western Political Thought*, Princeton, NJ, Princeton University Press. Cited in Barbara Nelson "Women and Knowledge in Political Science: Texts, Histories and Epistemologies", *Women and Politics*, 9, 1–25.

Sandercock, L., Forsyth, A. (1990), "Gender: A New Agenda for Planning Theory", *Working Paper 521*, Institute of Urban and Regional Development, Berkeley, University of California.

Tannen, D. (1990), *You Just Don't Understand: Men and Women in Conversation*, New York, NY, Williams Morrow.

Wekerle, G., et al. (1980), *New Spaces for Women*, Boulder, Westview Press.

21

Knowing Women/ Planning Theory

Helen Liggett

"The problem," Andreas Huyssen (1986, 53) says, "is the persistent gendering as feminine of that which is devalued." I wonder what he means by that. Radical feminists would explain the devaluing of the feminine by reminding readers that *Homo sapiens* (from the Latin, meaning "wisdom") identifies as human those who think alike. This tradition defined men while excluding women, who remained "outside" rationality. The devaluing of the feminine buttresses the edifice of male dominance by defining women in terms of the material, emotional, messy, and – in extreme cases – the evil aspects of the human condition. Huyssen argues that in the nineteenth century, equating mass culture with feminine imagery was enough to signal its danger in a huge bourgeois morality play concerned with keeping and maintaining reasonable order.

Yet feminist theory, particularly when surrounded by a postmodern aura, has been attracting attention for several years within the avant-garde factions of conventional disciplines in the arts, humanities, and social sciences. "Feminism" and feminist theory panels at national conferences draw large crowds. These signs of life suggest a reversal and also represent the expectation that there must be something new here and that the listener for one is not going to miss out on it. So what is it?

"It" is not the answer to the dream for a new intellectual configuration,

Reprinted by permission from *Planning Theory* 7/8, 1992.

for something new under the sun, or for a morally clear space. Feminism in the most general terms seeks to develop a sense of women's own subjectivity (Harris and King 1989). What feminist theory in particular offers are the fruits of at least twenty years of serious scholarship formulated within a dual intellectual and political agenda. On the one hand it strives to formulate an alternative base from which to assess the structures of dominance within which knowledge is produced. On the other hand it also entails commitment to political change. In addition, feminist theory has always been a highly self-conscious activity, which means that the inherent instability of theory is constantly being advertised within it. Before talking about what being systematically "unreasonable," committing political change, and being reflective have to do with planning, I want to present a brief scheme of the most familiar forms of feminist theory.

Three levels of theorizing are generally recognized. Each provokes companion forms of political action; each has acknowledged shortcomings (Butler 1990; Ferguson 1988; Lloyd, 1984; Nicholson 1990).

1   Talk about equality is framed in terms of "rights" and "interests". These notions are defining characteristics of the classic liberal tradition and American political culture in particular. This approach emphasizes the possibilities and limitations of acting within the electoral system and through social movements (see, for example, Black 1989). The limitations of this approach lie in the tendency of corporate democracy to define individuals in terms of operative units. Thus, arguments that women should become workers or soldiers imply that other aspects of their lives that define them as women are no longer relevant to what they are. Further, representation in the classic liberal sense assumes a stable identity and homogeneous interests among women.

2   Talk about women's ways of thinking, or women's experience recognizes differences, albeit culturally based, between the forces that produce women's and men's identities. Carol Gilligan's work is most often cited in this context. Examples of political action following from this claim include the call within the women's peace movement for a nurturing foreign policy rather than a competitive one (see, for example, Harris and King 1989). Here the assumption is that women bring a different way of thinking to public issues. This position is weak if it assumes that the subjectivity of women is grounded in some prediscursive place or if it reads today's concerns into other ways of life such as Native American culture. "Women's voice" can provide the basis for political argument, but this tends to exclude men and further does not legitimate an alternative philosophy needed to articulate fully what Tronto (1987) calls a "politics of care."

3   Feminist theory drawing on philosophical traditions and particularly what is known as "French Feminists" is organized around a critique of reason, particularly the assumptions of thought that universalize men and exclude woman. Understandably, this level is most common in the academy and so action entails challenges to conventions within disciplines about what constitutes thinking as

well as the boundaries of that thinking (see, for example, Nicholson 1990). Here literature is the paradigmatic case, with the well-publicized struggles over including women and writers of color in the canon. The critique of reason allows women to expose the dynamics that produce their exclusion and even to show how male identity needs that which it excludes. But it has not yet succeeded completely in offering a way out of the impasse: Attempts to develop "women's writing" are embarrassingly derivative of the system they attempt to escape.

Looking at women in the streets, the three levels intermingle; distinctions collapse. Beginning with the suffragettes, women's political actions have been sustained by alternative versions of what reason was, of how women should act, and the use of the language of rights to express their interests. But the distinctions are still useful for asking how planning theory might be influenced by the epistemological challenges of feminist theory. In other words, much as feminists appropriate and transform ongoing debates and fashions in many systems of thought to illuminate their practical concerns, planning can in its turn use the insights of feminist approaches to good advantage. Some of this work is well under way; the following is only a brief overview of the possibilities (Sandercock and Forsyth [1990] have compiled an excellent bibliography).

1   Historically, planning has not been an equal opportunity employment center. Nor has there been an assumption that women's interests should be represented except as adjunct to the American middle-class (dream) family. Of course inner-city women had problems. There were "bad" women, and some women seemed hellbent on "interfering." As lately as 1988, Peter Hall captions a picture of Jane Addams with the patronizing comment, "The face of compassion and do goodism . . ." (p.41) but these were merely markers outside the borders of the principal disciplinary concerns of planning with bringing rational order to the built environment.

2   Thus obviously, a notion of women's experience as a basis for making plans did not exist. For example, transportation facilities are geared to male commuting patterns (Gale 1985). One can argue that streets last longer than social norms and that "the working woman" places more and different demands on the transportation system than were dreamed of when it was devised. In those days, we may be reminded, women stayed at home in their communities. What, then, to make of the fact that the building of these roads destroyed communities where women were supposed to be safely at home living their spatially integrated lives.

3   Jane Jacobs's warning comes to mind: If modernist urban planning in the guise of urban renewal continued on its current trajectory, then the cities will have problems "that no amount of revenues can solve." This comment is a nascent critique of reason in planning. It could be the start of something big by way of analyzing the limits of planning reason and the discipline's role in shaping familiar social and physical distinctions within "the segregated city" (Relph 1987).

This brings us to the present. Postmodern feminist theory interrogates the problem of epistemology in relationship to political practice. Two directions this inquiry is taking can inform planning: First, the move to understand how women (particularly women of color) develop strengths in cultural contexts that would disable them (Collins 1991); second, attempts to incorporate theories of textuality into thinking about action (Butler 1990).

If identities are ongoing projects formulated in the context of cultures that devalue women, it is also the case that these conventions must be *reproduced* in order to continue. Reproductive practices are political acts of feminist identity formation. Reproduction is not cloning, not totally determined, but subject to escape. Thus, new women in old places are polymorphously destined to change some of the conditions into which their daughters will be born.

Planning, with its own double identity as an academic discipline and a professional practice, can learn from this position at the same time that it offers many sites where reproductive processes occur. (1) Women brought in by the narrowest definition of equality, that is, under affirmative action policies, will challenge ways of thinking that excluded them. (2) Planning education can include systematic analysis of how information about the society is gendered. For example, talk about teenage pregnancy and abandoned women not only perpetuates the devaluing of women's experience, it also leads analysis away from more useful insights into the centrifugal forces that constitute the culture of survival in everyday life. (3) Reasoning within planning itself should be subject to analysis as a shifting practice, formed in relation to its context. A central question in feminist theory is whether there can be difference without hierarchy and exclusion. This can be adapted to question familiar oppositions within planning such as that between economic development and community life.

In summary, feminist theory offers a variety of tools with which to begin the work of knowing and reacting to the limits of current "realisms" in planning. Following in the tradition of advocacy planning and working with current concerns with equity and ethics in planning, feminist theory offers a foundation from which to shape and reproduce the discipline. Nothing is guaranteed, but if planning is increasingly limited to the demands of postindustrial capital as some analysts suggest, then feminist frameworks for constructing alternative normative injunctions (Butler 1990) should be warmly welcomed.

References

Black, R. (1989), *Social Feminism*, Ithaca, Cornell University Press.
Butler, J. (1990), *Gender Trouble: Feminism and the Subversion of Identity*, New York, Routledge.

Collins, P.H. (1991), "The Politics of Black Feminist Thought", Paper delivered as part of Assembly Lecture Series, Cleveland State University Cleveland, Ohio, 27 February.

Ferguson, K. (1988), "Subject Centerness in Feminist Discourse", *The Political Interests of Gender*, edited by Kathleen Jones, Anna Jonasdottir, London, Sage.

Gale, F. (1985) "Seeing Women in the Landscape: Alternative Views of the World Around Us", *Women, Social Science and Public Policy*, Sydney, George Allen & Unwin.

Hall, P. (1988), *Cities of Tomorrow: An Intellectual History of Urban Planning and Design in the Twentieth Century*, London, Basil Blackwell.

· Harris, A., King, Y. (eds.) (1989), *Rocking the Ship of State*, Boulder, CO, Westview Press.

Huyssen, A. (1986), *After The Great Divide: Modernism, Mass Culture, Postmodernism*, Bloomington, Indiana University Press.

Lloyd. G. (1984), *The Man of Reason: 'Male' and 'Female' in Western Philosophy*, Minneapolis, MN, University of Minnesota Press.

Nicholson, L. (ed.) (1990), *Feminism/Postmodernism*, New York, Routledge.

Relph, E. (1987), *The Modern Urban Landscape*, Baltimore, Johns Hopkins University Press.

Sandercock, L., Forsyth A. (1990), "Gender: A New Agenda for Planning Theory", *Working Paper 521*, Institute of Urban and Regional Development, University of California, Berkeley.

Tronto, J.C. (1987), "Beyond Gender Difference to a Theory of Care", *Signs*, 12, 644–662.

22

Planning in a Different Voice

Susan S. Fainstein

Feminist scholarship has provoked a rethinking of fundamental concepts and epistemologies in every discipline, including planning. Feminist critiques have both illuminated the assumptions permitting overt male domination and revealed covert biases. These critiques, in exposing patriarchal relations, have paralleled similar efforts undertaken from the perspective of racially subordinate and colonized peoples. Feminist thinkers, however, have also attempted to go beyond critical readings of history, geography, and science from the viewpoint of the oppressed to affirm different ways of knowing and modes of social intervention. In this respect their ambitions perhaps exceed those of other analysts of "difference."

In this brief essay I shall first describe the major elements of the feminist critique of patriarchy as they most bear on planning and then address the issue of a "different voice"; I next consider the ways in which such a claim can productively affect planning theory and finally, the dangers of too strong an emphasis on difference.

The Feminist Critique and Agenda

Fundamentally, feminist thought comprises an attack on male domination. Within the urban realm feminists have contended that men design cities to serve male needs (see Birch 1985; *International Journal of Urban*

Reprinted by permission from *Planning Theory* 7/8, 1992.

and Regional Research 1978; *Signs*, 1980; Wekerle, Peterson, and Morley 1980). Even when women occupy positions as planners, they do so on terms dictated by men, and they lack the power to reorient the planning project so as to accommodate the interests of women. Within the two most significant planning arenas – economic development and land-use regulation – accepted frameworks of analysis have inherent biases that isolate and denigrate women.

The dedication of most planning enterprises to economic growth and efficiency, defined by a system of accounting that recognizes women's productive and reproductive work only to the extent to which it is recompensed monetarily, incorporates an automatic bias. Devalorization of programs oriented toward women (for example, day care, transit) ensues from assessing the benefits of these programs according to the earnings of their beneficiaries, which are lower than those that would accrue to men as a consequence of, for instance, facilitating their journey to work. Needless to say, enhancing nonpaying reproductive labor, still primarily performed by women, is considered a contribution to consumption and constitutes a total loss within standard accounting systems.

The subordinate role of women within the economy is overlaid with the identification of women as abiding principally within the private rather than the public realm (Eisenstein 1983; Pateman 1988). The public-private distinction is reinforced by prevalent social constructions of women's particular role in biological reproduction (that is, the transformation of the biological fact of the female as bearer into the social norm of the woman as carer for the child). Within the planning apparatus, the reality of geographical separations combines with perceptions of appropriate activities and interventions. Residential zoning exacerbates the division of home from work emblematic of large-scale capitalism. Governmental capital programming accepts the view of social services as "soft" in contrast to infrastructure and buildings, which represent "hard" investments. The focus on central business district development and the opposition, posed by progressive as well as conservative planners, between downtown and neighborhood reiterates and reinforces the familiar distinctions between the male and female spheres. Segments of the left continue to display unalloyed hostility to the displacement of manual labor by clerical jobs; rather than pressing for improved female wages, many critics of urban revitalization demonstrate a bias in favor of male employment and the still prevalent belief that women's salaries represent a "second income".

Feminist planners seeking to overcome female exclusion would instead privilege the female viewpoint by focusing on issues most germane to the lives of women. These include the feminization of poverty, protection of abused women, equal pay for comparable work, and the provision of an infrastructure of social services allowing women greater choice of job locations and hours. This agenda would make improvement of the economic and social situation of women rather than "economic development" the criterion for evaluation of planning outcomes.

Theoretical Initiatives

The first phase of feminist theorizing constituted an attack on androcentrism and a reexamination of social categories from a feminist perspective. More recently, theorists have attempted to go beyond scrutiny of social relations according to Enlightenment values of fairness and rationality and to propose criteria that transcend Western dualisms. With the contention that women speak in "a different voice" (Gilligan 1982) has come an effort to articulate new theories based on a rethinking of the Western tradition. Along with theoretical inventiveness, feminism has produced a methodological eclecticism reflecting the inter-disciplinary nature of women's studies as well as a frequent rejection of the rationalistic framework of modern social science. Thus, feminist theorists have substituted psychoanalytic insights and cultural critique for positivism or Marxist dialectics; and they have employed openly subjectivist narratives and visual media in place of the standard "scientific" exposition.

Substantively feminist social theory has redefined concepts of freedom and justice. The work of Nancy Chodorow (1978) emphasizes the different outcomes of the oedipal crisis for boys and girls, resulting in masculine valorization of separation and feminine espousal of attachment. In a parallel formulation, Gilligan's male subjects sought fairness through a rational calculus, while her female ones argued empathetically; boys valued abstract justice, while girls stressed relationships. These "female values" of closeness and empathy contravene the classic definition of freedom as "freedom from," based as it is on acceptance of separation as a desirable state.

Hirschmann (1989), in an effort to develop a feminist theory of obligation, builds on these arguments:

> [Within the Enlightenment tradition] the necessity of consent to obligation must logically derive from the freedom of individuals and from the concept of freedom defined negatively (p. 1234). [But] women have been bound historically to an entire series of other obligations – child care most obviously – to which consent is not only often unavailable but often of questionable relevance. Are these "obligations" entirely invalid? Or do they suggest a need to redefine the concept of obligation itself (p. 1240).

An extension of these analyses to planning calls into question the rational model that justifies, at least retrospectively, most comprehensive planning. It also problematizes the system of legal regulation that provides the context for planning practice. The abstract calculations of costs and benefits on which the rational model operates offer no place for empathy and personal relationships, while systems of regulation, rooted in an adversarial concept of opposing parties, forgo the connections between people posited by feminist theory. Feminism implies intuitive, participatory approaches to gaining knowledge and nonrational (although not irrational) contextual solutions to planning problems. Feminist theory thus introduces a perspective that starts with concepts of communal relations and incommensurable values, that substitutes the development of consensus for adversarial approaches, that protects the weak and recognizes the importance of sentiment.

This approach seems to offer the possibility of a more humane planning practice than heretofore. However, it also contains blindnesses that can lead to unproductive dead ends. Indeed feminist planning, if it accepts too uncritically the premise of postmodernist thought, can easily result in a loss of the progressive values that inspired feminism at its inception.

Difficulties of Feminist Planning Theory

Feminist theory comprises part of the broader postmodernist post-structuralist thrust toward the rejection of totalizing discourse as necessarily exclusionary. The renunciation of rationalism as the foundation of such a discourse, however, presents serious problems for left planning. The feminist emphasis on connectedness and natural obligation, combined with a repudiation of objective measurement of costs and benefits, can have a strong conservative tendency. Opponents of equality, based in traditional bastions of authority, claim legitimacy based on organic conceptions of a society connected by natural bonds. Historically, the thrust toward resistance to oppression and efforts at progressive social transformation in the Western world derive from a rationalist logic that compares what is to an abstract formulation of what should be.

We can reconstitute Enlightenment concepts of rationality rather than dismissing them (see Harding 1990). Calculation of the distribution of benefits from a program; analysis of the effect of planning outputs on particular social groups; logical argumentation, if not a full-fledged cost benefit analysis; understanding concepts relationally – these are all approaches that do not require the jettisoning of the Enlightenment faith in reason, although they do call for the reconstruction of the scientific method. To abandon the possibility of rational assessment is to negate the epistemological basis of planning itself, which fundamentally assumes a capacity of the intellect to integrate information and measure prospective outcomes. An emancipatory planning calls for recognition of difference but within the context of an abiding hope for rationality.

References

Birch, E. (1985), *The Unsheltered Woman*, New Brunswick, NJ, Center for Urban Policy Research.

Chodorow, N. (1978), *The Reproduction of Mothering: Psychoanalysis and the Sociology of Gender*, Berkeley, CA, Un. of California Press.

Eisenstein, H. (1983), *Contemporary Feminist Thought*, Boston, G.K. Hall.

Gilligan, C. (1982), *In a Different Voice*, Cambridge, Harvard Un. Press.

Harding, S. (1990), "Feminism, Science, and the Anti-Enlightenment Critiques", *Feminism/Postmodernism*, edited by L.J. Nicholson, New York, Routledge.

Hirschmann, N.J. (1989), "Freedom, Recognition, and Obligation: A Feminist Approach to Political Theory", *American Political Science Review*, 83, 1227–44.

International Journal of Urban and Regional Research (1978), "Special Issue: Women and the City", 2.

Pateman, C. (1988), *The Sexual Contract*, Stanford, Stanford Un. Press.

Signs (1980), "Special issue: Women and the American City", 5.

Wekerle, G., Peterson, R., Morley, D. (eds.), (1980), *New Space for Women*, Boulder, Westview Press.

23

Some Thoughts About Difference and Pluralism

Beth Moore Milroy

Given their Enlightenment origins, it is problematic whether current planning theory and practice can incorporate and respect simultaneous and contrasting representations of reality. The conception of pluralism in planning and elsewhere is being challenged because it identifies the issue as needing to find ways to resolve differing perspectives held by essentially similar people. Some feminist theorists contend that the assumption of basic alikeness is a distinguishing feature of Enlightenment philosophies and masks the question of differences associated with gender on the assumption that all people aspire to be or are capable of being like privileged men. Because of their interest in questions of difference, it is possible that feminist theories could be a source of insights for planning theorists. My contribution here uses very broad brush strokes to sketch some aspects of this topic from my current perspective, one that I note in advance is long on questions and short on answers.

The core of the matter in feminists' theories seems to be whether differences among people – women and men, women and women, men and men – are believed to be "real" and, if they are, how they should be taken into account in practice. This is very difficult to determine. One really wants to know what *difference* means. Is difference a question of equality, a juridical matter? Or is it also existential, a question of one's

Reprinted by permission from *Planning Theory* 7/8, 1992.

fundamental origins sexually and perhaps racially, together with the symbols and images that help to inform self-concepts and actions? That is, do differences resulting in inequality flow from social structures? Or are differences also built into more fundamental structures (such as philosophy, symbolism, language) that combine to give one an understanding of oneself and one's relationship to the world – a state of being that could not be addressed by making everyone equal within a juridical framework.

These divergent approaches are both found within feminism, but they evidently adopt different starting points. The "equality" approach – a shorthand term – would probably have the weight of the majority of white, middle-class Anglo–North American feminists behind it. The "originative" approach (shorthand again) would garner little support there, but is common among similarly placed feminists in parts of Europe, especially France and Italy (de Lauretis 1989; Bono and Kemp 1991). Without implying that these two approaches exhaust the ways in which difference is being discussed among feminists today, they do represent two pivots around which rich insights concerning difference are being developed. Consequently, it will be important in theoretical and epistemological discussions to clarify to which feminist theory one is referring.

A second point about these two approaches is that both use concepts that seem foreign to planners. Feminists talk about patriarchy, bodies, violence, a politics that includes silence, an economics that includes domestic work, of Other, of negation, and so on. These concepts are well outside the usual planning lexicon but are vital to evolving one of the most basic categories of feminist scholarship and practice: gender. Therefore, it will be necessary to be open to new terminology in order to take advantage of this scholarship.

Gender as difference, as it is implied by each of the equality and originative approaches, can be briefly illustrated in turn and shown to differ from the approaches that planners take to pluralism.

Consider first the equality approach. Gender research has given most attention to the social process of engendering, the business of tying social practices to sex (see Connell 1987; or for a short explanation in a planning context see Milroy 1991). Feminists claim that engendering has been sexist and generates inequality. People who study engendering say that gender development is different for boys and girls and that more often than not, the processes lead to boys thinking, talking, and acting differently from girls. That is, little girls learn to be little girls by behaving, speaking, and thinking in culturally expected ways. Otherwise one would not recognize them as little girls. The same happens to little boys. In this sense gender is one element among many that constitute social relationships, often described as gender relations.

If this much is so, one might reasonably ask *why* the process is not the same for boys and girls. One hypothesis being explored is that because men control the most influential sociopolitical and cultural phenomena, they therefore control how phenomena will be valued relative to one another. They also decide how phenomena will be assessed as real or correct, because they determine the validation criteria to be used. These points are decided in ways that reflect men's experience.

Going a step further, one could ask how it is that women have not objected more than they have to substantial exclusion from these decisions. Feminists have looked for answers mainly in two spots. One is in certain behaviors sanctioned by our society – such as homophobia, patriarchy, and violence against women – that encourage women to be docile and compliant. It is argued that if men have the explicit or implicit right to control women's bodies through these practices, then they effectively exercise control over how gender is constructed. The other, and of course related, place to look is in the theory of knowledge. A cognitive-based theory of knowledge can rationally exclude the means by which to grasp one's oppression. While expressly not wanting to sound conspiratorial, one can still make the case that a system of domination, constructed over time by a group in society, would logically not make room for a way to explain the domination from within the system because the domination is, after all, its inner logic and *raison d'être*. This is a deconstructive insight and not specifically a feminist one. Breaking the cycle demands validation from outside that theory of knowledge. Feminists have achieved this largely through validating feelings and personal experiences as sources of knowledge or understanding that lie outside the conventional rational framework.

Many feminists believe that they have truly begun to identify major sources of inequality and victimization through these types of investigation. Their solutions have taken many forms but are principally of two types: first, vigorous, politicized resistance to domination and second, theorizing socially constructed gender relations. Above all, the principle of specificity is advised, if not always heeded. That is, the experience of women must be explored in specific historical and cultural contexts.

This approach to difference could serve other disenfranchised groups. The engendering process that results in the construction of gender has parallels in the constructions of class, race, and ethnicity (Scott 1986: 1069). A theory of knowledge that could incorporate and respect such contrasting representations of reality is needed. How to construct such a theory has not been resolved by any feminist theories of which I am aware.

Turning now to the originative approach, one finds a contrary conception of difference. One is asked to consider that sexual difference actually *does* contribute to the constitution of gender. It is posited that difference is constructed, as in the previous approach, but in this case one's sexuality is identified as part of the core of one's being and recognized as contributing to how one experiences and understands the world. The challenge of social life in this case is to make room for and validate images of being that are women's and entirely separate from those of men, indeed expressly not like them, over and above those that men have created. This is not to seek equality, then, but to seek to have one's existential difference recognized.

Some feminists who have pursued this line of thinking have concluded that certain ingredients are needed before such a challenge could be met. In particular there is a dearth of positive symbols for women. "Woman" is primarily symbolized in Western culture as a counterfoil to men – as a mother figure or as an object of male sexual fantasies. That is, the sexual difference of woman is mainly identified negatively as "not a man," or complementarily as the "other." In this sense women are not a sex (Irigaray 1985); and there cannot be equality in sexual or gender relations because there is a consciousness not of two sexes but of only one and its counterpart. "Women" evidently exist, and they obviously function in capacities other than these two, but Western cultural imagery and symbolism give force and identity only to those that coincide with men's imagery of women. To this extent it is doubtful that the imagery and symbolism valued by a male-dominated world can secure equality for women unless women become like men, taking on the imagery of men. But of course once women do this they are not women, but women being like men, and one falls into a paradox. New images of women being creative independently of men need to be developed by women and to be incorporated into the symbolism of the culture. Achieving validation of such new, positive images that might replace those based on negation will certainly present a tough political struggle.

Equality + Differences?

There is substantial hostility to such visceral conceptualizations of difference, which is understandable because they are so distant from the cerebral, monosexual thought typical of Western philosophies. Pluralism fits in better with current Western thought than do the evocative concepts of difference being developed in particular by European feminists.

One of the reasons for hostility is that at first glance the originative and related approaches seem to hark back to biological or psychological essentialism. I would like to stress that this so-called originative approach as I intend to convey it is not a form of essentialism. Specifically, it does not harbor the claim that women have particular qualities that men do not have, nor the claim that either sex has a fixed nature. What I wish to convey is that "difference" probably emerges from places far deeper than such matters as economy and jurisprudence do, from right within the very bases of Western thought, which in turn are platforms upon which ideas such as equality are built. I think equality captures certain values and is a historically variable concept just as, for instance, family is, that it too is constructed within a context. One of its values is the unified human subject, which many (including me) argue needs to be questioned. This suggests that, anterior to making women and men equal lies the question of where to conjure up – within our psyches, languages, myths, images of the good life, and so on – woman as a subject who has the potential to be equal to man, who already is *the* subject, the unified human subject. The claims of the originative approach are that until woman is a subject there is no way she can be equal, that in Western thought she is not a subject but always a predicate, and that she cannot become a subject by fiat. The approach requires constructing a new subject, probably from fragments of Western culture and also from newly created images. The relationships between women and men – but also among women themselves and among men – would be restructured. I don't think this building and designing can properly be labeled essentialist. For that matter, one could turn the tables and illustrate that Western philosophy is essentialist because the exclusion of "woman" as a fully fledged being is *essential* to its logical structure.

Coming back to the question of pluralism in planning theory, a number of insights can be drawn from the experiences of feminists. The Enlightenment foundations of planning theory are not threatened by the feminist equality approach, because it retains the idea that humankind is essentially equal and that it is social arrangements that create inequality. In principle, the repair of these arrangements can be effected within Enlightenment precepts so as to achieve equity, juridically, for all, based on the juridical concepts of those who determine what in society should be safeguarded. In planning theory this would entail including women in the range of people who determine what is important in society. The insights from feminist theorists that would be especially important would be those that show how gender contributes to defining social relationships, including power differentials, and thereby constricts the application of pluralist principles.

By contrast, the originative approach does not accept the axiom that people are naturally alike as in Enlightenment philosophy but instead posits fundamental difference of experience and sense of being. In terms of planning theory, the most important step for the time being would probably be to take the position, first, that alternative images of the good life must be actively encouraged and sought out; and second, that social technologies need to be fostered for working with more than one image at a time while resisting the urge to reduce one to another.

References

Bono, P., Kemp, S. (eds.), (1991), *Italian Feminist Thought*, Oxford, Basil Blackwell.

Connell, R.W. (1987), *Gender and Power*, Oxford, Polity Press.

de Laurentis, T. (1989), "The Essence of the Triangle or, Taking the Risk of Essentialism Seriously: Feminist Theory in Italy, the U.S., and Britain", *Differences*, 1, 3–37.

Irigaray, L. (1985), *This Sex Which Is Not One*. Translated by Catherine Porter, Ithaca, Cornell University Press.

Milroy, B.M. (1991), "Taking Stock of Planning, Space, and Gender", *Journal of Planning Literature*, 6, 1, 3–15.

Scott, J.W. (1986), "Gender: A Useful Category of Historical Analysis", *American Historical Review*, 91, 1053–75.

24

Feminist and Planning Theories: The Epistemological Connection

John Friedmann

The feminist project rests on the explicit recognition that gender and gender differences pervade all aspects of social life, including language, moral consciousness, and the categories with which we think. Because women have been and continue to be subordinated to men in both the public and private spheres, the feminist project is one of emancipation. This means the dissolution of patriarchal relationships.

Because the starting point of the feminist project is women's subjugation to men, the power dimension is a central concern of feminist practice. Several correlates might be drawn from this basic supposition:

1 Historical subjugation has created among women a subaltern culture, negative self-images, and a mindset that often accepts as natural what in fact is a social product of male domination. Emancipation requires a freeing-up, a liberation of consciousness, both of women and men.

2 Emancipatory processes require the empowerment – psychological and political – of women situated in their specific life situations.

3 Women's emancipation needs to be informed by an alternative vision of the

Reprinted by permission from *Planning Theory* 7/8, 1992.

Is this possible? "good society" from which the power to dominate others is absent, and in which difference and equality can coexist.

4   For emancipation to succeed, male habits of power must be broken, leading to new householding arrangements, a degendering of the division of labor, and social arrangements that acknowledge for both women and men a life of their own, without at the same time sacrificing that which they hold in common between them: the life in family, community, and nation.

Feminist epistemologies are an element in the continuing struggle for women's emancipation. They also enlarge our understanding of what constitutes valid knowing. They take knowledge from the philosophies of science into the field of everyday practice.

At present, no consensus exists on a feminist epistemology. Moreover, I do not believe that there ever will be one. Epistemological debates will continue. But over and above the din of contending views are two contributions from within the feminist project that are of signal importance to the theory of planning. (I should add that there is no consensus about the theory of planning either. Planning theory is part of the continuing "conversation of mankind" as Richard Rorty has called philosophy). The first contribution is that of Carol Gilligan and her colleagues on the question of gender differences in moral judgements (Gilligan 1982; Gilligan et al. 1988). The other is an essay on feminist social research by Judith A. Cook and Mary Margaret Fonow (1990; orig. 1986).

Gilligan's work is very well known, and I do not need to summarize it here. She argues for a way of moral knowing that is based on relationships of caring. She contrasts an ethics of caring with an ethics of justice, where hard judgements are made concerning right and wrong. According to Gilligan (whose conclusions are based on extensive empirical research), an ethic of caring that stresses contextual ways of knowing and contains an implicit preference for solidarity over individuality is more typical of women than of men (though neither justice nor care are notions, beliefs, and practices unfamiliar to the other sex).

Cook and Fonow's essay is an attempt to set out a feminist methodology (and hence a methodology oriented to women's emancipation) based on five principles: "(1) the necessity of continuously and reflexively attending to the significance of gender and gender asymmetry as a basic feature of all social life, including the conduct of research; (2) the centrality of consciousness raising as a specific methodological tool and as a general orientation or 'way of seeing'; (3) the need to challenge the norm of objectivity that assumes that the subject and an object of research can be separated from one another and that personal and/or grounded experiences are unscientific; (4) concern for the ethical implications of feminist research and recognition of the exploitation of women as objects of knowledge; and (5) emphasis on the empowerment of women and transformation of patriarchal social institutions through research" (Cook and Fonow 1990: 72–3).

What is the significance of these feminist contributions to planning theory? To answer this question we need to ask which planning theory is meant or, more properly, which *tradition* in theorizing about planning. In my book (Friedmann 1987), I identify a *radical* tradition in planning, which I call social mobilization, and which I presented as an amalgam of anarchism, utopianism, critical theory, marxism, and other forms of radical thought and practice, including feminism. The radical tradition of planning is planning from within civil society. As is well known, there is little agreement among the various strands of the radical tradition. But in one way or another, they are all concerned with an emancipatory project. For women are not the only disempowered group. Workers, people of color, ethnic outcasts, and subsistence peasants are all striving, though not always militantly, for their release from subjugation.

Radical planning is today very much on the agenda of political practice. It has become a universal practice. What is significant for these struggles involving the resistance of subaltern groups is that they must be carried out by the disempowered themselves. No one can "liberate" people from the outside. The image of breaking down the gates to the Bastille and releasing its prisoners is a false image. Empowerment must be seen as a process of collective self-empowerment.

What do the feminist epistemologies of Gilligan and her coworkers, and of Cook and Fonow, contribute to the tradition of radical planning? Gilligan is spelling out the moral contours of a "good society" in which an ethics of care and solidarity with the sufferings of others temper the acquisitive urge of an individualistic, competitive economy (Ruddick 1989). Those moral contours are part of the utopian vision toward which we direct our efforts. This is a hope beyond idealism and is rooted in the ongoing feminist struggles for women's equality in the increasingly inter-active private and public spheres of life. To the extent that women achieve substantial equality in these spheres and with equality, a public voice, women's moral knowledge will begin powerfully to inform everyday practices and policies.

Cook and Fonow's work contributes in another way. It teaches us a model of research that is compatible with emancipatory practices. Though not unique to feminism, the model is an important contribution in this specific formulation. Related models are those based on Paulo Freire's work on education for critical consciousness, as well as the action-research model of Orlando Fals Borda (1988). As others have noted, women's struggles for liberation parallel and often converge with emancipatory movements of other oppressed groups (minorities, disem-powered workers, peasants and so on). These struggles underlie the recent emergence of organized civil society as a collective actor in the public domain. Radical planning is planning with and for civil society, especially those sectors that have been silent and submerged. The aim of these movements is to rearrange relations of power and to bring into being a society that lives at peace with itself and its environment; has eradicated subalternity; and is striving for always greater justice, care, and community. In the movement toward such a society, there must be a joining of feminist and planning epistemologies and practice.

References

Cook, J.A., Fonow, M.M. (1990), "Knowledge and Women's Interests: Issues of Epistemology and Methodology in Feminist Sociological Research", in *Feminist Research Methods*, Boulder, CO, Westview Press.

Borda, O.F. (1988), *Knowledge and People's Power: Lessons With Peasants in Nicaragua, Mexico, and Columbia*, New York, New Horizon Press.

Friedmann, J. (1987), *Planning in the Public Domain*, Princeton, Princeton University Press.

Gilligan, C., et al. (1988), "Mapping the Moral Domain: A Contribution of Women's Thinking to Psychological Theory and Education", Cambridge, MA, Harvard University Press.

Gilligan, C. (1982), *In a Different Voice*, Cambridge, MA, Harvard University, Graduate School of Education.

Ruddick, S. (1989), *Maternal Thinking: Toward a Politics of Peace*, New York, Ballantine.

25

Feminist Theory and Planning Theory: The Epistemological Linkages

Leonie Sandercock and Ann Forsyth

An epistemology is both a theory of knowledge and a justificatory strategy. It frames questions such as who can be a "knower" (can women? can nonexperts?); what tests beliefs must pass in order to be validated as knowledge (only tests from observation, experiment, calculation, or tests based on experience?); what kinds of things can be known (can subjective truths count as knowledge?); the nature of objectivity (does it require point-of-viewlessness?); the appropriate relationship between the researcher and his or her subjects (must and can the researcher be detached, dispassionate?); and what should be the purpose of the pursuit of knowledge (Harding, 1987)?

Initially (from the early 1970s), feminist theorists' interest in epistemology was provoked by the apparent exclusion of women from the epistemology that has dominated the social sciences since the nineteenth century, that of positivism. Feminists have argued that traditional

Reprinted by permission from *Planning Theory* 7/8, 1992.

epistemologies have excluded women as "knowers" or agents of knowledge and denied women's life experiences as valid foci of study; that the voice of science is a masculine one; that history is written only from the point of view of men of the dominant class and race.

Since the late 1970s feminists have been proposing alternative theories of knowledge that legitimate women's claims as knowers. Some of the labels given to these feminist theories have included "feminist empiricist epistemology" and "feminist standpoint epistemology" (see Cook and Fonow 1986; Westkott 1979; Harding and Hintikka 1983; Harding 1986; Jaggar and Bordo 1989; Nielsen 1990) or, more simply, "women's ways of knowing" (Belenky et al. 1986). Most of the earlier feminist work began by wanting to make a better science by "adding women" to traditional analyses. More recently, feminists have challenged the privileging of scientific and technical knowledge at the expense of other ways of knowing, such as knowledge based on experience, or learning by doing.

Feminists argue for "connected knowing", by which we mean something like "the head *and* the heart", reason *and* passion, rationality *and* politics: in other words, an effort to transcend the dualisms and exclusions of positivist epistemology and to discuss the politics of theory and method and the origins and implications of our theoretical hierarchies. While feminists are certainly not the only, or even the first critics of positivist epistemology (see Feyerabend 1975; Kuhn 1962; Polanyi 1958), our work originates in response to an alienation from the methods of research and definitions of knowledge that denigrate or ignore women's experiences and refuse to consider the political content of knowledge creation.

The feminist epistemological project, thus defined, has clear implications for planning theory and practice. While the issue of *a distinctively feminist epistemology* remains a controversial one, to which we shall return, we suggest that a feminist perspective involves the relevance of the following ways of knowing in the practice of planning (see Sandercock and Forsyth 1990). First, talking: especially the importance of oral traditions, of storytelling, of "gossip" (see Belenky et al. 1986: 116). Second, listening, which Forester (1989) insightfully describes as the "social policy of everyday life." Third, tacit or intuitive knowing (see Keller 1983; Polanyi 1958). Fourth, creating symbolic forms (paintings, murals, music): These may be a more important way of communicating, especially in the process of community participation, than planners have been prepared to acknowledge. Finally, acting – or, as Jane Addams defined it in her Settlement House work in turn-of-the-century Chicago, "learning by doing" (Addams 1910, Dewey 1929). All of these ways of knowing are subject-related. It is we who do the talking, listening, acting, which reminds us of the partially autobiographical and thus gendered nature of knowledge. And once we acknowledge the validity of other than scientific and technical ways of knowing, we have to rethink other method-ological issues, such as how we go about research in planning.

The danger in discussing "the feminist epistemological project" however, and the problem inherent in much of the literature written between the mid-1970s and mid-1980s, was precisely the tendency to imply that there was *a* feminist social science, *a* feminist epistemology, *a* feminist research method. In fact there is much disagreement among feminist theorists on these questions (see Jaggar and Bordo 1989; Nicholson 1990) and three broad challenges have been issued to the very notion of *a* feminist epistemology since the mid-1980s. These challenges have come from women of color, non-Western feminists, and postmodern feminist philosophy.

Women of color and non-Western women have disputed the assumption that the category "women" is a unifying category capable of transcending differences in class, race, ethnicity, and sexual preference. They have argued, on the contrary, that feminist theory has been written by white, Western, middle-class women, unconscious of their own position and special interests as members of a dominant culture (see Collins 1990; Hooks 1984, 1989; Moraga and Anzaldua 1981; Narayan 1989). The significance of this critique should not be lost in the links with planning theory, for it suggests the urgency of developing a theory and practice of "planning for multiple publics", at the center of which is an acknowledgment and celebration of difference. This is likely to become one of the most significant themes in the rethinking of planning in the 1990s.

Postmodern philosophers have also drawn our attention to the problem of *a* feminist epistemology, which is that, just like the many theories it criticizes, it upholds too universalistic an assumption of gender (see Jaggar and Bordo 1989; Nicholson 1990). Unfortunately, the epistemology debate, as it has been influenced by postmodernism and poststructuralism, has become increasingly esoteric and increasingly inaccessible for women who are not full-time theorists to read and integrate into their lives and feminist political projects. Epistemology is a crucial issue for feminists and planners. While we do not want to argue for a distinctive feminist epistemology, we do want to insist that knowledge is inherently dialectical and that feminist inquiry has had, and should continue to have, emancipatory as well as critical power. There will be never be closure to these debates, precisely because knowledge is a social construction. The construction of meaning, involving as it does communication, will always involve politics and passion as well as science. It will always be an unfinished business. Planners must, finally, learn to live with unstable paradigms.

References

Addams, J. (1910), *Twenty Years at Hull House: With Autobiographical Notes*, New York, Macmillan.

Belenky, M., Blythe, C., Goldberger, N., Tarule, J. (1986), *Women's Ways of Knowing*, New York, Basic Books.

Collins, P. Hill (1990), *Black Feminist Thought*, Boston, Unwin Hyman.

Cook, J., Fonow, M. (1986), "Knowledge and Women's Interests: Issues of Epistemology and Methodology in Feminist Sociological Research", *Sociological Inquiry* 56, 2–29.

Dewey, J. (1980), original 1929, *The Quest for Certainty*, New York, Perigree Books.

Feyerabend, P. K. (1975), *Against Method*, London, New Left Books.

Forester, J. (1989), *Planning in the Face of Power*, Berkeley, CA, University of California Press.

Harding, S. (1986), "The Instability of the Analytical Categories of Feminist Theory", *Signs*, 11, 645–664.

Harding, S. (ed.), (1987), *Feminism and Methodology*, Bloomington, Indiana University Press.

Harding, S., Hintikka, M. (eds.), (1983), *Discovering Reality: Feminist Perspectives on Epistemology, Metaphysics, Methodology, and Philosophy of Science*, Dordrecht, Holland, D. Reidel.

Hooks, B. (1984), *Feminist Theory*, Boston, Southend Press.

Hooks, B. (1989), *Talking Back*, Boston, Southend Press.

Jaggar, A., Bordo, S. (eds.), (1989), *Gender/Body/Knowledge*, New Brunswick, NJ, Rutgers University Press.

Keller, E. Fox (1983), *A Feeling for Organism: The Life and Work of Barbara McClintock*, San Francisco, W.H. Freeman.

Kuhn, T. (1962), *The Structure of Scientific Revolutions*, Chicago. University of Chicago Press.

Moraga, C., Anzaldua, G. (eds.), (1981), *This Bridge Called My Back*, New York, Kitchen Table Press.

Narayan, U. (1989), "The Project of Feminist Epistemology: Perspectives from a Nonwestern Feminist", in Jaggar and Bordo (1989).

Nicholson, L. J. (ed.), (1990), *Feminism/Postmodernism*, New York, Routledge.

Nielsen, J. McCarl (ed.), (1990), *Feminist Research Methods*, Boulder, CO, Westview Press.

Polanyi, M. (1958), *Personal Knowledge*, New York, Harper and Row.

Sandercock, L., Forsyth, A. (1990), "Gender: A New Agenda for Planning Theory", *Working Paper 521*, Institute of Urban and Regional Development, University of California, Berkeley.

Westkott, N. (1979), "Feminist Criticism of the Social Sciences", *Harvard Educational Review*, 49, 4, 422–430.

Part VI

Ethics, Professionalism, and Value Hierarchies

Introduction

This final section includes three readings on planning ethics, community participation, and communication. Each addresses a shortcoming of the traditional, rational-comprehensive model of planning, whether it be the simplistic notion of serving the public interest, the lack of subtlety about ethical conflicts, the presumption of privileged expert knowledge, or the tendency to oversimplify and overgeneralize the causal relationships found in cities.

A profession is characterized by a common set of expert knowledge and methods, professional autonomy, and internal control over the certification and disciplining of colleagues; it also shares a set of ethics, both implicit and explicit. These characteristics apply equally to planning. We begin with the ethical principles of the American Planning Association, followed by a critique of them by William Lucy. Lucy admires the good intentions of the stated ethics, yet he is troubled by the simplistic and antiquated planning theory assumptions that underlie these principles. At the heart of the principles is the premise that the planner's primary obligation is to serve the public interest. Yet for years planners have challenged the "public interest" as being a naive, overly simplistic ideal. Serving the public interest often clashes with the planner's obligation to serve the client, the profession, and his or her own sense of self-responsibility. Lucy also challenges the simple call for greater citizen participation and comprehensiveness. He faults these ethical principles for neglecting the real conflicts, dissent, and trade-offs that exist in planning. The vagueness and technocratic optimism in these principles do not always coincide with the competitive and messy political realities of planning.

In addition to ethical questions, planners face basic choices about what value should be placed on public health and the quality of life. In particular, the growing interest in environmental protection requires planners to address environmental risks. Though there is no scientific consensus on the level of risk for various environmental hazards, much of the current effort in risk assessment is a technocratic quest to define "acceptable risk." Frank Fischer, in "Risk Assessment and Environmental Crisis: Toward an Integration of Science and Participation," originally published as an article in 1991, challenges this standard model on both technical and political grounds. By integrating concepts from citizen participation, social communication theory, and a critique of technical rationality, Fischer argues for a participatory approach to risk assessment. This alternative is not just risk communication, in which scientific experts present their privileged information to the lay public. Instead, this risk assessment approach integrates the public into the process of defining the agenda, setting values and discount rates, and giving legitimacy to the process. The result is a participatory methodology that both avoids some of the risk assessment failures of technocratic institutions and includes a wider range of political interests and social concerns.

We conclude with "Learning from Practice Stories: The Priority of Practical Judgment," in which John Forester argues that communicating through stories is central to planning. Like Healey (this volume), Forester draws upon Jürgen Habermas's theory of communicative-based knowledge to examine the shortcomings of traditional scientific knowledge in the quest to understand social complexity. Too often, planners overgeneralize and reduce planning situations to simplistic theories. Particularities of individual cases are rejected as trivial details – just as skeptics deride individual case study analysis as being methodologically anecdotal. Forester defends the importance of planners telling stories filled with rich detail, whose subtle complexity conveys much more practical information than do the facts of reductionistic scientific analysis. Personalized stories reveal values, interests, relevance, moral commitments, basic assumptions, and possible solutions. Forester observes that it was assigning stories of practicing planners that finally gave his students a clear picture of what planners actually do.

26

APA's Ethical Principles Include Simplistic Planning Theories

William H. Lucy

I am pleased that the American Planning Association (APA) has addressed the issue of ethical principles for planning. I am skeptical, however, about the appropriateness of the first five of the thirteen principles that the APA board of directors adopted.

Principles 1 through 5 concern me for several reasons. First, they deal with some of the most difficult subjects of political and planning theory. Second, in some instances they reduce complex subjects to a single sentence and thus run the risk of trivializing the profession. Third, some of the principles are contradictory, either within a single principle or between principles. Fourth, some of the subjects should not be included in a statement of ethical principles, because of the oversimplification that brevity requires, the controversial philosophical issues they address, and the questionable conclusions they express. A statement in the July 1987 issue of *Planning* (p. 35) heightens my concern about those matters. The statement reads as follows: "APA encourages the adoption of the principles in this Statement by legislatures through ordinances or statutes, by public planning bodies through incorporation into bylaws, and by employers of planners, who may include them in personnel manuals and other employment policy documents."

Reprinted by permission of the *Journal of the American Planning Association* Vol. 54, No. 2, 1988.

I can explain my concerns most clearly by commenting on each ethical principle in sequence.

1 Serve the Public Interest

APA quite properly advocates serving the public interest, but I do not know what APA intends by that. The most prominent opinion among political theorists seems to be that "the public interest" is a phantom, unless the phrase means only an accumulation of individual wants, the merits of which others have no public right to judge. That is not my view of the public interest. Defending a concept of public interest that one cannot define solely as an accumulation of individual wants is a major task of political philosophy. The single sentence in the APA statement of principles about serving the public interest may seem harmless, but I question whether it is useful unless we elaborate on it. Such elaboration, however, would elucidate the complexity of the task and thereby raise doubts about whether APA should really include it in a statement of principles. I believe debate about the public interest is essential to the future of the planning profession and to the nation. The statement of principles may discourage such debate, because some will conclude from the simplicity of its expression there that nothing remains to be discussed.

2 Support Citizen Participation in Planning

Citizens should have some participatory role between elections, including opportunities to initiate proposals and to review and comment on the proposals of others; but planners should be wary of the common defects in citizen participation. Participation usually does not come from a representative sample of the population. Often it reflects narrow self-interests rather than any larger sense of public concern, and more often than not it expresses the views of the wealthier and better-educated strata of society. APA's omission of any reference to the role of elections is unfortunate. While elections have many faults – including being too unfocused on planning issues to provide clear guidance – they do offer the widest forum for participation. They also lead to election of representatives whose functions include deliberation. One hopes that deliberation by elected representatives will at least occasionally produce greater insight than, say, a poll of a random sample of not very interested citizens. The appropriate role for elections, deliberative representation, leadership by chief executives and political parties, and participation by citizens by various means between elections are fundamental subjects for discussion and debate. We would do better to deal with those subjects in analysis and essays than in a brief statement of ethical principles.

3 Recognize the Comprehensive and Long-range Nature of Planning Decisions

One problem with the formulation of the planning process in principle 3 is that comprehensive and long-range planning are not consistent with serving a public interest that is "continuously modified" (a characterization given in principle 2) since broad and long-range planning intentions must adhere to more stable values. Perhaps APA's intent in principle 3 was to emphasize balance between careful attention to breadth and length of vision and the responsiveness that principle 2 emphasizes. The notions of balance and responsiveness are stretched beyond possibility by the additional injunctions in principle 3 to "continuously gather and consider *all* (emphasis mine) relevant facts, alternatives, and means of accomplishing them" and to "explicitly evaluate *all* (emphasis mine) consequences before making a recommendation or decision." Critics of "idealized" planning have consistently attacked such unrealistic demands as impossible to accomplish because planners have limited time, money, expertise, and decision-processing capacity. In addition, planners cannot consider all consequences, because there are no predictive theories about some consequences, theories about other consequences are inadequate, and knowledge needed to assess still other consequences is not available. Perhaps APA intended to present some notion of sufficiency. Indeed, principle 7 encourages such a hope, saying, "If the official has not sufficiently reviewed relevant facts and advice affecting a public planning decision, the official must not participate in that decision." Principle 3, on the other hand, suggests an image of ivory tower planners far removed from arenas in which officials must make decisions with insufficient time, information, or expertise, as usually happens with important decisions. Certainly it is excessive to make an impossible assignment an ethical injunction; but that is precisely what principle 3 does. APA should at least revise that principle to make it consistent with the "sufficiency" spirit of principle 7.

4 Expand Choice and Opportunity for all Persons

My own political preferences include expanding choices for disadvantaged persons, as suggested in principle 4, and doing so by changing restrictive policies, institutions, and decisions. But that requires restricting the choices of some persons rather than expanding them. If the material pie is expanding more slowly than the population is increasing, as has been occurring in recent years, that trend calls for some redistribution of benefits and some limitations on choices accompanying the redistribution if we are to expand opportunities for the disadvantaged.

Furthermore, environmental conservation in particular requires limiting choices, and those limitations must apply to the disadvantaged as well as to the advantaged.

5 Facilitate Coordination through the Planning Process

This principle at first seems intended merely to encourage open and timely dissemination of information. But I also infer from it that it assumes an unrealistically pleasant and cooperative context for planning. It promotes cooperation as a planning ideal. But the adjustments on behalf of the disadvantaged, which principle 4 advocates, may call for some public officials, including planners, to develop coalitions of support on behalf of change. Planners have finally begun to pay more attention to the importance of devising strategies to cope with opposition in competitive contexts. We should not place a label of "unethical" on strategies to overcome opposition to low-income housing, landfill sites, homes for retarded citizens, neighborhood parks, annexation, and progressive taxation, merely because those strategies recognize that voluntary cooperation may not produce the desired results. Sometimes we best promote the public interest by coping with competition and opposition. Emphasizing coordination as a planning ideal may reflect avoidance of competitive political realities.

I hope that APA will give the statement of ethical principles additional deliberation and that APA officials will consider revising or eliminating principles 1 through 5.

APA Ethical Principles for Planning

1   *Serve the public interest.* The primary obligation of planners and public planning officials is to serve the public interest.
2   *Support citizen participation in planning.* Because the definition of the public interest is continuously modified, the planner and public planning official must recognize the right of citizens to influence planning decisions that affect their well-being. They should advocate a forum for meaningful citizen participation and expression in the planning process and assist in the clarification of community goals, objectives, and policies in plan-making.
3   *Recognize the comprehensive and long-range nature of planning decisions.* The planner and public planning official must recognize and have special concern for the comprehensive and long-range nature of planning decisions. The planner and official must balance and integrate physical (including historical, cultural, and natural), economic, and social characteristics of the community or area affected by those decisions. The planner and official must continuously gather and consider all relevant facts, alternatives, and means of accomplishing them. The planner and official should

explicitly evaluate all consequences before making a recommendation or decision.

4   *Expand choice and opportunity for all persons.* The planner and public planning official must strive to expand choice and opportunity for all persons, recognize a special responsibility to plan for the needs of disadvantaged people, and urge changing policies, institutions, and decisions that restrict their choices and opportunities.

5   *Facilitate coordination through the planning process.* The planner and public planning official must facilitate coordination. The planning process should enable all those concerned with an issue to learn what other participants are doing, thus permitting coordination of activities and efforts and accommodation of interests. The planner and official must ensure that individuals and public and private agencies possibly affected by a prospective planning decision receive adequate information far enough in advance of the decision.

6   *Avoid conflict of interest.* To avoid conflict of interest and even the appearance of impropriety, the public planning official who may receive some private benefit from a public planning decision must not participate in that decision. The private benefit may be direct or indirect, create a material personal gain, or provide an advantage to relations, friends, groups, or associations that hold a significant share of the official's loyalty. An official with a conflict of interest must make that interest public, abstain from voting on the matter, not participate in any deliberations on the matter, and leave any chamber in which such deliberations are to take place. The official must not discuss the matter privately with any other official voting on the matter. A private sector planner who has previously worked for a public planning body on a plan or project should not appear before that body representing a private client in connection with proposals affecting that plan or project for one year after the planner's last date of employment with the planning body.

7   *Render thorough and diligent planning service.* The planner and public planning official must render thorough and diligent planning service. Should the planner or official believe s/he can no longer render such service in a thorough and diligent manner, s/he should resign from the position. If the official has not sufficiently reviewed relevant facts and advice affecting a public planning decision, the official must not participate in that decision.

8   *Not seek or offer favors.* The public sector planner and public planning official must seek no favor. The planner and official must not directly or indirectly solicit any gift or accept or receive any gift (whether in money, services, loans, travel, entertainment, hospitality, promises, or in some other form) under circumstances in which it could be reasonably inferred that the gift was intended or could reasonably be expected to influence them in the performance of their duties or was intended as a reward for any recommendation or decision on their part. The private sector planner must not offer any gifts or favors to influence the recommendation or decision of a public sector planner or public planning official. The private sector planner should oppose such action by a client.

9   *Not disclose or improperly use confidential information for financial gain.* The planner and public planning official must not disclose or improperly use confidential information for financial gain. The planner and official must

not disclose to others confidential information acquired in the course of their duties or use it to further a personal interest. Exceptions to this requirement of non-disclosure may be made only when (a) required by process of law, or (b) required to prevent a clear violation of law, or (c) required to prevent substantial injury to the public. Disclosure pursuant to (b) and (c) must not be made until after the planner or official has verified the facts and issues involved, has exhausted efforts to obtain reconsideration of the matter, and has sought separate opinions on the issue from other planners or officials.

10 *Ensure access to public planning reports and studies on an equal basis.* The public planning official must ensure that reports and records of the public planning body are open equally to all members of the public. All non-confidential information available to the official must be made available in the same form to the public in a timely manner at reasonable or no cost.

11 *Ensure full disclosure at public hearings.* The public planning official must ensure that the presentation of information on behalf of any party to a planning question occurs only at the scheduled public hearing on the question, not in private, unofficially, or with other interested parties absent. The official must make partisan information regarding the question received in the mail or by telephone or other communication part of the public record.

12 *Maintain public confidence.* The public planning official must conduct himself/herself publicly so as to maintain public confidence in the public planning body, the official's unit of government, and the official's performance of the public trust.

13 *Respect professional codes of ethics and conduct.* The planner and public planning official must respect the professional codes of ethics and conduct established by the American Institute of Certified Planners (AICP) Commission and by several professions related to the practice of planning. Professional codes commonly establish standards of professional conduct and include provisions that protect the integrity of professional judgment and describe the professional's responsibility to the public, clients, employers, and colleagues.

27

Risk Assessment and Environmental Crisis: Toward an Integration of Science and Participation

Frank Fischer

Introduction

It is commonplace today to say that we live in an advanced techno-industrial, or high-tech society. Science and technology now literally drive the modern industrial economy and, furthermore, have spread into every area of social and political life. To be sure, the advance of techno-logical development has brought with it much of what we accept as good in modern society. Technological artifacts have become so much a part of everyday life that we take them for granted. In this respect the belief in technological progress has itself become one of the basic modern world views, an ideology cutting across the traditional categories of both capi-talism and socialism (Fischer 1990).

Many of the most ardent enthusiasts of this ideology, particularly the so-called postindustrial theorists, see its beliefs to be the rationale for the

Reprinted with permission from the *Industrial Crisis Quarterly*, 1991, Vol. 5, No. 2.

ascent of a new technocratic elite destined to guide our political and our economic systems (Bell 1973; Brzezinski 1976). These writers see the need to extend science fully into the realm of political decision making (Platt 1969). The function of the technocratic elite would be to replace democratic political decision processes (based on conflicting interests) with a more technically informed discussion (based on scientific decision-making techniques). In the process, political issues would increasingly be transformed into technically defined ends that can be pursued through administrative means (Stanley 1978).

Although technocratic elites still remain formally subordinate to political and economic elites, their world view and decision techniques now play prominent roles in the governance of modern corporate-bureaucratic institutions, the dominant power structures of modern society (Galbraith 1967). This essay is about one of these technocratic methodologies: risk assessment. Before turning to the methodology, however, it is essential first to elaborate on the political context to which it is applied, namely, the increasing concern about technological hazards and their impact on the environment. Toward this end, the chapter proceeds in the following fashion: after first examining the central importance of technological progress and its fundamental crisis, the discussion develops the concept of "acceptable risk" as the techno-industrial response to the current situation. The technocratic character of the risk assessment methodology is then criticized in the context of a broader sociological perspective. The result is a proposal to examine the possibility of restructuring risk assessment to include a wider range of participants. The chapter closes with a call for the innovation of a participatory methodology and briefly explores some of the institutional and political implications of such an approach for expertise more generally.

Technological Progress and the Environmental Crisis

In spite of the aforementioned enthusiasm for technological progress, during the past two decades there has also been a growing recognition that advanced technologies have brought with them many dangers. Indeed, in various quarters of society there is a growing distrust of modern techno-industrial progress (National Research Council 1989: 54–71). In the face of nuclear power catastrophes, the death of oceans and rivers due to oil spills and other disasters, greater structural unemployment owed to computerized work, pollution and the greenhouse effect, the pervasiveness of toxic wastes, the rise of cancer rates, and the like, we have come to recognize that one of the prices paid for this technological advance has been a dramatic increase in risk, or at least the awareness of risk (Slovic et al. 1980; National Research Council 1989).

Such events have given both credibility and political influence to the environmental movement, which emerged in the 1970s as a response to these and other related events (Douglas and Wildavsky 1982). The result has been a much greater awareness of the impacts of modern technologies on the environment, coupled with a questioning of our blind acceptance of technological progress. Indeed, the more radical ecological groups in the environmental movement have raised basic questions about our very way of life. Proponents of the "green" philosophy see the solution in a return to smaller, less hierarchical technological systems, with a much greater role for people (Porritt 1984).

In terms of environmental and technological risks, these two competing world views have divided one of the most critical issues of our time into two deeply entrenched and opposing camps: those who argue that we live in "the safest of times," and those who see it as "the riskiest of times" (National Research Council 1989). The first of these views, the technocratic view largely proffered by industrial and political leaders, takes life expectancy to be the best overall measure of risk to health and safety, points to substantial increases in this measure, and shows that these increases run parallel over time with the growing use of risky chemicals and dangerous technologies. In fact, they argue that many of the contemporary hazards have decreased overall risk by replacing more dangerous ones. People are seen as becoming more and more worried about less significant risks.

By contrast, the number of people who believe that we live in the riskiest of times has increased dramatically over the past two decades. For these people, particularly those of the green persuasion, the world is on the brink of ecological disaster. Modern technology is seen to constantly generate new threats to the earth's life-support systems and thus in turn to the stability of social systems. Especially important to this argument are the synergistic effects of these problems. It is not just the appearance of new problems but rather the emergence of countless serious problems at the same time, for example, overconsumption of the earth's energy resources, the ozone hole, the toxic waste problem, contamination of rivers and oceans, the dangers of nuclear radiation, the rise of cancer rates, the destruction of rain forests, the rise of the earth's temperatures, escalating population growth, and so on. Even though people are seldom exposed to one risk in isolation from the others, there exists little empirical information on the interactive effects of these dangers. For such reasons, those who see a dramatic increase in risks call for tighter control over technology, including the abandonment of some technologies considered to be particularly risky (such as nuclear power and genetic engineering) and the need for the development and introduction of more environmentally benign technologies.

Despite this fundamental disagreement, or perhaps because of it, the struggle over this question has elevated the "search for safety" to the top of the political agenda (Wildavsky 1988). The quest for safety has emerged as one of the paramount political issues of our time, both as a prominent public concern and a leading topic in intellectual discourse (Fischer and Wagner 1990). In Germany, for example, it has led sociologist Ulrich Beck (1986) literally to define the postindustrial society as the "Risk Society."

The Techno-industrial Response: Acceptable Risk

Such concerns have forced the proponents of large-scale technological progress, corporate and governmental leaders in particular, to pay much greater attention to the regulation of advanced technologies. Indeed, the future of many new technologies today is believed virtually to depend upon the ability of regulatory institutions to restore public confidence in them. Numerous industrial and political leaders, in fact, express their concern about an emerging environmental philosophy that would oppose the introduction of all new technologies – even tested technologies – without *absolute* prior proof that they pose no risks, a view exemplified by such radical ecologists as Jeremy Rifkin (Tivnan 1988: 38).

This concern often reflects very concrete experiences, the nuclear energy industry being the example *par excellence* (Rosenbaum 1985: 227–34). What started out as one of the magnificent peacetime wonders of modern technology has been brought to a virtual standstill in the United States by the environmental movement and the assistance of such events as the accidents at Three Mile Island and Chernobyl. Sweden, moreover, now plans a total phase-out of nuclear energy altogether in the 1990s, thanks to powerful environmental agitation.

Stated straightforwardly, the stakes in this struggle are high, and the mandarins of technology have recognized the challenge. The primary response has been an attempt to shift the political discourse to the search for "acceptable risk." Toward this end, supporters of the modern techno-industrial complex argue that risk must be seen as a mixed phenomenon, always producing both danger and opportunity. Too often, they argue, the debate revolves purely around potential dangers (all too often centering on high-impact accidents with low probability, for example, nuclear meltdowns or runaway genetic mutations). Risk taking, in contrast, must be seen as necessary for successful technological change and economic growth, as well as the overall resiliency and health of modern society.

Playing it safe thus actually tends to reduce opportunities to benefit from new entrepreneurial chances. Even further, risk taking is itself said to be a fundamental source of safety. Like joggers who routinely risk heart attacks to improve overall health, societies must run short-term risks in order to expand future wealth and security (Wildavsky 1988). Moreover, the resulting expansion of wealth is said to make it possible for society to absorb the impact of greater disasters, thus directly increasing its overall levels of safety. In short, risk raises issues fundamental to the future of Western industrial societies and has ushered in a deep-seated political struggle to shape the very way we think and talk about it.

The basic strategy of industrial and scientific leaders has been to focus the risk debate on technical factors (Wynne 1987; Schwarz and Thompson 1990: 103–120). The approach is grounded in the view that technological dangers have been grossly exaggerated (particularly by the Luddites in the environmental movement said to harbor a vested political interest in exploiting the public's fears). The result, it is argued, is a high degree of ignorance in the general public about technological risks. The layperson thus tends to worry a great deal about the safety of air travel but thinks nothing of driving his car to the airport, which statistics demonstrate to be much more dangerous (Lopes 1987). Because this uncontrolled expansion of "irrational" beliefs is quite threatening to technological progress, often specifically manifested in the issue of financial investment, managerial elites have seen the need to counter this antitechnology trend driven by the ecological movement.

The answer is to supply the public with more objective (technical) information about the levels of risks themselves. That is, the "irrationality" of contemporary political arguments must be countered with rationally demonstrable scientific data. The solution is to provide more information – standardized scientific information – to offset the irrationalities plaguing uninformed thinkers, namely, the proverbial "man on the street." More recently, in fact, the task has become the focus of a new subspecialty of risk management known as "risk communication" (National Research Council 1989).

The task of generating such information has fallen to the most likely candidate, the managerially oriented decision sciences. These sciences are themselves largely the by-products of large-scale technological systems and their managerial requirements. Developed to help steer and manage such systems, they can appropriately be seen as the methodological embodiment of the technocratic world view and its strategies.

Risk Assessment as Technocratic Methodology

Risk assessment, then, is the modern technocratic response to the contemporary technology and environmental crisis. It is a methodological strategy designed to supply a technically rational basis for centralized regulatory decision making. The practice first emerged to deal with two different types of risks: geological risks concerned with the probabilities of earthquakes and their damages; and technological risk problems confronted by the U.S. space program (which, it must be remembered, was as much an organizational and managerial project as it was a technical feat). Its more contemporary methodological manifestations are largely by-products of its adoption and use by the nuclear power industry (Mazur 1980).

As a scientific model of rational decision making, risk assessment reflects an amalgam of managerial and engineering methodologies. The goal of risk analysis is to provide objectively standardized quantitative information about the reliability of a technology's performance (Coppock 1984: 53–146). Toward this end, it defines risk in terms of the physical properties of a technology and its environment. Like the engineering model upon which it is largely based, risk assessment proceeds from a fundamental assumption, namely, that a technological system (defined as an integration of physical and human factors) can be rigorously defined with a unitary concept of technical rationality (Schwarz and Thompson 1989: 102–122).

This means, more specifically, that physical risks exist separately from the symbolic context in which they are socially situated and that social perceptions of technological systems and their risks can be strictly excluded. Indeed, social perceptions are "irrationalities" that have little or nothing to do with technical knowledge. The goal, in short, is to isolate and measure the objective probabilities of technical failure in terms of intrinsic and extrinsic physical properties.

In analytical terms, risk is quantitatively expressed as the product of the estimated degree of harm (death or damage) a given technical failure would cause and its probabilities of occurrence (Wynne 1987; Irwin and Smith 1982; Covello and Menkes 1985). In complicated technological systems, probabilistic risk assessment involves first breaking the system down into various measurable components – materials, pipes, pumps, seals, coolants, fail-safe mechanisms; second, measuring the statistical probability of a failure of each of these dimensions – using past performance data, experimental assessments, and expert judgments; third, it means an examination of crucial environmental factors that might either precipitate or exacerbate a technical failure, such as geological fault lines (which might cause earthquakes), or climatic conditions such as wind patterns (which would influence the spread of dangerous particles, for example, radiation). Fourth, the foregoing factors, stated statistically as multiple probabilities, must be integrated through a modeling process based on decision-oriented event and fault trees. After calculating the various chains of probabilities to provide an overall estimate of system failure, the figure must be multiplied by the estimated damages. For example, the health effects of human exposure to the release of dangerous substances, such as chemicals or radioactive particles, are estimated with epidemiological, medical, and actuarial data to determine the long- and short-run damages to human well-being, latent as well as delayed.

The result is a set of objective statements that are to be the focus of regulatory deliberations about risk, thus replacing risk "perceptions" divined – so to say – by technically uninformed social actors, particularly those who lead environmental movements (Andrews, 1990). Indeed, the U.S. Environmental Protection Agency established quantitative risk assessment as the primary methodology for agency decision making (Russell and Gruber 1987).

Methodological Critique: Bringing in the Social Dimension

The method proved to be anything but a success. Although it produced a mountain of quantitative data, it altogether failed to reassure the public. Indeed, in many ways it has only worsened the situation. There are, in this regard, two problems: one formally grounded in technical considerations, the other in political realities. Both, it is argued here, result from the technocratic framing of the risk problem.

First, the technical problem. Given the complexity of technological systems, the task of generating quantitatively standardized estimates of risk requires the use of very narrowly specified empirical assumptions and analytical concepts, including the very definition of what constitutes a technology. This is not the place to go into technical details (concerning such matters as data limitations, units of analysis, issues concerning the delineation of various technical subprocesses, security of safety components, levels of professional expertise, and the like). Suffice it to say that analysts are forced to make many uncertain assumptions – sometimes even heroic assumptions – which are later masked by the precision of their risk statements. As Wynne (1987) puts it, the price paid for precision is often a high degree of hidden ignorance about the safety of technical systems (Conrad 1980).

This glossing over of empirical and analytical uncertainties has given rise to a good deal of disagreement among the experts themselves. Indeed, their judgments about these statistics often range from completely reliable to totally useless. Almost needless to say, this display of technical disagreements – featuring counterexperts criticizing experts – does nothing to assuage the public of its fears (Collingridge and Reeve 1986). Indeed, there is little doubt that the open display of disagreement among experts has only heightened public worries. To put it bluntly, risk assessment – on its own terms – has not only failed as a technical tool, it has also in the process exacerbated the very doubts it set out to assuage (Schwarz and Thompson 1990; Wynne 1987).

This brings us to regulatory decision making and the role of social and political factors. Technocratic contentions to the contrary, the argument that social factors are irrelevant to the objective assessment of risk is sociologically uninformed. There are three interrelated points to make in this regard. The first concerns the goal of regulation itself. Despite a long history of technocratic attempts to structure and control regulatory decision making, the regulatory process in a democratic society is fundamentally concerned with the interrelations between technical developments and social concerns (Meiers 1985). Once risk assessment's technical estimates are formally introduced as the basis for regulatory rule making, the methodology encounters a fundamental decision problem – namely, that the very social context it holds constant becomes a key focus in regulatory deliberations.

The regulatory process, in other words, seeks to examine the effects of technologies and risks not only in terms of their physical magnitudes and probabilities but also in terms of how these have a specific impact on the social and institutional contexts in which the technologies are embedded, both internally (the workplace) and externally (the social and natural environments). In more recent years, risk assessment has attempted to confront this problem more directly through the empirical identification of rules for determining acceptable risk (Slovic et al. 1982). The idea is to determine empirically the levels and types of risks people have already learned to live with and then to posit these as objective standards of "acceptable risk." Regulatory rules, then, can be objectively determined by empirical comparisons of risk estimates and the standards of risk acceptance. This, in fact, shores up the technocratic mission; people's subjective perceptions of risk, as well as their individual comparisons of risk, need not be directly solicited. The entire rule-making process can thus be governed by the techno-analytic methodologies of the decision sciences (Wynne 1987).

This reluctance to consider contextual factors directly, however, breeds major problems. The method is greeted with public distrust, even suspicion. It comes to be seen – correctly – as a managerial decision methodology strategically employed to gloss over and hide important social and political issues. The result is a political legitimacy problem. By denying legitimacy to the values and anxieties that arise from the social contexts in which technologies are situated, those who seek to regulate risk seriously jeopardize their own credibility by saying to people that their social experiences and searches for meaning do not count (Wynne 1987; Schwarz and Thompson 1990).

In contrast to the engineering orientation, then, the regulatory task of risk assessment in a democratic society has to approach its object of investigation in a very different way, which brings the discussion to the second point. The first step toward a solution is to be found in the theoretical redefinition of large scale technological systems. Rather than a complicated set of technically oriented relationships, we must much more broadly recognize such systems to be socio-institutional phenomena (Joerges 1988). Actually, large-scale technological systems are integrated sets of techno-institutional relationships embedded in both historical and contemporary social processes. They are complicated technical processes functionally woven together by networks of socioorganizational controls (Perrow 1984).

This reality bears directly on the empirical estimation of risk *and* the social perceptions of acceptable risk. With regard to the social perception of risk, much to the chagrin of the risk analysts, these institutional factors are discovered to play an essential role in the layperson's perception of technological systems. Social perceptions and understandings of large technological systems – those of workers and citizens in particular – are fundamentally rooted in their concrete social experiences with decision-making institutions and their historically conditioned relationships. Any single technical "event" or "decision" is in fact located within a continual socio-institutional process, which is itself an integral dimension of the large-scale technological system. For example, sociological evidence (as well as common sense) shows that workers cannot altogether divorce their responses to physical risks from their attitudes toward social relations in the plant, particularly those pertaining to managerial practices. If the workers' social relations with management are pervaded by mistrust and hostility, the ever-present uncertainties of physical risks in the plant are amplified.

For risk analysts, this amplification is subjectively irrational behavior (sometimes portrayed as rooted in a neurotic pathology). The cynics among them see this inclusion of social perceptions to be the result of a simple fact, namely that the social dimension is the only aspect of such systems that people are capable of understanding. The technical dimensions are beyond their intellectual reach (Douglas and Wildavsky 1984; Wynne 1987). This judgment has in fact led to a line of behavioral research concerned with the psychology of risk perceptions (Slovic et al. 1982; Slovic 1984). Researchers seek to determine how and why people attach social meaning – irrational meanings – to specific technologies. Why, for example, has nuclear power – in the face of favorable risk assessments – attracted such negative images?

But really how "irrational" is this behavior? Which brings us to the third point. Here I want to underscore the most obvious empirical perception pertinent to this issue, that is, the fact that over the past fifteen years we have more and more recognized the sources of technological hazards and catastrophes frequently to have been the result of institutional failures (Paté-Cornell 1990; Clarke 1989). The examination of such accidents as occurred at Three Mile Island and Bhopal, the explosion of the space shuttle *Challenger*, or the Exxon oil spill in Alaska, show them to be the consequences of untrustworthy or irresponsible organizational and managerial systems. Indeed it becomes increasingly difficult to find crises in which this is not at least partly the case (Dobrzynzki 1988; Lambright 1989; Vaughan 1990). Such events have scarcely contributed to the public's trust and confidence in management's ability to ensure reliably personal and environmental protection.

Thus, institutional and managerial factors are themselves very real sources of technological risk and uncertainty; and people often correctly perceive this, even if formal risk assessment chooses not to. As Wynne (1980: 188) nicely puts it, "uncertainties which are not acknowledged and dealt with full-frontally have a way of creeping back into social perceptions, perhaps dressed in a different language." From this perspective, social perceptions can just as easily be seen as sources of experiential knowledge that must be taken seriously (Fietkau 1990). This is particularly the case when they pertain to the kinds of situational circumstances that escape the broad social generalities typically sought by risk perception research.

To the degree that risk assessment has miscast this problem, it becomes itself a source of technological risk. Rather than being a technical issue plagued by social perceptions, the risk problem turns out to be as much a social question related to technical issues. Not only does the abstract language of risk assessment underplay the institutional-managerial context of technological systems, it also fails to recognize that they reflect larger normative concerns rooted in the society itself (Schwarz and Thompson 1990). Some, in fact, argue that a lack of credibility in our institutions and leaders is, in reality, the central factor driving the fear of technological systems, an argument central to the environmental movement.

Restructuring Risk Assessment: Toward a Participatory Approach

One should not underestimate the problem posed here: the search for a more democratic form of risk assessment confronts a number of the most sophisticated political and epistemological problems of our time. In epistemological terms, it is nothing less than the question of how to relate empirical data to norms and values – a very old question that continues to occupy philosophers (Hawkesworth 1988). In political terms, this question asks how we are to transform our increasingly techno-bureaucratic institutions into less hierarchical democratic structures (Fischer 1990). Indeed, in an age of technocratic expertise the question is critical; one can justifiably argue that the very future of democracy depends on it (Petersen 1984).

Within the scope of this chapter I cannot, of course, adequately supply answers to these challenging questions. I will thus attempt only to point risk assessment in a direction suggested by the foregoing critique. The first step, which should be apparent by now, is to move beyond the idea that technical knowledge, coupled with improved communications of empirical findings, can alone answer questions posed in the social and political world. Put more bluntly, it is finally time to recognize this to be the technocratic ideology that it is (Fischer 1990).

The challenge is to find ways to integrate technical and social data more comprehensively and meaningfully in both analytical inquiry and public discussion. In the case of the latter, I mean something more than calling for new forums in which experts present and discuss their findings with the public, largely the contemporary approach to risk communication (National Research Council 1989). In this scenario, science presents something of a *fait accompli*. By virtue of their "exalted" method, scientists command the privileged position in such forums; the intimidated public is relegated to the role of passive listener largely closed out of the discussion. In the end, as experience shows, the process only further breeds the kind of alienation that already presents risk assessment with its legitimacy problem (Nelkin 1984; Petersen 1984).

The solution is to be found in the invention of new institutional forums and methodological approaches capable of opening up the risk assessment process to nonexperts. Laypersons must be integrated into the process as part of a discussion of the social and institutional issues upon which quantitative and technical risk assessment calculations rest. This means building the much-needed social discourse into the phases of scientific research itself (Eldon 1981). Consider some more specific illustrations.

At the outset of risk assessment, a wider range of stakeholders must be built into the initial discussions of what the risk problem is in the first place: they must again be built into the search for risks; then again when it comes to the determination of the relative importance of risks and benefits and how they might be most meaningfully quantified and measured. Finally, their perspectives on the interpretations of the resulting risk estimates must be elicited. It is important to elaborate somewhat on each of these phases.

First, building the participants into decisions about problem definition is essential to an effective strategy of risk assessment, especially once we recognize the fundamentally social nature of technological systems. Important in the definitional problem, for instance, are questions concerning what the technology actually is, what are its significant components and connections, and what are its boundaries and external contexts.

For instance, in a complex techno-institutional system such as hazardous waste disposal (involving a cycle of activities ranging from production, collection, transportation, treatment and storage), how do we determine which actors and institutions are in the system and which are out? In some cases, of course, the answer is easy: The incinerator, for example, is an essential component of the system. But what about the production process? How much of that, if any, is to be included in the definition of the hazardous waste system? Some argue that we cannot adequately understand the process without including the industry that produces the waste, although analysis typically ignores this dimension.

Perhaps even more critical, once we recognize that the social dimension is itself a fundamental source of risk, it is again important to bring the social actors themselves into the process of identification and search for risks. In particular, workers familiar with the everyday operations of a plant have important experiential knowledge about how the socio-institutional structures and processes of the system actually function. Such concrete knowledge is of critical importance in the search for alternative sources of risk. Information of this type often cannot be obtained from management, and it certainly cannot be gleaned from the kind of abstract statistical analysis that has typically characterized risk assessment (Wynne 1987).

While the assignment of weights to risks and benefits sounds like a highly technical task, this process too is grounded in a large number of normative considerations. How, for example, are risks and benefits to be counted? If a benefit is intangible or not traded in markets, how should we establish price values for it? If the benefits will occur far into the future, how should their values be "discounted" to accord with the fact that money available only in the future is typically worth less than money available immediately?

Or, how does one attach numbers to the value of lives saved by a safety procedure? Should the value of each life be the expected future earnings of each person? Should we count as part of the program's costs all of the future medical expenses of the people saved? Should we add their children's schooling and medical costs – children they would not have had if they would have died without the vaccine? Should we count as benefits the taxes paid by the people we rescued?

Finally, citizens and workers must have important inputs into the process of interpreting the meaning and uses of an analysis. Especially important in this respect is the relationship of the findings to the specific circumstances to which they are to be applied. The production of generalized information about the risks of a technological system can never be more than guidelines that must be interpreted within the specific contexts to which they are applied. Wynne (1987), for example, has shown how centrally established regulatory rules about risk often produce enormous problems in their implementation. Because each technological system is located in a different geographical area with varying physical and social characteristics, there is no possibility for the rule to apply directly to specific facilities. In each case, then, the meaning of the data must be socially negotiated between the central authorities and the local officials. Without such normative negotiations, central rules are seen often to do more harm than good. Not only do they create a great deal of frustration among local participants, they themselves also become the sources of risks.

These are typical of the kinds of normative questions that underlie an otherwise technical analysis. The processes of empirical measurement, data collection and mathematical analysis – the processes typically identified as scientific risk assessment – are seen to be founded on a very wide range of crucial normative judgments. Rather than questions and issues merely brought to the scientific process by concerned social and political participants, they are in fact an inherent part of scientific risk assessment. Although scientists must grapple with these judgments, such issues can only be established by social judgments. In this realm, scientists have no epistemologically privileged position over the other members of society, although in fact they frequently make such judgments in the name of science (Stone 1988). These are societal questions and can be legitimately dealt with only through societal processes.

The advantage of such an integration rests on two fundamentally important contributions. First, it builds into the analytical process the stakeholders' pragmatic experiential knowledge about technical and institutional risks, and second, it addresses the essential issues of public legitimation and motivation. By involving them in these normative dimensions of the scientific process as it proceeds, stakeholders become cooperative participants in the formation of scientific arguments rather than mere passive listeners, the result of which is greater commitment to the analytical conclusions. That is the very objective risk assessment has been unable to accomplish.

Institutional Innovations

Clearly such an approach will depend on institutional and political change. Risk assessment, as a decision strategy, is a product of a bureaucratic system of governance; it is a tool designed to inform and guide hierarchically structured decision-making processes. The success of a more democratically structured practice of expertise ultimately depends on a more participatory set of institutions.

Experimentation with such participatory structures for risk assessment is not an altogether new idea in the United States. The 1970s showed a wide range of experiments in this direction. Important in this respect was the rise of the public interest science movement and such institutions as the Center for Science in the Public Interest. To support such efforts, the National Science Foundation established a program to foster the development of citizens' science. Largely judged to be successful, the program was designed to help develop and facilitate projects that sought to incorporate diverse points of view into science and technology projects, thus helping to assure the representation of all groups with substantial interests in project matters.

The most widely discussed, if not the most important, effort of this type was the city of Cambridge's Experimental Review Board, established to examine the risks of biotechnological research at Harvard University and the Massachusetts Institute of Technology. In this case, the Cambridge City Council appointed a broadly representative group of nonscientific citizens to assess the risks involved in recombinant DNA research within the city's boundaries. After many months of intensive work, the group issued a report that stunned the scientific community. As a Harvard Nobel Prize-winning biologist and critic of the citizens' commission asserted, "the result was a very thoughtful, sober and conscientious report" (Dutton 1984: 148). It was widely agreed, independently of disagreements over the commission's final conclusions (which largely supported the continuation of such research), that a representative group of nonscientists could grapple with a profoundly complex science policy issue and develop recommendations widely seen to be intelligent and responsible. As Dutton (1984: 145) put it, "such a twist in science policymaking was as unprecedented as the research itself."

During the same period, Congress formulated national legislation to bring science research policy more fully into the public domain. Precipitated in large part by widespread worries about genetic research, as well as by the public attention received by the Cambridge review project, Congress worked out plans for a freestanding national commission dominated by nonscientists to make regulatory decisions and to consider long-range policy implications. Senator Edward Kennedy, for example, stated at a Senate hearing in 1977 that "the assessment of risk and the judgment of how to balance risk against benefit of recombinant DNA research are responsibilities that clearly rest in the public domain. And it follows that these issues must be decided through public processes" (Dutton 1984). Although the legislation ultimately failed to become law, it had strong Congressional support and was widely seen to be model legislation for the public interest science movement. As the *New York Times* noted, politicians and public interest groups were now recognizing that the regulation of risk was too important to be left to the scientists alone.

Regrettably, such innovative efforts were beaten back by scientific lobbies and conservative politicians during the Reagan years of the 1980s. The argument was always the same: The layman simply cannot understand and responsibly judge complex technological issues. Such participation is said to be unrealistic, if not utopian. As a former president of the National Academy of Sciences put it, "most members of the public usually don't know enough about any given complicated technical matter to make meaningful judgments. And that includes scientists and engineers who work in unrelated areas" (Handler 1980). There is truth in such statements, but they tend unfortunately to refer to the purely technical aspects of such problems, obscuring the wide range of normative social judgments upon which such technical matters depend. Even more important, experiments such as those of the Cambridge Review Board and the National Science Foundation show this view to be premature, if not simply false.

It is also important to mention several efforts designed to supply deliberative methodologies that incorporate a wider range of stakeholders into the decision processes. One approach is "constructive technology assessment" (CTA), particularly as developed and employed in the Netherlands Organization for Technology Assessment. CTA is an attempt to find ways to open up the technological design process as it unfolds, rather than focusing attention solely on the impacts of a technology after they have appeared. Toward this end, CTA theorists have sought an approach to build a wider range of stakeholders into the various discussion phases involved in the development of new technological systems. Although too limited in scope to fully constitute a participatory research methodology, this work offers important insights into how to identify the points at which social discourse can effectively be introduced in technical design processes (Schwarz and Thompson 1990: 143–151; Smits et al. 1987).

As yet, CTA theorists have offered few methodological details on how the discourse around these decision points might be structured. The question of how to organize and conduct such discourses has itself in recent years begun to receive attention in other disciplines, particularly in the advancing field of conflict and dispute resolution. Especially important in this respect have been the efforts to develop mediation techniques for structuring and facilitating dialogues between contending stakeholders (Susskind and Cruikshank 1987). Indeed, there has been much experimentation with dispute resolution methodologies, especially in the settlement of environmental disputes.

Such dispute mediation techniques are essentially efforts "to use informal face-to-face negotiations and consensus-building to resolve disputes" (Amy 1990: 212). Typically, the practice involves the use of a neutral mediator to bring together the various interests deemed party to a dispute – community members, businesspeople, environmental activists, and government officials, among others – in an effort to shape a compromise agreement among the relevant participants. As an informal process designed to get contentious parties to sit down and talk through their differences, this approach has made some real advances. Experience has shown that it can in fact lead to better communication, cooperation, and consensus building.

But the methodology is not without problems. Careful investigation shows the technique to harbor a number of hidden biases. One important disadvantage concerns the problem of access to the mediation process. The supporters of the technique offer it "as a new form of citizen participation open to all who want to participate," although it is far from obvious that equal access in fact exists in practice. Mediators, it is discovered, frequently "play a pivotal role in deciding who is invited to participate, and they often opt to keep the number as small as possible to facilitate the process of coming to agreement" (Amy 1990: 222). Moreover, the criteria that they typically use to select the participants is their relative power. Powerful interest groups, particularly those capable of later impeding negotiated agreements, are encouraged to participate, while the less influential tend to be ruled out, if not ignored. Beyond the problem of access, power also provides some of the participants with fundamental advantages at the bargaining table. One of the most important is the ability of those with the most resources to avail themselves of the best forms of scientific, technical, and legal expertise. As Amy (1990) sums it up, "despite the appearance of a purely informal process where people sit down to talk to equals," in practice it is often quite similar to "other political decision-making processes in which the special interests with the most power and resources have the most advantages" (224). The outcome is thus often a form of cooptation ratified in the name of participatory consensus. The issue, then, is less with the deliberatory techniques than with the legitimacy of the underlying balance of power. This suggests the need for a more radical orientation toward the distribution of power, the implications of which we take up in the next and final section.

Participatory Expertise

For those interested in democratizing the risk decision-making processes, the inequitable distribution of power and resources that differentiate the participants poses a fundamental challenge. As we have already seen, risk assessment, as a managerial decision science, is a product of a bureaucratic system; it is a tool designed to guide hierarchically structured decision-making processes. A more democratically structured practice of expertise would similarly require a more participatory set of institutions. This means new political innovations that can be brought about only through political struggles, particularly of the type advanced by participatory-oriented social movements, such as the ecology movement, grounded in a very different set of values (Friedmann 1987; Fischer 1990).

In the absence of a full-blown participatory social movement, we ask in this final section what kinds of political innovation the experts themselves might introduce to help overcome the barriers to participation. Toward this end, the first and most essential requirement would have to be a professional commitment, as least on the part of those committed to social change, to the furtherance of democratic participation and public empowerment. Such a commitment, of course, is not the sort of thing most scientists are accustomed to, or would even willingly welcome, as it clearly represents a challenge to their privileges and status. But as the sociology of science has made clear, social commitments are already imported into the research process (a point even more applicable to an applied goal-directed science such as risk assessment). A commitment to participation is therefore as much a matter of changing a social practice as it is disturbing the epistemological requirements of science (Weingart 1990).

Beyond the commitment must be the innovation of new methodological techniques capable of facilitating the development of participatory institutions and their practices. Here I refer to the kinds of discussion that take place in a public interest science center or a citizens' technology review board, as well as to the possibility of extending such participatory discourses to other societal institutions. Such a method would provide a format and a set of procedures for organizing the interactions between experts and the citizens they would seek to assist. One promising movement in this direction is the development of "participatory research" (Fischer 1990). Participatory research is a practice that has begun to take shape among alternative social movements, including alternative technology and ecological movements, especially in the Third World. Indeed, there is an international network of participatory research with its own publications (Society for Participatory Research in Asia, 1982).

To many conventionally trained scientists, both physical and social, the idea of participatory research sounds outrageously unscientific. But actually, in most ways it is only the scientific method made more time-consuming and perhaps more expensive, at least in the short run. Fundamentally, it is a progressive version of something already accepted as a methodology in the managerial sciences, namely, action research (Argyris 1985). Like action research, participatory research is designed as a methodology for integrating social learning and goal-oriented decision making. Where the former was eventually coopted by the managerial sciences to serve the rather narrowly defined needs of bureaucratic reform (typically defined as participatory management), participatory research is largely an effort to carry through on action research's earlier commitment to democratic participation (Reason and Rowan 1981; Fernandes and Tandon 1981; Kassam and Mustafa 1982; Merrifield 1989).

To be sure, participatory research is scarcely appropriate to all scientific contexts. Its most important applications pertain to problems involving a mixture of social and technical factors. Within this context it has emerged as an effort to restructure expertise to serve the requirements of democratic empowerment. Rather than providing technical answers designed to bring political discussions to an end, the task is to assist citizens in their efforts to examine their own interests and to make their own decisions (Hirschhorn 1979). Toward this end, it conceptualizes the expert as a "facilitator" of public learning and empowerment. Beyond merely providing data, the facilitator must also become an expert in how people learn, clarify, and decide for themselves (Fischer 1990). This includes coming to grips with the basic languages of public normative argumentation, as well as knowledge about the kinds of environmental and intellectual conditions within which citizens can formulate their own ideas. It involves the creation of institutional and intellectual conditions that help people pose questions and examine technical analyses in their own ordinary (or everyday) languages and decide which issues are important to them.

A particularly important feature of this integration process must be a better understanding of the relation of technical languages to public normative languages. For example, public debates, we are beginning to recognize, proceed more as social narratives than as formal inferential logics (Mink 1978; Fisher 1984; Stone 1989). While public narrative languages encompass elements of formal logic, in structure they are more like stories grounded in questions concerning the motivations and values of the political actors and technical experts involved in the ongoing deliberation, the way in which they conceive and behave in respect to the conflict, and so on (Weiss 1990). Such considerations it will be recalled, are the very sorts of social concerns that risk assessors have failed to appreciate (Wynne 1987).

To be sure, those who practice participatory research almost always underscore the difficulties that it encounters (Eldon 1981). Most of the problems, however, are social and interpersonal rather than scientific per se: it takes, in short, a lot of time, political commitment and interpersonal skill to build people into complex decision process.

But its practitioners also point to two important payoffs. One, it identifies very real and important dangers that hide behind the generalities buried in the technocrats' calculations. That is, it brings to the fore the very problems that have been overlooked by technocratic risk assessment. Every bit as important, participation in decision making helps to build both credibility and acceptance of research findings (Dutton 1984; Friedmann 1987), the most critical failure facing the contemporary risk assessment approach.

Finally, it is important to note that participatory research is already beginning to emerge in the assessment of hazardous risks. In recent years there have been a number of efforts to develop a community-based approach to risk assessment. Designed to facilitate empowerment, such experiments attempt to integrate citizen information methodologically into the analytical process (Wartenberg 1989: 23) The goal, as Chess and Sandman (1989) put it, is to avoid conducting "risk assessments in isolation from community concerns." Toward this end, community groups systematically "provide information to risk assessors about routes of exposure and the history of the environmental problem that can both increase the validity of the risk assessment." The results, as preliminary evidence suggests, are more effective identification and documentation of community concerns; a better understanding of the nature and degree of the hazardous risks confronting the community; an improved capacity to set action-oriented priorities; and greater input into public decision-making processes (Chess and Sandman 1989; Merrifield 1989).

By way of closing, it must be recognized that such a proposal will be criticized by many industrial leaders, politicians and scientists, as this approach will be seen as expensive, time consuming, inefficient and unscientific (the first three of which are surely true in the short run). But the long run suggests a different assessment. Given the failures of the technocratic approach, coupled with a way of legitimating new technologies, it would appear that a participatory approach may open the only avenue to a successful solution to this pressing problem.

References

Amy, J., 1990. Environmental dispute resolution: the promise and the pitfalls. In: N.J. Vig and M.E. Kraft (Editors), Environmental Policy in the 1990s. Congressional Quarterly Press, Washington, DC: 211–234.

Andrews, R.N.L, 1990. Risk assessment: regulation and beyond. In: N.J. Vig and M.E. Kraft (Editors), Environmental Policy in the 1990s. Congressional Quarterly Press, Washington, DC: 167–186.

Argyris, C., 1985. Action Science. Harvard University Press, Cambridge, MA.

Beck, U., 1986. Risikogesellschaft: Auf dem Weg in eine andere Moderne. Surkamp, Frankfurt.

Bell, D., 1973. The Coming of Post-Industrial Society. Basic Books, New York.

Brzezinski, Z., 1976. Between the Ages: America's Role in the Technetronic Era. Viking, New York.

Chess, C. and Sandman, P., 1989. Community use of risk assessment. Science for the People, January/February: 20.

Clarke, L., 1989. Acceptable Risk? Making Decisions in a Toxic Environment. University of California Press, Berkeley, CA.

Collingridge, D. and Reeve. C., 1986. Science Speaks to Power. St. Martins Press, New York.

Coppock, R., 1984. Social Constraints on Technological Progress. Gower, Hampshire.

Covello, V. and Menkes, J., 1985. Risk Assessment and Risk Assessment Methods: the State-of-the-Art. National Science Foundation, Washington, DC.

Dobrzynski, J., 1988. Morton Thiokol: reflections on the Shuttle disaster. Business Week, March 14: 82–91.

Douglas, M., 1982. Risk Acceptability According to the Social Sciences. Russell Sage, New York.

Douglas, M. and Wildavsky, A., 1982. Risk and Culture. University of California Press, Berkeley, CA.

Dutton, D., 1984. The impact of public participation in biomedical policy: evidence from four case studies. In: J.C. Peterson (Editor), Citizen Participation in Science Policy. University Press, Amherst, MA: 147–181.

Eldon, M., 1981. Sharing the research work: participatory research and its role demands. In: P. Reason and J. Rowan (Editors), Human Inquiry: a Sourcebook of New Paradigm Research. Wiley, New York.

Fernandes, W. and Tandon, R., 1981 (Editors). Participatory Research and Evaluation: Experiments in Research as a Process of Liberation. Indian Social Institute, New Delhi.

Fietkau. H.J., 1990. Accident prevention and risk communication in environmental protection: a sociopsychological perspective. Industrial Crisis Quarterly, 4: 277–289.

Fischer, F., 1990. Technocracy and the Politics of Expertise. Sage, Newbury Park, CA.

Fischer, F. and Wagner, P., 1990 (Editors). Technological risk and political conflict: perspectives from West Germany. Industrial Crisis Quarterly, 4: 149–154.

Fisher. W.R., 1984. Narration as a human communications paradigm: the case of public moral argument. Communications Monographs, 51 (March): 1–22.

Friedmann, J., 1987. Planning in the Public Domain. Princeton University Press, Princeton, NJ.

Galbraith, J.K., 1967. The New Industrial State. Houghton Mifflin, Boston, MA.

Handler, P., 1980. In science, 'no advances without risks.' U.S. News and World Report, Sept. 15: 60.

Hawkesworth, M.E., 1988. Theoretical Issues in Policy Research. State University of New York Press, Albany, NY.

Hirschhorn, L., 1979. Alternative services and the crisis of the professions. In: J. Case and R.C.R. Taylor (Editors), Coops, Communes and Collectives: Experiments in Social Change in the 1960s and 1970s. Pantheon, New York: 153–159.

Irwin, A. and Smith. D. et al., 1982. Risk analysis and public policy for major hazards. Physics and Technology, 13: 258–265.

Joerges, B., 1988. Large technical systems: concepts and systems. In: R. Mayntz and T.P. Hughes (Editors), The Development of Large Technical Systems. Westview, Boulder, CO: 9–36.

Kassam, Y. and Mustafa, K., 1982 (Editors). Participatory Research: an Emerging Alternative in Social Science Research. African Adult Education Association, Nairobi.

Knox, R., 1977. Layman is center of scientific controversy. Boston Globe, Jan. 8: 1.

Lambright, H.W., 1989. Government–industry relations in the context of disaster lessons from Apollo and Challenger. Paper presented at the Second International Conference on Industrial and Organizational Crisis Management. New York University, Stern School of Business.

Lopes, L.L., 1987. The rhetoric of irrationality. Paper presented at the Colloquium on Mass Communications. University of Wisconsin, Nov. 19.

Mazur, A., 1980. Societal and scientific causes of the historical development of risk assessment. In: J. Conrad (Editor), Society, Technology and Risk Assessment. Academic Press, New York: 151–157.

Merrifield, J., 1989. Putting the scientists in their place: participatory research in environmental and occupational health. Highlander Center, New Market, TN.

Mink, L.P., 1978. Narrative form as cognitive instrument. In: R.H. Canary and H. Kozick (Editors), The Writing of History: Literary Form and Historical Understanding. University of Wisconsin Press, Madison, WI: 20–49.

National Research Council, 1989. Improving Risk Communication. National Academy Press, Washington, DC.

Nelkin, D., 1984. Science and technology policy and the democratic process. In: C. Peterson (Editor), Citizen Participation in Science Policy. University of Massachusetts Press, Amherst, MA: 18–39.

Paté-Cornell, E., 1990. Organizational aspects of engineering system safety: the case of offshore platforms. Science, Nov. 30: 1210–1217.

Perrow, C., 1984. Normal accidents. In: F. Fischer and C. Sirianni (Editors), Critical Studies in Organization and Bureaucracy. Temple University Press, Philadelphia, PA: 287–305.

Petersen, J.C., 1984. Citizen participation in science policy. In: J.C. Peterson (Editor), Citizen Participation in Science Policy. University of Massachusetts Press, Amherst, MA: 1–17.

Platt, J., 1969. What we must do? Science, 28 (Nov.): 1178.

Plotkin, S., 1989. RATs to technology! Conflict, power and the crisis of industrial siting. Industrial Crisis Quarterly, 3: 1–16.

Porritt, J., 1984. Seeing Green. Blackwell, London.

Reason, P. and Rowan, J. (Editors), 1981. Human Inquiry: a Sourcebook of New Paradigm Research. Wiley, New York.

Rosenbaum, W.A., 1985. Environmental Politics and Policy. Congressional Quarterly Press, Washington, DC.

Russell, M. and Gruber, M., 1987. Risk assessment in environmental policy-making. Science, 236 (April 17): 286–290.

Schwarz, M. and Thompson, M., 1990. Divided We Stand: Redefining Politics, Technology and Social Choice. Harvester & Wheatsheaf, Hertfordshire.

Slovic, P., 1984. Behavioral decision theory perspectives on risk and safety. Act Psychologica, 56: 183–203.

Slovic, P. and Fischoff, B. et al., 1980. Facts and fears: understanding perceived risk. In: R. Schwing and W.A. Albers (Editors), Social Risk Assessment: How Safe Is Safe Enough? Plenum, New York: 75–98.

Slovic, P. et al., 1982. Acceptable Risk. Cambridge University Press, Cambridge.

Society for Participatory Research in Asia, 1982. Participatory Research: an Introduction. Rajkamal Electric Press, New Delhi.

Smits, R.E.H.M. et al., 1987. The possibilities and limitations of technology assessment: in search of a useful approach. In: Technology Assessment: an Opportunity for Europe, Vol. 1. Dutch Ministry of Education and Science/Commission of the European Communities/FAST, The Hague: 120–143.

Stanley, M., 1978. The Technological Conscience: Survival and Dignity in an Age of Expertise. University of Chicago Press, Chicago, IL.

Stone, D.A., 1989. Causal stories and the formation of policy agendas. Political Science Quarterly, 104(2): 281–300; also in: D.A. Stone, 1987. Policy Paradox and Political Reason. Scotts Foresman, Glenview, IL: 194–200.

Susskind, L. and Cruikshank, J., 1987. Breaking the Impasse: Consensual Approaches to Resolving Public Disputes. Basic Books, New York.

Tivnan, E., 1988. Jeremy Rifkin just says no. New York Times, Oct. 18: 38.

Vaughan, D., 1990. Antonomy, independence and social control: NASA and the space shuttle challenge. Administrative Science Quarterly, 35 (3): 225–257.

Wartenberg, D., 1989. Quantitative risk assessment. Science for the People, January/February: 19–23.

Weingart, P., 1990. Science abused – challenging the legend. Paper presented at the Seminar on Sociology of Science at the Inter-University Centre, Dubrovnik, May 7–21.

Weiss, A., 1990. Scientific information, causal stories and the ozone hole controversy. Paper presented at the Seminar on the Sociology of Science at the Inter-University Centre, Dubrovnik, May 7–21.

Wildavsky, A., 1988. Searching for Safety. Rutgers University Press, New Brunswick, NJ.

Wynne, B., 1980. Technology risk and participation under uncertainty. In: J. Conrad (Editor), Society, Technology and Risk Assessment. Academic Press, New York: 200–230.

Wynne, B., 1987. Risk Management and Hazardous Waste: Implementation and the Dialectics of Credibility. Springer, Berlin.

28

Learning from Practice Stories: The Priority of Practical Judgment

John Forester

Ten years ago, Peter Szanton wrote an insightful book called *Not Well Advised* about the problems of linking the research capacities of universities to the needs of our cities. Making those linkages work had been very tough, and Szanton wanted to explain what had happened, what wasn't workable, and what might yet work. In the closing chapter, "What Have We Learned?" in a short section entitled, "'Generalizability' Is a Trap," a striking passage says simply, "F. Scott Fitzgerald commented – on the writing of fiction – that if he began with an individual, he soon had a type, but if he began with a type, he soon had nothing." A similar rule, Szanton was arguing, holds for applied social research.[1] In recent years, several other authors have been exploring closely related themes.

In a popular book on the uses of history in policy analysis, *Thinking in Time*, for example, Richard Neustadt and Ernest May recommend a practical maxim they call the Goldberg Rule. They tell planning and policy analysts, "Don't ask, 'What's the problem?' ask, 'What's the story?' – That way you'll find out what the problem really is."[2]

In planning, Martin Krieger's *Advice and Planning* begins to explore the importance of stories as elements of policy advice, and Seymour Mandelbaum has always argued that our stories define us in subtle

Reprinted by permission from Frank Fischer and John Forester, eds, *The Argumentative Turn in Policy Analysis and Planning*. Durham, N.C.: Duke University Press, 1993, pp. 186–209.

political and social ways, expressing and reshaping who we are, individually and together.[3] And in political theory and philosophy, too, Peter Euben and Martha Nussbaum have argued that literature and drama, and tragedy most of all, can teach us about action, about ethics and politics, in ways that more traditional analytic writing cannot.[4]

In Nussbaum's view, for example, literature can give us a fine and responsive appreciation of the particulars that matter practically in our lives; literature, she suggests, can give us an astutely alert pragmatism, hope (with less false hope), a keener perception of what's really at stake in our practice; in effect, a realism with less presumptuousness about clean and painless technical or scientific solutions – be they the solutions of the hidden hand of the market or of the more visible fist of the class struggle.

The broader practical relevance of these writers' concerns is captured wonderfully by Robert Coles in *The Call of Stories*. The opening chapter, "Stories and Theories," provides a moving and resonant account of Coles's own early clinical training in psychiatry.

Coles introduces us to two of his supervisors: Dr Binger, the brilliant theorist who sought out "the nature of phobias," "the psychodynamics at work here," and "therapeutic strategies"; and Dr Lüdwig, who kept urging Coles to resist the "rush to interpretation" – the rush to interpretation – by listening closely to his patients' stories.

Coles writes that for thirty years he has heard the echo of Dr Lüdwig's words: "The people who come to see us bring us their stories. They hope they tell them well enough so that we understand the truth of their lives. They hope we know how to interpret their stories correctly. We have to remember that what we hear is their story."[5]

The important point here is *not* that psychiatric patients have stories – we all do – but that Dr Lüdwig was giving young Dr Coles some practical advice about how to listen, about how much to listen for, and about the dangers of rushing in "theory first" and missing lots of the action. Dr Lüdwig was giving Coles, and Coles is passing along to us, practical advice about learning on the job, about the ways our current theories focus our attention very selectively – as a shorthand, perhaps – but if we're not very careful, too selectively.

Coles recalls his mentor, physician and poet William Carlos Williams, on this danger of theoretical oversimplification. Williams said, "Who's against shorthand? No one I know. Who wants to be shortchanged? No one I know."[6] When we have practical bets to make about what to do and what might work, theory matters – but so do the particulars of the situations we're in, if we want those bets to be good ones, if we want not to shortchange others or ourselves.

But stories matter in the professional school classroom, too. In my undergraduate class "Planning, Power, and Decision Making" recently, my students read, as they typically do, a mix of planning case histories –

historical and theoretical material about power and powerlessness. But in this particular class, the students also read thirty to forty pages of edited interviews with planners who were graduates of our program.[7] These interviews were produced in the format that Studs Terkel has used in his many books: The interviewer's questions were edited out, and what remained, in our case, were planners talking about their real work – its difficulties, surprises, rewards, and, of course, frustrations.

The result in the classroom was striking: "Now I can tell my mom what planners really do; it's not all one thing, but this is it; now I can tell her." Another student said, "This was the most practical thing I've read in three years in this program!"[8]

Several other students had similar reactions. Somehow, the profiles had "grabbed" them in eye-opening and obviously effective ways. But why had that happened? What was so striking, so catching and effective, about those stories told by planners about their own work?

Of course, the stories were concrete and descriptive, and not abstract, theoretical, and full of unfamiliar language, but that was no explanation. The same was true of the historical material I'd assigned. Something much more important than "concreteness" was at work here, with implications reaching far beyond the classroom, as this essay will argue.

Consider this classroom experience in the light of recent empirical and ethnographic work on policy analysts and planners. Typically, such work involves not only interviews with planners and analysts but also observations of, and perhaps even participation in, various formal and informal meetings in the "policy process" – including, for example, planners' and analysts' own staff meetings.[9] Beginning to assess how much happens politically and practically when analysts and planners talk, and listen more or less well to others talk, this literature suggests that in actual practice, planners tell and listen to "practice stories" all the time.

Is it possible, then, that analysts and planners at work learn from one anothers' and other people's stories in ways subtly similar to the ways my students were listening to and learning from the practice stories they had read in class? Taking this question seriously can lead us to *watch* in planning and policy meetings in new ways, and to listen in new ways, too, to the stories that analysts tell at work, in their dealings with outsiders and with one another. Three questions about these practice stories quickly arise. First, what do planners and analysts accomplish in their telling of stories? Second, what kinds of learning from such story-telling are possible and plausible? And third, what does such storytelling have to do with the politics of planning and policy analysis?

These are the questions explored in the following sections. First, we examine an excerpt from a profile presented in the classroom. Second, we look closely at a segment of an actual city planning staff meeting – a segment in which the planning staff listen critically to, and reconstruct, a practice story told by the planning director. Third, we consider an essentially Aristotelian argument about the ways we learn from practice stories on the job (and more broadly as well).

Learning from Practice Profiles

How do we learn from the practice stories told by practitioners in their own voices? The following selection comes from an interview profile of "Kristin," a recent professional school graduate. Kristin had been describing a lengthy process of meetings she had held with residents and commercial interests in a neighborhood to discuss zoning issues – to allow concentrated, possibly mixed-use, commercial development and to prevent residential displacement, too. Out of the process came a proposal that went to the city council, twice. Kristin put it this way:

> At the [second] meeting, there was movement toward an agreement, but a councilman made a motion to drop the height by thirty feet in all of the areas, and it undid the whole thing. It upset the balance we had worked out. The developers jumped to their feet and rushed to the microphones and said, "Look, we worked with the planning staff long and hard to determine these heights, and they're not just drawn out of thin air. They're related to densities and uses, and these are the numbers that work. You can't just go in and chop!"
>
> Fortunately, the council listened to the voice of reason and they agreed, but very hesitantly. They didn't want to, but they agreed, since it was only a land-use plan and wasn't the actual zoning itself. Since the zoning was to be decided later, the council figured, "If we want to change our minds, we'll do it then." And they let the plan go through.
>
> We'd built a consensus and it really was very fragile, because different groups had very different ideas from the start. When we went to City Council for the second time, we thought, "OK, now we have it, because now everyone's happy, and we're sure everyone's happy." Then the process breaks down a second time, because of this idea of heights. The people who were really affected were satisfied, but because of one voice, the process stopped. It was just a lot of delay, a lot of frustration, and a lot of uncertainty. I really thought the whole thing was going to just come apart.
>
> [And] I hate to say this, because it sounds terrible, but in the end it almost doesn't matter. When our office goes to the Planning Commission, we go with staff recommendations. Although we take into consideration a lot of what goes on, in the end we don't really need to have a consensus because we only present the staff position. It's up to the citizens and the developers and other interests to come and present their own perspectives to the commission. In this city, our staff position doesn't carry the greatest weight. We can work on something for a very long time, but if someone

comes into a Planning Commission meeting and makes a statement, they'll just undo what we've spent months working at. If we take long, hard months and go through the process of building consensus, in the end it almost doesn't matter. I don't think the Planning Department's work has a lot of clout.

I've been very disillusioned. Of course people are going to be self-interested, but I was surprised at the degree to which that's true, and at how people work very long and very hard simply to protect their own interests. The City Council is just an extremely political place. This is the first planning job I've had, and I often find myself wondering, "Is this how it is, or is this how it is here?" Most of the planners I talk to are fresh out of school and they say the same thing.

Still, there are little successes. We just relocated a government facility that the government provided and expanded, and it didn't really stand in the way of our plans for the area to try and transform it. We got in on time on that and helped to get them a place that was more appropriate, and everyone sort of won. It's those little things that make me feel that maybe in the long run I can make a difference. In the long run, it's the little day-to-day things that come up that give you a chance to make a neighborhood a more pleasant place to live in. The small things make up for other things. I say, "OK, I'll put up with certain things because that's the price I have to pay to be able to do the other small things that do have an effect."

It's also been a learning experience. This is my first job, and even though sometimes I'm not real happy with the way things go, I'm still learning a lot about politics.[10]

Now, how do we learn from such stories and what do we learn? Kristin's account tells us much more than the simple facts of a case. We learn, first of all, a good deal about her: her disillusionment, her sense of satisfaction with the "little successes." We learn about her expectations and her awakening to the politics of the planning process – and as readers we're obviously invited to compare our expectations of the process with hers, perhaps to be awakened in the same way.[11]

We learn about the vulnerability of planners' efforts: "We can work on something for a very long time" and "someone" can "just undo what we've spent months working at." We learn about a plausible, if uneasy view of planners' roles ("Although we take into consideration a lot of what goes on, in the end we don't really need to have a consensus because we only present the staff position" to the Planning Commission); and we learn about what this view of her role implies about the encompassing politics of planning. So, she says, "It's up to the citizens and the developers and other interests to come and present their own perspectives," and having expressed this view, Kristin wonders if, and doubts that, the Planning Department's work "has a lot of clout."

And there's more, from insights about timing and politics ("Since the zoning was to be decided later, the council figured, 'If we want to change it, we'll do it then'") to Kristin's own sense of realism and hope ("This is my first job, and even though sometimes I'm not real happy with the way things go, I'm still learning a lot about politics"). What Kristin has learned can be a lesson to us, too.

Yet many people appear to believe that we learn nothing from practice stories that is not simply unique and idiosyncratic. For years it seemed, for example, that the distinguished practitioner turned academic Norman Krumholz doubted the value of writing up his ten years of experience, as the city of Cleveland's planning director, trying to make equity planning work. The urgings and encouragement of his many colleagues and friends notwithstanding, Krumholz suspected that his and his staff's experience would be too unique, too particular, too much "just about Cleveland" for others in other cities and towns to learn much from or to find really relevant.[12]

Krumholz's suspicions were fueled by an academic culture that often judges any work not conforming to canons of systematic social science as guilty before proven innocent. "Physics envy" in social research is alive and all too well. The point here is not to scapegoat positivism but to note that the imperial effects of social science narrowly construed have often terrorized both graduate studies and social inquiry more generally. We forget too easily that science is a cultural form of argument, not a valueless, passionless use of magical techniques.[13] Anthropology, for example, is a social science from which few would doubt we can learn, and it would be silly to dismiss anthropology, and perhaps history, too, because they're typically not "scientific" in the experimental, culturally conventional sense.[14] The point here is not to argue against hypothesis testing when it is possible, not even to argue for a desperately needed broader conception of social research, but to pursue the question of how practitioners learn and develop good judgment in practice – especially in applied and professional fields like the design and policy-related professions.

In practice, clearly enough, the real-time demands of work allow for little systematic experimentation. Just as clearly, practitioners at work engage in what we might call "practical storytelling" all the time – telling, for example, what happened last night at the meeting, what Smith said and did when Jones said what she said, what the budget committee chair did when the citizen's action group protested the latest delay, what happened with that developer's architect's last project, and so on. In practice situations we find stories and more stories, told all the time and interpreted all the time, sometimes well, sometimes poorly; but we find relatively few controlled experiments.[15]

We're likely to find far more stories, too, in practice settings than we will find opportunities to "try things out," to test our bets, to move and reflect in action, as Donald Schön so powerfully describes it in *The Reflective Practitioner*. Faced with such stories and paying careful attention to them, planners and policy analysts do seem to learn in practice about the fluid and conflictual, complex, always surprising, and deeply political world they work in.

But how do they do it? What does it mean to pay careful attention to these stories and so to learn from them? How can we explain and dignify the ways planners and analysts can learn practically and politically as they listen to these stories?

Practice Stories Told and Listened to in Practice

To explore how practice stories might work in actual planning and policy settings, we can sit in, for example, on a city planning agency's staff meeting. Here we see not only that the professional planners tell one another practical, and practically significant, stories all the time but also that they're creating common and deliberative stories together – stories about what's relevant to their purposes, about their shared responsibilities, about what they will and won't, can and can't, do, about what they have and haven't done.

To see how such common and deliberative stories can work, let us turn to a brief extract from a planners' staff meeting in a small city. We can think of listening in on a staff meeting as a way of getting inside the "organizational mind" of the planners, getting to know both how they perceive the situations they're in and how they begin to act on the problems they face.

In this case the staff numbers roughly half a dozen professionals. The meeting followed a recent election in which the mayoral challenger, who lost narrowly, had run a campaign vigorously attacking the successful incumbent's planners – the planners holding this meeting. As the transcript suggests, the staff feel, to say the least, unappreciated and misunderstood by the public. This segment of their conversation follows:

VINCE *(director):* I think the Mayflower project [an apartment complex] was pivotal. That's the first time that we took a very high profile position on a very unpopular issue. We were outvoted on council seven to three; we were pushed right to the center of that controversy. We tried to hold what we thought was the right line, and we really lost a great deal of support in the general public because of our position.

I think that was the first real bad one. And it gets blended in with the Northside. I think the Northside's the second one where we've been hurt, where those people who are afraid and concerned are really, really angry. And Lakeview Park's another one, although I don't think we're taking the heat for that one.

GEORGE (*community development planner*): I think we are.

KAREN (*housing planner*): I think we are too.

PAT (*assistant director*): I mean, I don't hear anybody saying, "The Board of Public Works really screwed up."

VINCE: It's interesting, because it wasn't our screwup.

KAREN: But we *never said* it wasn't our screwup. We never pointed the finger to the screwup.

VINCE: My perception is that people just think about any kind of change, and then they think about planning, and then they think about planners, and . . . somehow we're tied to everything.

BILL (*senior planner*): It's guilt by association.

KAREN: If something goes wrong, the planners did it. If something goes right, the City Council members claim credit for it.

VINCE: *That's* the kind of problem I think we have to address. Ms. Smith here has been saying, "You've got to come out," and you have too, and many of you have been saying, "We've got to answer this, we've got to answer this." And I've always said, "No, we *don't* – because we don't want to get into a cursing war with a skunk; you know, you just get more heat that way."

But now I think *we have to*. I think we have to set out a strategy over the next year or two of how we're going to sell the department and how we're going to position ourselves to get to those people whose minds aren't already made up. I mean, you'll never get Samuels [a local journalist] to think we're good guys, but there are a lot of people influenced by Samuels and the crap he's saying. If we could get to them with reason and explain to them what our job is and how we came to the conclusions that we've come to . . .

GEORGE: What about the concept of developing something like a position paper for the individual projects, like the Mayflower project, that would be very much a synopsis but at least it would state when it came to the department, what the developers' request was, what our recommendation was, what the council did, you know, a "who struck whom" sort of thing, and what the key issues were for the neighborhood, and how it turned out?

And the staff members here go on to discuss these issues.

Now, quite a bit is happening in this working conversation. The director tells a story about their efforts, what they have been up against, what they have tried to do. It has a time line; the Mayflower project was "pivotal"; "that was the first real bad one," he claims. And he connects that experience to others – the Northside and Lakeview projects. And he does more; he characterizes the people involved: They're "afraid," "concerned," and "really, really angry." He does not just describe behavior, he socially constructs selves, reputations: the kind of people – he is claiming – that the planners have to work with.

But the director is doing much more than that, too; he is telling a complex story, in just a few lines, about the allocation of responsibility and blame: "We tried to hold what we thought was the right line." "We took a very high profile position on a very unpopular issue." "We really lost a great deal of support." But, on Lakeview, "I don't think we're taking the heat." But then, when two of his staff think instead that they *are* taking the heat for it, the director says, "It's interesting, because it wasn't our screwup." So a story unfolds here about the courage of convictions, about the tension between commitment to a professional analysis and the desire for public support, about astute or poorly played politics, and also about "guilt by association," the vulnerability of the planning staff in a highly politicized environment.

This conversation begins with a working story of effective and vulnerable practice, practice that is strategic and "contingent" (as planning professors and consultants now say), and the conversation includes the retelling of this story, developing it so that a moral emerges: a lesson and a point, a clarification of the situation the planners are in and a clarification of what they can now do differently and better as a result.

The director speaks the most here, but he does not just tell a story to an audience; the planners together – with differences in their positions, power, and influence, to be sure – work to develop their own story, for it is, after all, the story they are willing and practically able to construct together.

So the housing planner echoes a pervasive problem in planning when she focuses on a particular irony of their practice: "If something goes wrong, the planners did it. If something goes right, the City Council members claim credit for it," and the director responds to her, affirming and building on her moral claim about the allocation of credit and blame: "That's the kind of problem . . . we have to address."

So he proceeds to reconstruct and present their working history again: "Ms. Smith here has been saying, 'You've got to come out' [more publicly]," and "Many of you have been saying, 'You've got to answer this,'" but "I've always said, 'No, . . . we don't want to get into a cursing war with a skunk.'"

And then he tells the staff he has changed his mind, so their collective story is changing: "But now I think we have to. We have to set out a strategy . . . to sell the department . . . to get to those people whose minds aren't already made up."

And the community development planner does not just take that as a personal tale of the director's change of heart. He takes it as a working story about where they are, practically speaking, as a staff, so he brings up a strategy to be considered: "What about . . . developing something like a position paper for the individual projects?" And he goes on to sketch his idea for the staff's consideration, for their deliberation.

What we see here, even in this short stretch of conversation from a staff meeting, is very rich, morally thick, politically engaged, and organizationally practical storytelling. But the point here, of course, is not that planners tell stories, for everyone tells stories.

In planning practice, though, these stories do particular kinds of work: descriptive work of reportage; moral work of constructing character and reputation (of oneself and others); political work of identifying friends and foes, interests and needs, and the play of power in support and opposition; and, most important (here in the staff meeting, for example), deliberative work of considering means and ends, values and options, what is relevant and significant, what is possible and what matters, all together. Values and ends are not just presumed, and means and strategies alone assessed by the staff; what matters and what is doable are explored, formulated practically, together.

Most important, these stories are not just idle talk; they do work. They do work by organizing attention, practically and politically, not only to the facts at hand but to why the facts at hand matter. In any serious staff meeting, for example, these stories are ethically loaded through and through. They arguably ought to be relevant, realistic, and sensitive to the staff's political history, and respectful of important values at stake; and always alert, too, to the idiosyncratic wishes and strong feelings of community residents and public officials, planning board and city council members alike. So, carefully telling these practice stories and listening perceptively to them are both essential to the planners' work of astutely "getting a take" on the problems they face.

In their meetings, then, the planners do not simply tell individual tales, they work together (as they work with others in other meetings) to construct politically shaped, shared "working" accounts – commonly considered, deliberative stories of the tasks, situations, and opportunities at hand. In these stories the planners not only present facts and express opinions and emotions, they also reconstruct selectively what the problems at hand really are. And they characterize themselves (and others) as willing to act in certain ways or not, as concerned with *these* issues, if not so much with those, as having good or poor working relationships with particular others, and so on.[16] So not only do we tell stories at work, but our stories tell a good deal about us as well.

We began by exploring the ways we learn from planners' accounts of their own practice. But that problem of learning from practice stories appears to be widely shared among professionals of all kinds who must listen to and interpret the stories they hear from their patients and clients: the developer wanting to build, the neighbor wanting to protect his or her neighborhood, the politician wanting some action from the planning department, the planning board member asking why more hasn't been done (and done more quickly) on a given project. What professionals generally, and planners particularly, face in such cases are complex stories, and if they do not learn from them – and quickly – they are likely to find themselves in serious trouble.[17]

But we still have not answered the central question here: How do planning analysts learn from such practice stories, and how do they learn politically and practically from such storytelling if they obviously do not do it through systematic experimentation? How do planners and policy analysts learn from other people's practice stories when they cannot do much hypothesis testing on the spot?[18] Or, better, perhaps, what image of practical and political learning can provide us with a fresh view of these questions if the imagery of learning through experimentation is not really apt in practice?

Learning and the Ethics of Friendship

When we ask how planners and professionals learn on the job, we want to know how they come to make practical judgments under conditions of limited time, data, and resources. We are not asking how scientific professionals can be; we are not asking how well they remember certain methods courses they took in school. We are after the ways they learn in the thick of things, in the face of conflict, having to respond quickly – not how they learn in the course of sustained research.

We should remember that when professionals learn on the job they have to make judgments of value all the time.[19] They have to find out not only how things are working but what is working well or poorly. They must learn not only about what someone has said but about what that means, why that is important, or why that is significant – all in the light of the inevitably ambiguous mandates they serve and the many, also ambiguous, hopes and needs of local residents.

With little time, and facing the multiple and conflicting goals, interests, and needs of the populace and their more formal clients, planners have to "pick targets"; they must set priorities, not only in their work programs but every time they listen to others as well. They cannot get all the facts, so they have to search for the facts they feel matter, the facts they judge significant, valuable. So whether they like it or not, they are practical ethicists; their work demands that they make ethical judgments – judgments of good and bad, more valued and less valued, more significant and less – again and again as they work. Ethical judgments, however embarrassingly little they may be discussed in planning schools, are nevertheless inescapable and ever present in practice. Really value-free professional work could well be literally what it says: value-free, worthless, without worth.

But what image, then, can help us make sense of the ways planners learn in practice as they listen to the stories they hear, and learn politically from them, too? Perhaps the simplest answer here is that we learn not just from scientific inquiry but also from friends.

We learn from friends – and we need to probe here our intuitions about friends and friendship to consider how we learn from planners' stories and how we learn, as planners (and practitioners more generally) on the job, when we work with others, when we listen carefully to others, paying careful attention to their stories.[20]

The point here is not, of course, that planners are, can be, or should be intimate friends with everyone they work with; the point is rather that if it is not clear how we learn from stories in practice settings, then we should think about the many ways we can and do learn from friends. Five related points deserve our attention here.

First, we learn from friends not because they report the results of controlled experiments to us but because they tell us appropriate stories, stories designed to matter to us. "Appropriate stories" are not appropriate in some ideal sense; they are appropriate to us and to the situations we are really in – insofar as our friends can bring their knowledge, empathy, thoughtfulness,[21] and insight to bear on our particular situation, needs, and possibilities. When we go to a friend with something important, we expect that friend not to respond with small talk and babble but with words and deeds, with little stories (sharing, confirming, reminding, consoling, perhaps encouraging) that can help us to understand practically and politically what it is (and is not) in our *power* to do.[22] These stories are typically narrative and particularized, not formal, logical proofs, however argumentative our friends may be. So, for example, when the director quoted above tells the story not only of having wanted to avoid "a cursing war with a skunk" but of his change of mind, it is a story directly appropriate to, and responding to, the staff's problem of vulnerability.

Second, we learn from friends because we use their words to help us see our own interests, cares, and commitments in new ways.[23] They help us to understand not just how the world works but how we work, how we are, who we are – including what sorts of things matter to us.[24] They help us to understand not only how we feel but what we value, not only "where we're at" in the moment but how we are vulnerable, dependent, connected, haunted, attached, guilty, esteemed, or loved, and so in many ways how we are related to the world not simply physically but significantly, in ways that matter to us and to others.[25]

We look in part, too, to friends to be critical (in ways we can respond to), to think for themselves as well as for us, not simply to condone or agree with our every crazy or ill-considered idea.[26] So in the staff meeting the housing planner does not let the director off the hook about getting the "heat" for the Lakeview project, even though he thinks "it wasn't our screwup." She points to the staff's own responsibility: "But *we never said it* wasn't our screwup. We never pointed the finger to the screwup" – whether or not pointing a finger would have been effective.

Third, we learn from friends because they do not typically offer us simplistic cure-alls or technical fixes. They do not explain away, but rather try to do justice to, the complexities we face. They do not reduce complexities to trite formulas; they do not make false promises and sell us gimmicks, even though they might encourage us and might not tell us everything they think about what we are getting into if they are confident that we will do what needs to be done once we get going. Friends recognize complexity, but as pragmatists concerned with our lives, our practice; they neither paralyze us with detail nor hide details from us when they know details matter.[27]

But if they do not offer us technical fixes, what *do* friends offer us? Certainly not the detached advice of experts, for they do not typically invoke specialized knowledge to tell us what to do. Instead, they help us to see more clearly, to remember, to see in new ways, perhaps to appreciate aspects of others or ourselves or our political situations to which we have been blind.[28] So in the staff meeting, the housing director's moral tale is poignant and powerful, capturing part of the bind the staff is in (and setting up the director's response): "If something goes wrong, the planners did it. If something goes right, the City Council members claim credit for it."

Her insight teaches us about the complex rhetoric of democratic politics and participation, its ideals and its ironies. So listening here, we might be less wishful but more astute, less purist but more committed to doing what we can. We can gather from these stories, too, the differences between better and worse deliberation, between more and less inclusive participation, between a more or less "fragile consensus" (as Kristin put it)[29]

Listening here, we can understand more about how power and rationality interact, about how what seems well founded may never come to pass, and about how planners' and citizens' good ideas can be watered down, lost in a bureaucracy, held hostage to one politician's campaign. These stories might nurture a critical understanding by illuminating not only the dance of the rational and the idiosyncratic but also the particular values being suppressed through the euphemisms, rationalizations, political theories, and "truths" of the powerful.[30]

Fourth, we learn from friends because they help us to deliberate. When we are stuck, we turn to friends, if we can. When we need to sort out what really matters to us, we turn to friends – close at hand or, perhaps, in our imaginations. We look to friends to remind us of what matters, of commitments we have lost touch with, of things we are forgetting in the heat or the pain of the moment. We learn about our relevant history and our future possibilities of practice. We learn, too, about better and worse (and so, without calling it that, about ethics) as we consider our friends' judgments about how to act on our more general goals in the particular and often surprising situations we face. And enriching our capacity for deliberation is part of what the profiles of planners do, part of what practice stories on the job do.[31] If we listen closely, not to the portrayals of fact in these stories but to their claims of value and significance, we discover an infrastructure of ethics, an ethical substructure of practice, a finely woven tapestry of value being woven sentence by sentence; each sentence not simply adding, description by description, to a picture of the world, but adding, care by care, to a sensitivity to the practical world, to a richly prudent appreciation of that world.[32] So in the staff meeting, again, the community development planner does not let the director stew in his own juices; he suggests a strategy for the staff to discuss and consider: a position paper for projects.[33]

Fifth, and finally, we learn from these practice stories as we do from friends, because they present us with a world of experience and passion, of affect and emotion, that previous accounts of planning practice have largely ignored.[34] These stories ask us to consider not only the consequential outcomes of planning or the general principles of planning practice, but the demands, the vulnerable and precarious virtues required of a politically attentive, participatory professional practice.[35] These stories enrich our critical understanding if they allow us to talk about the "political passions of planning" – the academic undiscussables of fear and courage, outrage and resolve, hope and cynicism, as planners (and other professionals, too, of course) must live with them, face them, and work with them.[36] If we cannot talk about these political passions, how could we ever talk about any critical practice at all? We would be left with passionless fictions of "correct politics," fantasies either of smooth incrementalist bargaining or "above it all" problem solving, which might inspire illusions of rational control but would hardly be true to anyone's experience. These politically passionless accounts of planning practice might be soothing and might promise a lot, but they would hardly inspire any confidence and hope about the challenges of planning, today and always, in the face of power.

How, then, can we learn from practice stories? We can learn practically from such stories in many of the ways we learn practically from friends. Both help us to see anew our practical situations and our possibilities, our interests and our values, our passions and our "working bets" about what we should do.

The argument here is hardly without precedent; the notion of friendship lay close to the heart of Aristotle's *Ethics*. Aristotle distinguished several types of friendship, ranging from forms in which friends simply provide one another with utility or pleasure to a form in which friends seek out not just the pleasures or benefits of association but far more: one another's virtues and excellence (their "real possibilities," some might say today).[37] The type of friendship from which we should con-

sider learning is therefore not the friendship of long affection and inti-
macy but the friendship of mutual concern, of care and respect for the
other's practice of citizenship and full participation in the political world.
This is the friendship of appreciation of the hopes and political possibilities of the other, the friendship recognizing, too, the vulnerabilities of
those hopes and possibilities.[38]

But, of course, neither friends typically, nor stories generally, promise
– much less provide us with – decision rules for all situations. We get no
gimmicks, no key to the inner workings of history, no all-purpose techniques for all cases. Instead, we seem to get detail, messiness, and
particulars.

That messiness of practice stories is an important part of their power.
To some degree, of course, the messiness is the message.[39] But that is far
too simple a formulation. That messiness is important because it teaches
us that before problems are solved, they have to be constructed or formulated in the first place. The rationality of problem solving and the
rationality of decision making more generally depend on the prior practical rationality of attending to what the problem really is – the prior
practical rationality of resisting the "rush to interpretation," of carefully
listening to, or telling, the practice stories that give us the details that
matter, the facts and values, the political and practical material with
which we have to work.[40] If we get the story wrong, the many techniques
we know may not help us much at all.

Consider, finally, a skeptical challenge: is all this about practice stories,
and by extension practical arguments, "just about words"?

No, certainly not. We have explored here what we do practically with
words as we work together. In studying ordinary work we always face
the danger that we will listen to what is said and hear words, not power;
words, not judgment; words, not inclusion and exclusion; "mere words,"
and not problem framing and formulation, not strategies of practice. An
Italian friend and colleague of mine put this worry beautifully recently
when he wrote to a mutual friend and colleague, "No doubt, it is important to understand how [planners] behave in municipal offices. This is
important for the sociology of organization and bureaucracy, for the
analysis of policy, etc., and also for understanding a portion of planning
implementation in practice. But for planning theory and practice it is less
important than an apple [was] for Mr Newton; in the end the apple is a
metaphor, while what [planner] Brown says in his office – it is just what
he says in his office!"[41]

But what planner (or policy analyst) Brown says in the office is not just
what he or she says, though it is that, too: what Brown says also embodies
and enacts the play of power, the selective focusing of attention, the
expression of self, the presumptions of "us and them," and the creation
of reputations – the shaping of expectations of what is and is not possible,
the production of (more or less) politically rational strategies of action,

the shaping of others' participation, and much more. What planner or architect Brown says involves power and strategy as much as it involves words.

So our ears hear sounds. A tape recorder records what is said. Children might identify the words. But the challenge we face, as planners and policy analysts more broadly, is to do more: to listen carefully to practice stories and to understand who is attempting what, why, and how, in what situation, and what really matters in all that. That challenge is not just about words but about our cares and constraints, our real opportunities and our actions, our own practice, what we really can, and should, do now.

Acknowledgments

This chapter benefited from comments of faculty and students who responded thoughtfully to its previous incarnation as an evolving lecture at the University of Illinois, Urbana-Champaign, the State University of New York at Buffalo, the University of Puerto Rico, and Cleveland State University. Thanks also to Pierre Clavel, Ann Forsyth, Davydd Greenwood, Jim Mayo, and John Nalbandian for critical comments.

Notes

1   He summarized results in this way:

> *Third-party funders of [policy and program] advice (and especially federal agencies) tend to seek not merely useful truths, but useful truths of general applicability. They expect in this way to maximize return on their investment. Consultants suffer from the same temptation. . . . The intention is reasonable, but the results are poor. All communities believe themselves special, indeed unique. They want their advisors to address their particular concerns, not the problems of some category of communities to which a federal agency assigns them. The result is that where third-party funders insist on work whose results will be "generalizable," city agencies lose interest, fail to cooperate, or flatly resist. . . . And Fitzgerald's irony holds: solutions to the problem of a particular city do prove useful elsewhere. Many urban problems are widely shared. Good solutions, therefore, do have wide potential. And urban officials across the country are linked by a profusion of professional associations . . . most of which meet regularly on national, regional, and statewide bases, and which also publish journals. News of useful innovations is thus conveyed in the least threatening and most convincing way – by the reports of fellow professionals . . . "Generalizability" will come, don't strain for it.* (P. Szanton, *Not Well Advised* [New York: Russell Sage Foundation, 1981], 159–60)

2   R. Neustadt and E. May, *Thinking in Time* (New York: Free Press, 1986), 274, 106.

3   M. Krieger, *Advice and Planning* (Philadelphia: Temple University Press, 1981); S. Mandelbaum, "Telling Stories" (Typescript, 1987); cf. P. Marris, "Witnesses, Engineers, or Story-tellers? The Influence of Social Research on

Social Policy," in H. Gans, ed., *Sociology in America* (Beverly Hills: Sage, 1990).

4   See P. Euben, *The Tragedy of Political Theory* (Princeton: Princeton University Press, 1990); and M. Nussbaum, "Finely Aware and Richly Responsible: Literature and Moral Imagination," in her *Love's Knowledge* (Oxford: Oxford University Press, 1990); see also Nussbaum's *The Fragility of Goodness* (Cambridge: Cambridge University Press, 1986), especially chaps. 2 and 10 and Interlude 2.

5   R. Coles, *The Call of Stories* (Boston: Houghton Mifflin, 1989), 7.

6   Ibid., 29.

7   The interviews were done by Linda Chu, a master's student working with me, and Linda and I created a set of practice stories, loosely called "Profiles of Planners" (Ithaca: Cornell University Department of City and Regional Planning, 1990).

8   As the professor, frankly, I did not know whether to laugh or cry. I thought much of what I had assigned for the previous ten weeks had been quite practical!

9   See, e.g., H. Baum, *Organizational Membership* (Albany: State University of New York Press, 1990), M. Feldman, *Order Without Design: Information Production and Policy Making* (Palo Alto: Stanford University Press, 1989); J. Forester, *Planning in the Face of Power* (Berkeley: University of California Press, 1989).

10   From J. Forester and L. Chu, "Profiles of Planners," 63 (Typescript for classroom use, Cornell University, Department of City and Regional Planning, 1990).

11   Cf. M. Nussbaum's arguments regarding literature and moral imagination, especially "Finely Aware and Richly Responsible."

12   See N. Krumholz and J. Forester, *Making Equity Planning Work* (Philadelphia: Temple University Press, 1990).

13   An extensive literature discusses this point; see, e.g., D. McCloskey, *The Rhetoric of Economics* (Madison: University of Wisconsin Press, 1985); on applied social research see J. Gusfield, *The Culture of Public Problems* (Chicago: University of Chicago Press, 1981).

14   At some point every year at Cornell, I find myself attending one seminar on qualitative research in which a question arises from the audience: "Since you haven't tested any hypotheses in a systematic manner, how can you claim to have made any contribution to knowledge?" And I find myself then, barely restrained, asking the skeptic, "Are you really willing to say that the fields of history and anthropology – whose practitioners do not typically test hypotheses in a controlled manner – have made no contribution to knowledge? No contributions to knowledge from ethnographic work? From historical research? Really?" "Oh no, no, no," comes the answer, "that's not what I meant . . ."

15   Don Schön shows us how practitioners "reflect in action" as they make moves, evaluate the results of those moves, and reconsider the working theories that guided those moves – as they consider what to do next. But the learning processes Schön focuses on presume a good deal of practical knowledge on the practitioner's part. Before moves can be refined – lay the school out this way or that way; expand the program this way or that way

– the practitioner needs to have taken a role in an institutional and political world. Not only are the roles typically ambiguous, but the political world is fluid as well. We need to explore how planners learn as they listen and, significantly, learn far more than the facts. See D. Schön, *The Reflective Practitioner* (New York: Basic Books, 1983); and his edited, *The Reflective Turn: Case Studies in and on Educational Practice* (New York: Teacher's College Press, 1990).

16   Just how much is to be attended to, probed, not missed, responded to sensitively, and appreciated as significant in these stories is not typically obvious at all. Because these profiles and practice stories show us the vulnerability of planners' best-laid plans to much larger forces beyond their control, they echo the themes of the classical tragedies. If political theorists and ethicists can explore literature and theater as rich and vital sources of ethical and political teaching, surely we can turn to the richness of professional practice profiles and practice stories to teach us about the possibilities of ethically sensitive and politically astute planning practice. See especially here the work of Nussbaum and Euben, cited above.

17   For more general work on narrative and story, see R. Alter, *The Art of Biblical Narrative* (New York: Basic, 1981); B. Bettelheim, *The Uses of Enchantment: The Meaning and Importance of Fairy Tales* (New York: Vintage, 1976); R. Coles, *The Call of Stories* (Boston: Houghton Mifflin, 1989); S. Deetz, *Democracy in an Age of Corporate Colonization* (Albany, State University of New York Press, 1992); P. Euben, *The Tragedy of Political Theory* (Princeton: Princeton University Press, 1990); J. Gusfield, ed., Kenneth Burke: *On Symbols and Society* (Chicago: University of Chicago Press, 1989); S. Hauerwas, *Truthfulness and Tragedy* (Notre Dame: University of Notre Dame Press, 1977); A. MacIntyre, *After Virtue* (Notre Dame: University of Notre Dame Press, 1981); M. Nussbaum, *Love's Knowledge* (Oxford: Oxford University Press, 1990); S. Terkel, *Working* (New York: Avon, 1972); and S. Terkel, *Race: How Blacks and Whites Think and Feel About the American Obsession* (New York: W. W. Norton, 1992).

18   We can do some hypothesis testing on the spot, as Don Schön (*The Reflective Practitioner*) has shown with his analysis of the moves that enable reflection in action. We seem, though, to learn a good deal more, and to reflect upon a good deal more, than Schön's account encompasses.

19   The planners not only have to make value judgments "in their heads," they must make value allocations as they speak and make practical claims about what their listeners or readers are to take as important and noteworthy.

20   Cf. M. Sandel on the epistemology of friendship in his *Liberalism and the Limits of Justice* (Cambridge: Cambridge University Press, 1987), 181. See Iris Murdoch's fascinating discussion in *The Sovereignty of Good* (London: Ark/RKP, 1970) of attention to virtue and the Good; also Nussbaum's concern with Aristotelian practical judgment and deliberation in *Love's Knowledge*.

21   Cf. Hannah Arendt:

[Thinking] does not create values, it will not find out, once and for all, what "the" good is, and it does not confirm but rather dissolves accepted rules of conduct. . . . The purging element in thinking, Socrates' midwifery, that brings out the implications of

the unexamined opinions and thereby destroys them – values, doctrines, theories, and even convictions – is political by implication. For this destruction has a liberating effect on another human faculty, the faculty of judgment, which one may call, with some justification, the most political of man's mental abilities. It is this faculty to judge particulars *without subsuming them under those general rules which can be taught and learned until they grow into habits that can be replaced by other habits and rules.*

The faculty of judging particulars (as Kant discovered it), the ability to say "this is wrong," "this is beautiful," etc., is not the same as the faculty of thinking. Thinking deals with invisibles, with representations of things that are absent; judging always concerns particulars and things close at hand. . . . If thinking, the two-in-one of the soundless dialogue, actualizes the difference within our identity as given in consciousness and thereby results in conscience as its product, then judging, the by-product of the liberating effect of thinking, realizes thinking, makes it manifest in the world of appearances, where I am never alone and always much too busy to be able to think. The manifestation of the wind of thought is not knowledge; it is the ability to tell right from wrong, beautiful from ugly. And this indeed may prevent catastrophes, at least for myself, in the rare moments when the chips are down. ("Thinking and Moral Considerations," *Social Research* 38 [1971]: 445–46)

22 Sandel (*Liberalism and the Limits of Justice*, 181) writes, "Where seeking my good is bound up with exploring my identity and interpreting life history, the knowledge I seek is less transparent to me and less opaque to others. Friendship becomes a way of knowing as well as liking. Uncertain which path to take, I consult a friend who knows me well, and together we deliberate, offering and assessing by turns competing descriptions of the person I am, and of the alternatives I face as they bear on my identity. To take seriously such deliberation is to allow that my friend may grasp something I have missed, may offer a more adequate account of the way my identity is engaged in the alternatives before me."

23 We may come to reconsider, for example, how we "rank" interests (to keep to a utilitarian language). Cf. F. Michelman, "Law's Republic," *Yale Law Review* 97, no. 8 (1988): 1493–1537; and J. Forester, "Envisioning the Politics of Public Sector Dispute Resolution," in S. Silbey and A. Sarat, eds. *Studies in Law, Politics, and Society*, 12: 83–122 (Greenwich, Conn.: JAI Press, 1992).

24 Cf. C. Taylor on qualitative distinctions and our identities in *Sources of the Self* (Cambridge: Harvard University Press, 1989).

25 Cf., possibly, *Befindlichkeit*, "care and situatedness," in Heidegger and feminist notions of relationship.

26 It could be productive to generate further synonyms here: mapping the ways we know we can make judgments that we would want friends to help us reconsider. Cf. discussions of self-command in decision theory, e.g., T. Schelling, *Choice and Consequence* (Cambridge: Harvard University Press, 1984) and weakness of will, e.g., A. Rorty, *Mind in Action* (Boston: Beacon, 1988) and M. Nussbaum, *Fragility of Goodness* (Cambridge: Cambridge University Press, 1984). Can we read or listen to practice stories without sliding from "understanding" them to "accepting" them at face value, thus losing any ability to be critical of the practice they (re)present? Again, thinking about how we listen to friends might be helpful, for we seem no

more to agree with or accept blindly whatever a friend says than we expect a friend blindly to agree with or accept whatever we (again blindly, rashly, mistakenly) say. Cf. "Can Phenomenology Be Critical?" in J. O'Neill, *Sociology as a Skin Trade* (New York: Harper and Row, 1972).

27　The lesson here is not that situations determine actions but that practical rationality depends on a keen grasp of the particulars seen in the light of more general principles and goals. By taking practice stories more seriously, we (ironically) make decision making less central to practice, making the prior acts of problem construction, agenda setting, and norm setting more important. Cf. Murdoch (*The Sovereignty of Good*, 37) here, undercutting decision-centered views.

28　Cf. Nussbaum, "Finely Aware," 160, on moral learning, seeing anew, and "getting the tip," where she cites L. Wittgenstein, *Investigations* (New York: Macmillan, 1968), 227e, on learning judgment.

29　Perhaps, too, we learn about the differences between dominated talk and "real talk," and all its contingencies, as Mary Belenchy et al. have described it in *Women's Ways of Knowing* (New York: Basic Books, 1986), 144–46.

30　Cf. here the work of M. Foucault, *Power/Knowledge: Selected Interviews and Other Writings, 1972–1977*, ed. C. Gordon (New York: Pantheon Books, 1980), and J. Habermas, *The Theory of Communicative Action* (Boston: Beacon, 1984), on discourse and power.

31　Roughly following Richard Bernstein's *Beyond Objectivism and Relativisim* (Philadelphia: University of Pennsylvania Press, 1983) and Seyla Ben Habib's "Judgment and Moral Foundations of Politics in Arendt's Thought," *Political Theory* 16, no. 1 (February 1988), this line of argument tries to bridge the work of Habermas (*The Theory of Communicative Action*) and Nussbaum (*Love's Knowledge*).

32　Iris Murdoch says, "If we consider what the work of attention is like, how continuously it goes on, and how imperceptibly it builds up structures of value round about us, we shall not be surprised that at crucial moments of choice most of the business of choosing is already over. This does not imply that we are not free, certainly not. But it implies that the exercise of our freedom is a small piecemeal business which goes on all the time and not a grandiose leaping about unimpeded at important moments. The moral life, on this view, is something that goes on continually, not something that is switched off in between the occurrence of explicit moral choices. What happens in between such choices is indeed what is crucial" (*The Sovereignty of Good*, 37).

33　In addition, such practice stories provide empathetic examples as well as abstract arguments about what ought to be done. They allow us to learn from performance as well as from propositions. Iris Murdoch puts this powerfully: "Where virtue is concerned, we often apprehend more than we understand and *we grow by looking*" (ibid., 31).

34　The works of Howell Baum and Charles Hoch are outstanding exceptions here. See, e.g., Baum's *Invisible Bureaucracy: The Unconscious in Organizational Problem Solving* (Oxford: Oxford University Press, 1987); and Hoch's "Conflict at Large: A National Survey of Planners and Political Conflict," *Journal of Planning Education and Research* 8, no. 1 (1988): 25–34.

35　We should consider applying the Foucauldian move of restoring or resurrecting or even reconstructing "subjugated" experience not only of suppressed and marginalized and dominated groups but of ordinary planners seeking to attend to issues of public welfare, inclusion, need, and suffering. Cf. Foucault, *Power/Knowledge: Selected Interviews and Other Writings, 1972–1977*, ed. C. Gordon (New York: Pantheon Books, 1980).

36   These stories – whether profiles of planners or practice stories actually told on the job – also engage our emotions and passions, allowing us to learn through them, to pay attention through them, too, to consider "how I might have felt in that situation," and help us recognize feelings we might not have recognized as relevant. These stories inform our repertoires of attentiveness and responsiveness; they teach us through empathy and identification; we learn about situations and selves – our selves – as we imagine being in the situations presented, as we ask, "Would or could I have done that? What should I have done?"

37   So commentators are careful to show that Aristotle's conception of friendship as an ethical ideal does not compromise broader claims of justice. And similarly, I claim that we can learn from the stories of planners in a way that speaks to the possibilities of justice, that does not compromise justice for the interests of a particular relationship.

38   The most helpful discussions of these issues – the relationship of story and literature to deliberation, ethics, and practice – are in the work of Martha Nussbaum, whose essays on this subject have been most recently collected in her *Love's Knowledge*. In related work, Nussbaum writes, for example,

> *[The Greek tragedies] show us . . . the men and women of [the] Choruses making themselves look, notice, respond, and remember, cultivating responsiveness by working through the memory of these events . . . and their patient work, even years later, on the story of that action reminds us that responsive attention to these complexities is a job that practical rationality can, and should, undertake to perform; and that this job of rationality claims more from the agent than the exercise of reason or intellect, narrowly conceived. We see thought and feeling working together . . . a two-way interchange of illumination and cultivation working between emotions and thoughts; we see feelings prepared by memory and deliberation, learning brought about through pathos. (At the same time we ourselves, if we are good spectators, will find this complex interaction in our responses.) When we notice the ethical fruitfulness of these exchanges, when we see the rationality of the passions as they lead thought towards human understanding, and help to constitute this understanding, then we may feel that the burden of proof is shifted to the defender of the view that only intellect and will are appropriate objects of ethical assessment. Such a conception may begin to look impoverished. The plays show us the practical wisdom and ethical accountability of a contingent mortal being in a world of natural happening. Such a being is neither a pure intellect nor a pure will; nor would he deliberate better in this world if he were.* (*The* Fragility of Goodness, 46–47)

39   But is it silly to say that the messiness of case histories and profiles is an important part of their message? After all, planners face enormous social problems; what sense can it make to argue that they and we learn about practice, good practice, through messiness, complexity, and particular detail rather than through general rules, universal maxims, and all-purpose

techniques? Nussbaum recognizes clearly the *suspicion* that meets the suggestion, and indeed the tradition "that defends the role of poetic or 'literary' texts in moral learning." Tackling this suspicion head-on, she writes, "Certain truths about human experience can best be learned by living them in their particularity. Nor can this particularity be grasped solely by thought "itself by itself." . . . [It] frequently needs to be apprehended through the cognitive activity of imagination, emotions, even appetitive feelings; through putting oneself inside a problem and feeling it. But we cannot all live, in our own overt activities, through all that we ought to know in order to live well. Here literature, with its stories and images, enters in as an extension of our experience, encouraging us to develop and understand our cognitive/emotional response" (*The Fragility of Goodness*, 186).

40   Cf. Murdoch's *Sovereignty of Good*. C. W. Churchman once described (in class) the pragmatist's theory of truth as follows: "A is B" (the car is red, the housing is substandard, it is raining) is to be read, "A ought to be taken as B" – thus taking descriptions to be pragmatic and selective actions, not correspondence-like statements picturing a brute reality. Nussbaum's concern goes further – to the very identification of B – issues which can hardly be discussed here. See, e.g., C. W. Churchman's *Design of Inquiring Systems* (New York: Basic, 1971) and *Challenge to Reason* (New York: McGraw-Hill, 1968).

41   LM to PH, June 22, 1990.

Index